Race and Reproduction in Cuba

Race in the Atlantic World, 1700–1900

SERIES EDITORS

Richard S. Newman, *Rochester Institute of Technology*
Patrick Rael, *Bowdoin College*
Manisha Sinha, *University of Connecticut*

ADVISORY BOARD

Edward Baptist, *Cornell University*
Christopher Brown, *Columbia University*
Vincent Carretta, *University of Maryland*
Laurent Dubois, *University of Virginia*
Erica Armstrong Dunbar, *Rutgers University*
Douglas Egerton, *LeMoyne College*
Leslie Harris, *Northwestern University*
Joanne Pope Melish, *University of Kentucky*
Sue Peabody, *Washington State University, Vancouver*
Erik Seeman, *State University of New York, Buffalo*
John Stauffer, *Harvard University*

Race and Reproduction in Cuba

Bonnie A. Lucero

The University of Georgia Press
ATHENS

Published by the University of Georgia Press
Athens, Georgia 30602
www.ugapress.org
© 2022 by Bonnie A. Lucero
All rights reserved
Set in 10/12.5 Adobe Caslon Pro Regular
by Kaelin Chappell Broaddus

Most University of Georgia Press titles are
available from popular e-book vendors.

Printed digitally

Library of Congress Cataloging-in-Publication Data

Names: Lucero, Bonnie A., author.
Title: Race and reproduction in Cuba / Bonnie A. Lucero.
Description: Athens : The University of Georgia Press, [2022] | Series:
   Race in the atlantic world, 1700–1900 | Includes bibliographical
   references and index.
Identifiers: LCCN 2022014512 | ISBN 9780820362762 (hardback) | ISBN
   9780820362779 (paperback) | ISBN 9780820362755 (ebook)
Subjects: LCSH: Fertility, Human—Cuba. | Women—Cuba—Social
   conditions. | Ethnology—Cuba.
Classification: LCC HB959 .L83 2022 | DDC 304.6/320951—dc23/
   eng/20220602
LC record available at https://lccn.loc.gov/2022014512

To the women in the struggle for reproductive justice

CONTENTS

List of Illustrations ix
Preface xi
Acknowledgments xv

INTRODUCTION Centering Women in Cuba's Demographic Dilemma 1

CHAPTER 1 Women's Reproduction in Law and Public Policy
The Birth of Racial Hierarchy in Sixteenth- and Seventeenth-Century Havana 26

CHAPTER 2 From Unwanted Infants to Useful Vassals
Institutional and Legal Protections for Expósitos and Their Racial Limits in the Eighteenth Century 50

CHAPTER 3 For the "Propagation of Slaves"
Enslaved Women's Reproduction on Plantations at the Dawn of Abolitionism, 1780s–1820s 74

CHAPTER 4 Preserving White Infant Life
Women of Color and Charitable Institutions amid Demographic Shift, 1820s–1830s 97

CHAPTER 5 From Regulating Slavery to Policing Enslaved Wombs
In the Twilight of the Slave Trade, 1830s–1840s 138

CHAPTER 6 "No Race Can Substitute Black Africans"
Reproducing Slavery after the Criminalization of the Slave Trade, 1850s–1860s 165

CHAPTER 7 Reconstituting Slavery
Poverty, Exclusion, and Criminalization after Partus Sequitur Ventrem 191

CHAPTER 8   From the Art of Midwifery to the Science of Obstetrics
            *Consolidating White Male Authority over Pregnant and
            Laboring Bodies*   208
CHAPTER 9   Birthing a Better Nation
            *Pregnancy and the Racial Logic of Early Republican Population
            Management*   232
CHAPTER 10 Abortion in Law and Medicine
            *Racial Assumptions and Continuities from Republic to
            Revolution*   262
CONCLUSION Protection, Correction, or Liberation   301

            Notes   311
            Bibliography   351
            Index   377

ILLUSTRATIONS

FIGURES

1.1. Spanish violence against Native populations, including mothers and babies, early sixteenth century   29
1.2. Map of Havana showing location of San Francisco de Paula Hospital, circa 1762   43
4.1. Diagram illustrating two procedures midwives were allowed to perform   113
4.2. Sample Inscription Form for Abandoned Infants, requesting information about race and color   120
4.3. White Expósito at the Casa de Maternidad de la Habana, ca. 1830s   134
8.1. Curette and Uterine Dilator, designed by Dr. Rafael Weiss   229
9.1. Foundlings Between Empires   233
9.2. Prize-winning babies, 1919   249
9.3. First prize in the 1919 Fertility Awards   250
9.4. Medicalization of Breastfeeding   254
10.1. The torno at Havana's Casa de Maternidad, early twentieth century   277

TABLES

3.1. Sex ratios of slave cargoes entering Cuba, 1790–1815   91
4.1. Patient outcomes by race and legal status at San Francisco de Paula Women's Hospital, 1835   109
4.2. Maternal and infant deaths in the diocese of Havana, 1843   110
6.1. Sex ratios of population of color, by legal status, 1861   177
9.1. Expósitos admitted to maternity department by race, 1900–1922   259
10.1. Women defendants in fertility crimes cases, 1914–1927   274

PREFACE

For a long time, I told myself that this project originated with an archival discovery. While finalizing the work on my first monograph, *Revolutionary Masculinity and Racial Inequality*, and making forays into the research for my second book, *A Cuban City, Segregated*, I found myself sifting through the mountains of unprocessed papers in an off-site repository associated with the Archivo Provincial Histórico de Cienfuegos. I stumbled on a huge number of criminal abortion cases dating to the early 1960s, a small number of which inform the final section of chapter 10 in this book. Although my goal for that trip was to gather material for the social history of urbanization, I paused to take a closer look at these files. The apparent paradoxes of my discovery were not lost on me. Here was evidence of the criminalization of women's reproductive choices during a period typically associated with women's liberation. Here was evidence that the most vulnerable women, impoverished women of color in the countryside, were precisely the ones hardest hit by the weight of the law precisely as the revolution declared the end to racism, mobilized women, and implemented a sweeping agrarian reform. It struck me as almost equally paradoxical as my experience growing up in a country that, while progressively gutting *Roe v. Wade*, routinely pats itself on the back as the home of feminism, a place of gender equality, and that sometimes cites the oppression of women as a pretext to invade other countries, as it did in 2003. Thinking through the significance and potential implications of these cases, I imagined a historical inquiry exploring how laws and policies governing reproduction intersected with systems of racial oppression in a society that, in many ways, was known for its role in pioneering progressive reproductive politics.

And for a while, it was exactly that—an academic exercise. But what we choose to write often reveals a lot about who we are, not just as intellectuals, but as people trying to make sense of our lives and world. Over the years I spent researching and writing this book, the subject matter was transformed from a topic of intellectual and theoretical concern into something entirely different—

something as historical as it was intensely personal. After gaining privileged and yet hopelessly incomplete access to pieces of the stories featured in this book, I became truly haunted by the horrors, the pain, the suffering so many women have had to endure for becoming pregnant, seeking to exercise autonomy over their bodies, or trying to have and parent their children on their own terms.

These women's stories have made me think and feel differently about the sexual and reproductive moments that punctuated my own origin and upbringing. They lent new meaning to my own experience of being abandoned by my father and raised in poverty by a single mother besieged by her own emotional demons, sexual traumas, and reproductive struggles. They have allowed me to appreciate the inexorable systemic forces shaping this tumultuous journey, even while recognizing their horrifically personal character and impact.

Writing this book has also underscored to me that, despite considerable change in the prevailing view and treatment of women, we have made alarmingly little progress in dismantling the structures of sexual violence and coercion that gave rise to many situations examined in these pages. While encounters with Cuba's infamous *pajeros* were all too common, a few years into the archival research for this project, I experienced an attempted sexual assault at one of the archives, which prevented me from continuing my work there. This not only influenced the sources that eventually ended up in this book, but it also redefined the meaning of my engagement with the material, especially as that experience retriggered numerous parallel traumas from my youth.

My research on the history of women's reproduction has also lent a peculiar intensity to interactions that would under ordinary circumstances feel quite forgettable. Toward the beginning of my journey through this project, one of my closest friends became pregnant. When I visited her, she reflected on pregnancy as an incredibly transformative experience—I think most women could agree about that. But she also made this claim: "You will never truly understand what it means to be a woman until you become pregnant and give birth." That statement was as jarring to me then as it remains now, but writing this book helped me discover why: it conflates womanhood with motherhood, a notion that has historically justified punishing women who conduct their lives outside the conventional bounds of motherhood. In part, this book recognizes the women who, in one way or another, attempted to disaggregate womanhood from motherhood.

The fear, pain, grief, and despair that echoed so loudly through the archival record have only become more real to me throughout this process. Like many women, I have endured reproductive events in my own life and body, as well as embarking on the long road of healing from past sexual and intimate traumas. Even while this book was in process, I experienced reproductive events whose emotional and physical intensity changed my relationship with this content. I felt panic at the prospect of having to raise a child alone. I negotiated restrictions on access to basic reproductive health care. I suffered the disappointment of watching an ultrasound screen reveal an unviable pregnancy and the unbearable misery of carrying it inside of me until my body could finally expel it. I felt the pain of miscarriage as I lost a baby I wanted and watched in disbelief as the father walked away before the bleeding had even ceased. And throughout all this, I have also felt the oppressive weight of other peoples' designs on my reproductive body, as various men pressured me to keep a pregnancy I could not bear, left me to grieve in silence and solitude, and demanded that I terminate a pregnancy that I wanted to keep.

Through those lived experiences, I came to appreciate the subject of this book in new ways, feeling in my own body a fraction of the pain and grief that can be triggered with pregnancy and pregnancy loss, and understanding that my position of privilege prevented me from truly fathoming the depths of the suffering endured by the women in this book. And it also made finishing this book an almost intolerably agonizing experience, as each keystroke conjured the terror, pain, and grief of the constellation of women's reproductive experiences across time and space. Grappling with the weight of these stories, I struggled with the reality that none of us could ever know how intensely they grieved, the emotions and physical sensations that drove them to give up their children, or how fiercely they fought for the lives of their fetuses, infants, and children, and clung to their own. Although a book such as this can never truly do justice to the lives and struggles of these women, I do hope that, in some way, recounting their stories contributes to a more empathetic and just world.

And now, just one day after the State of Texas has finally succeeded in its long battle to ban abortion, I offer this book as a window to the unnecessary suffering it will cause and possibly a blueprint for how we can fight it.

B. Lucero
Houston, Texas
September 2021

ACKNOWLEDGMENTS

I wish to acknowledge the generosity and intellectual engagement of scholars, archivists, and friends for their role in the conception, development, and completion of this book. I am indebted to Sally Kenney, who afforded me the rare privilege of a postdoctoral fellowship at Newcomb College Institute and generously sponsored research in Europe and Cuba. My year at Tulane provided me the time and space to think through, write, and obtain feedback on earlier versions of this book. My time at Newcomb restored my energy by extending access to an intellectual community and environment grounded in feminist ideology and praxis, and allowing me to participate in projects that restored my faith in the transformative potential of academic scholarship. It also afforded me the life-altering experience of working with incarcerated women, many of who shared experiences of sexual and intimate trauma similar to those recounted here. I owe a great debt to María de los Angeles Meriño Fuentes and Aisnara Perrera Díaz, who were exceptionally generous in sharing references they found during their extensive and prolonged work in the Archivo Nacional de la República de Cuba. Their support and collaboration was pivotal to developing the robust range of primary sources from the nineteenth century. Thanks, too, to Elizabeth O'Brien, who has consistently been a supportive and encouraging friend and colleague, always willing to share her expertise. The historiographical and bibliographic projects we undertook were essential in formulating my ideas about how this book fit into the broader field of the history of women's reproduction. I am also grateful for my friend and colleague Dr. Juan Coronado, who, in addition to giving his enduring friendship, also helped me access articles and books that my institution could not provide. I also want to thank Cassia Roth for patiently reading my earliest attempts at broaching this subject matter, and for graciously providing conceptual and historiographical suggestions.

I am grateful to the anonymous reader who saw both value and potential in an earlier version of this manuscript, which I had submitted to my editor, not because it was ready, but because I could no longer write about death, grief, and suffering after losing my own pregnancy. That person's careful attention resulted in feedback that was generous, kind, and generative, which is precious indeed in academia. Thanks also to a final anonymous reader, whose generous, constructive, and measured comments helped usher this book towards editorial approval. A final thank-you to my editor, Nate Holly, who has been consistently kind, responsive, and reasonable through this process. I am truly grateful for his respect and professionalism.

Race and Reproduction in Cuba

INTRODUCTION

Centering Women in Cuba's Demographic Dilemma

From its colonial inception, Cuban society was defined by a fundamental demographic conflict. Imperial authorities envisioned the island as a white Hispanic colony. Yet, the demographic realities of colonial life proved more complex than colonial settlement projects. Spanish explorers arrived not to a virgin island devoid of inhabitants but one populated by well-established communities of Indigenous inhabitants. Conquest hinged on the brutal and violent destruction of those lives, just as early Spanish colonization relied on the extraction of labor from survivors. Just a few decades after their arrival to Cuba, Spaniards had decimated Native populations by disease, enslavement, and violence, causing a precipitous demographic collapse.

The near eradication of Cuba's Indigenous inhabitants only exacerbated the fundamental demographic conflict. The destruction of Native populations left the colony devoid of labor, rendering Cuba even less desirable for Spanish settlement. The discovery of gold in Mexico and silver in Peru pulled Spanish settlers toward the mainland, leaving Caribbean settler populations to stagnate further. The Spanish population in Cuba declined by around 80 percent between 1520 and 1540. The low population density in the Caribbean's largest island left Spanish dominion vulnerable to piracy and foreign attacks, including one in 1538 and another in 1555. Assaults such as these periodically bolstered migration schemes and urban fortification projects, but concerns about underpopulation continued to plague Spanish colonization.[1]

Over the next 150 years, Cuba's population grew, but not in the ways metropolitan elites desired. Following the near eradication of the Indigenous population, the enslavement of Africans and their descendants emerged as a core pillar of colonial society. Despite Spain's tight control over the early slave trade, the majority of Cuba's laboring people were Black or brown. In this context, the ongoing anxieties about Cuba's supposed underpopulation hinged on the assumption that the number of *white* inhabitants was insufficient.

Concerns over the racial and ethnic composition of Cuba's population intensified in the late eighteenth century. Sweeping changes across the Atlantic World transformed a predominantly white settler colony into a majority Black slave society.[2] As the Seven Years' War (1756–63) raged in Europe, the British occupation of Havana (1762–63) opened the floodgates of the slave trade into Cuba. British slave traders expanded their existing commercial ties to the island's capital, importing more slaves during that eleven-month occupation than arrived the previous decade. Although the slave trade to Cuba temporarily contracted when Spain regained possession of the island in 1763, the gradual liberalization of commerce ensured its resurgence and growth. Between 1765 and 1784, annual slave importations to Cuba averaged only a few hundred, but these figures rose precipitously after the 1789 royal decree granting free trade in Spain's American colonies. The number of slaves toiling on the island more than doubled between 1774 and 1791.[3]

Although sugar cultivation expanded in the second half of the eighteenth century, slavery did not dominate Cuba until the Haitian Revolution (1791–1804).[4] With the collapse of French St. Domingue, Cuban planters scrambled to take advantage of soaring world sugar prices. The number and size of Cuban sugar plantations increased significantly at the turn of the nineteenth century, as did the demand for enslaved labor. The sheer magnitude of the slave trade into the island catalyzed a demographic shift. Cuba's white population lost its numerical majority as early as the 1790s.[5] At the dawn of the nineteenth century, Cuba had not only replaced St. Domingue as the world's largest sugar producer, it had also emerged as a significant importer of enslaved Africans. By the 1840s, the enslaved population alone outnumbered whites.[6]

In the face of Cuba's turn-of-the-century demographic shift, the island's economic and demographic agendas were fundamentally at odds. Its economic trajectory, centered on the extraction of labor from people of African descent, increasingly undermined its demographic identity as a white settler colony. Planters exerted insatiable demands for African captives, as they expanded their sugar plantations and fueled their own emergence as the island's economic elites. However, intellectuals feared that the ever-increasing importation of African captives would "Africanize" Cuba and thereby threaten the island's "Hispanic" identity. They worried that a majority-Black population imperiled their own privileged positions in the island's social and racial hierarchies and speculated that a Haitian-style slave revolt would inevitably demolish colonial rule, annihilate whites, and institute so-called Negro rule in Cuba. The eruption of several slave uprisings during the 1790s, and later the Aponte Rebellion in 1812, which drew direct inspiration from Haiti, fueled these fears. Managing the island's population came to hinge on an irreconcilable set of agendas—to advance the economic interests of a colony increasingly dependent on sugar and slavery while sustaining Cuba's white Hispanic identity by controlling the growth of nonwhite populations and maximizing that of the white population.

Existing scholarship posits that Cuban political and intellectual elites addressed these demographic concerns by attempting to regulate the quantity and type of people *entering* the island. They implemented two key policies. One policy centered on promoting migration and settlement of white families in Cuba. Although such a policy had long been a core element of Spain's imperial project in the Americas, "white colonization" assumed heightened significance in late eighteenth-century Cuba, where it became central to efforts to offset the growing Black population and restore Cuba's white majority. By the early nineteenth century, the Real Sociedad Patriótica, a society of creole intellectuals dedicated to promoting economic development, had established a Junta de Colonización Blanca (White Colonization Board) dedicated to fomenting the settlement of honorable (i.e., patriarchal) white families in Cuba. With funds drawn from a head tax on every male slave imported to the island, the board provided paid passage to Cuba, land grants, and temporary subsidies to encourage white migrants to relocate from Europe and the Americas to one of the growing number of fledgling white colonies across the island.[7]

A second policy focused on mitigating Black population growth by restricting the slave trade into the island. Cuban intellectuals like Francisco Arango y Parreño of the Real Sociedad Patriótica and later José Antonio Saco, a deputy to the Spanish parliament, famously advocated prohibiting the importation of enslaved Africans to preserve the island's Hispanic heritage and preempt slave rebellion.[8] Saco envisioned the abolition of the slave trade as part of a racial agenda linking whiteness to political reform: "we have no other alternative: whiten, whiten, and make them [Spanish authorities] respect us."[9] Spanish authorities initially attempted to silence these recommendations, even exiling their proponents. However, eventually they caved to international pressures. In addition to the 1817 antislaving treaty, Spain entered a second treaty with Great Britain in 1835 and later criminalized the slave trade in an 1845 penal law.[10]

What unified both these policies was their focus on the forced and voluntary migration—principally of men—as the primary agents shaping Cuba's demographic future. White colonization, which centered on recruiting able-bodied white male laborers, whose patriarchal responsibilities would ensure their reliance on wage work, promised to offset the growth of the enslaved population and promote economic development through agriculture. The logic of abolitionism drew on the assumption that Black men posed an imminent threat to the colonial racial and labor hierarchy rooted in slavery and white supremacy. Although male migration exerted considerable influence over the size and composition of the colonial population, it was by no means the only factor influencing the island's demographic trajectory.

Race and Reproduction presents a counternarrative to the male-normative perspective that dominates Cuban demographic history, instead centering women and specifically women's reproduction in the island's population politics. Biological reproduction, including conception, pregnancy, childbirth, breastfeeding, and other physical acts of motherhood (as well as the rejection of those roles), played a critical, though until now underappreciated, role in the evolution and management of Cuba's population. Although men certainly contributed genetically—and at times in other ways—to procreation, the principal protagonists of these actions were women, and the main sites were their bodies.[11]

The primary question guiding this book is how the twin demographic goals of white population growth and nonwhite population management shaped women's reproduction from the onset of colonization through the early years of the Cuban Revolution. This problem relies on the observation, well supported by existing scholarship, that demographic anxieties, and specifically the valuation of whiteness over Blackness, persisted well after the fall of slavery and Spanish colonialism.[12] Though this desire for whiteness might have been expressed in evolving discourses and with greater or lesser tenacity, it nonetheless remained a constant in Cuban history and in the policies and practices designed to manage women's reproduction.

Elite men, including judges, physicians, philanthropists, and public officials, intervened in women's reproductive lives in racially specific ways. Pronatalism defined interventions involving white women's reproduction. Colonial authorities advanced this agenda primarily through patriarchal protection aimed at saving the lives of white infants and harnessing the fertility of white mothers. When it came to women of color, interventions usually fell into two categories: exclusion and punishment. These two approaches defined both interventions aimed at extracting enslaved women's reproductive labor and mitigating population increase among free women of color. The specific methods employed to control women's reproductive lives did not always advance the overarching demographic goals in clear-cut ways. Nevertheless, white supremacy shaped tangible differences in the treatment of women and their infants across racial lines, and those reproductive outcomes were crucial in sustaining racial hierarchies through moments of tremendous political, economic, and social change.

Reproduction over Four Centuries

This book takes a *longue durée* approach to study women's reproduction in Cuba. The narrative begins with the early colonial period, following the sixteenth-century demographic collapse of Cuba's Indigenous population. Between the mid-sixteenth century and the late eighteenth century, Spanish colonial policy focused on increasing the white population through public, religious, and private investment in charitable institutions for women and infants.

The narrative ends with the long process of decolonization. I define this period as beginning in the final third of the nineteenth century, with the eruption of anticolonial struggle and the inauguration of gradual slave emancipation, both of which eventually spelled the demise of Spanish rule. I end this period, perhaps unconventionally, in the early years of the revolution—a moment of vindication, according to Fidel Castro, for the independence previously truncated by U.S. intervention, and also a watershed in the treatment of women's reproduction. During that period, the importance of legal status gradually faded, but race remained a salient factor shaping maternal and infant welfare services, pregnancy outcomes, and access to family planning.

The centerpiece of this book, though, is the hundred years between the rise of plantation slavery in the 1780s and its ultimate demise in the 1880s. During that period, colonial authorities, planters, and Creole (white Cuban-born) elites negotiated their economic reliance on slavery with their desire to preserve Cuba's Hispanic identity through the gradual demise of the transatlantic slave trade. Attitudes, understandings, laws, policies, and approaches to women's reproduction became irrevocably racialized during this hundred-year period in ways that both drew on early colonial foundations and shaped postcolonial trajectories in Cuba, reverberating through the birth of the republic and far beyond. For this reason, this book devotes the most sustained attention to the long nineteenth century.

During precisely this period, the paradox of demographic desires and regimes of labor extraction gave rise to a broad range of legal, institutional, and medical approaches to women's reproduction. These interventions exemplified the strongest and most explicit disparities along the lines of race and legal status. Although these approaches were often fraught and contradictory, they converged in their general paternalism and protection toward white women and exclusion and penalization of women of color. The racially specific logics and legacies of that reproductive landscape, though born of the colonial project, permeated subsequent historical periods. They persisted despite even the most monumental historical changes, surviving colonization and anticolonial struggle, economic boom and bust, and reform and revolution.

EARLY COLONIAL PERIOD

Research on colonial Cuba prior to the consolidation of plantation slavery has addressed women's reproduction through the lens of sexuality and marriage and that of unwanted or abandoned infants (*expósitos*, lit. exposed ones). Both these bodies of work have underscored the centrality of concerns over status, especially legitimacy, honor, and racial purity. Colonial subjects negotiated their place in the social hierarchy principally through the Roman Catholic Church, especially through formal ecclesiastical marriage and baptism. As scholars of women and gender in colonial Latin America have shown, both these sacraments were sites of ongoing struggle. Among honorable white families, a woman's sexuality, choice of partners, and the circumstances of her pregnancies significantly impacted her and her family's social standing. Negotiations of honor, legitimacy, virginity (and threats to it such as seduction, elopement, and deflowering), and marriage often hinged on racialized fears of miscegenation.[13]

Concerns over racial purity and legitimacy also influenced attitudes toward pregnancy, childbirth, and parenthood. Studies of childhood, especially infant abandonment, expose how both honor and status shaped women's reproduction.[14] In this regard, Havana's first foundling asylum, the Real Casa de Expósitos (Royal Asylum for Abandoned Infants), became an outlet for the unwanted children of white women who became pregnant due to illicit (premarital, sacrilegious, incestuous, adulterous, or interracial) sex.[15]

This book situates the Casa de Expósitos within a broader tradition of colonial charity. Institutions like the San Francisco de Paula Women's Hospital, established in the seventeenth century, and the Casa de Beneficencia, from the late eighteenth century, harnessed both ecclesiastical and local colonial authority to serve the spiritual, subsistence, and medical needs of impoverished women and unwanted infants. All of these institutions intervened in women's reproductive role in colonial society, whether more explicitly by providing physical care to expósitos, or more tangentially through providing spiritual and medical care to impoverished women and preparing orphan girls for marriage. They also all placed formal or de facto racial restrictions on access to services, while relying on the labor of enslaved and free women of color. With chronic budget shortfalls and woefully inadequate funding, these institutions covered deficits by imposing racial restrictions on admission to slow the ballooning demand on benefits, and exploiting the labor of women of color. Both measures supported white population growth while exerting a negative effect on the African-descended population. Employing women and mothers of African descent in these institutions redirected their reproductive labor away from their own children toward nourishing white children at the same time the institutions withheld benefits to Black mothers and infants.

Race and Reproduction analyzes this racially specific support against the backdrop of the law. The letter of the law criminalized fertility control and prescribed harsh sanctions. However, as in other Latin American colonies, there is little evidence that colonial authorities in Cuba implemented these laws to prosecute women for infanticide, abortion, or infant abandonment, at least not initially.[16] Instead, this research suggests that racially restrictive social welfare institutions afforded white mothers reprieve from the potential impact of criminal law by providing them a range of noncriminal and decriminalized options for their unwanted pregnancies and infants. Simultaneously, they denied the same options to women of color, who became the subjects of criminal investigation with greatest frequency by the mid-nineteenth century.

PLANTATION SLAVERY

A focus on women through the lens of family carries over into the scholarship on Cuba's period of plantation slavery. Studies of this period explore family formation among enslaved and free women of color since the late eighteenth century and especially the period of gradual emancipation, as well as the professional roles of free women of color in the realm of midwifery in the nineteenth century.

One of the overarching tropes in the scholarship on family is the notion that marriage was an institution for white elites, while informal unions prevailed among less privileged sectors. A 1776 royal pragmatic further required spouses to be of equal social status, reinforcing a racialized economy of marriage. Verena Martínez-Alier's classic study of the ways race and class shaped nineteenth-century marriage patterns showed how racial endogamy continued to prevail among the white population, even as sexual relationships outside the bounds of marriage often transcended race.[17] These racialized patterns of intimacy became entwined with stereotypes about the alleged immorality of people of African descent and most especially the sexual availability of Black and mulata women. Within this framework, the desire for racial improvement was encapsulated in the mulata women's desire for intimate relations with white men illustrated so vividly in the nineteenth-century lithograph series "Vida y muerte de la mulata."[18]

A growing body of scholarship explores family formation practices among enslaved people. María del Cármen Barcia traced enslaved families and social networks through notarial records.[19] Other historians employ ecclesiastical marriage and baptismal records from the late eighteenth and nineteenth centuries to reconstruct the enslaved family. María de los Angeles Meriño Fuentes, Aisnara Perrera Díaz, and Karen Y. Morrison have elucidated how enslaved women and men appropriated the sacraments for their own familial goals.[20] Historians of other slave societies are beginning to interrogate the ways sexuality and intimacy have constituted slavery beyond the family, sexual violence, and racial hierarchy.[21]

Scholars in Cuba also explored enslaved women's approaches to motherhood during the crucial period of gradual emancipation, following the 1870 free-womb law. Meriño Fuentes and Perrera Díaz challenge the stereotype that enslaved women lacked maternal sentiments by examining their legal strategies for achieving freedom during the decade of the 1870s.[22] Building on that study, Camillia Cowling compares enslaved women's legal claims making in Havana and Rio de Janeiro (Brazil) after the free womb laws.[23] This pathbreaking work examines enslaved women's legal petitions to gain their own and their children's freedom after 1870 in Havana.

Race and Reproduction situates these free-womb-era claims within a much longer history of enslaved women's efforts to assert autonomy over their bodies and advocate for their families within evolving legal, institutional, and political frameworks governing both slavery and reproduction. It begins with the claim, prevalent in studies of slavery and reproduction in other Atlantic World societies, that elite approaches toward enslaved women's reproduction responded to the shifting legality of the slave trade. Katherine Paugh shows how colonial authorities in Barbados manipulated reproduction in response to the transition from slavery to free labor. The salience of enslaved women's childbearing came to the fore following the abolition of the slave trade in the British Empire in 1807, when reproduction became the last remaining legal mechanism for sustaining slavery.[24] Diana Paton suggests that, while Jamaican planters did not pay much attention to enslaved reproduction before the onset of political abolitionism, they did consider it after 1789, and especially following the 1807 ban on the slave trade. Thereafter, both planters and colonial officials intervened to increase reproduction by reducing workload for pregnant and mothering slaves, among other reforms. During the period of apprenticeship between 1834 and 1838, however, planters changed course, actively rejecting pronatalist policies because they saw no economic benefit from enslaved infants and children, even as the state continued to push pronatalism.[25] Scholars of Brazil have made similar arguments, highlighting the importance of the 1831 ban on the slave trade, the 1850 end of the slave trade, and the 1871 free-womb law as key turning points shaping elite attitudes toward enslaved women's reproduction.[26]

Race and Reproduction reveals a more complex relationship between abolitionism and reproductive politics in Cuba, where a wide gulf separated abolitionist law from planters' persistent reliance on the clandestine slave trade. Initially, talk of abolitionism in the British Empire fueled preliminary discussions among Cuba's colonial elites about how to increase enslaved women's reproduction. However, planters continued to rely on the slave trade, with only momentary and uneven adjustment in their approach to slavery immediately following abolitionist legislation. Pronatalist proposals and policies in Cuba echoed their counterparts in the British Caribbean and North America, where historians document a range of diverse tactics from monetary incentives to physical punishments to force enslaved women to conceive and birth new generations of slaves, once servitude became an inheritable condition through the womb.[27] While some Cuban slave owners instituted pronatalist reforms, the interventions remained voluntary and inconsistent.

The real change occurred in the approach of colonial authorities, who by the 1830s became proponents of pronatalism to sustain the future of slavery. While this general conclusion aligns with Paugh's findings, the methods by which they pursued this goal appear, at least according to existing scholarship, decidedly unique to Cuba. Between the 1830s and the 1860s, colonial authorities not only deregulated slave ownership, but they attempted to extract enslaved women's reproductive labor through criminal prosecution. A small number of criminal cases involving enslaved women suspected of infanticide and later of other fertility crimes presents a fascinating counterpoint to research on other Atlantic World slave societies, like Brazil, where the institution of slavery appeared to insulate enslaved women from legal interventions into their reproductive lives.[28] These cases simultaneously suggest that enslaved women in Cuba, like their counterparts in other Atlantic slave societies, approached pregnancy and childbearing with their own cultural perspectives and social goals, even within the violently restrictive regime of slavery.[29]

Race and Reproduction shows how the prosecution of enslaved women coincided with persisting institutional extraction from and exclusion of women of color, both enslaved and free. Institutions like the women's hospital and the Casa de Maternidad relied on the reproductive labor of women of color as wet nurses, caregivers, and midwives to sustain white infant life. Yet, these same institutions denied services to women of color. This duality shows how both criminalization and exclusion defined elite approaches to the reproduction of women of color, even as the ultimate demographic goals diverged by legal status.

The themes of criminalization and exclusion also characterized the experiences of women of color laboring in reproductive care, including midwifery and wet nursing. As in other Atlantic slave societies, the care of women during pregnancy, childbirth, and postpartum in Cuba emerged as a profession of African-descended women—as did the nourishment of infants.[30] The racialized nature of reproductive labor in the colonial context meant that the professionalization of medicine not only extended male scientific authority to the historically female realm of reproductive care, as occurred in many European contexts, it was also an acutely racial process that specifically targeted women of color.[31] As scholars of Cuba have observed, the consolidation of white male authority over pregnancy and childbirth in Cuba paralleled an ongoing struggle to supplant Black women midwives and practitioners.[32]

Many of Cuba's budding *parteros* (male midwives, later called obstetricians), like their counterparts in mainland Spanish America, traveled to Europe (first Spain, and later France) for obstetric training, since neither obstetrics nor gynecology was in the medical curriculum in Cuba until the second half of the nineteenth century.[33] However, important differences distinguished developments in Cuba from the rest of the region. The enduring centrality of slavery, which, in Cuba outlasted every other Spanish American colony, meant that Cuban obstetrics developed intimately bound to the preservation of that institution—especially through the extraction of reproductive labor from enslaved women. In this way, it mirrored other second-slavery societies, like United States and Brazil, where the expansion of slavery in the nineteenth century coincided with Atlantic abolitionism.[34] Much of local physicians' practical experience about pregnancy and childbirth derived from plantation physicians, employed by slave owners to manage enslaved women's reproduction. Thus, the professionalization of obstetrics in Cuba aligns with Deidre Cooper Owens's finding that the development of gynecology in the United States hinged on access to and experimentation on the bodies of enslaved and immigrant women.[35]

In Cuba, though, the gradual development of obstetrics forced physicians to rely on women practitioners. As this book shows, physicians consciously sought to recruit white women to serve as formally licensed midwives and later as nurses, while erecting barriers to Black women's access to training and licensing. Like their counterparts in Brazil, Cuba's emerging cadre of physician-trained white women health care practitioners were gradually incorporated into late nineteenth- and twentieth-century maternal and infant medical care.[36]

The subjection of women of color midwives to the surveillance and authority of white male physicians formed part of a broader set of practices aimed at protecting white women's fertility. Like the regulation of wet nursing also discussed in this book, physicians rationalized the regulation of midwifery by scapegoating women of color for white women's poor pregnancy outcomes. They argued that wet nurses neglected and mistreated their white charges while also transmitting immorality and illness. Black midwives, they claimed, harmed white women, fetuses, and infants through their alleged ignorance, malpractice, immorality, and even malice. By disparaging the reproductive labor of women of color, and vilifying the women themselves, physicians and their allies framed the imposition of their own authority over pregnancy and childbirth as a way to protect white women and their infants, through the marginalization, displacement, and criminalization of midwives, wet nurses, and other women of color historically involved in the realm of reproduction. By analyzing this evolving medical landscape, *Race and Reproduction* shows how the penalization and exclusion of women of color was profoundly intertwined with the supposed protection of white women.

POST-EMANCIPATION PERIOD

As Laura Briggs shows in her study of late nineteenth-century Puerto Rico, the consolidation of white male medical authority over pregnancy and childbirth paved the way for further state interventions in women's reproductive lives.[37] Nowhere is this insight more evident than in early twentieth-century maternal and infant welfare interventions in Cuba, which formed part of a broader set of eugenic population management projects. Nancy Leys Stepan observed that eugenics arrived to Cuba by way of obstetrics, whose protagonists drew on their French training to implement the science of homiculture in the early republican period.[38] Tiffany Sippial shows how Cuban reformers understood prostitution regulation and venereal disease prevention as a matter of public health with evident demographic significance.[39] Armando García González, Raquel Álvarez Peláez, and Consuelo Naranjo Orovio elucidate the broad range of eugenic measures Cuban public health reformers implemented from premarital health certificates and racially selective sterilization.[40] Daniel Rodríguez further shows how public health campaigns aimed at addressing infant mortality formed part of a broader nationalist medical agenda during this very period.[41] These important studies reveal how Cuban physicians assumed an active role in shaping the size and racial composition of the national population, in part through interventions in women's reproduction.

Such interventions were by no means unique to Cuba. However, the demographic anxieties inspiring these discussions and interventions in Cuba grew out of the particularities of the island's political and economic history. Cuba's protracted transition from colony to republic largely coincided with the gradual emancipation of slaves over the final third of the nineteenth century. The late arrival of both independence and emancipation in Cuba distinguishes the island from its West Indian neighbors, as well as from its mainland Latin American counterparts, where slavery and colonial rule ended a half century earlier, respectively. And although the timing of Cuba's emancipation mirrors other second-slavery societies like the United States and Brazil, Cuba stood alone in the tenuous, halting, and truncated path to political independence. The island endured more direct and sustained U.S. military intervention and occupation than any other country in the Americas except Puerto Rico. The strong U.S. presence in the early twentieth century also shaped the island's medical profession, as aspiring physicians increasingly looked to the United States, as opposed to France, for medical training, research, and publication opportunities.

Perhaps because of these political and economic idiosyncrasies, discussions in early republican Cuba about the size and racial composition of the national population brought together ideas from the British Caribbean, the United States, Europe, and Latin America. The early onset of maternal and infant health interventions in Cuba mirrors developments in post-emancipation societies in the British Caribbean. As Juanita De Barros shows, maternal and infant welfare reform formed part of colonial efforts to manage the size and health of the post-emancipation populations in Barbados, Jamaica, and Guyana. There, as in Cuba, fears of population decline resurfaced in the late nineteenth and early twentieth centuries, albeit for very different reasons.[42] As in former Spanish colonies, Cuban approaches to maternal and infant welfare drew on long traditions of charitable institutions, which combined public, private, and religious authority.[43] But their twentieth-century iterations were very much aligned with state modernization projects.[44] Cuba's simultaneous reliance on white immigration and prophylactic public health and social welfare interventions focused on mothers and infants mirrored developments in mainland Latin America.[45] The emergence of coercive reproductive policies such as premarital health certificates, sterilization, and eugenic abortion evince the presence of more biologized notions of race, which appear to shape regions with pronounced U.S. influence: Cuba, Puerto Rico, Mexico, and the United States–Mexico borderlands.[46] Prostitution regulation and efforts to suppress the so-called *trata de blancas* (white slavery) also surfaced across the region.[47]

DECENTERING FAMILY

As this review of the historiography reveals, much of the existing scholarship has broached the history of reproduction in Cuba through the lens of family and childhood, whether by studying marriage and baptism patterns, parental claims, or eugenic policies and medical interventions. This work is certainly significant for understanding the institutional, moral, and scientific context in which reproduction occurred, but it has also tended to conflate family with reproduction. The former, which historians have often studied through marriage records, presumes a stable social unit with established kinship ties, such as husband-wife. Marriage, and to a lesser extent other heteropatriarchal arrangements, like concubinage, have served as a proxy for sex and, by extension, procreation, both of which are assumed to occur therein.

Despite the implicit recognition of intimacy and child-rearing within and beyond marriage, family and reproduction are not interchangeable. In Cuba, as elsewhere, family has long transcended blood relations, often encapsulating ties of spiritual filiation, fictive and ethnic kindship, child circulation, and adoption, with an emphasis on the selection of partners and the existence and rearing of children.[48] Similarly, an intimate union did not necessarily beget pregnancy, as some families throughout history have struggled with infertility.

Simultaneously, the lens of family can gloss over the social complexities of pregnancy and childbirth in family formation, thereby minimizing the role of women's bodies and bodily experiences in the production and survival of offspring. After all, not all pregnancies ended in the birth of a live, healthy infant. Miscarriage, stillbirth, and neonatal death were and remain common outcomes of pregnancy. And childhood illness and puerperal complications claimed the lives of countless infants and mothers.

Nor were all pregnancies necessarily intended or wanted. Women themselves sometimes determined that carrying a pregnancy to term, giving birth, or keeping a child was untenable, often because these competed against prevailing expectations about family. For some women, mainly those from more privileged social positions, illicit conception threatened to expose pre- or extramarital sex. Women in such positions risked the destruction of their public reputations and their current union or future marriage prospects if they did not hide or terminate the pregnancy, or abandon or destroy the infant. For more impoverished women, unintended pregnancy meant additional financial burden that may have jeopardized their own livelihoods and that of the children they already had. For enslaved women, giving birth to a child under slavery usually entailed the inhumane denial of parental rights, an abuse some women refused to accept.

Employing the lens of reproduction allows us to examine pregnancy and childbearing within a broad range of circumstances—within and beyond the bounds of traditional family. Indeed, it is premised on the recognition that, throughout the period under study, as today, notions of family were often at odds with the realities of women's reproductive lives. *Race and Reproduction* thus recognizes but decenters the role of family in reproduction, instead reorienting the focus toward women.

Decentering family is particularly significant for understanding the relations between race and reproduction in Cuba's colonial and postcolonial past. Ann Laura Stoler argues that intimate matters, such as parenting, breastfeeding, domestic service, and the care of orphaned and abandoned children, were central to imperial governance of racial difference.[49] As Franz Fanon demonstrates, colonialism shapes the moral and material conditions of decisions about reproduction, in ways that perpetuate the devaluation of Blackness and the valorization of whiteness in intimate life.[50]

Another advantage of this approach is that it brings into the frame themes previously only marginal to the scholarship on Cuba—for example, family planning, especially contraception and abortion. This paucity of research is particularly noteworthy considering how pronounced these topics have been in scholarship on mainland Latin America and even in Puerto Rico and the British Caribbean during the first half of the twentieth century.[51] What little scholarship exploring family planning in Cuba focuses on the second half of the twentieth century, especially the period after the Cuban Revolution of 1959. The only English-language monograph exclusively dedicated to reproduction in Cuba is Elise Andaya's *Conceiving Cuba*, an ethnographic study of abortion following the collapse of the Soviet Union. Rachel Hynson addresses this topic in a more limited way for the early revolutionary period, positing that women faced heightened restrictions on their reproductive freedoms during the early 1960s. She uses this to suggest that U.S. women enjoyed greater access to reproductive health care than their Cuban counterparts.[52] However, without concrete basis in prerevolutionary Cuba, neither the chronological nor geographical dimensions of this comparative argument hold up.

Race and Reproduction employs a broader conceptual and chronological frame to reveal how medical and legal attitudes toward abortion were complex and changed over time. By examining early twentieth-century discussions of abortion, it shows that, much as in Brazil, Peru, Mexico, and Puerto Rico, elite physicians in early twentieth-century Cuba articulated a strong pronatalist agenda that included opposition to abortion and contraception as a core tenet. Although it is evident from the persistence of such vocal opposition that plenty of physicians and midwives did condone and perform abortion, it is nonetheless noteworthy that some of Cuba's leading obstetricians pushed judicial authorities to do more to suppress criminal abortion, especially as a broader range of women gained access to that procedure over the first decades of the twentieth century. The medicalization of pregnancy and childbirth, opposition to abortion, and the prohibition of contraception converged with the expansion of policing to foster unprecedented state intervention in women's reproductive lives. That these developments also emerged in Cuba supports the argument that punitive measures defined interventions in the reproductive lives of women of color.

Official attitudes toward abortion began to change in the 1930s. As economic crisis made pregnancy and childbirth increasingly untenable even for white families, medical and legal circles began to consider poverty as a valid justification for abortion. Although the poverty exemption did not ultimately make it into the final version of the Social Defense Code of 1936, a clause therein formally recognized the legality of therapeutic abortion—abortion performed by a licensed medical practitioner with the express purpose of saving the woman from imminent death. These discussions evinced modest efforts to liberalize abortion in an era in which wealthy white women continued to enjoy almost complete impunity, while the weight of the law fell heaviest on impoverished women and women of color. The letter of the law—and ongoing racial and class stratification in prosecution for fertility crimes—persisted through the early years of the revolution, until the informal liberalization of medical understandings of maternal health in the early 1960s.

By contextualizing postrevolutionary family planning within the longer history of medical and legal approaches to women's reproduction, *Race and Reproduction* challenges the notion that the revolution increased restrictions on abortion. On the contrary, it demonstrates how Cuba's medical and legal establishments adopted restrictive policies similar to those across the Americas in the first half of the twentieth century.[53] Moreover, instead of narrowing women's access to family planning, the revolution instead brought continuity with previous periods in the ongoing investigation of poor women and women of color for reproductive incidents. Nor are these continuities surprising. Analyzing actual criminal abortion cases, I show that Cuba's postrevolutionary approach to family planning aligned closely with patterns identified by historians of twentieth-century Latin America, where revolutionary governments often continued pronatalist policies of previous regimes.[54] Even still, the informal relaxation of abortion statutes afforded Cuban women among the broadest access to abortion in the hemisphere well before *Roe v. Wade*.

Sources, Methods, and Theoretical Frame

The decision to focus on reproduction rather than family influences the kinds of sources I employ throughout this book. Previous historians, particularly those working on the colonial period, relied heavily on ecclesiastical records, which remain at the margins of this study. After all, neither marriage nor baptism serves as a particularly strong indicator of women's reproductive experiences, especially among populations of African descent. For one, rates of marriage and baptism among people of color steadily declined, as the institution of plantation slavery became entrenched in Cuba.[55] Access to and participation in these sacraments reflected both positionality within the colonial system and, to a lesser extent, the relationship with Catholicism. Enslaved people's access to marriage and baptism hinged on the whims of slave owners. Despite laws and decrees mandating that slave owners baptize and permit marriage among slaves, they did not always conform, especially when it might have exposed their violation of antislaving laws or increased their tax burden through census records.[56] Moreover, baptism does not encapsulate the many pregnancies that ended in outcomes other than birth.

Instead, *Race and Reproduction* relies on a range of historical sources to reconstruct women's reproductive experiences in Cuba: primarily on archival research in national, provincial, and local repositories across Cuba, and secondarily on archives in Spain and the United States. The sources cluster around the book's three main threads: law, social welfare, and medicine. My analysis of these three sets of sources focused on exploring the evolving ways legal theorists, medical practitioners, policy makers, and philanthropists attempted to regulate women's reproductive potential in service of particular social projects and demographic aspirations. Collectively, these sources reveal the broader connections between women's reproductive experiences and the overarching white supremacist racial order, of which patriarchy and class stratification were core pillars.

LAW

The first thread follows the legal frameworks governing women's reproductive bodies, particularly as they concern pregnancy and fertility control. Laws criminalizing infanticide and abortion lacked explicit references to race. However, certain iterations of the laws included implicitly racialized language, such as the reduced sentences prescribed for crimes committed in defense of a woman's honor. Part of this story necessarily involves synthesizing and tracing the evolution of laws that regulated women's reproduction. To do this, I consulted the published texts and commentaries on the legal frameworks applied to Cuba over the years, including the Siete Partidas (Seven-Part Code); the penal codes of 1822, 1850, and 1870 and the Social Defense Code of 1936. However, the story moves beyond a simple reading of the law by analyzing the evolving relationship between the letter of the law and the ways local authorities in Cuba understood and applied it (or undermined it), often in racially specific ways. I accessed the practical meanings of the law through police investigations and judicial proceedings involving women accused of fertility crimes. This kind of analysis reveals an acutely racialized legal landscape in which police investigations and criminal court cases involving infanticide, for example, usually targeted impoverished women and women of African descent. Indeed, the legal framework governing women's reproduction transcended the small number of legal statutes directly addressing pregnancy and its termination. I therefore consider legislation, such as slave codes and abolitionist treaties, and later labor policies concerning working mothers, which sometimes included guidelines on pregnancy, childbirth, and motherhood.

SOCIAL WELFARE

The second thread concerns the resources and institutions dedicated to the social welfare of pregnant women, mothers, and babies. I explore public, private, and ecclesiastical investment in charitable institutions, social programs, and other humanitarian projects to save unwanted infants, protect vulnerable mothers, and reduce infant mortality. The surviving records of institutions such as the San Francisco de Paula Women's Hospital, the Casa de Expósitos, and the Casa de Beneficencia provided a point of departure for understanding the social and demographic desires undergirding the creation and practical management of these establishments.

Of particular importance are the institutional records of the Casa de Beneficencia y Maternidad. This institution and its predecessors (the Casa de Expósitos, the Casa de Maternidad, and the Casa de Beneficencia) produced a significant volume of documentation. An 1823 inventory of the Casa de Expósitos tabulated in its archive thirteen books of baptismal records, seven books of breastfeeding logs, one book of financial records, and one file containing 258 loose sheets detailing ecclesiastical matters.[57] The majority of this archive has since been lost, so the historical reconstruction of this institution offered here is at best fragmentary. It is based mainly on the records of the Fondo de la Casa de Beneficencia y Maternidad, housed at the Archivo Nacional de la República de Cuba, a collection of miscellaneous documents, the better part of which are financial records, and a small portion of which were transcribed and published in Evaristo Zenea's 1838 history of the Casa de Maternidad. A significant portion of the records that appear in the archival catalog are no longer available, sometimes due to their deteriorated condition or misplacement.

I also consulted records dispersed through various collections at the Archivo Nacional de la República de Cuba, including Miscelánea de Libros, Gobierno Superior Civil, Real Consulado de la Junta de Fomento, Intendencia General de Hacienda, and Consejo de Administración, and the Fondo Antonio Bachiller y Morales at the Biblioteca Nacional de Cuba José Martí. Included, too, is a small volume of institutional documents housed at the Archivo General de Indias in Sevilla, Spain. I obtained further information about individual cases of expósitos surrendered to the institution from the records of the Audiencias of Santo Domingo and Santiago de Cuba, as well as notarial protocols in Cuba's Archivo Nacional.

A crucial aspect of this examination involves interrogating who gained access to those resources and who remained on the margins. In some cases, the exclusion of Black families was explicit, as it was in the founding documents of Havana's foundling asylum and in the recurring efforts to identify and restrict the benefits available to Black infants. In other cases, the racial boundaries were more implicit, though no less evident. The science of puericulture prescribed a wide range of state interventions to ensure the welfare of pregnant women and infants, all of which advanced the eugenic goal of "improving" the Cuban population through the production of more healthy white or white-passing babies. Reconstructing the explicit and more often implicit racial parameters of initiatives like these, I show how social welfare interventions served as a foil for increasing the white population through the protection of white infants and mothers, while denying the Black families access to such assistance. What is more, these institutions consistently relied on the reproductive labor of women of color midwives, wet nurses, and caregivers, who faced surveillance and blame for outcomes often beyond their control.

MEDICINE AND PUBLIC HEALTH

The third thread traces the medical and public health approaches to pregnancy and childbirth. Professional organizations like the Academy of Medical, Physical, and Natural Sciences of Havana and governmental agencies like the Secretariat of Sanitation and Beneficence and Infant Hygiene Commission provided a point of departure for charting the impact of medical professionalization of ideas and interventions in maternal and infant health. I supplemented that work with analysis of historical publications concerning forensic medicine, medical curriculum, and medical dissertations. I also examine demographic and health data, particularly for the later periods under study.

My analysis of these records starts from the premise that plantation medicine—slave owners' employment of white male physicians to manage the health and reproduction of enslaved labor forces—was a crucial foundation for medical legitimacy in Cuba. I trace the gradual consolidation of medical authority over women's reproduction, in particular, through the professional war white male physicians waged against Black women midwives. This racialized and gendered struggle began in the early nineteenth century with formal education and licensing requirements being imposed on midwives and with physicians' active racial agenda to encourage white women to join the profession as their subordinates. With the consolidation of obstetrics education in the late nineteenth century, physicians attempted to enforce their monopoly on women's reproductive health care by invoking their scientific authority to influence the racial dimensions of judicial prosecution of fertility crimes. In particular, they denounced practitioners, often women of color, who did not submit to their medical authority. I also chart the emergence of a professional code of ethics centered on pronatalism, in which elite physicians' racialized assumptions about women's reproduction drove opposition to family planning. Tracing these practices into the 1960s, this thread shows how the extension of medical authority was premised on a clear racial hierarchy among practitioners and reinforced disparate access to and quality of care among women by race and class.

RE-CENTERING WOMEN IN THE HISTORY OF REPRODUCTION

Most of the surviving archival sources privilege the perspectives of white male physicians, judges, philanthropists, and policymakers. These elites orchestrated racially specific interventions into women's reproductive lives to advance their own social and demographic projects, often neglecting or even actively silencing what women thought, felt, and experienced. Yet, rather than merely provide an account of the often-repressive practices they enacted on women's bodies, this book seeks to access the voices, perspectives, and experience of women themselves.

Vestiges of women's lives surfaced in the accusations, speculations, and prescriptions of lawmakers, judges, physicians, government officials, and philanthropists. These legal judgments, correspondence from charitable institutions, medical policy debates, and other elite white male-authored sources against the grain all reveal the power of women's reproductive bodies to occupy the attentions of some of the world's most powerful men. But women also spoke, even if their voices were often heavily mediated within the male-dominated archive. Women told their own stories in court testimonies, handwritten notes attached to abandoned infants, and in midwives' and healers' petitions and ads. These and other sources reveal how women continually claimed autonomy over their reproductive lives despite intensifying surveillance.

A woman's ability to make her voice heard, just like the kinds of reproductive experiences she faced, was conditioned by significant power disparities along the lines of race, class, and legal status. The literate and educated wives of Havana's creole elite recorded their thoughts and recommendations in their journals, deemed significant enough to be archived with the records of charitable institutions. By contrast, enslaved women often relied on scribes, notaries, or benefactors to transcribe their stories, which rarely evaded distortion. *Race and Reproduction* pays close attention to these power disparities, seeking to amplify the voices and experiences of African-descended and impoverished women where possible.

My approach is inspired by the long tradition of Black feminist thought, and especially the growing body of work on reproductive justice, in its central focus on the intersections of white supremacist racial hierarchy and gender relations of power. I take as the principal point of departure Dorothy Roberts's argument that reproduction has been a critical means of racial oppression and offers a possible route to liberation.[58] An entire generation of scholars of reproductive justice has demonstrated that race has historically impacted and continued to affect the life chances of Black women and their children through medical racism, efforts to circumscribe access to assistance, and an unyielding willingness to criminalize and punish.[59] I apply these insights to explore the strategies women employed to have children on their own terms, to limit their fertility, and to parent their children on their own terms.

Translating the reproductive justice framework to Cuba means accounting for historic differences in understandings and experiences of race across the Atlantic World. Even as the intensity of slavery and white supremacy transcended political and imperial boundaries, cultural differences distinguished prevailing discourses of race and inequality in the United States and Latin America. Whereas explicit reference to race has long prevailed in U.S. discourse, it has been less socially acceptable in Cuba, especially following the outbreak of anticolonial struggle, when raceless nationalism began to dominate the discursive landscape.[60] References to race are often implicit and embedded in alternate idioms, such as honor, patriarchy, class, and education.[61] Thus, this book pays close attention not only to the explicit references of race that sometimes surfaced in discussions about women's reproduction, it also decodes more subtle references to race by unpacking the racial meanings and implications of references to other forms of social inequality that in Cuba have historically been bound up with racial hierarchy.

Elite men's racially specific interventions into the realm of reproduction meant that women experienced pregnancy, childbirth, and motherhood in fundamentally different ways according to their race, legal status, and class. Elite efforts to defend white women from external harms to their ability to conceive, carry a pregnancy to term, and birth a living, healthy child, and to sustain their infants meant that, even as their choices were still constrained by patriarchy, white women often enjoyed a broader range of options and support than did nonwhite women.

The sectors most often vilified were women of African descent—wet nurses, midwives, and even poor mothers who abandoned their infants. Protecting white women and infants from these potential harms came in the form of controlling, restricting, and punishing women of color—imposing formal training and licensing requirements on midwives, regulating the care and nourishment of infants, especially when it involved wet nurses, and imposing and reimagining racial restrictions on access to charity. All these projects were premised on the gradual consolidation of white male authority over the previously female realms of pregnancy, childbirth, and motherhood. However, this inclination toward patriarchal protection of white women also undergirded the reluctance to prosecute white women suspected of fertility crimes, whether through the codification of honor as an attenuating circumstance for fertility control or simply a willingness to excuse or exculpate privileged women for their crimes of passion. Indeed, this investment in maternal and child welfare, which began in the colonial period, in many ways served as an antidote to punishment and correction, a tendency that carried forward through the twentieth century.

Elite men's racialized and gendered notions about reproduction had very different consequences for mothers and infants of African descent. The primary lens for this population was corrective, whereby interventions focused on enforcing the kind of reproductive behaviors that advanced prevailing economic and demographic agendas, and punishing women who failed to conform. Under slavery, this meant extracting future generations of slaves from the wombs of enslaved women through perpetually ineffective pronatalist policies, and later through criminal prosecution. More broadly, for free women of African descent, it manifested as seemingly endless limitations on access to assistance and support, exclusions that perpetuated poverty, exacerbated maternal and infant death, and brought impoverished and grieving mothers of color disproportionately under the spotlight of police investigation and criminal prosecution.

The exclusion and neglect that free women of color and their babies faced throughout the colonial period became the new norm applied on the entire population of African descent after the abolition of *partus sequitur ventrem* (a child's status follows that of its mother) in 1870. Without the legal distinction of slavery, poverty became the vehicle for the courts to target women of color, while race remained an evident, if unspoken factor in poor women's access to state benefits and reproductive health care. In short, tracing these three threads shows how competing claims on women's reproductive bodies not only drew on entrenched racial assumptions and agendas but also actively reinforced the political and social structures upholding white supremacy and patriarchy in Cuba.

All these interventions contributed to broader demographic trends, but their immediate outcomes did not always align in the most obvious ways with the prevailing demographic desires among island elites. Whereas elites subscribed to the desirability of increasing the white population, only some policies directly advanced this goal in practice. On the one hand, access to medical and social welfare institutions—hospitals, foundling asylums, maternity homes, and birthing clinics—certainly provided white women a broader array of options when it came to unwanted or complicated pregnancies. Although foundling asylums were usually plagued with high mortality rates, especially early on, they saved at least some white infants who likely would have died of exposure or outright infanticide, thereby contributing at least marginally to white population growth. Medical establishments, too, likely saved the lives of some white mothers and infants, especially in later periods following the introduction of asepsis and antisepsis. On the other hand, the reluctance to prosecute white women for fertility crimes invalidated the legal deterrents for committing abortion and infanticide. That white women largely evaded the weight of criminalization would have theoretically had a negative impact on white population, even despite the limited power of laws to shape behavior.

Similarly, the prevailing desire to mitigate the growth of the free Black population seemed to directly inform only some policies and restrictions on the reproduction of women of color. Excluding women of African descent from charitable institutions, for instance, reduced their options to care for their pregnancies and children, likely exacerbating morbidity and mortality. However, disproportionately criminalizing women of color suspected of fertility control aimed to deter these fertility control practices. By penalizing women of color more severely than white women, judges theoretically contributed toward higher fertility rates among a population elites considered undesirable, even as excluding them from resources would have mitigated that impact.

These apparent paradoxes between demographic desires and policies demonstrate that there was more at stake than simply increasing or controlling fertility. The variation in the way demographic agendas surfaced in reproductive policies vis-à-vis women of different racial backgrounds, legal conditions, and social statuses evinces that elites were as deliberate about the methods they employed as they were about the outcomes they pursued. Authorities in the realms of law, medicine, and public welfare all converged in their view of women's bodies and reproductive capacities as in need of male guidance and control. However, the racially specific ways they attempted to assert control reveals an ideology in which violence, coercion, and punishment were acceptable means for controlling the reproduction of women of African descent while milder interventions were preferred to encourage and coax white women to conceive, carry their pregnancies to term, and keep their infants alive.

The picture that emerges from these histories confirms the overarching valuation of white reproduction and devaluation of Black reproduction unless it held tangible economic benefits for elites. However, by analyzing interventions in law, public policy, and medicine, this book exposes contradictions and fissures in the demographic logics governing those desires. Ultimately, it demonstrates that while elites sought to increase white women's fertility, they did so through protective interventions aimed at sheltering white women from the consequences of their own actions and at saving their babies. By contrast, the prevailing approach to the reproduction of women of color centered on punitive measures and exclusion rather than protection. Even when elites took a temporary interest in enslaved women's reproduction, punishment, coercion, and surveillance were the primary tools for extracting reproductive labor. Colonial and postcolonial projects to regulate women's reproduction exposed the legal and social boundaries between populations whose humanity colonial authorities recognized and deemed worthy of saving, and those who existed merely to toil.

Chapter Outlines

This book unfolds chronologically. The first two chapters examine colonial legal and institutional interventions in women's health and reproduction prior to the late eighteenth-century consolidation of plantation slavery. Chapter 1 lays out the key laws governing pregnancy, explaining how colonial racial ideas gave laws made in Spain new meaning in Cuba. Even though these laws criminalized and prescribed harsh sentences against abortion and infanticide, neither Indigenous women nor white women faced criminal prosecution. By tracing the establishment and early institutional history of the island's first women's hospital, the chapter posits that charity superseded criminalization as the principal approach to women's reproduction by the mid-seventeenth century. The fact that the hospital explicitly discriminated on the basis of legal status and secondarily race foreshadows the centrality of white women in colonial pronatalist schemes.

Chapter 2 then traces key institutional and legal reforms aimed at helping *expósitos*, the designation given to abandoned children of unknown parentage. It introduces the Real Casa de Expósitos, established in Havana in 1711 to raise expósitos. Much like the women's hospital, the Casa de Expósitos erected clear boundaries of race and legal status, explicitly excluding the children of African-descended women. Yet, the original intention to serve whites only proved difficult to enforce. Moreover, the institution heavily relied on African-descended women—as wet nurses, caregivers, laundresses, midwives, and healers—to preserve white infants and mothers. By the late eighteenth-century, demographic transformations linked to the rise of plantation slavery lent unprecedented urgency to the defense of racial exclusivity, leading to additional exclusionary measures. Among these, colonial authorities imposed racial limits on a 1794 royal mandate granting expósitos legitimacy. The racial restrictions on both charitable services and legal protections for expósitos show how colonial authorities invested in white infants to the exclusion of nonwhite ones, aligning with colonial aspirations to increase the white population.

Chapters 3 through 7 examine legal, institutional, and early medical interventions in women's reproduction during the one hundred years between the consolidation of plantation slavery and its ultimate demise in the late nineteenth century. Chapter 3 surveys a variety of legislative projects and policy initiatives focused on regulating enslaved women's reproductive potential between the rise of Cuba's sugar plantation economy in the late eighteenth century and the first restriction on the slave trade to Cuba in 1820. It reveals a continued reliance on the clandestine slave trade as planters failed to mitigate slavery's deleterious impacts on enslaved women's reproductive lives.

Chapter 4 shifts focus to consider three parallel racial shifts in the legal and institutional approach to free women's reproduction following the consolidation of plantation slavery. It charts the start of efforts to regulate midwifery, justified as a measure to protect white women's pregnancies and infants. The simultaneous expansion of charitable services included not only white infants but also their mothers, all while reinforcing the racialized exclusion of children of African descent. The formal legal recognition of honor as an attenuating circumstance in fertility crimes in the 1822 penal code paved the way for white women to be protected from criminal consequences. Together, these three strands evince how protecting white women was entwined with excluding and controlling women of color.

Chapter 5 returns to the experiences of enslaved women. It charts a critical turning point in the role of the colonial state in enslaved women's reproductive lives during the 1830s and 1840s, as Spain entered its second antislaving treaty in 1835 and moved to criminalize the slave trade with an 1845 penal law. In the face of mounting restrictions on the slave trade, colonial authorities in Cuba shifted their focus from policies that encouraged planters to implement pronatalist reforms to interventions that directly affected the reproductive lives of enslaved women.

Chapter 6 assesses efforts to preserve the institution of slavery by increasing enslaved reproduction. Colonial authorities shifted their focus away from regulating slave owners, instead continuing to focus on criminalizing enslaved women not only for infanticide but for a range of alleged fertility crimes not covered under the relevant penal code. Colonial authorities sought to address the systemic demise of slavery by coercing enslaved women, rather than pursuing structural change in the labor regime.

Chapter 7 examines the continuities and changes in elite approaches to enslaved women's reproduction during the gradual transition from slavery to free labor. Planters continually endeavored to retain control over enslaved women's freeborn children, despite the shifting legal terrain of the free-womb law. They attempted to exploit enslaved women's reproductive labor, for example through wet nursing. Debt bondage remained a form of de facto enslavement but also became an added barrier to accessing charitable institutions. Racial exclusion from the expanding array of charitable services for infants and mothers created the conditions for racial disparities in criminalization to survive the transition from slavery to free labor.

Chapters 8 through 10 focus on Cuba's post-emancipation period, from the end of the anticolonial struggle to the early years of the Cuban Revolution. Chapter 8 reconstructs the racialized and gendered terrain of culpability for poor pregnancy outcomes during the final decades of the nineteenth century, as Cuban obstetricians professionalized amid war and nation building. Physicians readily blamed midwives for maternal and infant death in childbirth and puerperium, even supporting criminal prosecution. When it came to members of their own profession, however, they refused to apply a similar standard of responsibility, though they did appear to condemn physician-assisted abortion. Likewise, they also used their scientific authority to challenge judicial proceedings against white women accused of infanticide. These disparities in physicians' assessment of responsibility align with the overarching tendency of elites to protect white women by penalizing women of color, while also showing how obstetricians exploited this racialized approach to women's reproduction to advance their professional status.

Picking up on the thread of elite physicians' opposition to abortion, chapter 9 charts the development and consolidation of a pronatalist medical agenda among elite physicians, amid shifting demographic realities and concerns. Cuba's population declined over the thirty years of anticolonial struggle. While women of all backgrounds continued to control their reproductive potential alone and through a range of practitioners, Cuba's leading obstetricians envisioned newly medicalized forms of contraceptive and abortion as threats to white fertility specifically. Fearing these technologies would further deplete the white population, these elite doctors further restricted contraceptive and abortion access, as part of a broader nationalist project to maximize the white population. During the early republican baby boom, demographic anxieties expanded the conversation on race to include issues of morality, illness, and disability. The desire to produce a robust, productive, and orderly national population framed the development of maternal and infant welfare reforms that occurred under the umbrella of homiculture. These interventions evince the characteristic protectionist approach to white women's reproduction through the expansion of social benefits and the regulation of the reproductive labor of women of color. They also show the centrality of formally trained and licensed white women practitioners to the supervision and "correction" of reproductive practices of impoverished women and women of color.

Chapter 10 traces the liberalization of attitudes toward women's reproduction in three historical moments between the early republic and the first years of the Cuban revolution through the lens of abortion access. State approaches toward abortion in the first two-thirds of the twentieth century evinced alarming continuity in the prosecution of poor women and women of color, such that the 1965 reform likely afforded these groups unprecedented reproductive autonomy.

A Note on Names

Diverging from the conventional preference for surnames, I refer to certain historical actors by their first names when it makes logistical sense to do so. For example, I use first names when a single case or vignette involves multiple individuals with the same last name, as occurs frequently with situations involving enslaved people (who often carried the owner's surname). I also typically use first names for enslaved people who received different surnames over the course of their lives due to changes in ownership. In addition, it makes sense to use first names over surnames when discussing expósitos, most of who were assigned the surname Valdés.

There is also a political rationale behind my choice. The convention of using surnames, in my view, reflects the exclusionary character of the historical profession, which is built on centuries of scholarship focused on wealthy white men. The use of patronymics privileges patriarchal lineage, decentering women. For enslaved people and their descendants moreover, last names often denoted possession, as when a slave owner imposed their own last name on their slaves, or European understandings of African ethnicity based on ports of embarkation, as in the case of nation-based names, such as Congo, Carabalí, Lucumí, and Arará. Retaining those colonial naming traditions reifies the commodification of their existence. Although first names were also problematic in the cultural erasures they perpetuated, especially on African peoples, I find these to be the less offensive choice in terms of their appropriation and everyday use.

I note where I have altered names. Where late nineteenth- and early twentieth-century documents provided only initials for anonymity, I created names to make the narratives more readable. In documents from the 1930s and beyond, I changed names to protect the privacy of people who might still be alive.

CHAPTER ONE

Women's Reproduction in Law and Public Policy
The Birth of Racial Hierarchy in Sixteenth- and Seventeenth-Century Havana

Motherhood was at the very core of colonial understandings of womanhood in Cuba.[1] Based primarily on the Roman Catholic belief in Mary's Immaculate Conception, colonial society afforded women two paths to honorable existence: that of virgin, pure and fully devoted to God, or that of mother, a role that, if undertaken within the bounds of marriage, could provide redemption from the stain of sex.[2]

Despite religious prescriptions and social ideals, sex and pregnancy frequently occurred beyond the bounds of marriage. Part of this pattern can be explained by the unequal access to the sacrament of marriage—impoverished people and people of African descent married at much lower rates than wealthy whites. But out-of-wedlock pregnancy also occurred among the most privileged social classes. And when it happened, it chafed against the status-conscious, racially circumscribed desires of elite families. Marriage immediately following an illicit conception could repair the damage premarital pregnancy did to the woman's honor. But in some situations, such as adulterous, sacrilegious, or incestuous sex, or sex between two individuals of different races or statuses, marriage was often undesirable if not outright impermissible.

As the de facto institutional cornerstone of reproduction, marriage had profound implications not just for the woman's individual and familial status but that of her offspring as well. Consequently, decisions over marriage partners were tightly bound to not only issues of status and class but most notably of race. Thus, the fierce battles colonial subjects fought for legal recognition of their legitimacy, purity of blood, and legal whiteness all had material implications for their social standing and economic prospects, not least of which was their eligibility and desirability for marriage.[3] Disputes between women, their families, and the state over the choice of marriage partners, so endemic to the colonial period, often encapsulated negotiations over race and status. Such concerns rendered interracial marriage socially taboo even before it was legally banned in the eighteenth century. Consequently, illegitimacy became entangled with miscegenation.[4]

In cases of illicit sex not reparable by marriage, pregnancy became a visible sign of the woman's dishonor. To uphold their public reputations, some women sought to terminate the pregnancy or disavow it by hiding, destroying, or abandoning the progeny. In addition to shame and social stigma, poverty could also compel women to take similar measures to avoid adding to families they were already struggling to support. At all these junctures, race and legal status shaped the choices available to women, inflected their experience, and often determined the consequences of their decisions.

In the Spanish Empire, legislation punishing infanticide or the termination of pregnancy drew on the precedents governing personhood in thirteenth-century Castilian law. One of the first legal references to neonatal death appeared in the Fuero Juzgo, a set of laws enacted by Castilian monarch Fernando III in 1241. The law afforded inheritance rights only to fetuses considered to be "alive," a state that required the baby to survive birth, receive baptism, and live for "ten days, more or less." Mothers of baptized infants who died after ten days were entitled to inherit the property their late newborns would have inherited from their fathers.[5]

Concerns over inheritance also dominated the laws concerning pregnancy and infancy in the Siete Partidas, compiled during the reign of Alfonso X of Castile (1252–84). To ensure paternity, the law defined a legitimate birth as one occurring at least six months after marriage, and as many as ten months after the death of the father, and it restricted widows from remarrying in the year after the death of their husband.[6] In case of a twin birth, the male would receive primogeniture if the infants were of different sexes, and it would be divided among the babies if they were of the same sex.[7] So-called monstrous births, or births of babies that did not have discernable human form, were ineligible for inheritance.[8]

Importantly, the Siete Partidas offered a legal framework governing unwanted pregnancies and infants. Parricide laws criminalized the intentional killing of family members, including fetuses, newborns, and children, without regard to race or legal status. Infanticide, abortion provoked by consuming herbs or violently injuring the belly, and infant abandonment resulting in infant death could be punished with death.[9] If the infant survived abandonment, the law prescribed the loss of parental custody.[10] This rigid criminalization of women's fertility control practices and the harsh sentencing guidelines theoretically aligned with colonial demographic projects centered on population growth. By rescuing these emergent and fledgling souls, colonial administrators could grow the colonizing population while advancing its spiritual mission to bring more souls into the Catholic Church.

Conceived and written in a European context, these same laws and beliefs governing women's reproduction assumed new meaning in the context of Spain's ethnically and racially diverse American colonies, especially Cuba. Despite the rigid criminalization and stiff sanctions prescribed by the law, evidence of criminal prosecution for fertility control remained exceedingly rare throughout the first three centuries of colonial rule. The apparent impunity surrounding the loss of pregnancies and infant life extended to both elite and laboring populations, but for starkly different reasons within an emerging racial logic. Spanish men evaded prosecution for causing pregnancy loss, and infant and maternal death among Indigenous populations not only because of the weakness of the state, but also because of a profound ambivalence over the humanity of Native people. By contrast, the failure to prosecute white women owed not to apathy, but rather a paternalistic desire to protect them from themselves and society.

Building on this sentiment, colonial authorities developed an alternative approach to defending white fertility, centered on charity. The island's first formal institution for the care of women, the San Francisco de Paula Charity Hospital for Women, established in 1665, was a key part of that project. Through this institution, the colonial state invested in the health of poor white women, on whose reproductive labor the colony relied. This hospital marked the beginning of a much longer history of racially selective pronatalism.

Native Reproduction and the Law

The year after the Spanish Conquest began in eastern Cuba, Spanish authorities issued a set of laws to govern the treatment of Indigenous people. The Leyes de Burgos (1512) prohibited encomenderos from sending pregnant women to the mines or to labor in the fields after around four months of gestation, instead prescribing lighter work assignments such as domestic service or pulling weeds. It also afforded Indigenous mothers three years for breastfeeding, during which period they could not be used in labors that would "harm the infant." After that point, they could be legally required to work in the mines or fields.[11] This stipulation followed the precedent set by the Siete Partidas, which afforded mothers primacy over their children until the age of three years, by which time they were supposed to be weaned.[12] In 1513, several amendments augmented the protections available to Indigenous families, including protecting Native women married to Native men from serving in the mines unless they or their husbands chose to do so, mitigating the workload of children under age fourteen, and enforcing patriarchal control over unmarried Indigenous women.[13]

By their own admission and detailed throughout their chronicles, Spanish conquistadores flouted the law, inflicting unimaginable violence and cruelty on

FIGURE 1.1. Spanish violence against Native populations, including mothers and babies, early sixteenth century. Bartolomé De las Casas, *Illustrationes de Narratio regionum Indicarum per Hispanos quosdam devastattarum* (Francofurti: Sumptibus Theodori de Bry, & Ioannis Saurii typis, 1598), 47, 55. Library of Congress, Rare Book and Special Collections Division.

Native families, including pregnant women, mothers, and children. Franciscan Friar Bartolomé de las Casas recounted how they "entered the villages and did not even leave children, nor old people, nor pregnant women or new mothers behind without gutting them and cutting them to pieces.... They took the babies by their legs, tearing them from their mothers' breasts and smashed their heads on the rocks." In other cases, conquistadores reportedly threw babies into rivers, laughing as they drowned. Others drove their swords through both the babies and their mothers.[14] Spaniards also attempted to transport Native people to Hispaniola from neighboring islands, including nearby eastern Cuba, to labor in the mines, a gender-selective process that likely exacerbated the disruption of Native families and reproduction. "There were more than five thousand souls, [but] there is not a single baby: they killed all of them by bringing them to the island of Hispaniola after they saw the Natives of that island died off."[15] Violence against pregnant women, mothers, and babies, depicted in a series of images published by de las Casas, reduced the Natives' ability to reproduce future generations (fig. 1.1).

Although fertility rates for the period before 1511 are largely unknown, archaeological evidence as well as anecdotal evidence from Spanish chronicles suggests the existence of a thriving Native population on the island prior to Spanish arrival. For instance, the high proportion of children, particularly those under age four, in an excavated funeral cave at Marién in western Cuba (dated prior to contact), suggests strong fertility rates among Native populations in that part of the island, even as infant mortality remained high.[16] Those findings are consistent with the discovery of large numbers of children at other pre-Columbian funeral cave excavations, including those at Cayo Salinas, Bacuranao, and Perico.[17]

The violence of conquest and encomienda likely contributed significantly to the overall suppression of Indigenous fertility. By even the most conservative of estimates, the Native population of Caribbean islands like Cuba had plummeted to a fraction of its precontact size by the 1540s.[18] Without abundant forced labor, the gold output all but collapsed.[19] The encomienda system likely reduced the ability of Native women to conceive by separating them from their partners and communities. Moreover, the excessive physical labor and violence Native women faced under the encomienda likely imperiled any pregnancies and made it difficult to care for their infants and children. According to de las Casas, encomenderos "did not give the men or the women anything to eat besides herbs and things without substance; the milk dried from the new mothers' breasts, and all their babies died shortly thereafter as a result; and because the men were separated and never saw the women, reproduction ceased." De las Casas described the encomienda's impact on Indigenous women on the mainland, where mothers were "burdened with heavy loads . . . and unable to carry their babies because of the work and their own weakness from hunger." In desperation, these enslaved women "tossed their infants out on the roads, where infinite babies perished," a fate that Cuba's Native women likely shared as they endured the encomienda.[20]

Other Native women tried to escape the horrors of the encomienda with death. Although Cuba's Native populations may have practiced infanticide prior to the arrival of Spaniards, the causes and scale changed significantly after their arrival.[21] "Reduced to a state of slavery," some Native inhabitants attempted to flee, taking refuge in more remote parts of the island to avoid the certain death that awaited them in the mines; but others committed suicide and infanticide. Still others "strangled themselves in despair. Parents hanged themselves together with their children, to put a speedier end to their misery by death."[22] Infanticide and suicide further reduced the Native population, already ravished by violence, overwork, and disease.

De las Casas's indictment of the Spanish Conquest may have exposed some of the atrocities conquistadores committed, but it fell short of forcing accountability. Despite rigid laws prescribing capital punishment for the murder of an infant, there is no archival evidence that any conquistadores faced legal consequences for slaughtering Indigenous infants and violently precipitating abortions in Native women during the conquest or subsequent encomienda system. On the surface, the disparity between the severity of metropolitan (i.e., made in Spain) fertility control laws and the impunity with which Spanish conquerors murdered pregnant Indigenous women and their babies appears dissonant with colonial reliance on nonwhite labor.

Why did metropolitan authorities fail to bring abortion and infanticide statutes from the Siete Partidas to bear on conquistadores, or even on Indigenous women? Why did they fail to enforce the protections afforded by the Leyes de

Burgos? Part of the answer certainly lies in the short reach of the metropolitan state. Indigenous women likely avoided prosecution because metropolitan authorities, in addition to prioritizing the conquest over Indigenous survival, lacked the institutional structure to enforce the law. Yet, the absence of a definitive state presence prior to the consolidation of Spanish colonial rule only explains the lack of legal cases involving women's reproduction. It does not explain the dearth of moral outrage. Did the Spanish government even consider the violently induced miscarriages and bloody infant murders as abortions and infanticides?

The gap between the letter of the law and its lack of implementation also exposes the failure of metropolitan laws to account for the racial and ethnic diversity of conquest and colonization. The cross-racial character of these crimes baffled metropolitan laws, designed for a more racially homogenous society than the ones emerging in the colonies. After all, the main perpetrators of abortion and infanticide of Indigenous women's pregnancies and infants were in fact Spanish men, whose triumphant narratives of personal victory on behalf of the fatherland apparently overshadowed the brutal realities of their atrocities.[23] Conquistadores were also likely shielded from criminal culpability because their actions formed part of what their government understood as a just war.[24] The racial and gender privilege implicitly granted to Spanish men sheltered them from harsh judgments of their carnage. Such privilege was probably augmented by the fact that they enacted their violence on women and children who were dehumanized as savages and infidels, in addition to being dismissed because of their racial, ethnic, religious, and, in the case of women, gender difference.[25]

Part of the power behind laws criminalizing abortion and infanticide was that they codified moral outrage over violent fetal and infant death. But these feelings of moral outrage were premised on an understanding that infants, and even some fetuses, were human beings with rights. What happened to this assumption in a context of racial, ethnic, and religious Otherness? The impunity with which conquistadores slaughtered Native infants hints at the circumscribed definition of humanity that governed Spanish attitudes toward nonwhite fetuses and infants, a limitation that would become ever more apparent as the colonial period wore on.

Part of the impunity likely also stemmed from a lack of foresight about the potential demographic, and by extension economic implications of mass abortion and infanticide against Indigenous populations. Spanish chroniclers tended to discuss the reproductive lives of Indigenous women without referring to their demographic implications, as if pregnancy and childbearing had little to do with population, or occurred with such ease that it needed no safeguarding. Of the populations he encountered in Santo Domingo, De las Casas marveled that Indigenous women gave birth with very little difficulty or pain. They barely showed any suffering beyond an occasional grimace. Once they gave birth, they washed the baby in the river, breastfed it, and then returned to their activities.[26] He also noted the high frequency of twins and other multiple births, an observation later repeated by subsequent Cuban historians.[27]

Historians during the colonial period largely avoided the issue of Indigenous reproduction, limiting their commentary to family formation and women's folk healing. According to Dr. Antonio de Gordón, who wrote *Medicina indígena de Cuba y su valor histórico* (1894), Cuba's Indigenous societies eschewed marriages between blood relatives and women refrained from sexual intercourse during menstruation and after birthing.[28] According to Antonio Bachiller y Morales, Indigenous healers, known as *bohiques*, employed betún (naphtha) to treat ailments of the uterus, and tobacco and sassafras to address menstrual cramps and other ailments of the womb. They also used *cebadilla* (possibly black hellebore) to help expel the placenta or dead fetus from the uterus; and used the leaves of a plant known as *xutola* (possibly the ceiba, or cotton tree) for pregnant women.[29]

Although these snippets of Indigenous society seem to take Native women's ability to conceive, birth, and rear children for granted, it is clear that the conquest and encomienda system had significant implications for Indigenous women's reproductive lives, which in turn, fundamentally shaped the demographic future of Cuba's Native communities. In a context defined by violence, epidemic disease, and forced labor, soaring morbidity and mortality rates likely affected vulnerable populations—including pregnant women and young children—disproportionately.

Accounts of Spanish administrators and ecclesiastical authorities reveal that a limited number of Indigenous communities survived the encomienda, which began its gradual demise with the passage of the Leyes Nuevas (New Laws of the Indies) in 1542. Archaeological evidence suggests that some Native communities survived in parts of Cuba until at least the seventeenth century.[30] However, the total population of Indigenous inhabitants had been so diminished that "recuperation and reproduction of a socially discernible Indigenous group" was no longer possible. Spanish authorities also recognized that, despite the survival of small numbers of Indigenous inhabitants, the demographic collapse meant that Spaniards could no longer rely exclusively on Natives as a source of labor.[31]

Cuba's sixteenth-century demographic collapse marked a turning point in the island's history. Without labor, and no major economic activity, the island of Cuba offered little incentive for Spanish settlement. The arrival of Spaniards to the mainland further eroded Cuba's population. The conquest of New Spain (1519–21) transformed Cuba from a destination for Spanish colonists to a feeder colony for New Spain. The expansion of the Spanish conquest to Peru (1531–36) and the exploration of North America via Florida (1538) further diverted Spanish migration away from Cuba, toward the mainland where precious metals and labor remained abundant. Although population figures for this period are inexact, some historians estimate that Cuba's population declined by 80 percent in the two decades after the fall of Tenochtitlán.[32]

Yet, by the time the demographic impacts of the conquest and encomienda entered the awareness of colonial authorities, they had already found an alternative to Indigenous labor: African slavery. Within two years of Diego Velázquez's arrival to the island, Spaniards imported the first enslaved Africans to Cuba from Hispaniola. Larger transatlantic cargoes of enslaved Africans began to arrive in the 1520s.[33] By 1532, when one Spanish official estimated that no more than five thousand Natives remained in Cuba, the number of Africans had already ascended to five hundred.[34] Spanish authorities continued to request greater numbers of Africans to supplement the dwindling Native population.[35] The emergence of enslaved Africans and their descendants as the primary laboring population only exacerbated white apathy toward Indigenous women's reproduction. In instances in which Indigenous women terminated their own pregnancies or killed their own infants, criminal prosecution seemed immaterial considering the early employment of enslaved labor.

This general apathy toward women's reproduction as a mechanism of growing the laboring population seems to have extended to enslaved Africans in the sixteenth century, suggesting that the natural increase of laboring populations was not a principal concern in early colonial Cuba. A 1526 royal decree (*real cédula*) proposed rewarding enslaved Africans for their loyalty and service to whites with the right to marry (an enslaved woman) and monetary compensation after "serving a certain time" and even recommended that the wife and children be declared free.[36] Such an ordinance would have essentially treated enslaved Africans as potential settlers, but it is unclear what effect, if any, it had on colonial practice in Cuba. In fact, slaveholders in the sixteenth-century Spanish Caribbean may have interpreted such an ordinance in ways that discouraged slave marriage, fearing that the sacrament might free their slaves.[37]

It appears that whatever confusion over the hereditary nature of slave status was cleared up by the mid-sixteenth century, affirming the principle, inherited from Roman law, of *partus sequitur ventrem*, that a child's status follows that of its mother. Such appeared to be the case in a 1563 law included in the Leyes Nuevas, which afforded Spaniards who had children with enslaved women the right to *purchase* the child's freedom and gave priority for sales to parents over other parties.[38] This seemingly haphazard array of mandates suggests the lack of a clear policy toward the reproduction of enslaved women in early colonial Cuba. So long as slave owners could obtain royal licenses to acquire new slaves via the transatlantic slave trade, there was little material incentive to protect enslaved women's reproduction.

White Women's Reproduction in Law and Practice

A dearth of recorded abortion and infanticide cases for much of the early colonial period suggests that impunity surrounding these crimes also extended to white women who practiced fertility control. However, in contrast to the complete disregard colonial authorities had for the reproductive violence afflicting laboring populations, white women's ability to avoid prosecution did not stem from apathy toward the fate of white infants. On the contrary, colonial authorities expressed growing concern over the reproduction of the island's white population following the mid-sixteenth-century consolidation of Spanish rule in Cuba—first in the health and welfare of impoverished women, and later over the fate of unwanted white infants. This attention toward white women's fertility makes sense given the colonial project to foster white population growth. However, even as the draconian legal statutes against abortion and infanticide were implicitly directed at harnessing white women's reproductive potential, white women's fertility control practices rarely prompted police investigation, and even more seldomly landed in the courts. Indeed, between the late eighteenth and early nineteenth centuries, only a small number of infanticide cases, and even fewer abortion cases, ever made it before a judge. Convictions for these offenses remained even more unusual.[39]

If colonial authorities were so concerned with white population growth, then why did laws criminalizing abortion and infanticide result in similar impunity across racial lines? That the colonial state remained relatively weak and limited through the sixteenth and seventeenth centuries does not explain the absence of fertility crimes cases when courts were hearing cases for other crimes. Instead, it is more probable that white women evaded prosecution for fertility crimes in part due to disparities between the letter of the law and popular understandings of pregnancy and childbirth.

For all but the final decades of the colonial period, the crime of abortion, though explicitly recognized by the law, remained largely beyond the reach of criminal courts or ecclesiastical tribunals. In part, this impunity owed to the limitations in scientific knowledge of pregnancy and reliance on spiritual concepts such as ensoulment and animation. Prior to 1869, termination of pregnancy after ensoulment—that is, the process through which the fetus developed a soul—was punishable by excommunication, according to canon law. However, ensoulment remained largely undefined through much of the colonial period, sometimes invoking the concept of animation, an early stage of ensoulment in which a fetus acquired a rudimentary "nutritive" soul, though not yet a "rational" one.[40] According to Aristotle, animation occurred forty to ninety days after conception, depending on the fetus's gender, a notion that continued to influence Catholic thinking through the eighteenth century. In the late eighteenth century, some theologians began to posit that ensoulment could occur as early as conception, a belief that materialized in some parts of Latin America in an obsession with baptizing unborn fetuses and even surgically extracting them from their deceased mothers' bodies to perform the sacrament.[41]

The murky and shifting spiritual terrain surrounding pregnancy complicated the enforcement of laws criminalizing abortion. Roughly aligning with Catholic thought, the Siete Partidas distinguished between abortions committed before and after fetal animation. Although the precise definition of an animated fetus remained debatable, Italian priest Thomas Aquinas and others argued for delayed animation—the theory that an embryo does not have a rational soul and therefore is not yet alive. Abortion of an animated fetus merited capital punishment; abortion of an inanimate fetus or embryo was punishable by five years' banishment. Also relying on the woman's knowledge of her pregnancy, this law afforded at least four months to terminate pregnancy before incurring the maximum penalty.[42]

The Siete Partidas theoretically distinguished between abortion and infanticide based on the fetus's estimated gestational age. The crime of infanticide required the infant to be sufficiently developed to have a "human form" (as opposed to a "monstrous" shape) and survive long enough to be deemed alive—a period ranging from twenty-four hours to ten days. Nevertheless, interpretations of the law evinced ongoing confusion about the practical difference between abortion and infanticide, and between a fetus and a newborn. Law 13 of the Toro (Bull Laws), promulgated in 1505, clarified the distinction between infants who were killed after birth and fetuses that were aborted. If the infant was born prior to term, as indicated by the date of the marriage (presumably the only time when conception could legitimately begin), then the birth was not considered "natural or legitimate." The law defined "abortive births" as those in which the infant died fewer than twenty-four hours after expulsion from the uterus and without baptism.[43] Infants who were born "completely alive," lived at least twenty-four hours, and were baptized before death were said to be legitimately born, rather than expelled through abortion or miscarriage. Spanish laws defined viability of the fetus as necessary in order for the infant to have any rights—a notion that was common to most laws governing abortion and infanticide in Western Europe and China.[44]

Given early modern medical knowledge, these distinctions between embryo, fetus, and infant, and between not yet alive, alive, and deceased, relied almost exclusively on women's bodily knowledge and experiences. In essence, the only indication of pregnancy, besides a woman's own word, was the time since last menstruation (although amenorrhea is not necessarily indicative of pregnancy), and quickening, the point in a pregnancy when a woman could feel fetal movement—typically between the fourth and the sixth month after conception. By extension, the legal distinction between infanticide and abortion also remained malleable. Even as the medical notion of viability (the ability of a fetus to survive independently outside the womb), came to prevail over spiritual concepts of ensoulment in the eighteenth and nineteenth centuries, police and jurists seemed to conflate abortion and infanticide and often used the terms "fetus" and "infant" interchangeably.

Authorities also blurred the distinctions between ordinary reproductive events and criminal acts. It was often difficult to distinguish the intentional murder of an infant from stillbirth and neonatal death, particularly given the paltry medical knowledge on pregnancy and childbirth at the time. The intentional death of a viable fetus through voluntary expulsion from the uterus was criminalized as abortion, though existing science did not offer a reliable way to distinguish between spontaneous miscarriage and induced abortion.[45]

Further adding to the confusion, pregnancy and childbirth were regarded as private matters, to be managed by women and their female family members within the home. As one Cuban physician later explained, Cuban women traditionally preferred to entrust themselves to another woman during their pregnancies and labors, rather than "exposing themselves to the glances of a person of the opposite [sex], even if they were dressed in the character of a physician." Generally, the woman's mother or another woman who had already birthed a child would attend to her, and from this tradition emerged the profession of midwifery.[46] Such private matters presented obvious challenges when it came to evidence of criminality. As one legal theorist noted, evidence of infanticide was notoriously "imperfect and doubtful," thwarting most investigations if suspects could even be identified.[47]

These spiritual and juridical uncertainties about pregnancy and childbirth afforded women some leeway when it came to their reproductive choices. In fact, women in the early stages of pregnancy commonly understood their condition as a retained menses, a medical ailment that could be corrected with herbal remedies. These folk remedies often included juniper, cinnamon, saffron, rue, aloe, among other ingredients understood to possess abortifacient properties.[48] Rather than provoking an abortion, these remedies were understood to restore a woman's "obstructed" or "suppressed" menstruation and by extension to restore her health.[49] Natural abortifacients remained widely available and were later incorporated into a variety of elixirs marketed to cure "diseases peculiar to women" by "bringing down the menses," among other medical miracles.[50] Some of the nineteenth-century drug names marketed included Bismatriz, Las Píldoras de Ao, and Purgante Leroy No. 4.[51] "Abortion," as we now understand it to be the intentional termination of a pregnancy, regardless of the time elapsed since conception, remained murky legal terrain into the late colonial period.[52] Given that the Catholic Church's formal position of life since conception did not emerge until Pope Pius IX's 1869 *Apostolicae Sedis moderationi* bull, women who practiced fertility control in early stages of pregnancy typically avoided legal sanctions.[53]

Honor and the Racial Logic of White Women's Impunity

On top of these conceptual and logistical reasons for generalized impunity, white women in particular likely evaded criminalization because of their privileged positions in the patriarchy. Paternalistic attitudes casting white women as weak, dependent, irrational, and unintelligent contributed to men's desire to downplay their indiscretions, rather than punishing them. Lawmakers and judges may have experienced significant cognitive dissonance between their professional duty, as jurists, to prosecute and sentence offenders and their symbolic roles as patriarchs, white male heads of household obliged to protect white women.[54]

Perhaps more than anything else, the impetus behind this paternalistic protection also hinged on the assumption that white women practiced fertility control primarily, if not exclusively, to salvage their honor. From this vantage, white women were little more than victims of the failures of their own patriarchal protectors to shield them from the predations of other men. After all, colonial gender ideologies premised women's honor on sexual purity, a condition with evident implications for reproduction.[55] The concept of honor forced women into a relation of patriarchal dependence, conditioning their economic survival and social value on marriage with a man who could provide for and protect them and any children they might bear. Enforcing women's virginity until marriage, and fidelity within it, was understood to guarantee that a woman bore children fathered by her husband, and thus that the correct man assumed the financial burden. The related concept of legitimacy—often conditioned on whiteness in colonial Latin America, thus rewarded children conceived within marriage with favorable legal status, while the label of illegitimacy punished both women and their out-of-wedlock offspring for sex considered illicit.[56]

However, chastity until marriage followed by marital fidelity was not always possible. Certainly, it was often unavailable to women and girls living in more precarious circumstances. Given the stark gendered relations of power defining colonial societies, including Cuba, seduction, kidnapping, and deflowering by predatory men constantly threatened honorable women's sexual purity.[57] Even though abduction and elopement cases sometimes stemmed from women's agency over their romantic decisions and intimate lives, these actions could still wield destructive consequences for the woman as well as her family.

For unmarried women, pregnancy became the physical symbol of illicit sex. It marked an unwed woman's nonconformity to prevailing codes of female honor and cast her as dishonorable. If marriage did not immediately follow, pregnancy could have catastrophic social consequences, destroying a woman's reputation, her family's social standing, her eligibility for marriage, her entire livelihood. Typically the woman was saddled with the social and economic consequences of extramarital and otherwise dishonorable sex acts, while the father of the child often escaped the consequences.[58] These risks meant that some women had ample reason to hide or terminate their pregnancies or destroy the newborns.

This fundamental dilemma between the lived realities of women's intimate lives and the gendered social expectations placed on them became so definitive in the Spanish Empire that it inspired a well-known sonnet:

> Dos tiranos juzgaron de tu suerte,
> Amor contra el honor te dio la vida,
> Honor contra el amor te dio la muerte.[59]

> Two tyrants judged your fate,
> Love over honor, she gave you life,
> Honor over love, she gave you death.

The sonnet reflected a broader concern among elite families in colonial Cuba that illicit conception pitted a woman's supposedly natural "feelings of motherly love" against her obligation to defend her own and her family's honor.[60] Women who allowed their "carnal passions" to overcome their concern for honor could be tempted to hide the shame of the pregnancy by committing infanticide.

In this context, the question of whether or not to punish abortion and infanticide pivoted on a tug-of-war between the socially constructed demands of honor and the moral outrage prompted by infanticide. Spanish legal thought erred on the side of paternalistic protection of honorable women. White women also likely benefited from a general attitude of paternalism and pity, given the inherent conflict between prevailing social expectations that they remain sexually pure and the omnipresent threat of their sexual victimization. Although the letter of Spanish penal law would not explicitly codify honor as an attenuating circumstance until the nineteenth century, as we will see in chapter 4, it is evident that the concept shaped the application of earlier statutes. After all, canon law afforded leniency for honor-induced infanticide. This exception likely extended to single women who conceived out of wedlock.[61]

Cuba was certainly not unique in the dearth of criminal abortion and infanticide cases during the early colonial period.[62] What distinguished Cuba's colonial context from the metropolitan one on which the laws were founded, however, was that race in large part defined which women were understood to be honorable. Honor was synonymous with whiteness in early colonial Cuba. Thus the protection from prosecution on the basis of honor would have only been available to white women—not to Indigenous or African-descended women. So long as the white population remained wealthy and unequivocally privileged, sexual or reproductive indiscretions could be handled privately, without damaging the woman's or the family's public reputation. Thus, white women who fell under patriarchal authority in early colonial Cuba were insulated from external interventions from the state, such as a criminal process.[63]

However, as Cuba's impoverished white population expanded in the seventeenth century, whiteness became necessary but insufficient to signify honor. Multiple officials commented on the lack of social distance separating even the most privileged sons of conquistadores from Havana's landless poor.[64] With intimate unions typically more flexible and racial boundaries more porous among the lower classes, the physical and social proximity between the growing poor white population and the free population of color threatened to undermine the colonial social hierarchy through miscegenation. The question was not whether such intimacy would occur, but how authorities could manage it while still preserving the racial order underpinning the colony, especially as the gender imbalance among the white population remained significant.

Poverty coincided also with the growing prevalence of single white women and unwed white mothers. Thus, an increasingly urgent need emerged to provide an outlet for white women to shed the physical markers of their dishonor. Rather than giving impetus to penal approaches to women's fertility control, these paternalistic attitudes toward white women contributed to the emergence of a fledgling network of public services for white women and their children. In the absence of patriarchal authority, the state readily intervened, though not with law, but rather with charity.

Poor Women and the Patriarchal State

In 1665, ecclesiastical authorities established Havana's first hospital for women. Charitable institutions generally dedicated to poor relief proliferated in the Spanish Empire in the sixteenth century, following a series of poor laws aimed at controlling begging and vagrancy. Havana's San Juan de Dios hospital (formerly Hospital Real de S. Felipe y Santiago), established in 1603, formed part of this tradition. Those efforts expanded to target specific populations of poor people, including women and later orphans.[65] San Francisco de Paula Women's Hospital was founded at the peak of this expanded charitable project.

It was constructed in a marginal neighborhood on the southeastern part of the city, a liminal area considered unhealthy due to its proximity to Havana Bay. This neighborhood was already home to small property owners of diverse racial backgrounds. The hospital was bounded by parcels owned by men and women of African descent, including the *moreno* Antonio Jimenez and his wife, Gracia Ramírez, whose small estate and humble guano house wound up in the hands of ecclesiastical authorities charged with constructing the hospital. Among other African-descended property owners in the vicinity were morena Antonia Bañón, and a mulata by the name of María.[66]

The hospital began as a modest enterprise, directed by a single priest acting as chaplain, and staffed by a nun and an enslaved woman. Starting with just four beds, the institution's tiny staff provided free services to a growing population of impoverished women residing in Havana. As a point of comparison, around the mid-seventeenth century, when the women's hospital was established, San Juan de Dios Hospital boasted one hundred beds, thirty clergy, and treated eight hundred patients annually, though some estimates placed that number in the thousands due to immense population growth and port arrivals.[67]

San Francisco de Paula was established during a period of significant population growth in Havana. The number of households in the city skyrocketed over the second half of the sixteenth century, from under 50,000 households in the mid-1550s to nearly 600,000 around 1610.[68] Much of this population growth derived from male migration. Women represented just 20 to 30 percent of Europeans arriving to Cuba, as Spain continued to rely on individual initiative to fuel migration in the seventeenth century rather than implementing family migration programs to populate its colonies, as the Dutch and Portuguese did.[69] Even as men continued to outnumber women, marriage and family formation over Cuba's first century of colonial rule seems to have supplemented female migration to the point that the number of women in Havana justified the establishment of a new hospital.

San Francisco de Paula was not strictly a "medical" institution in the contemporary sense of the term. The provision of actual medical services was limited by the relatively inchoate state of medical knowledge, the limited number of medical personnel, and lack of training and licensing in early colonial Cuba. The majority of doctors in Cuba during the seventeenth and eighteenth centuries had earned bachelor degrees in Spain. However, licensing requirements were not firmly implemented on the island until the reestablishment in 1711 of the Real Tribunal del Protomedicato, a body of physicians appointed to regulate medical practitioners, similar to a medical licensing board. The eventual establishment of this body followed nearly a century of unregulated medical practice following the demise of an earlier protomedicato in 1632.[70] The seventeenth and early eighteenth centuries were characterized by a shortage of trained doctors in Havana. In a 1664 petition to the metropolitan government, colonial authorities requested more doctors, claiming that only one was then serving the entire city. Ten years later, local authorities reiterated their request, which remained unattended until 1728.[71] Aspiring Cuban doctors had to travel to Mexico to study medicine prior to the establishment of Havana's first university.[72]

The establishment of the Real y Pontificia Universidad de San Gerónimo de la Habana in 1728 marked a major milestone, contributing to a gradual increase in the number of Cuban-trained surgeons. However, limitations were pronounced when it came to women's health. Formal training in obstetrics and gynecology was not in the medical curriculum until the late nineteenth century, leading to significant gaps in knowledge over women's bodies among the very sectors increasingly claiming authority over them.[73]

Nor did San Francisco de Paula serve as a maternity hospital. Pregnancy, childbirth, and puerperal care remained the domain of female family members or midwives, who most often visited their clients in their homes well into the twentieth century. Birth attendants and midwives were almost exclusively female until the nineteenth century. Metropolitan laws governing the profession of midwifery dated back to the fifteenth century but had little impact in Cuba, where one of the first recognized practitioners was an Indigenous woman known as Mariana Nava, who obtained a license without formal education or examination in 1609.[74] At least ten white women were known to practice midwifery in seventeenth-century Havana, albeit without formal title. The protomedicato certified the first woman to practice midwifery by examination only in 1698. Nevertheless, African-descended women quickly came to dominate the midwifery profession, even as they remained excluded from formal examinations and licensing. By 1750, a royal decree required midwives to obtain formal training and licensing, and even though the mandate remained unfulfilled for decades, it marked the beginning of a gradual struggle by white male surgeons and physicians to claim authority over pregnancy and birthing care, in which San Francisco de Paula features prominently.[75]

If the hospital addressed women's reproductive disorders at all, it was likely limited to severe conditions, distressed pregnancies, difficult or obstructed births, and puerperal complications. Given obstetric knowledge at the time, such conditions would have been mostly untreatable even by the most skilled physicians.[76] Childbirth was treacherous for even the most privileged women, including royalty.[77] The most vulnerable impoverished women would have fared much worse on arrival at the fledgling San Francisco de Paula, in what many disregarded as a colonial backwater. If women went to the hospital for birth-related complications, they likely understood the dire state of their condition and it is probable they sought spiritual salvation for their fetus rather than medical care. The eighteenth-century publication of several manuals on cesarean section in Spanish America support this interpretation. Such major surgery was almost certainly a death sentence until well into the latter nineteenth century, and the procedure was often performed when the laboring woman had already died or was believed to have died. The purpose of the surgery, then, was not to save the life of the mother, or even the fetus, but rather to extract the fetus from the mother's womb in time to administer the sacrament of baptism and save the infant's soul, according to Roman Catholic belief.[78]

An early constitution of San Francisco de Paula explicitly prohibited hospital staff from admitting patients with contagious diseases, though it required them to care for patients who contracted those illnesses while already in the hospital. If fully enforced, this rule would have excluded large numbers of women suffering from early colonial Havana's most common afflictions—smallpox, measles, leprosy, and especially yellow fever.[79] Rather than enter the women's hospital, women infected with contagious disease were ejected from the city, in conformity with the Leyes Nuevas. During the yellow fever epidemic of 1649, patients suspected of the illness were sent several miles outside Havana to a few houses designated for contagious patients.[80] By 1714, the San Lázaro hospital for lepers was established outside the city walls.

Diseases of poverty likely accounted for a significant share of the hospital's patients. San Francisco de Paula was established around the same time as colonial authorities began construction on the city walls in 1674. A major investment that lasted into the eighteenth century, these physical barriers aimed to fortify Havana against the external attacks that had plagued the city throughout its early history. But such major infrastructure projects concentrated large numbers of male laborers within a relatively confined space. Moreover, the hospital was located mere blocks from the militia barracks, which in 1681 housed more than eight hundred men (fig. 1.2). The growing male population of soldiers and laborers in Havana probably also fueled the proliferation of prostitution. Syphilis and other venereal diseases thus likely contributed to the hospital's patient load.[81] The Havana city council minutes regularly mentioned the scourge of tuberculosis in the sixteenth and seventeenth centuries as well.[82]

Indeed, the surviving evidence paints a bleak picture for the prospects of San Francisco de Paula patients. In its early years, the actual medical care available to patients appears to have been very limited. In fact, although the founding documents mention a doctor's obligation to visit patients at the hospital each morning, the institution may not have had a designated medical practitioner on staff until the 1760s.[83] It is likely that that women arriving to the hospital were already severely ill and came there to die. Only in 1695 was Havana's first institution for convalescence established, suggesting low expectations for survival for much of the seventeenth century.

According to hospital records, an average of seventy-five patients died each year in the final decades of the eighteenth century. Surviving data do not include the patient's race, cause of death, or even the total number of patients admitted each year, so we can draw only limited conclusions from these records. However, the elevated number of deaths in 1783 and between 1791 and 1795 coincided with outbreaks of yellow fever and smallpox, which suggests that the hospital likely overlooked its own prohibition on the treatment of epidemic disease.[84] Moreover, the number of available beds during this period ranged between twelve in the early 1770s to seventy-eight at the end of the century, so we can assume that mortality rates were fairly high. Data from the mid-nineteenth century suggest that less than one-third of the patients who were admitted to the hospital were released alive within the year, and this rate would have likely been worse a century earlier, before the publication of early midwifery texts, the smallpox vaccine, and the invention of the stethoscope. From these rough sketches, it appears that much of the work the hospital's ecclesiastical staff did for its impoverished patients was less medical treatment and more end-of-life

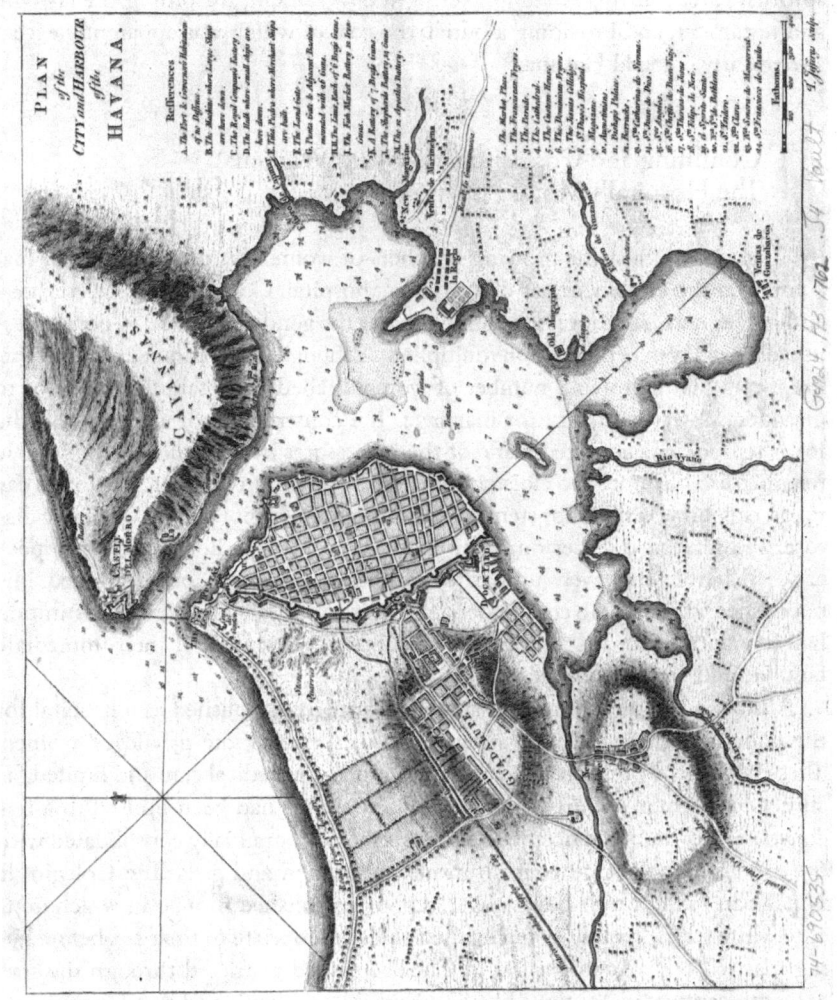

FIGURE 1.2. Map of Havana showing location of San Francisco de Paula Hospital, circa 1762. Thomas Jefferys, plan of the city and harbor of the Havana (London, 1762). Library of Congress, Geography and Map Division.

spiritual care. It involved administering the sacraments, recording the last will and testament, and providing a burial, the cost of which was apparently excessive in early colonial Havana.[85]

Confining and Correcting Wayward Women: The Hospital's Moral Function

It was not just the growing numbers of women residing in Havana that compelled the establishment of a women's hospital. Colonial and ecclesiastical authorities may have developed an inkling of the gendered effects of poverty, especially as Havana's population multiplied. Although population data are sparse, it appears that a growing number of women hailed from families too poor to provide a dowry sufficient for marriage. The construction of a convent in the 1630s temporarily assuaged some of these pressures by providing an honorable religious establishment to cloister unmarried women.[86] However, starting in the 1640s, economic difficulties stemming from unstable labor supply, epidemic disease, and increased duties on sugar drove more Havana households into poverty.[87] Whether they were unmarried, orphaned, widowed, or abandoned, impoverished women who could not gain admission to such a religious institution had few options for sustaining their livelihood, particularly if their immediate family could not or would not assist.

Although San Francisco de Paula was formally established as a hospital for the poor, it initially included separate wards serving more privileged women. These wards likely reflected the meager options for medical care and limited facilities for women in early colonial Havana, which had been limited to a few convents. However, the hospital's focus on the poor gradually consolidated with the establishment of other institutions for women and girls. The Colegio de Niñas San Francisco de Sales was a "school" established in 1680 in which non-elite white girls as young as ten learned skills appropriate to their sex before being married off.[88] As migration to Cuba remained restricted through the seventeenth century, institutions like San Francisco de Paula and San Francisco de Sales demonstrated that colonial and metropolitan authorities took seriously the role of women in the colony's demographic future.

The hospital also appears to have warehoused women whose conduct violated colonial gender norms. Because the city had no penal institution for women until the Casa de Recogidas San Juan de Nepomuceno was established in 1746, the hospital became a place of confinement for *recogidas* (lit. removed), a term encompassing a wide range of women who were institutionalized, usually against their will for their gendered transgressions. By 1688, the recogidas ward also contained several divorced women.[89] Some of these women were committed by their own families, when their husbands or fathers deemed them insolent to male authority, or otherwise incorrigible.[90] Others were sentenced by ecclesiastical tribunals to reclusion due to criminal conduct or immoral behavior, such as prostitution and adultery. In that regard, the hospital doubled as a Magdalene house. In 1674, for instance, Bishop Gabriel Díaz Vara Calderón reported that he had confined twenty-one mulatas at the hospital for being "public sinners." However, these women managed to escape the institution within several months.[91]

Thus, for much of the hospital's first century of existence, the women interned at the San Francisco de Paula hospital comprised a mix of infirm women too poor to afford private care and likely too sick to expect recovery, and women whose lifestyles transgressed moral expectations. The coexistence of these two populations alludes to the hospital's dual function in colonial society. It provided relief to impoverished women, who lacked sufficient patriarchal protection from fathers or husbands. Simultaneously, the hospital confined women whose conduct threatened the social and moral order of colonial society. This dual purpose reflected early modern beliefs about the entwinement of moral and physical ailments, particularly when it came to women. Drawing on Iberian precedents, San Francisco de Paula likely served as a place of both relief and confinement, of treatment and correction.[92] By removing both these populations from the public sphere, this institution helped cultivate and sustain a physically and morally sound population of women, whose role remained wedded to marriage and motherhood. In that regard, San Francisco de Paula laid an important foundation to ensure that colonial charity supported and advanced the colonial order.[93]

Given the institution's moralizing and corrective premise, it is no coincidence that race, class, and legal status played a paramount role in determining if women could access the hospital's services, and the kind of care they received. The most pronounced boundary, from the outset, was that of legal status. The hospital served both white and nonwhite patients, so long as they were not slaves. The inclusion of free women of color suggests that racialized anxieties about the alleged excessive fertility of Havana's free Black population had not yet emerged. That enslaved women were denied admission to the hospital is also significant. There was certainly a precedent for discrimination in access to charity, dating back to fifteenth-century Castile, which pegged worthiness for assistance to honor.[94] In the colonial context, however, the basis for discrimination was less honorability and more legal status and, later, race, as we will see in chapter 2.

The exclusion of enslaved women from the only institution focused on women's health set a clear boundary on state involvement in the regulation of slavery. By this exclusion, colonial authorities assigned the health and survival of enslaved women as the responsibility and expense of the owner. Using the logic of private property, this rejection of public responsibility over enslaved women implicitly amounts to a lack of financial support for the survival and reproduction of the enslaved population, by then the most important labor force on the island. But excluding enslaved women also served as a commentary on racial and legal limits of both womanhood and worthiness for assistance. In fact, the institution's early governing documents include an explicit prohibition on admitting enslaved women, even if their owners agreed to pay the costs.[95]

Although the hospital's formal policies maintained rigid eligibility restrictions barring enslaved women, the realities of the hospital appeared much more complex. Surviving documentation suggests that, in addition to patients and recogidas, the hospital also confined a third group of women known as *depositadas*. These were women of African descent, usually enslaved, who were sentenced to forced labor on behalf of the state as punishment for a crime, preventative incarceration during criminal investigations, refuge from abusive owners or during legal disputes with their owners, or even as a form of "treatment" for women found to be suffering from "hysteria." Tribunals and courts often designated charitable institutions, like San Francisco de Paula, in addition to public works and infrastructure projects, as the *depósitos*, or places for such women to be deposited.

Interning depositadas in the hospital established a precedent for extracting unfree labor to supplement the small staff of charitable institutions, which consistently struggled with meager budgets and ever-increasing demand. By the eighteenth and especially nineteenth centuries (see chapter 4 and 5), it became standard practice to deposit enslaved women, *emancipadas*—women legally freed following the capture of clandestine slave ships after 1817—and even free women of color in charitable institutions. In this way, the early use of the hospital as a gendered penal institution normalized the subsequent use of the courts, and especially criminal conviction, as mechanisms to control and extract labor, primarily directed at women of African descent.[96]

The uneasy coexistence of white women patients and recogidas and Black depositadas provided a powerful source of friction over the institution's early history. Since the mid-eighteenth century, many reform efforts focused on negotiating the hospital's mission as a charity hospital for the care of poor women regardless of race with its role as a colonial institution implicitly charged with upholding racial and social hierarchies. In the 1750s, for instance, institutional authorities advocated for a major expansion project that would more than double the hospital's capacity by adding seven more beds. The proposed expansion would not only serve more women but would provide services appropriate to patients' race and status. Institutional authorities argued that the expansion was necessary in order to properly separate white women patients from the "inferior ones," an argument that royal authorities certified in 1760.[97] The expansion plans included creating an entirely new wing of the hospital, upstairs, exclusively for the care of white women. Women of African descent would be relegated to the old wing. The project also included plans to build two additional spaces apart from the patient wards. One of these was a separate living quarters for the head nurse (*maestra*). The other was a holding area for the "depositadas."[98] Although the English occupation of Havana (1762–63) disrupted the construction, the project was eventually completed after Havana returned to Spanish control following the Treaty of Paris in 1763.

Just a few years later, another reform effort aimed to distance the hospital from its de facto penal function, a shift with racial as much as moral undertones. In a 1761 petition, institutional authorities sought to expel depositadas from the hospital, a reform they justified in economic and moral terms—not only were these women prisoners a burden on the hospital's modest coffers, but they also allegedly perturbed the institution's moral climate to the detriment of its white patients. The chaplain believed that providing "decent separation that it is just to have between some and others," as well as housing the women prisoners elsewhere, was necessary for maintaining "better order" at the hospital. He also insinuated that removing the prisoners would free up resources and space to treat the growing number of women in that city "obliged by their poverty and abandonment to seek their health and remedy at this House," the only institution founded to serve women. Under the chaplaincy of Rafael del Castillo y Sucre (1762–73), depositadas were removed and placed in jails around the city.[99]

While institutional authorities struggled to uphold racial distinctions and an air of moral rectitude, the realities of Cuba's colonial slave society complicated these efforts. By the end of the eighteenth century, for instance, the intendant mandated that the hospital serve refugees from St. Domingue, which had erupted in revolution in 1791, as well as admitting women classified as royal slaves; this requirement contradicted the prohibition on admitting slaves.[100] Institutional authorities later successfully petitioned the Real Hacienda to pay for the care of royal slaves.[101]

By 1812, the institutional constitution formalized existing policies prohibiting the admission of enslaved women and codifying the racial segregation of patients. Not only were white patients physically separated and located above (on the second floor) patients of African descent, but their hospital admissions were recorded in a separate book. It also appears that female visitors were allowed, presumably to keep company and elevate the spirits of patients, while male visitors were prohibited. The 1812 constitution makes a conditional allowance for the admission of enslaved women given "some powerful reason of need," seemingly in a servile capacity for the care and company of white patients.[102] Even before this regulation, the hospital admitted at least one enslaved woman, who died after twenty-three days. The hospital then successfully petitioned the government to pay the costs of her hospital stay.[103]

With women prisoners theoretically no longer housed at the hospital, institutional authorities evidently saw a need for supplemental labor. The 1812 constitution also formalized the use of enslaved women's labor in the everyday operation of the hospital. According to the constitution, two enslaved women labored at the hospital—one assigned to the kitchen and the other to washing, cleaning, and other patient care. The article describing the duties of the hospital's enslaved female labor force also notes that, in the event that one of the enslaved women should die, another should be acquired to fulfill the same duties.

The hospital's early status-based exclusion from charity offers a counterpoint to the pronatalism that some scholars have argued guided early colonial attitudes toward enslaved people as early as the sixteenth century. It is true that, by the late seventeenth century, regulations explicitly discouraged slave owners from impeding slave marriage and from selling spouses away from each other.[104] However, there was a gap between law and practice. There is ample evidence of brutal violence against enslaved women in the seventeenth century, evincing that slave owners not only cared little for the health or well-being of these women but also discounted their humanity. In the 1630s, a female slave owner faced criminal charges for whipping an enslaved woman to death.[105] A remarkably similar case occurred in 1681, when another female slave owner whipped her enslaved woman to death as she begged for mercy from the Virgin Mary.[106] In the second instance, no record survives of criminal charges being filed, suggesting a declining value placed on enslaved women's life. Gendered violence extended to men, as well, for instance, in the use of castration as a punishment for enslaved men.[107]

The reproductive consequences of this violence on enslaved women and men was stark. A late seventeenth-century census of Jesús del Monte, a Havana neighborhood just outside the city walls reveals just four babies born to a population of 950 enslaved people. As a point of comparison, the same neighborhood counted 122 babies born to the 551 free inhabitants (both Spanish and free people of color).[108] Although the data do not include the gender ratios of those populations, the miniscule number of babies born to enslaved women in that community suggests that placing the health of enslaved women in slave owners' hands had a terrible impact on the lives and fertility of that population. Banning enslaved women from admission to the hospital formed part of this broader apathy toward their reproductive lives.

Colonial authorities in Cuba took the lives of some infants more seriously than others. The impunity with which Spanish conquistadores harmed pregnant Native women and their babies demonstrated that Spain's evangelical mission neglected the souls of Native fetuses or infants. Although more research is needed to illuminate the reproductive experiences of Indigenous women during Cuba's early colonial period, a brief survey of Spanish chronicles shows that low fertility rates likely played a significant role in the inability of the Native population to recover from demographic collapse. The impact of the Spanish Conquest and colonization on Native populations foreshadowed a deeper apathy that would manifest with regard to the reproductive potential of laboring populations until the late eighteenth century.

The seventeenth-century establishment of the San Francisco de Paula Women's Hospital marked an important turning point in the charitable treatment of women in colonial Cuba. It not only evinced a concern with women's morbidity and mortality, it also evinced the growing importance of status distinctions in who was deemed worthy of relief. Moreover, the hospital established a precedent for the blurred boundaries between illness, criminality, and labor extraction that would come to define charitable institutions in colonial Cuba.

Though in its early years the hospital's impact on women's reproduction may have been limited to enforcing women's morality and social roles, San Francisco de Paula cast a long shadow in the centuries to come over the reproductive lives of many poor women. The hospital building itself and its plaza became key sites of maternal and infant death and abandonment. In the same vein, San Francisco de Paula became central to development of obstetric and gynecological knowledge in Cuba. In the 1820s, it became the site of Cuba's first midwife training school, the Academia de Parteras (see chapter 4), and by the 1880s, Cuban medical students began practical obstetrical and gynecology rotations at the hospital for the first time (see chapter 7).

The hospital's most immediate impact, though, lay in the moral, correctional, and punitive agendas embedded in its operation. The hospital simultaneously privileged the relief of honorable (white) women and relied on the labor of Black women. These racial and legal restrictions on access to charity and laboral practices would define subsequent charitable institutions, including the Casa de Expósitos.

CHAPTER TWO

From Unwanted Infants to Useful Vassals
Institutional and Legal Protections for Expósitos and Their Racial Limits in the Eighteenth Century

Shortly after the women's hospital was established, ecclesiastical authorities sounded the alarm over abandoned infants.[1] Throughout the sixteenth and seventeenth centuries, it was common for infants to be abandoned at the doorsteps or gates of convents, churches, and public hospitals, like San Francisco de Paula. Private residences also became sites of abandonment. However, by the late seventeenth century, as Havana's impoverished population continued to grow, abandonment in public places—including streets, plazas, gardens, parks, and beaches—was more pronounced and visible.

Infant abandonment appeared to be socially frowned on but was not criminally prosecuted. Moral outrage over infant abandonment stemmed from the naturalization of motherhood: mothers who abandoned their babies were said to violate "the laws of nature and love" that they should feel toward the "fruit of their wombs." In rejecting motherhood, they were "ignoring their conscience." The helplessness and innocence of infants further accentuated the heinousness of abandonment: "having hands, they cannot eat, having a mouth, they cannot ask, and having feet, they do not know how to walk." Any attempt to expose "the lives and souls of their infant children, unable to do for themselves, to so many risks" was considered a violation of a woman's natural motherly duty.[2]

Harrowing accounts began to circulate by the late sixteenth and early seventeenth centuries about the perils unwanted infants faced.[3] Stories abounded of live infants left to die in the dangerous morning dew and the discovery of tiny corpses mangled by wild animals. Many women allegedly carried their babies to vacant fields. There were "many and frequent cases" of women tossing babies "while still alive into wells" or into the sea. Still others abandoned their infants "out on the doors of certain houses, leaving them exposed for the dogs to tear to pieces and eat."[4] According to ecclesiastical authorities, it was common for women to abandon their unwanted babies in public places, where their exposure to the elements often accelerated their early demise. These unwanted infants abandoned by their parents became known as expósitos (lit. exposed ones).

The term *expósito* existed in the Iberian Peninsula prior the colonization of Cuba and had historically been a source of intense social stigma. Although parents abandoned children for a wide range of reasons, one of the most acknowledged was that the child resulted from premarital, adulterous, or sacrilegious sex. Consequently, the expósito label became associated with dishonor, illegitimacy, and, in the colonial context, with racial impurity. All these presumed stains on the expósito's reputation posed legal obstacles in education, employment, and social acceptance among elites. Seventeenth-century royal decrees suggest that even the most fortunate expósitos in the Spanish Empire, excluded from formal education, could hope only for a life of labor or impressment.[5]

Official attitudes toward expósitos began to shift by the eighteenth century, with expósitos in Havana gaining important institutional and legal protections. The Casa de Expósitos, a charitable institution designed to save unwanted infants, was established, and the metropolitan state later codified certain legal rights for expósitos. With these and other reforms, Cuban scholar José Torres Pico argues, the status of expósitos improved markedly through the eighteenth and early nineteenth centuries.[6]

However, if the restrictions on access to the women's hospital were any indication, it is probable that some babies benefited from these protections more than others. Institutional records, real cédulas, decrees, and individual petitions by expósitos reveal how both reforms aimed to save the lives of white infants specifically. The Casa de Expósitos explicitly prohibited the admission of infants of African descent, while exploiting and regulating the labor of women of African descent in the care of white infants. The extension of key legal protections, moreover, was premised on a racially specific definition of expósitos as white or at least white-passing (seemingly white, *al parecer blanco*). The legal protection of expósitos, including the default racial designation of expósitos as white, coincided with more rigid policing of racial boundaries in access to charity. The exclusion of abandoned African-descended infants from the legal category of expósito and its material benefits aligned with and advanced colonial demographic projects to foster white population growth while also policing the exclusivity of legal whiteness.

To Protect the "Man of the Cradle": The Creation of Havana's Casa de Expósitos

Between the late seventeenth and the early eighteenth centuries, various individuals and groups began to lay the foundation for a charitable institution specifically dedicated to abandoned infants. As early as 1687, Bishop Diego Evelino Hurtado de Compostela founded Cuba's first Casa de Expósitos, at the Nuestra Señora de Belén Church to rescue abandoned infants. The hospital was staffed by women of African descent who were charged with raising and educating unwanted children.⁷ The establishment was short lived, promptly being replaced by the Convento Santa Teresa. After Compostela's death in 1704, his successor, Fray Gerónimo Valdés, undertook to relocate the establishment to "a more populous neighborhood" where it could be more beneficial to the Catholic faith and the state. A royal decree of May 16, 1705, granted approval to establish the new institution.⁸ The following year, colonial administrators established the Department of Abandoned Children (Departmento de Expósitos) and construction began on a building closer to the city walls, on Oficio Street at Ricla Street.

The new institution, the Casa de Expósitos, known colloquially as the Casa Cuna (lit. Cradle House) opened in 1711.⁹ Havana's Casa Cuna emerged as Cuba's first charitable institution specifically dedicated to receiving and caring for infants surrendered by their parents. It was the third such institution in Spanish America, following ones in Lima and Santa Fé de Bogotá.¹⁰

The Casa Cuna significantly expanded the role of the colonial state in managing women's reproduction. Prior to the eighteenth century, state interventions in women's reproduction were largely limited to moral projects aimed at reinforcing heteropatriarchal family through marriage, including the reclusion of impoverished and wayward women at the women's hospital. Although laws criminalized infanticide, there is no evidence that colonial authorities enforced them. As one philanthropist later observed, "the wisest laws are not enough to avoid fatal disasters."¹¹ A charitable institution for unwanted infants offered a way to influence women's reproductive decisions through assistance, rather than the punitive threat of the law.

Indeed, the Casa Cuna offered a noncriminal alternative to abortion, infanticide, and public abandonment. According to Valdés, the institution was "very necessary" considering the great lengths the Havana elite had gone to "conceal the [moral] lapses caused by need or by their own fragility." Rather than punish, the Casa Cuna sought to shield disgraced mothers from the deleterious social consequences of illicit conception by allowing them to safely and confidentially surrender "the innocent and unfortunate children born of frailty, seduction, and poverty."¹² In that way, it seemingly recognized the exorbitant pressures on white women to maintain their public reputation of sexual purity, providing an escape for those who faltered. It also offered mothers a possible future for their infants. Rather than live a life of poverty and disgrace, infants surrendered to the institution would receive basic care: nourishment, clothing, and shelter. They would gain access to certain privileges, including the possibility of education and the surname Valdés in honor of the founder.¹³ Records from the late eighteenth century reveal that a small number of babies were registered in the institution on the day of their birth, suggesting that the Casa provided shelter for unwed pregnant women seeking to give birth in secret.¹⁴

Early on, the hospital was staffed by Black women; the institution also had a church, infants' ward, chaplain's chambers, and wet nurses' quarters.[15] It is unlikely coincidental that the Havana city council recognized the dearth of midwives at the institution and entertained at least two petitions from women (who appear to be of African descent, from Havana) for permission to practice their profession in the city.[16] Given the demographics of midwives in colonial Cuba, the African-descended women staffing the institution were likely a mix of wet nurses, caregivers, and midwives.

Proponents of the Casa Cuna proclaimed its victory over infant abandonment and infanticide. Shortly after the institution opened its doors, Valdés reported that the Casa had "remedied these harms." Within eight months of its opening, six or eight abandoned infants who were being cared for elsewhere were admitted into the institution.[17] Yet, the institution's founding documents reveal clear racial limits to the charitable services it offered. In his petition to the king requesting royal sponsorship, Valdés assured his potential benefactor that the Casa Cuna would serve only white families, excluding "the children of slave women, mulatas, and morenas."[18] In essence, Valdés framed his request for official recognition and financing of the Casa in terms of the exclusive benefits it bestowed on Havana's white population.

The racial exclusions governing the Casa Cuna exposed the demographic anxieties nearly a century prior to the consolidation of plantation slavery at the turn of the nineteenth century. Colonial Havana was an intensely multiracial, multiethnic society from its inception. Slavery had quickly emerged as a central pillar of its economy, wherein enslaved African men and women performed a wide variety of economic tasks.[19] While the number of enslaved Africans in the city continued to grow, a free population of color promptly emerged. As early as the mid-sixteenth century, gendered patterns of manumission and urban economic opportunity ensured that women outnumbered men among the urban free population of color. By one estimate, nearly two-thirds of all slaves manumitted in sixteenth-century Havana were women, most of whom were still of reproductive age when they obtained freedom.[20] Children age five and younger—often of mixed racial status—were also overrepresented among Havana's manumitted population, suggesting that white male slave owners may have freed some of the children they sired with enslaved women.[21] In the context of robust reproduction across racial and legal lines, the gender and age demographics of Havana's population of African descent help explain why Valdés excluded people of color from his pronatalist charity project. Limiting the benefits of social welfare to white infants would advance Spanish colonization of the island by increasing both white women's fertility and white infants' survival.

The Casa Cuna accepted both male and female infants, but a powerful gendered logic undergirded the charitable endeavor. Concerns over cultivating a desirable and productive (white) population meant an implicit gendering of infants as males, future farmers and heads of households.[22] As one Cuban philanthropist mused, "the man of the cradle" had to be protected and nurtured until "age could strengthen him such that he could hold his own."[23] In other words, women's acts of fertility control were understood as directly effecting Cuba's future population, somehow envisioned as male. The masculinization of expósitos eclipsed a broader neglect of female infants through the eighteenth century. Only in the second half of the eighteenth century did colonial authorities even entertain the idea of establishing an institution for abandoned girls, who the king ordered should be raised in a religious institution [Beaterio] in which prostitutes (*mujeres relajadas* and *mujeres mundadas*) were also housed.[24] Such a project treated unwanted girls as a liability. It foreshadowed how institutional care of female expósitos centered on control and containment rather than development, to ensure marriagability or prevent moral contagion.

Such acutely gendered attitudes toward unwanted children reflected a desire to transform them into what Carlos II called "useful vassals" for the colony.[25] While similar anxieties over fertility control practices had periodically erupted throughout much of the rest of the Atlantic World, they assumed heightened significance in colonial Cuba because of the precariousness of the colonial project, and later because of concerns about the racial demographic balance of the island. Cuban intellectuals envisioned expanding the island's white population as critical for economic prosperity and agricultural productivity.[26]

The majority of infants who entered the Casa fit the institution's preordained mission of saving white infants conceived out of wedlock. The Casa's registry book records infants of varying socioeconomic statuses in the eighteenth century. Some infants were handed over with expensive and luxury items, while others lacked evidence of material advantage.[27] One institutional administrator explained that women who abandoned infants conceived through illicit sex, whether extramarital or with a priest, typically supported their illegitimate offspring by either anonymously donating money for their care or magnanimously agreeing to raise them as their own. Although many infants came from well-off families, a smaller number of infants arrived at the Casa due to poverty and illness. A third group relied exclusively on the institution for survival and care.[28]

Authorities lacked complete control over the race of infants surrendered to the Casa. The *torno* (turnstile, lit. wheel)—a revolving window accessible from outside the building—enabled parents or their proxies to deposit unwanted infants anonymously. A traveler to Cuba later described the torno—in use until the mid-twentieth century—as a "sort of receptacle, with three or four compartments, which turns on a pivot. One side of it is open to the street, and in it the wretched parent lays the more wretched baby,—ringing a small bell at the same time, for the new admittance. The parent vanishes, the receptacle turns on its pivot,—the baby is within, and, we are willing to believe, in merciful hands." Witnessing for the first time a mother surrendering an infant via the torno, the traveler noted the "cautious approach, the frightened countenance, the furtive act, and the great avenging pang of Nature after its consummation." She imagined that the "helpless mother" would be "weeping at home, and begging, through long years, to be allowed to seek and reclaim" her child.[29]

The anonymity of the torno likely contributed to the admission of racially mixed babies into the institution. One likely example was the 1734 surrender of Francisca Sales y Valdés through the torno. Institutional authorities turned baby Francisca over to an external wet nurse, a single mother likely of mixed race named María de Flores, for breastfeeding. Although wet nurses typically suckled infants for two years, María raised baby Francisca until the age of twelve, when she was married off. In her will, María referred to Francisca as her daughter. Years later, Francisca's son petitioned to uphold his mother's status as an expósita, overriding any blood ties to the racially suspect María that would impede his eligibility for public office.[30] Although the Council of the Indies granted his request, the racial suspicion about María not only demonstrates that the institution relied on the labor of women of African descent but also implies that mixed-race infants sometimes permeated the racially restrictive boundaries of the Casa.

Another such exception was the surrender of Ana Josefa to the Casa Cuna in January 1750. In her baptismal record, the priest described the baby girl as a "mulatica." However, Ana Josefa was not raised in or by the institution. Instead, Casa authorities baptized her and turned her over to her godmother, parda libre María Candelaria, who cared for her for free, without support from the institution.[31] The fact that a small number of mixed-race babies passed through the Casa makes sense within the broader negotiations of legitimacy and legal whiteness occurring in the eighteenth century.[32] Since expósitos suffered the social stigma of their presumably illicit conceptions and lacked solid legal protections through much of the eighteenth century, it seemed that the stakes of enforcing the racial exclusions mandated in the institution's charter remained relatively low. Yet, it is notable that the institution did not invest in the survival of Ana Josefa, instead baptizing her and giving her away to a woman of color to raise, without the conventional wet nurse's salary. Such an arrangement suggests that, in contrast to white-passing infants of probable mixed-race heritage like Francisca Sales y Valdés, for light-skinned infants of color, the institution provided access to the sacrament of baptism and possibly a foster placement, but little or no material support for their survival.

A "Warehouse" of "Ephemeral Babies"

Although the establishment of the Casa de Expósitos marked a major watershed in state investment in the survival of unwanted infants in Havana, the institution suffered from serious limitations. The Casa was supposed to be "a place of refuge for the innocent and helpless orphans and a supplement to the watchfulness and obligations that their criminal parents abandoned." But for many decades after its founding, it had instead become what one critic described as "a warehouse and cemetery destined to receive ephemeral babies who are bound to disappear in but a few days from their painful existence, or a nursery of pernicious vermin who should be locked up for the safety of the neighborhood."[33] It became known for its "miserable conditions" and "excessive mortality."[34] Institutional records indicate mortality rates up to 79 percent in the first two decades. More than half of the infants admitted during the institution's first year in operation did not survive even one month, while more than a fifth of the remaining infants did not make it to six months. Between 1711 and 1752, 176 infants survived long enough to celebrate their fifth birthday (152) or to be reclaimed by their parents (24).[35]

High mortality rates were not unique to Havana's Casa Cuna. Expósitos at similar institutions across the Spanish Empire also perished in large numbers.[36] In Havana, the poor outcomes likely stemmed from a combination of factors, including high turnover among institutional leadership, chronic financial woes, and by the mid-eighteenth century, overcrowding.

Administrative and financial challenges plagued the institution in its early years. In the first nine years of the Casa's existence, there were 6 different chaplains, including several who did not last more than a year.[37] Compounding the turnover was the chronic lack of resources, and according to some critics, financial mismanagement. Eighteenth-century institutional records and correspondence suggest that the Casa suffered from inadequate funding during its early years, a shortcoming that likely exacerbated the unlucky fate of many of its infants. In his initial petition to the King for "royal sponsorship" of the institution, Gerónimo Valdés requested the allocation of a portion of local tax revenue to fund the institution's charitable activities, including the maintenance and education of the babies.[38] Although the King issued a royal order on November 15, 1713, congratulating Valdés for his work, he stopped short of providing the material support the institution needed. The "tightness of [His] royal coffers" apparently did not permit him to grant funds directly.[39]

Although local notables donated money and resources to construct the buildings, the institution relied on local authorities to allocate tax revenue to cover everyday expenses including paying wet nurses and caregivers, clothing the infants, and burying them when they passed away. Both the state and the Church remained austere. Despite several royal orders mandating support for the institution, both local government and ecclesiastical authorities fell short of making additional funds available to the institution.[40] On the institution's establishment, a royal order directed Valdés to consult with the captain-general to allocate funds to support the institution. When monies still failed to materialize, another royal order deflected to the colonial authorities and the Church, ordering the Bishop to form a committee with the members of the city council to allocate resources to sustain the Casa. However, funding remained an ongoing struggle, as even minor requests required numerous petitions, months and years of petitions, and multiple decrees from the king.[41]

By the middle third of the eighteenth century, demand on the institution surged amid massive population growth. Havana had become one of the most important shipyards in the Americas and a primary crossroads of trade in the mid-eighteenth century.[42] By the 1740s, Havana was the third most populous city in Spanish America—with a population just over seventy thousand. Only Mexico City and Lima boasted more inhabitants.[43]

It was in this context of urban expansion that Administrator of the Casa Cuna, Tomás de Heredia, petitioned to the captain-general of Cuba to request an increase to the Casa's budget. Although the government had recently increased the Casa's annual budget by 1,000 pesos, "it was not sufficient given the increased number of children" as well as the larger staff needed to care for them. Heredia had already made several requests in 1742 and again in 1744 to increase the budget. Despite the unprecedented wealth circulating in the city, and notwithstanding his repeated requests, Heredia had not had any success securing additional funds from the state. The following year, he reiterated his request, asking the captain-general to increase the Casa's budget from 1,000 pesos to 2,000 pesos annually.[44]

Over the next two years, the Casa received several major concessions from the king, but these failed to produce tangible improvements in the outcomes for abandoned infants. In December 31, 1755, the king granted 2,000 pesos to cover the Casa's "urgencies." The following year, he ordered another payment of 18,803 pesos to cover debts accrued between 1729 and 1756.[45] However, as one member of the governing board later noted, these supplements "were not enough to cover the necessary expenses and avoid the excessive mortality that the abandoned infants experienced."[46] By failing to provide adequate funding, he implied, the state was at least partially responsible for the infant death.

While institutional administrators blamed chronic budget shortfalls for high mortality, some critics suspected ineffective governance and ineptitude as the root of the Casa's problems. "The prosperity or poverty of the Casa," wrote one critic, "has depended not on the system that it needs, but on the intelligence and greater or lesser zeal of the chaplain."[47] In the 1750s, the chaplain apparently struggled to manage the Casa's finances, resulting in significant shortcomings in the care of the abandoned babies. For instance, in 1756, the king ordered payment of 38,880 pesos from liquidated assets with interest promised to Casa back in 1714. Nearly a decade later, Casa administrators had still not collected those funds, apparently due to the chaplain's "indolence" or because of confusion over the origins of the money and the deaths of those administering it.[48] Accounts of the state of the Casa in the 1750s Casa revealed its "deplorable" state, poor governance, and the abandonment of the children once they reached five years.[49] In response, metropolitan authorities ordered reforms including the acquisition of at least eight wet nurses to tend to newborns surrendered to the institution, the creation of a governing body and the drafting of bylaws to help run the Casa Cuna.

Surviving records suggest that financial mismanagement likely exacerbated problems with the institutional budget. For instance, by the 1780s the institution boasted an endowment of nearly 100,000 pesos but struggled to cover basic costs.[50] In 1783, as the leadership complained of insufficient resources, the budget also revealed that the chaplain received a 100-peso raise in his salary.[51] Such fiscal practices likely contributed to the shortage of resources available for the care of the babies.

The Casa's ongoing woes reflected more than just its meager budget and apparent financial mismanagement. Perhaps the most significant factor weighing on the institution was the rising costs of maintaining a growing number of abandoned infants. In the first half century of its existence (1710–53), the institution served 938 babies, according to baptismal records. However, nearly double that number (1,801 babies) received the sacrament in the decade of the 1790s alone. In the next six years (1800–1806), an additional 1,574 infants entered the Casa.[52] Clearly, the number of unwanted infants in Havana was growing as the population expanded, and the Casa's financial and administrative practices failed to keep pace.

A "Mark of Disgrace or Lesser Worth"

For expósitos fortunate enough to survive their early years, the presumption of illegitimacy posed challenges for their full acceptance in honorable white society. Such was the case for María Manuela, surrendered to the Casa in 1752, and eventually married to a city councilman in Havana. Despite her whiteness and incorporation into the local elite, she faced shame and humiliation for her supposedly illegitimate birth. Expósitos like María Manuela had two main legal avenues for obtaining legitimacy. The first required their parents to marry or their married parents to recognize them. Of the more than 1,800 babies surrendered to the Casa in the 1790s, only 14 entries evinced a change in the child's status due to marriage or parental recognition.

The second pathway to legitimacy involved *gracias al sacar* (lit. permission to take [leave from racial impurity]) applications, petitions produced when individuals attempted to purchase legal legitimacy.[53] Such gracias al sacar petitions offer some insights into the lives of Cuba's most fortunate expósitos. Most petitioners surrendered to the Casa were the illegitimate children of white mothers with honorable public reputations, but their petitions relied exclusively on the patronage of male relatives.[54] For instance, María Manuela's husband sought to end the social rejection and humiliation he and his wife suffered due to her unknown parentage, so he filed a gracias al sacar petition on her behalf. The successful petition to legitimize María Manuela was one of only five successful cases in which expósitos admitted to the Casa in the 1790s achieved legal legitimacy through gracias al sacar. All of these petitions were undertaken by men on behalf of their mother, wife, or daughter.[55] Some lucky expósitos like María Manuela went on to live privileged lives despite their status, gaining formal recognition or economic assistance from their parents, inheriting property, or even marrying into privilege.[56]

REDEFINING THE CATEGORY OF EXPÓSITO

While individual expósitos like María Manuela might have experienced trajectories of upward mobility, the status and life prospects of "seemingly white" expósitos remained tenuous.[57] Gracias al sacar petitions could be denied. Marriage proposals were not certain. Laws did not protect expósitos against discrimination or exclusion.

A series of late eighteenth-century reforms began to address the legal, material, and social precariousness expósitos faced. The reformist currents gained impetus as the Enlightenment stirred fears across the Spanish Empire that more populous, developed, and industrialized empires would overtake it.[58] The 1762–63 English occupation of Havana only exacerbated these fears, after nearly two centuries of pirate attacks had whittled away at Spanish colonies in the Caribbean.[59] In response, the Spanish monarchy sought to reinforce metropolitan control over the colonies through the Bourbon reforms. Prevailing accounts of eighteenth-century Cuba suggest that these reforms materialized in militarization and liberalization of trade.[60] But a series of measures to improve the reproduction and survival of white populations, in addition to the adoption of family colonization schemes to populate certain fringe areas of the Spanish empire, suggest that population management was equally significant.[61]

Among the most significant reforms was a mandate to define the legal status of expósitos, codifying certain rights, privileges, and benefits as wards of the Crown. One of the most important benefits expósitos gained was legal equality with legitimate children. In 1772, both the city council and the Council of the Indies ruled that infants at Havana's Casa de Expósitos be treated as legitimate. In the 1790s, metropolitan authorities extended this ruling to all expósitos, regardless of where they were surrendered or abandoned. A January 1794 royal decree consolidated this right by declaring that "abandoned children without known parents be treated as legitimate" for all civil purposes.

The same 1794 decree also prohibited discrimination against individuals who had been abandoned as children, mandating that the label should not be used as a "mark of disgrace or lesser worth." This "hombres buenos" designation entitled them to unrestricted access to charitable institutions, unless the establishment required its members to be conceived and raised within a "true and legitimate marriage." The decree also enabled individuals who had been abandoned as infants to marry into honorable families, and to sue for "insult or offense" individuals who called them any of the multitude of derogatory names related to illegitimate birth, including a "son of a bitch, illegitimate, bastard, spurious, inbred/incestuous, or the product of adultery." Such offenders would be required to retract their statements before a judge and would be subject to the same fines as if they had insulted a person who had not been abandoned. Finally, the decree protected individuals who had been abandoned as infants from facing punishments involving public humiliation, lashes, or hanging, unless their crimes would ordinarily merit such sentences. The decree essentially gave individuals abandoned as infants the same basic protections afforded to honorable free people, in case they descended from illustrious families.[62]

In more racially homogenous parts of the Spanish Empire, like the Iberian Peninsula itself, the benefits and privileges prescribed in this pragmatic would have transformed the status of the vast majority of expósitos. As the cornerstone of honor, legitimacy granted access to education, the clergy, public office, marriage into upper-class families, and more. However, in the context of colonial Cuba's multiracial society, it had the potential to be far more subversive. Even though Cuban foundling asylums openly discriminated on the basis of race, infant abandonment clearly transcended class and racial boundaries, a fact that even ecclesiastical and institutional records corroborate. Thus, granting legitimacy to expósitos in Cuba was tantamount to erasing, or at very least muting, the racial differences that doubtless characterized abandoned infants as a category of people. As Ann Twinam argues, by granting legitimacy to expósitos, the decree also extended the racial benefit of the doubt to expósitos.[63] In turn expósitos had a legal foundation to argue for legal whiteness, with all its accoutrements.

Scholarship shows how colonial subjects attempted to use this metropolitan mandate to secure material and social benefits for themselves and their family members. Upwardly mobile expósitos filed a flurry of petitions in the years after the 1794 decree, requesting the adjustment of their status to facilitate admission into institutions such as schools and religious establishments, and occupations such as the clergy, military, and government, which excluded illegitimate children and people of doubtful racial purity.[64] Some of these petitions stretched the letter of the mandate so as to make it barely recognizable, such as a 1797 request by an expósita to extend legitimacy and legal whiteness to her children, whom she raised presumably out of wedlock.[65] However, scholars have not yet uncovered hard evidence of how it impacted expósitos of African descent. To what extent did expósitos of mixed racial heritage in Cuba benefit from this decree?

"A CLASS TO WHICH HE DOES NOT BELONG": EXPÓSITOS AND THE RACIAL LIMITS OF ROYAL PRIVILEGE

The 1794 royal decree hit Cuba at a time of intense economic and demographic change. For the forty years preceding this royal decree protecting expósitos, the racial demographics of Cuba were transformed as Spain's century-old policy of tightly restricting the slave trade to ports across Spanish America gave way to an unrestricted trade in human captives. During the eleven-month British occupation of Havana during the Seven Years' War, an unprecedented 12,000 enslaved Africans arrived on Cuban shores. Once Spain regained the Cuban capital in 1763, metropolitan authorities inaugurated a gradual process of trade liberalization. That process culminated in February 1789—just five years before the royal redemption of expósitos—when metropolitan authorities issued a royal decree granting free trade in slaves throughout the Americas.[66] By the 1790s, Cuba's white population had lost its numerical majority. With thousands of slaves arriving each year to Cuban shores, creole elites expressed fears of the so-called Africanization of the island.[67]

In the context of the Africanization scare, decrees that afforded expósitos legal honor and legitimacy had potentially radical consequences for Cuba's racial hierarchy. Their application in Cuba set in motion a process of redefinition of what an expósito was and who could qualify as a member of that redemptive legal category. Cuba's foundling asylums had historically served white infants to the exclusion of Black infants, but authorities defended these racial boundaries with increasing ferocity once the island's demographic shift was underway. Access to those institutions and to the *expósito* label itself remained markers of immense privilege. As noted above, Havana's Casa Cuna was established along explicitly exclusionary lines as an institution dedicated to saving white infants, not infants of African descent.

Ultimately, the law as applied in Cuba reinforced racial distinctions and upheld the racial privileges of white children born of unfortunate or disgraced circumstances. The case of José Narciso Bravo illustrates how the implementation of the 1794 decree in Cuba hinged explicitly on race. Mere days after Carlos IV's decree, José Narciso appeared before a local judge petitioning for the formal recognition of his status as an expósito so that he could obtain admission to school.[68] Colonial law required legal whiteness for a broad range of activities and privileges, including public office; certain prestigious occupations, such as physician, lawyer, and notary; marriage with white people; entrance into the clergy; and admission to university.[69] Since expósitos were recorded in the baptismal records as children of unknown parents, their whiteness, even if phenotypically pronounced, was always conditional, and they often carried the label of "al parecer blanco/blanca."

The 1794 decree should thus have granted José Narciso the right to admission. José Narciso presented to the judge official documents and testimony from five individuals, all of who corroborated his origin story, which began nearly twenty years earlier when his parents abandoned him. In November 1777, Pedro Antonio Bravo and his wife, Soledad Méndez, found the newborn on their doorstep in Santiago de Cuba, where there does not appear to have been a formal casa de expósitos at this time. They took him to the parish priest, who baptized him as an expósito born on November 22, 1777, with Pedro Antonio and his daughter, Petrona, as his godparents. Pedro Antonio and his family raised the baby for three years, employing a wet nurse named Isabel Barales. The Bravo family came on hard times in the child's third year of life, requiring both husband and wife to labor in the fields. They turned the child over to Juana de Fuentes, so she and her husband could provide the appropriate religious instruction; José Narciso then grew up with the Fuentes family.[70] All these details of José Narciso's case aligned with the standard definition of an expósito.

Nonetheless, by late February 1794, the court denied José Narciso's request to validate his status as an expósito under the 1794 decree. The judge cited José Narciso's reputation as a *pardo*, an individual of mixed race, as the reason for his ineligibility. The court noted that the label of expósito "refers to white people, a class to which he does not belong."[71] This decision aligns with a broader current in the racial management of expósitos in Cuba, which by the late eighteenth century even required expósitos to submit to a medical examination to determine if they were white or not, before obtaining a copy of their baptismal record. Such a policy indicates that the conditional racial designations assigned to abandoned infants could be amended if their physical characteristics later revealed African ancestry. Thus, even as the 1794 royal decree expanded the privileges of legitimacy to expósitos who were likely not born of legitimate unions, this decision placed practical limits on who could enjoy that royal exception. In essence, the local courts conflated legitimacy and whiteness.[72] They were not willing to extend the privileges of expósitos to a person who they understood to be of African descent. José Narciso was therefore forced to prove his *whiteness*, not just his expósito status, to meet this legal threshold required for attending school.

Undeterred, José Narciso appealed the lower court's decision. His case did not challenge the court's interpretation of eligibility for the label of expósito. Rather, José Narciso disputed the court's assessment of his race. He claimed that the lower court had erred in assuming that he was "the son of a pardo," instead insisting that he was white. He argued that the Bravo family was not his biological family as the court had erroneously assumed. Rather, these "poor and helpless" people raised him for his first three years after his biological parents, who he insisted were white, had abandoned him. His misfortune of being raised by a pardo, he argued, should not preclude him from pursuing his studies. The judge did not agree. By August 1796, the appeals court also ruled against José Narciso, categorizing him as a pardo and excluding him from the protected group of expósito.[73]

The reluctance of the local courts to grant José Narciso's request evinces a growing racial anxiety in Cuba, which was likely particularly acute in the island's eastern region. Cuba's white population lost its numerical majority in the 1790s at the same time as the island's creole elites watched neighboring St. Domingue erupt in slave rebellion (1791–1804). French slave owners and free people of color flocked to Santiago de Cuba, often bringing slaves with them. In that context, Santiago's creole elite likely felt the urgency of policing the boundaries of whiteness, as the courts did with José Narciso.[74]

José Narciso escalated the case all the way up to the Real Audiencia de Santo Domingo, the highest appeals court with jurisdiction over much of the Spanish Caribbean. There he told the court that he was "not trying to pass" but rather trying to reveal the truth that he was white, so that he could serve God. Although the surviving court transcript is too deteriorated to read, a José Narciso Bravo later appeared on the rolls of the Convento San Basilio, suggesting that the audiencia may have eventually ruled in his favor.[75]

Whatever the racial heritage of his biological parents, however he imagined his racial identity, and regardless of how his society treated him, José Narciso built his entire case on his whiteness. This whiteness, in his estimation, entitled him to enjoy the privileges of legitimacy, according to the king's 1794 decree. As he interacted with the courts, however, José Narciso's insistence on his whiteness helped lay bare the racial limits of these broader efforts to save babies. Just as the Casa Cuna aimed to rescue white infants, the royal privileges granted to all expósitos were limited to white infants.

Three years after the original mandate, metropolitan authorities issued another royal decree, reminding authorities to correct the ongoing discrimination against expósitos. This law was published in Cuba in October 1797.[76] However, it appears unlikely that colonial authorities willingly extended such benefits to expósitos of color amid the heightened racial anxieties of the late eighteenth century.

Expanding and Regulating Charitable Institutions

A second set of reforms sought to improve the prospects of expósitos and orphans by expanding and regulating charitable institutions. In 1794, the same year the metropolitan authorities granted expósitos legal protections, ecclesiastical authorities founded the Casa de Beneficencia outside Havana's city walls. The institution provided charitable relief to needy populations, including paupers, the mentally ill, and orphans aged six and older. (This was two years prior to a 1796 royal decree calling for such an establishment.) Its early inauguration in Havana appears to have been one of several measures aimed at reducing mortality due to the overcrowding that plagued many Casas de Expósitos across the Spanish Empire.[77] Previously cast out onto the streets once they attained the age of six, these children could now theoretically gain admission to a separate institution that would continue providing food and shelter, and they even had a chance of receiving a basic education.

While the institution provided some access to trades education and apprenticeship for boys, its approach to girls appeared to focus on grooming for marriage and motherhood. The girls' department taught orphans how to become the morally upright white mothers the state desired.[78] The Casa de Beneficencia provided a dowry for at least some of its female residents.[79] Unwanted orphan girls could be transformed into marriageable young women and future mothers. This gender-segregated educational program seemingly brought the racialized pronatalism of colonial charity full circle. It extended the pronatalist role of its predecessor establishments, the Colegio de Niños San Ambrosio and the Colegio de Niñas San Francisco de Sales, as well as other charitable institutions, including the San Francisco de Paula Women's Hospital and the Casa Cuna.

Additional institutional reforms came with the 1796 royal decree, which included a *reglamento*, or set of bylaws, to govern Casas de Expósitos across the Spanish Empire. Its major reforms encouraged the surrender of unwanted babies at designated institutions. One vital directive centered on protecting women or other individuals abandoning infants from the threat interrogation, investigation, and criminalization. According to the order, many infanticides had resulted from the abandoner's "fear of being discovered or pursued" by authorities while attempting to abandon an infant at an asylum. This fear drove some individuals to expose the infant, for example on a country road or field, where it would die, or to kill the infant outright. To mitigate these fears, the king ordered local authorities to refrain from detaining or questioning any individual "day or night, in the countryside or in town carrying an infant who they claim they are bringing to a Casa de Expósitos." If the official were concerned about the infant's safety, the most he could do would be to accompany the individual to the asylum to ensure the infant was dropped off safely.[80] This measure likely aimed to reduce the barriers women faced when surrendering unwanted infants, thereby decreasing public abandonment.

Since the decree was evidently written with metropolitan conditions in mind, some of the regulations were unrealistic in the colonial context. One of these was the mandate to establish additional Casas de Expósitos in parishes where mothers most commonly abandoned their infants. Establishing facilities about every 21 to 25 miles, would help reduce the long journeys newborns faced and ensure that surrendered infants had prompt access to wet nurses—improvements that would help reduce mortality.[81] While the recommendation made sense in theory, it presumed a regular network of population centers outside the capital and provincial hubs. This was simply not the case in eighteenth-century Cuba, where Havana and a handful of other cities, including Santiago, were relatively spread out. One charitable institution seemed to function as both a Casa de Expósitos and a Casa de Beneficencia in Guanabacoa, a town 10 miles outside of Havana, in the late eighteenth century. However, surviving documentation does not permit a clear picture of how provincial cities addressed unwanted children or the extent to which the problem existed.

Yet, selective implementation of the 1796 guidelines likely advanced existing racial agendas in charitable institutions. For instance, while metropolitan authorities sought to ameliorate fear of prosecution for surrendering an infant at foundling asylums, local authorities gained renewed power to prosecute individuals who exposed their infants or abandoned them at places other than designated asylums. "All forgiveness and excuse ceases for abandoning babies, especially at night on the church doorstep or at the homes of private individuals or in hidden places, which results in the deaths of many infants." Individuals who abandoned infants in that manner "will be punished with all the severity of the law." The person could be eligible for a reduced sentence if they informed the priest immediately after abandoning the infant.[82] In the context of the racial restrictions on admission to the Casa, this rule essentially opened the door to the disproportionate criminalization of mothers of African descent.

Indeed, as part of this increased interest in penalizing public abandonment, the guidelines required private citizens to report to local ecclesiastical authorities any infants abandoned at their homes. They then had the option of raising the infants on their own, so long as they were "de buenas costumbres y honesta familia" (honorable white families) and had the means to provide for the infant's care and education, as they would not be eligible to receive a stipend from the parish. The caregiver had the right to relinquish custody of the infant at any time without penalty, but if they failed to notify the proper authorities, they too could face criminal prosecution.[83]

Authorities in Havana took these guidelines seriously, at least by the middle third of the nineteenth century. Together, the order to prosecute individuals who abandoned their infants in public places and the requirement to report anyone abandoning babies transformed the way local authorities engaged with pregnant women and new mothers. Beginning in the mid-nineteenth century, military authorities and police began documenting and investigating what had previously been a routine aspect of urban life: the discovery of abandoned infants, dead or alive, in public spaces across the city. When authorities began considering fertility control practices as crimes, the women bearing the brunt of this criminalization were impoverished women of color (see also chapter 8).

Other reforms, such as those perceived to impact white families, encountered resistance. Among these were the directives regarding parental custody rights over abandoned children. It had become customary for some families in Cuba to surrender their newborn to the Casa as a temporary solution to problems of honor or poverty. Parents sometimes returned to reclaim their surrendered children, either recognizing them as their own or claiming them through adoption. There was precedent for parents to "orchestrate private ceremonies where they first 'abandoned' infants and then 'found' and 'adopted' them."[84] This practice, recognized by institutional authorities and recurrent in legal petitions and custody claims, persisted through much of the colonial period, only periodically prompting backlash.[85]

The implementation of the 1796 decree would have halted this practice. The regulation established that parents who abandoned their infants lost all custody and rights to those children. Parents would not be able to reclaim those children except by judicial order proving paternity, and only when authorities judged it in the best interest of the child. Parents who abandoned their children due to extreme poverty fell under an exception that allowed them to reclaim their children later.[86] By codifying the loss of custody following infant abandonment, this regulation marked an effort to reduce abandonment as a solution to temporary problems. However, in the context of Havana's Casa de Expósitos, such a reform would discourage certain white families from surrendering their infants. Institutional authorities appear to have disregarded this rule. The practice of surrendering infants and children "temporarily" persisted well into the twentieth century, especially during periods of economic hardship, evincing the dire need for services such as nurseries, childcare, maternity leave, and foster care (see chapter 9).

The collective thrust of the regulations prescribed in the 1796 decree pushed infant abandonment toward designated institutional spaces, most especially Casas de Expósitos. However, authorities in Cuba implemented these reforms in ways that advanced existing racial boundaries on access to charity. The criminalization of public infant abandonment disproportionately impacted women of African descent amid ongoing racial restrictions in access to charitable institutions. By contrast, the crackdown on "temporary" infant surrender was likely perceived as a deterrent for white families. Even though this reform would have alleviated some of the overcrowding and financial strain, institutional authorities appear to have disregarded it, possibly fearing it might increase public abandonment of white infants.

Race, Gender, and Culpability: Black Wet Nurses and White Infant Death

One set of regulations in the 1796 royal decree that resonated in Havana involved management of wet nurses. The new bylaws required institutions to employ only healthy and honorable women as wet nurses but explicitly barred the employment of abandoned infants' own mothers. Eligible women were to have sufficient means to support themselves and the child until the child turned six years old. Whereas the bylaws appeared to encourage the use of white women through the racially coded requirement of honor, the poor pay, low status, and social stigma of the job tended to perpetuate the employment of impoverished or enslaved Black women, in the Casa and beyond it.[87] The bylaws also formally recognized the role of physicians in the care of abandoned infants, leaving to the doctor's discretion how long the infant would breastfeed.[88] In essence, these interventions sought to whiten the female staff directly tending to expósitos while also subordinating them to the supervision of white male medical authorities.

Institutional authorities had historically relied on the labor and bodies of women of African descent to care for the white infants. Its founding documents established that the hospital would be staffed by Black women, who would raise and educate the children. In addition to a room for the children, and another for the chaplain, the building was supposed to contain a room for the wet nurses.[89] Black women performed the most essential and intimate care, as midwives, wet nurses, and caregivers to the surrendered white infants. Through much of the eighteenth century, chaplains used enslaved women as wet nurses to care for a limited number of babies raised inside the Casa, paying each enslaved woman's owner a nominal fee. However, the number of surrendered babies increased dramatically, especially during the late eighteenth century. As the number of expósitos exceeded the capacity of internal wet nurses, the chaplain began farming infants out to wet nurses outside the institution—generally impoverished women of color earning as little as one real per day. As early as the mid-eighteenth century, the majority of babies surrendered to the Casa spent their first year in the care of a wet nurse beyond the walls of the institution. Almost all of the babies sent away to wet nurses died.[90]

For much of the Casa's existence, institutional administrators blamed infant death, morbidity, and moral corruption more generally on these women.[91] The alleged failures and misdeeds of wet nurses had emerged as a recurring complaint, in particular from the mid-eighteenth century onward. One critic attributed the high death rate among surrendered infants to the lack of care and attention received from the wet nurses, who came to the Casa only to collect their earnings, sometimes even after the infant had died. Other reports claimed that external wet nurses failed to report the deaths of infants they were nursing so they could continue to collect the four pesos a month. As early as 1767, authorities in Havana demanded greater vigilance over the predominantly Black wet nurses so they could reduce expenditures for feeding the infants.[92]

The question of who was best endowed to care for white infants remained unanswered. White women were sometimes perceived as too weak or sickly after childbirth to breastfeed, with their delicate constitutions producing thin breastmilk lacking the necessary nutrients.[93] Yet, apart from the allegations that Black wet nurses did not do enough to save their tiny white charges, there were myriad claims that implicated the unsuitability of Black women to nurse white infants. One institutional administrator claimed that Black wet nurses produced milk that was "too strong" for white newborns to digest.[94] In other slave societies in the Americas, physicians feared that the physical and emotional brutality of slavery reduced the quality of enslaved women's breastmilk.[95] Given the racial and gender dynamics of the hospital's economy of care, wet nurses offered a convenient scapegoat for the persistently high infant mortality rates and other institutional problems, including chronic budget shortfalls and overcrowding, that continued to plague Havana's Casa de Expósitos.

Pressures mounted toward the end of the eighteenth century. Whereas the Casa Cuna limited admission to between forty and seventy infants per year prior to the 1780s, the number of infants deposited in the years thereafter rose significantly to more than two hundred annually.[96] In one five-year period, the chaplain distributed over three hundred expósitos among enslaved and free wet nurses outside the Casa. Looking back on this practice, one institutional administrator at the dawn of the nineteenth century remarked that "everyone knows that infinite numbers of children perished in that way." The few lucky enough to ward off death survived "only by coincidence" or because their parents provided for them from afar.[97] In 1788, Carlos III issued a decree urging the institutions to exercise more caution when arranging for care outside the asylum. The decree specifically emphasized the importance of placing the infants in situations that would help them learn the skills necessary to be "useful vassals."[98] Yet, even babies raised in the Casa did not fare much better, with their odds of survival just one in six. Most surrendered infants died before their first birthday, whether they received care inside or outside the Casa.[99]

Authorities at Havana's Casa Cuna apparently struggled to implement the reforms mandated by the 1796 bylaws, especially the ones regarding the care and breastfeeding of expósitos. However, institutional authorities evidently continued to rely on women of African descent, even as they reiterated their desire to pay a small amount to "poor but honorable wet nurses" who could undertake infants' care until they could be weaned, or even until they could be trained in a trade. Despite this early allusion toward a desire for white wet nurses, wet nursing remained closely associated with women of African descent.[100] The disparity between the kinds of women Casa administrators imagined would serve as wet nurses and the ones who actually served became the source of ongoing concern through the nineteenth century.

While institutional authorities complained about wet nurses' endless faults and orchestrated varying schemes to control them, the survival of the Casa depended on the labor of these and many other Black women. Indeed, some administrators attempted to generate additional income by purchasing enslaved women. For instance, at the dawn of the nineteenth century, one petition called for the purchase of a hundred enslaved women, whom administrators proposed to employ in the production of cigarettes on-site at the Casa de Beneficencia. In an agreement with the Real Factoría de Tabaco, the Casa would receive a quarter of the proceeds from the cigarettes produced by the enslaved women.[101] This arrangement became another source of revenue for the Casa over the next several years.[102] Nevertheless, an 1806 letter reveals that the institutional budget continued to fall short, which prevented the institution from employing the staff necessary to save many of the children housed there.[103]

The central role of Black women within this charitable enterprise remained both the institution's saving grace and a convenient point of criticism. In 1813, the Havana City Council ordered a routine inspection of the San Francisco de Paula Women's Hospital, the San Juan de Dios Charity Hospital, and the Casa de Expósitos. During two routine inspections of the Casa, the inspector expressed "horror and scandal" at the conditions and the treatment afforded to the babies. The Casa staff allegedly treated the "indecent offspring" with the "greatest disaster," even though they had been sent there to receive "Christian charity to fill the absence of their parents and save this disgraced portion of the human race."[104]

The inspector's report was damning. It characterized the chaplain as unsuitable for the job because he prioritized his many obligations outside the Casa over maintaining order and hygiene in the Casa itself. "The first time we went to visit, [the chaplain] was not at the Casa," the inspector wrote. "And what we found were six very young children in the greatest abandonment." They reported seeing children sleeping on the wooden floorboards "without even rags on which their tender bones could rest." They further saw three children who they characterized as "pale and sick" and found out from "some women" at the Casa that two more children were receiving care outside the institution—one beyond the city walls and the other in Guanabacoa. The inspector also criticized the wet nurses. During their initial visit, they reported seeing "three Black women who said they were wet nurses, who did not have much milk and the little they gave was of minimal substance because insufficient care is given to their nutrition."[105] The committee made suggestions to improve the poor treatment afforded to the disgraced children in that Casa.

The chaplain came the next day to see one of the committee members, promising that everything would be fixed by the next visit. On returning to the Casa twelve days later, the committee members reported that "things remained in the same state of neglect and disaster as before." In fact, several children had died in the interim. "We do not need to search for any more heartbreaks," the inspector concluded. "This house, consecrated to humanity, cannot continue in this state that it is in." The committee urged the city council to "take serious measures."[106]

Just days later, the chaplain penned a fourteen-page letter responding to the allegations. He claimed to be "embarrassed and offended" by the report. He expressed disbelief that the inspectors could have given "such a mistaken report" attacking him for no reason, and worse, that the city council paid any attention to the report that would tarnish his good name.[107]

The chaplain could not deny some of allegations but insisted that these disorders did not demonstrate a lack of care. He admitted, for instance, that some of the children were indeed naked, covered only by handkerchiefs to protect them from the mosquito infestation. Nevertheless, he insisted that the Casa staff, including his mother and sisters, gave proper care to the babies, a claim that insinuated that he had implemented a racially tiered system of care in which white women supervised Black women. The expósitos received "more and perhaps better [care] than in the homes of some middle-class families," the chaplain wrote. "There is no house, however orderly it is and no matter how exquisite the cleanliness and even the delicateness of its owner, that if a visitor enters at a bad time or arrives unannounced, that the house would not be dirty or un-swept, the children naked, the servants unkempt and maybe even the owners or the lady of the house in some nudity." As heads of household, he argued, the councilmen should understand all this.[108]

The chaplain further boasted that the Casa had never been in better shape than it was under his leadership. Beginning in 1806, the chaplain's immediate predecessor reduced the practice of arranging external care for the babies whose parents did not return for them or who were not otherwise adopted.[109] Instead, he began to raise the babies in the Casa itself. The Casa required internal wet nurses to reside and remain within the Casa, a policy separating the women indefinitely from their own children. The limited number of internal wet nurses still required each woman to breastfeed multiple infants. In 1806, six wet nurses cared for sixteen babies in the Casa; each wet nurse earned a salary of twelve pesos and food and shelter for them and their helpers. That same year thirty-two children received care outside the Casa by women who earned four pesos and some clothing.[110]

When the chaplain assumed the directorship in 1807, he continued providing internal care for the infants, though he emphasized the supervision of Black wet nurses by white staff, including physicians and his own family members. He enlisted his mother and sisters to help care for the surrendered infants, moving them into the establishment with him. He claimed that these women took great care to keep the Casa clean, to provide clothing and cots for the children, and to feed the Black wet nurses enough. They served as "second Mothers for the abandoned infants, holding them in their arms every day and spending sleepless nights, caring for and attending to them with an affection that everyone acknowledges."[111] The chaplain asserted that his mother's age and experience raising a large family afforded her valuable knowledge about childhood illnesses. Using "home remedies that experience has taught her," she frequently cured surrendered babies afflicted with common illnesses. "Several physicians with good reputations" (Dr. Tomas Romay, Dr. Juan Carrilla, Lic. Jose Cometan, D. Nicolas Valses and others) attended to the children when they became sick, further demonstrating the chaplain's compliance with the 1796 bylaws.[112]

Despite the chaplain's "improvements," the Casa remained a veritable cemetery. The chaplain cited budgetary constraints as well as external failures as causes of the persisting high mortality rates and abysmal conditions. Due to budgetary limits, wet nurses cared for multiple expósitos, a fact that likely contributed to poor outcomes. Faced with the "invincible difficulty of breastfeeding so many infants," such wet nurses were unable to give each baby the "care and concern of a mother."[113] In fact, one institutional administrator claimed that each wet nurse could support four newborns by supplementing breastmilk with other forms of nutrition. He recommended cow's milk sold on the street, and liquids made with rice flour or other easily digestible food, feeding practices later found to cause fatal enteritis.[114] Even if the institution hired enough wet nurses to reduce the number of breastfeeding babies per woman, the institutional board of directors speculated that the number of servants and employees would be too great to manage and supervise effectively.[115]

The chaplain argued that the failure of ecclesiastical authorities to comply with the 1796 bylaws' mandate to establish additional foundling asylums meant that too many surrendered infants arrived in poor condition. He lamented that many of the children "get sick and also that many of them die despite all the vigilance and care." Such high mortality was "inevitable" because of the general destitution of mothers surrendering their infants. The babies admitted to the Casa were "commonly the children of impoverished mothers or [mothers] who for whatever reason have had to hide or have tried to hide their pregnancies." As a result, many of the babies "are born sick and weak." Some babies arrive already "dead, and others without hope of recovery," wrote one casa administrator at the turn of the nineteenth century.[116] They often arrive at the Casa only after long journeys, exposure to "morning dew," and "other mishaps." The chaplain explained that many infants "are surrendered with blood spewing from everywhere, others barely born and naked, and others with humors and blood so tainted that all the care and attention given to them is not enough." Still other infants succumbed to diseases contracted before their arrival.[117]

Given the institution's abysmal reputation, many impoverished or disgraced mothers continued throughout most of the colonial period to abandon their infants on doorsteps rather than relinquish them to uncertain fate within the Casa Cuna.[118] Newspapers reported countless newborns "left dead at the Churches and convents," among other public places across the city. Those babies received common burial in the general cemetery.[119] Regardless of where mothers surrendered their newborns, death claimed most. The generalized aversion to surrendering infants to institutional custody, as well as the persisting prevalence of infant abandonment and infanticide, underscored the Casa Cuna's limitations in saving the island's masses of unwanted white babies. Despite the institution's limited reach, its existence still exemplified the fundamental disparity in the way colonial authorities approached white women's reproduction with protection and assistance, while penalizing and policing women of color.

The thinly veiled racial guidance on selecting and managing wet nurses likely validated the chaplain's claim of institutional effectiveness. Surely, if the regulation specifically addressed shortcomings in wet nursing, then his culpability was mitigated. Yet, despite the explicit discussion of wet nursing, the remainder of the long list of regulations confirmed that metropolitan authorities well understood that wet nursing was not the only, or even the most salient, issue when it came to the mortality of expósitos.

During the eighteenth century, ecclesiastical authorities expanded Havana's fledgling network of charitable institutions with two new institutions, one for unwanted infants and the other for orphans. Despite the appearance of benevolent humanitarianism, these institutions were not founded to serve all children. Expanding the racial boundaries governing the San Francisco de Paula women's hospital, the Casa de Expósitos explicitly excluded the children of African-descended women, regardless of legal status. This exclusion ensured that, when confronted with unwanted pregnancy, only white women enjoyed the institution's noncriminal alternative to abortion, infanticide, and infant abandonment. By excluding children of color, the institution channeled its meager resources into saving white infants.

Although the care they received at the Casa likely gave surrendered infants a greater chance at survival than publicly abandoned ones, mortality rates remained stacked against them. Successive institutional administrators complained that inadequate funding deprived the institution of the resources and staff it needed to save infant lives, but direct funding remained scarce. The Casa came to rely increasingly on the unfree labor of women of color, not just for everyday operations, including breastfeeding and caring for infants, but also for additional revenue. The centrality of Black women's labor remained a pillar of institutional survival as well as a constant source of contention, as institutional administrators and external critics blamed wet nurses for high infant mortality rates.

In the late eighteenth century, metropolitan authorities mandated a series of reforms to improve the fate of expósitos by bestowing legal rights and protections aimed at curtailing discrimination against them and regulating the way charitable institutions cared for them. These reforms arrived to Cuba precisely as the rise of the plantation economy, acute growth of the slave trade, and the demographic shift generated acute racial anxieties in Cuba. Within this context, colonial authorities implemented the reforms in racially restrictive ways. As a result, colonial authorities imposed racial boundaries on the legal category of expósito, which came to refer only to abandoned white infants.

At an institutional level, the 1794 establishment of the Casa de Beneficencia distributed some of the demand by caring for orphans, including those who aged out of the Casa de Expósitos. Though theoretically open to children regardless of race, the Casa de Beneficencia served a racialized and gendered function by grooming abandoned white girls for marriage and motherhood. With racial restrictions already in place at the Casa de Expósitos, moreover, metropolitan mandates prompted a resurgence in racialized scapegoating and control against the women of color whose labor had long been central to the institution's survival. All these efforts evinced a clear priority on the part of the colonial state: supporting the growth of the white population by saving white infants and transforming them into useful vassals for the Crown.

CHAPTER THREE

For the "Propagation of Slaves"
Enslaved Women's Reproduction on Plantations at the Dawn of Abolitionism, 1780s–1820s

Between the late eighteenth and early nineteenth centuries, the problem of fertility emerged as a cornerstone of preserving slavery in Cuba. The rise of a sugar plantation economy accentuated the demographic reality that Cuba's enslaved population—like most others in the Caribbean—was not self-sustaining.[1] Enslaved people perished at astounding rates. Recently arrived captives experienced high morbidity due to exposure to a new disease environment during "seasoning."[2] Those who survived faced grueling regimes of forced labor. To be sure, enslaved people in Cuban sugar plantations typically toiled six days each week and as many as twenty hours a day during harvest time.[3] The everyday violence and brutality of slavery also contributed to high mortality rates among plantation slaves.[4] They suffered high disease rates, poor sanitation, and inadequate health care.[5] Under this brutal regime, mortality rates averaged between 10 and 12 percent annually, reaching as high as 18 percent on certain plantations. On arrival, the average enslaved person survived just seven or eight years in Cuba.

Yet, high mortality alone does not fully explain the demographic realities of Cuban slave populations. There were simply not enough babies being born to replace the huge numbers of enslaved people dying. As one traveler observed, a "notorious excess of deaths over births" characterized the island's enslaved population.[6] In part, low fertility stemmed from a gender ratio skewed hopelessly in favor of males. Planters insisted on the superiority of male labor, leading to greater demand for male African captives.

Looming over Cuba's burgeoning slave society were the abolitionist currents sweeping the Atlantic World in the late eighteenth century. The 1772 Somerset case, which effectively prohibited slavery in Great Britain, marked a turning point that reverberated well beyond Britain. Although Spain did not ban slavery on the peninsula until 1837, slave owners and their sympathizers across the Spanish Empire evidently understood the implications of such a judicial milestone, especially considering Britain's long-standing position as the premier slaving nation. By the 1780s, the abolitionist movement was well underway in Great Britain—first among religious sectors and subsequently expanding to the secular realm with the 1787 establishment of the Committee for the Abolition of the Slave Trade. British banks continued to finance slaving expeditions, but in an era in which Great Britain dominated the trade in slaves, abolitionists' mounting successes were a foreboding omen for Cuban planters.

In the context of these opposing circumstances, the long-standing legal principle of *partus sequitur ventrem* (lit. "that which is born follows the womb") vested enslaved women's bodies with unprecedented symbolic and material value. This legal principle derived from Roman slave law and found expression in the Siete Partidas, a thirteenth-century legal code.[7] This legal framework for generational slavery figured prominently in the debates surrounding the legal status of fetuses in late eighteenth-century Cuba.

Elite interest in enslaved women's intimate lives surged between the late eighteenth-century consolidation of plantation slavery and Spain's first antislaving treaty in the early nineteenth century. Prior to this period, colonial law and social welfare reforms largely neglected enslaved women, instead focusing on saving white infants. However, the rise of abolitionism forced authorities to consider alternatives to the slave trade for supplying the insatiable demand for slaves. This economic calculation pushed enslaved women's wombs to the very center of policy debates about the regulation and future of slavery in Cuba.

Early proposals to harness enslaved women's reproductive labor hinged on three pronatalist reforms: balancing sex ratios among slave cargoes and on plantations, extending marriage and familial rights to enslaved people, and ameliorating the conditions of slavery to incentivize reproduction. Proponents framed these adjustments as a form of insurance against impending restrictions on the slave trade. Nonetheless, slave owners continued to rely on importation, rather than reproduction, to meet their short-term labor needs. Colonial authorities enabled that dependence through their ambivalent attitudes toward antislaving legislation and, later, their general tolerance for the clandestine traffic in slaves. Although the reforms largely went unheeded, the idea that enslaved women could reproduce slavery proved transformative, as schemes to capitalize on enslaved childbearing became a permanent fixture in debates, attitudes, and later practices of slavery.

Enslaved Women, Reproduction, and the Law

The early sparks of Atlantic abolitionism coincided with heightened interest in enslaved women's reproductive potential in Cuba. As early as the 1780s, Spanish authorities sought to reinforce the legal foundations of generational slavery. Part of this agenda entailed preventing the small number of enslaved women from securing freedom. In 1784, Carlos III issued the *código negro carolino*, which prohibited the manumission of enslaved mothers. If realized, this provision would have overturned a statute in the Siete Partidas that offered pathways to freedom for slaves related to the owner, including enslaved women who had breastfed their owners' children and "hermanos de leche" (lit. milk siblings), enslaved children who shared the breast of their enslaved mother, while she nursed her owners' children.[8] Such policies formed the foundation of metropolitan efforts to exploit the reproductive labor of enslaved women.

Yet, like much of the legislation regulating slavery and the slave trade that followed, the código negro carolino was riddled in contradictions, particularly when it came to its implications for women's reproduction. The same code contained a clause prohibiting slave owners from owning the children they fathered with their enslaved women. Although the code was never implemented in its entirety, local courts sometimes applied part of the law to free enslaved children fathered by their owners.[9] Thus, the code implied contradictory roles for enslaved women's reproduction within the institution of slavery. The conflicting agendas contained in the código negro carolino illustrate a pattern that became central to the regulation of slavery in Cuba at the turn of the nineteenth century: enslaved women's ability to conceive and birth future generations of slaves afforded the possibility of legal and spiritual rights, while simultaneously crushing it with the violent seizure of their reproductive autonomy and parental authority.

In 1786 Cuba's governor issued a decree that afforded fetuses the same proportion of freedom as their mothers, when they initiated *coartación*, a process in which enslaved people purchased their freedom in installments. However, the Council of the Indies overturned this decree, ruling instead that a pregnant woman's status as a *coartada* applied only to her and not to her fetus. However, subsequent legislation reinforced *partus sequitur ventrem*, theoretically challenging that ruling. Still, enslaved mothers who attempted to apply their status as coartada to their children seldom succeeded.[10] These attempts to limit the pathways out of slavery for the offspring of enslaved women demonstrates how metropolitan authorities monetized women's reproductive potential.

These efforts to reinforce partus sequitur ventrem, by keeping children born to enslaved mothers in slavery, implied that the authorities saw in enslaved women's reproduction a potential source of profit for slave owners and for the colony more generally. Given metropolitan restrictions on the slave trade to Cuba, the turn toward enslaved women's reproductive potential underscored how the late-eighteenth-century growth of Cuba's sugar economy produced an insatiable demand for enslaved labor. Harnessing enslaved women's reproductive labor offered a potential long-range solution to supplementing the enslaved labor supply. However, it appeared only to make sense within the context of limited importations.

ENSLAVED REPRODUCTION AS LIABILITY

Attitudes toward enslaved women shifted as Spain liberalized the slave trade. In 1789, metropolitan authorities issued two decrees that seemingly prioritized importation rather than reproduction to meet demands for enslaved labor. A royal decree issued in February 1789 removed historic restrictions on the importation of slaves to Spanish American ports. The Free Trade in Slaves Act opened the floodgates of the slave trade to Cuba, communicating to planters that they could address high slave mortality by importing unlimited numbers of captives from Africa.[11]

This same legislation also specifically addressed the gender ratios of slave cargoes. Article 6 stipulated that "the Slaves should be of good stock, a third at most female, and the other two[-thirds] male."[12] Scholars have interpreted this clause as a mandate to import more enslaved women to help balance plantation populations.[13] However, the use of the phrase "at most" suggests that this article was less interested in balancing gender ratios than ensuring the importation of "useful" slaves. The same article defined desirable slavery through the exclusion of "unuseful, contagious, or chronically ill."[14] The cap of one-third for female slaves, moreover, suggests that metropolitan authorities viewed being female as an impediment for an enslaved person's usefulness.

This ambivalence on gender and reproduction among slaves became even more acute in a second decree, issued just a few months later, in May 1789. The Real Cédula sobre educación, trato y ocupaciones de esclavos, a set of laws that came to be known as the Código Negro Español (Spanish Black Code; hereafter, 1789 code), provided guidance on how to treat enslaved people. Recognizing "certain abuses not aligning and even opposing the system of legislation" and other dispositions on slavery, the order mandated wide-ranging protections for enslaved people; these largely reiterated existing orders, decrees, ordinances, and other policies. In light of the liberalization of the slave trade just months earlier, under which the enslaved population was projected to "grow considerably," the purpose of the code was to compile existing rules into a single document to facilitate compliance across the Americas.

The 1789 code treated slaves as implicitly male. For instance, in an article outlining the kinds of labor slaves should perform, it declared that "the first and principal occupation of the Slaves should be Agriculture and other labors of the countryside." It also instructed owners or plantation managers to assign slaves work that was appropriate to their "age, strength, and robustness." At the same time, the code instructed owners that they could not force female slaves to work, an exemption that also extended to elderly slaves over age sixty and children under age seventeen. Additional restrictions applied to the use of enslaved women, including a prohibition on employing them in labors not appropriate to their gender, those in which they have to mix with males, or as day laborers. Owners who employed enslaved women in domestic service, moreover, were taxed two pesos each year.[15] These restrictions on the use of enslaved women suggest that the prohibition from forcing them to work applied only to agricultural or plantation labor. By reinforcing the existing association between slavery and agriculture, and exempting women from working alongside men, the 1789 code seemingly validated the preference for male slaves. It further disincentivized the importation of females by taxing their use in domestic labor, which would have been among the few labors appropriate to their gender.

Even as the 1789 code seemingly cast agricultural labor as the work of enslaved men, it explicitly addressed marriage and childbearing. For instance, it called for owners to promote marriage among their slaves, "to avoid illicit contact between the sexes." It also instructed owners not to interfere if one of their slaves sought marriage with a slave from another plantation. In the event such a marriage occurred between two slaves on different plantations, the 1789 code declared that "the woman should follow the husband." To that end, it instructed the enslaved man's owner to purchase the woman, and if a disagreement arose, it also gave the woman's owner the right to purchase the husband. The code outlined owners' responsibility toward enslaved children as well. In that regard, owners were required to feed enslaved children even as the restrictions on the use of their labor theoretically applied until they turned seventeen. The 1789 code prohibited owners from setting enslaved children free to rid themselves of these costs, unless they bequeathed to the child sufficient money or assets so they could provide for themselves without assistance. In other words, it framed the birth of an enslaved child as the start of a financial burden with which owners would be saddled for at least seventeen years, without being legally permitted to extract agricultural labor.[16]

In the context of the 1789 code, enslaved women were a major liability for slave owners. It not only restricted the ways owners could use enslaved women's labor, it also prohibited them from obstructing enslaved peoples' marriages. In turn, marriages would theoretically open the door to reproduction. Any child born to an enslaved woman was the financial responsibility of the owner. Since owners were required to pay medical care and hospital stays for their ailing slaves, as well as burial costs, the high rates of maternal mortality would have further exacerbated the presumed burden of enslaved women's reproduction.[17]

In that vein, it is perhaps not surprising that one of the threads in the 1789 code is an emphasis on sex segregation of slaves. Enslaved men and women were not to work alongside one another, were not to mingle during festivities, and were to live in separate housing. While the decree offered a religious justification of preventing extramarital sex, all of these mandated elements of keeping enslaved women away from enslaved men were major impediments to slave agency in marriage, as well. Either way, if enslaved men and women could not come in contact with one another, then owners could avoid some of the perceived financial burdens associated with their union. Of course, the 1789 code does not directly address the very real issue of intimacy across racial and legal boundaries, including rape by slave owners, which resulted in many enslaved children.[18]

GENDER RATIOS AND MARRIAGE AMID RISING SLAVE IMPORTATIONS, 1789–1804

While neither the 1789 decree nor the 1789 code seemed overly concerned with promoting enslaved reproduction, conversations in Cuba reflected stronger interest in natural increase. Among Cuba's earliest pronatalist proposals emanated from creole reformers deeply invested in the development and expansion of the island's sugar economy. Such discussions took place within organizations such as Havana's Sociedad Económica de Amigos del País, a learned society formed by educated creole elites interested in advancing the agricultural and industrial future of the island, the closely related Royal Development Board (Real Junta de Fomento de Agricultura y Comercio), and the Consulado de la Habana. Bringing together some of the most highly educated members of the creole elite, these societies shaped policy through recommendations to colonial authorities. The severe gender imbalances characterizing the enslaved population struck creole elites as a major obstacle to increasing slave fertility.

Among Cuba's earliest proposals addressed the stark imbalances in gender ratios among plantations slaves. Many sugar planters maintained predominantly, if not exclusively, male slave labor forces on their sugar plantations, believing that they could extract more high-intensity labor from men than from women. One 1795 proposal raised in Havana's Sociedad Económica de Amigos del País outlined simple changes to taxation policy to increase demand for female captives. An apparent response to the two-peso tax the 1789 code applied on the use of enslaved women in domestic service, this plan suggested a six-peso head tax on the importation of male captives. The proposal's author, Francisco Arango y Parreño, a prominent Creole planter and intellectual, also recommended fining plantations with enslaved populations less than one-third female. By taxing the importation of male captives and making it more expensive to maintain predominantly male slave populations, he reasoned, planters would be more amenable to purchasing female captives, thereby increasing the potential for procreation.

Predictably, the prospect of heavier tax burdens and fines met with criticism. Opponents argued that such measures would unduly burden slave owners, suggesting that simply allowing enslaved people to marry was sufficient incentive for procreation. Despite opposition, metropolitan authorities eventually adopted a head tax on male captives, funneling the revenue to support white colonization projects via the Junta de Colonización Blanca.[19]

In another attempt to address the problem of gender ratios, Cuban reformers sought to underscore the unique utility of enslaved women to plantation owners. With the 1791 outbreak of the Haitian Revolution, Cuba's Creole elites envisioned enslaved women as a stabilizing influence over the demonstrated dangers of the island's predominantly male enslaved population. Cuba's increasingly male and African-born population resembled the enslaved population that eventually transformed France's most profitable colony into the world's first Black republic. Cuban Creole elites feared that enslaved people in Cuba would follow suit, employing their military experience to launch an uprising to overthrow slavery and exterminate whites.

Some Creole elites believed that importing enslaved women could reduce the risk of slave revolt by providing a sexual outlet for enslaved men and a disincentive to rebel.[20] Havana planter and member of the Sociedad Económica Juan Manuel O'Farrill declared that "the greatest solace" an enslaved man could have was "that no one could impede him from choosing a female companion to his misery." Members of the Sociedad Económica seemed to agree. In July 1798, Arango y Parreño encouraged planters to teach enslaved men to "love property," arguing that "giving them a woman, and giving them children" would "reduce the interest [male] slaves may have in changing their unfortunate fate."[21] Another observer speculated that enslaved women could help reduce mortality rates. "An increase in the number of female slaves," one traveler observed, would be "so useful in the care of their husbands and their sick companions," thereby prolonging their lives.[22] Companionship, and later family, would bind enslaved men to the plantation, providing a disincentive for armed revolt.

Both these measures—increasing the proportion of female slaves and encouraging marriage—formed part of a 1795 "Instructivo para suavizar la suerte de los negros esclavos" (Guide to improve the lot of the Black slaves) issued by the Royal Development Board. This ironically named set of recommendations sought to augment slave owners' wealth by encouraging procreation among the enslaved and investment in the survival of enslaved children. In addition to urging planters to increase the number of females on their plantations, the guide directed them to comply with their obligation as Catholics to "moralize" their slaves by avoiding the "horrible and brutal sins" of illegitimate sex and encouraging "lawful procreation" within marriage. While the notion that honoring the sacrament of marriage formed part of slave owners' religious duty was evident in the 1789 code, the 1795 guide explained the material advantages of this measure, namely new enslaved generations. By encouraging slaves to marry, planters could increase natural reproduction, thereby conserving "the principal that was invested in the initial acquisitions" of slaves.[23]

Part of the board's argument in favor of slave marriage hinged on an apparent hostility toward the moral absolutism of metropolitan legislation mandating segregating the enslaved by sex. The argument featured multiple references to the impracticalities and economic disadvantages of preempting contact between enslaved males and females. The 1789 code had called for gender-segregated living quarters for all unmarried slaves, reducing the opportunity for sexual intercourse.[24] Some planters sought to enforce abstinence by maintaining exclusively male slave populations or imposing gender segregation.[25] One planter reportedly locked all the young enslaved women on his plantation in a barracoon in case "Christian persuasion" failed.[26] Others cited the supposedly polygamous nature of Africans and their descendants, claiming that allowing slaves to marry would only promote the sin of adultery.[27] According to the board, such morally absolutist practices hindered planters from reaping the full economic benefits of slavery. Encouraging marriage, they implied, offered a middle ground between slave owners' moral obligations and their financial interests, while also contributing toward colonial wealth through reproduction in slavery.

Although proponents of slave marriage often rationalized their economic arguments in moral and religious terms, some critics recognized the potential abuses of this pronatalist strategy. In the late 1790s, Cuban priest and intellectual José Agustín Caballeros argued that "masters have an obligation of conscience to give spouses to those slaves inclined to matrimony." However, the sacrament of marriage was not merely up to the whim of the slave owner. He warned that planters should allow but not force their slaves to marry, a distinction that recognized that some planters might exploit the sacrament to increase their wealth. He also rejected moralist arguments to exclude enslaved people from the sacrament of marriage, positing that denying enslaved men access to sex, whether by intentional gender segregation or by failing to purchase sufficient numbers of enslaved women, would only exacerbate their alleged sexual deviance, producing "masturbators, perverts, and sodomites."[28] Most of all, though, marriage allowed intimacy, which in turn brought clear material advantage to Cuban slave owners. Citing William Wilberforce, Caballeros argued bluntly that marriage would "assure in our island the multiplication of the negros by the lawful way of marriage."[29]

More so than moral concerns, however, an aversion to legal responsibilities informed planters' attitudes toward slave marriage. Likely because of the legal rights marriage afforded the enslaved, planters and their allies resisted the proposed measures to encourage slave marriage for procreative purposes. Within the Sociedad Económica, critics of pronatalist mandates emphasized the need for "softer" measures to promote the "propagation of slaves" on plantations. Rather than encouraging marriage, they suggested an array of policies they considered less intrusive on slave owners' property rights and autonomy. These included exempting from taxation the sale of field slaves, obliging the owner of a male slave who married a female slave on another plantation to sell the male to the wife's owners if that owner wanted to buy him, and to reward with royal recognition slave owners who promoted the highest number of slave marriages and births.[30] Perhaps unsurprisingly, most of these proposed measures were already required under the 1789 code. In essence, a vocal contingent of the Sociedad Económica resisted any regulation of slavery beyond the bare minimum required by existing law.

Even though these discussions of reproducing slavery remained largely if not entirely theoretical, it is noteworthy that the proposals both referenced and transcended metropolitan law. In particular, the explicit reference to slave "propagation," the rejection of the religious and moral justification of sex segregation, and the reframing of better treatment as a means for increasing fertility marked significant colonial innovations on metropolitan law. It took several decisive blows to the slave trade and slavery itself in neighboring empires before these colonial discussions eventually resurfaced in metropolitan law.

TOWARD A PRONATALIST AGENDA IN METROPOLITAN LAW

Spanish posture regarding enslaved reproduction began to change as a major legislative threat to the slave trade shook the British Empire and revolution erupted across the French Empire. The first in a series of bills proposing to abolish the slave trade appeared before the British Parliament in 1790. Although these legislative efforts were not successful until 1807, they evinced the impending demise of the trade for what was then the largest slaving nation.[31] The outbreak of the Haitian Revolution in 1791 not only stoked fears of Africanization among Cuba's creole elites, but it also led to the abolition of slavery within French territories, and the eventual birth of the first Black republic in 1804. While the Haitian Revolution created the void in the world sugar market that fueled the expansion of the Cuban sugar plantation economy and plantation slavery, it also issued a stern lesson about the possible consequences of relying on the slave trade to import a labor force acquired primarily through war.[32] Both these developments led metropolitan authorities to anticipate issues with Cuba's reliance on the slave trade, whether due to commercial restrictions or from fears of racial uprising.

On April 22, 1804, metropolitan authorities issued another royal decree regarding slavery, seemingly upending the gender, marriage, and child-rearing provisions issued in 1789. For one, it eliminated the one-third cap on the importations of female captives, instead charging the governor and other colonial officials with correcting the gender imbalance on plantations. It mandated importing female captives (and limiting the importation of male captives) to estates with exclusively or majority-male slave populations until "all [the slaves] who so desire are married."[33] The order instructed the captain-general to make planters understand that these policies, in addition to being their "just and conscious obligation," were also in their self-interest. Increasing the number of female slaves promised to benefit planters "by augmenting the number of their slaves, and improving their condition, without the continual expenditure of resources on the purchase of African captives to replace those who die."³⁴ In essence, this decree addressed the problem of high mortality by instructing colonial authorities to exploit enslaved women's reproductive potential, in anticipation of restrictions to the slave trade. While this decree reframed enslaved women's reproduction as a potential source of financial gain, it also sought to preempt enslaved women and men from appropriating these protections to advance their own familial and reproductive agendas. The decree warned colonial authorities not to publish the regulations to prevent enslaved people from finding out and demanding compliance.

These evolving metropolitan regulations on slavery allude to an emergent pronatalist agenda at the turn of the nineteenth century. The new policy consisted of three key pillars: balancing the gender ratios of slave cargoes and on plantations, encouraging marriage as a mechanism of licit sex, and requiring owners to provide basic care to slaves and their children. Yet, metropolitan authorities also seemed eager to maximize the number of slaves imported in the years before the slave trade's projected restriction. Indeed, this last initiative gained impetus in 1791, when the king issued a new decree extending the free trade in slaves to additional colonies and removing any stipulations about sex ratios on slave cargos. In a seeming admission of failure, the decree empowered slave traders to decide for themselves the numbers of males and females in their cargoes, in order to meet the perceived demand at the disembarkation site.³⁵

These early discussions about enslaved women echoed ongoing dialogues in the British Empire. West Indian planters blamed enslaved people for the low fertility rates, citing practices of polygamy that allegedly exacerbated gender imbalances, infertility due to high rates of venereal disease that slaves allegedly acquired through promiscuous sex, and child-rearing practices including prolonged breastfeeding and abstinence after childbirth, which had roots in some African traditions.³⁶ They preferred replacing slaves through importation rather than reproduction or even adopted an antinatalist approach, discouraging pregnancy and child-rearing as a distraction from agricultural labor.³⁷ By contrast, British abolitionists cited the deleterious effects of slavery on women's ability to conceive and give birth to healthy children.³⁸ These observations laid the foundation for public debates on pronatalist policies that included plans to ameliorate certain aspects of slavery to raise the notoriously low fertility rates of enslaved women in the Caribbean.³⁹

Aware of the debates and policy initiatives in the British Empire, Creole elites and colonial administrators in Cuba and metropolitan officials in Spain proposed many of the same ideas to sustain slavery at home.⁴⁰ Pronatalist recommendations emerged in Cuba periodically beginning in the late eighteenth century largely in response to fears about the demise of the slave trade. At the turn of the nineteenth century, proposed reforms evinced significant inconsistency and vacillation and ultimately gained little traction on the island. As long as the slave importations remained plentiful, planters viewed pronatalism as a second-rate, inconvenient way to generate labor supply.

The impending abolition of the slave trade in the British Empire revealed to Cuban planters, and indeed to the entire Spanish Empire, the fragility of the institution on which their wealth relied. Anticipating instability in the supply of African captives, Creole elites turned to women's reproductive potential as a way to ensure the future of slavery in a time of uncertainty over the persistence of the slave trade. The rest of this chapter examines the extent to which this pronatalist agenda materialized in practice.

The unwavering emphasis in the 1804 decree on reproducing slavery foreshadowed a major blow to the slave trade just a few years later. In 1807, British abolitionists secured their first major legislative triumph with the passage of the Slave Trade Act, which banned slave trafficking throughout the empire. Although the British ban did not technically prohibit slave voyages to Cuba, British companies could not legally engage in the trade, which imposed the first real limitations on the slave trade to Cuba since the Spanish Crown had liberalized it in 1789. Because the British had dominated the trade after the Portuguese monopoly faltered in 1640, the law severely curtailed the supply of African captives in the years immediately after it became effective. In 1802, 10,752 African captives entered Cuba, 7,202 of which arrived on British ships. By 1807, the number of captives entering the island dropped to only 732, the majority of whom arrived on ships sailing under the U.S. flag. The following year, 791 captives entered Cuba, all on ships flying the Stars and Stripes.[41]

The 1807 British ban on the slave trade intensified Cuban debates about the role of women's reproduction in ensuring the future of slavery. Fearing the potential end of the slave trade to Cuba, political elites from Havana brought their concerns to the Spanish parliament.[42] The discussion centered on the role of enslaved women's reproductive potential in sustaining Cuba's enslaved population in the absence of regular shipments of African captives.

However, the British ban also appeared to embolden abolitionist sentiment among some sectors. One Spanish deputy, Manuel García Herreros, speculated that Cuban planters would perpetrate severe abuses against enslaved women to force them to reproduce. Buttressing his claim, he cited "the shameful measures that are [already] employed so that [enslaved women] procreate," in violation of "all of the laws of decency and of modesty." In light of these concerns, he argued that *partus sequitur ventrem* should be eliminated.[43]

Predictably, this proposal met with harsh censure. Arango y Parreño, for one, dismissed his colleague's insinuation that planters would exploit enslaved women's reproductive potential. Instead, he posited that planters could not reasonably rely on enslaved women's reproduction to sustain their slave labor forces because of the heavy financial burden and uncertain rewards of pregnancy, childbirth, and child-rearing. "The slave who is pregnant or who has recently given birth," he wrote, "is useless for many months, and in this long period of inactivity, her nourishment should be greater and of higher quality. This privation from work [and] this higher cost of [sustaining] the mother come out of the owner's pocket. Out of [his pocket] also come the ongoing expenses of the newborn, which are often in vain, and on top of that are the risks that these run to the lives of the mother and child." Considering these expenses, Arango y Parreño claimed that slaves born on plantations cost more by the time they are able to work than slaves acquired through the slave trade. Therefore, "there is no, nor could there be, any interest in encouraging enslaved women to give birth, and the *horrors* that García Herreros suggests are imaginary," he argued.[44]

Apart from claiming that reproduction was too costly, Arango y Parreño also argued that the demographic realities of Cuba's enslaved population limited the possibility of natural reproduction on plantations. He explained that enslaved women typically "sold for a third less than the males," and even though "the prices of the females have risen" in recent years, "they never equaled that of the males."[45] According to Arango y Parreño, enslaved women's lower valuation contributed to the gender imbalance, because slave traders trafficked predominantly males. "In the last fifteen years, many fewer females than males have come; so few have come that there were scarcely enough" to satisfy the demand for domestic servants among urban white families. He observed that "there is not a plantation that has the same number of women as men. Moreover, there are very few that even have women at all."[46] He asked rhetorically, "can the species multiply where females are lacking?"[47]

Arango y Parreño insinuated that reproduction itself was not the problem. He noted that, among urban slaves, fertility rates remained high—a claim he likely extrapolated from the higher proportion of female slaves in urban areas. The problem centered on the particular gendered geography of Cuban slavery: whereas the predominantly male slaves on rural estates could not reproduce without more women, the predominantly female population of urban slaves allegedly reproduced in excess. Given this demographic reality, Arango y Parreño argued that the importation of female captives was the necessary precondition for creating a self-sustaining slave population.[48]

Disparaging his colleague's apparent nod toward Catholic moralism, Arango y Parreño also retorted that certain planters' attempts to impose decency through maintaining exclusively male labor forces or imposing sex segregation had only exacerbated low fertility rates among slaves. "Until very recently, our moralists frowned on keeping both sexes in our rural buildings, without first contracting marriage," he noted. Arango y Parreño thought that the moralist argument his colleague used to propose ending *partus sequitur ventrem* was inconsistent. García Herreros and other moralists argued for the protection of enslaved women from immorality but believed that "it was not sinful to condemn to perpetual celibacy those who had been born into and lived in absolute polygamy," Arango y Parreño argued, deploying racialized stereotypes of African societies as sexually deviant.[49] Turning his opponent's claim to morality on its head, Arango y Parreño declared that "what should horrify Mr. García Herreros are the brutal, but necessary consequences that followed and follow from such absurd scruples."[50] Arango y Parreño's strident reaction suggests that, prior to direct restrictions on the slave trade to Cuba, it may have been cheaper and more convenient, in the view of certain Cuban planters, to purchase new African captives than to create conditions conducive to natural reproduction.

Given these observations, Arango y Parreño argued that abolishing the slave trade without "the other resolutions that should accompany it" was premature. He posited that the proposed policy would "leave whites without the means necessary for their subsistence or development or to protect themselves from falling victim to the corrupting swarm of urban Blacks and mulattoes."[51] Instead, Arango y Parreño maintained that increasing the number of enslaved women on Cuba's plantations was the most realistic solution to the Cuba's labor problem. As Cuban delegates pled their case to the Spanish parliament, the number of captives entering the island recovered to its pre-1807 peak by 1815. However, the 1807 British ban marked the beginning of the end of the transatlantic slave trade on which Cuban wealth increasingly depended. Cuban planters' worst fears materialized just two years later.[52]

"Natural" Reproduction Following the 1817 Antislaving Treaty

Spain's first antislaving treaty with Great Britain, signed in 1817, would theoretically end the legal slave trade to Spain's colonies, including Cuba, by 1820. With that bilateral agreement, the legal trade in slaves to Cuba was set to expire just three decades after Spain liberalized the slave trade to its American colonies in 1789. The deliberate three-year delay was to give planters time to shift away from dependence on the slave trade and toward an alternative means of sustaining their enslaved labor forces, such as reproduction.

The metropolitan government then issued additional guidance to reinforce or amplify the pronatalist mandates of the 1804 decree. A judge in the Spanish parliament communicated precisely this to the Spanish Ministerio de la Hacienda in January 1817, just months before the treaty became official, when he recommended that the metropolitan government require "as an indispensable condition" that one-third of the captives on any slave ship destined for its colonies be female.[53] This slightly revised late eighteenth-century policy that stipulated that *up to* one-third of captives should be female.

In 1818, Captain-general José Cienfuegos acknowledged instructions that he was to "persuade property owners to provide their estates with females and promote marriage among the slaves, because ultimately the trade would have to end."[54] Later that year, metropolitan authorities recognized that the one-third quota had not produced the desired results. They instructed the intendant of Havana to impose a four-peso tax on the importation of male captives and to reward slave owners with ten pesos for each female captive they imported, reiterating the need to "promote marriage."[55]

Despite these tacit echoes of pronatalist policy, the metropolitan posture on slavery proved remarkably inconsistent with the pronatalist guidance of 1804. The same year of the antislaving treaty, the metropolitan government issued a separate decree freeing the African captives of the *Dos Hermanos*, a slave ship captured by French corsairs off the coast of Cuba in 1795. Of the captives disembarked and sold in Cuba, sixty-seven were women. Significantly, metropolitan authorities voluntarily freed these enslaved women at precisely the moment in which enslaved women's reproductive potential theoretically became foundational to the survival of slavery. In fact, although women comprised only one-third of the captives onboard the ship, they were the majority of the Africans traced through the case. However, what is even more striking about the resulting legal proceedings was that the decree also granted freedom to any children those women birthed during their illegal enslavement. At least nineteen eligible children, between four and twenty years old, were traced and freed, after herculean efforts by their mothers and other family members.[56]

While metropolitan authorities seemingly neglected their own pronatalist mandate, developments in Cuba suggest that the treaty fostered important changes in planters' behavior—at least in the short term. Following announcement of the treaty, demand for female captives spiked. Female captives imported into the island increased from 20 percent annually between 1811 and 1816 to roughly 25 percent between 1816 and 1820.[57] The price of enslaved women also rose, though the average price never equaled that of the males.[58] This increase in the proportion and price of female captives imported into Cuba was temporary and fluctuated significantly after 1820. However, the mounting restrictions against the slave trade over the next three decades roughly correlated to periodic increases in the importation of female captives, likely valued for their reproductive potential.[59]

African captives continued to pour into Cuba via the clandestine slave trade, but as slaving came under closer scrutiny, enslaved women's reproductive potential became more valuable. The birth of an infant to an enslaved mother represented a material increase in the wealth of the slave owner—one more slave to toil in the fields, one more piece of property to be sold for a profit, one fewer captive to be clandestinely purchased from illegal slaving ventures.

In the wake of the antislaving treaty, metropolitan and colonial authorities began to consider other causes of low fertility, beyond the imbalanced sex ratios. One traveler noted in 1828 that "as difficulties are thrown more and more in the way of importation of slaves from Africa, a greater attention is paid to pregnant females, to preserve the stock of the plantation."[60] Some planters evidently experimented with previous recommendations to allow marriage between slaves. However, many of these slave owners recognized that simply encouraging procreative sex would be insufficient to overcome the poor pregnancy outcomes, high infant mortality, and practices of fertility control. On some plantations, planters offered certain concessions in "commiseration of female slaves in that delicate situation." Some pregnant women received exemptions "from labor for a month before and after the birth, to nurse themselves and the child, and have hours of the day for months after for the same purpose, during which others are at work."[61] As one traveler observed, if they received "relief from labor during pregnancy," they might be able to carry their pregnancies to term and keep their babies alive.[62] However, for other enslaved women, these so-called concessions amounted to nothing more than a hole in the ground to accommodate their bulging bellies during beatings.[63]

Other slave owners expanded surveillance over pregnant slaves and enslaved mothers in an effort to curtail enslaved women's practices of fertility control. One slave owner created a "lying-in hospital" and nursery for enslaved newborns on his coffee plantation, which facilitated the supervision and care of ninety-five enslaved children under age ten.[64] Another slave owner created a plantation hospital on his estate, placing his wife in charge to ensure that the enslaved infants were "more carefully and skillfully nursed." Though the hospital was apparently short lived due to the "negroes [being] anxious to have their children in their huts," the plantation owner boasted of the low mortality rates among his enslaved population.[65] These efforts to foster higher fertility among enslaved women and lower mortality rates among enslaved infants supposedly resulted in "Creoles [being] reared in much greater numbers than formerly," according to one traveler.[66]

Some slave owners attached incentives and punishments to enslaved women's reproductive lives. One slave owner reportedly promised freedom to mothers who bore six children who survived infancy. The same owner threatened enslaved mothers with punishment if their children died.[67] At least a few planters across the island seem to have applied some of these pronatalist practices, though never to the exclusion of importing African captives via the clandestine trade. The parish priest of the newly established town of Cienfuegos administered twenty-four marriages involving people of African descent, between 1821 and 1830, the majority at the behest of slave owners. During the same period, he baptized 374 people of African descent, most of whom were slaves. By the mid-1820s, locally born enslaved infants outnumbered African-born adults in the local baptism records—reflecting both the growing secrecy surrounding the introduction of new African captives, as well as the search for domestic alternatives to the transatlantic slave trade.[68]

With such emphasis on ameliorative measures, so-called good treatment became the paramount idiom governing pronatalist reforms of slavery.[69] In fact, the pronatalist practices employed by a small number of planters in the 1820s became the basis for new recommendations aimed at preserving the institution of slavery on the eve of renewed restrictions on the slave trade. As the price of contraband slaves crept higher beginning in the 1830s, the Royal Development Board proposed ameliorating the conditions of enslavement to foster reproduction, a recommendation it had pushed unsuccessfully years earlier.[70] In 1832, Arango y Parreño petitioned the Spanish monarch, emphasizing the importance of convincing slave owners that encouraging natural reproduction among their slaves was in their best interest.[71] Given the "true interest" slave owners have in "the procreation of their slaves," he wrote, "it is indispensable to treat them well." He proposed implementing broad ameliorative measures.

Some of his suggestions would have directly affected enslaved mothers, granting them exemptions from hard field labor for enslaved women during the last six to eight weeks of their pregnancies, reduced corporal punishment for women, and access to the sacrament of marriage. As before, he reiterated his recommendation that planters "avoid separating married couples," take measures to "help husbands not abandon their families," afford enslaved women the "necessary modesty," and also concede to pregnant slaves and new mothers "the relief that their situation demands."[72] Arango y Parreño's insistence on ameliorating the conditions of pregnant slaves and enslaved mothers echoed earlier recommendations, which planters had apparently failed to implement in any meaningful way.

Arango y Parreño also proposed a series of incentives for both enslaved women and their owners to increase fertility rates. Enslaved women would be offered both nominal monetary awards and time off from labor to encourage them to birth large numbers of babies and keep them alive to working age. An enslaved woman who bore four live infants, for example, would be rewarded with relief from fieldwork and double the period of rest afforded to other enslaved women. If an enslaved woman birthed six live infants, she would also receive a monthly stipend to be increased for each additional child who survived more than six years.[73] Incentives directed at owners included prizes for plantations with the highest fertility rates, and fines for plantations with the lowest birth to death ratios. Arango y Parreño proposed a 3,000-peso annual prize to the plantation owner who achieves the largest number of slave births in proportion to deaths, as well as a second prize of 2,000 pesos to the second-highest number of slave births to deaths. He also proposed imposing a fine of 500 pesos on the plantation owner with the most deaths to births, and 200-peso fine to the second-worst death rate.[74] Even as the Royal Development Board revived many of these recommendations from previous discussions, it took a shift in the material reality of the slave trade before some planters began to change their practices.

Just a few years later, another reform-minded creole, Andrés de Zayas, proposed a series of measures to alleviate the conditions of pregnant and nursing slaves. These included gradually relieving them from certain labor as they approached their due date and then exempting them from heavy labor for the first few months while they were breastfeeding. He offered all these recommendations not as reprieve for enslaved women, but rather as an incentive to encourage reproduction.[75]

While the 1817 treaty reinvigorated earlier pronatalist discussions among defenders of slavery, others interpreted it as the beginning of the end to slavery. Reviving earlier concerns about the reproductive coercion of enslaved women, Cuban priest Félix Varela proposed a free-womb law as early as 1822.[76] Although such a law did not materialize until a half century later, Varela's idea evinces the tensions between efforts to preserve slavery and the demographic anxieties that accompanied the accelerating growth of the enslaved population in nineteenth-century Cuba.

Between Protection and Coercion: Assessing Pronatalism under Slavery

Proponents of such pronatalist reforms were quick to proclaim the success of these recommendations. According to O'Farrill, thanks to the society, "female slaves are now sought after, when before, very few came, and those who did come did not have buyers beyond urban families seeking domestic servants, and always with long waiting periods and for a third less [cost] than the males."[77] Yet, closer scrutiny suggests that the successes of these policies were more limited.

The myriad recommendations and policy initiatives to balance the gender ratio of Cuba's enslaved population failed to alter the broader preference for male captives. Broader island-wide figures suggest a slight decrease in gender imbalance between the late eighteenth and early nineteenth centuries (table 3.1). In 1771, one in every nine enslaved people in Cuba was female. Nearly a half century later, in 1817, that ratio had changed only marginally to one in every seven. Much of that change owed to high proportions of female captives imported in the years leading up to 1820, when the first Anglo-Spanish antislaving treaty became effective.[78]

Yet, when we consider geographical distribution, this pattern changes. Females remained a minority among rural enslaved populations. A survey of fourteen plantations between 1798 and 1822 revealed an average gender distribution of 87.56 percent male to 12.44 percent female slaves. La Divina Pastora and San Miguel sugar mills employed exclusively male enslaved labor forces with extremely skewed age distributions. On those two plantations, 100 percent of the enslaved people were between the ages of sixteen and forty.[79] A third plantation, near Trinidad, employed an enslaved labor force of more than seven hundred, all of them male. The planter locked these enslaved men in a barracoon during

TABLE 3.1. Sex ratios of slave cargoes entering Cuba, 1790–1815

Year	Percent Female	Year	Percent Female
1790	33.75	1805	20.66
1793	22.24	1806	21.68
1795	29.17	1807	29.37
1796	18.57	1808	30.95
1797	19.85	1809	26.82
1798	14.27	1811	27.27
1799	18.84	1812	26.77
1801	21.86	1813	25.54
1802	32.13	1814	27.08
1803	29.13	1815	33.86
1804	29.66		

Source: Pablo Tornero Tinajero, *Crecimiento económico y transformaciones sociales: Esclavos, hacendados y comerciantes en la Cuba Colonial (1760–1840)* (Madrid: Ministerio de Trabajo y Seguridad Social, 1996), 60–61.

their hours of rest.[80] This decided preference for male captives manifested in higher prices for enslaved men than for enslaved women, who typically sold for between 66 and 90 percent the typical price of a comparable male slave at the dawn of the nineteenth century.[81]

In rural areas, particularly those where sugar was the principal economic activity, the gender imbalance grew significantly worse in the late eighteenth century and only improved marginally in the early nineteenth century. A survey of twelve sugar-producing regions in western Cuba demonstrates this. There, the enslaved population became more heavily male between 1800 and 1808, when the ratio changed from 308.7 males for every 100 females to 316.5. The female population rebounded slightly by 1817 to 313.2.[82] At least some of this recovery owed to the significantly more balanced gender ratio among the young population (under age seventeen). For that population, the ratio improved from 181.2 males for every 100 females in 1800 to 167.6 in 1808. However, the overall ratio remained extremely unbalanced, with an even higher preponderance of males among the working age population (over seventeen years old), evincing ongoing reliance on the slave trade. In 1800, the sex ratio of the enslaved population between age seventeen and forty was 378.1, and for the population over age forty, it was even higher: 409.1. By 1808, the seventeen to forty age range became more balanced with a gender ratio of 300.1, while the population over age forty showed even greater *im*balance with a gender ratio of 478.4.[83]

A similar pattern emerged in baptismal records. According to baptismal samples from rural Havana at the end of the eighteenth century, the proportion of baptisms performed on females was just one-third in 1790, and it further declined to less than 15 percent in 1798.[84] This decrease in proportion of baptisms performed on African women, though not a definitive indicator of gender ratios in slave cargoes arriving to Havana, does suggest that the Free Trade in Slaves Act of 1789 favored the importation of male captives. This pattern makes sense given the proliferation of sugar plantations and the marked preference Cuban planters demonstrated toward male labor forces.

Because enslaved men sold for higher prices than did enslaved women, slave traders continued to transport as many male captives as possible. Slave traffickers destined for Cuba sometimes brought cargoes with fewer than 10 percent female captives, according to the limited data on captives' gender available through the SlaveVoyages Trans-Atlantic Slave Trade Database. In 1813, for instance, a shipment of slaves entered the port of Santiago de Cuba with only 8 percent female captives. In 1855, a cargo with only 4 percent female captives arrived at Cabanas. Although these examples are outliers, female captives rarely exceeded one-third of the new Africans entering Cuba. During the period of unrestricted slave trade to Cuba between 1790 and 1807, the proportion of female captives hovered between 21 and 33 percent of official totals of Africans imported into Cuba.[85] The atypical demographic distributions associated with heavy reliance on the slave trade, specifically the preponderance of males over females among the enslaved population, produced low fertility.

When it came to encouraging marriage, Cuban slave owners also fell short of reformist recommendations. Planters remained reluctant to allow enslaved people to marry, in part because the sacrament vested enslaved husbands and wives with certain legal rights. For instance, the 1789 code obliged planters to provide appropriate housing for married couples on their own plantation, or by arranging for the sale or purchase of a slave's spouse, or at least visitation, if another person owned them.[86] Apart from recognizing enslaved people as spiritual beings, these obligations undermined the totality of control slave owners could enact over their human chattel, thus reducing the probability of compliance.

Data from twelve sugar-producing areas suggests that, on average, marriage rates increased between 1790 and 1808. In 1790 and 1800, average marriage rates for the areas sampled hovered just above 14 percent. That proportion increased to 23.9 percent in 1808. In some regions, the increase was more dramatic. In Bauta, for instance, not even 9 percent of the enslaved population was married in 1790, but by 1808, 35.9 percent was reportedly married.[87] The proportion of enslaved women who was married increased by a greater margin than did the overall enslaved population. Of the fourteen regions surveyed, an average of 30.5 percent of enslaved women were married in 1790. This percentage increased to 35.5 in 1800 and reached 52.9 in 1808. In Bauta and Sibarimar, 83.1 and 75.1 percent of enslaved women were married.[88]

Figures from four districts in the western half of the island between 1791 and 1796 show low rates of marriage among the enslaved population. In Bahía Honda, a coffee-growing region of what is now the westernmost province of Pinar del Río, the enslaved population had the lowest marriage rate of the four districts—just 14.8 percent. In Yaguaramas, a cattle-ranching area in what is now the central Cuban province of Cienfuegos, the rate was similar, with just

15.9 percent of the enslaved population recorded as married. In the two Havana districts for which data are available, the rates were much higher—29.7 percent in the neighborhood of Jesús, María y José (an extramural neighborhood adjoining Espírito Santo) and 22.5 percent in the more marginal district of Jibacoa, where cane cultivation would later take hold. In the more rural districts, marriage rates for enslaved people lagged far behind those of the free population of color and the white population. In the most urban district of Jesús, María y José, the marriage rates were roughly even across free and enslaved people of African descent (ranging between 29 and 29.7 percent) and only slightly lower than rates for the white population (35.5 percent).[89] By 1827, average rates of marriage among enslaved people across Cuba hovered around 1 in 207, according to census records, declining even further to 1 in 347 by 1831.[90]

Proposals to ameliorate slavery also failed to produce meaningful change for enslaved people. Although advocates of amelioration believed that reducing the brutality of slavery could help lower the high mortality rates and encourage procreative desires, planters typically prioritized maximum labor extraction over the welfare of enslaved people, especially since they retained access to the slave trade. Mortality rates still hovered around 8 percent annually, even as creole reformers repeatedly recommended reductions in the intensity of work regimes and limits on the types and severity of punishments owners could mete out to their slaves without judicial approval.[91] Even as amelioration proposals continued to emphasize the importance of familial preservations, like the prohibitions on selling young children away from their parents, the ongoing disruption of the enslaved family likely factored heavily into the persistence of low fertility rates.[92]

Amelioration failed to address many of underlying causes of low fertility, including enduring stresses on enslaved women's reproductive health. Low ratios of women to men on Cuba's sugar plantations may have reduced the probability of conception, but enslaved women's fertility, maternal health, and pregnancy outcomes all suffered under the traumas of the Middle Passage and slavery. Female captives typically suffered higher rates of sterility compared to enslaved women born in the Americas.[93] Infertility in African-born women may have even increased their vulnerability to the slave trade, but the physiological shocks of their capture and transatlantic voyage likely contributed to and aggravated reproductive ailments in captive women.[94] The everyday brutality of slavery exacerbated the already high rates of sterility among recently arrived women captives. Inadequate nutrition and strenuous work rhythms likely contributed to amenorrhea and other conditions that depress fertility and significantly reduced enslaved women's ability to conceive, in many cases rendering them sterile.[95]

If conception occurred, maternal health suffered due to inadequate nutrition, strenuous work rhythms, and physical violence, resulting in miscarriages, stillbirths, and high neonatal mortality. Police records from Havana and other Cuban cities frequently reference the discovery of newborns, many evidently premature, on public roads, gutters, public latrines, near bodies of water, and at church doors and cemetery gates.[96] High rates of infertility among the small numbers of women and poor pregnancy outcomes due to the brutality of slavery contributed to depressed birth rates. According to the 1827 census, which imperfectly based the number of births on recorded baptisms, the birth rate for the enslaved population hovered around 4 percent annually.[97] Even when compared with the lowest mortality estimates, more than twice as many enslaved people died as were born in Cuba during the sugar boom.

Enslaved women who managed to carry to term and birth live infants often faced insurmountable obstacles preventing them from caring for their newborns. Planters routinely separated enslaved families, selling wives away from their husbands and children away from their mothers. Baptismal records from the central Cuban town of Cienfuegos show that after the antislaving treaty went into effect in the 1820s, some infants born to enslaved people owned by one owner were listed as the property of another owner. In the years immediately following the 1820 ban, the parish priest of the newly established town baptized at least three infants born to enslaved women owned by one white planter and listed the infants themselves as the property of another man. These baptismal records, like most others involving enslaved people, did not include information on the infants paternal lineage. It is possible that the owner of the infant also owned the father. However, since the status of the mother determined that of the infant, this scenario seems unlikely. Given the large number of enslaved infants born to that planter, the discrepancy in ownership likely evinces a local trade in infants born to enslaved mothers.[98] Within the shifting legal context of the slave trade, the institutionalized exploitation of enslaved women's wombs was already beginning to materialize.

If enslaved women somehow kept their babies, they often faced new demands on their labor, including being hired out to white families or even charitable institutions as wet nurses. A survey of western Cuban newspapers reveals thousands of advertisements for enslaved wet nurses, some with their newborns, others without.[99] The Casa Cuna, and later the Casa de Maternidad, employed dozens of enslaved wet nurses, who lived on site, most likely without immediate access to their own babies. The owners of those enslaved women received up to thirty pesos for each month of breastfeeding.[100] Enslaved wet nurses breastfed white babies, often to the neglect of their own infants. In fact, ads for the sale or hire of enslaved women for use as wet nurses peppered the pages of Havana's newspapers in the late eighteenth and early nineteenth centuries. One advertisement auctioned off a fifteen-year-old girl for 300 pesos without her (likely deceased) newborn. Another ad scandalized a British traveler decades later: "Wet nurse, two months since giving birth, with her baby or without it!"[101]

While the conditions of the slave trade and slavery negatively affected fertility, pregnancy outcomes, and infant survival, enslaved women themselves also exerted influence over their own reproductive lives. Some enslaved women practiced fertility control strategies like prolonged lactation, terminating their pregnancies, committing infanticide, and abandoning or neglecting their infants to avoid producing children who would suffer the same condition of servitude (see chapter 5).[102] All these factors converged to depress enslaved women's fertility rates and to make pregnancy, childbirth, and infancy outcomes particularly poor for enslaved people.

Uneven implementation by colonial authorities and broad noncompliance by planters meant that pronatalist mandates had minimal impact on fertility rates. In fact, baptismal records suggest that the proportion of free to enslaved birth rates actually declined between the late eighteenth and early nineteenth centuries. Karen Y. Morrison's sample of baptismal records involving individuals of African ancestry in the Havana parish of Espíritu Santo shows a declining proportion of births to free mothers. During the second half of the eighteenth century, just over half of African-descended infants with recorded baptisms were listed as the children of enslaved mothers. That proportion rose to 56 percent in 1800. By 1820, 60 percent of African-descended infants baptized were the children of enslaved women.[103] Moreover, an increasing proportion of these enslaved babies did not have a father listed in their baptismal record, suggesting an extramarital birth. In the second half of the eighteenth century, a quarter of enslaved babies baptized in Espíritu Santo were recorded without a father. This percentage increased by nearly half by 1820. More than likely, some of this difference resulted from the consolidation of legitimacy as the domain of free people, and especially of whites in colonial Cuba, which led priests to omit paternal designations for enslaved children (and children of African descent more generally) even when it was known. However, the growth in illegitimate birth is so dramatic that it appears to undermine the presumed relationship between marriage and fertility that undergirded much of the metropolitan legislation.

Other fertility indicators suggest enslaved women's reproduction fared worse in sugar-producing zones. Data from thirteen sugar-focused zones shows a considerable decline in the proportion of enslaved children. In 1790, an average of 9.1 percent of the enslaved population in that sample was under age seven. That percentage declined to 7.1 in 1800, and reached 5.2 in 1808. That year, just 2.9 percent of the enslaved population in Batabanó (Matanzas) were young children. The greatest decline occurred in Macuriges (also Matanzas), where 1790 figures were as high as 12.2, and plummeted to 3.2, by 1808.[104] Overall, the average number of children per enslaved woman declined from 0.5 in 1790 to 0.4 in 1808. In one area, that figure dropped as low as 0.1 children per enslaved woman, and in another three areas, it was 0.2.[105]

Prior to the nineteenth century, neither metropolitan nor colonial authorities seemed immediately concerned with enslaved women's reproduction. In fact, the legal frameworks governing slavery in the late eighteenth century actually suggested an antinatalist approach that framed enslaved women as a liability for slave owners precisely because of the financial burden of reproduction. However, the rise of Atlantic abolitionism in the late eighteenth century, and its eventual arrival to Cuba by the 1810s, compelled changes in this attitude. As the Haitian Revolution fueled the expansion of Cuba's sugar plantation economy, the prospect of restrictions on the slave trade forced colonial elites to confront the reality that natural decrease defined the island's rural enslaved population.

Only as the British Empire moved closer to legal abolition in the first decade of the nineteenth century, however, did colonial and metropolitan governments consider how to sustain the island's enslaved population without the slave trade. In this context, colonial and metropolitan law began to reflect the belief that enslaved women's reproductive potential was key to the survival of slavery in an age of abolitionism. The Spanish government began to issue pronatalist guidance concerning enslaved people just three years before the passage of the Slave Trade Act in Great Britain, reigniting colonial discussions about pronatalist reforms within the institution of slavery.

The pronatalist reforms proposed by colonial elites involved balancing sex ratios, promoting marriage, and encouraging more humane treatment of slaves. However, these provisions largely failed in their pronatalist objectives. Part of the problem involved a demonstrable lack of urgency. After all, the foundation of pronatalist policy stemmed from the 1789 slave code, a document that predated the arrival of abolitionism to Cuba and largely lacked consequences for violations. As one traveler noted, "the law was never framed with any reasonable prospect of it being enforced; it never has been enforced, and, what is more, it never can be enforced against the planters who are the transgressors of it; because in fact these are the men who are entrusted with the execution of it."[106] Even the implementation of the first Anglo-Spanish antislaving treaty in 1820 failed to inspire their compliance in the long term because planters quickly discovered the flaccidity of Spanish efforts to enforce it. Slave owners largely ignored the provisions for encouraging marriage among enslaved people and allowing families to remain together. Enslaved women were routinely "torn from their children," as planters' short-term economic calculations continued to shape the way they managed their enslaved labor forces.[107]

With the persistence and growth of the clandestine slave trade after the renewal and reinforcement of Spain's antislaving treaty in 1835, colonial and metropolitan authorities concurred in two key realizations. First, they began to understand that the mere existence of enslaved women was insufficient to foster reproduction. Second, they also started to appreciate that changing planters' practices might require a stronger state intervention in slavery.

CHAPTER FOUR

Preserving White Infant Life
Women of Color and Charitable Institutions amid Demographic Shift, 1820s–1830s

In the early nineteenth century, the legal regime governing women's reproduction in the Spanish Empire began to change with the passage of two key sets of laws. First, in December 1821, metropolitan authorities announced the Ley de Beneficencia Pública de España (the Spanish Law of Public Beneficence), which was extended to Cuba in February 1822. The law marked one of the first formal state interventions in what had been, for much of the colonial period, an ecclesiastical domain. It called for the creation of secular governing bodies and bylaws to regulate charitable institutions and guide chaplains. It also issued guidance on a range of issues pertaining to the care of expósitos. It required that children be registered when they were admitted to the Casa de Expósitos, and encouraged institutional administration to prioritize external caregivers, returning to a practice that previous chaplains had tried to eliminate. The law also enabled Casa authorities to award full custody to caregivers if they requested it and prohibited the return of children to their parents.[1]

Among the most significant of the law's mandates, however, involved the unification of what had previously been three separate charitable institutions in the Spanish Empire: the Casa de Expósitos, the Casa de Beneficencia, and the Casa de Refugio. Although the first two institutions had operated in Cuba since the eighteenth century, the third institution, which sheltered unwed pregnant women from the seventh month of pregnancy through postpartum, may not yet have existed in Cuba at this time. Significantly, the law also called for the creation of a "school of obstetrics" within this maternity ward to train midwives. Sometime after the creation of such schools, the law declared that "no woman will be permitted to practice said art in the towns without having studied in it and at least having acquired the corresponding title, following examination."[2] Through these provisions, the Law of Public Beneficence reinforced, codified, and extended what had been a de facto approach to women's reproduction in Cuba: the patriarchal protection of women.

This framing of women as vulnerable and needing protection extended to a second major legal intervention: the 1822 penal code, the first Spanish penal code. One of the most significant reforms this new penal code introduced involved the codification of honor as an attenuating circumstance in fertility control crimes. In regards to infanticide, article 612 prescribed the same treatment for individuals who killed an immediate family member as for ordinary murderers. However, it made an exception for "single women or widows who, having an illegitimate child and not having been able to give birth in a *casa de refugio* nor being able to abandon it at the appropriate authority, kill [their infant] within the first twenty-four hours after birth to cover up their fragility." The law afforded judges discretion in determining the main motive of the infanticide and instructed them to apply this exception only for "uncorrupted women who had good reputations before the crime." Instead of the capital punishment, a woman convicted of *honoris causa* (for the sake of honor) infanticide would be subject to a sentence of fifteen to twenty-five years in prison and banishment from the town where she committed the crime.[3] Thus honor-induced infanticide became a privileged exception to parricide laws.

The 1822 penal code also introduced protections for women accused of abortion. First, the law distinguished between abortion committed with and without the woman's consent, positing that not all pregnancy terminations resulted from a woman's intentional action. Article 639 detailed an array of scenarios in which a third party would face criminal charges if they performed an abortion, even if their methods were ultimately unsuccessful in terminating the pregnancy. "Anyone who voluntarily and knowingly procures a pregnant woman's abortion by employing foods, drinks, physical violence, or any other analogous method, without her knowledge or consent, will suffer a reclusion of two to six years, if unsuccessful, and six to ten years if it was successful." If the woman consented to the abortion, the practitioner would be subject to one to four years reclusion if the procedure was unsuccessful and four to eight years if it was successful. Penalties were higher for medical practitioners who operated without a woman's consent. Physicians, surgeons, pharmacists, male midwives, or female midwives faced five to nine years if the procedure was unsuccessful or eight to fourteen years if it caused the termination. This shift reframed the expectant mother as a potential victim in need of state protection and enabled the prosecution of third parties, such as abusive partners and negligent medical practitioners, for the loss of a woman's pregnancy. The law also prescribed significantly reduced penalties for abortion if committed by the mother—four to eight years in prison or, in the case of an "uncorrupted" single woman or widow, only one to five years in prison.[4]

Even though the letter of the law did not include explicit reference to race, it assumed powerful racial meanings in the context of colonial Cuba's nineteenth-century slave society. Fertility crimes did prompt unprecedented state attention in the form of police investigations, across boundaries of race and legal status.

However, white women and free women of color had vastly different experiences under the 1822 penal code.

Colonial authorities continued to see white women as victims in need of protection, shielding them from prosecution in the courts, and expanding charitable services for them and their infants. Protecting white women and infants also served as a pretext for corrective, punitive, and exclusionary measures against women of color. Colonial authorities undertook the regulation and surveillance of midwives, which they framed as another protective measure to defend white women and their unborn infants from the alleged quackery of racialized women healers. The regulation of midwifery marked a pivotal change that later enabled colonial authorities to enforce the penal code's criminalization of unlicensed medical practice, which as later chapters will show, disproportionately targeted the women of color who practiced this profession. Charitable institutions simultaneously pushed for more zealous racial restrictions on charity. As a result, women and infants of color remained excluded from assistance, exacerbating their poverty and sometimes ensnaring them in the judicial system.

"A Profession that Could Be So Useful in Able and Masterful Hands"

Common to both the Law of Public Beneficence and the 1822 penal code was an emphasis on the regulation of midwives. The former established a mechanism for training midwives, who would, in turn, be subjected to greater state supervision via medical examination and licensing requirements.[5] The latter criminalized practitioners, including midwives who intervened to terminate pregnancy or kill newborns. The law criminalizing abortion committed "without the consent of the woman" evinced this understanding that midwives and other medical practitioners bore responsibility for the outcomes of a pregnancy. The same assumption also appeared to influence the infanticide law, which specifically addressed instances in which the murder was committed by someone other than the mother.[6] These broader conceptions of the parties involved in reproduction reflected an emerging recognition that it was not just the pregnant woman who had a stake in controlling the outcome of the pregnancy, and it was not just the pregnant woman who could affect its outcome. The principal justification for this redistribution of blame was the perceived need to protect white women from the negligence and malpractice of women of color midwives.

Together, these laws theoretically protected pregnant women from a range of potential threats. They would have criminalized abusive husbands for causing miscarriage. They would have also given pause to relatives or partners who might feel compelled to pressure a pregnant woman to abort or commit infanticide to salvage the family honor or to preempt the financial burden or social obligation of marriage. Such laws also made practitioners criminally liable for interventions that caused miscarriage or infant death and mandated educational measures aimed at preventing these kinds of "mistakes."

However, in practice, laws criminalizing third-party interference in women's pregnancies and childbearing formed part of a more general crackdown on reproductive health practitioners, especially midwives, as Cuba's medical establishment professionalized. Among Cuba's leading physicians, consensus gradually emerged that poor pregnancy outcomes were not necessarily always the premeditated criminal acts of "unnatural mothers." Rather, in some cases, expecting mothers suffered terrible tragedies at the hands of the people who attended their pregnancies and deliveries.

If midwives were to blame for poor pregnancy outcomes, then colonial authorities had a responsibility to regulate the profession more stringently. Even through licensing protocols had supposedly governed the profession since before Spanish colonization of Cuba, colonial authorities appear to have relaxed their enforcement of such requirements for midwives, due to a shortage of practitioners. Even after a Real Tribunal del Protomedicato (medical board) was established in 1711, the qualifications to serve as a midwife in Cuba were fluid. In fact, in that very year of 1711, a petition arrived to Havana authorities requesting that a twenty-three-year-old midwife named Blasa Romero be released from her prison sentence and banned from leaving the island due to the "shortage of women trained in said [midwifery] art." Three years prior, she had been convicted of the public scandal of cohabitating with her boyfriend, a military officer. Promising that Blasa would live "honestly and collectedly from then on," the petition also asked authorities to commute her prison sentence, even as they continued to prosecute her boyfriend for violating the precepts of the church.[7] Later that month, the city council also heard a petition from Agüeda de Barga, a resident of Havana, who declared herself skilled and capable in the art of comadre de partera. She requested permission to be examined so she could practice her profession.[8] Between 1701 and 1788, surviving records from Havana document the formal licensure of seven midwives.[9]

Beyond the women who sought formal license, much larger numbers of women practiced midwifery without formal training or title. Prior to the 1810s, lax enforcement of licensing requirements enabled midwives to circumvent the typical requirements of purity of blood, honor, and legitimacy governing other professions, such as physician. As a result, women of African descent came to dominate this profession in colonial Cuba.[10]

The professionalization of medicine in the late eighteenth and early nineteenth centuries in Cuba gave renewed impetus to formal examination and licensing requirements for medical practitioners, including those attending pregnant women. Although obstetrics and gynecology did not emerge as distinct fields of medical training or specialization in Cuba until the late nineteenth century, the most privileged Cuban physicians gained exposure to these fields in their advanced medical training abroad, especially in France. Drawing on those experiences, they brought to island the concept of parteros, male midwives. As precursors to obstetricians, parteros became central figures in overseeing the pregnancies and deliveries of enslaved women on Cuban plantations by the early nineteenth century, and very likely also attended impoverished women at San Francisco de Paula hospital and the Casa de Maternidad.[11] The emergence of the partero signaled the beginning of a much longer process in which white male physicians projected themselves as authorities and overseers of medical practice and healing more generally.

Precisely as a few white male physicians began fashioning themselves as parteros, Havana's Tribunal del Protomedicato renewed its efforts to regulate midwifery. In 1824, the medical board appointed two white male "professors in the art of obstetrics" to train and oversee midwives in Havana. Dr. Domingo Rosaín had studied under renowned Spanish obstetrician Francisco Lubián before establishing a midwifery academy. Francisco Alonso y Fernández, who started his medical career in the Spanish armed forces, was summoned to Havana to serve at the San Ambrosio Military Hospital, before offering the first obstetrics class for medical students.[12] And according to the medical board, they were "publicly known for their competence and positive results." These two men were charged with creating a course (cartilla) to train midwives beyond their "ordinary practices." That year, Rosaín—who then boasted the title of "Fiscal de Parteras"—published Cuba's first training manual for midwives, *Examen y cartilla de parteras, teórico práctica* (1824), which became the main text for the course. Ultimately, the course would prepare midwives to take the exam with the medical board.[13]

Although Rosaín and Alonso y Fernández gained formal authority from their new titles, their status within the medical profession proved more precarious. They invested significant energy in justifying their involvement in work that was not only historically female but also predominantly Black. Attempting to regain the respect of their peers, these early *comadrones* framed their interventions in midwifery as a form of patriarchal protection of white women from the abuses of women of color midwives. While these physicians did claim their own professional expertise, they relied even more heavily on discrediting midwives as unskilled and racially inferior.

Arguing for stricter licensing requirements for midwives, white male physicians claimed that the prevalence of unskilled women of African descent within the profession imperiled the lives of white infants and mothers. In a series of letters to Havana's medical board in fall 1824, Rosaín, decried the "blind imbecility" of midwives, arguing that these women were responsible for maternal mortality, miscarriage, stillbirth, and neonatal death. Because of the "abandonment and criminal indifference" with which authorities had typically regarded midwifery, these untrained practitioners had allegedly "sacrificed so many victims," including "mothers and those who ceased to be such (i.e., ones whose fetuses or infants died)." He argued that it would be "of use to the public" to enforce training and licensing requirements on the profession.[14] The medical board apparently found such critiques compelling. Tacitly referencing the 1822 penal code, they called for unlicensed midwives to be brought to justice by imposing the appropriate sentences to punish their "incompetence."[15]

For Rosaín, the threat of criminal prosecution was insufficient. Writing once again, he lamented the high incidence of maternal death during pregnancy, childbirth, and puerperium. But this time, he emphasized the moral and spiritual harms untrained midwives caused. These women inflicted "frequent disgraces and fatal occurrences" on expectant mothers, "both physically and morally." Most troubling was the death of infants without the spiritual salvation of baptism. These negative outcomes, he claimed, were "all the result of the ignorance of the midwives, who know no other principles than ordinary practice with their repeated absurdities."[16]

While the loss of life proved insufficiently compelling, the appeal to spiritual urgency apparently resonated with medical authorities. The protomedicato petitioned the captain-general for permission to establish a formal course of study for midwives. The petition found favor with colonial authorities. In his approval letter, the captain-general, Francisco Dionisio Vives y Planes, vowed to "extirpate the abuses" the protomedicato and Rosaín had denounced, putting an end to the "sad results that daily result from the imbecility" of midwives and reducing "the number of mistakes and their deplorable effects" they commit.[17]

Echoing many of Rosaín's arguments, Vives amplified the view that regulating midwifery was necessary to protect white mothers and infants from the intervention of Black women. Much like Rosaín and the Protomedicato, Vives denigrated midwives as ignorant, incompetent, immoral, impoverished, and by extension Black. Following Rosaín's lead and reproducing verbatim some of his phrases, the captain-general attributed the loss of maternal and infant life to the fact that midwives drew their ranks from "only the most uneducated and abject portion of the population," a characterization that drew on the social marginalization of Black women in colonial society. According to the captain-general, these women had "neither knowledge nor qualities [*calidades*]."[18] The captain-general's use of the word "calidades" significantly invoked a historic tie between the notion of quality and racial purity/whiteness. According to Vives, midwives also served a spiritual role, which demanded moral purity and religious devotion. Seemingly contradicting his argument that midwives caused poor pregnancy outcomes, he observed that midwives were expected to administer the sacrament of baptism to babies "born with little hope of life." Such an important spiritual responsibility required the practitioner "to be a good Christian, charitable, prudent, [and] cleanly."[19] Black women, he argued, did not possess these qualities. On the contrary, he declared, "the women among us who dedicate themselves to this profession" lack the "sweetness of character and [good] manners" necessary for the job. He assumed that the pregnant women and infants in need of protection from these midwives did possess decency, honor, and sensibilities, racialized attributes typically associated with white womanhood.

As he insinuated in this implicit comparison of Black women's supposed immorality and white women's perceived moral purity, Vives conflated pregnancy with white women's vulnerability. The expectant mother Vives conjured was a woman who required delicate care and sympathy in her "fragile state." Thus midwives needed to be "very exact and careful with the women giving birth, attending to them with pleasure, taking charge of consoling with affectionate words the ones who are truly afflicted in their state, letting them know the desire they have to alleviate their pains." Vives also emphasized midwives' duty to defend the privacy and honor of white expectant mothers, some of whom sought to give birth in secret to avoid public dishonor. It was the midwife's responsibility, according to Vives, to refrain from talking directly or indirectly about them, observing the greatest "stealth," and attempting to forget even their names, "since it is often through a lack of precaution that a [woman] who enjoys a good reputation is discovered, which is also the responsibility of the Midwives."[20] Vives believed that only white women could be entrusted with such important duties.

This racial argument emerged with particular clarity in the preface Vives wrote for Rosaín's midwifery textbook. Therein, he argued that the presence of Black women was a "fatal flaw" in the midwifery profession in part because of his (largely mistaken) assumption that they negatively impacted the pregnancy outcomes of white women, with grave consequences for the island's demographic future. To address this problem, he suggested the recruitment of white women to the profession. He asked: "Why do the white women of this City not dedicate themselves to practicing this Art? Do they believe that this profession degrades them? Ha!" He argued if white women considered "that there is no field of medicine that more directly impacts the health and life of individuals of their own sex, they would hurry to rescue the afflicted humanity with their knowledge." In doing so, white women could prove their worth: "There is nothing that society values more than those individuals who care about the well-being of their fellow creatures."[21] In pushing white women toward midwifery, Vives underscored an important shift in gender roles emerging in the early nineteenth century. Privileged white women gradually carved out space for themselves in the public sphere, especially in areas related to Christian piety and motherhood, such as charitable institutions. However, the frustrated, almost pleading tone of his appeal suggests that most white women were reluctant to enter a profession as gruesome, gory, and laborious as midwifery.

The hostility Vives expressed against Black women midwives also hinged on the emerging understanding that midwifery required knowledge and skills that not all women had or could grasp, especially as obstetricians gained new medical and anatomical knowledge and developed new surgical techniques. Yet, according to Vives, "the generalized belief [was] that no knowledge or qualities are necessary to practice it." Consequently, he felt the profession had become overrun by untrained, predominantly Black women, whose "almost absolute ignorance" and "blind imbecility" allegedly "disgrace a profession that could be so useful in able and masterful hands."[22]

Vives insisted that, in fact, midwifery did require significant skill. Because a midwife had to "have an exact knowledge of the parts upon which she works," "an idea of the fetus," and "the laws that govern its development," white women were in a better position to exercise the profession competently, Vives insinuated.[23] Midwives were required to provide "all the necessary assistance" to help a laboring woman deliver her baby and to intervene by supplementing her efforts if the birth did not progress naturally. They were also expected to provide prenatal care to the expectant mother during her pregnancy and delivery, and prevent issues that "could result in the premature expulsion of the fetus inside her womb [*fruto que lleva en sus entrañas*]." According to the captain-general, all these duties required "continuous study," something that most midwives in early nineteenth-century Cuba simply did not have.[24]

The lack of formal education was not unique to midwives. In colonial Cuba, formal education opportunities for girls and women were extremely limited, even at the most basic levels, let alone for more advanced or professional training. Although wealthier families could afford to pay for private tutors and "honorable" white families of more modest means had the option of sending their daughters to Havana's recently established Colegio de Niñas San Francisco de Sales, formal education for girls of working-class or poor families was decidedly limited in the early nineteenth century. Most education for girls focused on domestic skills to prepare them for their future roles as wives and mothers. Opportunities were even more limited for girls of African descent due to racial segregation and school admission exclusions. And access to formal professional instruction for women—beyond domestic skills—was essentially nonexistent.[25] The assertion that pregnancy and childbirth were legitimate areas of professional specialization that required skill and formal training was tantamount to arguing that Black women had no place in the historically Black and historically female profession of midwifery.

The racialized and gendered implications of this argument were not coincidental; they were indicative of the ways Cuba's emerging class of medical professionals understood, internalized, and deployed the Enlightenment-era conflation of knowledge, authority, and expertise with whiteness and maleness.[26] This redefinition of midwifery as a potentially respectable, skilled profession emerged precisely as elite Cuban physicians began accessing specialized training overseas, especially in France, a leader in obstetric innovation. To carve out a space for themselves in Cuba's medical establishment, physicians had to create a need for their services. By casting midwives as "clumsy and coarse interlopers" who commit "abuses and errors" every day against "poor expectant mothers," physicians could claim the role of heroes by facilitating regulation and formal training.[27]

Yet, as Rosaín himself later admitted, the state of the Cuban medical profession did not permit the replacement of "evil midwives" with physicians or surgeons. There simply were not enough doctors in Cuba, much less ones specializing in obstetrics.[28] Early efforts to address the shortage of maternal health specialists included midwifery examination and, later, training for male medical students. In October 1825, Francisco Alonso y Fernández, then serving as professor of anatomy and surgery, proctored one of the first public exams for male midwives, though just fourteen students stood for the exam.[29] By 1830, Dr. Alonso offered the first obstetrics class for medical students in the Havana's newly inaugurated Anatomical Museum (Museo Anatómico de La Habana), located in the San Agustín Convent, which shortly moved to the San Ambrosio Military Hospital. There, he instructed his students, including Nicolás José Gutiérrez (who later replaced him), in human anatomy through demonstrations with cadavers and wax replicas. Alonso also framed his endeavors as a humanitarian quest to save "the enchanting sex and the innocent baby," descriptors that undoubtedly revealed his understanding that the primary beneficiaries of his work would be white mothers and their children.[30]

With limited obstetric training for medical students, medicalization of pregnancy and childbirth relied first on licensing midwives. Though he recognized this dependence, Rosaín sought to exert greater control over the "quality" of people entering the profession, in part by providing formal training. For this, Rosaín sought to establish the Midwives' Academy (Academia de Parteras). In summer 1827, Rosaín wrote to the Real Sociedad Económica (then called the Real Sociedad Patriótica de la Habana), of which he was a member, and requested a dedicated space in the Francisco de Paula Women's Hospital for midwifery classes, and materials necessary for teaching, including an artificial pelvis, and six copies of his book.[31] Although Rosaín had already garnered the protomedicato's endorsement and captain-general's approval to oversee midwives, his petition for access to the women's hospital is significant because it would allow for practical training with live female patients.[32]

San Francisco de Paula gave Rosaín and his prospective students access to the bodies of Havana's most vulnerable women. In addition to attending impoverished women, as originally mandated in the institution's founding documents, the hospital also continued to warehouse incarcerated women while lifting or only conditionally enforcing the prohibition on admitting enslaved women. In fact, after free women of color, the next largest category of patients admitted in the 1830s was enslaved women.[33] Situating the academy within the charity hospital aligns with broader regional uses of enslaved and impoverished women as training sites for nineteenth-century medical practitioners.[34]

Likely recognizing access to the bodies of vulnerable women as crucial for the development of medical knowledge and authority, the Sociedad Económica approved Rosaín's petition. Writing on behalf of the sociedad, Francisco Arango y Parreño applauded this idea. "While we move toward having an adequate number of Professors well instructed in the art of midwifery," he wrote, "it will be of great utility that the women who now practice it so blindly acquire the knowledge that [Rosaín] desires to provide them."[35] Francisco de Paula's maternity ward became home to the Academia de Parteras Santa Lutgarda in 1827.

Following the establishment of the academy, race remained a point of contention in women's access to midwifery training and licensing. Metropolitan regulations required women to be widowed or married, provide written consent from their husbands, present recommendations proving their good conduct and morality, and demonstrate their purity of blood. The profession's bylaws in Cuba omitted the provision about purity of blood.[36] However, Cuban women did have to be over the age of thirty, and "of good customs" as sworn to by their priest or judge to gain admission to the course. These requirements alone would have been enough to disqualify most women of African descent and poor women, groups with markedly lower rates of marriage.[37] Despite these obstacles, some women of African descent did gain admission to the academy, only to find that the midwifery course itself was segregated. One group was open to white women and the other to women of color, with each group meeting on different days.[38] Moreover, the professor could expel students who failed to comport themselves with "the necessary moderation and respect" or who failed to attend classes.

The course lasted two years, with six months of class each year. At the end of each course, eligible students would sit an exam; those who passed would receive as their reward the cost of the exam, paid from the course fund, or from the Sociedad Patriótica. Students could take the exam at any time after enrolling in the course. They could also petition for a provisional license for one year after they started attending classes. However, after the first month of classes, no one could practice midwifery without the appropriate license from the medical board. Students who did would face a fine of eight pesos, or incarceration in the Casa de Recogidas the first time authorities caught them, and double those penalties each subsequent time. The fines would be dispersed equally to the accuser, local authorities, and the course fund. The medical board approved the bylaws in September 1827.[39]

In the first class of midwives, seventeen women solicited provisional licenses, fourteen of them of African descent.[40] One of these women, María del Cármen Alfonso, advertised her services in the *Diario de la Habana* later that year, announcing that she had obtained the title of Master in the Art of Midwifery from the medical board, and offered her services on Obrapía Street in Havana.[41] Women who solicited these provisional licenses were likely experienced midwives, who had learned their skills through apprenticeship and practice. The high proportion of women of African descent who solicited temporary permission to practice reflected their predominance in the midwifery profession. Moreover, even as Black women faced disproportionate obstacles to accessing training and certifications, they still composed roughly half of the women obtaining formal licenses for much of the nineteenth century, a statistic that suggests an even greater number practicing extralegally.[42]

The cost, eligibility requirements, and assessment associated with midwifery training and licensing created a mechanism through which white male physicians manipulated who could legally practice midwifery. In particular, the moral and economic restrictions imposed by formalizing midwife training and certification placed women of African descent at a disadvantage for obtaining licenses. As a case in point, even though fourteen women of African descent obtained provisional licenses in 1828, the *Guía de Forasteros* listed only four women of African descent practicing midwifery in 1834. In 1837, five of the nine midwives were Black women, none of whom coincided with the initial group of women with provisional licenses, and only one of whom had passed the exam in 1828.[43]

It is noteworthy that aspiring midwives in Havana did not have consistent access to the academy. In 1833, for instance, the academy halted its annual courses due to a cholera epidemic, which temporarily diverted the hospital's beds to patients affected by the outbreak. Rosaín apparently continued offering classes from his home for some time, but midwifery training remained inconsistent, as epidemic disease and other emergencies periodically shuttered operations at the women's hospital.[44]

Unlicensed midwifery persisted despite efforts to regulate the profession. Throughout the 1840s, authorities in Spain and Cuba reminded practitioners of licensing requirements. An 1842 royal order reinforced the need for formal training and examination, prompting the appointment of Dr. Joaquín Guarro as head of obstetrics. He established a new midwifery course outside the women's hospital.[45] But just two years later, the medical board again barred midwives from practicing without formal training and a license. Citing a royal order concerning the inspection of medical training, he declared that "no person in the islands of Cuba and Puerto Rico will practice the faculties of medicine and surgery, now including the branches of dentistry, blood-letting and midwifery, without having the corresponding title issued by a competent authority."[46] Part of a larger project of medical professionalization, this order also mandated specific punishments for individuals practicing without a license: "those who practice any branch of the science of healing without the legal title, or exceed the faculties that it concedes, will be issued, pending competent summary investigation by a local judge, a fine of 100 pesos the first time, or in case they cannot pay it, a month in prison; the second time 200 pesos or two months in prison, and for the third time 300 [pesos] or three months in prison," not including whatever penalties they incurred for any fatal results.[47]

In some cases, authorities revoked licenses as punishment for crimes or perceived transgressions. In the 1840s, for example, the African-descended woman María Pilar Poveda, who worked as a skilled midwife in Matanzas, was barred from practicing her profession after a tribunal convicted her of being an accomplice in the major slave uprising known as the Conspiración de la Escalera (Ladder Conspiracy).[48] Nonetheless, women of African descent continued to represent more than half of the women officially practicing midwifery through the 1840s: eight of twelve midwives in 1840 were Black women, seven of twelve in 1841, and eight of thirteen in 1845.[49]

Midwifery regulation erected significant bureaucratic and economic barriers to one of the only skilled professions in which Black women could earn a decent living at the same time charitable institutions closed their doors to Black women and children. Although the education and licensing requirements applied to women regardless of race, the eligibility criteria implicitly privileged white women, and the time and cost of midwifery courses disproportionately limited poorer women and midwives serving poorer clientele from obtaining the required certifications.

The Medical Utility of Patriarchal Protection

Since physicians emphasized poor pregnancy outcomes as one of the most significant reasons for introducing these reforms, it makes sense to ask what impact, if any, these new training and licensing requirements had on patient experiences and outcomes. Although reliable maternal and infant mortality statistics are unavailable for this period, data from the women's hospital suggest that mortality remained a defining experience for patients at San Francisco de Paula. Figures from the 1830s show abysmal mortality rates, with nearly as many women dying as were "cured" (table 4.1). In 1836, for example, the mortality rate was 35 percent, more than three times higher than at other public hospitals that year. According to the Sociedad Patriótica, the women's hospital "ordinarily presents an excessively high mortality rate; since [patients] really resort to it when terrible and incurable illnesses drive the patients to find their sad lurch where they can take their last breath of a miserable life tortured by the most lamentable disorders. As such, despite the care and assiduousness with which they are attended, medicine rarely triumphs" over their lifelong afflictions.[50]

TABLE 4.1. Patient outcomes by race and legal status at San Francisco de Paula Women's Hospital, 1835

	Admitted	Cured	Died
White	7	4	6
White prisoners	3	2	0
Free colored	21	13	12
Slaves	10	5	2
Prisoners of color	7	7	1
TOTALS	48	31	21

SOURCE: Real Sociedad Patriótica de la Habana, *Memorias de la Real Sociedad Patriótica de la Habana. Redactadas por una comisión de su seno.* Tomo II (Havana: Oficina del Gobierno y Capitanía General, 1836), 141.

Patient outcomes differed over race and legal status. Figures from 1835 show the lowest proportion of casualties for incarcerated white women. Free women of color had the highest number of deaths, as well as the highest number of patients admitted to the hospital, likely a result of the high rates of poverty and the lack of affordable medical care. Outcomes for enslaved women were significantly more favorable than for free women of color, possibly reflecting an interest by slave owners in preserving their productive and reproductive labor.[51] The data do not disaggregate by cause of death, so it is unclear how much of this mortality resulted from pregnancy, delivery, or puerperium, thereby making it difficult to consider the impact of training. If subsequent data is any indication, pregnancy and childbirth likely represented only a tiny number of cases, if there were any at all.

Official collection of island-wide birth and death statistics did not emerge until the late 1880s, following an 1885 law requiring it. However, local efforts to collect medical statistics began as early as the 1840s, following an 1842 declaration by the Junta Superior de Sanidad de la Isla de Cuba urging local authorities to collect data on mortality rates and causes of death as a means of developing public health policy. The 1845 publication of *Ensayo estadístico de la mortalidad en la diócesis de la Habana: Año 1843* by Dr. Ángel J. Cowley is among the first compilations of local medical data, including cause of death.[52] The data came from two key sources: six public institutions, including five charity hospitals and the Depósito de Cimarrones, and ecclesiastical records compiled by twenty-five parishes in addition to that of Havana and its surroundings, which were likely based on burials.

Each parish presented causes of maternal and infant death in ways that do not aggregate well. Still, it seems there were three key causes of maternal death and two main causes of fetal or infant death (table 4.2). Inflammation of the uterus (metritis), uterine hemorrhage (metrorragia), and childbirth were the three main causes of maternal death noted. Stillbirth and neonatal tetanus were the two main causes of infant death. The causes of death that appeared most

TABLE 4.2. Maternal and infant death in the diocese of Havana, 1843

| | Maternal Death | | | | | | Infant Death | | | |
| | Childbirth | | Metritis (inflammation of the uterus) | | Metrorragia (uterine hemorrhage) | | Neonatal Tetanus | | Stillbirth | |
Town and Ecclesiastical District / Cause of Death / Race	White	Of Color	White	Of Color	White	Of Color	White	Of Color	White	Of Color
Guanabacoa	0	3	2	2	2	0	20	23	—	—
Jaruco	—	—	—	—	—	—	7	12	—	—
Santa María del Rosario†	—	—	1	0	2	0	3	4	—	—
Santiago	0	3	0	3	1	1	32	52	0	—
Bejucal‡	—	—	1	0	—	—	9	15	1	2
Matanzas	2	1	—	—	3	0	33	69	1	0
Trinidad	2	1	0	3	2	1	8	23	1	0
Cienfuegos	1	2	—	—	—	—	11	12	—	—
San Antonio de los Baños	—	—	0	1	1	1	22	24	—	—
Villa Clara	3	1	4	0	6	0	136	81	—	—
San Juan de los Remedios	4	0	1	1	—	—	5	7	—	—
Sancti Spíritus	2	0	3	0	1	0	20	35	—	—
Güines	1	0	—	—	1	0	26	14	0	2
Jíbacoa†	0	1	1	1	—	—	6	4	—	—
Cárdenas	0	2	1	2	2	1	5	11	—	—
Guamutas	2	1	—	—	—	—	11	6	—	—
Álvarez†	1	0	—	—	—	—	12	2	—	—
Quemado de Palma†	0	1	—	—	1	1*	5	14	—	—

Macuriges	2	0	3	2	0	1	28	27	—	—
Managua†	—	—	—	1	1	1	5	4	—	—
Quivicán	—	1	0	2	—	—	19	26	—	—
Pinar del Río	2	0	3	1	0	0	20	36	—	—
Las Pozas†	—	—	—	—	—	—	5	5	—	—
Guanajay	0	2	2	0	4	—	8	20	—	—
Cano	1	1	0	1	0	0	5	12	—	—
Subtotal of ecclesiastical districts in Bishopric of Havana	23	20	22	25	25	10	461	568	—(2)	—(4)
Parish of Havana City and surrounding areas†	1	0	9	9	5	3	97	178	—	—
TOTAL	24	21	32	34	30	13	559	746	13	15

SOURCE: Ángel J. Cowley, *Ensayo Estadístico-Médico de la Mortalidad de la Diócesis de la Habana Durante el Año de 1843* (Havana: Imprenta del Gobierno y Capitanía General por S.M., 1845).

— Category not included in data.

* The total provided does not correspond to the values provided in each column, suggesting either an error in recording or a miscalculation. Since a value of one is listed for white women, and a total value of two is provided, it is likely the value for women of color is misrecorded and should be 1 instead of blank.

† One or more months not included in data.

‡ Includes January.

consistently throughout the data were metritis for women and neonatal tetanus for newborns, but not all institutions and parishes reported these.

In the entire city and district of Havana and its surroundings, only one single death was attributed to childbirth. Nine white women and nine women of color were said to have died of metritis, and another five white women and three women of color were listed as having died from metrorragia. These figures seem extraordinarily low considering the 454 white women and 606 women of African descent included in the data from Habana. For infants in Havana, the incidence of neonatal tetanus was very high: 97 of the 725 white children and 178 of the 930 children of color died of this illness. No stillbirths are included, even though this cause of death emerged among police investigations for the same period (see table 4.2). The near absence of causes of maternal death from the records likely indicates that women who died during pregnancy, childbirth, or from complications thereafter were counted as deaths by other or unknown causes, if they were included at all in the cause-of-death statistics.

Likewise, institutional data (all from Havana) show a striking absence of deaths attributed to pregnancy, childbirth, and neonatal illness. The lack of recorded deaths related to pregnancy and childbirth makes sense for institutions serving exclusively males, such as the military hospital, the San Juan de Dios Charity Hospital, and the Depósito de Cimarrones. It even appears plausible in the context of specialty institutions, such as the San Lázaro hospital for lepers, and the Hospital of Dr. Belot, which seemed to serve primarily patients afflicted with yellow fever. However, it is noteworthy that pregnancy and childbirth do not appear as causes of death in the institutions serving women, either. In fact, data from the San Francisco de Paula Women's Hospital do not include a single death related to pregnancy or childbirth.[53]

Given the state of obstetric knowledge at the time, Rosaín's training program could not have completely eliminated maternal and infant mortality. Midwifery training in Cuba evinced the limitations of obstetric knowledge, which, as Nora Jaffary observes, had advanced remarkably little from previous centuries.[54] Effective preventive measures for the most common causes of maternal mortality (uterine hemorrhage, puerperal fever) and infant mortality (neonatal tetanus) did not emerge until the widespread adoption of asepsis and antisepsis measures in the late nineteenth century, and treatments for those afflictions did not exist until the use of sulfa drugs and penicillin in the twentieth century. Obstetric training would have also failed to address obstructed births and eclampsia, since the procedure known as artificial premature birth emerged in Cuba only in the late nineteenth century, and cesarean section was almost always fatal for women in Cuba prior to the turn of the twentieth century. Similarly, prior to the development of effective treatments for syphilis and tuberculosis, stillbirths linked to in utero transmission would have remained high, as late nineteenth-century Cuban physicians noted.[55]

Preserving White Infant Life 113

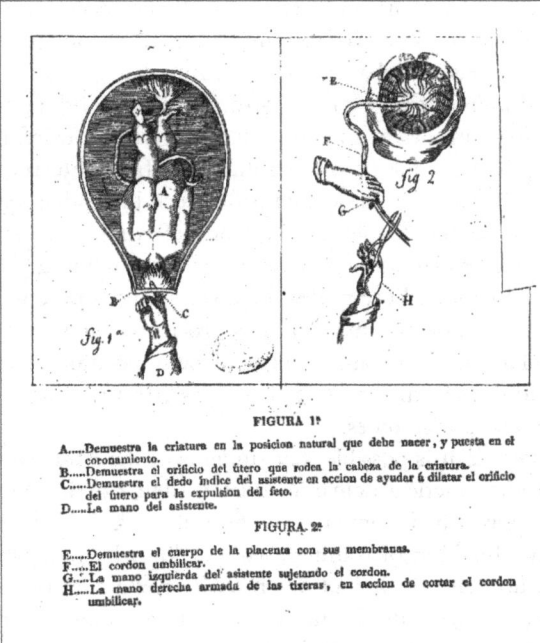

FIGURE 4.1. Rosaín's midwifery textbook outlined procedures that midwives were allowed to perform, including these two. Domingo Rosaín, *Examen y cartilla de parteras, teórico práctica* ([Havana?]: Oficina de Don José Boloña, impresor de la Real Marina, 1824).

A more plausible explanation for the low rates of reproduction-related maternal and infant deaths recorded at San Francisco de Paula Women's Hospital is that few impoverished women sought formal medical treatment there for pregnancy and childbirth. Most women continued to give birth at home, attended by female family members or midwives. Even when they experienced complications, such as infection or hemorrhage, or their infants were stillborn or became sick with common afflictions such as tetanus, midwives were more accessible than medical establishments. Such reproduction-related deaths only emerge in the documentary record if they were disclosed to ecclesiastical authorities on turning over the cadaver for burial.

This raises the question of what exactly midwifery students were doing in their training. Rosaín's textbook covered basic themes such as the kinds of situations midwives should expect to attend; rudimentary anatomy of women's reproductive parts including the pelvis and reproductive organs; a simple overview of pregnancy, the fetus, and birth; and a description of common complications, such as miscarriage, fetal deformity, and molar pregnancy. The majority of the work is descriptive, with only a few instances of explicit instruction for midwives. The textbook provided instruction about how midwives should attend to births, cut umbilical cords, and administer baptism if necessary (fig. 4.1). Beyond the use of plant extracts like almond oil and aceite de palo, neither Rosaín's 1824 text, nor a subsequent 1854 manual, prescribed sanitary measures, such as hand washing, instrument sterilization, or hygienic conditions of the environment.[56] Adoption of such practices remained contentious in Cuba even a half century later.

A second area in which Rosaín offered explicit instruction involved the numerous circumstances requiring midwives to summon a surgeon. In brief, if there was any complication, the textbook prohibited midwives from intervening and instructed them to call a doctor. These included breech birth, delivery complications, miscarriage, and others.[57] This emphasis on deferring to a doctor seemed to cast midwives as attendants whose main purpose was to bring patients with complications to doctors, whose professional status and reputation relied on access to patients for the development of new procedures and treatments. This supports Ana María Carrillo's argument that the imposition of licensing requirements for midwives formed part of physicians' effort to gain access to women's pregnant and laboring bodies.[58]

Given the manual's limitations, it is possible that students of the Midwives' Academy did not perform any practical deliveries during their training but rather used the bodies of impoverished women at the hospital to learn and be tested on women's anatomy. This kind of training, without knowledge about asepsis or antisepsis, would not have likely had much positive effect on pregnancy outcomes. Moreover, the mandate for midwives to refer complicated cases to surgeons was at best moot and at worst detrimental to pregnancy outcomes if it were actually enforced, since there were not enough doctors trained in obstetrics, by Rosaín's own admission, to provide any semblance of coverage. Thus, in this early struggle to subordinate women of color midwives to the medical supervision and authority of white male physicians, the patriarchal protection of white women's reproductive potential served as little more than a pretext.

Expanding the Social Safety Net for White Women: From Casa Cuna to Casa de Maternidad

While physicians claimed to protect (white) women and their pregnancies from the alleged dangers of untrained women of color midwives, metropolitan and colonial authorities expanded assistance for white women by mandating reforms on charitable services historically administered by the Roman Catholic Church. Article 41 of the Law of Public Beneficence, which required the unification of charitable institutions serving expósitos, orphans, and pregnant women, provided the foundation for the creation of Cuba's first formal Casa de Refugio for unwed pregnant women and mothers. This shelter would take the form of a distinct department within institutions serving a broader clientele of needy women and children.

The law specified that the explicit purpose of such a maternity ward was to "avoid infanticide, and salvage the honor of the mothers" by sheltering unwed pregnant women and new mothers.[59] To be eligible for admission, a woman had to be in the seventh month of pregnancy or beyond, unless "just and serious cause" required their admission prior, or they paid or earned their subsistence with labor. If admitted, unwed women could hide their pregnancies and give birth in secret to avoid the public shame associated with out-of-wedlock pregnancy.[60]

In Cuba, the consolidation of charitable institutions serving women, infants, and children found early expression in the creation of a new unit at the Casa de Expósitos—the first formal department for unwed pregnant mothers in Cuba. With the sizable bequest the institution received following the death of Doña Antonia María Menocal in 1820, institutional administrators at the Casa Cuna added a new charitable department called Maternity. The maternity ward offered a place where pregnant women could seek shelter to hide their extramarital pregnancies and secretly give birth. These women could then surrender their infants into charitable custody. The lactation department would then provide wet nurses and care for the unwanted infants, allowing their mothers return to their lives with their public honor intact.

By the early 1830s, the Casa de Maternidad (Maternity Home), also known as the Maternidad de María Santísima y San José, was established following a decade of discussion and negotiation involving metropolitan authorities, the colonial government, and ecclesiastical authorities.[61] The new institution recognized both its predecessor establishment, the Casa de Expósitos, with a portrait of Fray Gerónimo Valdés, and the principal benefactor making the new establishment possible, with a portrait of Doña Antonia María Menocal. As mandated in the Law of Public Beneficence, the Casa de Maternidad had three departments—maternity, breastfeeding (through age two), and children (until age six). As a whole, the institution aimed to save from certain "premature death" by abortion, infanticide, or abandonment "the innocent and unfortunate infants born of frailty, seduction, and poverty."[62] The maternity ward, in particular, sought to fulfill that mission by sheltering unwed pregnant women who might commit abortion, infanticide, or infant abandonment to salvage their honor.[63]

Havana's Casa de Maternidad served women in the advanced stages of pregnancy as well as ones who had already given birth at home. In contrast to the Law of Public Beneficence, which granted eligibility to women seven months pregnant, the Casa's bylaws limited access to women whose pregnancies were *eight* months along or further. The bylaws also extended eligibility to indigent women who gave birth at home but lacked the resources to sustain themselves postpartum. Like other charitable establishments, the Casa de Maternidad also drew distinctions on the basis of "morality and conduct," a mechanism to separate patients by class and status.

Despite this hint that the Casa might serve women of dubious morality, the bylaws depicted an institution that focused overwhelmingly on honorable white women. Echoing the Law of Public Beneficence, the Casa de Maternidad's bylaws provided important protections for women admitted to the establishment, notably guarding their privacy and anonymity to ensure their public honor remained intact. The maternity ward was to be completely separate from other departments and guarded by "the most inviolable secrecy." Department staff were prohibited from asking questions or soliciting information about "the private conduct of these sheltered women." Any employee who violated this vow of secrecy was subject to immediate termination. Adding onto the provisions of the Law of Public Beneficence, the bylaws permitted women to enter the establishment in disguise and under assumed names to protect their identities.[64]

The bylaws required women to make a decision about what to do with their child within twenty-four hours of birth. Although the law distinguished only between keeping the child and surrendering it to the institution, the bylaws provided a much broader menu of options. Women who had the "necessary qualities" could opt to serve as wet nurses, which would enable them to breastfeed their child (and others) while receiving ongoing subsistence from the institution.[65] Women could also pay for a private wet nurse, which the institution would procure according to the mother's request. Women who chose to keep their infant or surrender it to the institution would be discharged fifteen days after birth, except in extenuating circumstances. Women who experienced particularly difficult labors might be allowed to stay in the institution longer, on a doctor's recommendation. Women who became sick from childbirth had access to an infirmary where they could receive treatment from the staff physician. However, if their affliction was caused by anything other than childbirth, the bylaws required them to be sent to San Francisco de Paula Women's Hospital.

In contrast to the Law of Public Beneficence, the bylaws did not make reference to a midwifery school. But it required a medical doctor trained in surgery and midwifery to be on staff. In addition to treating ailing pregnant women, infants, and children, and maintaining an infirmary with a crew of "servants," this staff physician was also assigned to examine the breastmilk of wet nurses.[66] The "servants" were required to alert the doctor of any complications, so he could attend the "most difficult births" and those "against nature." These provisions suggest that the majority of the care of pregnant women and delivery of babies was done by midwives, who were not explicitly named as such in the bylaws. Though part of that labor was likely performed by enslaved women, an additional source of labor came with the establishment of a new midwifery course at the Casa de Maternidad in 1842. Midwifery students, both white and Black, likely attended patients in the maternity ward as part of their "training" under the supervision of Dr. Guarro.[67]

The expansion of charitable services to include not just infants but also pregnant women evinced an emerging recognition of fetuses as colonial subjects and the uterus as a site of political intervention. As Martha Few points out, these views, which had roots in the late eighteenth century Spanish religious and medical thought, framed the woman as the bearer but not the owner of the uterus.[68] These ideas likely informed the emergence of the Casa de Maternidad as one of the first formal institutions overseeing medical childbirth in colonial Cuba, where interventions in pregnant women's bodies were increasingly understood within the demographic projects of the time.

The creation of the Casa de Maternidad marked a decisive preference for charitable assistance over criminalization but also suggested a broader recognition of the limits of the 1822 penal code. In fact, the institution's bylaws even afforded women admitted thereto a form of legal immunity: her "discovery" within the institution could not be used as "legal proof against her," nor was anyone allowed to furnish information about her to the authorities.[69] Reflecting on the institution's creation, one administrator lamented that, even with the severest of laws, the best policing, and the highest degree of morality, thousands of children were in danger of "cruelly being cast aside abandoned without remorse by their parents."[70] The only other conceivable option, according to Casa philanthropists, was to ameliorate the stigma attached to seduction by providing shelter to pregnant women and save, by offering to raise them, the "disgraced" children of impoverished and illegitimate unions from "premature death."[71]

But who benefited from such a benevolent humanitarian approach? While the selfless language employed by Casa authorities suggests purely philanthropic interests in saving fetuses and infants from abortion and infanticide, in fact, unspoken racial assumptions undergirded these notions of charity and child welfare. The very fact that the Casa blossomed into a public institution in the 1820s, growing from its roots in seventeenth- and eighteenth-century medical and charity establishments, is significant, given the profound demographic changes shaking the island at the turn of the nineteenth century.[72] The rapid expansion of the sugar plantation system and the corresponding expansion in the importation of enslaved Africans ushered in one of the most significant demographic shifts in the island's history as a predominantly white settler colony morphed into a majority-Black slave society. It is also no coincidence that the establishment of the institution overlapped with the final years of a period of active, government-sponsored white colonization over the first decades of the nineteenth century.[73] The interest in reproduction and fertility in this context was a symptom of rising anxiety about the growing Black population, the supposed transformation of Cuba's racial identity, and the limitations of a demographic policy exclusively fueled by immigration.

The decision to extend the Casa's services to pregnant women hinged on several implicitly racialized assumptions about why women committed acts of fertility control as well as the reasons for the high mortality rates among the infants white women abandoned. According to the Casa's governing board, disgraced women often resorted to "violent remedies" to hide or end their pregnancies, or to escape the consequences of having an illegitimate child. As a result, these women frequently committed infanticide, or, when they "abstained from such cruelty," they tried to hide, ignore, or terminate their pregnancies. As a result, "their children are born sick, defective [*viciados*], or at least so weak that no amount of attention and care is enough" to save them. Another issue stemmed from the long journeys infants had to endure before arriving at the Casa. Most towns lacked the infrastructure to care for abandoned infants, even temporarily. Parish priests and town councils failed to allocate funds to feed, clothe, and transport the infants comfortably to the Casa. Consequently, many infants arrived "unclothed, hungry, and dirty" after their "delicate constitution" was exposed to a treacherous journey "in a basket, or if there are many, in a horse-drawn carriage" whose "violent movement they seldom survive." The governing board of the Casa de Maternidad argued that serving pregnant women would help reduce the excessive mortality rates among surrendered infants by allowing women to give birth inside an establishment equipped to care for newborns.[74]

The rationale for the expansion hinted at a subtle contradiction in the institution's mission. Here was a charitable institution for needy pregnant women and unwanted infants that explicitly concerned itself with defending women's honor. Women who had honor to lose most often held some sort of class privilege. Precisely these women enjoyed the broadest range of choices with regard to their unwanted pregnancies. Their families might have enough influence to pressure the father of the child to marry the expectant mother, or enough money to sue him, or even pay another man to marry her before she gave birth. Wealthier families might also have the resources to help the woman hide the pregnancy, give birth secretly, and give the infant up without damaging her public reputation. Wealthy women were in the best position to preserve their own and their family's honor and status by preventing their private indiscretions from tarnishing their public honor without committing abortion or infanticide.[75] In essence, most women who would have been considered honorable did not need an institution like the Casa de Maternidad.

By contrast, the women with the greatest need for such assistance were impoverished, a group that included both white and African-descended women, who largely fell outside prevailing notions of honor. Poor women typically had fewer resources at their disposal and often did not enjoy the luxury of hiding their indiscretions in the private sphere, nor could they always prevent sexual predation by men.[76] For this group of women, concerns about honor and future marriage prospects were mostly secondary to the concern of economic subsistence, especially for unwed women who lacked access to steady financial assistance from men.[77] For these women, abortion, infanticide, and infant abandonment were among the only alternatives to mothering in poverty. The institutional fixation on women's honor seemed to contradict the provision of services most needed by poor (presumably dishonorable) women.

This apparent contradiction revealed an evolving deployment of the concept of honor in the context of women's reproduction. By the early nineteenth century, an emphasis on honor was more about restoring the link between whiteness and elevated status than it was about investing in the reproduction of elite women. The creation of the maternity ward showed the colonial state's investment in harnessing the reproductive potential of impoverished white women to increase the colony's white population. This project hinged on downplaying class distinctions that had historically relegated poor white women to inferior status. By bringing impoverished white women under the umbrella of honor, the Casa not only invested comprehensively in the survival of white infants, from before birth through early childhood, it also reinforced racial boundaries between white and Black.

In fact, the Charity Board (Junta de Caridad), a governing body composed of some of the most powerful men on the island, created a set of rules that permitted only certain types of people to be admitted to the Casa de Maternidad.[78] This policy diverged from other charitable institutions that, in their discourse, promised to open their doors to "all classes of beings." The institution created partnerships with other charitable establishments, including the Paupers' House (Casa de Mendigos), where they redirected women who did not fit the standard they created.[79] Precisely as the letter of the law afforded greater leniency to white women, this group also gained access to a new set of public services, available only to them. Thus, the prevailing approach to white women's reproduction entailed providing services to shelter them from the social consequences of unintended pregnancy, in turn protecting their infants from abandonment or death. By focusing its mission on salvaging honor as a means to curtail fertility control, the institution targeted the same group of women who gained protection under the *honoris causa* exemptions: white women. The Casa's professed interest in protecting infants, thus, cannot be separated from ongoing racial transformations and anxieties defining turn-of-the-century Cuban society.

The Racial Boundaries of Charity

Around the time the Casa Cuna was reborn as the Casa de Maternidad, the institution also attempted to exert greater control over eligibility by implementing measures to enforce existing racial exclusions with greater rigidity. In the 1830s, institutional leadership discussed the "serious inconveniences" allegedly caused by the presence of children of African descent within the institution.[80] Admitting such children, they argued, exacerbated long-standing budgetary woes. Rising numbers of unwanted infants surrendered to the facility led

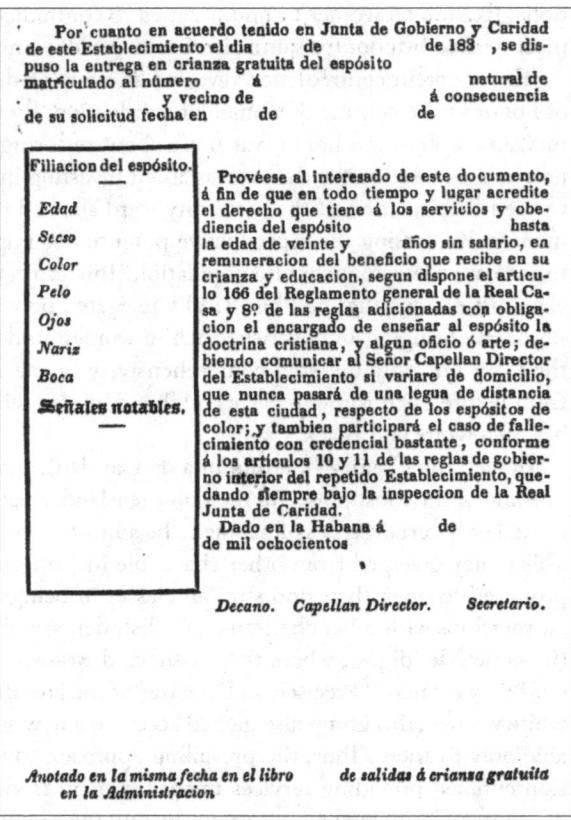

FIGURE 4.2. Sample inscription form for abandoned infants, requesting information about race and color. Evaristo Zenea, *Historia de la Real Casa de Maternidad de esta Ciudad* (Havana: Oficina de D. José Severino Boloña, Impresor de la Real Marina, 1838), 294.

to soaring expenditures and growing budget deficits. Amid this worsening fiscal status, institutional leaders saw the need for drastic changes to ensure that there were enough resources "to liberate [the existing infants] from death."[81]

The presence of infants of African descent within Havana's Casa de Expósitos was not altogether new. Although its predecessor institution, the Casa Cuna, had been founded with the explicit purpose of serving white infants, infants of mixed and unknown racial backgrounds entered the establishment (see chapter 2). Notably, the bylaws of the recently established Casa de Maternidad had no explicit racial requirements for eligibility. The intake form for the admission of expósitos into the institution, moreover, included a line to designate the infant's skin color as well as other physical characteristics associated with race, such as eye color, nose shape, and hair texture (fig. 4.2). However, the bylaws technically prohibited institutional staff from questioning those surrendering the child about its background or circumstances, a clause that carried forward from the 1796 decree. This prohibition would have theoretically banned questions about the infant's race or parentage.[82] However, institutional staff did assign race on the basis of phenotype, often denoting the conditionality of their designation with the phrase "al parecer blanco/blanca" (seemingly white), or in much rarer instances, "al parecer de color" (seemingly of color).[83] These records demonstrate at least a small number of racially mixed infants within the institution.

Despite these precedents, the complaints about the presence of African-descended infants found sympathetic ears within two new secular advisory councils that had been recently convened as required by the Law of Public Beneficence: the Charity Board, a board composed of prominent white men appointed to advise the director (chaplain) of the Casa and manage institutional finances; and the Piety Board (Junta de Piedad), composed of thirty prominent white ladies headed by the wife of the captain-general, and primarily charged with providing additional oversight of the care of children and fundraising.[84] As Sarah Franklin points out, charitable establishments created opportunities for elite white women to enter the public sphere.[85] But what impact did these women exert on the treatment of unwanted infants? An exclusionary one, as it turns out.

In January 1833, the leadership of the Charity Board met to discuss the "urgent necessity" of addressing the problem of the growing number of babies of African descent left at the Casa. The men had apparently brought the problem to the governor of the bishopric, Juan Bernardo O'Gavan, who proposed sending expósitos of African descent to nearby coffee and sugar plantations, where they would be raised and "receive the education appropriate to their class." The children would remain on the plantations until they reached age twenty-five, when they would be "emancipated." The committee discussed other solutions but decided that O'Gavan's idea was the best way to deter women of color from surrendering their unwanted infants through the torno. It not only promised to reduce the institution's expenditures but also "liberate the Ladies of the Piety Board from caring for and attending to certain abandoned infants who were never part of the establishment's mission."[86] To these men, the solution to the growing number of Black expósitos was enslavement.

The proposal seemed to address simultaneously three demographic problems that elites had. First, it provided a mechanism for plantation owners to acquire new slaves, as mounting restrictions on the slave trade threatened access to new captives and unbalanced gender ratios combined with the brutality of slavery ensured that mortality continued to surpass fertility among rural slaves (see chapter 3). Second, it could slow the growth of the free population of color by enslaving abandoned infants of color, or otherwise deterring free women of color from seeking assistance in keeping their children alive. Third, it contributed toward white population growth by freeing up institutional space and resources previously committed to expósitos of color to assist a larger number of white infants.

The logic of the proposal hinged on profound anxieties over the acutely gendered geographies of Cuba's demographic shift. The island's enslaved population, in general, and the rural enslaved population in particular, continued to be majority male, with men accounting for roughly two-thirds of all slaves (see chapter 3). By contrast, urban populations of color skewed more female, with enslaved women more likely to gain freedom than enslaved men. These gendered demographics of urban slavery and freedom lead to the growth of a sizable population of urban free women of color in Havana by the early nineteenth century.[87] Within this context, institutional leadership perceived the presence of children of color within the Casa de Maternidad as a serious misallocation of already scarce resources—ones they believed should serve white women and infants.

However, the proposal to place abandoned infants of color on plantations to free up space and money for white infants raised serious questions for colonial authorities and even some members of the Casa leadership. Among the challenges was a legal principle at the heart of the institution of slavery: *partus sequitur ventrem*. Colonial authorities recognized this contradiction. In the margins of the original memo appeared a note, dated February 26, advising the civil governor not to approve the proposal: "Expósitos of color are free people, and they should not be confused by working with and like slaves on rural plantations until a certain age, nor can they be subjected to an unnecessary emancipation, or exposed to the prospect of remaining slaves forever; and consequently, I believe that Your Excellency cannot adopt the proposed measure."[88] The proposal was denied.

The fact that such a scheme clearly violated established laws did not stop it from becoming the topic of intense debate among various groups of institutional leaders. The Piety Board women unanimously rejected the proposal, but on opposite grounds, claiming that it did not do enough to exclude children of color. Although they did not see a problem with enslaving free babies, they found fault with the presumption that they would arrange care for the expósitos of African descent on their own plantations. In addition to being "a great burden to them" to take responsibility for those babies, "they see it as impossible to oblige their own slave women, who barely attend to their own children, to care for other babies who are alien to them."[89] This objection pointed to the dire politics of reproduction on Cuban plantations, where pronatalist efforts had largely failed to produce self-sustaining slave populations.

Even as O'Gavan's proposed enslavement of expósitos of color failed to gain traction, institutional leadership remained perturbed by the presence of infants of African descent. The Charity Board appointed a new committee to report on the "abuse of introducing babies of color into the pious establishment." By June 1833, committee leadership, including Mariano de Arango and Domingo de

Aguirre, reported back to the director and the Charity Board. They noted that the "inconveniences" of having Black babies in the Casa were indeed "grave," although the exclusion of those children would be "diametrically opposed" to the institution's charitable mission.[90]

Instead of excluding children of color outright, the committee proposed placing financial conditions on admitting Black children. To ameliorate the "inconvenience of the excessive number of abandoned children of color," the Casa would require nonwhite children to compensate the institution financially for their care. The institution could create an "entirely separate department" for children whose "color, hair, or other indicators are clearly marked by their origin." Those children would be required to "learn a trade to pay the Establishment the [money] spent on their maintenance and education."[91] The Casa provided an option for parents to reduce or eliminate their children's debt by paying all or part of the costs.[92] However, given the poverty that likely afflicted free Black families who abandoned their children, this option was rarely viable. In essence, then, the committee proposed admitting children of color conditionally through an arrangement that would trap them in debt. Such a policy aligned with a longstanding Iberian tradition of tiered poverty relief, in which "worthy" poor received assistance, while "unworthy" poor were forced to work to earn benefits.[93]

The committee boasted the numerous advantages of their proposal. First and foremost, it would reduce the number of Black children surrendered to the institution by making the fate of the baby so unbearable that a childhood in poverty, or even death, would seem preferable. Thus, the Casa could indirectly deny Black children admission by making it unaffordable for Black women and unconscionable to mothers who wanted their free offspring to remain free: "With this soft measure, the abandonment of people of color will be greatly diminished and this purely charitable Establishment will not incur in the contradiction of closing its doors to creatures so worthy of their compassion."[94] The policy also assured an additional source of unfree labor, a valuable resource amid chronic financial woes.

The proposal was adopted by the Charity Board and promptly approved by the governor. Ultimately, by transforming expósitos of color from a financial burden into a revenue source, the committee, the institution, and colonial authorities sent a clear message about the boundaries of charity: the only mothers and infants worthy of true state protection were white ones—a missive consistent with prevailing preoccupations about expanding the island's white population.

FEMINISM AND RACIAL EXCLUSION

The women of the Piety Board were incensed by this new policy. They believed that debt bondage was not harsh enough to deter Black mothers from surrendering their infants. In November 1833 they appointed a separate women's committee to report on the "difficult problem of determining what would be convenient to do with the abandoned Black children, in a way that would simultaneously satisfy humanity as well as the justice, policies, and mission of the institution."[95] The committee, headed by the Countess of Fernandina and Paula de Chávez, reportedly shared the "pious feeling to shelter and adopt orphans without regard to color" but believed "precautions" were necessary to "ensure the discrete and equitable accomplishment of this."[96] They argued that "exposing" the Casa to the "exclusive domain of the heterogeneous castes" would violate the institution's "founding spirit," referencing the Casa Cuna.[97] For this reason, they judged the recommendations of the men's commission insufficient.[98] They insinuated that the Charity Board had failed to consider some of the advantages Black families stood to gain by surrendering their infants to the Casa. These benefits outweighed the costs of debt bondage, they suggested, rendering the approved policy essentially useless.

The women's report disparaged Black women as morally depraved, a condition that engendered a domino effect from sexual promiscuity to excessive fertility to maternal ineptitude and finally to infant surrender. About the sex lives of Black women, the report claimed "that perhaps half of colored women live with their personal affairs in the street, with absolute liberty." Not deterred by education, public opinion or even religion, these women were apparently driven by "the whims of their [sexual] appetites."[99] With such hypersexual lifestyles, Black women allegedly became pregnant often and had children in great numbers.

These statements pathologizing Black women's sexual and reproductive practices invoked an entire body of racial and gendered stereotypes about the perceived social dangers of free women of color, especially in Cuban cities. The 1827 census calculated the birth rate among the free Black population as only slightly higher than that of the white population—one birth for every six women of African descent, versus one birth for every seven white women.[100] However, elite discourse emphasized the dangers of Black reproduction. According to prominent Cuban intellectual Francisco Arango y Parreño, Black women in urban areas caused "the greatest damage to us [white Cubans]" with their excessively high fertility rates.[101] These women, "all of whom have offspring" and the majority of whom have "numerous children," are vectors of "all kinds of vices, laziness and lewdness being the most common." Most troublesome of all, all of these women have "the ability to liberate [those children] and to free themselves." The result, concluded Arango y Parreño, was the concentration of "an infinite number of people of color in our towns."[102] Surveying Havana's population by race and legal status, he noted that in Havana "the damage is so great that free people of color nearly equal the number of slaves, and together, both classes [exceed] the [number] of whites." He also noted that the number of baptisms was twice as high for people of color as for whites. Although this last observation did not consider that many of the baptisms of people of color most likely were of enslaved adults, it seemed to corroborate white elites' broader fears that free Black women's allegedly excessive fertility threatened Cuba's white population.[103]

Reproducing this logic, the women's report further argued that the poverty of free Black families made it impossible for them to sustain such large families. "People of color all live, with very few exceptions, in the greatest destitution," the report stated. "To alleviate the great strain" additional children posed on the family economy, many parents surrender their infants, "even those born of legitimate marriages" to the Casa.[104] Thus poverty compounded the effects of Black women's alleged moral depravity, threatening to overwhelm the institution with unwanted Black children.

The report also insinuated that some devious enslaved women, and quite possibly even some slave owners, abused the institution as a pathway to freedom for their babies. Because laws prohibited institutional authorities from inquiring into an expósito's background, surrender potentially afforded enslaved mothers a way to circumvent generational slavery, provided they could get their child into the Casa. The report alleged that enslaved women, "greedy by nature" and "nearly devoid of human feelings," would produce infinite numbers of children if they "knew they could freely surrender them to be maintained and raised much better than in her power." But enslaved mothers were not alone. The report alleged that it was also not unknown for severe slave owners to order the abandonment of their slaves' children, "to free themselves of the expenses they incur."[105] With no checks on legal status, the Casa de Maternidad threatened to undermine *partus sequitur ventrem*.

Also potentially "abusing" the institution was a new category of Black women known as emancipadas. Per the 1817 antislaving treaty, emancipados were Africans illegally trafficked to Cuban shores and captured by antislaving authorities. Although technically free, they remained wards of the state, usually confined in public institutions, where they labored for the state. This ambiguous status often prevented emancipadas from mothering any children they might have had during the Middle Passage or subsequent custody. If children of emancipadas survived, they sometimes landed in debt bondage arrangements vis-à-vis the state, but the women's committee feared they might end up in the Casa de Maternidad or the Casa de Beneficencia. It would be "too violent," they argued, to allow pregnant emancipadas "the unlimited ability to come from Guinea with the right to freely populate our House of Piety." If the Casa did not develop policies to avoid the admission of such babies, the committee feared that the institution would be filled up with the abandoned infants of enslaved African women, with no space left for white babies.

The women's committee argued for "strong restrictions" on the admission of

Black children to the Casa. Without such restrictions, they argued, "the proportion of them [Black children] to white ones would undoubtedly become ten to one." Because the Casa did not charge rent and had capacity to serve only "a limited number of infants," failing to restrict the admission of Black children would leave whites "excluded from the benefit." Such an arrangement could not possibly be "rational and equitable" and threatened the Casa with "monstrous inequality."[106] By equating the admission of Black infants with the exclusion of white infants, the women's committee exploited a logical slip common to exclusionary arguments across time and place: extending relief to the subordinate group was conflated with harming the privileged class.

Issuing a bold challenge to the authority of the all-male Charity Board, this report articulated an early vision of feminism that was premised on racial exclusion.[107] For the women's committee and the broader Piety Board that ratified the report, charitable relief of expósitos could function only if the institution was limited to individuals worthy of assistance. Definitions of worthiness hinged on race and legal status. Free Black women were deemed unworthy because of their alleged immorality, which was believed to cause "excessive" fertility. For unfree women, unworthiness hinged on the perception that they exploited charity to bestow on their children a legal status that did not belong to them. Authorities deemed excluding these populations from assistance as essential for serving white women and children.

MOTHERHOOD ACROSS RACE AND LEGAL STATUS

The men of the Charity Board did not take kindly to the challenges posed by their female counterparts. They rejected the women's claim that they should have been consulted on the matter and disputed the charge that they had not considered the severity of the situation. "We all recognize the grave inconveniences that color difference presents in our country," the men argued, claiming that they took it seriously in their report. They claimed their policy to be "very judicious, very legal, and very humane." They scolded the women's board, arguing it should have proposed "new and more adequate means of minimizing or diminishing the cited inconveniences," rather than simply criticizing the approved policies and painting an "exaggerated picture" of the circumstances.[108]

The men took issue with the women's claim that admitting Black children to the Casa would subject the institution to a "suspicious invasion" of Blacks. They reiterated their position that "distinctions of color" were incompatible with the Casa's mission to "save the lives of infants who would perish without help." The men also reminded the women that the Casa was not just a facility for pregnant women but also one for birthing and for raising the abandoned children, undercutting the Piety Board argument that the principal mission of the Casa was to serve elite women's honor. Finally, the men's commission appealed to the women's Christian sentiments, reminding them that, in Heaven, "such distinctions are unknown."[109]

Much of the men's rebuttal centered on reframing Black women's sexuality and reproductive practices to downplay the likelihood that they would surrender infants. For one, the men disputed the women's conflation of sexual promiscuity and bad motherhood, arguing that maternal sentiment was natural to all women. Though they agreed that the "promiscuity" of Black women was "infinitely greater" than that of plebeian white women, they did not believe white women would necessarily "have greater affinity for their children than colored women."[110] After all, "there are infinite loose women who love their children with so much and at times greater tenderness than those who are not [licentious]."[111] Turning the women's argument on its head, the men posited that Black women's presumed immorality actually gave them one fewer reason to surrender their children, precisely because they did not have any honor to lose.[112]

The men also contested that poverty made free people of color abandon their children with greater frequency. Although "it is true that among people of color there is a higher number of poor people," they claimed that poverty was not really a major consideration during the first year of an infant's life because mothers "do not make any other expense other than the milk which nature deposited for this purpose in the mother's breasts." The men ludicrously asserted that mothers of color do not spend much money, "as they keep [their children] naked and with crude nutrition in contrast to whites, who have to dress them and nourish them with a certain decency." The men's committee seemed not to consider how single mothers might earn money to support themselves and their infant. Nevertheless, they judged that "the pain of abandoning their children" would outweigh whatever "small and insignificant expense" they could avoid by surrendering their infants.[113]

The men's commission found something universally female about motherhood: "maternal love created by nature to safeguard the weak existence of man is equal in every species of human." They argued that neither immorality nor racial difference detracted from maternal instincts. Freedwomen "do not stop being mothers just because they are African and loose."[114] They observed that the number of women of any class who "get to the extreme of putting out the flame of maternal love in their hearts by abandoning their children" was relatively low. To support their claims, the men's committee offered the example of free African women, who were "as easy as beasts in their union with our sex." Yet, "we see nevertheless that the population grows considerably, and this would not happen if the mother did not take care in raising her children."[115] Essentially, the men's committee posited that maternal love was inherent in all women, which translated to population growth.

All these rebuttals led the men's commission to reaffirm their approved policy that African-descended children pay their expenses at the Casa through apprenticeship work. They argued that this policy would serve as "a very powerful deterrent" to Black children being left with the Casa "because it is known that mothers of color count on the support of their children in their old age, and they cannot want to be without that in the long term as they should take a long time to reimburse the Casa" for their expenses.[116] In truth, of all the children in the Casa between September 1833 and April 1834, thirty-four were white and only two were of African descent (one mulatto and one moreno), figures that refute any claim that the Casa was under siege from an impending Black "invasion."[117] By 1835, metropolitan authorities issued a reminder of the 1794 decree granting legitimacy to all expósitos and declared that the legal benefit applied to all expósitos "without exceptions."[118] Legal protections, however, did not guarantee admission to the Casa. By 1836, institutional correspondence shows an ongoing effort to place expósitos of color with private families, who, it seemed, would extract a few decades of domestic labor from each infant they took.[119]

EXCLUSION AMID CONDITIONAL ACCEPTANCE

The new policy of conditionally admitting children of African descent into the Casa fell short of dismantling racial exclusion. In part, the ongoing racial exclusion owed to structural barriers preventing certain categories of women from accessing the institution. In this regard, alarmist fears about emancipadas supposedly exploiting the Casa de Maternidad for the benefit of their children could not have been further from the practical realities most of these women, as a class, confronted. Emancipadas with babies and young children often found themselves in the Casa not as beneficiaries but as unfree laborers. In fact, by 1840, a royal order made the Casa de Beneficencia the sole depósito de esclavos in the city of Havana. The Royal Development Board, a council composed of prominent (slave-owning) Creole notables of Havana, characterized the policy as "new proof of the esteem" the Crown held for their charitable work.[120] From there, the board, which oversaw the city's charitable institutions as well as the administrative processes governing emancipados and runaway slaves, assigned the emancipados different duties, from street paving to service in the Casa de Maternidad.

Irrespective of whether they had young children, many emancipadas were forced to labor at one of the charitable institutions, often in capacities whites deemed "appropriate to their sex." Some of these emancipadas were assigned to the Girls' Department of the Casa de Beneficencia, where the director complained that they allegedly corrupted the little white girls, infecting them with "shameful vices," including promiscuity and licentiousness.[121] Others were assigned directly to the Casa de Maternidad. One emancipada named Paula, "number 354," who arrived to Cuban shores in July 1840 with her new baby on the captured ship *Negrito*, labored for nearly two years in the Casa de Maternidad before obtaining her freedom papers. It is unclear whether she was allowed to leave the Casa thereafter.[122] By the mid-1840s, there were so many babies interned at the depósito in Havana that the administrator petitioned to exempt that institution from accepting "young children and unuseful ones."[123]

In fact, it was unlikely that emancipadas ever escaped the custody of the Real Hacienda, let alone with their children.[124] One emancipada named Rita, "number 212," captured in 1845 aboard the clandestine slave ship *Planeta*, was confined in the Depósito de Cimarrones with her son, José Eligio. Rita became ill and died shortly thereafter.[125] Unlike white orphans or children of convicts, however, José Eligio did not gain admission to the Casa de Beneficencia on his mother's death. Instead, an infantry captain took custody over him, essentially impressing him into the military.[126] Another emancipada Luiteria, who arrived on Cuban shores aboard the schooner *Ninfa*, was remanded to the Depósito de Cimarrones, a holding cell for escaped slaves, along with her small child, Julián. Julián died in custody in September 1844.[127] A similar fate befell the emancipada known as Gertrudis, seemingly employed at the Casa de Maternidad as a wet nurse in the late 1860s. Her baby Miguel perished in November 1867.[128] By the mid-1850s, the Junta de Fomento even requested that 2,500 pesos from the emancipados budget be allocated directly to the Casa de Beneficencia, presumably to pay for the maintenance of the growing number of emancipados from whom the institution extracted labor.[129]

The children of enslaved women also confronted seemingly insurmountable barriers to accessing charitable assistance. In 1849, the governing board denied a petition to admit the legally free mixed-race child of an enslaved woman. In late December 1848, the morena Dolores Villafranca gave birth to a child conceived after a "small misstep," presumably with a white man, whose identity remained undeclared in the child's baptismal record. Dolores secured freedom for the baby a few months later through an act of charity from a "protective hand." The baby's freedom papers denoted that a white man named Manuel Sainz had paid fifty-one pesos to liberate the child, a reduced price usually reserved for the freedom of a fetus in utero. By September 1850, Dolores appealed to authorities on behalf of her child, "obsequiously implor[ing]" that her baby be admitted into the Casa de Maternidad. However, the Casa's Governing Board rejected her request, ruling that it violated its policy of accepting only true expósitos, without any family members capable of raising and educating them. The board argued that baby Manuel did not qualify because he still had his mother, a woman whose enslaved status, by definition, would prevent her from raising and educating her free son.[130] This decision aligned with the women's committee argument for excluding the children of slaves but fell short of the men's recommendation to fine the owner 500 pesos.[131]

Casa authorities did not enforce the policy as stringently on white families. For instance, in June 1841, the Casa welcomed five white children after their father was convicted of murder.[132] The same year, a white father snatched his child from a wet nurse employed by the Casa, after months of the infant's mother visiting the wet nurse's home regularly. The scandal, and the ensuing debates about custody rights that it provoked, revealed the existence of white children who did not meet the classification of expósito but still gained admission into the institution.[133] Casa authorities noted that, legally, parents who abandoned their children lost custody and all parental rights over them and therefore surrendered the option to reclaim them or request at any time for their children to be returned to them. However, a parent who went before a judge to prove paternity may be eligible to make a claim when it was in the best interest of the child.[134]

In practice, it was relatively common for impoverished white parents to request their children be admitted to the Casa, only to attempt to collect them later.[135] For instance, the white man Manuel Rodríguez requested that his two-year-old daughter, Petrona Josefa, be admitted to the Casa, explaining that he was destitute. He suggested that one of the "infinite slave women" incarcerated at the institution would be able to take care of her "without cost." Expressing pity for the man's situation in a letter to Gerónimo Valdés, Mariano de Arango wrote of the urgent need to implement his plan for a new institution for impoverished families, especially considering the "growing poverty" afflicting the city.[136] The policy of exclusively admitting expósitos into the establishment, selectively applied by race, afforded Casa authorities a mechanism by which to enforce racial exclusion without overtly announcing it as such.

The various governing boards and commissions guiding the institution found other ways to refuse to admit children of African descent who otherwise appeared eligible. One such technicality was the claim that nonwhite children brought the risk of disease and contagion. In 1841, for example, the director of the San Lázaro charity hospital appealed to local authorities to transfer eight children born there to sick patients to the Casa de Maternidad. Most, if not all these children, appear to be of African descent. The hospital director identified one of them explicitly by name, race, and sex as the "negrita Salustiana Crucet," whose mother, Merced Marqueti, had died in the hospital and whose father, the moreno León Crucet, remained in the hospital. Salustiana and her two siblings lived at the hospital alongside their father, who it seems had an incurable illness, possibly leprosy. Several of the remaining children had been born to mothers with close ties to slavery, as indicated by the hospital director's description of their relatives, friends, and comadres.[137]

The hospital director noted that most of these children required breastfeeding and care beyond what the hospital could provide. He also inquired about policy, asking if in general babies born to patients should be sent to the Casa or remain with their mothers. If they were to remain with their mothers, he requested additional resources to sustain them. According to a physician's report, all except one of the children were "healthy and well-nourished." The only one found to be ailing was Salustiana, who the doctor claimed suffered from a "predisposition to leprosy." Salustiana was transferred to the San Francisco de Paula Hospital for Women, where she would be less likely to become exposed to the illnesses common to the lazaretto. The healthy children were ordered to be transferred to the Casa to be breastfed by a wet nurse that did not nurse other children.

However, the Maternity Board, a council charged with advising the director on matters pertaining to the maternity ward, opposed the order to admit the seven healthy children, claiming that the possibility of contagion was reason enough. A committee appointed by the Maternity Board and headed by Evaristo Zenea expressed its regrets, saying that it wanted to be able to admit "the disgraced children of Lazarinos" to the Casa "without insurmountable inconveniences" so that their "honorable and Christian work" could liberate the children from the "evils of their parents' disgrace." Nevertheless, the committee concluded that admitting the children would be "irreconcilable with the existence of the Real Casa." They warned that the children would cause "so many and such grave inconveniences," and such harms could "destroy from its foundation an establishment that relies on the generosity of the sovereign who protects it as well as the charity of the citizens of this privileged soil."[138]

The committee claimed that the Casa had insufficient space to keep the children separate, as instructed in the transfer order. They also argued that there were not enough wet nurses, and it would be impossible to find enough women to comply with the mandate that each of the seven children have its own wet nurse, who did not nurse any other children. They claimed that potential wet nurses would not "subject themselves to the risk, however remote, of catching an illness," and that even if they did, "their owners will not want it, if they are slaves, nor their relatives and families if they are free." The committee argued that even bottle-feeding the babies would impose an undue burden on the Casa, because there was still the problem of finding caregivers to attend to the children. "Surely it would not be useful nor charitable to transfer them to a place in which it would be very difficult if not impossible to give them the care to preserve their lives," the committee warned.[139]

Besides the supposedly insufficient resources, the committee also opposed the children's admission because of the "fear of infection." Conflating genetic ailments with contagious disease, the committee claimed that the children were predisposed to their parents' diseases and that most probably had leprosy. Even if the children themselves were not symptomatic, the committee still worried about the risk of contagion. The committee even questioned if the children's absence from the hospital would negatively affect the parents.[140]

The committee even appealed to an external medical board, the Superior Board of Medicine and Surgery, for guidance. That board supported denying the children admission to the Casa de Maternidad. However, they also rejected the possibility of the children remaining at the hospital because of the risk of contagion. Instead, the board suggested the seven children be placed at a charitable or religious establishment with more space, or "entrusted to women in private homes in the city and in neighborhoods beyond the city walls," as arranged by the Casa de Maternidad. All of these options would remove the children from their parents and make visitation nearly impossible. The last option also presented problems with finding caregivers. Eligible wetnurses were notoriously difficult to recruit since the wages were insufficient to cover the women's own subsistence, let alone enough for them to produce high-quality milk to nourish a child.[141]

Over a month later, the hospital director was still searching for women willing to take the children. One woman, Doña Francisca del Castillo, had offered to take in several of them to work for her. Possibly suspecting the indenture of their children, some of the ailing parents rejected that solution, instead summoning friends or relatives to provide temporary care, despite their own poverty. The director favored this arrangement for its financial benefits. "To indulge the patients," he wrote, "I turned over the children to the mentioned godmothers which resulted in a savings to this hospital" of the costs associated with those children.[142]

Not all the parents had friends or family who were able to take in their children. After his wife, Merced Marqueti, died in the same hospital, León Crucet had nobody to take care of their three children. Nonetheless, he opposed the internment of his children with Doña Castillo. The surviving documentary trail does not reveal what happened to Salustiana and her two siblings.[143] What is clear, however, is that none of the eight children was accepted to the Casa de Maternidad, an outcome that upheld the institution's racial exclusivity without explicitly revealing the racial rationale.

Once Casa authorities identified race as a central concern for treating abandoned infants, authorities elaborated policies to define who was Black, and to distinguish the way Black and white infants were treated. "Having experienced many cases in which the abandoned infants are presented as white when they are baptized, but later turn out to be mulatto, and vice versa, seeming to be mulattoes they later turn out to be white, without being able then to determine the true color," the rules required Casa employees to wait until the infant was six months old before inscribing their baptism in the Casa records in order to list them in the appropriate book for their status.[144] Moreover, Black children were to remain under the supervision of the Casa until the age of twenty-five, apparently as a measure to avoid "the number of mulattoes and Blacks being too numerous in the Establishment."[145] While whites would live within any distance of the establishment, Black children could not reside more than one league from the Casa, "with the goal to be able to attend to them easily and to avoid the enslavement of mulattoes and Blacks."[146]

By the late 1840s, the Casa de Maternidad housed more than six times as many white babies as babies of African descent. Between 1847 and 1848, the number of white babies increased by twenty-seven, while the number of babies of African descent remained at nineteen. The Casa admitted twelve infants of African descent and released four, and eight died.[147] Institutional records from 1848 lack any reference to race, an implicit indication of whiteness. Most of the children in those documents were surrendered because of poverty, rather than honor.[148] My research uncovered only one letter authored by a woman of African descent soliciting the admission of her grandchildren during this period, and institutional administrators did not record their answer to her petition.[149] This evidence suggests a subtle evolution in the Casa's mission from protecting privileged white women to upholding the racial privilege of vulnerable white women through the exclusion of Black families.

The demographic implications of these racialized charity policies were consistent with prevailing anxieties surrounding the growing Black population in Cuba's slave society. Discouraging the admission of Black infants through policies requiring them to pay for their own maintenance by working effectively prioritized white infants over Black infants. Thus, the Casa addressed fertility control among the white population, while dismissing infanticide among the Black population unless they could pay with money or labor. Moreover, by identifying the preservation of elite, white women's honor as one of the key objectives of the institution, the Casa implicitly denied shelter to women deemed to lack honor: Black women. Both these policies combined to ensure that white women had a safe space to deliver illegitimate babies without risking their own honor, and that white infants would be protected by the public, thus discouraging fertility control in the white population. In contrast, by denying Black pregnant women shelter and by imposing restrictions on the admission of their infants, the Casa essentially refused to address fertility control among the Black population. More surviving white babies, as the women's council earlier alluded, was necessary for balancing the ever-expanding numbers of enslaved Africans imported into the island.

Both the regulation of midwifery and the racial restrictions on charity evinced a focus on protecting and assisting white infants. This shared racialized vision is

FIGURE 4.3. White expósito at the Casa de Maternidad de la Habana, ca. 1830s. This same image also appears in Zenea, *Historia de la Real Casa* (1838), 8. The shared imagery suggested a common emphasis on saving white infants. Domingo Rosaín, *Examen y cartilla de parteras, teórico práctica* ([Havana?]: Oficina de Don José Boloña, impresor de la Real Marina, 1824), cover.

encapsulated by the use of the same image of a white baby in both Rosaín's midwifery textbook and Zenea's history of the Casa de Maternidad (fig. 4.3). This same agenda also informed reforms to the letter of the law.

Honor and Victimhood: White Mothers under the 1822 Penal Code

Just as defending white women's honor was at the core of the establishment of Havana's first maternity ward and ensuing efforts to exclude infants of color from charitable benefits, so too did it shape laws criminalizing fertility control in the new 1822 penal code. The formal recognition of honor as an attenuating circumstance in fertility crimes provided the foundation for stark differences in the way women experienced state intervention thereafter.

The code included specific guidance on which women qualified for this consideration. According to the letter of the law, the attenuating circumstance applied only to single women or widows who conceived illegitimately, not to married women who conceived via adulterous sex. As one Spanish legal scholar later pointed out, the exemption also did not account for cases in which individuals other than the mother committed infanticide to salvage the mother's honor. A common scenario involved mothers protecting their daughters by destroying the evidence of their sexual dishonor.[150] Moreover, women who sought reduced sentences had to prove that they were unable to give birth in a charitable establishment or to relinquish the child to an asylum after birth. They also had to prove that they were honorable in the first place and committed the crime to preserve their reputations. Finally, attenuating circumstances applied only if the woman committed the crime within the first twenty-four hours after birth, a requirement that, like the others, was difficult to prove.[151]

Despite the explicit restrictions on the kinds of women who could invoke *ho-*

noris causa exemptions, this benefit could apply only to women who had honor to lose in the first place. Although class and religious differences likely marked those boundaries in the peninsula, it was race most of all that delineated the boundaries of honor in nineteenth-century colonial Cuba's slave society. As we saw in the realm of charitable institutions, the colonial state extended resources and protections to impoverished white women with the purpose of upholding the honorability of colonial white womanhood, across class lines, as a mechanism of enforcing racial boundaries vis-à-vis free women of color. When applied to the 1822 penal code, this conflation of whiteness and honor would have enabled impoverished white women to invoke the *honoris causa* exemption, even if they did not necessarily meet the standard of honorable birth or conduct.

Certainly, the short-lived penal code prompted discussion about honor and the law. Legal scholars remained divided about the potential implications of allowing honor as an attenuating circumstance for fertility crimes. In their 1842 legal text, *Librería de jueces, abogados y escríbanos*, Spanish jurists Florencio García Goyena and Joaquín Aguirre wrestled with this ambivalence. They argued that "it is necessary to admit that human civilization is the principal cause of infanticide, not the perversity of a father or a mother." Because dishonorable pregnancy was "an object of shame and opprobrium," women are compelled to commit infanticide. If this were not the case, they speculated, "surely" a woman "would not have had the barbarous courage to bloody herself on a newborn." In this vein, they admitted that considering honor in infanticide or abortion cases "would incline anyone in favor of the mother, who in no way can be believed to be the perpetrator of such a homicide with intention."[152] Framing fertility control as a desperate attempt to preserve honor, these legal scholars cast white women as incapable of rational decision-making and thereby less responsible for their behavior. Nevertheless, García Goyena and Aguirre also envisioned the law as a deterrent for criminal acts, claiming that shaming women who partake in "the excesses of carnal passions would produce demoralization a thousand times worse than the rigors of the law."[153] In essence, even though they recognized the immense social pressures on unwed pregnant women, García Goyena and Aguirre advocated for accountability rather than leniency.

These outcomes do not appear to have materialized in practice. Instead, a small sample of police investigations in Havana between the publication of the 1822 penal code and the 1850 implementation of a new penal code shows that state intervention transcended racial boundaries. In the nine police investigations of infant abandonment unearthed for this period, both white and African-descended babies appear. The earliest such case dates to 1842—well after the implementation of the penal code, suggesting a delay in enforcement, a gap in the documentary record, or both.[154] Five of the cases are from 1846, lending further credence to the unevenness of these records. Despite the shortcomings in this sample, it is noteworthy that five of the seven cases with explicit racial designations involved abandoned infants classified as white or seemingly white. Only two cases involve infants of color, including one investigation following the abandonment of two babies.

These investigations reveal just how limited the understanding of pregnancy and childbirth was among the white male authorities investigating these possible "crimes."[155] While the investigations were labeled as possible infanticides, the characteristics of the cases are far more suggestive of poor pregnancy. All but one of the cases involved infants already deceased on discovery. This pattern, which also defined later investigations, indicates that the deaths most likely resulted from stillbirth, difficult delivery, or neonatal morbidity, an interpretation borne out by the fact that medical examiners determined death by "natural causes" in the majority of cases. The cases are also indicative of poverty. That many of the deceased infants were abandoned at or near religious establishments, though adhering to legal mandates, likely indicates that the parents were too poor to afford burial. Consequently, these investigations hint at the emergence of a criminalizing lens through which police viewed impoverished women's reproduction.

Police investigations of infant abandonment and suspected infanticide transcended race, but there is no evidence of significant racial differences in prosecution or conviction, since most cases of fertility control did not reach the courts. Legal impunity remained the norm for white women, particularly for those who would have fallen under the protective *honoris causa* clause. Among impoverished white women, however, fertility control did provoke police investigations—a marked departure with the past. However, the lack of prosecution also appears to have extended to free women of color, as well.

While police intervention in reproductive matters, including those of white women, was certainly a novel development, investigation did not necessarily correspond to criminal charges being filed, much less prosecution or conviction. On the contrary, very few of these investigations ever insinuated criminal intent, instead describing cause of death as "natural" or "nonviolent." Such designations would have ended the case without elevating it to the courts.

There is some anecdotal evidence that cases involving white women arrived to the courts. One judge made reference to "numerous examples of the crime of infanticide" appearing before his court, many precipitated by women's desperation to "avoid the stain and dishonor that comes to them for offending public customs."[156] However, the judge explicitly framed these cases to invoke the *honoris causa* clause and would have likely influenced the courts to dismiss the case. My research did not reveal evidence of conviction, or sentencing of white women under the 1822 penal code. The surviving archival record does suggest, however, that patriarchal protection continued to prevail over criminalization and punishment as the colonial state's main approach to white women's reproduction.

In the early nineteenth century, lawmakers, philanthropists, physicians, and others increasingly understood protecting white women to be important in saving white infants. Four transformations were specifically aimed at protecting white women's reproductive potential: the regulation of midwifery, the establishment of Havana's first maternity ward, efforts to exclude women and children of African descent from charitable institutions, and the codification of reduced sentencing for honor-induced fertility crimes. The result was a more comprehensive approach to protecting white infants through direct care of unwanted white infants as well as paternalistic interventions designed to assist white women through legal loopholes and toward social welfare benefits. The expanded humanitarian assistance fit within a broader paternalistic view of white women as helpless victims, incapable of rational decision-making, and hopelessly dependent on men. That these changes roughly coincided shows how colonial authorities continued to privilege patriarchal protection over criminalization in their pronatalist policies toward white women.

However, protecting white women came at a high price for women of African descent and their families. The humanitarian approach to white women relied on systematically excluding Black children and mothers while creating unprecedented opportunities for elite white women to claim authority in the public sphere. Moreover, framing white women as victims both of social conditions and medical malpractice, rather than as criminals in their own right, hinged on reorienting criminal culpability toward Black women reproductive health practitioners. This racialized bifurcation in regulating women's reproduction laid a crucial foundation that endured well into the twentieth century and beyond. Although the 1822 penal code does not appear to have subjected white women to criminal prosecution for fertility crimes, it was nonetheless a turning point in the way colonial authorities approached women's reproduction.

CHAPTER FIVE

From Regulating Slavery to Policing Enslaved Wombs
In the Twilight of the Slave Trade, 1830s–1840s

In 1839, an enslaved African woman known as Merced Conga faced criminal charges for infanticide and attempted suicide. Just twenty years old when she appeared in court, Merced was undoubtedly smuggled into the island as a girl or young woman sometime in the 1820s or 1830s, after the first Anglo-Spanish antislaving treaty went into effect. During precisely that period, mounting restrictions on the slave trade forced planters to reimagine how they managed their enslaved populations. Unwilling to heed colonial administrators' proposals to import more enslaved women and to ameliorate their conditions, Cuban planters sometimes turned to the courts to enforce their ownership over enslaved women's wombs.

Merced's owner told police that the enslaved woman had drowned her two young daughters, Loreto and Margarita, in the creek near the plantation on which she labored as a slave. Her owner's son, Romualdo, appeared just as Merced waded into the creek, where the bodies of her two babies floated face down. Romualdo later recounted how he launched himself into the creek to pull the two lifeless girls out of the water. He tried to resuscitate them, "hanging them upside down and making every effort to return them to life [but] it was all useless."[1] Both Loreto and Margarita were dead.

Merced's owner reported to authorities that she had murdered her two children and had even made an attempt on her own life, and she was taken into custody. Charged with infanticide and attempted suicide, Merced awaited her hearing in the local jail. In a summary proceeding that does not appear to include testimony from the accused, a local judge found Merced guilty of infanticide and sentenced her to life in prison.[2] Merced eventually was returned to her owner's dominion—after a long, traumatic journey through the appeals process.[3] Her winding trajectory through the courts offers greater insights into the legal thought informing judgments against enslaved women, as well as the rationale behind the kinds of sentencing judges gave in these cases.

Merced's encounter with the criminal courts is part of a sample of five surviving infanticide cases against enslaved women under the 1822 penal code, scattered throughout a sprawling collection of miscellaneous documents occupying several thousand cubic feet in Cuba's Archivo Nacional. The enslaved women traced in these cases were certainly not the only ones to appear before the courts for fertility crimes during this period, or more generally. The surviving records of Cuba's early nineteenth-century courts are extremely fragmentary. The courts did appear to be quite familiar with infanticide cases (see chapter 4), even if most of those proceedings evaded the archival record. The five cases discussed here are almost certainly not the only cases of enslaved mothers' encounters with the law, either. On the contrary, the fact that one of these cases confounded two enslaved women of the same name who both apparently faced similar charges of infanticide suggests that the actual number of women appearing before the courts was much greater. Additional cases against enslaved women as well as police investigations across racial and status lines exist for the period under the 1850 penal code.

Despite these limitations, this small set of surviving cases offers keen insights into the racially specific ways colonial authorities approached women's reproduction during this crucial period. These surviving cases appear to suggest that the 1822 penal code led judges to prosecute infanticide in earnest for the first time in Cuba's colonial history. When paired with the sample of early police investigations of infanticide discussed in chapter 4, these court cases indicate that Cuban authorities did enforce the fertility control laws after the publication of the 1822 penal code. The timing of the earliest surviving infanticide cases in Cuba (1830s) roughly aligns with the date range in which already-independent Spanish American countries and provinces adopted the penal code, including El Salvador, Bolivia, Veracruz, Colombia, Ecuador, and Costa Rica (1826–41).[4] The fact that the courts actually convicted these women of infanticide distinguishes Cuba from most other Latin American societies, where enforcement and prosecution remained rare until the early twentieth century.[5]

On closer examination, it appears that the penal code may have not been the principle impetus for prosecuting fertility crimes after all. At least one of the judges during this period explicitly invoked the Siete Partidas, not the 1822 penal code, in his judgment.[6] Indeed, the 1833 death of Spanish king Fernando VII set off civil war in the peninsula, as well as the return of the laws of the old regime until the passage of the 1848 code in the peninsula and the 1850 penal code for Cuba and Puerto Rico.[7] Thus all the surviving infanticide cases in this sample postdate the nullification of the 1822 penal code. So, if not the 1822 penal code, then what prompted this sudden prosecution of infanticide?

The timing of these cases against enslaved women vis-à-vis abolitionism offers a clue. Although the existing documentary trail does not indicate when, exactly, the criminal courts began to prosecute enslaved women for fertility crimes, it is surely no coincidence that all five surviving cases date to the period after 1835, when Spain entered its second antislaving treaty with Great Britain. Given this blow to Cuba's slave trade, a renewed emphasis on reproducing slavery makes sense. The colonial state, by way of the local courts, began to intervene in the relationship between slave owner and enslaved mother as reproduction became increasingly pivotal to the future of slavery in Cuba. Even as police investigated fertility crimes seemingly irrespective of race, this selective prosecution along the lines of race and legal status suggests that it was not the penal code, but rather the 1835 antislaving treaty, that prompted judges to prosecute infanticide cases involving enslaved women.

These cases collectively complicate the conventional narrative that colonial elites in Cuba privileged enslaved women's productive labor over their reproductive potential.[8] Admittedly, decades of pronatalist decrees from metropolitan authorities remained ineffective in shaping the overarching attitudes and behaviors of Cuban slave owners. Mandates about gender ratios, marriage rights, and "good treatment" in the 1789 slave code and pronatalist mandates in 1804 and 1817 were practically unenforceable in Cuba. Moreover, colonial authorities' lax enforcement of the first antislaving treaty had essentially communicated to planters that they could continue to expect slave importations. With the emergence and growth of a robust clandestine slave traffic, most planters prioritized short-term labor extraction over maintaining their labor forces long term, believing that they could extract less work from females and judging their ability to become pregnant as a liability. Nevertheless, there is evidence that *some* planters instituted procedures to promote enslaved women's reproduction, viewing it as a mechanism for increasing their property and wealth. However, the decision of whether or not to implement pronatalist measures was at individual planters' discretion.

What colonial authorities did not leave to planters' discretion, however, was how to manage enslaved women who were unable to procreate enslaved children, or those who refused to do so. Judges at varying levels of Cuba's legal system meted out a wide range of sentences, from physical punishment to life in prison, often with no relation to what the law prescribed. In several cases, defenders invoked insanity defenses to secure reduced sentences for enslaved women. However, after lengthy investigations and judicial proceedings, judges ultimately returned enslaved women to their owners, where they were expected to resume their productive and reproductive duties.

Yet, the legal interventions of the late 1830s were more than a symptom of changing attitudes. They suggest a more active state role in enforcing enslaved reproduction, as the future of the slave trade became increasingly precarious. However, colonial authorities did not simply reiterate metropolitan decrees as they had in the past, nor did they extend the patriarchal protective measures afforded to white women to enslaved women. Instead, they resorted to criminal prosecution of enslaved women. This shows a willingness to impose punitive measures to coerce enslaved women to sustain the institution of slavery, even to the point of encroaching on slave owners' property rights, all while essentially refusing to hold slave owners themselves accountable.

The courts' initial intervention in the relationship between slave owners and enslaved mothers set off a struggle over who wielded the ultimate authority over human chattel—negotiations that went well beyond the island of Cuba. By 1842, a new slave code formalized state authority over slavery, and even included sanctions against planters who failed to comply. Planters, who had grown accustomed to the lax or nonexistent enforcement of antislaving laws and slave codes, did not allow these interventions to go uncontested. The ensuing struggle between state authority and individual property rights enveloped enslaved women's reproductive lives for the next several decades.

"The Demand for Males Is Much Greater": The Limits of Pronatalism after the 1835 Antislaving Treaty

In the half century since the rise of Cuba's plantation economy, the legal regimes governing slavery had operated more as a set of recommendations than enforceable laws. Planters had grown accustomed to wielding almost total authority over their enslaved workforces. Pronatalist mandates periodically issued by metropolitan authorities had failed to yield significant changes in the conditions of enslaved people, much less their fertility rates. Not even the end of the legal slave trade in 1820 had compelled planters to change their practices. Gender ratios remained hopelessly skewed in favor of males on most sugar plantations. Moreover, while planters commonly boasted of how well they treated their slaves, their allusions to "good treatment" were mostly rhetorical. The persistently high mortality rates afflicting the enslaved population suggest that overwork and brutal punishment remained far more common than moderation and restraint.

Even as some slave owners voluntarily adopted certain pronatalist measures, the general resistance to reproduction as a mechanism of preserving slavery surfaced in planters' steadfast reliance on the slave trade. In 1833, on the heels of one of the island's worst cholera epidemics, planters resorted not to reproduction but to importation to replace the thousands of enslaved people who succumbed to the disease. The number of captives disembarked on Cuban shores soared to unprecedented levels.[9] Based on this experience, colonial and metropolitan authorities could be sure of one thing: recommendations and guidelines, however often repeated, were insufficient to sway planters from their steadfast reliance on the slave trade.

The response to the second antislaving treaty in 1835 further underscored the rift between metropolitan prescription and colonial practice. Between 1835 and 1841, the annual number of captives entering the ports of Havana and Matanzas declined from over fifteen thousand to under nine thousand.[10] However, just as in the aftermath of the first antislaving treaty, this decline was both superficial and short lived.

Despite the temporary dip in slave importations, the demographic profile of African captives forcibly imported into Cuba changed remarkably little during these critical years of heightened restriction on the slave trade. The U.S. consul, Nicholas Trist, a well-known apologist for slavery, estimated that no more than 20 percent of African captives entering Cuba during the same period were female.[11] Others estimated that the gender ratio was even more extreme. According to the British consul, the slaving ship *Empresa*, which was intercepted by the British navy in 1836 as it headed for Cuban shores, carried just 47 female captives in a total cargo of 384. Irish abolitionist Richard Madden estimated that male captives outnumbered females more than four to one, a gender imbalance worse than that in St. Domingue prior to the Haitian Revolution.[12]

The gender disparity among African captives stemmed from more than just the supply side: Cuban planters, too, exerted influence on the gender ratios of slave cargoes. According to British abolitionist David Turnbull, the imbalance owed to the "selfish and sordid views of the planters, who, flattering themselves that the slave-trade is to be perpetual, and finding that more labour can be extorted from the thews and sinews of the one sex than the other, have offered to the slave-trader the necessary premium to encourage this unnatural disproportion."[13] On nearly every Cuban plantation, "the demand for males is much greater than for females, [so] the proportion between the sexes is nearly three to one ... in favour of the masculine gender." Because the slave trade to Cuba continued via clandestine channels well after the imposition of antislaving treaties, "the consequent cheapness of young Bozals at the barracoons, make it more for the interest of the planter to keep up the numbers of his gang by purchase than by procreation."[14] On most plantations "natural increase is disregarded." Instead, planters preferred to "import the stronger animals, like bullocks, work them up, and then seek a fresh supply."[15] According to this logic, planters extracted labor from their slaves immediately, expecting that the slave's life would be short. They viewed the need to invest in maintaining a pregnant slave and her infant as a burden.

In part because of these calculations, the price of female slaves remained lower than that of male slaves in most areas and most years in the first third of the nineteenth century, reflecting planters' general preference for men. Although prices for enslaved women began to increase as restrictions on the slave trade mounted, they only sporadically equaled the price of males and only rarely exceeded it. During the periodic pushes to import more female captives, planters' preference for men occasionally resulted in slavers accumulating a surplus of unsold captive women. In a letter intercepted by English authorities, an agent in one Cuban merchant company dealing in clandestine African captives observed that "the vessels which have lately arrived have brought a large proportion of females, which we have not been able to dispose of at any price." In the same letter, he recommended that his supplier "endeavour to embark the smallest possible number, or none, in order that we may dispose of the cargoes to advantage."[16] The assumption that male captives would sell at higher prices drove companies like this one to continue supplying disproportionately male cargoes, even as colonial and metropolitan authorities pushed for greater gender balance.

Planters preferred male captives for other reasons as well. Certain planters did not allow any enslaved women on their estates, speculating that the presence of both sexes would "give rise to immoral behavior" among them.[17] This "prejudice founded on 'religious scruples,'" attempted to force "the slaves to celibacy, under the pretext that vicious habits were thus avoided."[18] Such appeals to Catholic values conveniently ignored guidelines encouraging slave marriage.

As male captives continued to outnumber females in the cargoes arriving to Cuban shores, the gender imbalance on the island's plantations widened. According to the 1827 census, Cuba's total slave population numbered 286,942—183,290 males and 103,652 females. However, foreign travelers who visited plantations in the years thereafter revealed a much greater gender disparity among the rural enslaved population. Turnbull noted that, "however great this discrepancy between the sexes may appear, it is, in point of fact, not nearly as great as that which is borne out by my own personal observation and researches." In all of his travels across the island, he claimed not to have come across a single plantation with a gender ratio even close to the one in the 1827 census. Turnbull observed that some Cuban planters were "so totally regardless of every human sentiment, save the sordid sense of their own pecuniary interests, that they people their estates with one sex only, to the total exclusion of females." He claimed that it was "notorious" for certain estates to have "600 or 700 negroes upon them, from which the softer sex is entirely excluded." On plantations like these with exclusively male slave populations, planters sought to "prevent the nocturnal wanderings of the men, by locking them up in their plantation prisons, called also barracoons, as soon as their daily labour is concluded."[19]

One such plantation located in Cienfuegos employed seven hundred enslaved people, "not one of whom was female." To prevent uprising, the estate manager "has taken to locking up the men, during the short period allowed for needful rest, in a building called a barracoon, which is in fact, to all intents and purposes, a prison."[20] Nor was that plantation unique. Madden also wrote of the general scarcity of enslaved women on plantations, where fewer than a third of the population was female, and numerous plantations had enslaved workforces that were entirely male.[21] Several sugar plantations between Bejucal and San Antonio de los Baños had similar gender ratios among their enslaved populations, which were usually one-third or less female. On Santa Ana, there were 30 enslaved women in a total slave population of 90; of 161 slaves laboring on La Pita, 48 were female, one of whom had given birth to the estate's only enslaved infant in a year that claimed the lives of five enslaved people. At another neighboring sugar plantation, 70 men and 30 women composed the enslaved population, two of whom died in a year with not a single birth. On the Alexandria plantation near Havana, there was "no increase by births, but a very great decrease by deaths."[22] In 1835, the total slave population of the town of Matanzas and its surrounding countryside was 31,045, of whom only 9,835 were female.[23]

Despite the general preference for enslaved males on Cuban plantations, antislaving wording in the 1835 treaty seemingly prompted at least some planters to explore opportunities for purchasing enslaved women. In April 1836, for instance, one plantation owner wrote to the Royal Development Board requesting to purchase ten to twelve of the sixty or more enslaved women that governing body possessed in the form of seized assets from the demolished Cangre sugar mill. The planter offered to pay the taxes owed on them, and noted that he needed the women to aid in repairing his sugar mill along the Río Blanco del Norte.[24] The offer, which was considerably lower than market value, likely hinged on the assumption that the enslaved women were more of a burden than an asset to the board.

The board's response to the planter, however, reveals competing ideas about the value of enslaved women. The board denied the planter's request. Not only was the offer too low; the board expressed concerns that the planter would purchase the "cream of the crop" (la flor de ellas), making it difficult to sell the rest. This comparative valuation of enslaved women likely hinged on perceived fertility. Some of the women were mothers, accompanied by at least one of their young children. Other women in the group likely fell outside of their reproductive years, making them less desirable. Given these considerations, the board preferred to sell all the women and their children as a group, or at very least in randomly assorted smaller groups.[25] However, not everyone agreed with this valuation of enslaved women's reproduction. Although the board encouraged the use of enslaved women as breeders to reduce Cuba's reliance on the slave trade, some planters argued that the cost a planter incurred in sustaining a pregnant slave and her infant exceeded the cost of acquiring a fresh captive via the clandestine trade.[26]

There is no mention of male slaves seized from the same plantation. It is possible that their former owner selectively paid taxes to subject his least valuable assets to seizure, but it is more likely that whatever adult male slaves the board had seized had already been sold off at a favorable market price. Either scenario indicates a lower value placed on enslaved women.

In another instance, around 1840, the Royal Development Board received another group of enslaved people from the Real Hacienda to advance road construction projects. The group of slaves included Margarita, and her two young children. Asked if she was married, she reportedly replied that she was not. Deciding that it was not "convenient to have slave women or slave children as small as these," the board auctioned off these three. The buyer allegedly discovered later that the enslaved woman was married to an enslaved man, Feliciano, from the same gang. He petitioned the board to cede the husband to him or issue him a refund for his purchase "to avoid separating the marriage."[27] Likely suspecting the board's desire to sell off "second-class hands," this planter may have invoked the slave code to acquire a male slave in addition to the enslaved woman he had already purchased at reduced price.

Initially, it seemed that the buyer would get his wish. The board determined that "slave women are not very useful in hard labor like street construction," so it was preferable to sell off Feliciano, rather than refund the buyer. The board set the price at $389, the price at which it had acquired Feliciano, if the buyer could present a marriage certificate for Feliciano and Margarita. However, neither the buyer nor the slaves themselves were able to obtain the marriage certificate, because the couple had contracted their marriage in Pipián, a small village halfway to the Ciénaga Zapata. The board annulled the auction, which entitled it to repossess Margarita and her two children, though the documentary trail does not reveal the actual fate of Margarita, Feliciano, or their children.

As these vignettes suggest, the periodic proposals to encourage reproduction had little effect on gendered attitudes about slavery. Planters resisted paying full price for enslaved women preferring to obtain them for free or at minimal cost. By extension, initiatives to import more enslaved women, which had circulated at least since the 1780s, seemed slow to take root and gained urgency only during panics following the tightening of antislaving legislation.

"With the Intention of Avoiding the Servitude of Her Child": Prosecuting Enslaved Women's Reproductive Agency

Although its effect on the slave trade was rather minimal, the 1835 treaty did prompt changes in elite attitudes about enslaved women. One such change involved growing doubts about enslaved women's relationship to pregnancy and motherhood. As fertility rates remained exceedingly low, universalizing presumptions about women's natural maternal sentiment eroded into a growing suspicion that enslaved women actively rejected motherhood as an act of defiance against the institution of slavery. Encapsulating this increasingly powerful assumption, French doctor Henri Dumont, who practiced plantation medicine in Havana and Matanzas, wrote of the "terror" enslaved mothers felt at the thought that their children would share their same condition of servitude.[28] Such fears allegedly drove enslaved women toward nefarious practices to avoid conception, terminate their pregnancies, and murder their infants. The image of the enslaved woman who killed her children to save them from slavery came to dominate prevailing perceptions of enslaved motherhood at precisely the moment when Atlantic abolitionism delivered a material threat to slavery's future in Cuba.[29]

This trope of the murderous enslaved mother was omnipresent in criminal prosecutions of enslaved women for infanticide. Surviving cases following five enslaved women accused of fertility crimes featured remarkably similar trajectories to the one recounted early on in this chapter. The accused women, who ranged in age from the mid-teens to early thirties, faced lengthy criminal proceedings after their owners reported them to local authorities. In most cases, judges initially sent the women to either the Francisco de Paula women's hospital or the insane asylum to await trial. However, the directors of those institutions found ways to deny the women admission, despite their theoretical mandate to serve "all types of beings."[30] Instead, most of the enslaved women who stood trial for fertility crimes awaited their court dates in jail.

All the women were ruled guilty at one point or another, even when the evidence did not support the allegations. Judges at varying levels of Cuba's legal system meted out a wide range of sentences, from physical punishment to life in prison. In several cases, defenders invoked insanity defenses to secure reduced sentences for enslaved women. Such sentences rarely ended with those prescribed by the law. In fact, most of these cases ultimately resulted in the enslaved women being returned to their owners.

These women's winding trajectory through the courts offers insights into the legal thought informing judgments against enslaved women, as well as the rationale behind the sentencing judges delivered. In particular, the cases expose how pronatalism in the name of salvaging the institution of slavery helped rationalize unprecedented state intervention into the relationship between slave and slave owner. Even more importantly, the outcomes of these cases illustrate just how limited the state's reach was, especially when it came to changing the ways slave owners approached the institution of slavery, and the way colonial institutions themselves functioned vis-à-vis ingrained practices of racial exclusion.[31]

A year after local police detained Merced on her owner's plantation, threw her in jail, and summarily convicted her of infanticide, the enslaved woman came before an appeals judge. Opposing the life sentence handed down by the lower court, Merced's defender argued that the enslaved woman's "mental state of idiocy" rendered her "without moral liberty in her actions." This condition absolved her of any responsibility for or understanding of her crime. Such a defense played into nineteenth-century ideologies of racism, which hinged on intelligence as the exclusive domain of whites, but it also relied on a clear racial bifurcation in the perceived reasons women committed infanticide.

Indeed, the appeals judge himself contrasted Merced's case with the conventional white-normative understanding of honor-induced infanticide. The judge first observed that some mothers' desperation to preserve their honor drove them to take up "the bloody dagger of parricide." Although few records of such infanticide cases survive today, the judge noted that the "annals of the court offer numerous examples of the crime of infanticide, in which unnatural mothers violated with cold insensitivity one of the most sacred natural Laws of the propagation of the human species" in desperate attempts to salvage their honor.[32] However, the judge noted that Merced's case had little, if anything, to do with honor.

Rather, the judge accepted the defender's claim of Merced's alleged "idiocy." He based this on Merced's seemingly nonsensical answers to his questions during her interrogation. When the judge asked her why she had killed her children, and if she had done so because her owners had mistreated her, Merced answered that she "did not know how to work well" and that "she had no other reason." Merced informed the court that her owners did not punish her in excess, and she was able to get enough to eat. However, she also stated that she "did not know if her owners wanted good or bad for her children" nor "if it is good or bad to have drowned her daughters." Concluding that Merced suffered from insanity, the judge revoked the sentence of the lower court.

The judge entertained a number of sentencing options. He initially considered committing Merced to the insane asylum, as the defender had suggested. However, the Casa de Beneficencia, which then housed a small department for mentally ill people, refused to admit her, enumerating the inconveniences that would result from her presence in the institution. The women's ward of the insane asylum, the director wrote, lacked even a single vacant room. In addition, he claimed that the institution was already so understaffed that the two employees locked patients in their rooms at sunset. He speculated that Merced would need a dedicated staff person to care for her and prevent her from escaping under the cover of darkness. He suggested placing her in a more secure institution, by which he likely meant jail.

Next, the judge considered sentencing Merced to ten years of labor in the San Francisco de Paula Women's Hospital. However, he observed that "her presence would be detrimental and very alarming to the poor sick women," who already endured enough suffering. These women, he speculated, "would live in continual fear and shock at such a guest [as Merced], fearing and justifiably so that she would commit a similar act against them to the one she did to her two daughters." Therefore, he concluded that it "would be too impractical, or at least very dangerous" to allow Merced to work in the women's hospital.[33]

Ultimately, the appeals court returned Merced to her owner after she had apparently regained her sanity. Rationalizing this decision, the judge posited that the slave owner's "self-interest" would compel him to offer the most efficient and effective treatment of Merced's mental illness, and offer the best chance to "return her to reason and restore her brain and mental faculties to their perfect and true equilibrium." He apparently did not consider that the very conditions of enslavement might have contributed to her affliction. The decision to return Merced to her owner reflected the growing barriers Black women faced in accessing the emerging public services. However, in the context of mounting restrictions on the slave trade into Cuba in the late 1830s and 1840s, the decision also represented a more material consideration hinging on property rights—the ownership of Merced, her labor, and the future potential of her womb.

In light of the material implications of Merced's sentence, the insanity defense becomes more suspect. After all, Merced's ambivalence over her owner's intentions toward her daughters and her mixed feelings about her decision to end their lives do not seem so irrational in the context of slavery. Could Merced's comment about not knowing how to work well enough have been an allusion to feelings of inadequacy under the harsh labor regime of slavery? Could her uncertainty over her owner's intentions towards her daughters lay in her mental calculation of the future suffering her daughters would face as they grew up in bondage? Was Merced alluding to a simultaneous sense of despair for the end of her children's lives and a feeling of relief that they would not live the torture she had suffered? The judge seemingly never entertained these questions, nor did he seriously consider the subjectivity of the enslaved woman he interrogated.

The judge's inability to make sense of Merced's answers, or his willful ignorance about her experience, prompts questions about who benefited from the insanity defense. Accepting the insanity defense offered the judge a legal pretext to exempt Merced from prison time, sparing the state the expense of her subsistence. With mounting racial exclusions in charitable institutions, Merced had no other place to go but back to her owner, who would continue to exercise his legal right to exploit the remaining years of her life.

Surviving court records from that same decade reveal that at least four other enslaved women faced criminal charges for committing infanticide and attempting suicide. The case of the sixteen-year-old enslaved girl Ciriaca de la Rosa illustrates these patterns without much more detail. In 1832, in Havana's Jesús María neighborhood, authorities apprehended Ciriaca on suspicion of trying to kill her eight-month-old baby and then attempting suicide. After spending months in jail during her criminal trial, the judge found Ciriaca guilty, sentencing her to be returned to her owner for correction, a penalty that included twenty-five lashes.³⁴

Sometimes, authorities pursued cases in which the alleged perpetrator of the infanticide had already died. In October 1837, in the Havana neighborhood of Guadalupe, Don Ramón Vélez Herrera informed police that his mother had discovered the body of the enslaved woman Isabel, drowned in a well near her house. They suspected that Isabel's son, Fernando, also lay at the bottom of the well. Authorities ordered a group of enslaved men on the plantation to descend into the well to extract the corpses. The slave owners expressed shock at Isabel's apparent parricide and suicide. The enslaved African woman was "the most reasonable of the house." She was the "first to get up to call the other slaves to summon them to their labors," but the morning of the ordeal, another enslaved woman, named Rita, had told him that Isabel's hut door was ajar and she was missing. Although authorities interrogated the other enslaved people on the estate, no one offered any answers, and the criminal proceedings tapered off.³⁵

The trope of the enslaved woman who committed infanticide apparently was so widely accepted that some slave owners used it to cover up their own crimes against their slaves. Fitting this mold were the 1837 criminal proceedings against a thirty-year-old enslaved African woman, Teresa Lucumí, accused of slitting her toddler's throat and attempting suicide. Teresa's owner later recounted to authorities how the enslaved woman had secretly stolen a knife from the kitchen in anticipation of committing the murder. Early on the day of the crime, she allegedly sequestered her son away from the main plantation house. Setting eyes on the boy, she declared, "we are all going to die." She then grabbed him and sliced the kitchen knife clean through his throat, killing him instantly. She allegedly threw his body behind a patch of coffee plants.

Then Teresa reportedly tried to kill herself.³⁶ But the details of Teresa's attempted suicide were even more farfetched. Her owner claimed that she first tried stabbing herself to death, only to be thwarted by a dull knife. Then she tried to hang herself, but could not find rope. Such methods, which were more commonly associated with men in Cuba, seem unlikely, considering the owner's claim that she had just murdered her child with a knife.³⁷ Frustrated in her attempts, Teresa allegedly lay herself to rest behind a patch of banana trees on a neighboring coffee estate, determined to die right there. However, the estate owner, Buenaventura Piedra, found her and allegedly convinced her to seek medical treatment. Instead of taking her to the doctor, he delivered her to the stocks.³⁸

The elaborate story ended with the enslaved mother's gruesome confession, wherein she allegedly admitted to brutally murdering her child and trying to kill herself several times. The enslaved mother was "resigned to die and did not want to serve her owners anymore." The confession supposedly included Teresa's statement that her owners treated her well, gave her enough food and clothing, and did not punish her in excess. Buenaventura corroborated this story.[39]

Local authorities ordered Teresa's transfer from the city of Nueva Paz (then part of Havana province, now southern Mayabeque province) to the women's prison in Havana, once her health was sufficiently "out of danger."[40] A month later, Teresa appeared before a judge in the capital, where she faced charges of infanticide. The judge read the confession that Teresa had allegedly given to local authorities back in Nueva Paz and asked her to verify it. Teresa informed the judge that she had never been allowed to make a statement before a local judge or any other authority. Although she had repeatedly asked to speak with police "to tell them what her owners had done to her and her small child," they ignored her requests and even threatened her.[41]

Teresa recounted the fateful day in her own words, filtered through the understanding and shorthand of the court scribe in Havana. She testified that some time prior to the death of her son, her mistress, Josefa, had left on vacation for several months. On her return, Josefa confronted Teresa, accusing her of having sex with Josefa's husband. Teresa testified that Josefa "asked her how many times she had slept with her owner." Teresa denied the allegation, telling her mistress that she had not shared a bed with anyone other than her small son. Josefa apparently did not believe her and indeed became angrier. She even tried to entrap Teresa by asking to borrow money, which would "prove" the enslaved woman had received payment for having sex with her owner. It seems probable that Josefa suspected that her husband had fathered Teresa's son.

Teresa recounted how her mistress's hatred toward her grew to the point of worsening physical violence. Josefa "continually gave her bocabajos"—a sexualized physical punishment that apparently involved severe lashing of the buttocks. Teresa showed the judge the resulting deep scars. In the midst of these ongoing beatings, Teresa pleaded with her mistress to transfer her and her son to a new owner, even finding a buyer on her own. However, her mistress only tortured her with more "bocabajos."

One day around lunchtime, Teresa went to the kitchen to collect the table scraps to feed her son, but she could not find him. An enslaved man working in the kitchen told her he had seen their owner take the boy out to the chicken coop earlier that day. Teresa walked outside, only to discover her son's decapitated corpse behind a patch of coffee plants. She started to scream and run, when her owner grabbed her, covering her mouth. He told her not to scream and that the situation could be "fixed." Her owner took her to the neighboring coffee plantation and, with the table knife he carried with him, cut her throat. She tried to fight him off, but her owner slashed her throat again, and Teresa fell to the ground. Her owner then cut some leaves off some nearby banana trees and threw them on top of her body to conceal it, and left.

Later that afternoon, she heard dogs barking and people talking. She assumed it was her owner coming back to finish killing her. Teresa dragged herself away to hide but encountered the neighbor's child. She begged him not to tell his father, who was friends with her owner. The next day in the afternoon, one of the neighbor's dogs forced her from her hiding spot, and the neighbor saw her. He asked her why she had killed her son and cut her own throat, and she told him that her owner had done it. The neighbor told her not to say such things, because her owner could "lose everything." He brought her to the main house and summoned the authorities, warning them that Teresa was trying to frame her owners for her crimes.

Without collecting testimony from Teresa, the local judge had found her guilty of infanticide. He concluded that Teresa's crime was so egregious that she had "undoubtedly incurred" the death penalty. However, owing to "her young age and the rusticity of her race," the judge reduced her sentence to one hundred lashes and ten years in prison, during which time she would be shackled with a ball and chain, breaking rocks for street paving.[42]

Teresa's defender appealed the local judge's decision, arguing before the Audiencia de la Habana that the enslaved woman should be absolved of all blame and punishments because she did not commit the crimes. He pointed out a major conflict of interest in the evidence presented against Teresa. The key witnesses for the prosecution were Teresa's owners, who were possibly implicated in the crime, and their neighbors, who were close friends with Teresa's owners. None of these individuals had actually witnessed firsthand the alleged crime, despite their detailed testimony. The defender argued that there was more evidence to support Teresa's account—that her owners murdered her child and attempted to kill her. Then, "having no other means of saving themselves," they framed Teresa and convinced their neighbors to corroborate their claims with fabricated testimony.[43]

Next, the defender argued that even if Teresa had committed the crime, that the sentence was extraordinarily harsh, especially considering the "cruelty and inhumanity" her owners subjected her to. He implored the judge to reflect on the "desperation of a poor creature condemned to such endless suffering," as well as "her ignorance and imbecility" as attenuating circumstances. If anyone deserved punishment, he argued, it was Teresa's owners. "Perhaps if they would have treated her with the moderation and kindness the law and religion demand," the defender speculated, "we would not have witnessed such fatal accidents, which are direct consequences of the desperation to which her owners' barbarism drove her." For that reason, he argued, the Teresa's owners deserved six years in prison in addition to forever losing their right to own slaves.[44]

At that point, the documentary trail becomes muddled. The audiencia seems to have merged two similar cases, each involving a different African-descended woman named Teresa, both accused of the crimes of infanticide and attempted suicide. Both women had deep scarring across their throats, evidently from knife wounds or noose lacerations. One of them was an African-born enslaved woman called Teresa Lucumí, discussed above. The other was in a Cuban-born free Black girl in her early to mid-teens, allegedly suffering from mental illness. While physician's reports from earlier in the court record verified the enslaved Teresa's severe scarring on her buttocks, the younger Teresa lacked those particular marks.

The judge sentenced the younger Teresa to institutionalization in the insane asylum until she regained her senses. However, when the director of that institution refused to admit her, the judge transferred her to the San Francisco de Paula Women's Hospital. After six months, the hospital director informed the judge that the younger Teresa's worsening state of insanity posed "grave inconveniences to the hospital." Without any way "to contain a furious crazy woman," the director claimed that her presence harmed the sick treated therein. Curiously, he lamented that "if she were a slave" then she could easily be returned to her owner for "treatment." The director implored the judge "to exonerate the Hospital San Francisco de Paula" from the "heavy burden" of keeping the younger Teresa. By summer 1841, the judge ordered her relocation to the insane asylum.[45]

Although the documentary trail ends before revealing whether the insane asylum actually admitted the younger Teresa the second time around, the judge's insistence on committing her to a public institution evinces important differences between the treatment of women of reproductive age, based on their legal status. Whereas the courts returned both enslaved women, Ciriaca and Merced, under their owners' control despite their probable culpability in their crimes, the younger Teresa seemingly remained confined to public institutions, where her sexuality and reproductive potential could be restricted. We may never learn the fate of the elder Teresa, but it is probable she was returned to her murderous owners who probably evaded legal consequences for violently abusing and attempting to kill her, and (likely) murdering her son.

The investigation and prosecution of both women marked an important shift in the legal authority over women's reproduction and over the enslaved population more generally. Until the late 1830s and early 1840s, slave owners expected to enjoy total dominion over their slaves. Although the 1789 slave code theoretically bestowed certain rights on enslaved people, in practice few enslaved people arrived before a judge prior to the late 1830s, whether to claim legal rights or to face legal consequences.[46] As metropolitan authorities renewed and tightened restrictions on the slave trade, they also carved out greater authority over the everyday practice of enslavement.

This seemingly confounding outcome resulted from a confluence of three key processes. First, although enslaved women's race implicitly excluded them from *honoris causa* defenses spelled out in the 1822 penal code, defenders representing enslaved women seemed to invoke a different defense strategy more aligned with prevailing racialized and gendered assumptions about enslaved women: the insanity defense. Attorneys invoked two types of insanity: "idiocy" and "mental derangement" or "madness." Individuals who suffered from idiocy supposedly lacked intelligence, were bereft of judgment, and easily gave in to their passions. Idiocy could either be innate or could develop with age or illness. By contrast, mental derangement resulted from a continuous disruption in a person's intellectual faculties, which usually lasted a long time.[47] Judges often found this latter defense compelling and attempted to send the enslaved women to either the insane asylum or the women's hospital to work while supposedly receiving treatment. However, the directors of these institutions routinely refused to admit enslaved women. Rather than keep them in jail, where they could not serve their productive or reproductive purposes and where they supposedly drained public coffers, judges sent the enslaved women back to their owners.

By convicting these women, but ultimately returning them to their owners, the courts adjudicated the fundamental contradiction between the humanity of enslaved people and their legal status as property. In trying fertility cases involving enslaved women, the courts intervened in the relationship between property owners and their possessions, simultaneously acknowledging the enslaved woman's fundamentally human status as bearer of life and recognizing her human capacity to violate the law. Yet, the very definition of her criminality hinged on her simultaneous status as property. Her crime was not that she took a life, but rather that she deprived her owner of her own body and the additional lives she could bring into the world. While the insanity defense recognized the human need of enslaved women for medical and psychological care, barriers on access to public institutions ensured that labor extraction, rather than humanitarian assistance, conditioned their presence therein. Relinquishing any public responsibility in the care and correction of enslaved women, judges ordered their return to the very conditions that jeopardized their and their children's lives. In doing so, the courts reinforced the sanctity of private property and the private responsibility of slave owners to administer the care they deemed appropriate.

Deregulating Reproductive Management: Toward a New Slave Code, 1841–1844

Although there was not yet much explicit legal basis for the intervention of the courts in these cases, the tightening restrictions on the slave trade began to foster legal reforms that would not only authorize but require judges to assume this degree of authority. Just as the paper trail of Teresa's case ended, metropolitan authorities discussed a new set of laws to govern the institution of slavery in Cuba. Interim Governor Antonio García Oña introduced to the Gobierno Superior Civil a draft slave code in July 1841, which would have obliged planters to relieve pregnant slaves from work during the last trimester and for six months after giving birth.[48] The proposed law would have also imposed severe penalties on slave owners who committed infractions, including fines of up to 400 pesos, and even the possibility of incarceration. Although the draft revived many of the regulations that had formed part of the 1789 slave code, this version was unique in that it punished slave owners for failing to comply.

With the discussions of a firmer slave code already underway, the appointment of Jerónimo Valdés as Cuba's new captain-general in late 1841 delivered another powerful blow to slavery in Cuba. Valdés cracked down on the clandestine slave trade to Cuba, ordering stricter enforcement of antislaving laws, and imposing new barriers on the disembarkation and sale of African captives in Havana by closing certain slave markets and banning the registration of foreign ships under the Spanish flag. These impediments to the clandestine slave trade coincided with an abrupt increase in the price of female slaves of reproductive age, who temporarily outpriced males.[49]

Captain-general Valdés also sought information about the best practices for sustaining enslaved populations, independent of the clandestine trade. In February 1842, he surveyed fourteen prominent Havana slave owners, inquiring about planters' standard practices for managing their enslaved populations. The results of this "Survey on the Reform of the Hygienic, Moral, and Nutrition System for Slaves" would be used to inform discussion of the new slave code. Two of the eight questions were about families and reproduction. One of these requested information about the "most convenient system for regularizing the customs and morality of married slaves." It asked if married slaves were permitted to live in their own huts, and at what age enslaved children should be returned to their parents' supervision. The other question concerned the standard regimens of care provided to enslaved women who were pregnant, giving birth, or had recently given birth, and to their babies.[50] It queried about the nutrition, duties, and working hours assigned to enslaved women at various stages of reproduction as well as the role they should play in the care of their infants. It also asked about the most appropriate design for the nursery. The answers to these questions would serve as the foundation for parts of the new slave code.

Twelve planters responded to the survey.[51] Many of these planters clearly suspected the captain-general's pronatalist agenda. Most of the respondents described regimens of care that began before conception and lasted through the postpartum period. Respondents wrote that enslaved families should live together in their own huts as opposed to sleeping in gender-segregated barracoons, a measure likely intended to stimulate procreative sex. One planter noted that, despite their security, the barracoons were "somewhat oppressive," and he preferred to keep his slaves calm by providing plenty of good food and establishing strong order and vigilance.[52] Another planter described a rectangular building whose single locking exterior door provided the security of a slave barracks, but its individual rooms for families allowed the enslaved father to "enjoy the benefits of a property-owning head of household."[53] Several planters mentioned the practice of keeping young and single women locked in a separate building to prevent supposed immoralities. Others discussed the role of religion in curbing bad habits, such as polygamy, which they presumed to be widespread among slaves.

Most planters claimed that they assigned pregnant slaves to a reduced workload with shorter working hours, longer breaks, and easier work in what they called "light chores."[54] According to Sebastián I. de Lasa, "when the slave-women are pregnant, one should undoubtedly reduce their workload, just like during breastfeeding."[55] However, planters differed on when they granted a reduced workload, the extent of the reduction, and the duration of this benefit. Most did not adjust enslaved women's workloads until the final months of pregnancy. Joaquín Gómez noted that once pregnant slaves reached their last months of pregnancy, they performed "simple tasks, of which they only do what they want." Apparently, the only reason for assigning them this work was to get them to exercise, since their work was not assessed or scrutinized. He noted that this system had yielded "favorable results."[56] On plantations owned by José Manuel Carrillo, pregnant slaves received an exemption from "all heavy labor as soon as they get to the final months of their pregnancies." Even still, he assigned these women to what he called "soft jobs," like helping in the nurseries.[57] Some planters suspected that enslaved women lied about their pregnancies to gain access to the workload reductions. According to Juan Montalvo, enslaved women on his plantations "frequently, say that they are [nine months along] when they are really only four or five months pregnant, and in this way they spend the rest of the time in laziness, and this is allowed so as to avoid any misfortune."[58]

Some planters reported providing accommodations around four or five months, when pregnancies became visible. For instance, Domingo de Aldama noted that "every slave women who becomes pregnant ceases to perform [field] labor by the fourth or fifth month of their pregnancy." Between about the fourth month and the eighth, pregnant slaves worked in the *batey* (owners' residence). After that, "she does nothing and she is only obliged to sweep occasionally and meander."[59] One planter claimed that as soon as an enslaved woman reported her pregnancy, he reduced her workload. Others monitored enslaved women's menstrual cycles to ascertain when they might be pregnant. For instance, Joaquín Muñoz Izaguirre noted that, on his plantations, medical staff did just this. "The head nurse should be in touch with the enslaved women and inquire about the suspension of their menstruation," he wrote. Once an enslaved woman on his plantation became pregnant, she was to be "treated with marked deference." As she advanced in her pregnancy, the enslaved woman gained access to more benefits. "After the fifth month, she should be exempted from all work," the planter wrote.[60]

However, most planters who mentioned an exemption from work for pregnant women noted that enslaved women were still responsible for domestic duties in the owners' house. According to one planter, enslaved women "do nothing more than help with cleaning and sweeping" after reaching their final month of pregnancy. Another planter justified these activities as beneficial to the enslaved woman, claiming that it would "prepare her for an easy labor."[61] Some planters moved pregnant slaves to the nursery in their final weeks of pregnancy to await their labor. On most plantations, enslaved nurses attended the births of pregnant slaves. One planter noted that he called a physician when complications arose: "When she goes into labor, if all is well, she is attended by the nurse ... and if there is any difficulty, a physician is called to the estate so he can operate according to his art."[62]

For the first forty days after birth, the *cuarentena* (lit. Lent, quarantine), most planters reported that enslaved mothers remained with their babies in the nursery. They were exempted from work and received higher-quality food and in larger quantities. Jacinto González Larrinaga noted that, on his plantations, enslaved mothers received generous portions of well-seasoned food after giving birth.[63] Typical rations included chicken broth during labor and meat or poultry thereafter. Some planters included chocolate and wine as well. The regimen Carrillo described was common. On his plantations, enslaved women "should be treated with the utmost care" in the forty days after birth. In addition to "providing them with the best rations," Carrillo exempted enslaved mothers from field labor "so they dedicate themselves to the care of their newborns."[64]

After the cuarentena, most planters required enslaved mothers to resume work, though with some accommodation to allow breastfeeding, such as reduced working hours and longer or more frequent breaks. However, the type, intensity, duration, and location of postpartum duties varied by owner. On Ignacio Herrera's plantations, enslaved women resumed work after forty days but were assigned jobs near the nursery. After six months, they were returned to field work but were entitled to reduced hours to allow breastfeeding.[65] Juan Montalvo reported that, after forty days, mothers began work two hours later and finished two hours earlier than other slaves and had an extended midday break to nurse their children. They received this accommodation as long as they were breastfeeding, "which they prolong as much as possible," according to Montalvo.[66]

Some planters described more extensive periods of relief for enslaved mothers. Rafael O'Farrill wrote that enslaved women on his plantation "remain exclusively dedicated to nursing their children for two or three months." After that time, he ordered them back to work but assigned them to jobs near the nursery so they could breastfeed periodically.[67] Domingo de Aldama claimed that he ordered his staff to take "all precautions necessary to avoid any misfortune to the woman or her baby." He denied them nothing "that could deliver a good result, whether in medicines or food as well as clothing and shelter for the mother and child." Enslaved women on his estates returned to work forty days after birth, laboring "a half day on the batey in light jobs," during which time mothers were allowed to attend to their babies "two or three times." He noted that he allowed enslaved mothers to remain with their babies if they became ill. When the baby grew teeth and began to walk, at around twelve to fifteen months, enslaved mothers received "a gift of four pesos and a piglet to raise" and were "sent back to work in the fields with the rest of the slaves, but always permitting them some time to check on their babies, and excluding them from night work." He also reported offering "certain rewards" to enslaved mothers who took good care of their babies.[68] Carrillo noted that other planters offered enslaved women "certain privileges according to the number of children they have, including exemptions from work."[69]

By the time the captain-general distributed his survey in 1842, the planters also indicated that it was standard practice to centralize the care of enslaved babies and children. One or more women, usually older slaves, supervised and prepared food for children up to age six or seven in a separate *casa de criollos* (nursery) on the plantation. Most planters described the nursery as a standalone building that was covered, dry, and well ventilated. In some cases, it included an additional ward for enslaved women in advanced pregnancy. One slave owner described the nursery on his plantation in San Antonio de los Baños as being as large as the infirmary, with hard, low beds. It was staffed by one or more enslaved wet nurses who attended to all enslaved children younger than seven years; they also breastfed enslaved infants in the absence of their mothers.[70] One planter specifically recommended cement floors to prevent pregnant women from eating dirt (a common symptom of nutritional deficit), and an enclosed outdoor space where the children "can walk around but cannot leave." He also recommended providing buckets for bathing.[71] In the nurseries, babies typically were fed rice, wheat, or cassava flour mixed with cow's or goat's milk, in addition to breastmilk.

Some planters boasted of the size and modernity of their plantation nurseries. Aldama observed that the nursery "should be big enough to accommodate all the children, dry and clean and ventilated with some space outside so the children can run freely, and according to their number." He employed "a slave woman of certain age and discernment" to attend to the enslaved children while their mothers worked. On one of his plantations, he boasted that the nursery had a large fenced area attached to it where the slave children "run all they like." On another plantation, he paid "a free woman to take care of them" including taking the children on walks.[72]

Other planters described more rustic facilities. Juan Montalvo claimed that with nurseries he found it "convenient to cut the luxury that is sometimes the son of vanity and harms the principal objective, which is the nutrition and care of the children." The children should be "well fed and housed" and "have appropriate clothes for winter." He insisted that "very few will perish if the physicians of the plantations have the intelligence and zeal necessary" to avoid lockjaw or infant tetanus, and get through the period of teething.[73] Another planter simply combined the housing for enslaved women with the nursery.[74] Most planters agreed that enslaved babies should be raised in the nursery until of age, when they would be returned to live with their parents and put to work. However, one planter argued that enslaved children should "never be under the direction of the parents," a categorical statement likely rooted in fear of infanticide.[75]

The nurseries that cropped up on Cuban plantations simultaneously represented the institutionalization of earlier amelioration efforts as well as a concerted effort to supervise the rearing of future slaves. A French traveler described the nursery on one Matanzas plantation as "a large cage where they lock the Negro children while their parents go to work. The little Black devils roll all naked in the dust and frolic around us, asking us for a penny, while the guardian, trapped with them, flashes us a broad smile, while braiding a straw mat."[76] A North American traveler commented during his visit to a Cuban plantation that "the nursery is also quite an important place, and is highly amusing to visit, for here the future hopes of the plantation are cared for."[77] He imagined this idyllic space as a joyful respite preceding the ordinary brutality of slavery. He reported seeing the enslaved children "running and tumbling over each other in great glee.... They all appear to be happy and jolly, and make as much noise and have as much fun as would satisfy any 'radical' in the States." Importantly, however, he admitted that the "poor things, they happily know nothing of the hard lot in store for them."[78]

Several of the surveyed planters wrote with pride about the pronatalist measures they had implemented. José Manuel Carrillo boasted that "it would be difficult to conceive of other more prudent and correct [measures] to obtain the diverse ends of conserving and augmenting the slaves" than the ones he employed on his plantation.[79] Many aspects of this regimen of care for enslaved pregnant women and babies aligned with the medical standard of care that physicians recommended to planters. A plantation medical guide published in the 1860s detailed an augmented nutritional regimen for breastfeeding mothers and their enslaved children, as well as safety and hygiene precautions for the nursery. Its author instructed planters to ensure that the nursery was free from sharp objects that could hurt the babies, that the area remained clean, and that the beds or cots for the new mothers were low to the ground to avoid injury to babies who fell. It also advised that the enslaved nurse should be responsible for preparing meat stew for new mothers, rice for children, and mush or porridge for babies. She was also responsible for bathing the babies.[80] This guide's emphasis on reducing dangers betrayed a prevailing assumption that at least part of the nursery's function involved protecting enslaved infants from the neglect or intentional harm their mothers could inflict on the babies themselves, and by extension on the future wealth of the planter.

Some observers quickly proclaimed the success of these ameliorative measures. José Antonio Saco declared in the early 1830s that some planters had increased their slave labor forces without purchasing new captives by introducing precisely these pronatalist reforms. Despite persisting imbalances in gender ratios, some planters reported increased fertility rates and decreased mortality rates among their enslaved populations.[81] By the 1840s, members of the Royal Development Board noted that, "over the last twenty years," slave owners had undertaken "a very favorable change" in the way they managed their plantations and the "correction" of their slaves. This sudden shift toward these "truly humanitarian ideas" coincided with the growing "difficulty of replacing laborers bound for agriculture, due to the cessation of the slave trade." Within this context, some slave owners began to take considerable pride in their immaculate nurseries and the "well-kept" slave labor. Cultivating the image of the "happy slave," these planters congratulated one another on their humane treatment of their slaves and their refrain from the more carceral and violent aspects of slavery.[82] While the slave breeding operations that emerged on some Cuban plantations were never significant enough to impact demographic trends, this understanding of enslaved women's pregnancies and infants as future laborers helps explain why some slave owners might denounce their own women slaves for infanticide.

Not all respondents offered such favorable replies to the questions concerning care of enslaved pregnant women and infants. A few planters replied with marked annoyance, demonstrating their resentment at what they believed to be the state's incursions into their property rights. The Marqués de Arcos answered the question on pregnant women and children by informing the captain-general that he implemented whatever measures he believed would benefit him: "I will limit myself to say to Your Excellency that, on all these matters, as well as the housing and care of the babies, whatever seems to me most suited to humanity which is happily combined with my own interests, is what is done on my plantations."[83] Along the same lines, the Count of Fernandina suggested that whatever regulations the captain-general might issue regarding the care of pregnant slaves and enslaved mothers would likely be ineffective and poorly received: "the interest of the owners does much more than anything that can be prescribed by the best laws." After all, he noted, "public sentiment vituperates the cruel slave owner" and his "own self-interest . . . inspires his humanitarian sentiments." From his point of view, "there was no need for extraordinary orders."[84] Wenceslao de Villa Urrutia declined to discuss pregnant women and babies, stating outright that he "only answered the most sensible questions." He closed his letter with a lengthy diatribe of what he viewed to be the dire consequences of the state's interference into slave owners' property rights. By protecting slaves and punishing slave owners, he argued, the government effectively undermined the entire premise of the institution of slavery.[85] Even planters who answered the questions expressed hesitation over codifying their practices into a law. José Manuel Carrillo, for instance, wrote of the dangerous consequences of an obligatory set of laws.[86]

In November 1842, mere months after these planters registered their complaints, the captain-general published the new slave code, *Reglamento de esclavos de Cuba*. The 1842 slave code, which became effective January 1, 1843, renewed many of the provisions in the 1789 code, such as encouraging slave marriage and keeping slave families together. It obliged owners of male slaves to keep families, including children under age three, together or sell them all to a third party. It also added four articles on the treatment of enslaved infants and children. Among these, the 1842 slave code obliged slave owners to construct a nursery—"a house or special room where the children of slaves could be watched by old slave women while their mothers worked."[87] Other provisions addressed feeding and caring for enslaved babies while their mothers were working, and clothing children. The code also stipulated that planters should remove enslaved mothers from field labor if their infant fell ill while still of breastfeeding age.[88]

The 1842 slave code also featured other provisions that essentially called for state intervention in the relationship between slave and owner. Because the slave code formally subjected the relationship between slave owner and slave to the authority of the colonial legal system, it extended the entire legal system to cover enslaved people, treating them as subjects who not only could claim legal rights but also face legal consequences for their actions and perceived transgressions. Indeed, article 42 of the code required slave owners to turn over to the courts enslaved people who committed "more serious offenses," including crimes that merited more severe punishments than slave owners could lawfully mete out. Furthermore, article 48 charged local authorities with enforcement of the laws.[89] Together, these provisions split the jurisdiction over enslaved people's lives between the slave owner and the state, with the former in charge of addressing minor offenses, and the latter retaining authority over more egregious violations.

As much as planters feared this partition of authority would strip them of their power and mire them in legal suits brought by their slaves, in practice much graver consequences loomed for enslaved people, particularly those whose bodies could bear new life. The slave code subjected enslaved women's reproductive lives not only to the whims of their owners but also to the often equally prejudiced decisions of the courts. In so doing, it implied important changes in both the meaning and application of fertility control laws. Under the 1842 slave code, legal theorists would have to consider for the first time how race and legal status might impact existing legal frameworks on women's reproduction—laws that metropolitan authorities had developed specifically with white women in mind. Given the broader context of Atlantic abolitionism, there was ample reason to halt enslaved women's practices of fertility control, though the rationale for regulating their reproductive lives differed substantially from the interests in white women's wombs. Legal theorists, therefore, would have to depart from the centuries-old practice of writing these laws through the implicit lens of whiteness. They would have to consider how to apply laws criminalizing abortion and infanticide to women whose race alone excluded them from the category of honorable, and whose legal status of enslavement rendered their children the property of private citizens.

Dividing the authority over enslaved people also would have forced various branches of the local state to contend with the profound contradiction of attending to people whose enslavement denied the very humanity on which their rights and responsibilities rested. The courts would have to mediate the investigation, judgment, and sentencing of enslaved women accused of fertility crimes through the lens of slavery—both the property rights of the slave owner and the future of the institution as a whole. Local civil and ecclesiastical authorities, too, would have to determine how to attend to individuals whose womanhood ordinarily warranted patriarchal benevolence and charity, but whose race and legal status allowed the repudiation of state responsibility. All these emergent challenges to the theory and practice of the law would have created a legal foundation that could mire many more enslaved women in long legal battles like the one Teresa faced. In essence, the 1842 slave code formalized the state's coercive and punitive power to compel enslaved women to reproduce.

The colonial government maintained its course even as slave owners across the island expressed outrage over the 1842 slave code. The eruption of one of the island's most significant slave uprisings—the Ladder Conspiracy (Conspiración de la Escalera)—in 1843 amid an emerging multiracial anticolonial movement against Spanish rule, however, forced the colonial government to reconsider. Colonial authorities placed some parts of Cuba under martial law, unleashing a "bloody reign of terror" against enslaved men and women, extracting testimony and confessions through fear, violence, and torture. One form of torture, which gave name to the uprising, involved brutally beating suspects tied facedown on a ladder. Hundreds of Black men and women faced brutal execution or other reprisal in 1844 for their alleged roles in the uprising.[90]

Within this context of colonial repression, slave code reform provided a way to cultivate and consolidate the loyalty of Cuban sugar planters, a relationship crucial to the preservation of Spanish rule in Cuba. By late February 1844, a new captain-general more sympathetic to slave owners' immediate interests reached out to the Royal Development Board leadership for advice about the 1842 slave code. He cited "various observations indicating that the reform or modification of certain [laws] would be convenient."⁹¹ The board promptly appointed a committee of three prominent slave owners: the Count of Romero, the Count of Cañongo, and Antonio María de Escovedo.

Predictably, these men rejected what they saw as the state's encroachment into their dominion over their human chattel. Their report to the president complained that the new slave code undermined their authority, thereby causing discipline problems and inciting slaves to rebel. In particular, they took issue with six provisions: article 3, which limited the hours of slave labor on Sundays; article 23, which set caps on the number of hours worked per day and mandated minimum periods for rest and sleep; article 32, which gave the state authority to force the sale of a slave subjected to mistreatment; article 41, which limited the types and severity of physical punishment slave owners could administer; article 43, which stipulated that only the owner, majordomo, or foreman could administer punishment; and article 44, which subjected slave owners to fines for violating the slave code.⁹² The planters claimed that these provisions "manifest a visible tendency to dampen the dominating authority" slave owners enjoy over their slaves, "stripping, in the eyes of the slaves, the prestige that made them see their owner as a sole, absolute and legitimate power."⁹³ These planters speculated that, by undermining the complete dominion of slave owners over their slaves, the code essentially rendered the institution of slavery untenable.

They implored that the slave code be suspended and the laws reframed so they were not "rights slaves could claim." After all, they argued, the only way to truly "govern the colored race" was to implement "a bare and vigorous regime of superiority and predominance, in which whites and especially slave owners are vested with prestige that undergirds their moral power with physical force."⁹⁴ Affording enslaved people even the most minimal semblance of rights proved incompatible with this system of racial domination. Instead, the committee urged colonial authorities to forcibly remove or at least encourage the exodus of free people of color from the island, while extracting maximum labor from nominally free emancipados. The management of slaves, they proposed, should be left to slave owners, who should moralize their charges through religious instruction.⁹⁵

On this final point, the board agreed, but offered a few modest additions to the responsibilities of slave owners. In addition to Christianizing their slaves, the board's provisions required slave owners to feed, clothe, and provide medical care to them; restrict the presence and roles of free people of color on their plantations; report deaths or suspicions of unrest to local authorities; and employ at least 5 percent white people. This list of duties made no mention of keeping enslaved families together, or caring for pregnant women, new mothers, or their babies. In late May, the captain-general, then Leopoldo O'Donnell, adopted this minimalist version, which became known as the 1844 Ordinances Governing the Management of Slaves.⁹⁶

In effect, the 1844 ordinances rolled back many of the most important rights the 1842 slave code afforded enslaved people, and all but eliminated accountability for slave owners. These changes had significant consequences for enslaved women's reproductive lives. By limiting its guidance to the most basic requirements for survival, the ameliorative and pronatalist measures of the 1842 slave code faded out of official prescription, inviting unprecedented abuses. One foreign traveler noted that church marriage was relatively rare in Cuba, because of the inconveniences for slave owners, particularly in terms of their ability to sell or mortgage their slaves. Most "marriages" among enslaved people were performed by slave owners themselves and consequently carried "with them no legal rights or duties."[97] Another traveler noted that many plantations lacked female slaves entirely, but even on those with more balanced gender ratios, the slaves "do not increase," owing to the "mismanagement"—that is, the cruelty and excessive workload. "On a sugar estate employing two hundred slaves," he claimed, "I have seen only three or four children." Coffee plantations "where the slaves are deprived of sufficient rest, are also unproductive," he noted.[98]

Still another observer dismissed the premise of reproduction entirely, claiming that Cuban planters "know that it is much cheaper to import slaves than to breed them." Even when British antislaving patrols drove up "the price of an able-bodied" slave to $500, many planters still preferred to import clandestinely than to breed. By the 1850s, when the British had "relaxed" their vigilance, the price of a slave dropped to $250 or $300. With these conditions, one traveler observed that "the greater economy of keeping up the breed by importation is too plain to be overlooked." Consequently, there was little incentive to create "a self-sustaining system," and Cuban planters continued to pack their barracoons with "numerous bands of males and but a very few females, or ofttimes none at all."[99] Despite an increasingly volatile clandestine slave trade, planters continued to resist the "burden" of reproduction.

Facing mounting restrictions on the slave trade, colonial authorities in Cuba shifted their focus from policies that encouraged planters to implement pronatalist reforms to interventions that directly affected enslaved women's reproductive lives. The surviving documentary record reveals that, as planters continued to rely on the clandestine slave trade after the 1835 antislaving treaty was implemented, local courts pursued criminal charges against enslaved women for alleged fertility crimes. In those cases, local courts attempted to enforce not just a private claim to the reproductive potential enslaved women's wombs held, but also a public one, underscoring a powerful relationship between coercive reproduction and the colonial state's interest in slavery's survival.

Colonial authorities attempted to formalize and extend this pronatalist agenda through a new slave code that would have imposed unprecedented legal accountability on planters to ensure conditions deemed amenable to enslaved reproduction. While slave owners seemed to accept and uphold state interventions that criminalized enslaved women, they vehemently rejected the state's attempt to burden them with legal responsibilities or liabilities. Planters successfully demanded an overhaul of the legislation in 1844. The result was a reformed slave code that rolled back many of the most basic protections for enslaved women and mothers precisely on the eve of the Spanish criminalization of the slave trade.

CHAPTER SIX

"No Race Can Substitute Black Africans"
Reproducing Slavery after the Criminalization of the Slave Trade, 1850s–1860s

In March 1855, a little girl named Leocadia discovered a basket containing the body of a dead infant in the plaza of Havana's San Felipe church. When police questioned Leocadia, she said that the basket had come from a particular house on Aguiar Street. Arriving at that house, police found an enslaved African woman named Luisa, who worked as a domestic servant. The enslaved woman told them when interrogated that her owner had sent her there to give birth to her baby. However, her baby had become sick. At just eight days old, her daughter had succumbed to "el mal de los siete días" (infant tetanus). The grieving mother informed her owner of the infant's demise and prepared her deceased child for burial. However, unbeknownst to Luisa, the tiny cadaver was unceremoniously abandoned in public just a few hours later.[1]

Luisa's encounter with urban police emerges from a modest set of surviving archival documents tracing the investigation and prosecution of fertility crimes under the 1850 penal code. It consists of twenty-seven police investigations and three criminal cases between the implementation of the 1850 penal code and the Moret Law of 1870, which freed babies born to enslaved women. Luisa's case was one of nineteen dating to the 1850s. Although these were not the earliest instances of police investigation or criminal prosecution of infanticide, the sample from the 1850s is distinctive because it encompasses a broader range of reproductive incidents than the cases of the 1830s and 1840s (see chapter 5). Among these were instances of apparently unintended pregnancy loss and infant death, which police and judges viewed through the lens of criminality.

The letter of the law had little to say about such cases. The Spanish penal code of 1848, which was later revised and applied to Cuba and Puerto Rico in 1850, criminalized infanticide. Convicted individuals incurred the same penalties as for homicide.[2] The 1850 penal code also criminalized abortion, carrying forward the distinction between practitioners and patients already outlined in the 1822 penal code. Prescribed sentences ranged from seven months to twenty years in prison. A third party who intentionally caused an abortion with violence incurred the longest range of incarceration. In order of decreasing sentence ranges, the other crimes were as follows: causing an abortion without the woman's consent; causing an abortion with the woman's consent; and attempting to cause an abortion. If the third party was a medical practitioner, the law prescribed the maximum sentence in each category. Like the 1822 penal code, the penal code of 1850 also punished women for causing their own abortion or consenting to an abortion but allowed a reduced sentence if they did so to hide their dishonor.[3]

Nowhere in the 1850 penal code do natural neonatal death or miscarriage appear. In the annotated version of the 1848 code, Spanish jurists specified that, for the infanticide law to apply, the infant needed to be viable (able to live outside the womb). However, despite the conventional reliance on the docimasia to determine if the infant took its first breath, these jurists observed that neonatal death could result from a range of causes that had nothing to do with criminal intent on the part of the mother.[4] Moreover, they recognized the difference between provoked abortion and spontaneous abortion (miscarriage), which doctors of the time attributed to factors well beyond the pregnant woman's control, such as an injury, fall, fetal death, overexertion, or "strong moral emotions."[5] These cases, the jurists noted, "do not fall under the jurisdiction of the penal law." Judges were forced to rely on medical expertise to distinguish between miscarriage and provoked abortion, but, as these jurists noted, "the evidence is very rare in cases of this nature," and it was important to avoid assumptions based on "dogmatic tone" and "fanaticism."[6]

As Luisa's case suggests, colonial authorities did not stop at the letter of the law when it came to enslaved women's fertility. Instead, police investigated a widening range of reproductive events, signaling expanding state intervention throughout enslaved women's reproductive lives. Although colonial authorities had practically liberated planters from any pronatalist duties with the 1844 ordinances, metropolitan authorities criminalized the slave trade in 1845. With this prohibition, enslaved women's reproduction was reaffirmed as the only legal mechanism of preserving slavery in Cuba. While planters continued to rely on the clandestine slave trade, the growing popularity of plantation medicine—particularly the medical management of enslaved women's pregnancies, births, and child-rearing—suggests that some slave owners invested in reproducing slavery as well. However, the resurgence of criminal cases against enslaved women evinces both the minimal impact such investments had on enslaved fertility as well as the marked preference for coercion and punishment over incentives and encouragement. The seemingly frivolous legal pursuits against enslaved mothers signaled both the state's expanding presence in matters of slavery as well as planters' growing desperation to extract future generations of enslaved workers from the wombs of their human property.

"The Physiology of Increase": Plantation Medicine after 1845

In 1845, a new law repressing the slave trade arrived to Cuba along with a communication instructing colonial authorities to preempt any alarm and to foment the white population. In his reply, the captain-general noted that the "propagation of the Native-born Black race does not substitute the void caused by illness and death," since one in every five enslaved people died and the proportion of enslaved women to men was too low to foster reproduction. Consequently, he predicted that the enslaved population would suffer rapid decline. Within a year or two the losses to the treasury would already be considerable, since neither "good treatment" nor promoting marriage had significantly increased enslaved fertility.[7]

Worried that the law would ultimately result in the loss of the colony, metropolitan authorities authorized a new committee to advise on how to prevent the losses Captain-general O'Donnell predicted. The committee recommended financial incentives for planters who achieved increased reproduction and suggested the importation of enslaved women from Brazil to circumvent the prohibition on transatlantic slaving.[8] Under this scheme, planters who increased the number of marriages and infants born on their estates would receive direct monetary compensation, tax exemptions on enslaved women and children under age twelve, and tax reductions on enslaved men who lived with their wife and children. The benefits only applied to legitimate or legitimized children of slaves, a measure designed to further promote marriage.[9]

The emergence of several large-scale slave-breeding operations on western Cuban plantations around this time suggests that at least some planters implemented such pronatalist programs, though it is unclear the extent to which O'Donnell's proposal inspired them. As one traveler noted, "now that importation is more difficult, and labor is in demand," some planters have turned to "their own stock" and begun "to learn the physiology of increase."[10] Indeed, planters' interest in reproducing slavery gave impetus to plantation medicine. This new specialty applied medical interventions to maximize the profits planters could extract from their enslaved labor forces, including through "natural increase."

As Cuba's medical establishment professionalized, physicians became increasingly central to the extraction of enslaved women's reproductive labor, through the medical supervision of pregnancy, childbirth, and breastfeeding. Although physicians had been involved in managing enslaved labor forces on Cuban plantations since at least the late eighteenth century, these white male medical professionals had gradually displaced women of color midwives and practitioners in the supervision of enslaved women's pregnancies and childbirth on some Cuban plantations by the mid-nineteenth century.[11]

By the 1850s, several prominent physicians compiled their best practices for maintaining enslaved labor forces, based on years working on Cuban plantations. In many respects reminiscent of the pronatalist regimens prominent planters described for the captain-general in the 1840s, these plantation medical guides explicitly instructed on the medical management and reproduction of enslaved labor forces. However, they exposed a much longer history of medical interventions and experimentation of enslaved women's bodies, which became the basis not just of plantation medicine but the emerging field of Cuban obstetrics and gynecology.

One of the most well-known plantation medical guides appeared in Cuba in 1854, authored by a prominent surgeon, Honorato Bernard De Chateausalins. Trained in France, Chateausalins claimed eight years of experience as a surgeon on Cuban plantations, during which time he tended to more than one thousand enslaved women. A significant share of his guide advised planters on how to diagnose pregnancy, prevent miscarriage and abortion, and increase the survival of enslaved infants.[12] His recommendations focused on ensuring that enslaved women carried pregnancies to term, birthed live infants, and kept those babies alive through their most vulnerable years.

Chateausalins framed many recommendations as tools to entice enslaved women to carry their pregnancies to term through measures that resembled amelioration. "Once a planter discovers that one of his slaves is pregnant," Chateausalins wrote, "he should avoid giving her harsh treatment, [and] exempt her from those jobs that require the most strength." In the weeks after an enslaved woman gave birth, Chateausalins advised planters to allow the enslaved mother to rest and attend to her infant. "Planters who desire to conserve their slave babies and have their estates well populated should not only take good care of the baby, but also of his mother," he wrote. He recommended that they protect the enslaved mother from the weather and refrain from burdening her with strenuous labor. It is more beneficial for the planter "to sacrifice a few shifts than to expose his slave woman to death as a victim of his greed," he argued.[13]

These "concessions" were not just about reducing miscarriage, stillbirth, and neonatal death; according to Chateausalins, better treatment also reduced the likelihood of abortion and infanticide. He wrote that "the extreme rigor of slave owners, the unjust punishments of the overseers and foremen during [a woman's] pregnancy, jobs that demand of them in their sorry state the abandonment and neglect of their babies and many other reasons including the barbarity of the mother, push her toward this act of desperation and cruelty."[14] Chateausalins underscored the correlation between the ordinary tortures of slavery and enslaved women's desire to terminate their pregnancies.

By contrast, enslaved women receiving good treatment and care were more likely, in his opinion, to keep their pregnancies and raise their infants. He noted that "it is worthwhile to give her better food than before, and entertain her with trinkets and concessions to motivate her to keep the fetus and raise the new slave baby." On "every plantation where the owners show the slaves kindness, gentleness, and courtesy, one can find many happy little slave children whose mothers show their contentment through their songs and smiling faces," Chateausalins mused.[15] In emphasizing the power of amelioration, Chateausalins challenged planters to transcend the minimalist requirements of the 1844 ordinances.

Although he emphasized preventive measures, Chateausalins also admitted that some pregnancies would inevitably end in miscarriage. "Sometimes, despite all the precautions, ... the slave woman happens to arrive to the infirmary to miscarry, and oftentimes, after having miscarried." His long list of the most common causes of miscarriage in slave women included "weakness, heavy bleeding, fullness of the stomach, acute illnesses, severe, deep cough, imprudent inducement of vomiting, considerable hemorrhaging, venereal disease, licentiousness, uterine ulcers, hard labor, falls, beatings, especially those given with a whip, straining to carry or unload heavy objects, and finally all the diseases of the fetus."[16] Most of the external causes formed part of enslaved women's everyday lives, in which heavy labor and physical abuse were normalized. Nevertheless, this recognition of miscarriage did not appear to assuage physicians' suspicions about enslaved women's abortion practices, despite the difficulty of medically distinguishing between the two.

Even as Chateausalins advised planters to treat pregnant slaves with slightly more humanity, he also made it clear that such concessions could not be granted to just anyone. Indeed, he expressed contradictory views about enslaved women, at times portraying them as murderous thieves and unnatural mothers, and at other moments as liars trying to gain benefits to which they were not entitled. Some enslaved women allegedly "fake amenorrhea when they actually are not pregnant." In other instances, pregnant slaves would feign illness while withholding information about their condition in order to obtain medications known to have abortifacient properties. Chateausalins therefore instructed planters to ask enslaved women "if there has been or are any changes to her menstruation, such as lighter flow, excessive bleeding, difficulties, retention or suspension of menstruation" before giving certain medications since they could "could cause miscarriage." Chateausalins also observed that "it is a common thing among slave women to fear and even loathe the state of pregnancy, even aborting by way of some bitter herbs they know which have an infallible abortifacient effect."[17] Underlying these competing claims was an argument that the management of enslaved women's reproduction required specialized expertise.

Indeed, one thread running throughout his guidance on managing enslaved women's pregnancies was the need for white male supervision, especially once labor commenced. Chateausalins advised planters at this point to send the woman "immediately to the birthing room," where a midwife (most likely another enslaved women) would attend to her according to medical instructions. He recommended administering "a cup of very strong substance from time to time" to usher the labor along. In cases of prolonged labor, "beverage number 58 every two hours" was indicated—a potion consisting of precise amounts of cinnamon tea, absinthe, rue, juniper, simple syrup, opium, and castor oil. Apparently employed to induce uterine contractions, the same elixir was also used to "bring down the menses" when taken immediately after a "suppressed menstruation."[18] Yet, later studies revealed that the opium in this prescription was potentially harmful to the fetus because it suppressed respiration.[19]

Chateausalins urged planters toward patience rather than "calling too hastily a romantic surgeon whose operations make the situation worse by impeding nature's efforts." In his entire career, he had to use forceps or other medical instruments to birth only six or eight babies, and he delivered an additional four or five using manual interventions. Surgeons "have always regretted" surgery more than waiting, he observed.[20] The high risk of infection from obstetrical interventions and abdominal surgery outweighed the potential benefits, especially prior to the introduction of asepsis and antisepsis in Cuba in the 1890s.

Further guidance focused primarily on nutrition and disease prevention. Chateausalins insisted that breastfeeding offered the best chance of survival. He recommended keeping the mother and infant together for the first eighteen months. Once the infant had at least twelve teeth, the mother could wean it.[21] "Deplorable experience has demonstrated to me that by failing to observe this rule, many planters lose half of their little slave babies who die from teething-related accidents." When the mother was not able to breastfeed, Chateausalins urged planters to hand the baby over to an enslaved wet nurse, preferably one who was "young and healthy." The enslaved wet nurse "should have given birth around the same time as the baby's mother, her skin shall be shiny, which is a sign of health," and "she should be of soft manner, patient, and exempt, if possible, from drunkenness, promiscuity, and other vices common to slaves."[22] If no wet nurses were available, the baby could be given goat, sheep, or cow milk, either directly from the animal's teats, or in a sponge-topped bottle meant to imitate a nipple.

Even as Chateausalins emphasized the importance of breastfeeding, he warned planters that enslaved women could also harm the infant during this time. He depicted enslaved mothers as laden with vice, apathy, and evil intentions. For instance, if an enslaved woman was infected with contagious disease, including venereal disease, suffered from alcoholism, or was too promiscuous, her breastmilk could contaminate the baby. He instructed planters to "repress" any "excess licentiousness" to ensure that "their little slave babies grow strong." Chateausalins also blamed enslaved mothers for any breastfeeding difficulties; enslaved infants who struggled to latch onto the nipple did so because the mother was too "stupid and apathetic" to notice, and as a result, "the little slave baby becomes skinny."[23]

As enslaved babies grew, Chateausalins urged planters to continue monitoring the type and quantity of nourishment enslaved mothers gave to their babies to prevent potentially fatal gastrointestinal complications. He warned planters that enslaved women often fed their infants solid food too early, causing intestinal blockages, and death. They "almost always believe that breastfeeding is not enough for their infants," he claimed. As a result, they end up filling their babies up with plantains, yams, boniato, and other starchy foods, causing "incurable blockages because of the continuous excesses." He explained that "the lack of nourishment destroys the fragile health of those little ones; when [the mothers] hear them cry, they tend to give them solid food without thinking, and sooner or later that infallibly produces fatal consequences."[24]

According to Chateausalins, even when the babies were old enough to eat solid food, their survival depended on strict regiments of nutrition. "Any planter who wants to conserve the little slave babies had better try to prevent indigestion than cure it, and he will do so by watching them closely." He instructed planters to "personally ensure the type and quantity of [babies'] food" and to prevent unscheduled feedings. Most important of all, he recommended not "filling their weak stomachs with fruits like mangos, avocados, mamey" so the babies would not fall victim to indigestion.[25]

While Chateausalins was quick to blame enslaved mothers for their supposed failures, his descriptions of the everyday lives of enslaved mothers illustrates just how impossible it was for these women to tend to their children. Many slave owners had the "bad habit" of forcing enslaved mothers to return to work shortly after giving birth and "not allowing the mother [to] breastfeed her child more than once per day." With mothers occupied elsewhere by slave owners, solid food was the only alternative to nourish their infants during their extended absences.

The plantation medicine guide also addressed diseases commonly affecting enslaved infants, including infant tetanus, which according to Chateausalins, afflicted enslaved infants more than any other group.[26] To an extent, he recognized that the unsanitary and impoverished conditioned enslaved mothers faced on Cuban plantations contributed to high infection rates. "The slave huts on most plantations are in bad shape, full of holes." The location of these slave huts in "cold elevated places" was believed to be "especially harmful to children" because it exposed them to "the pernicious effects" of "strong winds day and night." Nor could this problem have an easy solution, according to Chateausalins, because enslaved mothers and fathers are "always busy working for their owner, [so] they cannot rebuild their houses like free people of color."[27] He also noted the scarcity of clean clothing, an observation others corroborated. According to one traveler, enslaved women "commonly get a coffee-bag to cover themselves; they cut a hole in the bottom of it for their head, and two holes at the corners for the arms."[28] Lacking other clothing, enslaved mothers often wrapped their infants in rags, rarely changing them. As a result, most enslaved infants spent "most of the night in their excrement." Likely unaware that infant tetanus was most commonly caused by infected instruments used to cut the umbilical cord, Chateausalins viewed unsanitary shelter and clothing as chief causes of infant tetanus.[29]

Rather than advise planters to provide better accommodations to enslaved parents and their infants, or time off to fix their huts, Chateausalins blamed enslaved mothers for exposing their babies to filth, disease, and vice. For instance, he charged that enslaved women who had ample clothing reserved it for "their own use" rather than clothing their infants. These "barbaric mothers" failed to swaddle their infants properly, thereby exposing their umbilical stumps to injury and tetanus infection. Beyond that, the "state of poverty and servitude" in which enslaved mothers lived contributed to their general "apathy" toward their babies. "Slave women generally have very little attachment to their infants," he wrote. "The unmarried ones in particular don't think of anything other than fulfilling the work required by the owner," he claimed, glossing over the fact that absolute servitude was the premise of chattel slavery. According to him, enslaved women lived "indifferently" and cared little about their babies, because they feel a "natural repugnance toward raising [babies] fated to work their whole lives to make a fortune for their owner," and as such they believed that "the owner should care for" them. He speculated that enslaved women would "often allow [their babies] to perish were it not for the punishments" applied in these cases. Overall, he concluded that the "negligence of slave mothers" was a principal cause of infant tetanus.[30]

This tension between enslaved women's productive and reproductive responsibilities captured so vividly by Chateausalins offered a compelling argument for expanding medical supervision of enslaved reproduction. Indeed, a different plantation guide instructed planters to augment their nurseries with additional departments for pregnant women and children who were weaned but not yet old enough to work on their own, beyond the main one dedicated to infants.[31] However, even in the most state-of-the-art nurseries, enslaved mothers and infants could not escape the grim realities of slavery. Indeed, Cuban physicians later criticized plantation nurseries for perpetuating many of the problems attributed to slave mothers. One physician decried the "inadequate nutrition" that cost more than half the babies their lives and the "barbarous treatments" to simple ailments caused by poor hygiene. Another doctor observed that enslaved nurses in charge of the nursery, in their "misery and ignorance" made whatever food they could to sustain the "poor beings deprived of maternal nutrition," but those little stomachs could not digest it. With the added scourge of infant tetanus, smallpox, tuberculosis, and other illnesses, these nurseries were "true human hecatombs."[32]

Although some of the recommendations in plantation medicine guides were later proven wrong or even harmful, the medical knowledge gleaned from enslaved women's bodies became the basis for maternal and infant welfare interventions in the late nineteenth and early twentieth centuries. The emphasis on breastfeeding over solid foods became the best practice for preventing enteritis, a leading cause of infant death. The notion that poor hygiene increased the risk of infant tetanus, though failing to acknowledge physicians' own role, eventually exposed the need for sanitation in childbirth and newborn care. Moreover, the suspicion that poverty and inhumane living conditions drove women to fertility control also continued to shape attitudes toward infanticide and abortion. Linking all these ideas were two overarching beliefs—that enslaved women were potentially harmful to fetuses and infants because of their alleged immorality, vice, disease, and malice, and that supervision by white male physicians and surgeons could offset these risks.

But how effective were these recommendations in their original goal of fostering natural increase among slaves? The results appear as uneven as the adoption of the recommendations. The mid-century emergence of large-scale slave breeding operations suggests that some Cuban planters indeed adopted the pronatalist measures outlined in plantation medical guides. A number of prominent planters boasted of fostering reproduction among their enslaved labor forces. On the Victoria sugar mill, in the jurisdiction of Colón in the western province of Matanzas, the owner reported that all 240 adult slaves were married. One Cuban observer noted that "the owner dedicates much attention to the propagation of his slaves and he has achieved it in such a way that allows him to complete the grind [of sugar cane during the harvest] without occupying more time than that between five in the morning and ten at night, at which hour everyone, including the [slaves] in the boiler house, retires to rest." The enslaved population on that plantation grew by 4.5 to 5.5 percent annually. In 1855, the nursery housed eighty enslaved children between one and ten years old.[33] On a plantation called Unión in the jurisdiction of Cárdenas, the gender ratio approached parity at 40 percent female. In a labor force of 598 slaves, 100 were children.[34]

One of Cuba's most notorious slave breeding operations was on the San José de Bainoa and Jesús María sugar mills in Matanzas province. The owner of those plantations, Antonio Santa Cruz de Oviedo y Muñoz, was a notable slave trader. When his son Estéban Santa Cruz de Oviedo inherited these assets, nearly four hundred enslaved people labored on both plantations. With antislaving legislation rendering the contraband activities of his father increasingly dangerous, Estéban shifted his focus from illegal slave trafficking to breeding slaves. He founded two new sugar mills, Santísima Trinidad and Vista Hermosa. By the mid-1850s, he had grown the number to more than one thousand on Santísima Trinidad alone.[35] Approximately three hundred slaves were children, including at least twenty-six sired by Estéban himself. Enslaved women on just that plantation collectively gave birth to approximately thirty babies each year, while deaths totaled around ten annually.[36] Other notable slave breeding operations existed on the Angelita and Juraguá mills, both outside of Cienfuegos.[37]

Enslaved Women's Reproduction as a Matter of "Public Interest"

As much as these individual cases evinced a concerted effort among some planters to extract enslaved women's reproductive labor, the demographic impact of these slave breeding operations was, at best, insignificant. By the mid-1850s, Ignacio González Olivares, a judge at the Real Audiencia Pretorial de la Habana, explained in no uncertain terms how pronatalist measures such as those outlined by Dr. Chateausalins, had failed to produce natural increase among Cuba's enslaved population. "It is evident that slave owners give their slaves healthy and abundant rations, and provide them care when they are sick," he wrote expectantly. "And yet, not only do they not increase, but they decrease in a manner truly frightful for the future of the Island of Cuba." The number of babies born was "infinitely" smaller than the number of deaths even under "ordinary mortality rates."[38]

A sense of urgency pervaded his observations. The contraband trade in captives had grown increasingly volatile, especially following Spain's 1845 criminalization of slaving. In peak years like 1841, twenty-seven ships carrying nearly 10,000 captives entered Cuban ports. In slower years, like 1845, the Havana commissioner estimated that fewer than 1,000 slaves landed on the island. Although an infusion of U.S. capital in the late 1850s temporarily wrought larger slave cargoes (as many as 30,000 in 1859), between 1841 and 1861 the island's total enslaved population declined for the first time since the sugar boom, from 436,500 to 367,400.[39]

In this context, the persistently low fertility rates among Cuba's enslaved population spelled economic disaster for an island almost completely reliant on sugar cultivation. "If slaves are necessary for at least certain jobs" but importation was illegal, the judge reasoned, then enslaved women's reproduction was the only way to preserve slavery. However, authorities first had to understand why birth rates remained low, despite the supposed provision of adequate rations, clothing, and medical care. "It is necessary to investigate the cause of this fatal result [of low fertility rates] and apply the convenient remedy so that we do not find ourselves within a very short time without the workers necessary to save the island from catastrophe," the judge declared.[40]

The judge concluded that the "excessive work" planters demanded of slaves disrupted reproduction. It seemed apparent to him that, in addition to "other reasons that should not be discussed in this type of communication," planters "mistakenly believe that they can demand all the work they want from a slave, so long as it is well dressed and nourished." This was precisely the message colonial authorities had communicated to planters when they approved the 1844 Ordinances. However, the judge sympathized with planters, noting that their "financial situation" obliges them to produce a greater quantity of sugar than can be "rationally demanded, given the number of workers they have." With few exceptions, they forced their slaves to toil for an "excessive" number of hours on plantations during harvest season. As slaves "decrease and become more expensive," he predicted that planters would only work their slaves harder. The result of this practice to be clear: overworking slaves shortened their lifespan and was "contrary to reproduction."[41]

Some planters had already begun experimenting with alternative forms of labor to supplement enslaved Africans. Chinese indentured servants began arriving to the island in the 1840s, and planters even imported a small number of Indigenous workers from the Yucatán Peninsula.[42] White colonization schemes also resurged during this period. However, the judge captured the broader preference for enslaved African labor when he wrote that neither Chinese nor European workers could replace slaves in Cuba's plantation economy. According to the judge, "the total lack" of enslaved Africans, given the current system of cultivation and production of sugar, "would inevitably produce the country's ruin."[43] Enslaved Africans and their descendants were still the preferred form of labor on Cuba's plantations, thus remaining a central pillar of the island's economy.

In light of planters' continued reliance on enslaved labor, the judge argued that firm government intervention to enforce pronatalist measures was necessary. "Expecting a remedy from slave owners themselves is useless, because pressing needs and naive errors almost always oblige them to sacrifice the future for the present," he explained. Rather than allowing planters to regulate themselves, he argued that the government, as the representative of "public interest," was obligated to defend the interests of today's public but also that of tomorrow, by "providing rules that require individuals to behave appropriately." There were, in effect, laws governing slavery, he observed.

Existing laws, though, had proven overwhelmingly detrimental to pronatalist aspirations, and the judge recognized this. The protocols outlined in the 1844 ordinances "were made for different times, when . . . the importation of slaves abundantly satisfied the demand for labor; when the opposition to slavery was not as pronounced as it is today that everything is done to discredit [the institution, even] exaggerating its evils."[44] The judge declared that Cuba needed a new approach to slavery that would bypass planters and gradually wean them from their reliance on the clandestine slave trade.

Cultivating a self-sustaining slave population in Cuba, the judge argued, required direct involvement by the colonial state. "A healthy intervention by the government," could manage slavery for "public benefit" while also assuring the slave "humane treatment, religious instruction, and a moderated workload, in addition to the healthy rations, clothing, and medical care that he already has." He suggested a set of laws similar to the one set forth in the May 31, 1789 royal decree. The judge argued that if the government actually implemented and enforced such laws, it could save slavery: "The number of babies born will be greater than the [number of] deaths. Instead of declining, they will expand the cultivation and production of our commodities, business will grow, wealth will increase, and foreigners will stop throwing in our face an institution that is no longer at odds with humanity and with progress."[45] This plan to regenerate Cuba's enslaved population and salvage Spain's international reputation recognized that the future of slavery lay in enslaved women's wombs.

The judge's appeal went unheeded. In fact, just two years later, in 1855 colonial authorities deployed these precise arguments to support a request to reopen the slave trade to Cuba. In letters to the Spanish minister of state, Captain-general José Gutiérrez de la Concha claimed that desperate conditions faced the island's sugar planters. Like his colleague at the audiencia, he concurred that "no race can substitute Black Africans" in assuring the wealth of the Island of Cuba. Echoing earlier recommendations, he argued that "natural reproduction" was the best remedy to expand the island's enslaved population. However, he noted one major obstacle in the way of creating a self-sustaining slave population: the "inconvenience that females are very scarce."[46] Demographically speaking, the captain-general was right. The enslaved population remained predominantly male, particularly in the western department, where sugar plantations, infused with foreign capital, continued to run profitably (table 6.1).

With the antislaving treaty renewed and fortified in 1835 and slaving recently criminalized in the 1845 Spanish code, the captain-general must have known that a favorable response to his request would be unlikely. The Spanish minister of state observed that the 1835 treaty prohibited only the acquisition of slaves in Africa and did not technically interfere with the sale of "legitimately acquired slaves." Thus, an inter-American trade in slaves was arguably permissible. Nonetheless, he speculated that British authorities would protest attempts to import slaves into Cuba, regardless of their supposed origins.[47]

Undeterred, the captain-general replied with a plea on behalf of Cuba's planters. Cuban slave owners, he claimed, were doing all they could to foster the reproduction of the African race—"buying all the women they could, encouraging marriage, attending to the females during their pregnancies and childbirths

TABLE 6.1. Sex ratios of population of color, by legal status, 1861

	Free			Slave			Emancipado			Total		
	Male	Female	Total	Male	Female	Total	Male	Female	Total	Male	Female	Total
West	66,461	73,308	139,769	191,243	127,532	318,775	4,500	1,761	6,261	262,204	202,601	464,805
East	42,566	43,508	86,074	27,479	24,299	51,778	219	110	329	70,264	67,917	138,181
TOTAL	109,027	116,816	225,843	218,722	151,831	370,553	4,719	1,871	6,590	332,468	270,518	602,986

SOURCE: "Censo de la población según el cuadro general de la comisión ejecutiva de 1861," in Centro de estadística, *Noticias estadísticas de la isla de Cuba, en 1862* (Havana: Imprenta del gobierno, 1864), 14.

with as much care as possible, rewarding them for keeping their children alive, and in sum doing all that is practiced in the United States [to ensure] the reproduction of the slaves."[48] Despite their supposedly faithful compliance to pronatalist mandates, all their efforts were for naught.

According to the captain-general, there were simply too few enslaved women to make natural reproduction viable. He lamented that many slave owners lacked foresight to import female captives prior to that point, "assuming that the treaties celebrated to repress the slave trade would be lightly enforced or illusory." If they would have acquired a proportional number of women to men before the treaties, he reasoned, then the number of slaves would have increased as it had in the United States. "It is too late now," he concluded. Given the gender ratios on typical plantations, there would be "no remedy to avoid that the Black race declines." Appealing to the benevolence of his superior, the captain-general expressed his helplessness: "neither property owners despite their keenest interest, nor the Government of this Island can do anything alone to augment the number of women." However, if the minister authorized the importation of enslaved women, then the enslaved population could achieve "a balanced proportion of men and women, so it can reproduce itself naturally and increase progressively."[49] According to the captain-general, natural reproduction required the importation of new captives, who he promised would be women.

Figures from around this time suggest that the gender ratio was not nearly as imbalanced as the captain-general claimed. In 1862, 60 percent of the island's total enslaved population was male. In the western portion of the island, which held the vast majority (86 percent) of the island's enslaved population, the proportion of males was slightly higher at 61 percent. Though imbalanced, these figures compared favorably to the gender ratios typically characterizing slave cargoes arriving to the island, which rarely exceeded 30 percent female. In more heavily urbanized areas, like Havana, the gender ratio approached parity, with only 51 percent males.[50] However, the captain-general likely meant to invoke the scarcity of females on plantations, particularly those that continued to import large numbers of captives. On that basis, he asked the Spanish minister of state to authorize the importation of enslaved women from neighboring slave societies, such as Brazil.[51]

The minister of state appeared to understand that this request was a mere pretext to circumvent restrictions on the slave trade. He pointed out that even with England's unlikely consent, the proposed plan did not guarantee improved gender ratios on plantations. Indeed, he speculated that plantation owners would still prefer to purchase male slaves, who they considered more productive than females, and slave traffickers would still import more male captives because of their higher prices. "Neither now, nor before, nor after," he wrote, "would [traffickers] run the risk of a slaving expedition to bring females, who are worth much less than males." The only way to encourage traffickers to bring females would to be ensure that authorities would permit their importation, and to allow them to bring three or four males as well. Such a policy would entail publicizing the implicit tolerance for illicit slaving, begetting corruption within the government and diminishing the prestige of the Spanish Crown. The minister's letter segued into a discussion of the disadvantages of tolerating the clandestine slave trade to Cuba, and recommended alternatives to remedy the island's alleged labor shortage.[52]

The gender ratios among captives imported since the passage of the first antislaving treaty suggested that the minister was right. After over a half century of failed policy initiatives directed at balancing the gender ratio of Cuba's enslaved population, clandestine slave ships still smuggled predominantly male cargoes, some as low as 4 percent female.[53] Indeed, one foreign traveler even remarked that "Cuba does not traffic much, like New Orleans, in second hand muscles [women]," which keeps up an "alarming preponderance of the male sex" on many plantations.[54]

"A Fatal Example for Slavery": Restoring State Authority over Enslaved Women's Wombs

As metropolitan authorities prepared for a transition to free labor, colonial officials clung fiercely to the potential of enslaved women's wombs, the final frontier for preserving slavery. Although the captain-general failed to regain access to a legal trade in slaves, judicial authorities seemed to heed the counsel of the audiencia judge by assuming a more direct role in enslaved women's reproductive lives. This intervention did not take the form of a new code of laws, as the judge had recommended. Rather, it emerged through shifting interpretations and implementation of existing laws, ones that assumed different meanings and had distinct consequences when applied to enslaved women.

One of the most significant developments concerned who held the legal jurisdiction over enslaved women's reproductive decisions. Slave owners had typically enjoyed almost complete authority over their slaves, including judging their behavior and punishing them. However, in the late 1830s and early 1840s, two important precedents emerged to support a more pronounced state presence in those decisions: the prosecution of a small number of enslaved women for infanticide, and the brief and wildly unpopular expansion of state authority prescribed in the 1842 slave code. While the 1844 ordinances had essentially halted this expanded state presence in slavery, the increasing urgency of reproducing slavery laid the foundation for its return in the late 1850s.

Criminal investigations evinced a resurgence of interest on the part of local authorities in the reproductive lives of enslaved women. In April 1851, authorities in Cárdenas investigated the discovery of an enslaved woman and her young son drowned in a well. The investigation proceeded despite that fact that the primary suspect was no longer alive. Police apparently suspected that the enslaved woman, Juana, had thrown her child, Juan Emeterio, into the well and then committed suicide in the same manner.[55] They found no evidence of murder-suicide but apparently never considered alternate explanations. Perhaps the child fell into the well and the mother tried to rescue her son. Such a narrative did not fit into prevailing perceptions of devious enslaved mothers. Although we may never discover what happened to Juana and Emeterio, investigations like this show ongoing elite concern with the loss of enslaved infants and children on rural plantations.

While the focus on enslaved reproduction on rural plantations was not new to the 1850s, there is also evidence that enslaved women in urban settings became subject to police investigation and even prosecution for fertility crimes by the late 1840s. The 1855 investigation of the enslaved woman Luisa following the discovery of her deceased infant daughter in urban Havana, recounted early in this chapter, illustrates this expansion in the geographic parameters of colonial interest in enslaved women's fertility. After authorities confirmed that the deceased infant belonged to Luisa, they questioned the enslaved woman's owner, who corroborated Luisa's testimony. She explained that she had been ill and had another slave who had just given birth, so she had sent Luisa to give birth in the home of one of her associates. However, the baby was sick, and it died before they could baptize it. Although she had requested that her son take care of the burial, she claimed that he was too busy to do so. The investigation ended when Luisa's owner died.[56]

This case followed a much different trajectory than the cursory investigations of Black infant abandonment and the drawn-out criminal proceedings against rural enslaved women. Investigations of Black infant abandonment typically yielded the least documentation, sometimes only a few sentences. By contrast, criminal infanticide cases against enslaved women produced substantial documentary trails (chapter 5). Although the police interrogated both Luisa and her owner, they did not pursue charges of infanticide. Nor did authorities throw Luisa in the depósito for preventative incarceration during the investigation. Evidently, the circumstances surrounding the death of Luisa's baby differed from similar cases involving rural slaves. In Luisa's case, her owner corroborated the infant's illness, rather than blaming her for the death, as rural slave owners often did. Though a single case is not enough to draw any definitive conclusions, the lower intensity authorities brought to this case possibly stemmed from the diverging attitudes about Black reproduction in terms of both legal status and geographic area. Whereas colonial elites often lamented the burgeoning (largely free) Black populations in urban areas, they seemingly obsessed over trying to raise the fertility rates on rural plantations to offset the growing restrictions on the slave trade. That even the accidental death of enslaved infants on plantations prompted criminal convictions, while urban slaves rarely prompted similar investigations and criminal proceedings, hints that these demographic pressures might have influenced both which infant deaths authorities investigated and the degree of criminality ascribed to the mother.

Luisa's case does, however, allude to an emerging consensus that managing the fertility of enslaved women required state intervention. In 1857, one of Cuba's most influential legal theorists, Félix Erenchún, argued that while slave owners should retain some authority over their slaves, the state could and should intervene in certain situations, including ones in which reproduction was at stake. When it came to cases of fertility control, he argued that slave owners should reserve the authority over enslaved women suspected of attempting abortion or infanticide. In those cases, he argued that enslaved women should not be subjected to public authority because of the "incertitude of the proof and the harm that could be caused to the owner." Instead, he recommended that owners issue the sanctions according to their property and economic interests and moral judgments.[57] In essence, he directed slave owners to take private responsibility for preventing infanticide on their estates. However, cases of abortion and infanticide that resulted in the successful termination of a pregnancy or death of a newborn warranted, and indeed required, state intervention in the form of a formal investigation and criminal proceeding.

Within this context, Cuban legal scholars began to offer racially specific guidance on how Cuban judges might interpret the supposedly colorblind laws, given the island's racially stratified slave society. For instance, the long-standing allowance for reduced sentencing for women who committed infanticide to defend their honor, recently recodified into law in the 1848 and 1850 penal codes, offered a fertile terrain for introducing considerations about race and legal status.[58] Although the absence of racial language clearly implied a focus on white women only, Erenchún made the racial limits of attenuating circumstances defenses more explicit.[59] He argued *honoris causa* crimes were the exclusive legal domain of women with honor to lose. According to Erenchún, the "reduction of the punishment when an abortion occurs to hide dishonor" is not applicable to cases involving women of African descent, because honor "does not exist among people of color with respect to the concept of legitimacy."[60] While some scholars have argued that enslaved people in other Latin America societies laid claim to honor in and beyond the courts, it appears that in the context of criminal prosecution for fertility crimes, honor remained out of reach for women of African descent in Cuba. There, judges appeared much more swayed by legal defenses emphasizing idiocy and insanity than honor.[61]

Regardless of the actual reason motivating infanticide or abortion, this categorical racial exclusion from honor made women of African descent ineligible for reduced sentences for *honoris causa* fertility crimes. Justifying this particularly punitive recommendation, Erenchún argued that punishing an enslaved woman to the fullest extent of the law was especially important if she committed the crime "with the intention of avoiding the servitude of her child." He opined: "without a doubt, this circumstance should not be taken into account ... for the reduction of the punishment, because this would be a fatal example for slavery."[62] Because any fetuses conceived in the wombs of enslaved mothers constituted potential future property of the slave owner, harsh sanctions against enslaved women who committed fertility control could drive slave reproduction. But Erenchún's logic relied on the conceptual conflation of Black reproduction with slavery. If followed, his interpretation, which lacked distinctions about legal status, would have similarly penalized free women of color, thereby exacerbating what white intellectuals saw as the island's terrifying racial imbalance. Punishing Black women more severely than white women in a time of profound anxiety over the "Africanization" of Cuba's population could make demographic sense only if Black women's fertility had tangible economic and property interests for slave owners. This required eliding free Black women from the discussion.

Even his recommendations about the treatment of fertility control among mixed-race unions revealed the conflation of Blackness and slavery. Specifically, he prescribed harsher penalties for abortions of pregnancies conceived through mixed-race and mixed-legal status unions. For example, he explicitly suggested stiffer abortion penalties against fathers of African descent when the mother of the fetus was a white woman, a union presumed to be violent and nonconsensual. He also indicated that among pregnancies resulting from sexual relations between slave and owner, enslaved fathers who impregnated white women slave owners merited harsher penalties than slave owners who impregnated enslaved women (by far, the more common scenario). In cases in which the abortion resulted from the union of a slave and another party (not the owner), the latter would be responsible for the value of the lost fetus as well as that of the mother, if she were to die.[63]

Some of these racially specific sanctions for fertility control in mixed-race unions appeared to respond to demographic anxieties surrounding the potential growth of the island's free population of color. Sexual liaisons between enslaved people and their owners constituted a potential weak point in generational slavery. Given *partus sequitur ventrem*, tougher sanctions against unions between enslaved men and white women seem consistent with attempts to curtail interracial unions that might produce free colored offspring, while also punishing Black men for claiming white women. In the far more common scenario involving enslaved women carrying their owner's child, mothers gained a minute degree of leverage and bargaining power over their status and that of their enslaved offspring.[64]

Amid many other hard-fought pathways to freedom, inter-status sex contributed to growth of the free Black population. Demographic data for the early nineteenth century indicate that the free population of color hovered around 15 or 16 percent. Censuses from 1827 and 1841 show free people of color constituted approximately 15 percent of the population, while in 1860 the figure rose to 16 percent. Although the rather constant proportion of free people of color in the island's population might seem to suggest continuity rather than change, the number of free people of color nearly doubled between the 1840s and the 1860s.[65] Women were overrepresented among this growing group of free people of color. Some estimates indicate that women constituted nearly two-thirds of the enslaved people freed in Cuba.[66]

Anxieties about enslaved women's reproduction remained pronounced through the 1860s, as the clandestine slave trade slowed. Ramón de la Sagra commented on the "scarcity" of babies born to slaves. He suspected the low number of slave births recorded in the parochial baptismal registers owed to the practice of abortion by enslaved women. According to de la Sagra, enslaved women knew of certain members of their community who prepared "very effective abortive drinks unknown to the whites."[67] The courts reasserted their authority in matters pertaining to enslaved women's reproductive lives, seemingly heeding Erenchún's demand to have no mercy on enslaved women. But they found not the malicious criminal activities described by de la Sagra but rather the poor pregnancy outcomes that were undoubtedly much more common.

An 1863 case involving the death of an enslaved infant on a plantation outside the central Cuban town of Camarones evinces how the lens of criminality prevailed even in cases of apparently unintentional death of enslaved babies. Authorities received word of the death of one-month-old Andrés, born to an enslaved woman on the plantation. According to the slave owner, the baby was so healthy they had not yet baptized him, as they expected him to survive.

When the local judge asked him if he suspected that the baby's mother had killed her newborn intentionally, he replied that he did not. He told authorities that he believed that the baby's mother, a sixteen-year-old girl called Lorenza, must have "suffocated the little Black boy accidentally" in her sleep. He characterized the young mother as "a very trustworthy slave and very rational." She possessed "a natural motherly sentiment." Finally, he testified that "neither he nor his family had ever witnessed any impulse that could have made her commit such a despicable crime."[68] He had heard from the other enslaved women who slept in the same room that the infant had started crying in the middle of the night, and that his mother had gotten up to breastfed him, and then returned to sleep. When authorities interrogated the baby's mother, Lorenza, she confirmed the narrative, and indicated that she had received good treatment from her owner.

The surviving documentary record does not reveal what became of Lorenza. However, it is telling that local courts pursued an infanticide investigation in a case in which even the slave owner recognized a lack of intentionality, one of the key measures of criminal responsibility in prevailing legal interpretations of infanticide statutes. This trajectory mirrored the case developed against Luisa, recounted earlier. Together, these police interventions in evidently noncriminal enslaved infant deaths suggest that the colonial state, even more than the planters themselves, pursued slave breeding as a cornerstone of a last-ditch effort to preserve slavery. These cases, in the context of Erenchún's racialized readings of the law, appear to reveal the relative ease with which jurists criminalized people of African descent. Under this emerging legal framework, Black women were criminalized for failing to uphold the dying institution of slavery with their reproductive labor.

A Pregnancy Feigned, a Pregnancy Hidden

On New Year's Day in 1865, police responded to a report from a plantation in the neighborhood of Príncipe that an enslaved woman had suddenly lost her pregnancy. According to the slave owner, twenty-four-year-old Isabel Frías had grown a "bulging belly" large enough to suggest she was in the later months of pregnancy. However, he noticed that her abdomen had recently decreased in size. He had confronted her, asking her "where her belly had gone." She had reportedly answered that she did not have a belly and had not been pregnant at all. Police took Isabel into custody on suspicion that she either had "exposed her fetus" (had a miscarriage or a stillbirth and abandoned the remains) or committed infanticide.[69]

After a lengthy investigation, during which Isabel languished in Havana's Casa de Recogidas, a local judge found her guilty of infanticide. The case against Isabel followed a similar trajectory as the cases against enslaved women in the 1830s and 1840s (see chapter 4). Like enslaved women before her, Isabel faced intense scrutiny over her reproductive life, as her owners understood the material benefits her fertility offered them. In both contexts, slave owners enacted their interest in enslaved women's reproductive lives by reporting suspected cases of fertility control to local authorities, thereby facilitating state intervention to enforce slave owners' claims to ownership over fetal and infant life.

However, unlike the investigations of the 1830s, the case against Isabel did not fall under abortion or infanticide laws. Although her owners framed their allegations in terms of infanticide, the details of Isabel's case suggest that if she had been pregnant at all, she likely miscarried, which did not merit criminal prosecution under the 1850 penal code. Infanticide required the infant to be sufficiently developed to be viable and born alive. Moreover, even if Isabel had procured an abortion, the medical knowledge was insufficient to prove that. Isabel's owner could muster no other evidence than his observation that Isabel's once-enlarged belly had receded. By his own admission, he had not seen her miscarry and had no knowledge of any fetal remains or afterbirth.

Despite these apparently flawed allegations, police promptly launched an investigation. Upon interrogation, Isabel denied any knowledge of a pregnancy. She told police that she was naturally a "barrigona"—a big-bellied woman. Police then questioned others on the estate. They interrogated the morena María de la Luz Nieves, who slept in the same room as Isabel. She allegedly told police that Isabel might have in fact been pregnant, though it is unclear on what grounds she based her assumption. At that point, police took Isabel into custody.

During the preliminary hearing, Isabel's owners told the court that, although they did not know who the father of the alleged child was, Isabel did have "amorous relations" with multiple men. Although there was no proof of these supposed sexual acts or of any alleged pregnancy, the judge ordered Isabel transferred to the Francisco de Paula Women's Hospital to await trial. However, the director of the women's hospital refused to admit her, requesting her transfer to the women's prison, the Casa San Juan Nepomuceno de Recogidas.

Isabel appealed the conviction. The ensuing investigation included a medical examination of Isabel, which allegedly revealed that she had, in fact, given birth, though it did not specify when. Still, the prosecutor attempted to ascertain the identity of the father of Isabel's alleged baby. He questioned other slaves on the estate, especially those perceived to maintain the closest contact with Isabel. He also questioned the neighbors closest to the estate for information about Isabel's alleged pregnancy, birth, and sexual relations. However, those encounters yielded little information.

In fact, the investigation provided more reason to drop the charges than to pursue them. For instance, one of Isabel's previous owners, a Frenchman named Eugenio Fource, testified that two years prior, when he owned Isabel, she had given birth previously and "raised her children like a good mother." He expressed surprise that Isabel would be implicated in such a crime, especially considering his opinion that Isabel's owner generally treated his slaves "very well." One of the enslaved men with whom Isabel previously labored testified that he had seen her give birth two years before the incident but had not seen her since she had been sold off. After all this, the court determined that "despite its diligence," it had not been possible to verify the identity of the "negro calesero" who carried on "relaciones" with Isabel.

Nonetheless, the court continued its search for incriminating evidence. The prosecutor again turned to Isabel, interrogating her once more. From her cell in the Casa de Recogidas, Isabel testified that she had only given birth once, when she was a slave of "Sr. Frías," and she denied engaging in sexual relations on her new owner's estate. The court then turned to the church, requesting information on Black or mulatto infants baptized during the window Isabel allegedly hid her pregnancy. The priest answered that only one baptismal record fit the description, but that the baby was listed as the legitimate daughter of a married free *pardo* couple. Next, the prosecutor attempted to find Isabel's alleged baby by surveying the enslaved newborns on the estate where she allegedly gave birth. They found no fetal remains or cadavers, nor did they discover Isabel's alleged baby living on the estate. Investigators found three babies among the enslaved population, all of whom had already been baptized, and no one connected with these babies had information about Isabel's alleged pregnancy or baby.

Apart from the medical examination, which could not give a timeline for the alleged birth, the investigation had failed to produce proof of pregnancy. With such a lack of physical evidence, the appeals judge reasoned that he had to rule out charges of infanticide. Nevertheless, he suspected that Isabel might have either abandoned her newborn or hidden her pregnancy, crimes that while not covered under the 1850 penal code, might have incurred some form of penalty under the Siete Partidas. Yet, even these lesser crimes did not seem to fit Isabel's circumstances. The courts usually pursued these crimes to protect the civil status of the baby, in cases that would result in the child losing legitimacy and family rights. In Isabel's case, however, neither condition applied. She was unmarried, so by definition the baby would have been illegitimate; and she was a slave, so there were few if any applicable family rights to uphold. The judge also considered applying laws governing the theft or kidnapping of a slave but determined that kidnapping one's own child would not fall under that law. Nor was theft by a slave against his owner punishable under that code. The judge resolved to consult the superior court, remanding Isabel to her owner's custody to await the court's order.

In retracing much of the lower court's investigation, the superior court found one new piece of information: an afterbirth was discovered in a nearby latrine. Although there was no direct evidence tying that tissue to Isabel, and she had been in custody for at least one week at that point, the judge concluded that "the slave woman had undoubtedly been pregnant and given birth." Yet, investigators had not found any baby and presumed that Isabel had killed her infant, or brought it to a charitable establishment, so that the "fruit of her womb would not follow" in her mother's servitude.

Isabel's defender argued for the complete absolution of his client due to insufficient evidence. After all, just because medical examiners found signs of childbirth, did not necessarily mean that Isabel committed a crime. Her owner's description of her bloated belly and alleged lactation could have been symptoms of any of a number of illnesses. Moreover, just because authorities discovered evidence of childbirth in a latrine did not mean that Isabel had given birth there or at all. The latrine was shared by many people, including other women who could have been pregnant. Moreover, Isabel's defender suggested that if she had killed her newborn, police should have found the newborn's body in the same latrine with the afterbirth. However, they made no such discovery, there or anywhere else.

In addition to the lack of direct evidence, the defender noted that there was no reason for Isabel to have violated her "dear love for her child." If Isabel's owners had a history of abusing her, the defender reasoned, then it would make sense that she would have attempted to "liberate her child from the suffering she endured." However, this was not the case. Isabel was, in the words of her defender, "a slave of a decent home, with religious, mild, and kind owners," and she enjoyed good treatment. Nor was Isabel married, so she had no motivation to hide adultery.

On the contrary, the defender depicted Isabel as a good mother, whose only motivation was the best interest of her child: "she desires the greatest good for her child, and for a slave, the greatest happiness is freedom." If the owner baptized and raised the child as free, then nobody would dispute this status. The defender speculated that Isabel had perhaps "conceived a white man's child" and sought to secure a better life for it. These aspirations may have compelled Isabel to relinquish the baby to the Real Casa de Maternidad so that it might "be considered white and free." The defender told the court that "all of this is very natural especially since Isabel is a negra criolla with the enlightenment born of her interactions with distinguished people such as the ones she serves." In his final plea, the defender told the court that "if the slave woman really gave birth to a child, there is every reason to believe that he lives hidden from her owners in search of his freedom, an intention that far from meriting censure, shows a mother worthy of applause." In essence, the defender framed Isabel's condition of servitude as an attenuating circumstance for her alleged crimes, an argument that Erenchún had explicitly dismissed.

The judge rejected this appeal. Although he ruled that the case for infanticide had no merit, he did not absolve Isabel of wrongdoing. Instead, he invoked an obscure Siete Partidas clause regarding the theft of slaves to condemn Isabel for allegedly hiding her pregnancy. He fined her 20 escudos and remanded the enslaved woman to the custody of her owner, where she would presumably be forced to bear children for him.

The judgment against Isabel is both significant and paradoxical. Alongside the tumultuous journeys Luisa and Lorenza experienced through Cuba's legal system, it offers a rare glimpse into the evolving intervention of the colonial state in the reproductive lives of enslaved women. Like earlier cases, these three instances show both private and public interest in the outcomes of enslaved women's pregnancies. However, unlike earlier cases, these instances show how negative pregnancy outcomes, even when evidently noncriminal, became the subject of state intervention through police investigation and even, in the case of Isabel, criminal prosecution. Isabel's conviction despite a clear lack of evidence illustrates an early example of the consequences of men's misunderstandings of pregnancy and childbirth, which led them to conflate poor pregnancy outcomes such as miscarriage, stillbirth, and neonatal death with intentional criminal acts such as infanticide and abortion.[70]

Yet, Isabel's case also presents an apparent paradox within the broader medical understanding of enslaved women's pregnancies. Around the same time of Isabel's lengthy criminal court proceeding, several manuals for plantation owners advised slave owners to be wary of enslaved women's claims that they were pregnant. They insinuated that enslaved women might feign pregnancy to gain access to certain privileges or benefits recommended for encouraging natural increase among slave labor forces on plantations. The 1862 *Cartilla práctica*, for instance, advised planters on managing the pregnancies of enslaved women on their estates. Although it observed that "neither the state of pregnancy nor that of puerperium constitute an illness," they should be brought to the estate manager's attention for his supervision. In particular, the manual warned that some enslaved women might feign pregnancy to obtain benefits such as relief from work. To avoid such "fraud," plantation managers were instructed to calculate the expected delivery date based on when the enslaved woman announces she "feels she is pregnant" and the approximate amount of time since her last menstrual period. In this way, the manager could help avoid handing out benefits to enslaved women who were not reproducing slavery.[71]

Advising planters to be skeptical of enslaved women's pregnancy claims, this plantation guide evidently attempted to reconcile production and reproduction by continuing to extract the maximum amount of labor from enslaved women while also expecting them to conceive, carry, and birth the next generation of slaves. What is so striking about this piece of advice, though, is its insinuation that enslaved women would feign pregnancy to obtain benefits, which typically included exemptions from heavy lifting and a modified workload aimed at preserving the pregnancy. Yet, if the case of Isabel, or that of any of the other enslaved women investigated or prosecuted for fertility crimes, is any indication, awareness of pregnancy brought surveillance and the very real possibility of criminal charges if anything negative were to happen, whether real or imagined.

These two extremes—counseling planters to be suspicious of enslaved women's claims of pregnancy and prosecuting an enslaved woman for allegedly hiding a pregnancy—converged at what must have been a time of panic for Cuban slave owners. As the very last clandestine slave cargoes arrived to Cuban shores in the late 1860s, the price of enslaved women reached all-time highs.[72] Although prices of enslaved women reflected a premium on childbearing years, enslaved infants still commanded prices approximately 5 to 10 percent that of an adult male at his prime, evincing a contradictory valuation on reproduction.[73]

Slave owners evidently saw reproduction as a gamble, one they were not likely to win. Medical research supported this conclusion. Physicians noted the high mortality rates among enslaved children in at least two studies, including one dating to 1862–63.[74] An 1867 publication calculated the mortality rate of enslaved children ages zero to ten at over 4 percent that year, while free children of color perished at 5 percent annually.[75] Another physician, claiming years of experience tending to slave labor forces on ten plantations, argued that the "terrible hygienic conditions" explained the "notable proportion of deaths" among enslaved children, with diarrhea being the most common cause of death. He also observed that enslaved women commonly suffered from gynecological ailments, especially endometriosis and venereal disease, particularly syphilis. Many enslaved women's pregnancies ended in miscarriage, which he attributed to reproductive disorders or to enslaved women's deliberate efforts to terminate their pregnancies.[76] Even the proportion of births to deaths among the entire African-descended population (including free people of color, who had a higher fertility rate) declined between 1846 and 1861.[77]

Writing in the late 1860s, one plantation owner complained that "negro women equally shrank from the pains and from the duties of maternity. She either contrived to have no children, or treated them as if she hated them." And despite the "immense trouble taken to encourage fertility by setting a reward on every child," not even one in every three pregnant slaves on his plantation "brought her offspring to maturity."[78] However, even as Cuban slavery was evidently in its death throes, the *Cartilla*'s close attention to enslaved women's pregnancies and a judge's willingness to convict an enslaved woman, without evidence, for stealing the fruit of her own womb from her owner, shows that enslaved women's reproduction remained a battlefield to the bitter end.

Scholars of Atlantic World slave societies suggest that prior to the demise of the slave trade, both planters and the colonial state showed heightened interest in enslaved women's reproduction between the implementation of slaving restrictions and the onset of gradual abolition, when the birth of enslaved infants brought discernable financial value.[79] These police investigations and prosecution of enslaved women during the 1850s and 1860s support that conclusion. Luisa, Lorenza, and Isabel were evidently not alone in facing the weight of the colonial state. Writing in 1867, José Antonio Saco noted a peculiar anomaly in the gendered breakdown of crime among enslaved people of African descent. Whereas free people regardless of race tended to evince higher rates of crime among men, Saco noted that enslaved men had lower than average rates of crime, while enslaved women had higher than average rates. "The statistical data do not give me any insight to explaining this difference; but it is possibly owed to, in part, infanticides that enslaved women commit," Saco observed.[80] These legal interpretations and their apparent impact on the racialized legal treatment of women suggest that the debate over women's reproduction and fertility control had fundamentally shifted in response to the changing conditions of slavery and the slave trade to Cuba. Whereas earlier discussions centered on saving the lives of (white) infants, authorities increasingly turned to controlling women's bodies, which aimed to defend the property rights of slave owners—even at the cost of demographic imbalance.

In the twilight of the transatlantic slave trade, colonial authorities faced mounting pressures from metropolitan authorities to preserve the institution of slavery. As access to African captives via the clandestine trade became increasingly uncertain following the 1845 criminalization of slaving, colonial authorities resurrected and expanded a pronatalist agenda that had been nearly a century in the making. Unwilling or unable to hold slave owners accountable for ameliorating the conditions of slavery enough to foster reproduction, colonial authorities and slave owners enacted this pronatalist agenda on the bodies of enslaved women through medicalization and criminalization. Planters employed physicians to maximize the extraction of reproductive labor from enslaved women's bodies. When they believed enslaved women had failed or refused their reproductive duties, planters appealed to the state. State intervention enforced coercive pronatalism by criminally prosecuting enslaved women suspected of fertility control. The paucity of evidence and the invocation of legal statutes outside the relevant penal code evinced the desperation with which colonial authorities and elites attempted to capitalize on enslaved women's reproductive potential to preserve slavery.

By the 1860s, it was evident that nearly a century of pronatalist policies had produced no measurable increase in the enslaved population. Although planters continued to rely on the clandestine slave trade to sustain their enslaved workforces, the number of captives arriving to Cuban shores tapered off over that decade. The last recorded slave ship arrived on Cuban shores in 1867, but the end of the slave trade to Cuba did not spell an immediate transformation in planters' management of slavery. Within three years of the last slave shipment's arrival, however, after stubbornly clinging to over a half century of failed policy initiatives, metropolitan authorities introduced gradual abolition.

CHAPTER SEVEN

Reconstituting Slavery
Poverty, Exclusion, and Criminalization after Partus Sequitur Ventrem

In 1870, as anticolonial insurrection spread across eastern Cuba, metropolitan authorities implemented the Moret Law, which inaugurated a process of gradual abolition of slavery. Nullifying *partus sequitur ventrem*, the law severed the ties of generational slavery. Although the law also granted freedom to the elderly, veterans of the Spanish military, and emancipados, it became known as the Free-Womb Law for its first two articles freeing babies born to enslaved mothers. According to those provisions, all babies born after the law's publication on July 4, 1869, were legally free. Babies born between September 17, 1868, and July 4, 1869, became property of the state, which would indemnify owners 125 pesetas. These benchmarks meant that, by late 1869, all babies born to enslaved mothers should have been free.

The Moret Law brought nominal freedom to thousands of infants across Cuba. The government estimated that 61,766 enslaved babies gained freedom between 1870 and 1877. Among other age brackets, more than half that number gained freedom, including a significant proportion of elderly slaves over age sixty. Between legal freedom and death, Cuba's enslaved population declined by well over 100,000 during those seven years.[1] By 1880, metropolitan authorities issued the Patronato Law, which transformed enslaved people into "apprentices" to be freed by 1888.

If other Atlantic slave societies were any indication, the onset of gradual abolition should have compelled colonial authorities and slave owners in Cuba to modify their approach to enslaved women's reproduction. Diana Paton shows that apprenticeship (1834–38) in Jamaica led planters to reject pronatalism, because they no longer saw economic incentive in supporting enslaved children.[2] Similar arguments have been made about the demise of pronatalism among planters in Brazil following its 1871 free-womb law.[3]

However, in Cuba, it appears that slave owners' responses were more varied, especially since pronatalist measures were never systematically applied. The Moret Law theoretically incited planters who had promoted enslaved reproduction to disengage from pronatalism. The declining number of African-descended babies being born during the 1870s supports this theory of declining interest in enslaved women's reproduction.[4] However, not all planters wrote off enslaved mothers or their free-womb children. Some scholars of Cuba have argued that the onset of gradual abolition did afford some enslaved people a way to influence their legal status and that of their family.[5] Enslaved mothers, in particular those in urban areas, appealed to magistrates to secure freedom for their children and themselves, often invoking sentimental constructs of motherhood to incur sympathy, as Camillia Cowling shows. But slave owners, judges, and magistrates routinely ignored abolitionist laws, frustrating enslaved mothers' persistent attempts to enforce the freedom of their free-womb children.[6] Planters' noncompliance with metropolitan mandates fits within a longer trajectory of resentment and resistance to state and church interventions in the authority of slave owners.[7] Although planters had long cast these weak and dependent beings as burdens, there was clearly a reason they fought so hard to retain control over free-womb infants and their enslaved mothers.

The commodification and exploitation of enslaved women's reproductive labor and their children persisted through the process of gradual abolition. Planters' ongoing interest in enslaved women and their free-womb children partly stemmed from short-term economic calculations. In slavery's twilight, slave owners were keen to extract income from their slaves, correlating to a surge in hiring out and coartación.[8] Although this was by no means a new practice, the end of *partus sequitur ventrem* likely gave further incentive for slave owners to extract wealth from the reproductive bodies of enslaved women and their free-womb children. The Moret Law transformed the economy of enslaved pregnancies but did not eliminate the economic value of reproduction. Regardless of her infant's fate, a lactating enslaved mother could make her owner money as a wet nurse, for instance. And although the Moret Law reduced the economic incentive to keep free-womb infants alive, if they survived, owners were entitled to extract labor from them until adulthood.

Both gradual emancipation and the final demise of the apprenticeship system, two years earlier than scheduled, in 1886, presented new challenges to enslaved women's reproductive freedom. Freedwomen struggled to reconstitute their families, but their pregnancies and infants often suffered under poverty. Excluded from public assistance, these women suffered miscarriages, stillbirths, and neonatal deaths that drew scrutiny from neighbors and police. Poverty and exclusion could be nearly as powerful as slavery and debt bondage in guaranteeing a captive labor force.

Enslaved Mothers and Child Custody under the Moret Law

The Moret Law garnered mixed reactions in Cuba. On some plantations, the prospect of freedom appeared to boost fertility and even reduce infant mortality, despite overall trends to the contrary. According to one plantation owner, enslaved women had more babies and cared for them more zealously than before. A few years earlier, he had complained that enslaved mothers refused to have children and were apathetic about or outright rejected their maternal responsibilities. "But all that is changed now," he declared after the Moret Law. "The nursery is crowded to an extent, and tended with a care never known before."[9] The promise of freedom had apparently surpassed all pronatalist measures in incentivizing enslaved mothers to have children.

Other slave owners proved determined to retain ownership over free-womb children. In fact, irregularities in baptismal records for children of color in the late 1860s and early 1870s suggest some slave owners evaded the law by obscuring the birthdates of babies born to their enslaved women. Some parish priests continued to classify babies born to enslaved mothers as slaves well after 1869, while others simply omitted these births from the baptismal records.[10] The 1875 discovery of two children held in slavery on one rural Matanzas plantation brought such practices to light. Neither child could be located in the baptismal registry. Closer inspection revealed that the children had been born in 1868 and 1869, and at least one of them was nominally freed through the Moret Law.[11] In another case, a slave owner fought to retain ownership of a baby born to one of his free-womb enslaved women, even though the infant had been baptized as free. It appears the baby had remained under the custody of the slave owner, who argued that the birth had predated the Moret law by a few days. He attempted to formally change her legal status to a slave years later.[12]

Although the practical freedom free-womb children enjoyed was clearly fragmentary, the Moret Law placed limits on slave owners' dominion over them. Article 6 mandated that free-womb babies remain under the apprenticeship of their mother's owner until the age of twenty-two. As apprentices, free-womb children technically could not be sold, a restriction some slave owners tried to undermine. In 1872, a slave owner liquidating his estate sold off his assets, including an enslaved mother and her four children. One was a free-womb child, then just three years old.[13] Though illegal, the sale would have documented ownership of the child, thereby assigning her slave status. To thwart the enslavement of her free child, the enslaved mother had to endure the separation of her family, by arranging for a free woman of color to foster.

Slave owners clearly resented that the Moret Law required them to assume the cost of raising freeborn children, without being able to own them outright.

Slave owners were legally obligated to provide food, clothing, medical care, and rudimentary education or training for freeborn children throughout the period of apprenticeship. Some slave owners simply rejected this burden. In 1871, for instance, a slave owner in Quivicán refused to pay for the burial of an enslaved woman's free infant, who had died at just ten days old. Metropolitan authorities responded the following year by decreeing slave owners' responsibility for burial costs until the child turned eighteen.[14] Cases like this remained common, even after a subsequent law granted freedom to apprentices whose owners failed to provide them basic care. Between 1881 and 1883, 3,766 apprentices obtained legal freedom under this clause.[15]

Still, slave owners stood to benefit substantially from the Moret Law. Although they were required to raise free-womb children at their own expense, the law entitled them to indemnification of those costs. Parents could pay to release the child from the apprenticeship. If they could not pay, the child's labor became the payment.[16] By transforming freeborn children into "apprentices," the law simultaneously empowered slave owners to extract labor from their young apprentices while forcing enslaved mothers and their babies into indebtedness with the owner.

Indeed, the apprenticeship provision widened the legal gulf between enslaved mothers and their newborns. One of enslaved women's only options to secure the practical freedom of their free-womb children was to obtain freedom themselves. Once freed, they would be able to earn money to indemnify their child's patron, thereby liberating them from apprenticeship. However, enslaved women who gained freedom actually lost the meager parental rights granted them under the Moret Law. Whereas the law prohibited slave owners from separating a freeborn child from its enslaved mother, colonial authorities decided this protection did not apply to freedwomen.[17]

Some enslaved women made unimaginable sacrifices as they attempted to liberate their freeborn children. In 1872, enslaved morena Isabel Casas was sold as a wet nurse. The transaction forced her to relocate to her new owners' residence, far removed from her own free-womb son. The child was sent to be raised by the morena Leocadia García. Though separated from and unable to breastfeed her baby, the arrangement offered Isabel a chance at freedom, which would enable her to reunite with her son. She had secured a promise from her new owner that she would obtain freedom after nursing his son for sixteen months. However, after that period, her owner extended her obligation an additional seven months. At this point, Isabel appealed to the governor. By the time authorities contacted Isabel's owner, the enslaved mother no longer resided there, and he claimed that he did not know where she was. However, he did admit to having promised her freedom and was prepared to honor his promise.[18]

Although it is unclear if Isabel Casas obtained the freedom she was promised and reunited with her baby, she was perhaps luckier than most. An 1875 petition by the enslaved María de la Cruz Morejón exposed a slave owner who refused to relinquish control over her and her children, even though she had purchased her freedom, and her children had been born free under the Moret Law.[19] Another mother who had obtained freedom appealed to authorities in 1876 to stop her former owner from selling her young daughter away to another city. In an 1876 query about whether a slave owner could sell the slave girl away from her free mother, the council ruled that the sale could take place because the Moret Law only prohibited the sale of children under fourteen years away from their *enslaved* mothers.[20] Thus the Moret Law protected slave owners' property rights over working-age slaves by deploying minimal parental rights as bait for enslaved mothers to remain in slavery.

The 1880 Patronato Law carried forward the paradoxical conditions of apprenticeship, generalizing them to all individuals then remaining in slavery. Enslaved people became *patrocinados* (apprentices), and slave owners became *patronos* (masters, or bosses). Like the Moret Law, the Patronato Law continued to require indemnification to former slave owners to liberate children from apprenticeship.[21] This continuity failed to dissuade slave owners from retaining hold over enslaved women's nominally free children. One mother attempted to negotiate her daughter's freedom. However, the slave owner refused the money she offered. The enslaved woman eventually prevailed by securing a judgment from the Junta de Patrocinados, a local board assigned to adjudicate disputes over the enforcement of the Patronato Law.[22] Another formerly enslaved mother, complaining that her former owner held her free-womb children captive, petitioned for legal custody in 1883, convinced that the law supported her plea. She lost her case. Only halfway through the period of apprenticeship did metropolitan authorities finally cede freed mothers the right to custody over their children.[23]

A Market in Milk: Enslaved Wet Nurses and Their Freeborn Infants

The arrangement that Isabel entered—sending her infant to be raised by a third party while leveraging her breastmilk for freedom—suggests that the end of generational slavery changed how some slave owners calculated the economy of enslaved reproduction. An enslaved woman's pregnancy could no longer amplify the enslaved labor force, but it could temporarily increase her economic value. Owners of lactating enslaved women stood to profit from the pregnancy regardless of the infant's fate. It had long been customary for privileged white families to turn their newborns over to the care of a Black wet nurse. Some Cuban doctors criticized this practice for the dangers it allegedly posed to white infants, speculating that the contaminated breastmilk of African women not only spread disease and immorality to white infants, but also contributed to their mortality.[24] Still, wet nursing remained the preferred method of infant care and Black women the most common to be hired.[25]

While slave owners could and did advertise their lactating slaves in newspapers and via informal channels, Havana's public institutions had consistently high demand for these women. The Casa de Beneficencia y Maternidad (formerly the Casa de Maternidad until its 1852 unification with the Casa de Beneficencia) was Havana's largest employer of enslaved wet nurses. Although institutional records mention artificial lactation as early as the 1830s, apparently the Casa de Maternidad did not institute such bottle-feeding during the nineteenth century. Medical opinion heavily favored breastfeeding, labeling it as "sacred" and without comparison to artificial alternatives, despite earlier opinions to the contrary.[26] Within the Casa de Maternidad itself, artificial lactation was never seen as a method that could, by itself, sustain an infant.[27] Such strong preference for breastfeeding meant a heavy reliance on wet nurses to sustain abandoned infants.

Records from the late 1860s suggest that the institution employed women of various backgrounds, including enslaved women, free women of color, and emancipadas, as internal wet nurses. In October 1867, there were seventeen *crianderas* (caregivers) attending twenty-eight infants in the breastfeeding department. Three of these women were hired as wet nurses that same month—two enslaved women and one free woman of color. Among these was the enslaved African woman named Marilina Conga, whose owner had sent her to the Casa to serve as a wet nurse with her one-month-old daughter. The parda libre, Antonia Rodríguez, stayed less than three weeks. She was replaced by the enslaved woman Natalia Hernández.[28] Records from November 1867 note the departure of Eugenia, an enslaved wet nurse. A few days later, the institution hired Epifania Conga, an enslaved wet nurse.[29] Of the thirteen wet nurses employed in December 1867 to care for eighteen breastfeeding infants, two were emancipadas, both listed with "owners." Occasionally, white women appeared in the breastfeeding department. These women most likely entered the establishment as *refugiadas* (women who sought refuge in the institution to give birth in secret). Their stays were usually brief, aligning with the policy allowing them to nurse their own newborn for the first fifteen days.[30] Da. Cástula García may have been one such woman, though she died of cholera within two weeks of giving birth.[31]

By the early 1870s, however, the demographics of the institution's wet nurses had changed. Records from 1874 indicate that the Casa de Beneficencia y Maternidad employed sixteen on-site wet nurses. All were enslaved women. Records show that the Casa paid the women's owners between seventeen and thirty pesos per month.[32] The account for February showed nineteen women laboring full-time in various capacities, including breastfeeding and caregiving.

The majority of them were enslaved women whose owners received their wages, eight were women of African descent of unknown legal status collecting wages directly, and one was a white woman. An additional twenty-two women received wages for nursing babies for only a few days that month, or performing other related tasks. Nine of these women were white; the remainder were women of African descent, including one emancipada.[33]

At least some of the women who labored at the Casa de Maternidad, including those employed as wet nurses, were assigned such work by a judge. When enslaved women filed complaints against their owners, judges sometimes placed them in a public institution, such as the San Francisco de Paula Women's Hospital or the Casa de Beneficencia y Maternidad. There they would labor on behalf of the institution while their owner indemnified the state for the slave's subsistence at a rate of one peso per day per slave until the case could be resolved. This happened to an enslaved woman named Francisca when she petitioned for her own and her children's freedom. Her owner, a married man, had kept her in a relation of concubinage for eight years on his plantation in Guanajay (southwest of Havana). She had given birth to several of his children, including a six-month-old daughter, whom she was then breastfeeding. She had arranged with her owner to search for someone to purchase her and her children, after her owner's wife, in a fit of jealousy, threatened to separate Francisca from her children. However, her owner had reneged on his promise, instead arranging Francisca's sale without her children. Francisca stated that she was too scared to lodge the complaint locally, for fear of her owner's wrath, as he was very influential in Guanajay. So, she petitioned instead to Havana's second *síndico* (legal protector of slaves), whom she had heard was a just man. The síndico noted that no clear policy existed with regard to Francisca's situation. He adjudicated the matter by sending Francisca and her daughters to the Casa de Maternidad y Beneficencia. Their owner would pay a one-time fee for each slave.[34]

Cases like Francisca's were likely not uncommon. In the wake of the Moret Law, a barrage of petitions were raised by enslaved mothers on behalf of their children.[35] Understanding the value of and demand for lactating slaves, judges helped staff the Casa de Maternidad with wet nurses, forcing them to sustain white infants as they awaited resolution. Rulings like this one show how the legal system had become instrumental in reconstituting gendered systems of reproductive labor extraction even outside of *partus sequitur ventrem*. Though such arrangements were hardly new, they became increasingly salient as the institution of slavery itself came to an end.

The preponderance of enslaved wet nurses at that institution raises questions about what became of their babies under the Moret Law. Though judgments like the one sentencing Francisca to labor at the Casa tended to keep enslaved mothers with their infants, not all the institution's wet nurses landed there by court order. Many more of the enslaved wet nurses breastfeeding the predominantly white expósitos of the Casa were employed through direct arrangements with local slave owners. And while there is evidence that at least one enslaved woman labored as an internal wet nurse with her baby, most records of enslaved wet nurses do not mention the women's babies at all.[36] What became of these babies born of free wombs?

Research on Brazil shows that the 1871 free-womb law there coincided with a marked increase in the number of African-descended babies surrendered at foundling asylums. In addition, scholarship shows that the end of slavery there coincided with a surge in child labor contracts involving the children of enslaved or freed women.[37] Although the Moret Law prohibited this separation, it is possible that slave owners in Havana, like their counterparts in Rio de Janeiro, surrendered freeborn infants to the Casa de Maternidad to avoid the cost of raising them. Moreover, if the complaints of the Piety Board at Havana's Casa de Maternidad were any indication (chapter 4), it is quite possible that the patterns of child labor scholars have described in Brazil also materialized in Cuba.[38]

Freeborn Infants and Havana's Casa de Maternidad amid Gradual Abolition

Just prior to the onset of gradual abolition, reforms at Havana's Casa de Maternidad chipped away at historic restrictions on the admission of Black infants. The racial restrictions that had formed part of the Casa de Expósitos since its inception seem to have become less prevalent following the institution's 1852 unification with the Casa de Beneficencia. That institution had formally permitted the admission of boys and girls of color since 1847.[39] By the 1860s, authorities at the Casa de Beneficencia y Maternidad developed an elaborate new system for ascertaining the race of expósitos precisely as generational slavery came to an end. Historically, the chaplain at the Casa de Maternidad decided an abandoned child's racial classification after hearing the doctor's recommendation. If the two disagreed, the chaplain would involve a third party and then record that racial classification in the margins of the child's baptismal record. Institutional staff had unofficially observed a six-month waiting period on assigning race, a measure to prevent admitting white-passing infants of color (see chapter 4).

When it came to recording race in the baptismal registry, however, rarely did the chaplain declare his decision unequivocally as either white or of color. Rather, standard notarial practice dictated the use of labels like "al parecer blanco/blanca" (seemingly white). This label cast doubt on the true racial identity of a person whose physical appearance qualified them as white. This important distinction between true white and seemingly white advanced the surveillance and policing of people of mixed racial heritage, whose social mobility further undermined the crumbling legal boundaries between people of African descent and white people. Authorities, and even white residents, retained the power to revoke a person's whiteness if their physical appearance or other aspects of their person eventually revealed their Blackness.[40]

Now institutional policy required certification of race from at least three individuals, including a physician. The governing board would then make a determination based on these opinions and issue an official document specifying the infant's racial classification six months after the child's baptism or arrival at the establishment. In cases of uncertainty, whatever its basis, the policy mandated that the abandoned child be classified as white. Moreover, the child had the right to appeal the governing board's determination at any time if they felt aggrieved by the decision.[41]

Although the committee eventually retained and codified the institution's old policy, the discussions leading up to that decision were mired in contradictions. The six-month waiting period emerged as a key source of contention due to disputes about the science of race. At one point, the committee argued that an infant's "true race" was immediately evident on birth. "In reality, it is a scientific error to suppose that in the first days of a human life, and even moments after having been born, racial characteristics are not perfectly determined to the point that a white person could be confused with a pardo, much less a Black person." The committee suggested that medical doctors perfectly agreed about the biological fixity of race, contradicting decades of practice. Yet, the committee nonetheless acknowledged that chaplains and other Casa staff who lacked formal medical training could not attain this level of scientific expertise. Therefore, a six-month waiting period was appropriate.[42]

Other contradictions were apparent, as well. While the policy institutionalized the role of professional medicine in the assessment of an infant's race, it placed equal weight on the opinions of men without medical training or scientific expertise. It insisted on the biological fixity of race but resurrected older beliefs that an infant's race was not necessarily evident from its first days of life. It demanded scientific certainty to ascertain the true race of an infant but also admitted the possibility of disagreement, error, and correction, with the prospect of appeals. This ambivalence over the place and extent of scientific authority highlights a tension between the emerging role of physicians and the more deeply entrenched professional authority of members of the colonial state, including institutional administrators and judges.

Following the adoption of this policy, the Casa de Maternidad registered a substantial increase in the number of children of African descent admitted between the 1860s and the 1880s, precisely the period of gradual abolition. Just prior to implementation of the Moret Law, at least a few of the breastfeeding babies at the Casa de Beneficencia y Maternidad were of African descent.[43] The baby boy named Tomás, alternately labeled a "párvulo de color" (colored infant) and a "son of an emancipada," for example, received care outside the institution from a woman named Irene Domínguez in 1867 and 1868. In October 1867, there were twenty-eight infants in the breastfeeding department and an additional thirty babies receiving care outside the institution. One of these was José Antonio, surrendered on September 30, and labeled by institutional authorities as "al parecer pardo" (seemingly pardo).[44] In November 1867 the institution also recorded that Miguel, the newborn son of the emancipada Gertrudis, died in the maternity ward on November 17, before he even reached two weeks old.[45] December's records reference the surrender of a baby girl named Dolores Amelia, whom institutional authorities labeled as "al parecer parda." Also listed that month was a baby girl born to Trinidad Peraza, who was later transferred to the insane asylum.[46] Although surviving records demonstrate the existence of a small number of infants of African descent within the Casa de Maternidad, they do not allow us to assess the extent to which slave owners surrendered the infants of enslaved mothers to the Casa de Maternidad.

By the 1880s, it appears that more children of color gained admission to the Casa. Institutional records from 1886, the year slavery ended, reveal that over 30 percent of infants admitted for breastfeeding were labeled as "of color." Despite that relatively high proportion of admissions, African-descended babies comprised just 10 percent of infants in the breastfeeding department. Institutional authorities explained away the difference by referencing the waiting period on racial classification. The proportion of babies of African descent in the breastfeeding and young children's departments "is in reality much greater," they claimed, because the practice of waiting a certain time before assigning race had fallen out of use and many were baptized as white, "which they are only in their baptism record."[47] However, this explanation does not account for similar gaps in admission and retention for older children.[48]

The discrepancy might also be due to racial differences in mortality rates associated with poverty and disparities in care. To be sure, mortality rates were highest among newborns and infants, many of whom were deposited at the institution by police after being abandoned in public, or after petitions from impoverished relatives, or surrendered in the middle of the night, often with "the classic signs of infant tetanus."[49] Although racially disaggregated mortality data are not available for these departments, one-third of all infants entering the breastfeeding department died. Permitting at least a portion of this overall mortality rate to include white infants, death alone is unlikely to account for the difference between admissions and permanence. Nor does the 4.5 percent mortality rate of children in the young children's department account for the decline in Black representation among the girls' and boys' departments. Only 10 percent of the boys over age five were of African descent. The disparities in the girls' department were even more striking. Just under 9 percent of the girls admitted were of African descent, and only 2 percent persisted. These disparities potentially indicate an informal policy of hiring these children out.[50]

However, it is also quite possible that the admission of significantly higher proportions of Black babies and children reflected increased rates of surrender for Black infants as slavery declined. Even the lower proportion of babies and children of color retained at the institution suggests a longer pattern of growth in Black presence in the institution, especially when compared with the tiny numbers of the 1860s. Compared with data from the 1830s, the proportion of infants of African descent had more than sextupled.[51]

Admission and persistence statistics by race unfortunately are not available for the period under the free-womb law or the Patronato Law. Registration books for expósitos of color are mentioned in other records, revealing that infants of color were, in fact, admitted to the Casa de Maternidad, despite institutional policies designed to exclude them. Unfortunately, those books appear to be lost.[52] The inscription books for white expósitos mistakenly contain entries for racially ambiguous infants, whose light skin led institutional authorities to record their race as "al parecer blanco/blanca." However, subsequent notes suggest that their white privilege was soon revoked when institutional authorities suspected their African ancestry. The notes indicate that those children were reinscribed in the registration book for expósitos of color, though it is unclear what became of these infants, whether they were allowed to remain in the institution, or the level of care they received.[53] Despite these archival losses, the evolution of institutional policies regarding racial classification offers insights into patterns of infant and child surrender during the gradual abolition of slavery.

Resurrecting Racial Exclusion after Slavery

As the numbers of expósitos of color reached all-time highs with the end of slavery, racial anxieties at the Casa de Maternidad again surged. In fact, in 1886, the very year that the Patronato Law ended the remaining legal remnants of slavery, philanthropists and colonial authorities attempted to resurrect discriminatory policies from the 1830s designed to exclude infants of African descent.

The director of the Casa, then Cornelius Coppinger, lamented what he characterized as the negative impact of abolition on his work at the Casa de Maternidad. "After careful study," Coppinger recommended that "a department entirely separate from the whites be created for the infants whose color, hair, and other features distinctively mark their [African] origin"; and second, though the Black infants should "be treated the same" as their white counterparts, Black infants incurred financial debts to the Maternity Home throughout their upbringing. When they reached the age of apprenticeship, Black children were obliged to pay the establishment back the money spent on raising them by learning a trade and then working for the benefit of the Casa, their debts and wages recorded in a special account book that the child had to carry on his person. The child would not be released from this arrangement, which was debt bondage in all but name, until the debt was fully satisfied.[54]

Reproducing verbatim some of the language from the official discussions of the 1830s, Coppinger noted previous objections about the logistical and moral difficulties of implementing the racial repayment plan, "which came to constitute a kind of slavery." Such an arrangement, some of his predecessors claimed, conflicted with the institution's supposed commitment to morality and charity. However, he implied that the policy of racial segregation had persisted until very recently. Coppinger reported that, although the institution racially segregated abandoned infants of color, the practice came under scrutiny with the abolition of slavery and associated metropolitan reforms granting people of African descent civil rights. He noted that "certain doubts" had emerged as to whether the establishment should continue the practice, "given the intensity of efforts to impose progressive ideas, and above all negrophilia." Coppinger was likely referring to metropolitan laws dismantling racial segregation in certain public places. He implied that the broader inclination toward racial integration, of which desegregating the charitable institutions formed part, stemmed from a desire to avoid looking bad in public. Coppinger's negative characterization of these reforms suggests that he faced unwelcome pressure, as the director of a public institution to align the Casa's policies with metropolitan integrationist mandates.

The inability to continue the overt racial exclusion of earlier periods contributed to what Casa administrators judged as the exploding numbers of Black infants in the institution. From Coppinger's perspective, such reforms had a negative impact on the work of the Casa de Maternidad. Coppinger noted that, with the racialized debt bondage system, the proportion of Black infants admitted to the Casa was significantly lower, resulting in "miniscule proportions" of African-descended children in the girls' and boys' departments of the Casa. However, the supposedly progressive ideas forcing the Casa to admit Black infants, Coppinger claimed, incentivized women of color to abandon their children. One-quarter of the 108 babies in the infants' department, were classified as infants of color—roughly the same proportion as in the 1830s when Casa authorities previously protested the excessive number of Black babies.[55]

However, Coppinger argued to the governing board that shifting political currents could not alter the rationale for racial segregation: "neither the abolition of slavery, nor the recognition of the civil rights of people of the African race, nor the just efforts to moralize it and deliver it from the ignorance in which it exists, are enough to make disappear the reasons, which the founders of the Real Casa de la Maternidad had for imposing the aforementioned conditions on continuing to admit infants of color." Coppinger proposed reinstituting racial segregation in the Casa de Maternidad, which relied on the medical assessment of an infant's race mandated in the 1860s.

He couched his proposal in arguments about the institution's inadequate resources and others about what he believed to be appropriate treatment according to social status. Citing space limitations, Coppinger decried the unhygienic conditions afflicting the 108 babies and 39 wet nurses residing therein. Making the conditions even worse, Coppinger claimed, was "the peculiar stench of the [Black] race." Coppinger not only took issue with the comingling of Black and white babies, he also noted with dismay the prospect that the establishment's general provisions afforded Black infants a standard of care too high for their social status. Because of an "unhealthy sentimentalism, abandoned infants are reared, without distinction of race or color, with luxury and bounty." According to his judgment, abandoned infants of color not only enjoyed better conditions than babies in similar orphanages outside the island, they also enjoyed a level of care even "few legitimate children of affluent families" could afford.[56]

His disapproval of the supposedly luxurious upbringing afforded to abandoned infants of color thus casts considerable doubt on his subsequent recommendation to reinstate racial segregation in the infants' department "without making any change in their regimen of care and preservation with that which is observed for whites."[57] A few weeks later, the governing board ratified the director's decision, concurring in his reasoning, and also noting that the measure was necessary due to the "growing number of infants of the colored race who enter this establishment daily," which posed additional hygiene concerns. After approving Coppinger's petition, the board even advocated additional measures to limit the admission of Black infants. A proposal to close the torno, raised in the same context as the reinstitution of racial segregation, promised to lend institutional authorities greater control over the kind of infant admitted to the establishment. Though not resolved at that time, such a proposition initiated what became a theme in the institution's discussions over the next sixty years: how to restrict admission to subjects deemed worthy of assistance.

The notion of worthiness was governed by a racial double standard. While white women's indiscretions entitled them to access charitable resources to protect their public reputations, perceived gendered transgressions by Black women were reasons to exclude their children. Underlying this logic was the assumption that unwanted Black infants existed due to the immoralities of Black women and the broader pathologies of the Black family, namely the propensity toward out-of-wedlock pregnancy and childbirth. Advocates of racial restrictions believed that extending assistance to such families imposed an undue burden on society and further encouraged immorality.

"Moralizing" formerly enslaved people reemerged around slavery's demise as a proposed solution to Black women's supposedly excessive fertility. One such proponent was José Plá, author of a pamphlet outlining the need to increase marriage rates among people of color. Like his predecessors, Plá linked marriage to procreation; but instead of framing it as a vehicle for population growth, he envisioned marriage as a moralization tool to reduce illegitimacy.[58] Over the final century of slavery, marriage rates among the enslaved had declined considerably.[59] According to Plá, the prevalence of informal unions among people of color produced "criminal offspring." Thus concubinage and other fleeting unions were "the seed of disorder." Promoting marriage, he argued, would help control the "promiscuity of sexes" and curtail the high number of illegitimate births contributing to infant abandonment and Black population growth.[60] While the institution of marriage had always implied an element of sexual control, its function had shifted from increasing enslaved fertility to supressing free Black fertility.

Precisely as institutional authorities resurrected racial barriers to admission, liberal currents swept through the Spanish Empire leading to the abolition of racial designations in official documentation. Article 1 of the *Ordenanzas para el gobierno de las casas reunidas de Beneficencia y Maternidad*, published in 1888, only recognized racial distinctions among the category of people who "because of their age and ailments are not able to dedicate themselves to jobs that provide a means of subsistence." Other protected categories, including expósitos and pregnant women, lacked explicit reference to race.[61] This regulation would have theoretically dismantled the Casa's new racial classification system.

How the Casa resolved this conflict between the integrationist law and the discriminatory currents of institutional leadership remains largely obscured by the documentary trail. Racially segregated admission records appear to have ended around 1900. However, the notes that sometimes accompanied the surrendered infants tended to emphasize whiteness. One infant surrendered through the torno in July 1886 came with a note explicitly indicating his whiteness and explaining that his mother had died and his father was too poor to care for the infant.[62] In other instances, whiteness was implied through allusions to legitimacy and formal marriage. "Obliged by the most absolute indigence," one man surrendered his one-month-old after his wife died. The father, a bricklayer with two other small children, had failed to find a private family to take the infant. He promised to return to collect the child when his circumstances permitted, but she did not survive to her second birthday.[63]

Other notes emphasized poverty and misfortune of single motherhood. One mother's "extreme poverty" prevented her from breastfeeding her baby at all. The mother promised to return for her "innocent child" once her health improved, but the baby died less than a year later.[64] Against the backdrop of Coppinger's zealous advocacy for racial segregation and exclusion, white babies continued to receive priority at the Casa during the final years of Spanish rule. The ongoing discrimination in access to charity reinforced the historic institutional mission to privilege the lives of white infants over those of Black infants.

The apparent resurgence of racial boundaries of admission was not unique to the late 1880s, nor was it confined exclusively to the Casa de Maternidad y Beneficencia. On the contrary, within the Casa, this debate had resurfaced repeatedly in times of demographic anxiety, such as 1830s and the 1860s. And efforts to exclude women and children of African descent also shaped the women's hospital and the insane asylum. Certainly these same currents help explain why neither institution was willing to admit enslaved women like Merced or Teresa (see chapters 5 and 6). But it did have new meanings in the final years of slavery. At least part of the historic rationale behind racial exclusion in charity had been that such institutions afforded enslaved mothers a mechanism to free their babies, thereby subverting the reproduction of slavery. However, with the bonds of generational slavery severed, this status-centered argument collapsed, exposing the centrality of whiteness to perceptions of worthiness.

Criminalizing Impoverished Mothers after Slavery

Exclusion from charitable institutions left formerly-enslaved mothers and their children deprived of much-needed assistance. The case of the morena María Caridad González Betancourt reveals the potentially fatal consequences of this discrimination. In June 1888, authorities detained thirty-two-year-old María Caridad on charges of attempted parricide after she allegedly threw her young child off a balcony. For some time, she had been sporadically suffering from mental illness. She had no relatives, but she knew who her child's father was and where he lived, even though her child had been baptized as the son of an "unknown father." She confessed that she had been admitted several times to the women's hospital due to the "attacks" she suffered, but this last time, they refused to admit her, claiming that "she was crazy." Records at the women's hospital confirmed that María Caridad had been admitted that past March, diagnosed with "hysteria," and discharged after only three days. According to the hospital administrator, there were no other references to the woman.

Suspecting María Caridad was criminally responsible for her actions, the judge sent her to jail, where she was to be under medical observation for two weeks to ascertain her mental state. After two weeks, the judge repeated his belief that María Caridad was criminally responsible but accepted the medical diagnosis of "mental derangement" and appointed a special defender. The records of the case end there. There is no mention of what happened to María Caridad's son. The charges of attempted parricide suggest the child did survive, but it is unclear if the child was placed with his father, or even if the man was located based on the information María Caridad provided. If not, it is possible the child was sent to the Casa de Beneficencia. Either way, he was evidently separated from his mother, whose recognized mental health condition remained untreated as she languished in jail.[65]

Police investigation and criminal prosecution for fertility crimes disproportionately penalized women of African descent due to their circumstances of poverty and exclusion. An 1878 investigation for possible infanticide suggests how poverty and lack of access to public assistance cast impoverished women's poor pregnancy outcomes as potential crimes.[66] Police responded to the discovery of a deceased newborn girl of African descent, only a day or so old at death, whose body was wrapped in linen cloth and abandoned at the gates of the Espada Cemetery in Havana. Citing the advanced state of putrefaction of the body, medical examiners could not determine the infant's cause of death. However, the case does not indicate any signs of external violence.[67]

Such experiences of neonatal death were certainly not exclusive to impoverished women of African descent. To be sure, other police investigations from this period involved infants labeled as white or without a racial label but who similarly died without external signs of violence.[68] However, anecdotal evidence suggests that women of African descent were disproportionately susceptible to poor pregnancy outcomes related to poverty. In 1893, Dr. Manuel Delfín observed that Black and mestizo women died in "extraordinary" numbers and at a much higher rate than men of African descent did. He attributed this gender-specific high mortality rate to their "lack of moral and material culture" and the poor hygiene, conditions that would have been particularly dangerous during childbirth. He also identified a declining birth rate among Black and mestizo populations, though he admitted that the statistics did not reflect the large number of children of color not inscribed in the official civil records.[69]

In a context in which the elite men in charge of Havana's charitable institutions serving women and children were reluctant to admit individuals of African descent, it is conceivable that the baby girl left at the gates of the cemetery would have had a different outcome if her mother had had access to assistance to ameliorate her poverty, address illnesses, and care for her pregnancy. Given the high mortality rates both at the women's hospital and maternity ward, the infant might still have died, but such institutions could have at least facilitated a proper burial, thereby preempting police involvement in an already tragic event.

The intertwined trajectories of exclusion from public assistance and criminalization of Black mothers reveal that, far from dismantling elite interference in Black women's reproduction, the abolition of slavery actually perpetuated and even intensified it. It also alluded to an important shift. In the absence of the legal divide between free and enslaved, the status-specific treatment of African-descended mothers and their children ceased to exist. The few protections and incentives previously afforded to enslaved women quickly evaporated, as the more coercive and punitive approach that had prevailed for free women of color became more racially generalized to Black women.

For the architects of Cuba's emerging nation, the stakes of limiting Black women's reproduction were high. Amid persisting fears of Black women's excessive fertility, the end of slavery threatened dire political consequences, especially given prevailing assumptions that a racially heterogeneous population was incompatible with self-governance and national prosperity. For some elites, the impending end of slavery doomed the emerging nation. "It is hard to say, but it is necessary to confess, that this population is not what is properly called a political society," wrote plantation owner Celestino de la Torriente. "It does not have the political nor the moral conditions for stability, social peace, nor wealth." From his perspective, Cuba's population, "well, simply is nothing more than a mosaic of races."[70] In a similar vein, Plá argued that the alleged immorality of formerly enslaved people threatened to fill the jails and prisons but would also poison society and revert Cuba into a primitive state.[71] Although Plá naturalized the supposed criminality of African-descended people, his allusion to racialized incarceration became more real than he could have imagined, as the case of Caridad, and countless other Black women after her, revealed.

The onset of gradual slave emancipation in 1870 changed the way slave owners approached enslaved women's reproduction. However, unlike in other slave societies like Jamaica and Brazil, it did not result in owners widely abandoning enslaved women and their children. On the contrary, some planters stubbornly clung to their control over enslaved women and their freeborn children, especially during the early years following the Moret Law.

These slave owners understood that while the Moret Law ended generational slavery, it did not immediately abolish the institution of slavery, or their access to unfree labor. In fact, slave owners continued to profit from enslaved women and their pregnancies by hiring them out as wet nurses, as they had historically done, but now with little or no economic incentives to keep their infants alive. Moreover, the free-womb law and its successor, the Patronato law, were both premised on reframing child enslavement as apprenticeship—in reality a form of debt bondage. These legal and practical innovations and reinventions of slavery laid the foundation for the limited ways formerly enslaved women and their children could experience freedom, even after the institution of slavery was, in name, no longer alive. The poverty and exclusion from public assistance that defined the post-emancipation lives of many women of African descent condemned their pregnancies, births, and motherhood to the criminalizing and disparaging lens of the police.

CHAPTER EIGHT

From the Art of Midwifery to the Science of Obstetrics
Consolidating White Male Authority over Pregnant and Laboring Bodies

In the final third of the nineteenth century, the professionalization of medicine catalyzed a dramatic expansion of public health innovation and development. As Daniel Rodríguez observes, this public health renaissance coincided almost exactly with Cuba's protracted struggle for independence.[1] The outbreak of the Ten Years' War (1868–78) marked the beginning of nearly thirty years of anticolonial struggle, which included the Little War (1879–80) and culminated in the War of Independence (1895–98). During those thirty years, Cuban doctors and surgeons produced a wealth of research on a range of ailments, from mosquito-borne illnesses (e.g., yellow fever) to infectious diseases (e.g., tuberculosis) to the bacteriological causes of infection. This research contributed to public health interventions targeting morbidity and mortality, often through hygiene and sanitation.

A critical yet underappreciated aspect of medical professionalization, though, hinged on the emergence of obstetrics and gynecology as distinct medical specializations in Cuba. This development built on the expansion of obstetric and gynecological training in Havana's medical school over the second half of the century. The first course in obstetrics, gynecology, and pediatrics entered the medical curriculum following an 1842 royal order secularizing education.[2] By 1853, fourth- and fifth-year medical students did a rotation at the women's hospital during their vacation months. Early on, students worked not with obstetrics or gynecology specialists but with general surgeons, like Dr. Fernando González del Valle, who completed their medical training entirely in Cuba and served the women's hospital among other professional functions. However, a growing number of Cuban physicians obtained advanced training in obstetrics abroad, especially in France and later the United States, where gynecological and obstetric training were distinct medical specialties with well-established curricula and faculty.

Like other Cuban doctors, obstetricians and gynecologists saw reducing mortality as a mandate for rebuilding the emerging nation.[3] Existing scholarship has tended to focus on efforts to curtail infant mortality, which stretched back into this period and emerged with renewed energy in the early republic. However, scholars have paid less attention to interventions concerning maternal mortality. Between the 1860s and the 1890s, Cuban physicians produced a wealth of research on wide-ranging topics, but many focused on improving maternal outcomes during pregnancy, childbirth, and postpartum. Some doctors studied common conditions afflicting pregnant and puerperal women, such as severe vomiting during pregnancy, and postpartum insanity. Other physicians explored labor and delivery complications, such as pelvic narrowness, breech birth, cervical obstruction, and the retention of the placenta. Still others focused on surgical techniques, such as embryotomy and cesarean section.[4] Common to all these studies was a focus on reducing maternal mortality through more precise medical interventions, ones that ideally preserved fertility.

The health outcomes of pregnant women commanded the attention of obstetricians in part because the anticolonial struggle was an intensely gendered process, one with profound implications for women's reproductive lives. War disrupted family structures by pulling male heads of household away from their homes, jobs, and communities and onto the battlefield, into exile, or into prison.[5] While some women also entered combat zones, the majority remained on the home front, where they faced food shortages, raids, and "reconcentration" (confinement of rural dwellers into concentration camps).[6] Insurgent men from a range of backgrounds similarly expressed paternalist desires to protect their wives, mothers, and daughters, as well as other women, from the harms of war.[7] As resources available to charitable institutions dwindled and eventually disappeared, mothers were the first and last line of defense for infants. Thus maternal outcomes were a critical factor in infant survival.

Early obstetricians were celebrated for their successes in saving the lives and reproductive capabilities of Cuban women. Among the more influential early Cuban obstetricians was Serapio Arteaga y Quesada, who in the 1870s had studied and then taught in Paris, where he explored the treatment of hereditary syphilis.[8] After returning to Havana, Arteaga became assistant professor of obstetrics at the University of Havana under Pablo Valencia y García in the early 1880s; Arteaga later succeeded Valencia as lead obstetrics instructor.[9] Although Arteaga held the role relatively briefly before his early death, he made a significant impact on the development of the field, especially through training future generations of Cuban obstetricians. With the establishment of the first independent obstetrics clinic in 1880, medical students watched as Arteaga pioneered a number of lifesaving procedures. In one instance, he saved a woman from a total hysterectomy by enlisting two of his strongest medical students to hold her upside down by her feet while he inserted his hand into her vagina to extract a dead fetus. On another occasion, he saved the life of a woman whose uterus had ruptured.[10]

Although the school closed in 1896, when most of its professoriate joined the war of independence, many of the clinic chiefs and teaching assistants studying under Arteaga and his contemporaries benefited from it and later became leading figures in obstetrics.[11] Among them was Gaspar Rafael Weiss Verson, who in 1888 published a paper claiming that white women's delicate anatomy made them more vulnerable to injury during pregnancy and childbirth than women of African descent.[12] Weiss Verson later went into private practice, catering to precisely the clientele he deemed most vulnerable. He helped found a policlinic that included a consultation service in women's health and childbirth in September 1892. There he pioneered techniques in artificial premature birth (see chapter 9).[13] Weiss Verson eventually separated from the policlinic and briefly ran a two-bed private clinic in his home.[14]

As Weiss Verson's career suggests, curbing maternal (and also infant) mortality hinged on often unspoken racial assumptions about which women and infants were most vulnerable, who was primarily responsible for the high mortality rates, and who could rescue them from the jaws of untimely death. It was, perhaps unsurprisingly, white women, especially those from the upper classes, and their children, whose deaths obstetricians found most alarming. But who was responsible when white women's pregnancies ended unfavorably? While judges appeared quick to investigate women after the discovery of fetal remains or infant cadavers, doctors insisted that fetal loss and infant death in those cases resulted from natural causes, which exculpated the women from criminal charges. In this way, they asserted their professional expertise vis-à-vis judges by challenging them to respect emerging but still blurry medical distinctions between criminal infanticide and stillbirth or neonatal death, and between criminal abortion and miscarriage.

While exculpating most patients, physicians blamed unlicensed midwives, often women of color, for allegedly causing preventable maternal and infant deaths. As part of a broader crusade against midwives, doctors vilified their female rivals not only for the poor pregnancy outcomes they allegedly caused, but also for their roles in providing abortions. Physicians did not appear to hold their professional peers to the same standard, even as maternal and infant deaths regularly resulted from their medical and surgical interventions, and as they provided abortions. Together, physicians' willingness to support the prosecution of midwives, condemn but not criminalize their peers, and completely exculpate white women evinces an emerging code of professional ethics centering a racially defined pronatalism. They enacted this through the patriarchal protection of white women from women of color healers and unscrupulous abortionists. Medical pronatalism was nationalist in that it implicitly advanced white population growth by opposing abortion; and it was self-serving, because it helped them advance their own professional status in the emerging nation.

Poor Pregnancy Outcomes: Criminal Acts or Natural Occurrences?

In the final third of the nineteenth century, infanticide cases increasingly came before local courts across the island. Judges relied heavily on medical examiners to produce forensic and medical evidence from the bodies of accused women, fetal remains, and deceased infants. Although pelvic examinations and autopsies were standard in most of these cases, compelling physical evidence of criminality remained rare. Most medical examiners, though usually lacking specific training in obstetrics or gynecology, appropriately reported that the available evidence was inconclusive. However, their inability to produce incriminating evidence frustrated judges and served as an enduring source of tension between the medical establishment and the courts.

The gradual professionalization of obstetrics in Cuba helped reinforce medical authority in these fertility crimes cases. In particular, the induction of obstetricians into the Academy of Medical, Physical, and Natural Sciences of Havana (hereafter Academy of Sciences, or academy) following its establishment in the early 1860s brought to bear the latest medical knowledge on questions pertaining to pregnancy and childbirth. Members of the academy served on discipline-specific committees, each responsible for providing expert scientific guidance to the state. The academy's legal medicine and public hygiene committee, from its inception complained of its "infatigable" workload. The large volume of reports and consultations requiring forensic medical expertise forced the academy to create a separate childbirth committee specially focused on obstetrics and gynecology. These two committees became clearinghouses, of sorts, for the interpretation and validation of the forensic medical basis for charges of infanticide, and later abortion cases against women, the majority of whom were white.[15] Between 1868 and 1915, as Cuban physicians consolidated their hold on a new field of medical science devoted to women's health, the committee published reports on more than two dozen of these infanticide and abortion cases, most of which involved criminal proceedings against women accused of infanticide. The physicians of the academy quickly wielded this new institutionalized status and relationship to the state to assert their authority as experts.

What implications did these medical-legal encounters have for women accused of infanticide? Initially, physicians appeared to disagree on the question of who bore responsibility for fetal loss and infant death among nonmedically supervised pregnancies. This lack of consensus emerges in a consultation on an 1873 case in which authorities in Pinar del Río charged a white woman with infanticide, despite no evidence of violent death. The charges centered on the claim that the mother failed to keep her infant alive after a difficult birth. The judge requested an opinion on whether a mother's failure to keep her newborn alive after a difficult birth could constitute infanticide. The question at hand boiled down to whether a mother could be criminally liable for delivering a baby who died shortly after birth.

The case prompted vociferous disagreement among the physicians of the legal medicine committee. On the one hand, Dr. Ambrosio del Valle argued that pregnancy and childbirth followed "natural law." Likening childbirth to other "natural functions" like digestion or breathing, he claimed that "all women are able to help and save their child." He noted that childbirth predated the creation of medicine, and women had always attended to themselves adequately in their "savage state," notwithstanding some "anomalies, which are the exception and not the rule." On the other hand, Dr. Rafael Cowley argued that not all women could save their newborns. He noted that certain known complications could injure the infant during delivery. He also noted that younger first-time mothers might not have the experience necessary to save their infants in these circumstances.[16]

Although the legal medicine committee periodically returned to this debate over the late nineteenth and early twentieth centuries, their consultations on infanticide cases suggest a default posture of patriarchal protection, not criminalization.[17] Indeed, the legal medicine committee was often a mitigating force in criminal proceedings, challenging the courts' propensity to convict on flimsy evidence. These physicians most often argued against convicting white women in infanticide cases, in numerous cases claiming insufficient evidence of criminal infanticide, and that cases were more consistent with poor pregnancy outcomes, such as miscarriage, stillbirth, or neonatal death. These interactions between judicial and medical authorities align with the observation that police and judges often misunderstood pregnancy and childbirth and tended to conflate criminal abortion and infanticide with noncriminal reproductive events (e.g., miscarriage, stillbirth, and neonatal death).[18]

Forensic medical investigation in infanticide cases usually hinged on two conditions: proof that the infant lived and breathed outside the womb, and evidence that the cause of death was artificial and violent.[19] For the first condition, the standard practice was for physicians to use a method developed in Europe called the docimasia, or hydrostatic test of the lungs, to determine if an infant had lived outside the womb. The test required the examining physician to remove the lungs from the thoracic cavity and place them in water. Lungs that floated in water and released air bubbles when submerged could indicate that the infant had breathed.[20] In addition to demonstrating that the infant had lived outside the womb, an infanticide conviction required proof of violent death (infanticide by commission). Certain medical legal specialists advocated for criminalizing maternal neglect (infanticide by omission), though the letter of the law did not recognize this distinction, and the charge was much less common than allegations of violent infanticide by commission.[21] To corroborate infanticide by commission, examining physicians had to rule out ordinary birth complications and common neonatal ailments, and show physiological evidence of violent death.

Most cases of infanticide on which academy physicians consulted lacked evidence of violent death. In cases with some circumstantial evidence of a possible crime, the committee tended to err on the side of caution when interpreting the medical reports. In an 1871 case involving an infant with a strip of linen wrapped three times around its neck, for instance, the committee concluded that nothing actually suggested death by strangulation. Court testimony suggested that the mother had endured a difficult and painful labor, and that the infant lived only for a half hour after being born. The committee pointed to the absence of redness or swelling around the neck, characteristic of strangulation. The committee's consultation, though indirect, undermined the court's case of infanticide against the mother.[22]

The legal medicine committee also challenged infanticide charges in an 1879 case against a white woman whose newborn baby girl was discovered with piece of cloth tied into a noose around her neck. In another instance, the Audiencia de Puerto Príncipe presented a harrowing narrative of a mother who violently asphyxiated her baby girl in the twenty-four hours after giving birth. In reviewing the case, the physicians on the legal medicine committee disagreed with conclusions, claiming that there were "numerous deficiencies and contradictions" in the expert documentation. The examination of the infant's body was incomplete, the autopsy did not provide any evidence in support of the alleged infanticide, and a number of other claims lacked proof. The committee therefore deduced that the conclusions drawn from the expert testimony "lack the scientific value needed for the clarification of such a delicate and difficult subject as infanticide."[23]

Even in cases involving what appeared to be a fatal injury, the legal medicine committee demanded that the courts prove that violence caused it. In early April 1893, authorities in the country town of Esperanza, in rural Santa Clara province, dug up what they initially believed were the remains of an aborted fetus, buried in a shallow hole in a pineapple grove. After performing the autopsy, the examining physicians concluded that the fetus was in fact a newborn infant, fully developed at nine months' gestation. With the umbilical cord yet untied, the physicians concluded that the infant died very shortly after birth. The state of the lungs suggested that the infant had breathed and lived outside the womb. There was no evidence of asphyxiation. The autopsy also revealed that the infant had a broken neck. Although the physicians did not note any external injuries to the infant's body, they speculated that the damage to the infant's spine caused its death. The examining physicians concluded that the death was "provoked and violent," likely the result of a violent manual strangulation.

The Criminal Court of the Audiencia of Santa Clara charged the infant's mother, a white woman with initials S.M., with infanticide. In her statement, the mother told authorities that she became pregnant by her boyfriend in November 1892 and had a fairly uneventful pregnancy until around April. In her estimation, she was about six months along when she began feeling labor pains shortly after carrying two large buckets of water. As her labor progressed, she left her parents' house to seek medical attention on April 4. However, when she arrived at the doctor's house, around midnight, only his girlfriend was home. Shortly after arriving there, she gave birth, seated on a stool. The mother told authorities that she was too dazed from the labor to know if the doctor's girlfriend tied the fetus' umbilical cord or not. The doctor's girlfriend told her that the infant took two breaths and then quickly died. She placed the infant's lifeless body on the stool until morning, then told the mother that they should bury the body right there in the yard. The mother told her that it was better to bury the body farther away, and the doctor's girlfriend took the body away. When authorities asked her if anyone had enacted violence on the infant, the mother answered in the negative.

The court requested the opinion of the Academy of Sciences regarding the cause of death. The legal medicine committee noted that the real question was how the fatal injury occurred. They offered a variety of scenarios involving violence—hanging, strangulation, a fall, or extensive pulling or turning to extract the body from the womb during birth. However, ultimately, they concluded that there was insufficient evidence to offer any definitive conclusions about the cause of the infant's death. They requested additional information about the circumstances of the birth and the state of the infant.[24] The court sent the mother's statement as well as a second autopsy report, created by a second set of physicians based on the first report and not on actual examination of the cadaver. The court informed the academy that they were unable to provide further information regarding the condition of the infant because, when they went to exhume the body from the cemetery, the infant was no longer in the grave.

After reviewing these documents, the committee determined that there was still not enough evidence to offer definitive conclusions in this case. The committee noted that the absence of the infant's body rendered the second autopsy report moot. The second set of physicians simply reiterated the information in the first report and added some of the legal vocabulary the committee had referenced in their first session. The second report left an unexplained discrepancy between the lack of physical injuries around the infant's neck and the conclusion of a death by violent strangulation.[25]

In other cases, the evidence pointed to multiple possible causes of death, including common pregnancy complications and neonatal illness, even as the courts pursued infanticide charges. For instance, in an 1887 case involving the death of baby Tranquilina Basallo, the evidence suggested that the baby had died due to neonatal tetanus. The baby's mother testified that she had given birth without incident to a healthy baby girl, who became ill at three days old. Her family corroborated her story. The autopsy report seemed to support the suspicion of tetanus, indicating a possible infection of the umbilical stump. When the medical examiner removed the swaddling on the belly, he also noted discoloration—a dark green color on the belly button and lighter green on the stomach and chest.[26] Although the medical examiners suggested tetanus as a possible cause of death, they also noted injuries that "inclined them to believe that the girl had received a blow to the head." Significant bruising and darkening around the neck led the medical examiner to posit that the infant had been strangled.

In their consultation on the case, the legal medicine committee characterized the autopsy report as "notably deficient," arguing that the report contained no evidence to support either tetanus or asphyxiation as causes of death proposed by the medical examiner. They noted that the trauma to the head could possibly explain the death, but there was not sufficient evidence to confirm it.[27] Such expert opinions certainly did not support conviction.

Other cases were so flimsy that the courts could prove neither a violent death nor a live birth. The committee pointed to such deficiencies in their consultation on an 1868 inquiry about a deceased infant discovered in the Havana neighborhood of Jesús María with severe head injuries. The committee answered that the state of putrefaction of the corpse precluded determining the cause of the wounds, the infant's race, how old it was, or how long it had been dead. Although they could not rule out that someone had bludgeoned the infant to death, the committee noted that it was equally plausible that stray dogs had devoured the infant's head. The cadaver appeared to be that of a full-term infant, but maggots had already infested the lungs, thereby corrupting the result of the standard docimasia and preventing physicians from determining if the infant had lived outside the womb. Noxious gases stemming from putrefaction were known to give fetal lungs buoyancy and lead to a false positive result confirming respiration and life in a fetus or stillborn infant. Therefore, the committee could not conclude whether the infant had been stillborn or born alive. Without a confirmed live birth, no medical evidence supported an infanticide case.[28]

Some judges pursued charges on even more dubious grounds. In 1888, judicial authorities in the district of Alfonso XII pursued an infanticide investigation based on the facial expression on the cadaver of an exhumed infant corpse. Authorities discovered the unmarked grave, noting the dirt over the surface had recently been moved. At about six inches down, they discovered a placenta. Directly below that, they found the cadaver of a seemingly full-term fetus, facedown in the dirt, without anything covering the body. They determined that it was the body of a newborn girl. She had no hair on her head, and her eyes were open and her tongue out, a description that became a topic of note in the ensuing investigation.

The medical examiner determined that the infant was full term and had likely been born alive. The body's decomposition made it difficult to determine if the infant had breathed. The examiner concluded that if the infant had lived at all, it was likely for a very brief time. He estimated that the infant died four or five days prior. The medical examiner immediately ruled out the common "accidents of birth" such as asphyxiation, innate weakness, umbilical hemorrhage, or pulmonary apoplexy, because the cadaver "did not show the characteristic signs" of those conditions. Instead, he fixated on the facial expression, speculating that the wide-open eyes and tongue sticking out of the mouth "if not evident signs, suggested death by strangulation." However, the neck and throat lacked signs of violence. He also noted that the umbilical cord seemed to have been ripped apart violently, and left untied.

The medical examiner suggested that the infant had likely presented as a breech birth. Although the lungs apparently floated in water, the examiner concluded that the advanced decomposition made the docimasia unreliable. The examiner noted that although the fetus's development suggested that it could have lived, neither a newborn's good formation nor its perfect development was sufficient for deducing that it lived outside the womb. He was unable to determine with certainty whether the infant lived, or how it died.

The legal medicine committee focused on the dangers of breech birth, especially when attended by untrained practitioners. Frequently in these cases, the committee explained, "inexperienced hands will pull on the limbs or on the cord, perhaps with the goal of bringing an end to the woman's suffering," but this bruises the limbs and ruptures the umbilical cord. In those cases, the babies take a few, incomplete breaths after emerging from the womb. Although their discussion insinuated that the infant in question had died naturally due to these causes, the committee concluded that the documents contained insufficient information to resolve the matter.[29]

All these cases have in common that physicians undercut the criminal charges against white women suspected of infanticide. In fact, of the fourteen criminal cases against mothers on which the legal medicine committee consulted between 1868 and 1895, only two involved women of African descent. The legal medicine committee did not support a single criminal infanticide charge until 1910, when members approved dubious medical evidence against a mixed-race woman in Jaruco after authorities allegedly found her fetus at the bottom of a latrine.[30]

After several decades of arriving at strikingly similar conclusions in their consultations on infanticide cases, members of the legal medicine committee began making firmer and more direct statements about the need for medical evidence to pursue a charge of infanticide. In response to an 1894 consultation requested from a judge in the district of Guadalupe following the discovery of a decomposing fetus, Dr. Luís Montané noted that the medical-legal inspection of fetuses was "one of the most delicate matters" appearing before the courts.[31]

Just a few years later, another member of the legal medicine committee, Dr. Tomás V. Coronado, expanded on Montané's message as he consulted on a case involving the death of what he alternately referred to as a fetus and an infant. Addressing the other committee members, he emphasized both the importance of maintaining scientific rigor in criminal infanticide cases, and the risks this kind of case posed to the scientist's reputation. "Fellow academics," he declared, "we are dealing with a case of one of the crimes that gives the greatest contingent of work to medical legal experts in all nations, and on the other hand, puts the reputation of the medical expert in grave danger." For Coronado, not only the practical difficulties of the fetal autopsy and examination of the mother but also the powerfully emotional nature of the crime imperiled the expert's prestige. Citing the French physician Paul Camille Hippolyte Brouardel, under whom he trained, Coronado explained that infanticide "exalts public sentiments, placing public opinion in a special state, predisposed to fall with its critiques upon the medical legal expert." To defend his reputation against the weight of public opinion, Coronado counseled physicians consulting on these cases as experts and examiners to "not form an opinion." Rather, they should "present a demonstration" supported by hard evidence. However, if it were "impossible to prove that the crime occurred," then physicians had a responsibility "to study the case carefully and offer a conclusion" based on an established scientific protocol.[32]

Coronado's remarks summed up the legal medicine committee's frustration with the way local courts handled fertility crimes cases. Apparently under pressure from judges, medical examiners sometimes offered conclusions that strayed from strict scientific analysis of medical and forensic evidence. In admonishing his professional subordinates to uphold scientific rigor, Coronado and his peers on the legal medicine committee vested themselves with a new responsibility to police the boundaries of the medical profession and defend its reputation vis-à-vis other professionals. While it is clear that the physicians on the legal medicine committee invoked science in part to buttress their own professional status and authority vis-à-vis judges, they also appeared to frame themselves as patriarchal protectors. And the demographics of the criminal cases they influenced show that white women were their primary beneficiaries.[33]

Criminal statistics from the end of the nineteenth century show remarkably low conviction rates for fertility-related crimes, including infant abandonment, infanticide, and abortion, especially considering the volume of police reports, investigations, and court cases involving those crimes. Only a small number of women were confined in Cuban jails at the turn of the twentieth century. Havana's Casa de Recogidas contained twenty women on charges of infanticide. An additional eight women were confined at municipal jails across western Cuba, including at Havana, Guanabacoa, Matanzas, and Güines. Records from central Cuba listed five women prisoners at municipal jails in Cienfuegos, Santa Clara, Sagua la Grande, and Remedios. An additional three women were confined at the municipal jail in Santiago de Cuba, in eastern Cuba. Of all these women, only two had been charged with fertility-related crimes. Eighteen-year-old white woman Elena Muñoz Romero, a native of Caibarién, was convicted of infanticide and incarcerated in the municipal jail at Remedios in November 1899. Teresa Milanés, a Black twenty-nine-year-old from Santiago was also convicted of infanticide and jailed at Santiago in September 1899.[34]

Given the medical establishment's involvement in judicial proceedings, these low rates of conviction—though not out of the ordinary for Latin America at this time—suggest struggle over who to blame for pregnancies that for whatever reason did not end in the birth and survival of a live child. Police and judges seemed willing to investigate and prosecute women for failing or refusing to procreate the next generation, although it is noteworthy that the majority of the cases on which they requested expert consultation did involve white women. This desire for reassurance might suggest the use of a higher standard of evidence for white women, who, historically were judged to require protection rather than punishment. That physicians opposed convictions in most cases involving white women seems to support this interpretation. These interactions between elite physicians and judges contributed to an emergent medical consensus that poor pregnancy outcomes were not necessarily the fault of pregnant women themselves, but rather that they were caused by untrained midwives, "interlopers" corrupting a noble profession.

"An Interloper in the Art of Midwifery": Policing the Racial Boundaries of Reproductive Medicine

As white male physicians sought to consolidate their place within the medical profession, they increasingly sought to discredit midwives, who historically performed much of the work surgeons now claimed for themselves. For the better part of a century, these doctors had publicly criticized midwives for their alleged ignorance and blunderous practices. They blamed midwives for poor birth outcomes, even if those outcomes likely could not have been improved with the most advanced medical techniques of the time. Initially, these critiques served to justify the imposition of medical supervision over midwifery through training and licensing requirements (see chapter 4). This nineteenth-century resurgence of medical hostility toward midwives formed part of broader movement across the Atlantic World in which formally trained white male physicians displaced traditional healers, who were most often women of color.[35]

Tensions intensified in the final decades of the century, as a growing number of doctors formally trained in obstetrics struggled to earn their livelihoods through private practice. This competition drove some Cuban physicians to participate in the criminal prosecution of midwives, whom they viewed as cheaper, less-skilled competitors stealing clients. While continuing to push for even stricter regulation of midwifery, physicians also argued that midwives were responsible for poor pregnancy outcomes. Their lack of training, some doctors claimed, caused them to rely on backward practices that harmed or killed mothers and infants.

Such a vague claim of malpractice emerged in an 1876 police investigation following the discovery of a deceased newborn in the Havana neighborhood of San Leopoldo. The medical examiner noted injuries to the neck and face, which he suspected were likely inflicted by extraction tools during the birthing process. The physician's examination suggested that the birth was mired in complications. However, he determined that the cause of death was suffocation due to "manipulations enacted by inexpert hands." With this simple turn of phrase, the medical examiner revealed his assumption that the person who attended the birth was not a physician but rather a midwife, an occupation women of African descent most commonly engaged in.

Given that the newborn's body was naked and wrapped in rags, the mother was likely impoverished. Thus, the medical examiner's assumption was probably true, provided that midwives were a much more affordable option than physicians. However, why the medical examiner conflated midwifery with a lack of medical skill is questionable, since even the best trained physicians of the time would have struggled to save the infant's life. By portraying the infant's death as the result of a midwife's medical malpractice, the medical examiner opened the door to the criminal prosecution of a Black woman. The police pursued an investigation, but none of the people whom authorities interrogated offered any information about a pregnant woman in the neighborhood. Although the case eventually tapered out without suspects or arrests, it foreshadowed how physicians weaponized infanticide laws against their rivals.[36]

Allegations of malpractice similarly informed an 1883 case, following the death of a pregnant woman and her fetus during childbirth. The victim was Martina Miranda, an impoverished thirty-nine-year-old of African descent and a first-time mother from Havana. Miranda worked as a domestic servant and she lived with her partner, the moreno Serapio Valdés, by whom she became pregnant.[37] Toward the end of her pregnancy, Miranda began feeling labor pains. After two days of contractions, the labor had not progressed, and Miranda had started to experience convulsions. She asked her partner to summon a midwife, a Black woman named Polonia Aragón.[38]

The midwife arrived at Miranda's residence that evening. However, by the morning, Miranda's labor had still not progressed. She was still in excruciating pain and was having trouble breathing. A strong odor suggested that the fetus had died in utero. Realizing the delivery was mired in complications, Polonia summoned a physician. He arrived late that afternoon, when the top of the lifeless infant's head was "not far from the vulva." The doctor prescribed an ointment, presumably to lubricate the vagina, and administered a drug used to induce labor by provoking uterine contractions (*cornezuelo de centeno*, an ergot alkaloid). Having spent just a few minutes with the patient, the doctor left, only instructing the midwife to give the woman soup and wine. Although Miranda's labor intensified enough to expel the infant's head and one of its arms, the poor woman had been in labor for days at that point. With her exhaustion and the complicated presentation of the fetus, the birthing process stagnated once again. By the time the physician returned the following afternoon, the fetus's arm and head were detached from its body, and Miranda had died what could only be described as an agonizing and torturous death, her womb still holding the decapitated body of her fetus.

Authorities apprehended the midwife and charged her with homicide by "reckless imprudence." In her court testimony, the midwife emphasized her charity toward the patient and the restraint she exercised in treating her. She explained that her patient's partner, moreno Serapio, summoned her that night, explaining that he "did not have the resources to pay for a midwife." However, the midwife agreed to help attend to her "free of charge," as she was "guided by her generous sentiments, as always in such cases." Although she recognized that she lacked the license and authorization to be a midwife, she framed her actions more as coaching her patient through the labor and seeking professional assistance, rather than intervening medically herself.

She pointed out that she summoned a physician and followed his instructions. The midwife explained to authorities that once the physician left, she did not leave her patient's side but did not touch her. When the patient went into labor later that evening, the midwife coached her through the contractions, without "allowing herself to go beyond that." However, the fetus presented arm-first, and since it was already "dead and rotten," when its arm and head finally emerged from the womb, they were swollen and putrid. "They fell into her hands, without her even pulling," she recalled.

The physician's testimony largely corroborated the midwife's account, but he blamed her for the outcome. He told the court that when he examined the patient, he deduced that she was in labor, but it was not progressing due to her weakness. After administering medication to induce contractions, he recommended that the midwife notify him of any developments. According to the physician, the midwife failed to notify him when the entire head emerged from the patient's womb that night. He testified that if he had been notified at that time, the "labor would have ended happily because of the resources of his art."

Although he blamed the midwife in his court testimony, the physician vacillated in his explanation of the patient's cause of death. At one point in his testimony, he claimed the woman had died because of her "natural weakness" as well as the protracted and painful birth, following a pregnancy filled with ailments and problems. The convulsions and bleeding, he explained, caused nervous exhaustion, resulting in death. However, the physician also speculated that the traction imprudently employed by the midwife only added to this. He opined that the midwife had undoubtedly pulled very hard to have torn the head and arm from the body. Even though the fetus "exhaled a foul odor" during his first exam, the state of putrefaction was not so advanced as to allow the tearing with light pulling. By his judgment, the midwife did not need to pull, because science had enough resources to extract the fetus without incident.

The medical examiner who performed autopsies on the mother and fetus seemed to concur with the attending physician. The fetal autopsy described a decomposing cadaver that lacked the characteristic signs of a live birth. The physician concluded that the fetus died before or during the early stages of birth, but that the arm and head were torn off with force. To verify this, the physician exerted pressure on the other limb, in an effort to imitate the force that a midwife might exert during labor, but the arm did not detach. The rest of the body, extracted after the mother died, did not have the same lacerations, but it was putrid, with a strong odor, and almost all the skin was detached and green, characteristic of decomposition. Following an autopsy of the mother, he concluded that although the fetus had died thirty-six to forty-eight hours before its expulsion, Miranda could have given birth by herself or with "a small intervention by expert hands."[39]

The district court at Guanabacoa submitted the case for review at the Academy of Sciences. The legal medicine committee disagreed with the autopsy conclusions, arguing that the labor was undoubtedly slow, but the report contained insufficient information to determine the true reasons it did not progress. They argued that it was impossible to assume that the woman or her baby could have been saved, even with timely medical intervention. They noted that the force necessary to tear the head and arm from the body must have been great, which suggested that Miranda likely would not have been able to give birth without medical intervention. Based on the information provided, they could not ascertain the cause of death.[40]

The courts responded to the committee's decision by sending more documentation, including a second statement by the physician, whom the judge had summoned back for further questioning. In his second round of testimony, the physician explicitly accused the midwife of practicing without a license and killing the patient through malpractice. He testified that when he arrived at the woman's room, he found a woman of color known as La Toña, an "interloper in the art of midwifery." The label "interloper" had come to represent an implicitly racialized and gendered practitioner who defied white male medical authority. Instead of merely receiving the fetus expelled naturally as instructed, the midwife exceeded her mandate. Guided by ignorance, she pulled the head and arm so hard that she completely separated them from the body. Exonerating himself from the poor patient outcome, he claimed that by the time he arrived, the patient's condition was so critical that extraction was impossible and a fatal end was almost certain.

The doctors of the legal medicine committee seemed to agree that the midwife had intervened forcefully. In addition to observing the great force likely exerted to detach the arm and head, the committee also noted the bruising all over the mother's bladder and surrounding areas, signs suggesting significant force to extract the fetus. Although the decapitation of the fetus may have aggravated the situation, there was insufficient evidence to prove that the midwife's intervention caused or accelerated the woman's death.

They emphasized the adverse circumstances of the pregnancy and the complications during the birth. The woman was already around forty years old, of "weak constitution," and had an "unnaturally narrow" pelvis. In addition, records claimed this was her first pregnancy, and malnutrition and poor living conditions exacerbated the situation. According to the committee, her residence was "completely devoid of the hygienic amenities that are so necessary and indispensable to life." Moreover, by the time she sought a midwife's assistance, Miranda's condition was already critical, with infection, convulsions, and difficulty breathing. The committee concluded that the many complications afflicting her slow and painful labor likely caused her death.

The legal medicine committee appeared reluctant to label the case a homicide not because of a desire to protect an unlicensed midwife, but because the outcome of the case reflected on one of their own. They noted that the midwife did summon a physician "since despite her limited or total lack of obstetric knowledge, she could tell she was dealing with a serious case" and that she "dared not" attend the birth alone. Since she subordinated herself to a physician's authority, any finding would likely implicate him as well. They even admitted that "a small intervention performed by masterful hands" might have saved the mother. While perhaps overly optimistic, this claim insinuated that the attending physician should have performed such an intervention. Did he withhold such assistance because the patient was poor and Black? Did he fail to act out of negligence? Although the documentary record does not reveal what became of the midwife, the case does show how the medicalization of childbirth rendered midwives particularly vulnerable in the event of poor patient outcomes. The one aspect of this relationship between physicians and midwives that seemingly protected midwives was the medical establishment's desire to protect its own—physicians—from potential culpability.[41]

By the late nineteenth century, however, physicians leveraged developments in the field of obstetrics to reframe their critiques in scientific terms. In the 1890s, critiques of midwives centered on specific causes of maternal and infant death, namely puerperal fever, a deadly postpartum infection, and neonatal tetanus, a bacterial infection usually originating at the umbilical stump. In an 1891 pamphlet, Gabriel Casuso decried the evils of "recibidoras" a vulgar name for unlicensed midwives, also called "interlopers." Casuso's description of recibidoras drew distinctions between formally educated and licensed midwives, who were more likely to be white and literate, and unlicensed practitioners, who lacked formal training and were more likely to be less privileged women and women of African descent. Women from the latter category, recibidoras, served pregnant women from all classes and backgrounds, much to Casuso's dismay. Most offensive to him was the use of unlicensed midwives by wealthy white women. He found it strange that women from the "best" classes of society, "people of true enlightenment, who are rightfully horrified by curanderos, submit themselves without any difficulty to the arms of a filthy woman that doesn't even know how to read."[42] According to Casuso, relying on a recibidora was tantamount to a death sentence, an accusation all the more damning when it afflicted the most demographically and socially desirable sectors.

Much of Casuso's horror stemmed from the high infant and maternal mortality rates. Puerperal fever deaths in Havana were, even by the most favorable accounts, more than ten times higher than they were in Europe. In December 1890, Havana recorded 9 puerperal fever deaths out of 347 births, a rate that physicians said was increasing.[43] Official statistics recorded 20 puerperal fever deaths for every 1,000 women in Havana, where the rate of deaths in London and Geneva were 1.5 and 1 per 1,000, respectively. Statistics for death by septicemia, which physicians mostly attributed to puerperal infection, were even worse. Dr. Vicente de la Guardia's statistics showed septicemia death rates as high as 59 per 1,000 during a three-month period he studied in Havana.[44] Casuso's data showed that, of the 350 births observed over another three-month period, 31 deaths resulted from septicemia.[45] Infant mortality, too, was dire. In 1892, one infant died nearly every day from neonatal tetanus in Havana. The introduction of antiseptic provisions through the 1890s had helped reduce this number to 250 infants per year. However, according to Casuso, the proper implementation of antisepsis by midwives could entirely eliminate this preventable illness.[46]

Casuso attributed these excessive mortality rates to the misdeeds of unlicensed midwives. The "excessive ignorance" of these practitioners, especially their failure to adhere to antiseptic practices, allegedly caused puerperal fever and neonatal tetanus.[47] Casuso recommended that pregnant women not under the supervision of a physician choose licensed midwives, rather than recibidoras. He had created a set of antiseptic guidelines for midwives to follow prior to attending any pregnant or laboring woman. This "Reglamento de desinfección para las comadronas" instructed midwives to keep their fingernails short and perfectly rounded, roll up their sleeves past the elbow, and wash their hands twice for five minutes each with a different cleansing agent, as well as disinfecting the woman's genital area. It also instructed midwives to apply antiseptic agents to the newborn's umbilical cord. Casuso had actually sent this regulation to the Superior Board of Sanitation (Junta Superior de Sanidad) to obtain approval for implementation, but the only response was to thank him for the recommendations.[48]

An 1895 case involving the death of a mother and her fetus from infection seemed to lend credence to Casuso's claim that midwives caused maternal and infant death by disregarding antisepsis and asepsis protocols. A judge in the district of Cerro, in Havana, requested a consultation from medical experts at the Academy of Sciences, on a case involving the death of a woman in labor and her fetus. The pregnant woman's husband called the midwife, who she claimed administered some "sachets" (likely cornezuelo de centeno) and other medicines. The woman bore a dead fetus the second night, already showing signs of fever. Her husband called a doctor, who arrived the next day and diagnosed her with puerperal fever. By that evening, her condition had further deteriorated, as gangrenous lesions appeared on her vulva. She died that night.

Examining physicians offered apparently conflicting opinions about the cause of death.[49] One physician claimed that the woman had succumbed to septicemia, but also that antisepsis would not necessarily have prevented the death. The other physician argued that the vulvar lesions could have been caused by a variety of afflictions. The judge sought the opinion of the Academy of Sciences to determine if the woman's death from puerperal septicemia following a normal birth and the death of the fetus during labor could be attributed to the intervention of the midwife, an unlicensed recibidora, whether by malice, reckless imprudence, or at the least with simple imprudence or negligence.

The reporting physician in this case was Dr. Casuso, who had obtained his bachelor's degree in Madrid and doctorate in Paris, after the Ten Years' War interrupted his studies in Havana. Having returned to Cuba after the Pact of Zanjón (1878), Casuso worked as a surgeon and served on the gynecology service in Havana's Hospital de Higiene for prostitutes. He later helped establish the first private gynecology clinic in the Jesús del Monte neighborhood of Havana and succeeded Serapio Arteaga as professor of obstetrics at the University of Havana.[50] He was known among his peers for implementing asepsis and antisepsis in abdominal surgery.[51]

Casuso argued definitively that the midwife was responsible for both deaths. He alleged that she had probably infected the woman with septicemia after attending to another infected woman and failing to observe antiseptic procedures. That infection, he argued, had killed both the mother and her fetus. Although the midwife likely did not act with malice, according to Casuso, she was guilty of reckless endangerment by practicing a profession without the necessary knowledge or license. But more so than negligence, the midwife was guilty of ignorance, since she could not even sign her own name.

The judge of the Real Audiencia recommended convicting the midwife of homicide by reckless endangerment, with a sentence of a year and one day in prison as well as a fine of five thousand pesetas. Casuso called the punishment "sensible." He denied getting any kind of pleasure from the woman's suffering and even suggested that she had likely acted in good faith and with charity. However, he opined that such punishment was necessary to end abuses by unlicensed midwives, whose errors cost lives.[52]

Much like the previous two cases discussed here, this 1895 case hinged on allegations of malpractice by an unlicensed midwife, who purportedly caused maternal and infant death. However, the conviction and sentencing of this practitioner, and the enthusiastic participation of a Cuban obstetrician in condemning her, set this case apart. The entire premise of the conviction rested on Casuso's claim that the midwife infected the pregnant woman, causing her and her fetus's death, which would have been easily prevented by a sanitation procedure that he had mapped out a few years earlier. The first part of his claim, though unproven, was entirely plausible—the onset of her fever as described in case notes was consistent with septicemia contracted during childbirth, with death typically following within three days. However, would the handwashing and antiseptic treatment of the woman's genitals, as outlined by Casuso in his 1891 regulation, necessarily have prevented infection? Would this woman and her fetus have survived if she had given birth in a hospital or clinic instead of at home?

Descriptions of Havana's obstetric clinic suggest not. Dr. Le-Roy, one of the first medical students to study at the obstetric clinic, described it as a "miserable hovel" tucked between the washroom and the morgue in the San Francisco de Paula Women's Hospital. The clinic, illuminated only by a few tiny windows and oil lamps, consisted of a patient ward reminiscent of a closet with four beds, a birthing room with two beds, and a conference room. From the facility's small covered porch, attendants threw excrement.[53] After dark, medical students lit matches near the patient's vulva to supplement the faint light in the birthing room.[54] A cramped, dimly lit, poorly ventilated place with numerous student observers could hardly provide the kind of aseptic environment necessary to prevent infection.

Moreover, although Casuso and many of his peers blamed midwives for failing to implement asepsis and antisepsis when examining pregnancy women and delivering their babies, ample evidence indicates that the problem was not limited to, or even primarily with, midwives. Cases of puerperal septicemia had actually become more common with the professionalization of obstetrics, which brought more frequent surgical intervention in pregnancy and childbirth.[55] Discussions among physicians in the Academy of Sciences show that some Cuban physicians were not familiar with asepsis and antisepsis. But it was not until 1891—the same year Casuso drafted the antiseptic protocols for midwives—that he and Rafael Weiss Verson published the first official piece on obstetrical antisepsis: a translation of Pierre Victor Adolphe Auvard's *De l'antisepsie en gynécologie et en obstetrique*.[56] Casuso himself admitted that physicians were not very "scrupulous" about observing antiseptic protocols during childbirth and that not even the doctors who proclaim themselves as specialists take all the necessary precautions with their hands and instruments.[57] A contingent of Cuban physicians even believed that asepsis and antisepsis were not legitimate practices. Dr. Montané, for example, recounted an interaction with a colleague who boasted that he used lamp oil when performing pelvic exams because "asepsis was a joke."[58] It was no wonder that even after the introduction of asepsis and antisepsis in Cuba, maternal and infant mortality rates from infection remained high, and only began to decrease in the early twentieth century, when sterilizing medical instruments became more generalized.[59]

Although such an anecdote certainly suggests some dismay at physicians who neglected antisepsis, midwives bore the brunt of the burden. A failed cesarean section in the 1890s exposed the double standard in accountability over poor pregnancy and birthing outcomes. A mulata woman brought in a pregnant patient with complications due to a breech delivery. Several physicians examined the woman and attempted unsuccessfully to extract the already-deceased fetus vaginally. Abandoning their efforts after three hours, the physicians then cut into the woman's abdomen, extracting the fetus in pieces. The woman died less than three days later.

The report does not provide details about cause of death, but the timing suggests the patient likely contracted an infection or suffered other complications during surgery, causing her to die. Abdominal surgery, especially a cesarean section, was a death sentence before the generalization of antisepsis and prior to the introduction of antibiotics and blood transfusion. Although a small number of cases note physicians extracting deceased fetuses from women, Cuba's first successful cesarean section, in which both fetus and mother survived, did not occur until 1900.[60] Patient deaths from surgical intervention appeared to be so common that by the late nineteenth century, some obstetricians suggested that surgeons resist performing any procedure until the patient was in imminent danger.[61] Ambrosio González del Valle's 1876 statement was still valid years later: "surgery is in reality the art of not operating."[62]

Despite the likelihood that the reporting physician himself caused the death, he blamed the mulata who brought the patient, labeling her an unlicensed midwife or recibidora. He protested "a thousand and one times against the intrusion of the so-called recibidoras." He claimed that early intervention by a physician, such as himself, would have saved both the fetus and the mother, because he could have performed a caesarean section. "Two lives sacrificed to ignorance," he lamented, implicating the midwife. The laws prohibiting unlicensed individuals from practicing the "art of childbirth" were "dead letter" without proper enforcement.[63]

Although cloaked in genuine concern about maternal and infant health, some of the outrage over unlicensed midwives undoubtedly stemmed from Cuban obstetricians' professional and financial precariousness. As in other parts of Latin America, Cuban obstetricians competed with midwives for access to patients, whose continued reliance on midwives meant low demand for obstetrics services.[64] Although obstetricians boasted years of theoretical training and formal degrees, their services were expensive, intimidating, and inaccessible to most women. The abysmal reputation obstetricians had gained likely did not help build their clientele. Administering high doses of chloroform as a form of anesthesia during labor and delivery, for example, occasioned numerous deaths in the late nineteenth century, but doctors continued to experiment with this drug as well as morphine.[65] Limited access to patients meant fewer pregnant bodies on which to practice their craft, innovate procedures and technologies, and more generally, establish themselves professionally. The vast majority of nineteenth-century Cuban women, quite simply, continued to prefer midwives.

Policing the Profession: Physician-Assisted Abortion

As physicians blamed midwives for poor pregnancy outcomes, they revealed an incipient belief among a sector of the Cuban medical establishment that they had a professional and patriotic duty to protect the fertility of vulnerable women. Yet, in some ways, the development of obstetrics brought more than the potential for improving pregnancy and birth outcomes; the same training also offered broader access to the knowledge, instruments, and technologies needed to perform a range of obstetrical and gynecological procedures, including ones that could terminate pregnancy. The dual potential of obstetrics to save maternal and infant life and to end pregnancies, independent of clinical indication, became a source of growing tension among Cuban physicians in the late nineteenth century.

While midwives, healers, and other practitioners had employed herbal remedies for centuries, the development of obstetrics brought new techniques and procedures, many with roots in therapeutic treatment of pregnancy and labor complications, to bear on the termination of pregnancy. By the mid-nineteenth century, and especially by the 1880s, cornezuelo de centeno (an ergot alkaloid derived from rye), emerged as a remedy to terminate unwanted pregnancy in Cuba. It was used as a labor accelerator in Europe as early as the Middle Ages, and in some parts of Latin America since the eighteenth century.[66] Explicit references to the drug do not appear in Cuba until the second half of the nineteenth century, following formal studies of its use in labor and delivery, including as a method of provoking miscarriage and artificial premature birth, in Spain.[67] Obstetricians had begun using this powder to help induce contractions in women whose labor did not progress quickly enough. However, the substance doubled as a de facto abortifacient.

By the 1890s, Cuban doctors developed new surgical instruments and techniques designed to treat certain pregnancy complications and postpartum conditions threatening the lives of the mother and fetus. A procedure euphemistically called artificial premature birth, was among those lifesaving interventions physicians used to treat gestational illness, such as uncontrolled vomiting, uterine hemorrhage, severe eclampsia, or what doctors called "extreme pelvic narrowness."[68] It typically involved provoking uterine contractions by injecting fluids into the cervix, or surgically dilating the cervix.[69] Advocates of the procedure boasted that it did not require destroying the fetus. On the contrary, artificial premature birth was medically indicated only for women whose pregnancies were seven months or further along. Medical curriculum therefore instructed Cuban physicians not to perform artificial premature birth unless other therapeutic methods had failed, but also advised they not wait until the patient was too critical.[70] Another technique, dilation and curettage emerged first as a treatment for incomplete miscarriage, in which fetal or placental tissue remained in the uterus, potentially causing infection.[71] Facilitating these lifesaving procedures were innovations in surgical instruments, including the modified curette and uterine dilator Weiss Verson presented in a U.S. medical journal in 1892 (fig. 8.1).[72]

Although these medical developments empowered physicians to perform lifesaving interventions, they proved controversial, not least because they blurred the lines separating legitimate clinical indication and criminal conduct. All these procedures and instruments could be used to perform abortions, which was criminalized under the 1870 penal code. Nevertheless, medical-legal specialists in the mid-nineteenth century noted exceptions for practitioners terminating pregnancy or inducing early labor to save the life of the mother. The letter of the law exempted from criminal culpability physicians performing the procedure to save the mother from "grave and *imminent* danger." This circumstance also appeared in the 1848 and 1850 penal codes, leading one Spanish medical-legal specialist to argue for a more liberal interpretation based on developing medical science. He cited the successful adoption of artificial premature birth in the United Kingdom, Germany, the Netherlands, Italy, and France, which in many instances had saved the lives of both mother and fetus. Based on those

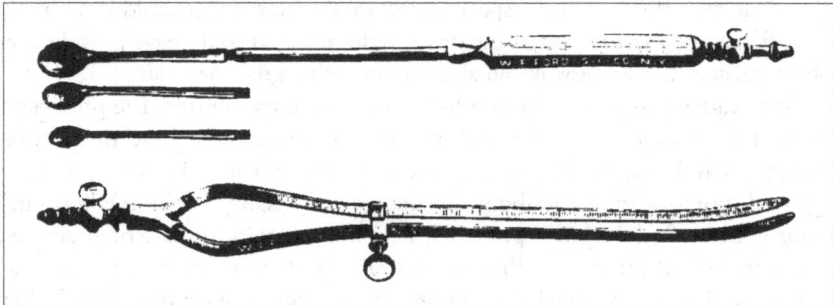

FIGURE 8.1. Curette and uterine dilator designed by Dr. Rafael Weiss. Rafael Weiss Verson, "A New Curette and a dilating uterine sound," *American Journal of Obstetrics and Diseases of Women and Children* 26 (1892): 360.

data, he argued that a physician had the legal right to provoke the expulsion of the fetus in situations that could later pose a threat to the life of the mother or child. One such conditions involved extreme pelvic narrowness, which in the mid-nineteenth century was typically treated with symphysiotomy or cesarean section, procedures that most often proved fatal to the mother. However, artificial premature birth after the seventh month of gestation when the fetus was considered viable, he argued, would easily save both lives.[73] Despite the insinuation that the fetus would survive, Elizabeth O'Brien observes that fetal death was often a foregone conclusion, suggesting that physicians used artificial premature birth to legitimize abortive procedures.[74]

Early pioneers of these technologies, including Weiss Verson, evidently faced criticism for the moral implications of their innovations. Assuming a defensive tone, Weiss Verson later explained that "in the course of its history, artificial premature birth has suffered multiple very harsh attacks, like no other obstetric procedure."[75] The techniques and instruments employed in the procedure could just as easily be used prior to fetal viability to provoke a miscarriage, whether considered therapeutic or not. Thus the technique Weiss Verson detailed also provided a blueprint for surgical abortion. It was precisely surgical innovations like these, amid acute anxieties about population, that fanned the flames of opposition to abortion among Cuba's elite physicians.

These tensions between medical development and legal responsibility reemerged in an 1884 criminal investigation of a physician who allegedly facilitated a medical abortion on a pregnant white woman.[76] In this case, the physician, Francisco González, had administered cornezuelo de centeno to a young woman who was pregnant, inducing a miscarriage. Authorities in Havana detained the doctor and launched an investigation, part of which entailed requesting a consultation from the Academy of Sciences. The judge of the Prado District asked the academy if the drug had a special effect on the uterus; if it could be properly classified as an abortifacient; if the dosage administered could have provoked an abortion; and if it did provoke an abortion in the pregnant woman.[77]

The academy assigned the case to the childbirth committee. The physicians on that committee answered that cornezuelo de centeno did have an effect on the uterus and that it could be classified as an abortifacient. However, they requested more information about the dosage and quality of the medication.[78] Shortly thereafter, the judge presented new testimony in the case of attempted abortion against the doctor. Pharmaceutical experts reported that the two sachets found each contained three grams of cornezuelo de centeno, which they described as a known abortifacient. The committee noted that the drug in question strengthens contractions that are already underway but does not produce them. They offered a perplexing explanation, claiming that in cases where a predisposition to miscarriage already exists, anything could provoke it. On the contrary, if a predisposition does not exist, not even the strongest factors can produce miscarriage. However, in the later months of pregnancy, they warned, abortifacients can have more powerful effects. Several of the physicians on the committee opined that the medical examiner's conclusions were too absolute and not necessarily borne out by the evidence. Sending the chemical reports to special experts failed to confirm that the powders contained cornezuelo to the exclusion of other compounds.[79] Without the woman's medical history, the legal medicine committee concluded that there was insufficient evidence to convict the doctor.[80]

This case was significant for two key reasons. First, when compared with the cases against midwives discussed earlier, it evinces a different standard of criminal culpability for women of color and white male medical practitioners. Whereas physicians appeared perfectly willing to assign midwives criminal responsibility for unintended poor birth outcomes, they seemed unwilling, despite their performance of moral outrage, to support the conviction of one of their own for intentionally terminating a pregnancy. Second, the case shows a consensus between elite physicians and judicial authorities that practitioners bore some responsibility in abortion. The fact that police investigated the activities of a white male medical professional and that the courts pursued a criminal case against him shows that even privileged white men might be held accountable for terminating a desirable pregnancy. That physicians discussed this case openly within a broader professional body of scientists evinced their willingness to make their antiabortion posture public.

Yet, the criminality of abortion seemed to hinge more specifically on the perceived racial dimensions of the pregnancy itself. In this regard, it is significant that Dr. González faced charges for terminating the pregnancy of a girl who was presumably white. His deed carried significant consequences not only for the woman and her family but also for the nation then in a brief intermission from a decades-long struggle for sovereignty in a time when self-government presumed whiteness.

Cuba's medical-legal community seemed to assume a correlation between abortion and whiteness. According to Dr. José Agustín Martínez, abortion was "a crime of civilization." He based his claim on a (dubious) assumption about which women practiced abortion and why. He argued that abortion was unknown among Black and mixed-race women, largely because their social status was so low that legitimacy and honor were not significant concerns. By contrast, white women's social status hinged on both honor and legitimacy. Dr. Martínez claimed (incorrectly) that illegitimate births had been highly uncommon among white families through Cuba's colonial period, during which time criminal abortion was "not a common practice." He claimed that illegitimate births had increased among the white population over the late nineteenth century, as moral laxity intensified.[81] The notion of abortion as a white woman's procedure seemed to heighten the stakes of Dr. González's practice, and it would continue to inform the stridently antiabortion postures of much of Cuba's medical community for the next half century.

With the professionalization of obstetrics in Cuba, elite physicians gradually carved out a role for themselves in the emerging nation. This role centered on advancing white population growth through protecting white women's fertility, especially reducing maternal and infant mortality, and condemning fertility control. Paternalistic protection for white women was most obvious in physicians' reluctance to support convicting them of criminal infanticide. Yet it also emerged certain physicians' active participation in prosecuting midwives for poor pregnancy outcomes. This professional antagonism rendered midwifery ever more perilous for women of color practitioners. Not so for (white) physicians, whose formal training and licensing did not necessarily beget significantly better patient outcomes during this period. However, they do not appear to have faced criminal charges in the way midwives did, even when their actions directly caused the death of women or their infants.

Instead, abortion became one limited area in which physicians considered holding their peers responsible, but only because of the implicit association between abortion and white pregnancy loss. Ultimately, these positions formed part of a pronatalist agenda tailored to the needs of the emerging nation, one that privileged the patriarchal protection of white reproduction through the professionalization of medicine.

CHAPTER NINE

Birthing a Better Nation
Pregnancy and the Racial Logic of Early Republic Population Management

In August 1898, mere days before the United States proclaimed victory over Spain following the Spanish-Cuban-American War, the New York–based magazine *Puck* published a political cartoon titled "A Trifle Embarrassed."[1] Cuba appeared alongside Puerto Rico, Hawai'i, and the Philippines, four crying infants in a basket. Each baby donned cultural accessories to denote its racial and ethnic Otherness, Cuba wearing the hat of an insurgent soldier. Two large white arms, labeled "Manifest" and "Destiny," place the basket at the entrance of the "U.S. Foundling Asylum." Casting Cuba as an unwanted infant was indeed an ironic rewriting of a historical moment orchestrated by U.S. military intervention to obtain an island that U.S. presidents had coveted for the better part of the century.[2]

A skeptical Uncle Sam and a concerned-looking Lady Columbia stand nearby. Columbia peers intensely at the babies in the basket, her body leaning toward them as she steps forward and reaches out. Uncle Sam stands stiffly back, his body turned away from the babies. He glances back, scratching his head in apparent confusion. Four white or white-passing children, labeled California, Texas, Alaska, and New Mexico play merrily in the background. The cartoon's caption features an exclamation by Uncle Sam: "Gosh! I wish they wouldn't come quite so many in a bunch; but, if I've got to take them, I guess I can do as well by them as I've done by the others!" (fig. 9.1). Invoking a racially charged paternalist obligation, Uncle Sam at once complains of the burden of accepting his new racially degenerate, revolutionary, and backward charges, even as he commits to the benevolent venture of civilizing them.

Mirroring the vulnerable and dependent status of the abandoned infant in the political cartoon, Cuba entered the twentieth century as an occupied land, ravaged by thirty years of internecine anticolonial warfare. Although thousands of people fought three wars to liberate their island from colonial rule, the United States usurped the Cuban army's victory over Spain, stripping the veterans who freed it and the statesmen who governed it of the independence req-

FIGURE 9.1. Foundlings between empires. Udo J. Keppler, "A Trifle Embarrassed," *Puck* 43, no. 1117 (August 3, 1898). (Keppler & Schwarzmann), centerfold. Library of Congress, Prints and Photographs Division.

uisite of modern manhood.³ The eventual birth of the Cuban republic in 1902 punctuated a much longer process of national identity formation in which Cuban elites struggled to redeem themselves and their nascent republic from the emasculating state of neocolonialism.⁴ While scholars have studied the role of politicians, creatives, and labor activists in this process, they have paid much less attention to Cuba's professional classes.⁵ Legislators, jurists, and physicians staked their claim in the emerging republic during the first three decades of the twentieth century by forging a population that truly embodied both civilization and modernity. Women's wombs were at the very center of this project, as the island's leading men of science recognized how managing pregnancy and childbirth was central to growing the citizenry and improving its quality.

In the context of these early republican demographic anxieties, physicians developed homiculture, a science dedicated to improving humanity through interventions at various stages of reproduction. Like their peers in other parts of Latin America and the Caribbean, Cuban physicians adapted homiculture to their multiracial context, often aiming to prevent racial "degeneracy" and promote whitening.⁶ While maternal and infant welfare measures aimed to reduce mortality rates especially among the white population, Cuban physicians also focused on increasing fertility. Though staunch opposition to family planning and demands for greater accountability for criminal abortion, physicians retained their paternalist character in "protecting" white women's fertility often at the expense of women's own ability to care for the infants they birthed. Ultimately, this posture suggests that despite the abrupt political ruptures with the colonial past, continuity rather than change defined state attitudes toward women's reproduction, especially when it came to the birth of future white citizens.

Resuscitating the Birth Rate: Family Planning in the Early Republican Medical and Moral Landscape

Cuban independence from Spanish rule came to a population ravaged by thirty years of internecine warfare. Birth rates declined during the period of anticolonial struggle, but most dramatically during the war of independence (1895–98). In 1860, estimations suggest that between 27 and 35 babies were born per thousand people in Cuba. By 1890, the birth rate had declined to just 19.4. As Cuba emerged from the war in 1898, it had plummeted to just 5.7. On average, there were 31,970 recorded births per year between 1890 and 1893. That figure declined by almost half during the war, when an average of just 17,204 births were recorded per year. Although the numerical value of these estimations is not precise because they are based on registered births, the pattern of decline during the final years of the nineteenth century is nonetheless striking.[7] In 1899, Cuba had the smallest proportion of children under age five of any country for which data were available, a reflection of the low number of births and high infant mortality during the war of independence. In fact, that year, there were 95,229 fewer children under age five than there were children ages five to nine.[8]

When combined with increased mortality due to war, famine, and epidemic disease, and population loss through emigration, Cuba's declining fertility rates had a marked impact on the overall demographic trajectory. Between 1861 and 1877, the rate of population increase declined from 18 percent per decade to just 5 percent, when it had previously ranged between 23 and 31 percent. The rate of increase rebounded slightly to 8 percent per decade following the Peace of Zanjón (1878). Whereas Cuba's population increased incrementally between 1877 and 1887 (by 110,003), beginning in 1895 the island lost roughly 30,000 each year until 1899.[9] By the time Cuba secured independence from Spain in 1898 and entered a period of U.S. military occupation in 1899, its population counted 58,895 fewer inhabitants than in 1887. This amounted to a population *decrease* of 3.6 percent.[10]

Unfavorable demographic comparisons with Puerto Rico, which had one of the highest population densities of the Americas, further exacerbated the urgency of these figures.[11] While U.S. authorities later interpreted these demographic comparisons as evidence of the pathological overpopulation of Puerto

Rico, the contrast was a source of shame for many Cuban authorities, who believed that Cuba's substantially lower population density fell far short of the demographic yardstick.[12]

The dawn of the Cuban republic to a declining population set the stage for key medical interventions aimed at increasing births. Early republican physicians actively intervened in women's reproductive choices, most often acting to circumscribe family planning options, even if it meant suppressing life-saving obstetric procedures. During the republic's first decade, Cuban medical authorities opposed the introduction of contraceptive devices as well as technologies they believed could be used to limit the birth rate, such as artificial premature birth. They also challenged judges to shift their focus from prosecuting impoverished women to pursuing charges against more privileged (white) women, who had historically enjoyed relative impunity for fertility crimes. Through these reproductive interventions, physicians attempted to implement their vision of a modern, civilized, white nation by increasing the birth of desirable babies. However, these policies ultimately contributed to an increase in unwanted pregnancies. The resulting harms disproportionately impacted impoverished women and women of color, who risked life-threatening complications and death from clandestine abortions and increasingly resorted to infant abandonment.

THE "UNFERTILIZER OF WOMEN"

For the nascent republic's leading physicians, ensuring the birth of future Cuban citizens required them to address women's efforts to limit their fertility. Asserting their medical authority to defend the emerging nation's future from the *lesa patria* crimes—crimes against the nation—that women committed, some of Cuba's most prominent medical doctors confronted emerging technologies that expanded the options available to women interested in family planning. This put them at odds with scientific developments in their own profession.

An early example of this opposition to the emerging science of family planning was a 1903 case in which a prominent Cuban doctor advised customs officials against allowing the importation of a foreign contraceptive device called the "unfertilizer of women." In September 1903 the customs administrator at Matanzas intercepted the medical device on suspicions of immorality. According to a physician's report, the "unfertilizer of women" consisted of three parts: a rubber bulb used as a kind of pump, an aluminum tube for injecting liquids, and a hardened rubber dilator, about 9½ inches long with four valves. The device allowed liquids or powders, presumably ones with spermicidal properties, to be introduced into the vagina. An instruction sheet and a recipe card with the name of Dr. Huter, Arzt. instructed the user to concoct an "antiseptic and highly astringent mixture" consisting of boric acid and other ingredients.[13] Although the instruction card seemed to advertise the device as contraceptive, Cuban physicians considered the injection of antiseptic solutions, including those containing borax, into the vagina as one of the common methods of clandestine abortion employed by midwives and unlicensed abortion providers.[14]

The customs official alerted the Academy of Sciences to his discovery and requested a consultation on the "morality" of the device. Dr. Jorge Le-Roy y Cassá argued that the device was "immoral because it opposes one of the highest ends of marriage, which is procreation and also relaxes morals." In referencing marriage and morality, Le-Roy y Cassá exposed his assumption that the device's primary clientele was white women. Framing the risk of pregnancy as a safeguard forcing white women's sexual propriety, he predicted that allowing a contraceptive device would encourage promiscuity. Seemingly conflating pregnancy prevention with pregnancy termination, he claimed that the device enabled women "such criminal means" to "satisfy their sensual appetites" by having non-procreative sex. Because the device empowered women to divorce sex from procreation, it threatened to undermine the moral foundation and demographic future of the republic.

Dismissing any potential therapeutic purpose in medicine, Le-Roy y Cassá argued that "the Unfertilizer of Women" would inflict significant harm on the nation. This claim rested on a particular vision of women's bodies as passive objects whose sole noble purpose was to reproduce. "The vagina," Le-Roy y Cassá explained matter-of-factly, "is a virtual conduit that only opens to give way to the penis in the moment of coitus or to the product of conception in the act of birth, or to the fingers or other foreign bodies that separate its walls with therapeutic or criminal intentions." Seemingly detached from the woman's consciousness and will, this vision of women's reproductive organs as vulnerable vessels called for male supervision and control.[15] Stepping into that role, Le-Roy y Cassá declared that, because the contraceptive device "was dedicated to impede one of the most important functions, which is the perpetuation of the species," it was necessary to ban its importation.[16]

Le-Roy y Cassá's unwavering opposition to this early contraceptive device formed part of the same emerging standard of professional ethics that vilified women of color midwives (chapter 8). Conflating nationalism with patriarchal moralism, the island's leading physicians cast themselves as defenders of Cuba's future citizenry. Efforts to circumscribe women's reproductive choices only became more pronounced during the early decades of the twentieth century. However, Cuban physicians were not interested in raising the fertility rate across the board. For the island's leading medical professionals, ensuring the future of the Cuban nation required ensuring the right kind of births to build a modern Cuban citizenry.

"LOOK FOR THE BABY KILLER IN THE UPPER ECHELONS OF SOCIETY"

In addition to their work in the medical field, physicians also attempted to enact their vision for the national population through the courts. Criminalization, one of the oldest, albeit least effective, mechanisms of regulating women's reproduction, remained a powerful tool in Cuba's new republic. Drawing on precedents in the late nineteenth century, physicians urged police and judges to reorient their prosecutorial efforts away from impoverished women of color and toward the women who, in their view, truly had a motive to commit infanticide: honorable (white) women. Such a recommendation failed to recognize how poverty was a powerful motive for infanticide, even as many of the cases suggested poor pregnancy outcomes due to extreme poverty, overwork, malnutrition, and disease, more than intentional violence. Yet, chipping away at wealthy white women's de facto exemption from criminal prosecution for infanticide had obvious demographic ramifications for the fledgling republic, whose elites believed it needed a larger and better quality population.

Dr. Tomás V. Coronado, for one, witnessed firsthand one of the problems plaguing that arena in his capacity as a member of the Academy of Sciences legal medicine committee. As a key medical expert advising judges on infanticide and abortion cases in criminal courts across the island, Coronado had noticed the preponderance of impoverished women among the criminal infanticide and abortion cases on which he consulted. The disproportionate prosecution of impoverished women for fertility crimes seemingly contradicted the prevailing understanding of abortion and infanticide as crimes generally committed by women to preserve their honor—that is, by white women from the upper classes. Whereas judges appeared more likely to request a formal consultation from the legal medicine committee in cases involving white women, these cases typically involved impoverished white women (see chapter 8). Yet these represented only a portion of the cases appearing before judges, who appeared less likely to hesitate when prosecuting women of color. Thus, according to Coronado, there was a gulf between the population who committed these crimes and the group who suffered the consequences. If legal consequences were meant to make the crime less frequent, then, this disparity proved even more troubling for the future of the republic. It essentially allowed wealthy white women to drive down the white birth rate by committing fertility control with impunity, while erecting punitive barriers for poor women and women of color to do the same. The ultimate demographic consequence of this socioeconomic and racial bias in criminal prosecution would be a darkening of Cuba's population in a time when elites considered whiteness as absolutely essential for self-government and modernity.

A 1907 infanticide case following the discovery of a deceased white infant offers a microcosm of the way race and socioeconomic status proved central to the confrontation between physicians and judges over the island's reproductive future. In July, Havana police had discovered the cadaver of a newborn near the Torreón de San Lázaro, a watchtower overlooking the waters of Havana Bay. Summoned to the scene, the physician on call at the Casa de Socorro observed that the newborn, who he determined to be a white girl, was full term and had recently died. His preliminary report describes a deep sunken bruise on the right side, another bruise on the right shoulder, and a fractured right clavicle. The entire body had meconium stains and the umbilical cord was not tied, suggesting that the death may have occurred prior to or during birth.

Despite the physician's conclusions, authorities detained a young Black woman, whom we will call Juana, alleging she had given birth to and then violently murdered a white man's baby. An autopsy performed by the medical examiner the following day corroborated the first physician's conclusions about the infant's race and sex. However, the medical examiner noted that there were no signs of violence around the neck, nor any traumatic injuries to the body, contradicting the first physician's report about the injuries to the shoulder and clavicle. He also added that the infant's body had not yet putrefied and was covered in blood, likely from the mother. He opined that the labor was likely prolonged, and the infant's head may have been stuck. In the majority of cases like this, "the new being comes out in a state of imminent death, dying often despite the efforts of an intelligent midwife, which was absent in this case." The autopsy report suggested the infant had died of natural causes, not violence.

A district court in Western Havana brought infanticide charges. The allegations, which assumed an infant of mixed racial heritage, contradicted the reports of both the physician on call and the medical examiner. Nevertheless, the court subjected the accused woman to an invasive medical examination to verify the circumstances of her pregnancy and birth. The examination revealed that Juana was still bleeding and in evident discomfort from a recent birth. The physician noted that her labia majora and other genital areas were "excessively sensitive," indicating that she was in considerable pain worsened by an intrusive pelvic exam. Inserting his hand into her vagina, the doctor even poked his index finger through the cervix. The doctor also squeezed the woman's nipples until they produced what he described as a thick milky substance. The doctor concluded that the woman had likely given birth five to seven days earlier and that the fetus was about six or seven months along. Although the doctor's report seemed to corroborate that Juana had recently given birth, it challenged the court's assumption that she was the mother of the deceased white infant. The infant in question was full term, not premature like the accused woman's fetus. Moreover, three physicians had now without hesitation labeled the infant as white.

The woman's attorney pressed this last point, requesting additional expert testimony from the physician involved in the autopsy. He asked if it was possible for a Black or mixed-race woman to give birth to a white baby. He also pushed for a definitive conclusion about the infant's cause of death. If the infant had succumbed to natural causes, as the autopsy report suggested, the courts had no grounds to pursue criminal charges. On the contrary, if the preliminary medical assessment that the infant had been subject to violence proved correct, then the courts would have to prove that the accused woman had, in fact, birthed the dead child, which appeared increasingly unlikely given the differences in race and gestational age.

In August, the medical examiner appeared before the court to address these and other questions about the case. Confident that existing science could provide clarity on all the attorney's queries, he again confirmed that the infant autopsied had likely died from a long and difficult birth, not violence. He also reiterated his doubts that Juana had given birth to the infant in question due to the difference in gestational age. On the question of race, the judge intervened, inquiring if the infant in fact "belonged to the white race, or if it could be mestizo," and if the autopsy could determine the race with certainty. The medical examiner replied that the infant was "al parecer blanca" (seemingly white), but added that if she were racially mixed, her parents would have had to be white and mestizo. In other words, the medical examiner essentially ruled out the possibility of a Black woman, like Juana, as the deceased infant's mother.

The following month, the judge asked several other physicians to consult on these racial questions. The medical consensus was clear in three short reports that unequivocally described the deceased infant as white and the accused woman as Black on both her maternal and paternal sides. Juana's supposedly pure Blackness meant that she could not have given birth to the deceased white infant. The judge remained undeterred, however. He then asked the doctors to determine whether Juana had given birth to a viable infant, which would make her legally responsible for its life. The doctors answered that she had a natural premature birth, but the medical examination of her body alone did not allow them to determine the viability of her fetus.

Although the gestational age of the woman's pregnancy remained an issue, the judge pushed back against medical opinion most stridently on the issue of race. Summoning the doctors to the court once again, the judge pushed them to modify the infant's racial label so he could pursue charges against the accused woman. However, none of the physicians altered their conclusion that the infant was white. One of them actually offered further explanation, noting that the "frosty white color of the skin, the rounded shape of the head, [and] its straight hair" all indicated that the infant belonged to the white race. In addition, he noted that the use of common scissors to dissect the cranial bones, was only possible given the "thinness of those bones proper to the white race." Also confirming the infant's whiteness was the absence the "mancha jaba," a marking supposedly characteristic of "mestizos atrasados" (lit. backward mongrels; or mixed-race people with more pronounced African ancestry). The medical opinion that the infant was "seemingly white," allowed only for slight racial mixture, as would occur with a union between a white man and a very light-skinned mestiza woman. Such a mix might not immediately reveal the racial mixture in its physical characteristics.

The judge's line of questioning betrayed a powerful urge to prosecute despite expert medical opinion that the evidence contradicted the allegations. The judge even resurrected the idea, common during colonial times, that an infant's true race required time to manifest, to cast doubt on the deceased infant's true whiteness. First, he asked whether "all individuals of the Black or mixed races have the color to which it respectively belongs from the first moments after birth." Such a question implied skepticism about the medical report describing the infant as truly white. The infant's medically assigned race would need to be false in order for Juana to be the mother. Nor did physicians allow for substantial change in the infant's phenotype over time, arguing instead for the biological fixity of race. "Pure Black or dark mestizos," one physician explained, "have the coloration proper or characteristic to their race from the first moment they are born," and although the color may be "weakened or pale" at first, it "intensifies after the first 24 hours after birth."

The professional opinions of multiple physicians undermined the credibility of the criminal case. By early October, the judge asked once again for medical certification of the race of the infant. On receiving yet another confirmation of the infant's whiteness, the judge requested a consultation from the legal medicine committee. He forwarded the various physicians' reports, a photograph of the infant's body, and another photograph of the mother for their review. Responding on behalf of the committee, Coronado confirmed the opinion of the medical examiner, arguing that the accused woman's Blackness disqualified her as the mother of the white infant. He based his conclusion on the various "scientific" properties of different races as they manifested in newborn infants.

Appealing again to beliefs about the delayed manifestation of racial mixture, the judge asked if "science" had "any positive indicator to distinguish which race a fetus belongs to from the first hours of its birth." Coronado responded in the affirmative, noting that exposure to light and processes of putrefaction during the seventy-two hours elapsed between the infant's birth and the autopsy would have made the "coloration more pronounced" in "the Black and mestizo races." In addition, "the complete desiccation of the hair during the indicated time would have shown the frizziness corresponding to the product of a Black woman and a white man, or a white woman and a Black man."

The judge also requested clarification about the distinctions between racially pure and mixed-race individuals. He questioned if "all of the mentioned characteristics are necessarily exclusive to fetuses of the white race, to the point that determinations can be made beyond any doubt," or if "all or some of these characteristics occur in fetuses of other races." Coronado answered that "in the pure races, ethnographic clues distinguish one from the other," but these signs did not exist for the "light mixed races." The characteristics typical of the white race, he explained, were "always found in fetuses of the White race, sometimes in light mestizos, but never in Black of dark mestizo [fetuses]." He also observed that the thickness of the cranial bones of a fetus of the Black or mestizo race would have required a different instrument to cut them.

For Coronado, the photographs of the infant's cadaver confirmed his scientific determination of the infant's whiteness. Coronado explained that in marriages involving people who are "seemingly white but actually mulatos," their offspring "reveal the racial impurity of the parents," which the deceased infant in question had not. Citing the absence of the "Salto atnís," a physical marker supposedly indicative of racial mixture, he argued that "the fetus autopsied belongs indisputably to the white race, since any mark of the African race it could have is completely erased, thus being a mixture of the fourth or fifth degree." As a result, Coronado was able to "dismiss any possibility that [the fetus] could be the child of a white man mixed with a Black woman." He even concluded that "if there is any racial mixture, it would be so remote that it authorizes us to assure without fear of being wrong that it belongs to the pure white race." Therefore, he resolved, a "Black woman could not have given birth to the deceased infant in question," a conclusion that exonerated the accused woman.[17]

While Coronado's ultimate conclusion favored Juana's acquittal, the physicians couched their arguments not as a defense of her innocence, but rather as a demand for recognition and respect for physicians' scientific authority. Indeed, for the legal medicine committee, the consultation was more than a matter of simply rectifying the science undergirding a single case. It brought to the fore a much more significant set of challenges facing the medical profession. Addressing the rest of the committee, Coronado lamented the stubbornness of some judges, who insisted on pursuing cases against the expert knowledge of medical professionals. "So it seems, fellow academics," he wrote, "that the commission of crimes brings to the spirit of the judges in charge of administering justice the will to find, always and with unflinching precision, the authors." However, because infanticide provoked intense emotional and moral reactions, the judges "tend to transform presumptions and coincidences into the fundamental basis for tremendous accusation that, in not a small number of cases, culminate in the sentencing of innocent people." Citing a notable medical legal expert from Buenos Aires, Coronado blamed "the little faith (to not say the disdain) with which judges and magistrates handle the indications of the medical legal experts called to make statements." He argued that judges often treated these physicians "not as the experts they are, but rather as mere witnesses who are often denied the respect and consideration they so deserve." This failure to heed the conclusions of medical professionals caused "true judicial errors."

Defending the status and rigor of his profession, Coronado boasted of the rigorous training provided in the medical school, where he served as faculty. "In the name of the Academy ... and as a professor of Legal Medicine in our University," Coronado claimed that the "the body of forensic doctors in this Capital, has members sufficiently enlightened so that their reports serve as an excellent guide for the just administration of the law." Their declarations "adhere so perfectly in this case with scientific precepts and are in agreement with the opinion of the most recent treatises of Legal Medicine" that Coronado himself "would not hesitate to make them his own."[18]

The implication of Dr. Coronado's report was that the judge was clearly prosecuting the wrong woman, scapegoating a Black woman rather than confronting the uncomfortable reality that a white woman had likely committed infant abandonment if not outright infanticide. The epigraph on his report, which quoted a stanza of a poem, implored judges to "look for the baby killer in the upper echelons of society, and not in the lower ones." Among poor people, the epigraph continued, "maternal love surpasses the conventions of a poorly understood honor."[19] Coronado's reference to upper- and lower-class women was not merely a class distinction; it was a racial one. The case report in which the epigraph appeared confirmed this by arguing against prosecuting a Black woman for the death of a white baby, whom the judge assumed to be her child, against medical conclusions. This racial distinction aligned with early republican intersections of race and class—elite women would have been understood to be white, despite the existence of a Black elite, while poor women, usually cast as racially and morally inferior, included women of African descent as well as white women.[20]

Coronado invoked these distinctions at a critical time in Cuba's early republic. Just a year prior, U.S. marines had invaded the island in the wake of the so-called Guerrita de Agosto, a political uprising stemming from the fraudulent 1905 presidential elections. By the time Coronado formed his opinion about the infanticide case, the second U.S. military occupation was well under way, intensifying the stakes of proving Cuban civilization. Urging the courts to shift their approach toward infanticide, Coronado contradicted nearly a century of legal reform, which had gradually introduced protections and loopholes for white women suspected of fertility crimes. His call to the courts acknowledged a fundamental contradiction between the state's racialized management of fertility control and the perceived demographic needs of the nation. The fact that the vast majority of infanticide cases coming before the courts involved impoverished women, many of who were of African descent or mixed racial heritage, was symptomatic of a broader tendency to conflate criminality with poverty and racial Otherness. Yet, the vulnerability of poor women and especially women of color to police surveillance and investigation also meant that the state took the greatest action to deter infanticide among a population historically designated as undesirable for the nation. On the contrary, middle- and upper-class white women—the group who simultaneously held the greatest potential to birth the kinds of citizens Coronado and his peers believed Cuba truly needed and who faced the most intense social pressures to destroy the evidence of dishonorable sex—were precisely the women who evaded the legal consequences of their actions.

Managing Cuba's Early Republican Baby Boom

While Cuba emerged from the war of independence with fewer people, fertility recovered remarkably during the first years of the republic. Over the first decade of the twentieth century, Cuba's crude birth rate increased by nearly 15 points, from 32.8 in 1899 to 47.6 between 1905 and 1909.[21] However, physicians identified two key problems that they believed were souring the positive impact of this early republican baby boom. First, while birth rates did increase, infant mortality remained high, stalling population growth. Second, some doctors believed that the wrong kind of babies were being born during this period, ones whose alleged racial, physical, and moral impairments would burden the nation, rather than contributing to its modernization.

In a 1909 study on this issue, Rafael Fosalba proclaimed that "the future of Cuba, as a political and economic entity, depends principally on the growth of a healthy population."[22] While many public officials and policymakers of the time saw white immigration as the answer to the nation's population problem, a small but vocal group of physicians and other professionals argued that a larger and better quality population started with improving the conditions of people already living in Cuba.

For Cuba's medical community, the problem of infant mortality was at the very core of the young republic's demographic debacle. In line with Fosalba's declaration, many of the physicians who contributed to this burgeoning field of medical inquiry concurred that infant mortality constituted a major threat to the future of the republic. Infant mortality was a national problem because it deprived the nation of future citizens. Physician Enrique Barnet articulated this concern with growing the Cuban population when he declared that "the future of the fatherland" rested on preventing children's cadavers from filling the cemeteries.[23] According to Domingo F. Ramos, the large number of infants and children lost each year presented a particularly "serious problem for the fatherland," since, in his view, population growth through natural reproduction was preferable to immigration.[24]

While most physicians framed the significance of infant mortality in terms of its impact on population size, many of them also declared a need to improve the "quality" of the national population. "It is not enough for us to maintain [the national population]," declared Ramos; "We need to augment the quantity and improve the quality of our citizens."[25] Ramos argued that the "social ideal should consist not only of obtaining a large number of births, but a large number of healthy children equipped for life in the new environment."[26] When physicians invoked the idea of health, they usually implied a desire to reduce or eliminate disability—physical, psychological, and, above all, racial. Premature births, births to unhealthy parents, or pregnancies and births in otherwise adverse conditions, Ramos warned, threatened to produce sickly, degenerate, or disabled babies. These future citizens, in turn, were more prone to become burdens on the state, occupying space and consuming resources in the asylums and prisons.[27] Likewise, Mario Lebredo wrote of the need to obtain "good and useful stock" and reduce the number of "sick and useless lives" weighing down the nation. He argued that both hereditary disease and poor health negatively affected the "national race and morality."[28] Lebredo argued that the "cruel" laws of inheritance justified severe policies such as castration and genital sterilization to prevent idiocy, imbecility, and foolishness.

Some physicians evidently questioned whether the early republican baby boom was providing the kind of babies Cuba needed. Jorge Le-Roy y Cassá, for one, observed that the fertility surge did not occur evenly across the population. In a study of fertility by race, Le-Roy y Cassá found that birth rates remained higher among women of color, while the number of babies born to the island's native white population failed to keep pace. More than half of the women (55.56 percent) in his sample of 270 women who had only one child were white. By contrast, 68 percent of the women who had more than one child were either Black or mestiza. Twice as many white women (42) as Black women (21) were without children. The 106 Black women in his sample bore an average of 3.33 children, mestiza women averaged 2.6 children, and white women averaged just 2.2 children. Even births of multiple babies were more common among Black women than among white women. Four Black women gave birth to five sets of twins and two sets of triplets, for a total of sixteen babies, while three white women gave birth to five sets of twins (ten babies).[29]

While the fertility of women of different races had long been a preoccupation among Cuban elites, Le-Roy y Cassá suggested that white women's low fertility was entering a critical decline and claimed that white women previously bore many more children. Citing the anecdotes of two late colonial-era authors, Le-Roy y Cassá depicted a foregone era in which white women routinely had families of ten, even up to twenty-five, surviving children.[30] He alluded to declining marriage rates and a growing tendency to remain single as a potential cause of white women's waning fertility.[31] Overall marriage rates declined from 7.33 in 1899 to as low as 4.7 in 1915.[32] By the end of the first decade of the twentieth century, one-sixth of native-born Cuban white women lived in "concubinage."[33] While marriage rates among Cuba's population of color had historically remained low, by the dawn of the republic, white women were marrying less frequently, a tendency that coincided with delayed childbearing and decreased fertility.

Equally concerning was the significant numbers of infants who died in their first year. Between 1903 and 1907, 29.26 percent of all registered deaths in Cuba were babies under the age of one year. Close to half (41.54 percent) of the total registered deaths were children under five years of age.[34] Statistics from Havana suggested that infant mortality had grown worse since the final years of the colonial period. Official statistics recorded 5,213 infant deaths between 1888 and 1891, representing an average of 19.9 percent of total deaths. The figure rose to 20.52 percent between 1903 and 1907, despite innovations in hygiene and sanitation. Children between one and five years contributed an additional 9.83 percent of total deaths.[35]

Other physicians expressed concerns over disability and birth defects. Dr. Alfonso Betancourt published his study of "monstrous births" (which included severe birth defects) in 1899. It was also noteworthy that Betancourt attributed these birth defects to U.S. military intervention (1898), reviving the nineteenth-century belief that strong emotion could disrupt pregnancy and interfere with fetal development.[36] A later study by ophthalmologist Juan Santo Fernández suggested that simply cleaning an infant's eyes with silver nitrate or citric acid in the moments after birth could help reduce the blind population by one-third.[37]

These concerns over the size and quality of Cuba's early republican population offered fertile ground for eugenic ideas to take root through the emergent field of homiculture. Derived from the French "science of investigating and applying knowledge about reproduction, conservation, and betterment of the human species," homiculture resonated across Latin America. But it found special audience in countries perceived to be suffering from "underpopulation."[38] As scholarship shows, homiculture took firm root in Argentina, Brazil, Mexico, and elsewhere by the late 1910s and 1920s. Cuban physicians imported and customized it earlier than most.[39]

A relic of the deep French influence in Latin American obstetrics and gynecology, homiculture arrived to Cuba at a moment when Cuba's wars of independence interrupted medical training and displaced Cuban physicians. Many of early republican Cuba's leading physicians studied obstetrics in Paris under French eugenicist and obstetrician Adolphe Pinard.[40] One of those men, Eusebio Hernández, studied under Pinard in the 1890s before returning to the island to teach obstetrics until the outbreak of the war of independence, during which he participated in the New York–based Comité Revolucionario Cubano. Following his homecoming to U.S.-occupied Cuba in 1899, Hernández quickly distinguished himself as one of Cuba's leading obstetricians, eventually earning the title of "father of Cuban obstetrics." He not only served as professor of obstetrics at the University of Havana, he and philanthropist Rosalía Abreu also founded Havana's first dedicated birthing clinic. Hernández and his former student, Domingo F. Ramos, who also studied under Pinard, later emerged as Cuba's leading architects of homiculture, first through their roles in the Secretariat of Sanitation and Beneficence, and later through the establishment of the Infant Hygiene Service.[41]

Hernández and Ramos helped institutionalize homiculture in Cuba. The creation in January 1909 of a new governmental agency, the Secretariat of Sanitation and Beneficence, centralized disparate efforts to improve public health and assist the island's indigent populations—one of the world's first public health services. This new administrative entity vested elite physicians with formal authority over public policies governing a broad range of initiatives, from the research on and campaigns against disease to the administration of asylums and public hospitals. At the helm of the new agency were men who built their careers on studying and regulating women's bodies. Prior to assuming his position as the first secretary of Sanitation and Beneficence, Matías Duque Perdomo had researched pregnancy complications, venereal diseases, and leprosy, as well as serving as director of the Special Hygiene Service (a government entity overseeing prostitution). After his short tenure over the secretariat, Duque Perdomo published one of Cuba's most comprehensive studies of prostitution as well as a book on puericulture.[42] The third secretary, Enrique Núñez de Villavicencio Palomino, had studied gynecology under Gabriel Casuso Roque. Before the war of independence, he was honorary physician at the San Francisco de Paula Women's Hospital, assistant at the Faculty of Medicine's Obstetrics and Gynecology clinic, and assistant professor of obstetrics and gynecology at the Practical School of Medicine in Havana.

Although the Secretariat of Sanitation and Beneficence would tackle morbidity and mortality writ large, a small group of physicians working within the secretariat focused on the welfare of infants—and by extension their mothers. Ramos, recently appointed to the secretariat's research and studies section, and his former professor, Hernández (director of the secretariat's homiculture projects) developed and introduced plans to implement this emerging field.[43] At the core of their efforts was the desire to enhance Cuba's demographic profile, and with it the nation's economic and political destiny.[44]

Ramos outlined sixteen key interventions framed under the umbrella of a hygiene campaign. Most notable were a specialized national campaign against infant mortality, on par with efforts against yellow fever and tuberculosis; specialized medical services and facilities for gynecology, obstetrics, and pediatrics; special asylums for pregnant and breastfeeding women, infants, and children; milk inspection; a full homiculture curriculum; and standardized data collection on pregnancy, childbirth, and infancy outcomes.[45]

Ramos's 1910 study seems to have played a pivotal role in expanding the secretariat's focus from conventional campaigns against infectious diseases to a more comprehensive vision of public health that included maternity care and infant welfare. Duque Perdomo's successor, Manuel Varona Suárez, acknowledged Ramos's influence in his realization that homiculture constituted "a very powerful aid to Sanitation." He credited the physician with demonstrating the significance of "infant hygiene" and creating a compelling case for implementing Hernández's homiculture plan.[46]

In late 1910, Varona created a new entity under the secretariat called the Homiculture Department. He appointed Hernández as technical director and Ramos as chief. In those capacities, Ramos and Hernández developed plans for a new building dedicated to implementing homicultural interventions focusing on pregnant women and infants. Throwing his support behind the project, Varona recommended that the building be named the Pinard-Hernández Homiculture Palace. In March 1911, Varona petitioned President José Miguel Gómez, proposing an appropriation for the homiculture palace, as well as other aspects of Hernández's and Ramos's plan: the creation of a national homiculture service, a homiculture course at the School of Medicine, a position for assistant professor of homiculture, a national board of homiculture, and the elevation of the department to a bureau of its own.[47]

By 1913, Varona's successor, Núñez de Villavicencio Palomino created a new agency, the Infant Hygiene Service, tasked with reducing infant and fetal mortality. He appointed Ramos to lead it. For Núñez, the social policies and medical facilities Ramos advocated promised to address what he called one of the most important sanitary challenges facing Cuba: the physical and moral betterment of its children "so as to guarantee strong and vigorous future citizens."[48] Challenging Cuba's reliance on white immigration, Núñez advocated a focus on biological reproduction: "it is more convenient for the safety and well-being of the Republic ... to conserve sons who love it than to attract foreigners who serve it."[49] Conserving future citizens required improving the health of the single most significant contributor to the island's mortality statistics: children under age five.

According to decree 441, which authorized Núñez to establish the unit, the Infant Hygiene Service was responsible for the "life, health, and welfare of human beings from their procreation up to the legal age for work [fourteen years]." The specific areas of authority included supervising midwives; inspecting and educating poor women during pregnancy and the first two years of child-rearing; regulating and inspecting wet nurses; overseeing and inspecting children's welfare institutions, such as asylums and crèches; conducting medical inspections of schools; vaccinating schoolchildren; regulating and quality-controlling the milk supply; caring for sick children; creating sanatoriums for "consumptive" children; collecting statistics on infant mortality and morbidity; overseeing the physical education of children, and assisting poor mothers during the first year after birthing.[50]

Sanitation and hygiene projects contributed to major reductions in the number of infant deaths. In 1899, the infant mortality rate was 22.47 percent; by 1907, it had slightly declined to 21.3 percent.[51] Incremental improvements in total infant mortality owed to significant progress in specific areas, such as infant tetanus, and to a certain extent, enteritis. For instance, in the 1870s, annual infant deaths from tetanus averaged 344. The greatest improvement came after independence, when for the first time the number of deaths from infant tetanus dropped below 100 per year—first in 1899, then consistently since 1902. By 1918, the number had dropped to zero.[52]

Homiculture in Action

At the core of Cuban homiculture was the desire to enhance the island's demographic profile, and with it the economic and political destiny of the nation, through targeted interventions at every stage of reproduction.[53] Building on the work of his mentor Pinard, Hernández proposed a subfield for each of the six stages: *prógonocultura* (heredity), *patrimatricultura* (parents before conception), *matrifeticultura* (pregnant woman and her fetus), *matrinaticultura* (birth, breastfeeding and weaning), puericulture (childhood, ages two to fifteen), and *postgenitocultura* ("manhood").[54] This developmental approach to the population problem suggested a comprehensive package of social reforms aimed at perfecting human reproduction from the selection of genes to the moral development of the citizen.

Uniting all these subfields was the belief that medically supervising women's reproduction was necessary to ensure the procreation of infants desirable for the nation. Public health campaigns, which involved medical interventions, education, public assistance, and more, often appeared well intentioned, rationalized through humanitarian arguments. However, they also revealed a penchant for protecting white women's pregnancies while correcting and punishing the sexual and reproductive choices of poor women and women of color.

PRÓGONOCULTURA: RACIAL IMPROVEMENT THROUGH THE GENERATIONS

Prógonocultura, the subfield of homiculture dedicated to improving heredity, made explicit the racialized demographic aspirations that had long defined Cuban population politics. Nowhere was this clearer than in the National Maternity and Infancy Competitions of the early twentieth century. Founded in

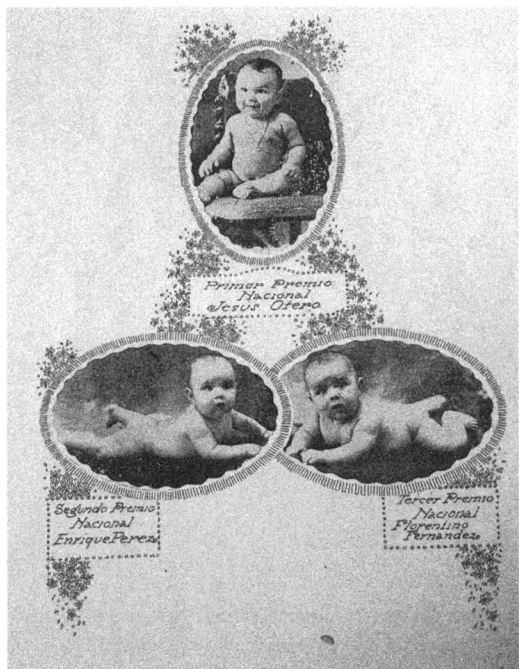

FIGURE 9.2. Prize-winning babies in the 1919 National Maternity and Infancy Competition. Secretaria de Sanidad y Beneficencia, *Servicio de Higiene Infantil: Concurso Nacional de Maternidad* (Havana, 1920), 30–31.

1914, the competition sought to integrate the ideals of hygiene and eugenics inside Cuban homes by incentivizing mothers to raise "strong, robust, and healthy children."[55] Each year, it offered monetary prizes in three categories deemed central to infant welfare and eugenic reproduction more generally: maternity and infancy, which celebrated the fittest babies and their mothers; homiculture, which included prizes for the cleanest houses and best personal hygiene; and eugenic reproduction, celebrating "strong and healthy family trees."[56] According to one administrator, the competitions held "exceptional importance for the future of the creole race," to find the "Cuban biotype and disseminate the norms of sanitation and hygiene."[57]

The 1919 competition lays bare the racial undertones of the Infant Hygiene Service's view of maternity, infancy, and reproduction. All the prize-winning babies were white or white-passing (fig. 9.2). White families also dominated the other prize categories. First prize in the category of poor families "who with less economic resources have their children inscribed and in school, and appear in the best health, upbringing, and hygienic education" went to a white couple with seven children aged between twelve years and nine months. Second prize went to another white couple with ten children, third to a mestizo couple with eleven children, and fourth to a white woman and mestizo man with nine children.[58]

FIGURE 9.3. This mestizo family with fifteen children captured first prize in the 1919 fertility award. Secretaria de Sanidad y Beneficencia, *Servicio de Higiene Infantil: Concurso Nacional de Maternidad* (Havana, 1920), 32–33.

First prize in the fertility awards went to a mestizo family with fifteen children aged between twenty-two years and three months (fig. 9.3). Second prize went to a white widow with eight children, and third to a mestizo couple with ten children, including one set of twins.[59]

The absence of Black families among the awardees for fertility suggests a preference for high fertility among white or white-adjacent families. The presence of mixed-race families among the awardees nods toward ideas about "racial improvement" through selective marriage and procreation. A photograph of the first prizewinners in the fertility category seemingly celebrates generational whitening by showing the predominantly white-adjacent mestizo offspring of a union between a Chinese-descended husband and an African-descended wife. The inclusion in the portrait of an older Black man, likely the maternal grandfather, further accentuates the supposed racial improvement (fig. 9.3). Only families with children within the bounds of legitimate marriage won awards, reinforcing an emerging medical belief that illegitimacy contributed to infant mortality.[60]

In disturbing ways, these contests echoed the incentives some slave owners offered their enslaved women for reproducing in the ways they desired. But it also underscored in more explicitly racial terms the trajectory elite physicians envisioned for the Cuban population. The contests encouraged racially selective patterns of procreation to influence the hereditary trajectory of the Cuban population. They celebrated white mothers and their white babies for producing exactly the kinds of citizens perceived to benefit the nation. They also rewarded families that demonstrated generational progress toward whiteness. In this vein, homiculture lent legitimacy and scientific authority to long-standing demographic desires for whitening.

PATRIMATRICULTURA:
THE FIGHT AGAINST CONGENITAL SYPHILIS

Adverse pregnancy outcomes often resulted from conditions afflicting the pregnant woman, such as disease, malnutrition, lack of resources, and inadequate rest. Thus a second point of homicultural intervention revolved around the parents' health and condition prior to conception, concerns that informed the field of patrimatricultura. A cogent example of this is the campaign to curtail congenital syphilis. Women who became infected with this venereal disease by a sexual partner prior to or during pregnancy, then transmitted it to the fetus in utero, often causing miscarriage, stillbirth, premature birth, or neonatal death. Physicians attempted to curtail syphilis-related infant mortality, in part, through an inchoate sexual education campaign, which outlined the dangers of venereal disease.[61] Since promiscuous and unfaithful husbands, including ones who had sex with prostitutes, were a common cause of women's infection, the campaign focused on teaching adolescent boys to avoid "risky" sexual partners. Although the campaign focused on educating boys, it blamed women as the root cause of congenital syphilis, instructing boys to avoid this source of contagion.

Other interventions involved medical examination to detect the disease prior to marriage and conception. Some physicians proposed requiring premarital health certificates to prevent the legitimate procreation of individuals plagued by transmissible diseases like syphilis and other physical and psychological afflictions.[62] More draconian proposals sought to curtail procreation among certain less-desirable and diseased populations through sterilization.[63] Efforts like these to prevent congenital syphilis marked a growing interest among physicians in addressing the nation's demographic future through interventions in the reproductive-aged population.

MATRIFETICULTURA:
SUPPRESSING CRIMINAL ABORTIONS

In addition to ensuring the conception of desirable pregnancies, homiculturalists concerned themselves with the state of pregnant women and their fetuses. Matrifeticultura sought to usher healthy pregnancies toward live births. Part of this agenda involved preventing premature termination. Physicians believed that criminal abortion represented a significant threat to the birth of live infants in Cuba.

To address this threat, Ramos proposed the complete protection of the child and mother. The main intervention he proposed involved legal and institutional reforms to protect pregnant women's right to hide unwanted pregnancies and to give birth in secret. He advocated restoring this function at the Casa de Beneficencia y Maternidad. He also implored Cuban lawmakers to adopt laws guaranteeing the secrecy and impunity of motherhood, "a right that civilization has conceded to the modern woman as a guarantee for infant life." According to Ramos, "only when all this is a reality will Cuban society be able to bid farewell to criminal abortion."[64] Those protections, were slow to materialize and largely limited to white families (see also chapter 10).

Although Ramos framed the campaign against criminal abortion as defending women's right to motherhood, the logic of the intervention politicized pregnancy by casting the fetus as a future citizen, whose fate and rights appeared to be more important than the mother's. Indeed, Ramos declared that abortion was the single largest cause of infant mortality in Cuba. His unconventional claim relied on a broad definition of infancy that also encompassed fetuses in utero. With that foundation, infant mortality encompassed not only accidental death through illness, injury, or natural causes, but also a broad array of fertility control practices, from contraceptive technologies to infanticide and abortion. Another prominent physician agreed, declaring that induced abortion and the murder in the act of childbirth "have increased to the extent that it is necessary to take them into question as a cause of infant mortality."[65] By conflating a fetus in utero with an infant and future citizen, homiculturalists rationalized a wide range of interventions on women's reproductive choices, restrictions that remained for decades.

MATRINATICULTURA:
PREVENTING ENTERITIS

As the campaign against criminal abortion suggests, homiculturalists took special interest in the mother's postpartum condition and conduct, a decisive factor in the infant's overall health and survival. This concern over the relationship between the mother and her newborn informed matrinatricultural interventions, such as the campaign to reduce enteritis. Infant mortality statistics revealed that this gastrointestinal condition, understood to result from improper nutrition in infants, accounted for the highest number of infant deaths in early republican Cuba. At the time, enteritis claimed as many children under age two as individuals of all ages who died of tuberculosis.[66] Physicians blamed mothers' tendency to give their babies "artificial nutrition," by which they meant foods or drinks other than breastmilk. One of the most common sources of infant nutrition was cow's milk, which in early republican Cuba was notoriously dangerous, because it was frequently adulterated or contaminated with harmful bacteria. Physicians also suspected that women commonly gave their infants solid foods prematurely, causing major problems with digestion.

While many doctors chastised poor and working-class women for their "ignorance," in reality many less privileged women were unable to breastfeed their infants because their economic situations forced them into employment outside the home. Economic need caused by low wages, high unemployment rates, and single motherhood also forced many pregnant women to work outside the home through the entirety of their pregnancies.[67] Working women often had to rush back to work shortly after giving birth to avoid termination. As a result, these working mothers were unable to breastfeed or otherwise attend to their children. Physician Enrique B. Barnet conjured a scene of "children, on death's doorstep, without parents to feed them, with deserted mothers who cannot provide the necessary care."[68] This circumstance forced them to rely on cow's milk and solid food to keep their babies alive while they worked.[69] According to one physician, an infant was more than twice as likely to die if its mother gave cow's milk instead of breastmilk. Among working-class women in certain industries, up to half of their infants died, with the highest rate occurring among the most impoverished families.[70]

Much of the campaign to address enteritis focused on encouraging breastfeeding. Targeting working-class women, physicians proposed policies to promote breastfeeding through education and advertisements about its benefits, establishing institutions and medical intervention for breastfeeding mothers, and providing monetary incentives. In practice, medicalizing breastfeeding had clear racial implications. It introduced an emerging sector of medical practitioners into the arena of infant care: nurses. Working under the supervision of white male physicians and often within medical institutions, these formally trained women, most of whom were white, intervened into the child-rearing practices of more impoverished women, many of whom were of African descent (fig. 9.4).

While breastfeeding initiatives specifically targeted working-class women, physicians believed that wealthy white women also failed to breastfeed their infants, albeit for different reasons, such as vanity.[71] The perceived unwillingness of privileged white women to sacrifice their beauty and lifestyle to nourish their infant had historically driven a high demand for wet nurses. But state regulation of wet nurses had been limited to charitable institutions, such as the foundling asylum. Physicians sought to extend some of these moral and health criteria by creating a registry for wet nurses, who had to undergo physical examination by a physician to obtain permission to work in this capacity.

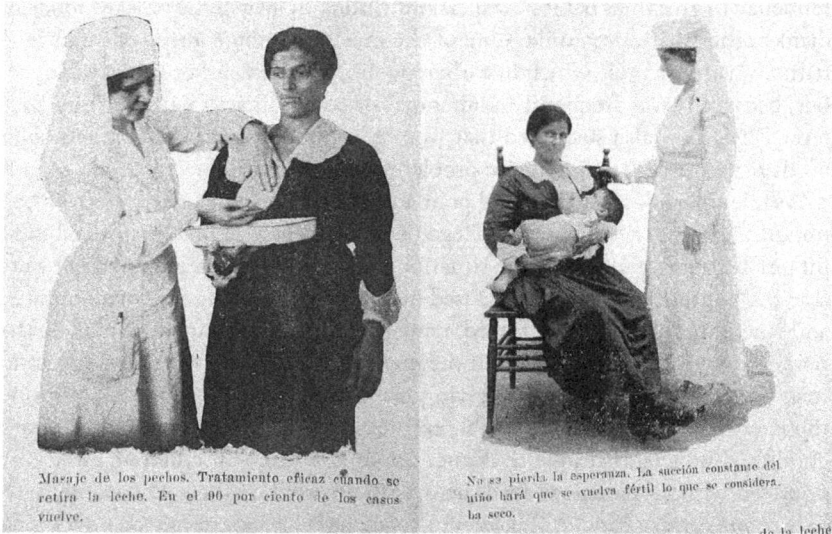

FIGURE 9.4. Medicalizing breastfeeding had racial implications. Secretaria de Sanidad y Beneficencia, *Servicio de Higiene Infantil: Concurso Nacional de Maternidad* (Havana, 1920), 15.

Working with the local health office in Havana, the Infant Hygiene Section assigned physicians as medical inspectors in each of Havana's districts. These physicians were "charged with and held personally responsible for" supervising pregnant women, infants, midwives, and wet nurses. For instance, medical inspectors were ordered to maintain a wet nurse registry, for reference by families requiring those services. To be registered, women had to obtain a health certificate describing their physical condition as well as the details of their last birth, including the place of birth, the midwife or physician who attended it, and the outcome of the infant. Medical inspectors also had the authority to collect samples of their breastmilk and to disqualify them or report them to the courts for perceived misconduct. This regulation of wet nurses mirrored historic attempts to control midwives, which also continued under the Infant Hygiene Section, through the creation of a census of midwives. Using this list as a reference, medical inspectors were responsible for supervising midwives' professional activities, advertising municipal midwives at tenements, and most importantly reporting "unauthorized or unqualified" practitioners to the courts when they intervened in childbirth, and informing the municipal midwife service of any misstep, inattention, or lack of skill exhibited by midwives. These interventions specifically aimed at protecting infants born to white women privileged enough to afford wet nurses and licensed midwives.

A parallel intervention involved the government regulation of cow's milk, the main source of artificial nutrition for babies. The Infant Hygiene Section assigned medical inspectors to scrutinize the quality of the food supply in their district, including milk.[72] Pasteurizing and inspecting cow's milk for quality and purity had the potential to reduce enteritis-related deaths with minimal imposition on the general population.[73] Such a reform extended the role of the nascent republican state as a patriarchal protector of Cuban infancy.

These reforms revealed an emerging consensus among Cuban physicians citing poverty and "ignorance" as the key indirect causes of the republic's exorbitant infant mortality rates, which usually stemmed from often-preventable afflictions.[74] Most especially, physicians blamed poor and working-class women—often women of African descent—for infant death. Whether impoverished working mothers or wet nurses serving elite families, these women allegedly failed to grasp the basic tenets of modern hygiene necessary to ensure a healthy pregnancy, birth, and baby. Thus many of the public health reforms they proposed involved the education, regulation, and supervision of these poor women's reproductive labor.

Medical inspectors also oversaw the health of pregnant women and children in their district. These physicians were to visit the homes of pregnant women every ten days to instruct on pregnancy and infant hygiene, as well as offer two hours of free consultations each for pregnant women and sick children. They were to maintain records on such populations, especially monitoring and rectifying the housing and hygienic conditions of poor mothers as well as the public and private institutions for children.[75] To advance these projects, the Infant Hygiene Section also formed a committee of citizens called the Association for the Protection of Infancy, whose responsibilities included fund-raising and local organizing. Members included prominent physicians as well as elite women. Subcommittees in New Havana, Vedado, and Cerro each established local crèches under the supervision of physicians and advised women's groups.[76]

Like the campaigns to address congenital syphilis, criminal abortion, and enteritis, many of the other proposals physicians constructed to improve the "quality" of Cuba's babies included hygienic education and protective measures for mothers and infants, in addition to expanding medical facilities.[77] Physicians commonly recommended that new institutions and laws protect mothers and children. Foundling asylums, breastfeeding consultancies, children's hospitals, leagues against infant mortality, aid to indigent mothers, maternity wards, and other measures to protect working mothers all surfaced as potential state solutions to infant mortality. Further legal protections for children could help combat "the odious effect of child neglect" and provide the "materially neglected child a safer existence under the protection of the State."[78] This was precisely the rationale undergirding the long struggle to support working mothers with childcare.

PUERICULTURA: CHILDCARE FOR WORKING MOTHERS

While interventions in pregnancy and breastfeeding emerged relatively quickly, puericultural reforms—those aimed at supporting children from age two to fifteen—were slower and more challenging. The long and frustrated struggle for access to childcare illustrates an important gap in homiculture's pronatalist policies. It also exposes a greater willingness on the part of physicians, and the state more generally, to intervene directly on women's bodies than to provide the support that they needed to raise their children on their own terms.

At the dawn of the republic, growing numbers of impoverished women were pushed into the formal workforce, forcing them to choose between earning their own meager living and raising their children. A letter from the director of the Casa de Maternidad y Beneficencia reveals that a significant number of these women confronted this impossible situation by surrendering "an infinite number of children" to that institution. The director claimed that 20 to 25 percent of the babies surrendered to the Casa had mothers who had previously appealed to authorities for childcare assistance. Poor women, forced to seek employment beyond their homes, had increasingly petitioned to admit their young children temporarily to the Casa de Maternidad while they worked or sought financial security.[79]

The director's observation pointed to the growing presence of women in formal employment in the early twentieth century. According to the 1899 census, 66,356 women (8.8 percent of the female population) were gainfully employed. That number increased to 73,520 in 1907. Though more women entered formal employment, the proportion of female wage earners relative to the total female population declined slightly to 7.5 percent due to the growing number of children. Roughly 70 percent of working women were engaged in some form of personal or domestic service, though a growing number took jobs in manufacturing. The proportion of female wage earners was significantly higher in urban areas (cities over 25,000), and highest (16.8 percent) in Havana.[80] Women entered the workforce in greater numbers due to increased economic need and shifting family structures, especially as large numbers of women were widowed in the war (51.2 for every 100 married women in 1899).[81] Marriage rates hovered between 7 and 8 percent between 1899 and 1904 before beginning a steady decline through 1915, when the rate was just 4.7 percent. The number of registered births roughly doubled between 1899 and 1919. However, the crude birth rate (number of births per thousand) increased only marginally in that period, from just over twenty-six at the dawn of the twentieth century to thirty in 1919, with a notable increase in the first years of the republic and a marked decline during World War I.[82]

Without maternity protections or childcare, working mothers with young children had few options. According to the director, these "mothers often have to leave their little one alone in their houses" or otherwise turn them over to the "mercenary hands" of a poorly paid babysitter while they work to earn their subsistence. Such practices subject the children to "all kinds of illnesses and vices rooted in a lack of supervision," at worst making them "dangerous" and at best "useless to Progress and the Nation." By refusing impoverished families childcare services, the director implied, the state was contributing to Cuba's population problem. In the most desperate cases, impoverished women resorted to one of the only state institutions dedicated to the care of infants: the Casa de Maternidad. But the institutional mission of the Casa did not align with the needs of these working mothers, who were unwilling to relinquish their custody rights.[83]

Moreover, the institution was historically overburdened and underfunded, resulting in abysmal outcomes for the babies in its care. Since at least the late colonial period, impoverished and working mothers periodically appealed to the institution to care temporarily for their children, either during the workday or for longer periods of financial hardship.[84] During the war of independence, a surge in the number of babies and children sent to the institution by the city council exacerbated the Casa's dire financial situation, negatively affecting the infants under its care.[85] At least half as many infants died as entered the Casa for most years in the decades leading up to the establishment of the republic. Some years (e.g., 1894, 1896, and 1898), the number of fatalities approached the number of infants admitted.[86] The military-ordered relocations and reductions in the institution's service during the war of independence likely contributed to exorbitant mortality rates in the latter two years.[87]

Although the Casa briefly received support from the city government during the U.S. military occupation (1899–1902), funding again declined with the inauguration of the republic, exacerbating the historic challenges the institution had faced (see chapters 2, 4, and 7). Institutional authorities began to protest the ongoing tendency of local government to send minors to the Casa during the U.S. military intervention and early republic, revealing a tension between the historic mission of the institution and the demands of a new era.[88] By the turn of the twentieth century, the institution predominantly served white families, with poverty-induced surrenders vastly outnumbering honor-related ones.

To alleviate some of these pressures, the director of the Casa proposed establishing a crèche. This new institution would be dedicated to "the daily care of poor children up to two years old."[89] This way, the burden on the Casa would be relieved, and childcare would be funded directly through a public institution designed for that purpose.[90] The crèche would care for the babies of working mothers, who could drop them off in the morning before work and pick them up in the evening after their shift. The director suggested placing such institutions in the island's industrial centers to provide childcare to the growing number of women working in manufacturing.

The crèche promised immeasurable benefits to the nation by expanding the available labor force and improving the moral and civic quality of future citizens.[91] For poor families, the crèche offered a suitable substitute for "irreplaceable maternal warmth." In this way, it would help "form an enlightened generation, removed from grotesque habits and phrases" they pick up from their surroundings at a young age, while the "good hygiene and nutrition will provide them with strength for the future." Moreover, the crèche would ameliorate the constant pressure on working women to care for and feed their children during the workday, thereby providing industry with more "workers disposed to work." In the long term, the Casa director speculated that government-sponsored childcare could actually decrease the burden on the treasury by providing parents an alternative to abandoning their children, which in turn would reduce the number of expósitos surrendered to the Casa. He even proposed a system of government-issued tickets identifying eligible parents and children to prevent "mendicancy and slacking by parents" and other abuses of public charity.[92]

Havana Mayor Juan R. O'Farrill responded to the petition favorably but noted that the city lacked the resources to reach all of Havana's impoverished residents. However, by placing the institution near the city limits, it could benefit "no small number of families that live crowded in the neighborhoods" bordering its projected site. Once the advantages of the service became apparent, they could consider placing subsidiaries in each of the city's poorer districts. These crèches were to be known as Consejos a las Madres de Familia.[93]

Despite the initial enthusiasm for a crèche, working families would have to wait another decade for Havana's first public childcare facility. In the meantime, unwanted infants continued arriving in ever-greater numbers to the Casa de Maternidad. During the first decade of the twentieth century, the number admitted to the Casa de Maternidad nearly tripled, but those of African descent fluctuated in the same range. The proportion of infants of African descent decreased over the first two decades of the twentieth century, suggesting that the institution still primarily served white infants (table 9.1). Correspondence by Casa administrators reveals that far greater numbers of unwanted infants were turned away due to lack of space and resources.[94]

A 1926 proposal to relocate the torno to a less conspicuous place suggests a strong police presence in the immediate vicinity of the Casa de Maternidad, which may have served as a deterrent or obstacle for certain populations to access it. Institutional leaders recognized that police, "ignorant of their mission," often interrogated and apprehended individuals attempting to surrender infants through the torno, despite late eighteenth-century laws prohibiting such interventions.[95] Police harassment would have certainly made infant surrender more difficult for women of African descent, who already shouldered the burden of

TABLE 9.1. Expósitos admitted to Casa maternity department by race, 1900–1922

	Total Admitted	Negro	Pardo	Mestizo	Total of Color	Proportion of Color to White	Died
1900	18	2	—	2	4	22.2	11
1901	24	1	1	1	3	12.5	16
1902	16	—	—	6*	6	37.5	9
1903	24	2	—	2	2	8.3	11
1904	29	3	—	5	8	27.6	14
1905	43†	2	1	—	3	7.0	21
1906	44‡	1	—	7	8	18.2	23
1907	46	—	—	6	6	13.0	15
1908	56	3	—	4	7	12.5	25
1909	47	1	—	4	5	10.6	21
1910	46	3	—	6	9	19.6	19
1911	60	—	—	8	8	13.3	29
1912	45	—	—	6*	6	13.3	22
1913	44	1	—	5	6	13.6	15
1914	49	2	—	2	4	8.2	33
1915	43	2	—	4	6	14.0	28
1916	34	1	—	3	4	11.8	21
1917	43	1	—	3	3	7.0	31
1918	45	1	—	6	7	15.6	31
1919	24	—	—	1	1	4.2	11
1920	41	—	—	1	1	2.4	15
1921	32	—	—	4	4	12.5	27
1922	52	4	—	2	6	11.5	31

SOURCE: Libro matriz general de la casa, books 2 (1886–1917) and 3 (1917–23), Fondo Casa de Beneficencia.
* One infant initially classified as mestizo was later reclassified as white. The "misclassification" in 1902 was reportedly "due to an illness that altered its color."
† Includes 3 "null" entries
‡ Includes 1 "null" entry

scrutiny and criminalization of their reproductive decisions. The torno was not relocated, possibly explaining, in part, the persistently low numbers of Black infants admitted to the Casa de Maternidad (table 9.1).

In the 1910s and 1920s, public and private investment significantly expanded the social safety net through key institutional and legal protections for mothers and children. While the Casa de Beneficencia y Maternidad remained the only public institution devoted to caring for abandoned infants, numerous other public and private institutions dedicated to the care of other groups of vulnerable children had emerged across the island by the 1920s. These included asylums for orphaned, impoverished, or vulnerable children, as well as correctional and preventative institutions for children deemed problematic.[96] The state also provided funding to public establishments across the island, supplementing private donations.[97] In addition, a foster care system operated with limited scope by the 1920s, although poor families remained suspicious of that system, because of a tendency to exploit the children.[98] Other institutions catered to pregnant women and infants. The Instituto de Homicultura Nena Machado in Matanzas, for instance, provided prenatal and postnatal care.

The most significant institutional developments occurred around crèches. Whereas Havana had not one crèche at the dawn of the republic, three privately run crèches had been established there by 1911. That number had grown significantly by the following decade. In the 1920s, the municipalities of Havana and Jesús del Monte had public municipal crèches. Additionally, the Secretaria de Sanidad sustained the Crèche Findlay, which initially served one hundred children, aged six months to six years before its expansion. Private crèches served babies in Marianao, Vedado, Cerro, and Barrio del Pilar. Crèches also cropped up in Santa Clara (Crèche General Machado); Reparto Lutgardita (Berta Machado); and Santiago de las Vegas (Crèche Antonio Maceo).

Elite women were at the forefront of the movement to organize and fund crèches.[99] In their advocacy for crèches and other protections for working-class women, these privileged women extended their moral and maternal authority into the public sphere, some even serving on national boards and commissions, like the National Commission for the Protection of Maternity and Infancy. Proponents argued that crèches educated and disciplined children "forgotten by fortune." Crèches allowed some working mothers to leave their young children in safety, but elite women argued that every tenement neighborhood should have a crèche to rescue *all* the children living in what these women saw as "schools of vice, immorality, and bad habits." Elite-supervised childcare facilities like these promised to moralize impoverished children, providing enlightened discipline. Instead of "hearing bad words and witnessing immoral scenes, they are regenerated physically and morally, so they can present themselves at the Asylums and Schools after getting out with their habits corrected."[100] By framing crèches as institutions capable of redeeming the offspring of impoverished families, these women carved out a central role for themselves in the betterment of the Cuban population.

Yet, even given public and private childcare facilities, infant abandonment remained a pervasive problem, suggesting that available facilities were insufficient or served particular populations over others. By 1917, the Casa de Maternidad's new bylaws explicitly recognized "children of impoverished parents unable to work," as well as abandoned infants (expósitos), poor orphans, and abandoned children without relatives legally obligated to care for them, as populations entitled to admission. Impoverished infants and orphans were eligible to receive breastfeeding through the institution, alongside babies whose parents paid for the service.[101] Such an extension in the eligible populations hinted at the unmet needs of impoverished families—caught between inadequate institutional support and moralistic prohibitions against family planning.

At the dawn of the twentieth century, elite desires to project the nascent republic as both civilized and modern manifested in acute anxieties over the size and quality of the national population. Fusing their patriarchal roles as protectors of and providers for women and children with their political roles as stewards of the nation, elite white male policymakers and physicians implemented a range of interventions in women's reproductive lives aimed at shaping demographic and health outcomes. Women's access to family planning was restricted in order to increase the birth rate, while expanded institutional and state support for impoverished mothers and babies sought to mitigate infant morbidity and mortality. Throughout the early republic, public health authorities celebrated mothers and families who conformed to their prevailing elite ideas of progress and civilization, promoting high fertility and whitening.

In trying to manage the number and kind of babies born on Cuban soil, physicians intervened in the most intimate reproductive decisions of women's lives. All these interventions implied expanded state surveillance and control over all aspects of reproduction, from conception to child-rearing. These interventions amounted to nothing less than a project of internal imperialism, as Cuba's educated white elites sought to "civilize" the reproductive practices of subordinated groups and rear the nation's unwanted children, all in service of the state.

Nancy Leys Stepan argues that homiculture introduced eugenics into Latin American population policies by way of obstetrics and infant welfare campaigns.[102] However, the vision of homiculture that Hernández sketched and the policies implemented following its institutionalization evinced remarkable continuity with colonial approaches to reproduction. The idea of deploying institutional support and medical interventions to manage women's pregnancies, births, and mothering was in fact older than the colony itself. Homiculture, however, provided the vocabulary and framework to rationalize expanded medicalization of pregnancy, childbirth, and motherhood. Indeed, Cuban obstetricians appropriated these tools to advance their own professional status, consolidate their roles overseeing women's reproduction, and cast themselves as protectors of the national population. Amid rigid limitations on access to contraception and persisting inadequacies in public support for mothers and infants, though, many women found themselves in the difficult situation of having to terminate their pregnancies.

CHAPTER TEN

Abortion in Law and Medicine
Racial Assumptions and Continuities from Republic to Revolution

In 1913, Dr. Tomás V. Coronado delivered a shocking speech on "a subject of great social transcendence" before his colleagues at the Academy of Sciences. Coronado was referring to an explosion of criminal abortions in Havana. He claimed that there were a "considerable number of young people who go to the hospitals and the medical professors' consults to get treated for genital hemorrhages, whose origin is certainly not unrelated to the probes [*sondas*] introduced into their uterine cavity for abortive purposes." His description of the genital trauma and hemorrhaging these young women suffered evinced a growing concern over surgical abortions, which usually involved the intervention of a physician or midwife.[1]

While Coronado's declarations startled many scientists in the audience, abortion for many of Cuba's leading obstetricians was not just a taboo medical procedure. Amid broader anxieties about the size and quality of the nation's population (chapter 9), Cuba's leading early republican physicians considered abortion, alongside neonatal tetanus and enteritis, as a major threat to the nation's infants. Fellow physician Le-Roy y Cassá classified termination of pregnancy as a crime against the nation.[2] He noted that "the considerable increase in the number of criminal abortions" threatened to "depopulate" Cuba. Citing the high number of criminal abortions performed in Paris and New York as a cautionary tale, he warned that the same pattern was unfurling in Cuba.[3] Dr. Eusebio Hernández estimated that Cuban women terminated approximately 25,000 pregnancies between 1903 and 1907. According to this estimate, the number of abortions exceeded the number of stillbirths (21,223) reported nationally between those years, and approached half of the number of children who succumbed to malnutrition (58,394) during the same period.[4]

Yet, physicians were not concerned just with the impact abortions had on the birth rate. Medical and legal discussions of abortion in the first half of the twentieth century reveal an implicit preoccupation with the kinds of women who were obtaining the procedure, namely that the typical abortion patient was a white woman of some means. The pathologization of abortion as a public health crisis and threat to the nation hinged on a host of racialized assumptions about how the termination of those women's pregnancies shaped Cuba's demographic future. In essence, the antiabortionism that emerged among Cuba's leading physicians relied on a racial logic that the procedure deprived the nation of the future white citizens it so desperately needed.

Cuban physicians were not alone in framing abortion as a medical and public health dilemma. The timing and tenor of Coronado's remarks was almost identical to similar speeches by physicians in other Latin American countries, including Brazil and Peru.[5] As Cassia Roth observes, the abortion debate was a "proxy for a larger discussion about the role of the physician" in society.[6] Certainly, Cuba's leading obstetricians negotiated their professional status through their public postures on abortion, as they did through interventions in contraceptive access and maternal and infant welfare reforms (chapter 9). But abortion debates in Cuba also reflected competing visions over the role of women and people of African descent in a country that had long struggled to define itself as both masculine and white.

Medical and legal debates about abortion periodically surged during the first two-thirds of the twentieth century, capturing national attention in moments of acute political crisis and social transformation. As Cuba emerged from its third U.S. military intervention following the "race war" of 1912, Cuban physicians sounded the alarm over what they believed to be an epidemic of criminal abortions, left unpunished. Under the 1870 penal code, implemented in Cuba in 1879 and still in effect during the early republic, prosecution of criminal abortion was rare. As technologies for pregnancy termination improved and became more widespread, physicians demanded greater legal accountability for criminal abortion as part of a broader pronatalist project aimed at protecting the fertility of white women on behalf of the nation.

More reformist approaches toward abortion surfaced in the 1930s, as Cuban women gained the vote, and ushered into public office the country's first female representatives in 1936.[7] The inclusion of a lone woman lawmaker on the committee charged with drafting the abortion law for Cuba's 1936 Social Defense Code, helped draw attention to the mounting pressures on poor and working families due to the economic crisis, which had catalyzed a wave of infant abandonment and abortion. In response, lawmakers drafted the most liberal abortion law in Cuban history, despite the omission of the proposed poverty exemption. Although the new abortion law afforded reduced sentences and expanded exemptions from criminal conviction, prosecution of criminal abortion actually expanded under the Social Defense Code.

Engendering a period of tremendous social and political upheaval, the Cuban Revolution promised to bring justice to workers, peasants, women, and people of African descent—precisely the intersection of populations that had long suffered the gravest reproductive injustices. Yet, with the prerevolutionary legal regime remaining intact through the early years of the revolution, doctors, police, and judges continued to investigate women's reproductive lives. As reforms like the literacy campaign and declarations against racism and sexism threatened to destabilize long-standing social hierarchies, elite men grasped at fertility and motherhood as sources of constancy as they clung to an idealized traditional family. Moreover, internal strife, foreign invasion, and threat of nuclear holocaust accentuated the need for Cuban women to continue birthing new revolutionary citizens. It was not until the worst political and social upheaval had subsided, following the 1961 Bay of Pigs Invasion and the 1962 Cuban Missile Crisis, that shifting mores crystalized an interpretive change to the letter of the law. By 1965, Cuba essentially decriminalized abortions through an expanded definition of women's health.

Juxtaposing these three moments underscores the incredible continuities in women's reproductive experiences over the first two-thirds of the twentieth century, even as political, economic, and social conditions evolved dramatically. Throughout all three of these periods, the women most likely to become ensnared in the criminal courts for abortion were precisely those whose precarious economic situations forced them to seek cheaper unlicensed practitioners or to attempt abortion themselves. These women, many of whom were of African descent, often came to the attention of police because of the complications they experienced, while privileged white women continued to enjoy broad access to professional surgical abortion with impunity. Such punitive approaches to the reproductive lives of Cuba's most vulnerable women shows remarkable continuity with nineteenth-century infanticide investigations and court cases.

A "Truly Scandalous" Number of Abortions

In early republican Cuba, pregnant women obtained abortions by various means, but the options available to them depended largely on their class and geographic location. More impoverished women tended to ingest substances understood to have abortifacient properties. Women with access to midwives had more options, including the injection of caustic fluids into the vagina, and the insertion of a hard instrument to mechanically dilate the cervix. Both types of abortions carried significant risks to the woman's health, and complications, such as hemorrhaging and infection, were evidently quite common. More privileged (white) women in urban areas had access to physicians, who could perform surgical abortions, generally dilation and curettage. With advances in medical technologies and the gradual development of obstetrics training in Havana's medical schools, surgical abortion became safer and more widely available, quickly gaining in popularity among women who could afford it.

These women were precisely the ones whose reproductive capabilities were perceived to yield the greatest benefit to the nation. The conflation of abortion with the loss of white infants often translated to a concern about honor-induced abortions. In a speech ominously titled "Criminal Abortions in Cuba," Dr. Domingo F. Ramos argued that abortion primarily stemmed from women's preoccupations about honor, historically an exclusively white domain.[8] He implied that the "defects and backwardness" stemming from colonial constructs such as honor compelled Cuba's most reproductively desirable women to have abortions, because white women continued to face tremendous social pressures to have children only within the bounds of marriage. Nevertheless, with "changing customs," extramarital and premarital sex became more common, or at least more visible, in Cuban society, even as the prevailing expectation of women's sexual chastity remained firmly entrenched.

According to Ramos, the conflict between women's lived realities and the ongoing social pressures to conform to antiquated gender expectations "compelled" a growing number of abortions, as women attempted to sustain their public honor. He encapsulated this race- and class-specific tension in his revised definition of criminal abortion. Criminal abortion was not just a miscarriage "provoked without a therapeutic indication," according to Ramos. It was an operation that the patient or a member of her entourage "decides to undergo," one in which "the life of a fetus or embryo is sacrificed to resolve a social or moral problem for the patient, who seems to have no other solution without causing greater harm."[9] This framing of abortion as a means to mitigate the social or moral consequences of sexual indiscretions exposes the core assumption underlying much of early republican antiabortion sentiment: that honorable white women saddled with out-of-wedlock pregnancy were the principle clients of the procedure.

Initially, concerns over the loss of future white citizens led concerned physicians to blame members of their own profession for contributing to the so-called abortion crisis. The prevalence of physician-assisted abortion revealed sharp divisions in Cuba's medical community about the procedure. Ramos explained that physicians in early republican Cuba held a wide range of attitudes about abortion. Some physicians believed that the artificial termination of pregnancy was simply another obstetric procedure and did not cause harm to anyone, because a fetus was not a person. Revealing his disdain, Ramos claimed that these physicians performed abortions to enrich themselves, without regard for the moral or societal implications. A second group of physicians held a more moderate position, supporting the criminalization of abortion with exceptions for certain circumstances, such as when a woman's honor was at stake. A third group of physicians were what he termed "extreme antiabortionists." Men in this camp, including Ramos himself, believed that abortion should be prevented at all costs, through the complete protection of mothers and children, including the approval of divorce, the establishment of secret maternity homes, and a guarantee of secrecy and impunity for mothers, punishable if violated.[10]

Physicians from this third group came to dominate the legal medicine committee, even raising the issue of criminal abortion to the academy's broader body of scientists. They advocated dismantling the historic impunity surrounding the procedure in favor of a system of vigilant policing and prosecution. Yet they tended to favor prosecution of practitioners, rather than abortion patients, for whom they often expressed patriarchally tinged pity. This position relied on a particular understanding of abortion. Although other methods of inducing abortion certainly existed, extreme antiabortionists seemed to refer specifically to surgical abortions—ones performed by a medical practitioner. Echoing one of his professors from his obstetrics training in Paris, Le-Roy y Cassá characterized abortion as "a professional crime" involving a midwife, doctor, or other person illegally practicing medicine.[11]

Extreme antiabortionism was partly based on the claim that advances in medical technology had rendered therapeutic abortion obsolete. About the inchoate state of nineteenth-century Cuban obstetrics, Ramos reminisced that "the surgeon had to decide [then] between killing the fetus to save the mother" or risking the death of both mother and fetus due to uterine rupture.[12] Cuban physicians employed then-acceptable surgical procedures such as craniotomy and embryotomy to try to save the woman's life by extracting the fetus.[13] However, by the late nineteenth and especially the early twentieth centuries, elite physicians began to argue that advances in the medical treatment of certain pregnancy-related ailments had rendered pregnancy interruption, including therapeutic abortion, essentially unnecessary. According to Le-Roy y Cassá, cardiac and renal conditions, and even certain psychiatric afflictions then understood as "psychosis," were no longer absolute indications to interrupt pregnancy.[14] His own dissertation research on severe morning sickness during pregnancy surveyed an array of remedies that could preempt the medical indication of abortion.[15] Further developments in antisepsis and Cuba's first successful cesarean section further challenged medical practices that sacrificed the fetus, even if it was to save the mother. Ramos concurred, claiming optimistically that advances in obstetric surgery could address most pregnancy and birth complications.[16]

Even as medical technology supposedly obviated abortion, the procedure was becoming increasingly prevalent in Cuba, especially in heavily urbanized areas, where the ratio of doctors to patients was highest. Lamenting "the rapid increase in the number of abortions" occurring in the capital, Le-Roy y Cassá declared that "right here in Havana, we all know that some colleagues disgracefully dedicate themselves to such criminal deeds."[17] Nor was physician-assisted abortion limited to Havana. One Cuban gynecologist recalled that an abortion clinic existed in Cienfuegos in the early 1920s—that it was well-known suggests a degree of complicity among certain physicians regarding pregnancy termination.[18]

Extreme antiabortionists argued that unscrupulous physicians performed abortion not out of medical necessity but rather to grow rich by charging exorbitant fees for the illegal procedure. Coronado decried: "it is truly scandalous the number of abortions that are done in our city, and what is even sadder, is that this crime, punished by the law, is perpetrated by some physicians for excessive sums of money."[19] Dr. Fernando Méndez Capote remarked that he frequently attended female patients who presented with postabortion complications. He shared Coronado's concern over the supposed abortion crisis in Cuba, proclaiming that he had "done well by bringing it to the Academy." He also reminded his colleagues that proof corroborated Coronado's statement even before he made it, and he specifically referenced a recent conversation among academy physicians about a doctor who performed abortions for a fee.

The increase in physician-assisted abortions raised serious questions about professional ethics. Le-Roy y Cassá attributed this problem to "the decline of professional standards that has disgracefully invaded some of our colleagues who practice [criminal abortion] with the same tranquility with which they would conscientiously perform it for a perfectly justified therapeutic purpose."[20] Worst of all, "nothing" had been done to resolve the criminal abortion crisis and scientists had barely even studied the problem, according to Ramos, who had previously authored a paper considering abortion a cause of infant mortality.[21] Abortions had evidently become so commonplace that they were "frequently committed with impunity," despite their criminalization under the penal code.[22] Ramos reminded his colleagues that the Academy of Sciences had failed to resolve the problem, even after Coronado raised it for the second time earlier that year.[23]

Some physicians pushed for the enforcement of antiabortionism as part of a professional code of medical ethics. This agenda favored direct involvement from the medical community in criminally prosecuting abortion. Coronado argued that the Academy of Sciences had a duty to address the so-called abortion crisis by taking "an active part in the prosecution of this deed." Broaching the topic in an address to the island's most prestigious scientists, he declared that "although it is too dirty a topic to be discussed by decent people, doctors have the obligation to sound the voice of alarm and protest against such scandalous deeds."[24] If a significant part of the problem lay in the medical community itself, he argued, then the onus fell on doctors, more than anyone else, to find a solution.

Although many physicians shared Coronado's moral concerns, the idea of imposing antiabortionism as part of the medical establishment's official agenda proved more controversial. In particular, Coronado's colleagues expressed significant concerns about the prospect of holding physicians accountable. Le-Roy y

Cassá, for instance, noted that although he and many of his colleagues knew of numerous physicians who performed abortions, criminal culpability was difficult to prove. In order to convict the perpetrators, the courts needed hard evidence, which was scarce in abortion cases. Advances in technique and sanitation had also made complications less common, further thwarting prosecutorial efforts, he explained. The dearth of evidence likely informed the scarcity of criminal cases under the 1879 code. Once abortion cases entered judicial purview, academy physicians could offer only their interpretations of evidence presented to them.

Other physicians pushed back on expanded medical involvement in criminal prosecution on the grounds that it threatened to compromise their professional relationship with their patients. Méndez Capote, for instance, admitted that physicians were among the only people who might be able to provide hard evidence of a crime required for prosecution. However, he opposed Coronado's suggestion that the academy require physicians to report suspected criminal abortions to authorities because doing so would further undermine patient trust in professional medicine. "In reality the situation of the doctor in this case is too difficult," he observed. From his perspective, abortion was "a secret that is not confessed but exposed, and it is understood that it should be kept [secret]." After all, the doctors and midwives were the only people who could help the women suffering from abortion complications, and that professional duty required some level of confidence. Moreover, even if the physicians provided evidence that a woman had an abortion, surgical techniques like dilation and curettage necessarily formed part of the obstetric curriculum in Cuba and had real medical indications, making it difficult to demonstrate a practitioner's "criminal intent." Just as it had been for the cases the academy consulted on, the bureaucratic processes of criminal investigation and prosecution proved to be yet another obstacle.

Other detractors opined that efforts to halt abortion were more suited to the medical school than to the courtroom. Le-Roy y Cassá considered that "educating and only educating" could "remedy such a fatal attack on the life of a new being," since women "almost always" paid for "their transgression against the laws of physiology with the loss of their health."[25] Méndez Capote, too, predicted that any intervention by the academy would be unlikely to "yield favorable results, because our professional class is prepared for all of these procedures" through the limited obstetric training they received in medical school. From his perspective, professors were in a stronger position to instruct future doctors in the ethical standards of pregnancy termination. Dr. Agustín de Varona concurred, arguing that, since the principal offenders were physicians and midwives, the medical school should take the initiative to instruct practitioners properly.[26]

While physicians trained in obstetrics and gynecology could see the urgency of Coronado's claim, other scientists within the academy found the discussion scandalous and inappropriate. Dr. Federico Grande Rossi, an infectious disease specialist, interjected that "people who do not perform surgery or obstetrics are tired of hearing about women who provoke their own abortions, inserting in themselves the probe by looking in the mirror." He opposed direct involvement by the academy, "because it will not have any results." After all, practitioners stood to accumulate great wealth by performing abortions, citing as evidence the case of a North American professor who worked only two hours a day and earned $700 or $800 per month just performing abortions. Another physician proposed that the academy write to the medical board to call attention to this professional moral issue, rather than taking action directly.[27]

Given this opposition from his colleagues, Coronado retracted his statement. He remarked sarcastically that in light of their complacency, the academy should "continue ignoring the increase in abortions in Havana as well as the existence of people who insert probes into women's uteruses to liberate them of the product they conceived."[28] Despite his apparent frustration, Coronado continued to push his colleagues, both inside the academy and beyond it, to take a firmer position against abortion. He petitioned the medical school to address the issue in its curriculum. However, the school leadership replied that the problem of abortions fell beyond its jurisdiction and suggested he take it up with the academy.

Several months later, Coronado again raised his concerns about Havana's abortion epidemic during a meeting of the academy, this time directing his ire at midwives instead of physicians. He reminded his colleagues about the "scandal" of pregnant "girls" who go to the hospitals with "probes that have been introduced into their uterine cavity with the goal of provoking an abortion." Although he was careful to note that "many doctors also recur to such a criminal deed daily," he reserved greatest consternation for the many "midwives who advertise solely for abortions." Abortion, he declared, is a "very grave social matter, and as such, it should be studied in the Academy and prophylactic measures proposed." Rather than wait "smiling for others to intervene," he implored the academy to "call the attention of our politicians and legislators about this criminal act and that they put in place measures to prevent it." With that, Dr. Coronado requested that the academy appoint a committee to investigate and denounce the actors, so that they could stop being "an accomplice to such an atrocious crime with its silence."[29]

The academy president opposed Coronado's motion. He argued— unsurprisingly to many members—that "nothing will be gained from opening a scientific discussion about criminal abortion," and that the academy should focus on concrete cases brought by courts, as it had for the last several decades. Coronado retorted that he was not suggesting that the physicians of the academy "denounce these crimes," a task he reserved for the police. However, he insisted that as doctors they had valuable information about where and how women obtained abortions. In particular, doctors working at hospitals for the poor, such as Hospital Mercedes and Hospital Número Uno, the two Havana hospitals with the highest mortality rates, allegedly knew the details of Havana's criminal abortion scene. By naming specific institutions, Coronado implied that the academy should require doctors working there to facilitate this information to authorities.

Although Coronado backtracked slightly on his initial motion, his insinuation that medical professionals should serve as police informants did not sit well with many at the session. Dr. Aristedes Agramonte interceded that requiring hospital directors to ask doctors to report the abortions they treat, so the judge can investigate the case, would be "counterproductive." As soon as these deeds are denounced, the women will stop seeking treatment at the hospitals, he forecast. A compassionate doctor, Agramonte argued, "will save many women who will not recidivate" due to the pain and humiliation of the procedure. In fact, the National Sanitation Committee had entertained but ultimately rejected a similar proposal to curb abortion on the grounds that the harrowing experience of abortion punished women enough, without the added threat of criminal prosecution. In essence, Agramonte suggested that, as a fledgling profession lacking the full trust of the Cuban public, the medical community could not afford to give patients further reason to avoid them.

Opposition also arose along moral grounds. Agramonte speculated that taking an explicit stance against abortion as a professional organization would commit the academy and its members to a moral position that not everyone shared. Invoking earlier commentary about the inevitable failure of the academy's direct intervention, Agramonte argued that cracking down on doctors would cause nothing more than scandal, since the academy "cannot prevent doctors or midwives who discredit the profession."[30] While numerous members agreed that physicians—and practitioners more generally—bore much of the responsibility for the rise in criminal abortions, the reluctance to assist in criminal prosecution underscored ambivalence over the ethical boundaries of the medical profession. To be sure, some physicians must have realized that committing to denouncing and prosecuting practitioners could affect their own professional practice and criminal accountability.

Confronting resistance even from fellow antiabortionists, Coronado's motion ultimately failed to initiate institutional action against criminal abortion. Nevertheless, the debates it prompted evinced a growing interest in state intervention in the reproductive lives of the island's most privileged women, whose wombs purportedly held the key to the nation's demographic fate. Within this broader frame of Cuban debates about population, Coronado's call to end abortion amounted to nothing less than an attempt to safeguard the whiteness of the island's future citizenry—a goal many physicians evidently supported. By shifting his focus from immoral physicians to intrusive midwives, Coronado conflated midwifery with criminal abortion. In so doing, he advanced his own moral agenda by channeling his profession's historical hostility against a rival group of practitioners to reinforce the professional authority of white male physicians, a contentious battle that physicians would continue to wage in the ensuing decades.[31]

While Coronado encountered opposition to holding physicians accountable, there appeared to be more support for prosecuting midwives. Many physicians found it easier to blame the abortion crisis on unlicensed midwives and "quacks," perpetuating patterns of scapegoating that had existed since the late nineteenth century.[32] As self-proclaimed "extreme antiabortionist" Ramos later observed, the medical profession lacked sufficient regulation to monitor the practitioners who perform abortion and prevent what he called "intrusions" from women who lacked formal training and licenses but posed as midwives. These so-called intrusions had become a "scourge responsible for the death and infertility of mothers, the sacrifice of many children, and almost the entirety of criminal abortions."[33]

According to Ramos, the activities of such interlopers confronted physicians with a "frightful dilemma," regardless of their personal or professional moral convictions: they could either perform the abortion or "let the patient try her luck." If the physician refused to perform the abortion, patients often resorted to more dangerous alternatives. The patient might "allow herself to be infected by one of the people who dedicates themselves to the abortion trade because they lack the conditions to exercise their profession honorably." Worse, she might "resort to something even more serious, if there could be something more serious, such as suicide or prostitution."[34] Ramos implied that physicians' expertise almost required them to perform the procedure to prevent the patient from falling prey to unlicensed, unskilled, clandestine practitioners. He alleged that midwives lacked the training and specialized skill necessary to perform the procedure successfully. In the best of cases, Ramos opined, midwives could assist physicians in their mission to safeguard the health and advance the "betterment" of the population. In this regard, Ramos defended physicians' moral high ground by scapegoating midwives, as alleged perpetrators of the vast majority of criminal abortions.

Although unlicensed practitioners undoubtedly performed many abortions, the focus on so-called interlopers eclipsed the undeniable involvement of licensed practitioners, both midwives and physicians. Le-Roy y Cassá recalled that, a few years earlier, authorities had denounced a woman who dedicated herself to performing abortions. On investigation, they found "proof" that she, a licensed midwife, worked for a doctor who provided surgical abortions to women who needed them.[35] Criminal prosecution evidently followed the path of least resistance by preying on the most vulnerable practitioners. As they had for nearly a century, physicians enacted their professional moralism by advocating for the prosecution of women practitioners while seeming to tolerate physicians and medical students who performed abortions.

Amid the broader focus on practitioners, a few physicians evinced a certain degree of ambivalence toward abortion patients. Some physicians approached these women with paternalism, characterizing them as vulnerable beings in need of protection. Firmly in this camp, Ramos suggested that the spike in criminal abortions in Cuba stemmed from the dearth of institutional and legal protections for pregnant women. According to Ramos, "remedies of a social character," more so than "the pharmacist's drugs or the surgeon's scalpel," would liberate physicians from performing such a "mutilating and murderous" procedure as abortion. Ultimately, offering assistance to mothers could save women from the "genital disability, suicide, or prostitution" that apparently awaited them after abortion.[36]

Other physicians espoused more disparaging moral judgments about abortion patients. Challenging the social welfare approach proposed by Ramos, Agramonte argued that the persistence of criminal abortion despite significant expansion in social and charitable services for pregnant women and infants demonstrated women's licentiousness and immorality. Maternal refuges and other institutions for "illicit conceptions," like the Casa de Maternidad, "do not serve any purpose" in preventing abortion "because what the women want is not to hide their dishonor, but rather to enjoy pleasure," he declared matter-of-factly.[37] According to Le-Roy y Cassá, women who terminated their pregnancies have "an even lower moral level than the physicians and midwives who facilitate the commission of this crime."[38] These harsh opinions favored a more corrective and punitive approach directed at patients.

The comments of early republican Cuba's most elite physicians reveal a widening rift within the medical profession about pregnancy termination. Coronado, Ramos, Le-Roy y Cassá, and other physicians articulated a position that centered vehement opposition to abortion as a cornerstone of a broader pronatalist agenda implicitly focused on harnessing the reproductive potential of the nation's white women. By contrast, their comments also exposed the existence of a significant group of physicians and other practitioners who performed abortion, apparently without moral reservations, as part of their everyday professional practice. The disparate status and earning potential of these two groups helps explain the diverging attitudes toward the procedure. Coronado and his colleagues formed part of the nation's medical elite and held professional appointments beyond their private practice, including as professors of medicine. Among the second group, by contrast, economic incentives of performing the procedure likely outweighed whatever moral reservations may have existed. In the context of early republican women's ongoing preference for midwife-attended homebirth, abortion provided a very real and necessary form of income and clinical experience for physicians whose primary means of income was private practice.³⁹ Even the most extreme antiabortionists understood these demands, which led many to steer away from actively targeting physicians.

Criminal Abortion in the Courts: Expanding Prosecution in the 1910s and 1920s

While physicians found midwives to be the most convenient targets, judges appeared to target abortion patients. Criminal statistics during the years leading up to Coronado's declaration of crisis suggest growing judicial intervention in women's reproductive lives, though very few convictions for criminal abortion. Between 1909 and 1913, Cuban courts heard seventy-two abortion cases, sixty infanticide cases, and eighteen infant abandonment cases against women, according to official judicial statistics.⁴⁰ None of the abortion or infant abandonment cases resulted in convictions, and only fourteen infanticide cases resulted in convictions during this period. Of all fertility-related crimes, infanticide earned the most convictions—thirty-one between 1909 and 1927, with nearly half of those concentrated in the first five years (1909–13). In 1914, five of the inmates at Havana's Jail for Women had been convicted of infanticide.

These data suggest unprecedented legal interventions in women's reproductive lives, but anecdotal evidence points to ongoing racial disparities in conviction, underscoring continuities with the late colonial period. Judges continued to grant leniency in cases involving honorable women. In 1927, for instance, authorities in the central Cuban municipality of Trinidad investigated a young woman named Josefa (known colloquially as Pita) for possible criminal abortion or infanticide. According to public rumors, she had given birth a few days earlier and had made the child disappear "in a mysterious way" to hide her dishonor. Pita confirmed the pregnancy, testifying that about a week earlier she had "suffered a fall in her home," as she was trying to tie her shoes while seated on her bed. She hit her hip and left leg, causing her to miscarry at five months pregnant. No one attended to Pita during her miscarriage, and she buried the lifeless fetus in the patio of her house.

Authorities ordered the remains disinterred for medical examination. The autopsy revealed no evidence of violence on the unviable fetus. They also inquired about a certain woman who had been seen around Pita during her miscarriage: Amparo Jimenez—allegedly the town midwife. Further investigation revealed that Amparo was not in fact a midwife, and she had not attended to Pita. Medical examination of Pita's genitals failed to reveal any evidence of trauma. Only after interrogating Pita and disinterring the fetus she had miscarried did authorities eventually conclude that no crime had occurred.⁴¹

While lower courts heard a higher volume of cases, involving a broader segment of the female population, the few fertility-related cases that arrived to Cu-

TABLE 10.1. Women defendants in fertility crimes cases before audiencias, 1914–1927

		Abortion	Child Abandonment*	Infanticide	Total
1914–1918	White	1	0	4	5
	Mestizo	0	0	2	2
	Black	0	1	0	1
1919–1923	White	3	0	3	6
	Mestizo	3	1	1	5
	Black	0	0	0	0
1924–1927	White	1	0	4	5
	Mestizo	2	0	2	4
	Black	0	0	1	1
TOTAL, 1914–1927	White	5	0	11	16
	Mestizo	5	1	5	11
	Black	0	0	1	1

SOURCE: Israel Castellanos, *La delincuencia femenina*, tables 110, 116, and 121.
* Additional child abandonment cases appeared before the correctional courts.

ba's higher courts tended to involve more privileged women. Republican audiencias, which served as appeals courts, did not record an abortion conviction against a woman until 1916, the year after Ramos published his report on criminal abortions. Even thereafter, abortion convictions remained sparse, with only five between 1916 and 1927. Three of these convictions occurred in 1926 alone. Only five misdemeanor infant abandonment charges resulted in conviction between 1914 and 1927. The courts convicted only two women of felony infant abandonment, one in 1918, the other between 1919 and 1923.[42]

The little demographic information available about the women involved in these cases suggests a judicial focus on patients over practitioners, and a tendency toward greater leniency for more privileged women. Most cases involved women of reproductive age, as opposed to older women (over forty), who would more likely have been practitioners. Most audiencia cases involved women labeled as white or mestizo (table 10.1). Although these women faced conviction from lower judges, the majority ultimately evaded legal consequences. These judicial patterns suggest an ongoing correlation between whiteness (or proximity to whiteness) and legal impunity.

Reproduction in Crisis: Abandonment and Abortion in the 1930s

The onset of the global economic crisis of the 1930s transformed the debate about abortion. As economic hardship descended on a growing numbers of families, a broad consensus emerged that poverty more than honor or vanity compelled unprecedented numbers of Cuban women to terminate their pregnancies and abandon their children. These were not the same kind of women physicians imagined decades earlier; they came from a broader segment of Cuban society, which included more working women and rural women. These women gained expanded access to surgical abortion as a greater number of practitioners, including midwives, learned to perform injection, dilation, and dilation and curettage procedures. Despite this apparent democratization of abortion, social status remained a key determinant of women's experience of reproduction. Impoverished women, rural women, and women of color, more likely to resort to unlicensed practitioners, also suffered more complications, which in turn brought them into the grips of the penal system.

Cuban families, and most of all mothers and their babies, quickly felt the impact of the global economic crisis. Plummeting demand for Cuban sugar, soaring unemployment, and declining wages placed unprecedented demand on women to make ends meet. Perhaps hardest hit were single mothers and illegitimate children, many of whom ended up on the streets. Growing numbers of these women resorted to prostitution to weather the crisis. More than seven thousand women were engaged in this occupation in Havana in 1931, and the majority of incarcerated women had been charged with this crime.[43]

Cuba's fledgling social safety net, which had long been viewed as a safety valve to prevent fertility control, faced unrelenting pressures. The expansion of social welfare services for mothers and infants, a continuation of early republican homiculture buttressed by feminist relief work, ushered into existence a number of charitable institutions precisely as the economic crisis hit hardest. The inauguration of new facilities for mothers and infants, like the Elvira Machado maternity hospital in 1930 (later renamed América Arias), for instance, suffered under the weight of economic crisis. In fact, the original plans included an entire department for pregnant women, which was axed by budget shortfalls.[44]

More established institutions, like the Casa de Maternidad, also struggled under soaring demand. The desperate state of impoverished mothers became strikingly clear in the surge in letters to the Casa de Maternidad.[45] Throughout the 1930s, impoverished women and their benefactors—the vast majority of whom were white—regularly petitioned the Casa director to admit one or more of their children, even if temporarily, while they attempted to improve their economic situation.[46] One of the requests in 1930 came from the president of the Humanitarian Charity Branch of the International Sunshine Society, who wrote of a pregnant working-class woman with two small children, living in poverty and hunger. She asked if the woman would be permitted to surrender her newborn and then return to collect her later when her economic situation is "no longer so precarious."[47] The director replied that infant surrender to the Casa was considered abandonment by their parents and relatives, and that status would be inscribed in the civil registry. Parents could not reclaim children they had abandoned without a judicial order confirming their paternity. He also informed the petitioner that the institution was no longer admitting minors, because of the "excessive number" of children already interned therein. The Casa could not offer the woman assistance.[48]

With austerity measures leading the Casa to deny the vast majority of petitions, some benefactors resorted to extremes to gain access to the shrinking benefits. One police lieutenant wrote that an impoverished white mother's poverty threatened to compel her toward prostitution if the Casa did not admit her newborn infant. Writing to the Mother Superior, the officer described a pitiful scene—a young Spanish woman whose husband had abandoned her at seven months pregnant. She was able to secure admission to a maternity hospital (possibly the América Arias Municipal Maternity Hospital) to give birth, thanks to the patronage of a prominent white widow. However, the officer expressed concerns that the woman's persisting state of poverty would drive her down the "path of evil." He requested admitting the baby to the Casa until the woman could be placed in a "decent home" likely as a servant.[49]

A rare petition from 1931 shows how white patronage and perceptions of propriety were central to Black women's attempts to gain access to institutional services for which they evidently qualified. Penning her petition from her humble home in the neighborhood of Cerro, a white widow recounted the "very sad" situation of a young parda woman, whom she was helping. The woman's husband had abandoned her in the "greatest destitution," with seven young children. She had initially moved in with a family member, sleeping on the floor with her children. Then the widow took her in but confessed that the meager income that she gained from her own children's wages was barely enough to sustain her own family. Attesting to the woman's "good conduct," the widow requested that the Casa director admit "two, or at least one" of the parda's children.[50]

Given the surge in demand, authorities in the Casa de Maternidad sought to deter infant surrender and restrict the number of infants who could access the charitable services. In 1930, the Havana newspaper *El Mundo* announced changes at the Casa de Maternidad, including the impending closure of the torno (fig. 10.1). That February, the Casa's governing board had approved a resolution to "suppress" the device that had historically afforded African-descended infants some access to the institution's services. Noting that the institution's founding documents did not explicitly require a turnstile, the board argued that closing the torno altogether would help ameliorate the devastating mortality rates among infants surrendered to the institution. At least half as many infants died as were admitted annually throughout the 1920s. In some years, the number of deaths nearly equaled the number of infants admitted.

The Casa director, Cándido Hoyos, claimed that the mortality of infants admitted through the torno was generally higher than that of infants surrendered through the front door—57 percent versus 49 percent. He argued that closing the torno would help diminish the "hecatomb" of infant mortality. Although the

FIGURE 10.1. The torno at Havana's Casa de Maternidad, early twentieth century. *Popular Mechanics Magazine* 33, no. 1 (January 1920): 718.

director justified closing the torno because of its potential to reduce infant mortality, the decision also permitted institutional administrators to exert greater control over which babies entered the Casa, precisely as demand peaked due to the global economic depression. It was no coincidence that Hoyos mentioned the hereditary defects and illegitimacy contributing to infant mortality among abandoned infants.[51]

Measures like closing the torno erected barriers to vital charitable services for populations perceived to be unworthy of assistance. Given the institution's history and its response to mothers' petitions, worthiness had definitive racial and class implications. A significant and growing gap remained between the quantity and kind of services available and the needs of impoverished women and women of color.

As the functionality of charitable services crumbled under the weight of the economic crisis, abortion appeared to gain renewed visibility. Between July 1933 and June 1936, the Audiencia of Havana heard 179 abortion cases—an annual average of 59 cases. During this period, the court rendered four judgments—two against midwives and two against nonmedical personnel—convicting three defendants. These figures represented a remarkable increase from the period between 1914 and 1927, when all audiencias across Cuba combined heard just 10 abortion cases (see table 10.1).

Forensic evidence suggested a much higher rate of abortion than the judicial statistics captured. In 1936, Havana's forensic medical service identified evidence of fertility-related causes of death in 304 autopsies, including 13 postpartum deaths, 7 abortions, 1 infanticide, and 283 "intrauterine causes." An additional 5 medical examinations revealed evidence of abortion. This forensic record thus identified 309 cases involving the termination of pregnancy.

Medical observation suggested that criminal abortion was even more prevalent than indicated in the forensic record. In a single Havana hospital, physicians documented 1,176 cases of abortion in one year. This figure included roughly 672 procedures completed after abortive work was initiated outside the hospital, and an addition 488 curettage procedures. For every 4,176 births, there were 1,176 abortions, or 28.1 abortions for every 100 births at that hospital, not including clandestine abortions. In a single private practice, there were 538 documented abortions.[52]

Even still, the number of abortions documented in hospital records paled in comparison to the total number of clandestine abortions. José Chelala-Aguilera estimated that 9,441 clandestine abortions were performed in the fourteen known abortion centers in Havana.[53] Altogether, Chelala-Aguilera estimated that 10,617 clandestine abortions were performed in the city of Havana in a single year.[54] Dr. Luis Alberto Rubio similarly observed major discrepancies in Pinar del Río in his role as provincial justice minister. Although no criminal abortion cases arrived at the courts, Rubio acknowledged that "these criminal practices occur daily," since "the majority of married couples" have declared an "unjust and criminal war ... against offspring." Rubio claimed that it had become "so common and natural to speak of the 'need to not have children'" that criminal abortion had effectively become "perfectly licit and authorized by social rules." As a vehement opponent of abortion. Rubio urged doctors, legislators, and police to be more vigilant in preventing "abortive practices."[55]

Local authorities prosecuted abortion with widely varying zeal across the island. While few provinces rivaled Havana in the sheer number of abortion cases, the Audiencia of Oriente heard fifty-eight criminal abortion cases between 1934 and 1936, resulting in the identification of twenty accused people, four arrests, and zero convictions.[56] In other jurisdictions, criminal prosecution of abortion remained rare or nonexistent. In 1936, for instance, Rubio revealed that the courts in Vuelta Abajo had not heard a single case of criminal abortion in three years.[57]

Some judges did seem to focus on the prosecution of practitioners, namely midwives. The Audiencia of Matanzas heard thirteen criminal abortion cases between 1934 and 1936. Judges brought charges against practitioners in three cases, resulting in the arrest of six midwives in 1934 and 1935. Although the midwives were eventually absolved, not one physician faced criminal charges.[58] The remaining cases failed to identify suspects after the interrogation and examination of women patients.

Just as Cuba's audiencias reported a tremendous increase in criminal abortion cases, so too did certain local courts. A small set of records from the Juzgado de Trinidad shows a surge in criminal investigations and criminal cases involving abortion, from just one in the 1920s, to nine between 1930 and 1941.[59] These cases help unearth the personal experiences of women who became ensnared in the cold statistical portraits. They also document the subtle interplay between medical and legal communities, revealing how the recommendations of extreme antiabortionist physicians began to emerge in judicial cases, even as continuities with previous periods remained.

Much like the police investigations of the late colonial period, many of the 1930s cases involved women who experienced apparently unintentional poor pregnancy outcomes at home without medical intervention. These reproductive events came to the attention of authorities only when a neighbor or witness denounced the woman, sometimes as part of a larger interpersonal conflict. In 1932, Trinidad police received report of a possible infanticide. Serafín told authorities that one autumn night, his neighbor, twenty-two-year-old Ramona, had given birth to a baby in her rural home. The next morning, he allegedly saw the woman's husband, Ramón, carry out of the house the dead infant wrapped in a sack. Serafín claimed that Ramón then buried the body on a remote part of the plantation. Serafín explained that he appealed to authorities more than two months later, because Ramón had attempted to frame him for killing the child.

Ramona told a completely different story. When the rural guardsman confronted her about Serafín's allegations, she recounted the events leading up to what appeared to be a miscarriage or stillbirth, though she did not directly acknowledge any pregnancy. The day prior to going into labor, she and her husband had left the house on horseback. The next day, she began hemorrhaging. However, the couple did not have enough money to call a doctor. Instead, she employed "various home remedies" to recover. Ramón told the same story, further adding that his wife "had not had any abortions of any kind."[60]

Testimony from community members suggested that this was not the first pregnancy Ramona had lost. Neighbors told authorities that they suspected that she suffered from an ailment that made it difficult for her to carry pregnancies to term. The rural guardsman investigating the case reported Ramona as "a woman, who owing to a certain illness, has had six miscarriages in a row." The miscarriage prior to the one investigated in the case had been treated by a doctor, but this time the couple did not have enough money to summon a doctor.[61] Ramona suffered the miscarriage in her home without medical assistance and, importantly for this case, without an educated male professional who could corroborate her story.

Despite this testimony, authorities ordered the remains exhumed for forensic investigation. Men with shovels dug up the entire area indicated by Serafín without finding anything—not even the sack mentioned in his denunciation. The dirt also lacked evidence of disruption. "In my judgment," declared the investigator, "we are dealing with a denunciation of pure revenge, since it is true that said woman had a miscarriage, but [the fetus] was two months [along] and it occurred by hemorrhage and blood clots."⁶² Although authorities eventually dismissed the investigation against Ramona, the allegations prompted what had to have been a traumatic intrusion into her most intimate reproductive experiences, in addition to subjecting her pregnancy to public scrutiny.

In the cases involving medically supervised pregnancies, the physicians themselves reported their patients to authorities. In one 1934 case, a physician reported one of his patients to authorities for possible criminal abortion without even examining her. Twenty-year-old Rosa miscarried her pregnancy at around four months gestation, apparently preserving the fetus in a bottle of alcohol. When she began to suffer complications in the days thereafter, her brother-in-law summoned a physician from a nearby town. The physician did not examine Rosa because he did not have the necessary tools, but he did conclude that she most likely suffered from a severe infection. He could not determine if the infection resulted from a simple miscarriage, as Rosa claimed, or from a criminal abortion. The doctor found it suspicious that the family had summoned him all the way from Güira de Melena, when the town of Manicaragua was much closer. The local judge pursued an investigation into potential criminal abortion. Authorities interrogated neighbors, who told them that Rosa had miscarried after falling while carrying water back to her house. Authorities still ordered the medical examiner to study the fetus to determine if evidence of violence or force would implicate Rosa in the purposeful abortion of the fetus. No evidence of violence was found.⁶³

In a 1930 case, a physician reported a patient for criminal abortion as revenge after the woman sought care through a midwife because she was unable to afford the physicians' fees. Felicia was about three months pregnant when she began to experience heavy bleeding. Her husband, Edom, summoned the town midwife, Eladia Mirabal, a woman of color. Eladia confirmed the pregnancy and informed the couple that Felicia was having a miscarriage. Felicia was skeptical, noting that she had not suffered any blow that could have caused that, but she received care from Eladia during her miscarriage.

Even after the fetus emerged, Felicia continued to bleed for several days, at which point Edom summoned a physician. On examination, the doctor noted that the woman's cervix had been displaced to the point where he could hardly find it. The cervical membrane also presented various lesions, which bled on touching them. The doctor suspected that an object had been inserted into the woman's vagina and caused the injuries. The doctor interrogated the ailing woman, asking how she had ended up in this condition. According to the doctor, Felicia told him that four or five days earlier, she had summoned her midwife, who informed her that she needed "some healing" and had performed a painful procedure with a rubber probe rigged with a metal wire at the end. She allegedly inserted this instrument into the pregnant woman's vagina, causing an abortion. The procedure hurt so intensely that Felicia had allegedly begged the midwife to desist. The doctor reported to police that the midwife in question was Eladia Mirabal, a woman of color.

During the investigation, authorities subjected Felicia to an invasive medical examination. The doctor concluded that she suffered from "advanced symptoms of Nervous Hysteria" and that the size and state of her uterus indicated that she had been three or four months pregnant. However, contrary to the original physician's report, he found no evidence of vaginal or uterine trauma. Instead, he suspected that the bleeding was likely caused by chronic endometriosis, a condition that had probably contributed to the miscarriage. A fetal autopsy, moreover, showed that the fetus did not show signs of trauma and was entirely whole. Thus, the forensic medical investigation supported Felicia's assertion that she had suffered a miscarriage, not a criminal abortion.

Further exploration revealed that the physician who attended Felicia had fabricated his initial report to police, likely in an attempt to crush his competition: the midwife Eladia. Felicia's husband later told authorities that both the midwife and the physician had visited Felicia several times during her treatment, and the physician had proposed a procedure for which he charged five pesos. A dispute over the price apparently resulted in Felicia's husband asking the midwife to perform it instead of the doctor. Eladia complied, attending Felicia for three days. Out the five pesos, and confronted with a woman who performed the same medical procedures as he did, the physician likely accused Eladia of performing an abortion as revenge for stealing his patient.[64]

Only one surviving case from this court during the period actually concerned actions that resembled criminal abortion. The case, which entered the courts in 1930, originated in an alleged abduction of a young white woman, Juana. In her initial testimony, Juana told authorities that she was in a relationship with her boyfriend, Ramón, when another man, Pedro Ferrara, seduced her. Enticing her with the promise of marriage, Pedro convinced Juana to "receive him in her home," where he "enjoyed her virginity." Pedro vanished before Juana discovered that she was pregnant from that encounter.

Juana attempted to hide the pregnancy from her mother, but her symptoms drew suspicion. Her mother, María, eventually took her to a doctor in Santa Clara to find out why she was feeling ill. The doctor promptly informed them that Juana was pregnant. Juana's mother then consulted with Alejo Gómez, "a friend of the house," who brought an assortment of medicines for Juana to take, saying that they would "make me better." Juana claimed that she took the medicines, not knowing what the result would be, but shortly thereafter, she experienced "a kind of flow, without seeing what it contained." María had arranged the abortion to clear the path for Juana to marry her boyfriend, Ramón. After the alleged abortion, Juana fled the home. With Juana no longer at home, María accused another man, Cecilio Cantero, of abducting Juana.

Juana later revealed that she had fabricated the harrowing story of seduction, abortion, and abduction at her mother's demand. Her mother had apparently been pressuring her to marry Ramón and pass the pregnancy off as his. However, she told authorities that she did not want to deceive Ramón and did not like him enough to marry him. Juana also confessed that her mother had forced her to conspire in accusing Alejo of dispensing abortifacients, when in fact he had not. An investigation later revealed the María knew of her daughter's affair with Alejo, which she vehemently opposed because he was a man of color. The judge concluded that "the mother, who belongs to the white race, seeing her daughter in a pregnant state, planned a way to provoke her daughter's abortion, which she herself denounced," blaming Alejo, with whom María maintained sexual relations according to public rumors. Alejo denied any wrongdoing but focused on denying any sexual contact with any of the people involved in the case, seeming not to know about any abortion drugs. However, both Alejo and María were charged with abortion and jailed.[65]

A similar concern over a woman's honor and virginity occurred in 1932, when a father, Rafael, denounced the slander of his daughter in the town of Güira de Melena. Apparently his neighbor, Hermogenio, had been talking in "dishonest terms" about his daughter Catalina, advising the girl's fiancé not to marry her because she had allegedly had an abortion. The allegation prompted a medical examination of Catalina. Noting a broken hymen and brownish discharge on the vulva and in the vaginal fluid, the medical examiner concluded that the girl was not a virgin. Authorities launched an investigation of Catalina's alleged abortion, but no evidence emerged.[66]

More than a mere increase in the number of abortion cases, these individual accounts help elucidate important changes and continuities in the ways legal authorities intervened in women's reproductive lives during a period of intense economic hardship. As in the late nineteenth century, local police in the 1930s saw potential criminality in a range of reproductive events. The prevalence among these cases of reproductive events that appeared to resemble miscarriages and stillbirths more closely than abortions and infanticides shows both ongoing gaps in judicial authorities' understanding of the physiology of women's reproduction and the severe limitations in the medical care in rural areas. Even still, physicians levied the courts and exploited women's reproductive crises to gain a foothold in rural areas, where midwives were the main source of pregnancy and birth care.

The small number of criminal cases involving claims of abortion often had very little to do with the actual criminal abortions occurring across the island. According to Chelala-Aguilera, the drastic disparity between the number of known clandestine abortions and the number of criminal abortion cases arriving to the courts demonstrated key problems with the way Cuba approached women's reproduction. He pointed to a total "lack of comprehension of the existing law," a claim with striking resonance in the criminal abortion cases surveyed above. Although most patients and abortion providers acted with impunity, impoverished women suffering from ordinary reproductive crises became ensnared in the courts. But Chelala-Aguilera also noted broader failures to attend to the realities confronting Cuban women. The state had failed to provide much-needed protections and resources for mothers and infants. Indeed, the cases above show that even basic medical care remained out of financial reach for most poor women. Perhaps most importantly of all, a lack of appropriate legislation regarding birth control condemned impoverished families to conceive more children than they could support, placing additional strains on already-limited charitable assistance. Such deficiencies produced "thousands of victims annually."[67] For Chelala-Aguilera, neither punitive approaches nor protective measures could effectively address criminal abortion without empowering women and families to prevent pregnancies they did not want and plan their families according to their circumstances.

Toward the Social Defense Code: Legal Debates on Abortion amid Economic Crisis

In the desperate economic and social situation of the 1930s, the moral landscape surrounding pregnancy and family planning began to shift. Lawyer Moisés Vieites, for instance, argued in 1933 that abortion should be decriminalized on the grounds that it was not an immoral act, but rather a merciful one, with the aborted being producing a great social benefit in certain circumstances.[68] This was a new position for him. Just seven years earlier, he had drafted a law to "prohibit the provocation of an abortion purposefully and illicitly of someone else, or help [a woman] to abort." His 1926 proposed law was significantly more lenient than the existing law, in that it targeted practitioners, rather than women and offered judges ample discretion in sentencing, from restitution to incarceration.[69]

Although his previous position was perhaps more liberal than average, the context of global economic depression in the 1930s clearly influenced his opinion in favor of decriminalization. Amid widespread depression-era unemployment, many families struggled to feed their children, and child delinquency became widespread. According to Vieites, within these circumstances, interrupting a pregnancy constituted a moral decision because it would prevent the birth of a child who would suffer from poverty. "What benefits does society gain from forcing an impoverished woman to bear children," he asked rhetorically.[70]

This argument about the morality of abortion within poverty proved controversial within Cuba's patriarchal society. Some hardline antiabortionists argued that women could avoid the problem entirely by abstaining from sex. However, Vieites pointed out that women did not always have control over their intimate lives: "if there is any act that can be classified as involuntary for the woman, it is coitus." After all, men commonly exerted "all kinds of forces and suggestions to obtain carnal access," exploiting women's social position, needs, and weaknesses with money, power, and seduction. Moreover, women were also subject to rape and other forms of coercive and nonconsensual sex. Vieites argued that since the woman suffered the consequences of having a baby more than anyone, she, and not society, should have the right to "judge and determine what would be best for her and the child."[71]

Vieites also argued that laws criminalizing abortion disproportionately punished poor women while failing to hold more privileged women accountable. "In thirty years of legal practice," he declared, "I have never seen a judgment against a woman of high social status." Instead, the courts punished "women of modest means, precisely the ones most in need of interrupting the pregnancy." For women whose wealth and influence enables them to hide the crime, "the sanction practically does not exist, despite its frequent consummation in high society and among the bourgeoisie." Based on these and other arguments, Vieites advocated for the legalization of abortion, so long as it is requested by the woman and performed by a physician.[72]

Such critiques informed a shifting legal conversation about women's reproduction, one that introduced new protections for women and mothers. Although the liberalization of abortion was a figment of a distant future, Cuban lawmakers were more willing to make concessions in protecting working mothers. One of the most important reforms came in 1934, with a law requiring employers to contribute to national maternity insurance, which afforded expectant mothers six weeks' paid leave from their employment.[73] This law offered an important protection for working mothers. However, it disproportionately benefited white women with the exclusion of domestic workers, who constituted nearly half of the female labor force, and among whom women of African descent were a majority.[74]

Feminist critiques also shaped understandings of women's reproduction in the 1930s. Ofelia Rodríguez Acosta's 1933 *La tragedia social de la mujer* powerfully rebutted biologically deterministic views of women's reproduction. Rodríguez argued that motherhood was a moral tragedy for women who became pregnant outside bourgeois society's social expectations. She advocated for birth control to enable women to have only the number of children they desired and could afford to raise.[75] Access to contraceptive remained elusive, not least because, like abortion, it was perceived to empower immorality while limiting the fertility of the most demographically desirable sectors.

Perhaps unsurprisingly, eugenic arguments offered the most compelling case for extending access to abortion. In 1936, Dr. María Gómez Carbonell, one of six women elected to the House of Representatives, introduced two bills that challenged the Cuban state's blind pronatalism. The first bill, on eugenics, puericulture, and homiculture, introduced on June 22, 1936, proposed establishing a national council of eugenics and puericulture to be responsible for issuing premarital health certificates required for legal marriage, providing pregnancy care, sponsoring childcare, and permitting euthanasia to "eliminat[e] at birth monsters or anomalous beings." The bill also proposed restricting fertility among the poor, and creating eugenics and puericulture courses for schools.[76]

The other bill, on protecting and defending Cuban children and adolescents, introduced on November 28, 1936, proposed extending earlier homicultural projects focused on social welfare, and "recogni[zing] prenatal rights."[77] Gómez Carbonell's parallel support for abortion and euthanasia for the poor and disabled, and what appeared to be an early rendition of "right to life" rhetoric, might appear contradictory. However, these positions aligned with Cuba's early republican tradition of eugenic pronatalism by permitting fertility-limiting measures for undesirable populations and supporting reproduction by desirable ones.

All three of these perspectives emerged to varying degrees in lawmakers' discussions as they drafted the abortion law for the Social Defense Code. The committee charged with drafting the law initially entertained a proposal that criminalized abortions, except under four conditions: when it was necessary to save the life of the mother; when the pregnancy was conceived as a result of rape, abduction not followed by marriage, or other violation; to prevent a serious hereditary or contagious disease from spreading to the fetus; and in cases of extreme poverty, provided the woman had already given birth to three living children.[78] This last exemption provoked the most vociferous debate.

For at least one member of the committee, these four exemptions were insufficient. Dr. Candita Gómez Calas de Martínez Bandujo, the only woman on the committee, argued that abortion should be regulated, not criminalized. She explained that regulation was about more than exempting certain circumstances from criminalization; it was about providing safe access to medical care. Like Vieites, Gómez characterized abortion as a moral choice under certain circumstances, and observed that under the current regime of criminalization, impoverished women suffered disproportionately. Whereas a wealthy woman could easily consult with a physician to "fix her situation," a poor woman often lacked sufficient resources to access such care. Instead, her economic situation forced her to "resort to a midwife, putting her life in danger." To avoid such stark inequities, Gómez insisted that hospitals should provide broad access to abortion and the law should exempt all women, "because there are certain circumstances that advise it."[79]

Some members of the committee appeared superficially sympathetic, but promptly objected that the nation needed population growth. Dr. Manuel Giménez Lanier, for one, recognized the "suffering of children born into poverty," but simultaneously invoked historic concerns about the population. Noting the need for "procreation and population increase," he recommended a compromise by making the sentences for criminal abortion "as light as possible." Dr. José Agustín Martínez, too, thought an exemption for "women whose poverty did not permit them to maintain children" was worthy of consideration, as long as the procedure was performed in a public hospital and with the father's permission. However, he opposed exemptions for abortion providers, who, he claimed, were "not as harmless as pregnant women, because they do [the procedure] for a price." Like Dr. Giménez Lanier, Dr. Martínez invoked concerns about population to justify his reservations about decriminalization. He reminded his colleagues of the stakes of procreation: "we are talking about a human being who has the right to life, who could become a useful man for Society in the future, an Einstein, a Lincoln, a Pasteur." He warned against adopting the extremes of the "Soviet model" (the Soviet Union had decriminalized abortion entirely in 1920). Instead, he proposed the committee study three key exemptions from criminalization: women who have more than three children; impoverished women; women who conceived out of wedlock.[80] Dr. Raggi also "sympathize[d]" with the poverty exemptions but concluded that it was "inoportune" for Cuba at that time.

However, the proposed poverty exemption provoked vocal opposition as well. A memorandum from the special codifying committee reiterated concerns about the national population, arguing that such a liberal law on abortion might be justifiable in an overpopulated country; but it "goes against the interests of the Republic, ever in need of an increase in population." But the memorandum went even further, claiming that permitting abortion violated Christian morals. The memo concluded that even if a poverty exemption for abortion were "defensible in the scientific or purely technical penal aspect," it was "not the most appropriate solution" for Cuba.[81]

Nor did Cuba's vice president, Dr. Federico Laredo Brú, who presided over the drafting of the code, accept the poverty exemption. He speculated that "98 percent of women who practice abortion do so not to avoid having more than three children, but to avoid having any at all." He instructed the committee that the proposed law should be based on the existing laws and should not introduce substantial revisions.[82] Such a law, he implied, would have to force Cuban women to comply with their responsibility to the nation by having as many children as possible.

Moving the matter to a vote, all the members of the committee—except Dr. Gómez—voted to remove the poverty exemption. Explaining her vote, she argued that wealthy women habitually practice abortion with the full knowledge of society, and this is tolerated without applying any sanction at all. Allowing impoverished women to obtain abortions without criminal penalty would help rectify the law's unequal application.[83] Although the committee registered her dissent, the proposed law—minus the poverty exemption—was approved and became part of the new 1936 Social Defense Code.

The law featured the lightest sentences for women of any abortion law in Cuban history, while maintaining similar sanctions against practitioners. An individual, including a physician, pharmacist, or midwife, who "caused an abortion or destroyed in any way an embryo" would face a prison sentence of six to twelve years if done coercively or violently, three to six years if performed without the woman's consent, and one to three years with consent. An individual who physically abused a pregnant woman, later resulting in a miscarriage, would face six months to three years in prison. A woman who caused her own abortion or consented to the procedure would face three to twelve months incarceration, unless she was attempting to protect her honor, which would afford a reduced sentence of one month to two years and a fine.

The final law reflected an incremental liberalization of abortion law that still maintained a racially disparate impact. Preserving two of the three exemptions from previous codes perpetuated the historic impunity of privileged women. Women who were able to afford medical care as well as those whose racial and class privilege vested them with honor could still expect to avoid criminal consequences for obtaining abortions. The new code's unprecedented eugenic exemption, moreover, would have theoretically allowed doctors to exert influence over the kinds of pregnancies they deemed eligible for termination. Omitting the poverty exemption meant that women of color, who were overrepresented among the poor and working classes, had no relief from criminal sanctions.

Opposition to Abortion Liberalization, 1930s

Why, amid such acute economic crisis, did Cuban lawmakers reject an abortion law that provided an exemption for poverty? One possible answer lies in the persisting belief among some white male elites that abortion deprived the nation of its most desirable future (white) citizens. After serving on the committee in charge of the abortion law in the recently approved Social Defense Code, one of the more outspoken opponents of abortion, Diego Vicente Tejera, argued that Cuba needed a much stricter law than the one his fellow lawmakers had just approved.[84] Two years later, Tejera published another essay equating abortion with murder.[85] He applied this definition to any stage of pregnancy, arguing that destroying an embryo early in pregnancy, even the first or second month, still constituted criminal abortion. According to Tejera, abortion at any stage of pregnancy under almost all circumstances was illicit and needed to be punished. He disputed many of the common defenses and proposed exemptions of criminal culpability for abortion, such as a woman's right to bodily autonomy, and the morality of abortion under certain circumstances, including when it was caused by concerns about honor or poverty.[86]

When it came to prosecuting criminal abortion, for instance, Tejera challenged the belief that low rates of prosecution owed to society's general repudiation of punishment. Instead, he blamed deficient policing.[87] He also disputed the disparate impact of antiabortion laws. While advocates of decriminalization like Vieites and Gómez cited the impunity enjoyed by privileged women, Tejera claimed that the law itself was not to blame, since it made no distinctions on the basis of class or wealth. Rather, it was "the idiosyncrasy of the Cuban people, that has not yet been swept of its colonial legacy, that has not recognized yet its civic duties, in a word, because it is not a population of citizens."[88]

Driving this absolutist opposition to abortion was a belief that the nation's demographic requirements exceeded women's and infants' needs. Tejera reiterated that the national need for population growth justified rigorous criminalization. "Society needs men," he proclaimed, and "a fetus is a future man"—a "human being in the making." Reminiscent of the "man of the cradle" argument of the 1830s, Tejera conflated reproduction with the birth of future male citizens. This framing not only erased girls but also cast women as mere vessels needed to birth men. For Tejera, abortion did not necessarily cause the fetus "personal damage" because it has not yet lived, but it did harm the nation in need of citizens.[89] For those reasons, he argued for the rigorous criminalization of abortion, with exceptions made only when the pregnant woman's life was at stake or in cases of rape.

Like Tejera, Rubio opposed leniency in cases involving honor or poverty. He argued that abortion to hide a woman's dishonor should not be permitted, because the woman engaged in the intimate deed in "plain consciousness that she is doing a reproachable act." The honor that she attempts to salvage through abortion "no longer exists," as "she herself threw [it] to the mud and besmirched [it]." Rubio went further, disputing exemptions in cases of seduction and underage sex, because the victim allegedly "submits herself voluntarily" and engages in the act with "absolute and plain dominion over her actions." Therefore, he argued that abortion is not justified if the future father refuses to marry the girl, since she "knew perfectly well the possible consequences" of "accepting the lover."[90]

Even moderate minds acknowledging the need for some exceptions to criminalization tended to pit women's rights against national interest. According to Martínez, the "right to abortion" did not exist. In the crime of abortion, he explained, "we are not dealing with the right of women to control their bodies, but rather the deposit that was made into her womb in the act of procreation." This "new factor"—the embryo—"intervenes in her absolute right to use and control her body." He argued that "it is necessary to protect" this new subject to preserve "the right to its own life" on which society depends.[91] In essence, the society's interest in increasing the national population superseded women's rights.[92] Tejera's demand for more zealous criminalization of abortion, regardless of honor, on behalf of the national population suggests that the early republican assumption that abortion was a white woman's crime persisted well into the 1930s.

Increased Prosecution, despite Legal Liberalization

Although Tejera criticized the new law's leniency, he must have been satisfied with its results. Following promulgation of the Social Defense Code, official statistics signal a marked increase in criminal abortion prosecutions. Between mid-1938 and mid-1939, Cuba's courts recorded 172 criminal abortion cases, in addition to eight infanticides and one "suposición del parto" (faked birth).[93] Between July 1940 and June 1941, the Audiencia of Havana alone heard 111 criminal abortion cases—roughly double the number on its dockets in the mid-1930s.[94]

This abrupt spike in criminal abortion cases reflected an expanded state role in policing pregnancy and childbirth, recently codified under the 1940 constitution. Article 43 formally subordinated motherhood and family "under the protection of the State." In some respects, this provision promised material benefits to mothers and their children. To be sure, it vested the state with the power to investigate paternity (article 44), which would make it possible to hold men accountable for providing for their children.[95] This reversal of men's historic impunity in reproduction likely prompted studies on the science of paternity, including a 1943 publication by criminologist Israel Castellanos.[96] It also correlated with the abolition of legal distinctions between legitimate and illegitimate children, removing the historic disadvantage of children born out of wedlock. Yet, codifying state authority over something so intimate as motherhood and family also laid the foundation for expanded external involvement in women's reproductive decision-making. Especially in the context of persisting pronatalism and eugenic emphasis on whitening, this expanded authority over the personal and intimate details of women's lives likely contributed significantly to the increasing number of abortion cases tried in Cuba's criminal courts after 1940.

Apart from facilitating expanded prosecution, the Social Defense Code had little material impact on the kinds of cases entering judicial purview. As in previous periods, surviving court cases reveal that the so-called abortion cases recorded in the official statistics included a broad range of reproductive crises facing mostly impoverished women. The unscrupulous physicians that anti-abortionists decried and the wealthy women who made use of their services remained beyond the law's reach.

Police continued to investigate involuntary miscarriages as potential criminal abortions. In 1937, for instance, a judge in the town of Trinidad heard a case involving a white woman, Zóila, who had given birth to a premature stillborn fetus. The woman had a history of reproductive distress, namely chronic hemorrhaging during her previous two pregnancies. In her testimony, she pointed squarely at the abusive treatment her husband, Candelario Bosch y Miranda, subjected her to as the principal cause of the stillbirth. Weak and anemic, Zóila had been prescribed several medications to withstand her pregnancy. She testified that Candelario refused to give her the medication, despite her pleas. On top of exacerbating her medical complications, Candelario declined to hire a female helper to assist his bedridden wife care for their five small children. He physically abused Zóila on numerous occasions throughout her pregnancy, and threatened violence against her on other occasions. These abuses caused Zóila to flee her home, taking her five children with her. The courts classified the case as an "abortion," even though the woman had carried the pregnancy well past twenty weeks. Nevertheless, authorities did not pursue the case.[97]

A 1940 case involving both an abandoned infant and a stillbirth on the same plantation was similarly processed as an abortion. The transcript of the case revealed that a private citizen had discovered a newborn baby girl alive, inside a burlap potato sack and, wrapped in two finer sackcloths. The infant had been abandoned late at night or early in the morning by the side of the Camino Real at the entrance of the Cedro Seco plantation. The man reportedly took the baby to his room, where he fed her. Interestingly, in this initial report, the phrases "of the white race" and "took nourishment well" were underlined in pencil, suggesting that the surviving infant's race and vitality were important factors for authorities.

Just hours later, at nine o'clock in the morning on the same estate, authorities arrived to the home of José Antonio Varona, a Black man, who had allegedly discovered a young woman with the cadaver of a newborn near his residence. The woman, twenty-two-year-old mestiza Bacilia Varona Cruz, admitted that the dead infant was her son. After she "exerted much force" carrying buckets of water, Bacilia felt labor pains. She later gave birth to a premature stillborn fetus without any assistance.

Bacilia's mother and sister, who lived with her, confirmed her story. The sister, twenty-four-year-old Higinia Varona Cruz, added that they did not have the money to send for a doctor or purchase medicine. The only reason anyone found out about her sister's stillborn fetus, she explained, was the "scandal" surrounding the abandoned white infant. Bacilia's mother, María Fausta Cruz Baez, claimed that her daughter "had no reason to hide her pregnancy, since it was publicly known in the neighborhood, and that the fetus was six or seven months [along] and her daughter did nothing to abort [it]." Bacilia herself noted that she lived far from the town, forcing her to rely on home remedies. She placed her stillborn son in a small box in the corner of her house in order to bury it later, but she continued to hemorrhage, forcing her to seek help. Everything is due to the "state of misery," that is, poverty, she found herself in.

Authorities prohibited burying the infant until a thorough investigation of the possible connections between the two cases could be undertaken. Investigators also recommended that the judge order the stillborn infant to be examined to determine whether he had actually been born dead, or whether Bacilia had "ingested a harmful substance" to induce abortion. An autopsy determined that the fetus was only six or seven months along. After abandoning the investigation of the stillborn child because of the advanced state of "putrefaction" of his cadaver, authorities concluded that the two cases could not be connected because the surviving infant was "of the white race, while the mother of the [stillborn] fetus is of the colored race."[98]

A 1941 case involving a fifteen-year-old mestiza, Brígida, who suffered a miscarriage revealed the combined duress of poverty and familial strife. Brígida, who lived with her mother, Eulogia Medina, on the El Infierno estate, became pregnant by her boyfriend, Anselmo Blanco Gómez, in January 1941. Despite her pregnancy, she continued her rigorous work schedule at El Infierno and other plantations, often requiring her to leave early in the morning and return late at night. Brígida testified that on April 2, at around two months pregnant, she fell, which provoked a miscarriage. Her mother described the product of the miscarriage: a little blob that did not exhibit development in the form of a human, nor bones, nor flesh, nor skin. Eulogia took the tissue and buried it by a post in the dirt-floored room of their shack due to "ignorance, not bad faith."

In July, her boyfriend denounced the crime to authorities, who launched a detailed investigation. The judge ordered a priest to preside over exhuming the fetus. On digging up the dirt floor of the girl's room, authorities found no trace of the fetus, which Eulogia and her daughter explained was a result of it being small and undeveloped. Authorities ordered the analysis of the dirt, again coming up empty-handed.

Following the conclusion of the investigation in August 1941, Brígida's sister, Clara Trina, known as "Trinita" Paredes, approached police with quite a different version of events surrounding the termination of Brígida's pregnancy. Trinita confirmed that her sister was indeed pregnant, but suggested that the fetus was much farther along than two months, given the "large belly" her sister exhibited. Trinita pointed not to an out-of-wedlock sexual relationship between Brígida and her boyfriend, Anselmo, but rather a longer history of sexual abuse perpetrated by their stepfather, Filomeno Rodríguez, in whose home the family resided. In fact, Trinita claimed that her sister never even had a boyfriend; rather she had become pregnant after Filomeno raped her. Trinita declared that she fled the house to live with her aunt and godmother because Filomeno "also wanted to perform carnal acts with her." Authorities do not seem to have taken seriously Trinita's declarations. The case records do not evince any investigation of the serious accusations against Filomeno.[99]

Surviving abortion cases from central Cuba underscore the limits of 1930s reformism. Omitting the poverty exemption from the new penal code only aggravated the acutely gendered and racialized impact of economic crisis. With austerity contracting the fledgling network of charitable services, impoverished women and mothers sought abortion as one of few options at their disposal to help them and their families survive the economic conditions. Zealous police and judges, emboldened by the letter of the law and assisted by physicians, hauled a growing number of these desperate women into the penal system. This prosecutorial zeal only amplified the negative impacts women suffered due to continued judicial ignorance over the physiology of reproduction. The apparently routine investigation of involuntary reproductive events through the punitive lens of criminality added humiliation to the grief women already suffered due to their reproductive losses, often inflicting further harm in attempts to collect medical and forensic "evidence." Even as reformers advocated for legal exceptions for economic hardship, impoverished and rural women, especially ones of African descent, continued to be threatened with criminalization for poor pregnancy outcomes.

The existence of parallel samples of criminal abortion cases dating to Cuba's prerevolutionary period, especially the 1940s and 1950s, suggest that the desire to use legal interventions to control impoverished women's reproductive lives persisted well beyond the cases discussed here.[100] In fact, extreme antiabortionism appeared to resurge in the late 1950s, as revolutionaries gained ground against the dictatorship of Fulgencio Batista. In a 1957 article published in the popular Havana magazine *Carteles*, eight prominent white male physicians decried the evils of "Malthusian practices," a euphemism for abortion. Abortion, which several physicians equated with the most heinous murder, threatened the woman's life, and imperiled Cuba's demographic future. Although a few physicians admitted the detrimental impact of poverty and social stigma, they offered only the Knaus-Ogino (rhythm) method as a tool for family planning, and only when absolutely necessary. The overwhelming consensus was that neither the most severe destitution nor the harshest social opprobrium could justify a woman's decision to deprive the nation of its future citizens. The birth of unwanted children, several physicians proclaimed, was nothing that the Christian charity of a new class of white women social workers could not handle. This article communicated an overwhelming consensus among Cuba's leading physicians that abortion was unacceptable under any circumstances.[101]

Why such an extreme position at this particular moment? And what happened to the plurality of views about abortion that had prevailed for much of the previous fifty or even eighty years? One possible answer lies in the resurgence of periodic demographic anxieties following Fulgencio Batista's 1952 coup. During the remainder of the 1950s, population growth declined and birth rates stagnated, likely exacerbated by internal strife on the island.[102] Yet, the physicians interviewed were also clearly concerned with the international reputation of the Cuban medical establishment. Over the 1940s and 1950s, the island had apparently gained somewhat of a reputation among North American women as a place where abortion was easily accessible, unlike in the United States before *Roe v. Wade*. Such a claim was advertised in certain U.S. newspapers, quite to the embarrassment of antiabortionist physicians in Cuba. The article officially rejected this "misinformation." Even as abortion advocates and providers clearly existed, adopting antiabortionism as the official position was deemed necessary for restoring the respectability of Cuba's medical establishment in a neocolonial context in which U.S. opinions mattered greatly.[103]

Physicians had apparently consolidated extreme antiabortionism as the official position of the Cuban medical establishment—a goal that Dr. Coronado had tried to achieve back in the 1910s. Yet, this public relations campaign to uphold the moral rectitude of Cuban medicine came at the expense of impoverished women, whose reproductive lives remained public fodder for police, judges, and jealous physicians. All the while, wealthy women within and beyond Cuba continued to enjoy relatively unfettered access to surgical abortion.

Investigating Miscarriage in Early Revolutionary Cuba

In November 1961, in a sleepy country village in the remote countryside of central Cuba, members of the National Revolutionary Police force detained the morena Felipa Acea, a midwife, on suspicion of performing abortions. Hours earlier, the medical staff at the local maternal and children's hospital had admitted a white woman, Clara, suffering from what doctors initially described as a "nervous breakdown." She claimed to be one of Acea's patients. Her initial examination revealed that the twenty-six-year-old wife and mother of three suffered from a high fever, massive hemorrhaging, and "hysteria." On closer examination, doctors discovered that she was suffering from a uterine infection.

Clara told the doctor that she had started to experience signs of miscarriage several days earlier, after falling while carrying two buckets of water. Spotting intensified to severe bleeding and cramping. When she began suffering high fever and ongoing pain, her husband took her to the maternity and infant hospital in Cienfuegos. There, doctors extracted the remains of her pregnancy. In her fever-induced delirium, Clara apparently insinuated that she had procured an abortion. She told her nurse that she "felt responsible for the miscarriage" and even though she was "sometimes incoherent," she accused herself, her husband, and "someone called Felipa." The hospital director summoned authorities to investigate.

When Acea's client emerged from the procedure, she faced interrogation by the police. Clara confessed to paying the town midwife, Acea, to perform an abortion, with her husband's knowledge. According to Clara, Acea demanded twenty-five pesos up front before initiating a multiday procedure. Clara recounted that the midwife had her lie down on a table and attempted to insert a piece of rubber through the vagina to dilate the cervix prior to the abortion. However, since the cervix was tightly closed, she used forceps. Clara experienced considerable bleeding, and the midwife inserted a wick to help drain the blood. The following day, Clara returned to the office to finish the procedure. The midwife attempted to perform a curettage procedure, inserted gauze into the vagina, and injected her with an unknown substance. She instructed Clara to remove the gauze once she was home and return the next day, since the cervix was still not fully dilated. When Clara returned on the third day, the midwife allegedly found the cervix still closed. Acea instructed her to return the next day, but instead Clara fell ill with a high fever and hemorrhaging. With Clara still delirious, the police detained her at the hospital and arrested Acea for the "crime of abortion." Clara confessed to the crime, but Acea denied involvement. Still, a local judge set bail set at 500 and 1,000 pesos, respectively.

Over the next month, judicial authorities obtained testimony from at least ten private citizens, in addition to expert reports from multiple physicians and police officers. However, the evidence remained inconclusive. In his testimony to the court, the hospital director noted that Clara had confessed to having an abortion multiple times, even after receiving a tranquilizer to calm her "nervous crisis." Nevertheless, a gynecological examination of Clara did not reveal injury to the cervix or surrounding tissue. Nor could anyone verify that Felipa Acea had treated Clara at any point. Clara's husband testified that the midwife Acea had not attended to Clara, nor did they even know her. He also noted that his wife had suffered similar states of temporary insanity, "spending several days talking like a crazy person" after her other pregnancies. A doctor who treated Clara speculated that her high fever likely caused a "mental crisis." The police investigator concluded that Clara had miscarried due to the heavy labor she, as a "country woman" had to perform. Both women posted bail by January 1962 as the investigation continued.[104]

Although it is difficult to ascertain whether Clara had miscarried or obtained an abortion from Felipa, it is evident that medical authorities were hypervigilant about abortion, particularly when midwives performed the procedures. According to the director of the Cienfuegos maternity and infant hospital, "the quantity of women who come to said Hospital with induced abortions is alarming." He was able to confirm that "people without scruples initiate the Malthusian practices and later send [the women] to said Hospital," where physicians are required to perform curettage procedures to save the patient's life. Although he could not "scientifically prove" it, "there are suspicions that what has been said is true."[105] This allegation evinced the remarkable continuity in medical thinking about abortion since the late nineteenth century, as physicians continued to claim the moral high ground in a crusade against practitioners whom they disparaged as quacks and interlopers performing botched abortion procedures.

It is also clear that revolutionary police and judges took allegations of abortion very seriously. Between 1960 and 1963, authorities investigated over two hundred suspected abortions in the jurisdiction of Cienfuegos alone, though that number reflects only the cases that survive in the provincial archive today. Authorities pursued full-blown criminal investigations for seemingly insignificant reproductive events. Throughout this period, physicians employed the term "prácticas maltusianas" as a euphemism for abortion. In the context of Cuba's budding revolution, the reference to English economist Thomas Robert Malthus seemed apt. After all, in his 1798 *Essay on the Principle of Population*, Malthus posited a link between poverty and fertility control strategies.[106] Surviving archival records reveal that the vast majority of Cuban women facing criminal charges for allegedly terminating their pregnancies were impoverished, uneducated, and rural, and African-descended more often than not.

Yet, for Thomas Malthus, poor people's efforts to stave off starvation by limiting family size were more than just a product of poverty. Infanticide, along with epidemic disease, famine, and warfare, served as natural mechanisms to check population growth. Even as Cuban physicians, jurists, and politicians invoked Malthus's name and theory, the intensity of criminalization suggests that they did not share Malthus's laissez-faire attitude toward population, let alone vis-à-vis reproduction. While Malthus imagined that exponential population growth in Europe would strain limited resources, authorities in 1960s Cuba worried about sustaining the revolutionary population, then under siege by hostile forces and foreign enemies. The early 1960s in Cuba were marred by exodus—of education professionals, wealthy business people, physicians, and even children.[107] If Malthus was right about poverty as a natural mechanism of population control, the intensely unequal postcolonial society that the revolution had inherited not only imperiled the birth of future generations of Cubans, it also jeopardized the very revolution itself.

In April 1961, for instance, revolutionary police were dispatched to Colonia Rosario to investigate "counterrevolutionary activity," following a denunciation of "weapons hidden to overthrow the Revolution." As they dug up the patio of the plantation house, they discovered a bundle of bloodstained rags containing fetal remains. Preliminary investigation revealed that the fetus belonged to the plantation owner's daughter-in-law, Mirta, who also lived there. The young woman told police that she had felt cramping after being thrown from a horse. Two physicians attended her. The first doctor informed her that she was starting to miscarry and gave her a medication to help prevent it, but the pregnancy could not be saved. The next day, the doctor informed her that she had retained the placenta and referred her to a second physician, who removed the remains of the pregnancy. Mirta's husband buried the fetus in their yard. Police turned over the fetus to the local morgue and initiated an investigation. Numerous witnesses corroborated Mirta's story. In a pelvic examination of Mirta, the medical examiner reported that he did not see signs of Malthusian practices, and the miscarriage was likely caused by a cist on her left ovary. Police concluded that the miscarriage was natural, not provoked, and ended the case, though not before bringing Mirta's miscarriage to the attention of her entire family and neighborhood.[108]

Authorities also pursued investigations following accusations by jealous spouses, rival neighbors, and dissatisfied associates. In April 1963, authorities in Cienfuegos received a detailed denunciation of an abortion. The denunciation alleged that a man named Zoilo had called a midwife to perform an abortion on his wife. The midwife, known as Petrona, visited Zoilo's house for three consecutive days. One of Zoilo's tenants, who rented a room in his house, had overheard the conversations with the midwife and told her daughter, Rosa, who in turn denounced the crime to authorities. Rosa demanded a thorough investigation of the crime, including an examination of Zoilo's wife by medical experts "as soon as possible so the symptoms of the abortion and pregnancy do not disappear with the passage of time."[109] Authorities opened an investigation into the crime and the identity of the midwife.

While authorities took the allegations very seriously, Rosa gave ample reason to believe that she reported the alleged abortion to avenge her eighty-year-old mother, Felina, of apparent abuses by Zoilo, her former landlord. According to Rosa's denunciation, Felina had been renting a room in Zoilo's home for several years, paying twelve pesos in rent. However, the Urban Reform Law of 1960, which prohibited landlords from charging rent for urban real estate, changed the dynamic between Felina and Zoilo. Felina now paid ten pesos to the revolutionary government, much to Zoilo's dismay. No longer receiving rent, Zoilo apparently resolved to oust Felina, reportedly demanding that she move out. When she refused, he denounced her to authorities for various reasons, claimed she was crazy and belonged in an insane asylum, and most recently prohibited her from using the only toilet in the house. Zoilo had even denounced Rosa and her husband to authorities for unknown crimes. In the midst of all this conflict, Rosa reported the alleged abortion.

Both Zoilo and his wife denied the charges. They told authorities that neither of them knew any midwife by the name of Petrona, and that the denunciation owed to personal conflicts between Zoilo and his former tenant, Felina. Felina corroborated her daughter's allegations but admitted that her hearing was poor. Although the allegations were dubious, authorities initiated a criminal investigation and subjected Zoilo's wife to a pelvic exam. The medical examiner found no evidence of abortive practices. However, the neighborhood Committee for the Defense of the Revolution (CDR) revealed that Zoilo's wife had visited a midwife on several occasions, then took fifteen days off from work. Although the CDR did not profess to know the veracity of the current allegation, they also reported that they had learned from a family member that Zoilo's wife had terminated other pregnancies, visiting a midwife known as Amancia Ramírez, who worked in the maternity and infant hospital. Authorities interrogated Amancia, who testified that she did not recall visiting Zoilo's wife, since she attends a large number of patients. The investigation ended with no convictions.[110]

Other abortion cases arrived to the courts after lovers' quarrels ended in vengeful accusations. In March 1962, Ramón, a resident of La Sierra, denounced his former lover Guillermina for getting an abortion after leaving him. He told authorities that Guillermina was about six months pregnant with a very advanced belly when she left him. The next time he saw her, she did not have the pregnant belly, and he suspected that she had an abortion. Guillermina denied the allegations, testifying that she fell while visiting her parents. When she began bleeding, she sought medical care and a doctor gave her medication. Sometime thereafter, she separated from Ramón, whom she claimed "mistreated women" and threatened to kill her if she left. Authorities ordered a medical examination of Guillermina, which revealed no signs of pregnancy or Malthusian practices. The police investigator concluded that Guillermina had indeed been pregnant while living with Ramón. He suspected that she had procured an abortion but could not prove it, so he closed the case.[111] That the investigator chose to include his unsubstantiated opinion of the suspect's guilt in the official case file underscores how the presumption of guilt fueled humiliating and invasive interventions into women's most intimate experiences.

The prevalence of physician-reported cases suggests that earlier recommendations to mandate reporting of suspected abortions had actually materialized by the 1960s. In January 1963, a physician at the maternity and infant hospital in Cienfuegos reported to judicial authorities that Moraima Acea Apesteguía was under treatment for uterine hemorrhage. Moraima told authorities that she was at a bembé party in the outlying Cienfuegos neighborhood of Pueblo Grifo when a machete fight erupted. In the commotion, she was thrown to the ground several times, causing her to miscarry. The ensuing investigation corroborated Moraima's story, thereafter focusing more on the chaos of the party. Apparently, the host, Mailén, was a person of "terrible antecedents" who engaged in prostitution. She frequently threw bembé parties attended by "criminal elements," including prostitutes, homosexuals, and other "individuals of dubious morality," including Moraima, who also allegedly practiced prostitution. According to the CDR, there had been numerous complaints about the "scandals" and prostitution emanating from Mailén's residence, but no arrests were made.[112] Nonetheless, the focus on the alleged immorality, gender transgression, and racial disorder underscored the disparaging attitudes authorities brought to bear on ailing women like Moraima.

Physicians apparently reported more than cases in which patients made direct allegations or confessions. In fact, they seemed to report to authorities even women who sought care for spontaneous miscarriages. In March 1960, for instance, doctors on call at the Centro de Socorro in Cienfuegos reported several patients who presented with abnormal uterine bleeding following miscarriage that was "spontaneous and purely casual." Although the law did not require criminal investigation in such cases, these physician reports nonetheless prompted the Cienfuegos Juzgado de Instrucción to file a record in each instance.[113]

Criminal convictions appeared rare in this sample of abortion cases. Nevertheless, the sheer volume of cases suggests that both medical and judicial authorities remained vigilant about possible abortions. The existence of so many abortion cases might seem like an anomaly in the context of a revolution explicitly committed to dismantling systems of class, racial, and gender oppression. Could this be evidence of a crackdown on abortion during the first years of the revolution? One scholar has recently posited that access to abortion initially became more restrictive during the early revolutionary period than in previous periods when women enjoyed broad access to abortion in Cuba. This supposed rupture with the past is used to suggest that the revolutionary government "increased state control over women's bodies and their reproductive decisions."[114] However, situating these cases within a *longue durée* narrative nullifies this claim. Certainly, the volume of surviving cases dating to the early 1960s is greater than previous periods. However, this aligns with broader patterns across the Americas, as law enforcement developed and criminal prosecution expanded over the twentieth century.[115] It also reflects the superior conservation in Cuban archives of more recent documents, compared with older records which are more inconsistent due to losses and accidents accompanying jurisdictional shifts and political transitions.

Perhaps more importantly, analyzing these cases against those from the republican period demonstrates remarkable continuities, rather than abrupt changes in women's reproductive experiences during the early revolution. The kinds of people and circumstances reflected in criminal abortion investigations and the way they arrived to the attention of authorities after the revolution were remarkably similar to those before it. Reflecting entrenched patterns dating back to the nineteenth century, authorities investigated a range of reproductive events. Most common among these were ones with no apparent criminal act, like spontaneous miscarriage and stillbirth, evincing the ongoing criminalization of poor pregnancy outcomes. But this approach did not affect all women equally. On the contrary, even before the twentieth century, reproductive events like abortion and miscarriage came to the attention of the state only when racialized poverty so limited women's reproductive options that their private matters became public. Financial constraints forced impoverished women to seek abortions from informal practitioners, raising the chances of infection, which then compelled them to seek emergency medical care at hospitals, where physicians denounced them to police. Impoverished and rural women, including many women of African descent, above all continued to face disproportionate legal interventions into their reproductive lives. Reproductive events also came to the attention of authorities often through rumors and personal conflicts, which more commonly encompassed private matters of pregnancy in impoverished communities, where women enjoyed less privacy due to social and physical proximity to their neighbors. These findings suggest that persisting demographic concerns, backed by an unaltered legal code, tempered the positive impact of the revolution's healthcare expansion for women and their families. Indeed, despite the transcendental political and economic change of the revolution, socialist attitudes toward women's reproductive duties remained remarkably similar to their capitalist predecessors, even as the state harnessed them toward different ends.[116]

The large number of criminal abortion investigations suggests that the triumph of the revolution did not immediately or dramatically dismantle the historic restrictions on women's reproductive choices. This interpretation aligns more closely with feminist scholarship showing the persistence of women's subordination through revolutionary change.[117] Difficulties such as reduced capacity to provide women's reproductive healthcare following the emigration of large numbers of ob-gyns, the struggle to provide affordable contraception, especially with the U.S. embargo, and the enforcement of antiabortion laws, contributed to the revolution's ultimate failure to dismantle longstanding reproductive injustices disproportionately afflicting impoverished women and women of color. Yet, it is striking that many of the denunciations occurred at women's interface with physicians and hospitals, suggesting that the revolutionary expansion of medical care into poor and rural communities may have been a double-edged sword for Cuba's poorest women. Elise Andaya posits that the ongoing criminalization of abortion contributed to a spike in abortion-related death as well as unwanted births in the context of the early revolution's baby boom.[118] But these cases also make it abundantly clear that Cuban women continued to seek and obtain abortion despite the state's efforts to suppress it.

The absence of criminal abortion cases after 1963 is perhaps no coincidence. This was the year that Cuban birth rates peaked, potentially forcing Cuban authorities to reconsider the material costs of pronatalism in a society in which the state promised to assume some of the burden of child-rearing. Shifting attitudes toward women's reproduction in the early years of the revolution became policy in 1965, when the revolutionary government adopted the World Health Organization's more expansive definition of health. This modification to the meaning of the 1936 abortion law enabled most women to obtain legal abortions through the existing exemption for procedures required for the woman's health.

This chapter underscores key continuities in the ways the Cuban state approached abortion between the early Cuban republic and the first five years following the revolution. Throughout this period, physicians, lawmakers, and jurists converged in a largely pronatalist posture that vilified abortion as immoral and detrimental to the nation, framing it as unacceptable under most circumstances. This persisting opposition to abortion drew on long-standing colonial gender ideologies, including the assumption that women only rejected motherhood to salvage their honor. The persistence of this belief accentuated implicit racial ideas undergirding antiabortionism, which many physicians viewed as one of the greatest threats to Cuba's white population.

Contrary to recent claims that abortion restrictions became more severe during the early 1960s, an analysis of the letter of the law suggests 1959 did not mark a turning point for women's access to abortion in Cuba.[119] Rather, the medical and legal debates surrounding the Social Defense Code, and its eventual adoption as law in 1936, reflected a concerted though ultimately frustrated effort to challenge extreme antiabortionism, as the procedure became more common across a broader social and racial spectrum of Cuban women. Analyzing surviving court cases shows that criminal prosecution persisted through the triumph of the Cuban Revolution, not as a rupture with the past, but as a response to the continuity in the letter of the law as well as ongoing anxieties about population.

Finally, the ways physicians and judges enacted their antiabortionist views reproduced racialized and gendered inequities among patients as well as reproductive health care providers. Especially as surgical abortion became cheaper and more readily available through midwives and nonprofessional practitioners, impoverished women and women of color bore the brunt of criminal prosecution, just as they had for infanticide during the nineteenth century.

Moreover, physicians also exploited antiabortion laws to denounce Black female midwives, whose ongoing provision of reproductive health care challenged the consolidation of physicians' authority over pregnancy and childbirth dating back to the 1820s. Although white male physicians routinely performed illegal abortions, medical doctors conflated clandestine abortion with midwives, who disproportionately faced legal consequences for providing these vital services. Thus, the de facto decriminalization of abortion in 1965 marked a major turning point for Cuban women because it dismantled the legal rationale for the historically racialized prosecution of patients and midwives. More work is necessary to explore how this new legal climate affected the status of women of color vis-à-vis the medical profession.

CONCLUSION

Protection, Correction, or Liberation

Pregnancy has historically held wide-ranging consequences for women and their families. Since the colonial period, honor, marriage prospects, economic status, individual aspirations, and so many other vital social and cultural contingencies all hinged on the circumstances of and power dynamics surrounding the sexual act resulting in pregnancy. Yet, decisions about whether and under what circumstances to conceive and how to handle pregnancy were rarely in the hands of women alone. Rather, nearly all segments of society laid claim to the potential of women's wombs. A woman's family, her spiritual community, and the man who impregnated her all had moral and material interests in decisions about the pregnancy. The state, too, laid claim to women's fertility as a determinant of one of the most valuable resources available: population.

Indeed, population was serious business since the very inception of Spanish rule. Long before the Argentine political theorist Juan Bautista Alberdi coined the now-famous expression "to govern is to populate" (*gobernar es poblar*) in the mid-nineteenth century, colonial and metropolitan authorities obsessed over the size and composition of Cuba's population.[1] And although the historiography does not necessarily reflect it, Cuban elites well understood that it was not just the immigration or importation of men that influenced population growth; it was also women's ability and willingness to become pregnant, give birth, and raise future subjects and, later, citizens.

From the moment Cuba became a multiracial colonial society, following the Spanish colonization of the island, elite interests in pregnancy hinged on three key variables: a woman's race, her class status, and, during times of slavery, her legal status. For much of the colonial period, concern over pregnancy and fertility control focused exclusively on white women, generally aiming to maximize the white population by increasing fertility and reducing fertility control practices. Initially, class distinctions played a major role in prevailing attitudes about white women's reproductive lives. During the first two centuries of colonial rule, policymakers focused on saving infants born illegitimately to elite white women. The reproductive potential of poor and laboring populations initially received much less attention. Spanish authorities demonstrated their apathy toward the reproduction of Native women in the impunity they afforded to conquistadores, who not only massacred pregnant women and infants but disrupted families to the point of making demographic recovery impossible.

Until the rise of plantation slavery in Cuba in the late eighteenth century, policymakers paid little attention to enslaved women's fertility control strategies and even less to their pregnancy experiences. Instead, elites uniformly pursued population growth, implicitly focusing on white women. As Cuba rapidly transformed from a predominantly white settler colony to a majority Black slave society over the second half of the eighteenth century, elites began to approach population management in a more explicitly racialized way. The prevailing demographic agenda became centered on white population growth across class distinctions, while simultaneously managing Black population growth based on legal status.

Because legal status passed from mother to child, women of African descent carried in their wombs the dual possibility of preserving Cuba's burgeoning institution of slavery and of accelerating the already-worrisome growth of the free Black population. Thus elites sought different outcomes for the reproduction of free women than they did for that of enslaved women. Whereas elites consistently sought to limit the growth of the free Black population, for the century following the late consolidation of plantation slavery in an age of abolitionism, a pronatalist agenda emerged to increase reproduction by enslaved women.

As the island's Black population surpassed whites at the turn of the nineteenth century, Cuban intellectuals sought to curtail what they deemed to be the excessive fertility of free women of color, particularly in urban areas. By contrast, with abolitionism rising in the late eighteenth century British Atlantic and arriving to Cuba by the early nineteenth century, enslaved women's reproduction became increasingly central to preserving slavery. As restrictions on the transatlantic slave trade mounted after 1817, colonial authorities actively encouraged procreation among enslaved women, whose wombs were seen as key to slavery's future.

These demographic anxieties did not merely melt away with the late demise of slavery. On the contrary, they assumed new shape and gained renewed urgency. After all, the gradual emancipation of enslaved people coincided with a protracted, halting, and truncated struggle for Cuban sovereignty that—despite achieving independence from Spain in 1898, ending U.S. military rule in 1902, and abrogating the Platt Amendment in 1934—did not fully materialize until the Cuban Revolution in 1959. During this period, an evolving group of national elites sought to shape the face of the national population and, by extension, the identity of the emerging nation. Population growth remained central to that project, and although racial language became less overt during the republican period, the aspiration for whiteness persisted. Thus, the long-standing demographic agenda that prioritized increasing the Cuban population through white population growth and Black population management endured through the republican years.

Various groups of Cuban elites operationalized these overarching demographic desires, in part, through interventions in women's reproduction. They approached pregnancy, childbirth, and motherhood in substantially different ways, and they sought to advance their demographic goals by using fundamentally different methods, both depending primarily on race. Whereas they sought to increase the white population through protection and assistance, they approached managing the Black population through punishment and correction.

These racially specific reproductive interventions reflected two competing worldviews when it came to the relationship between reproduction and population. One perspective, rooted in the Spanish Roman Catholic tradition, framed reproduction as women's Christian duty to bring new souls into the church. However, religious and social expectations demanded that women procreate only within legitimate Christian marriage.[2] This meant that any pregnancies conceived through illicit (premarital, adulterous, sacrilegious, or incestuous) sex could destroy a woman's honor. The need to preserve honor drove women to terminate pregnancies and abandon or murder infants to hide from public view the physical consequences of their sexual indiscretions. Although fertility control violated both Iberian law and religious principle, authorities viewed these women in the image of Eve—morally corrupt but deserving of grace. Based on this understanding, the solution to fertility control involved not legal prosecution or excommunication but extending Christian charity to unwanted infants and even their mothers. Protection and assistance, thus, became mechanisms of fostering population growth by mitigating the social consequences of illicit conception.

A second understanding, implanted in Cuba precisely during the late eighteenth-century consolidation of plantation slavery, was rooted in Malthusian perspectives linking overpopulation to poverty. The 1798 publication of Thomas Robert Malthus's *Essay on the Principle of Population* posited that reproduction naturally produced exponential population growth, which placed mounting pressure on land and resources.[3] According to this perspective, poor people's responses to poverty, such as limiting fertility through infanticide, helped slow population growth caused by unrestrained reproduction, thereby controlling the labor supply. Any interventions to mitigate poverty were seen as only exacerbating the problems of overpopulation, because they removed the natural constraints on fertility. Therefore, the solution was to refrain from ameliorating poverty and instead control poor people's sexuality.[4]

For much of Cuba's colonial period, protection and assistance defined the prevailing approach to women's reproduction, as authorities sought to increase the colonial population, which they implicitly envisioned as white. It informed the creation of charitable establishments with strong roots in the Catholic Church, such as the San Francisco de Paula Women's Hospital and later the Casa de Expósitos. However, prevailing attitudes about who deserved access to such assistance did not include women of African descent or their infants. Particularly as the African-descended population expanded through the eighteenth century, racial restrictions became increasingly central to managing Cuban houses of charity. Whereas the women's hospital originally served free women regardless of race, the Casa de Expósitos, established just a half century later, explicitly excluded certain abandoned infants from admission on the basis of race. And even though the implementation of this racial boundary was always imperfect, efforts to enforce it defined the history of the Casa and other charitable institutions.

Not coincidentally, white women's expanding access to charity coincided with efforts to liberalize fertility control laws in racially specific ways. At first glance, the reluctance to prosecute white women appears to contradict the demographic agenda of increasing the white population. After all, the impunity with which wealthy white women committed abortion was perceived as the principal cause of the dwindling size of elite white families in the late nineteenth and early twentieth centuries. However, within the context of Cuba's expanding network of racially restrictive charitable services, it is clear that the reluctance to prosecute white women did not reflect any lack of interest in maximizing white women's reproduction. On the contrary, it merely reflected a reluctance to deploy criminalization, specifically, to control white women's fertility, even as elites willingly applied it to women of African descent and impoverished women. This contrast reveals how Cuban elites applied diverging tactics to advance their demographic goals, depending on women's race and status. Whereas prosecution, violence, and coercion were deemed acceptable tactics for controlling the reproduction of women of African descent and impoverished women, they were apparently less socially acceptable for approaching more privileged white women. Instead, authorities sought to achieve white population growth in ways that aligned with the racialized patriarchal expectation to protect, rather than punish, white women.

This patriarchal protection of white women was the pretext for an expanding surveillance, regulation, and penalization of women of color, whose reproductive labor had historically been essential to preserving white infant life and tending to pregnant white women and mothers. In fact, physician-led regulation of wet nurses as early as the eighteenth century and midwives from the nineteenth century onward defined the professionalization of medicine. Claiming to protect white women from the alleged abuses of women of color served as a foil for consolidating white male authority over pregnancy and childbirth.

The second view, which linked overpopulation and poverty, shaped the treatment of mothers and children of African descent, most especially those with legal freedom. For this population, the overarching interventions wielded exclusion and penalization to control population growth. These patterns were most evident in racial restrictions on access to charitable institutions, which essentially left impoverished Black mothers and their children to suffer and die under the weight of their poverty, or somehow not have as many children. The emphasis on controlling sexuality emerged in the tendency to prosecute impoverished women of color for alleged fertility crimes.

This racialized criminalization of fertility control might seem to contradict the demographic goal of controlling the free Black population. However, when juxtaposed with the racialized exclusion from assistance, this willingness to prosecute women of color evinces an effort to enforce a unique form of reproductive control, which privileged reducing fertility by suppressing sexuality. Rather than disaggregating sex from pregnancy through family planning (or at least allowing for some flexibility for when illicit pregnancy inevitably occurred), racial restrictions on support services made pregnancy and motherhood as materially inconvenient as possible for the most vulnerable groups of women. In this context, women of color, particularly those whose economic situations remained precarious, had few alternatives to rearing children in poverty: they could try to prevent pregnancy by abstaining from sex or risk criminalization for practicing fertility control. This racially selective deployment of withholding assistance and threatening criminalization to control fertility was tantamount to punishing anything other than the demanded sexual behavior—in essence, an early manifestation of "abstinence-only" logic.[5]

This insight about how the reproductive control of women of African descent hinged on enforcing certain rigid sexual behaviors helps revise and expand prevailing scholarly interpretations of race and sexuality. Existing scholarship focuses mainly on the ways patriarchy has shaped the sexual control of white women, through constructs such as virginity, chastity, fidelity, and especially the institution of marriage. Such studies emphasize the racial hierarchy within Cuba's sexual economy, which manifested in lower rates of formal marriage among people of African descent, who married at declining proportions over the colonial and early republican periods. Within this framework, scholars have rightly observed the hypersexualization of Black women, who were cast as sexually available to white men, morally corrupt, and excessively fertile.[6] While this interpretation rightly captures the diverging sexual roles assigned to women across Cuba's racial spectrum, it presents white women as the principal victims of the patriarchy's sexual control, eclipsing the ways women of African descent were saddled with similar sexual expectations, albeit in different ways, under different conditions, and for different social purposes.

In fact, both white women and women of African descent, wealthy women and impoverished alike, faced pressures to abstain from out-of-wedlock sex. For

Cuba's most privileged women, public honor, which determined social status, marriage prospects, and so much more, demanded strict adherence to standards of sexual propriety. Fathers zealously guarded their daughters' virginity, warding off the predations of unworthy men, to protect the family's status and guard the daughter's reputation and eligibility for marriage. In turn, husbands were expected to provide for and protect wives in exchange for sexual fidelity. Even though the social status of white women remained closely linked to sexual propriety, elite society well understood that white women frequently violated these sexual ideals, whether willingly or involuntarily. A range of institutional, material, and social resources emerged to mitigate the consequences of white women's periodic sexual indiscretions by hiding resulting pregnancies from public view. Such mechanisms for forgiveness proved necessary for maintaining Cuba's colonial racial hierarchy by sustaining the reputations and privileges of white women and families.

For less privileged groups of women, honor proved less central, but standards of sexual conduct remained overwhelmingly similar, even as these women were afforded fewer protections. Outside slavery but especially within it, the disruptions to family and kin relations essentially precluded enslaved, free Black, and impoverished women from enjoying any of the patriarchal protections routinely afforded to more privileged (white) women. Depending on the moral and material whims of their owners, enslaved women faced gender segregation from enslaved men; coerced sex, marriage, and conception with enslaved men; and outright rape and sexual violence by white men. Free women of color faced similar sexual pressures, with pregnancy often meaning the end of employment, even as employment sometimes required sexual availability. At the same time that slave owners and employers restricted these women's ability to exercise sexual and intimate partnerships with the men of their choosing, men *not* of their choosing—especially ones with privilege and power—wielded disproportionate power over their sexual lives.

In a world in which pregnancy and motherhood were already financially and socially challenging, enslaved and free women of African descent faced overwhelming burdens on their reproductive lives. Enslaved women bore babies who were ripped from their arms. While enslaved women were expected and pressured to continue bearing children whom they had to surrender to slavery, free women of color faced mounting pressures to limit their fertility, which elites viewed as excessive and socially detrimental. Free women of color faced negative material consequences for becoming pregnant and having children, which included exclusion from support services and resources, poverty, and the threat of criminalization for fertility control. These negative consequences functioned to enforce abstinence as the only acceptable method of limiting fertility, even as this was not always completely within the control of women themselves, especially since Black women's bodies continued to be viewed as sexually available to white men. Given these paradoxes, many women of color confronted impossible situations.

When it came to enslaved women during the final century of Cuban slavery, the demographic agenda evinced a profound conflict between protective pronatalism and more coercive, punitive measures. Colonial and metropolitan authorities, planters, and physicians deployed an array of interventions to increase the enslaved population. A few of these interventions, such as recommendations that planters treat pregnant slaves less barbarically, applied the protectionist model to increase fertility. However, colonial authorities appeared to recognize a practical problem in applying the protectionist model to enslaved women, because shielding enslaved women from the violence of slavery required intervention in slave owners' property rights. This not only proved ineffective, as Cuban planters simply disregarded laws and guidelines and continued to rely on the clandestine slave trade, it also generated frictions between colonial authorities and elites, which troubled the fragile colonial consensus in one of Spain's last remaining American colonies.

Punitive or corrective interventions briefly coexisted with the clearly ineffective protectionist ones but far outlasted them. For example, one recommendation that emerged alongside the "good treatment" mandates was to emphasize Christian marriage. Although enslaved people's access to the sacrament required some cooperation from slave owners, its primary aim was to impose a particular model of monogamous intimacy, which planters imagined would increase the fertility of enslaved women by correcting their alleged sexual promiscuity, vice, and immorality.

Colonial authorities eventually abandoned protective mandates altogether for a more voluntary model premised on the belief that planters' would act in their own financial best interest by encouraging enslaved reproduction. Interventions then shifted toward purely punitive measures, including criminal prosecution of enslaved women for alleged fertility crimes. Colonial authorities had shifted the focus of their surveillance and enforcement from planters to enslaved women. However, in contrast to the courts' approach to free women of color, who often languished in prison where they could not reproduce, enslaved women were most often exploited for their reproductive labor in charitable institutions serving white women and children for months or even years before being returned to their owners. Remanding these enslaved women to their owners underscored the expectation that they resume their reproductive duties to help preserve slavery in an age of abolitionism.

The racialized duality of protecting white women and punishing women of color continued to shape post-emancipation reproductive interventions. As Cuba transitioned from colony to republic, historic anxieties over the size and quality of the national population resurfaced with even greater urgency. National interest in women's reproduction emerged most clearly in expanding maternal and infant welfare services. Within a broader public health campaign to address infant mortality and morbidity, physicians advocated for expanded state protections for pregnant women, mothers, and their infants, while also seeking to limit access to family planning technologies. These interventions were often premised on the ongoing surveillance, regulation, and criminalization of women of color wet nurses and midwives. Physicians framed these reforms as a means to protect white women and infants from suffering poor pregnancy outcomes. The limited gains in social welfare disproportionately benefited white families, while contraceptive restrictions were understood to promote higher fertility among white women, whose racial and economic privilege afforded them preferential access to medical care, including family planning.

Abortion, too, fell under this racialized pronatalism. By the early republican period, physicians decried a criminal abortion crisis, stemming from the growing involvement of physicians and midwives in medical and surgical pregnancy terminations. In this context, physicians debated the role of the medical profession in the prosecution of criminal abortion, ultimately targeting midwives, who were disproportionately women of color, and patients themselves. The medical uproar over criminal abortion reflected implicit racial assumptions about the kind of women who procured these procedures. References to honor suggest that physicians overwhelmingly understood abortion patients as white, precisely the kind of women whose babies they deemed so necessary for the nation. Physicians demanded that judges protect white women from the threat of abortion by prosecuting practitioners, while criminalizing women of color themselves for attempting abortions. All of these policies supported an implicitly racialized pronatalist nationalism emanating from Cuba's medical community.

As surgical abortion expanded beyond the privileged urban elite, medical and legal attitudes toward the procedure began to shift, particularly in the context of the global economic crisis of the 1930s. Feminist and Marxist-inspired critiques of the patriarchal oppression of women and the deleterious effects of poverty on pregnancy and children inspired architects of the 1936 Social Defense Code to write one of the most liberal abortion laws in the Americas at the time, even though the proposed exemption for poverty-induced abortions did not make it into the final version. While the law afforded lesser sentences and broader exemptions than the 1870 penal code, the courts heard far more abortion cases after the 1936 law's introduction than before it, and the majority of the accused were poor women. Although convictions remained rare, the 1936 law gave police and judges great latitude to intervene in ordinary women's reproductive lives, even during routine reproductive events like miscarriages. As they had before, physicians used the criminalization of abortion to pursue their ongoing rivalry against midwives, mostly women of color, through the courts. Poor women and women of color disproportionately bore the burden of criminalization within the broader context of exclusion.

The larger social implications of protecting white women and excluding and criminalizing women of color were clear. Condemning Black women to raise their children in poverty reinforced and strengthened the existing racial hierarchy and breathed new life into racist assumptions about people of African descent. Not only did poor, racially marginalized women make easy targets for police, judges, and physicians, who already assumed racial and moral degeneracy as a cause of poor pregnancy outcomes, but impoverished mothers with dependent children also ensured their availability and vulnerability in the labor pool. Moreover, children raised in poverty would face circumscribed life chances accompanying limited access to maternal attention, medical care, and educational opportunities, among other building blocks of social mobility.

The triumph of the revolution in 1959 promised to address these historic inequities through expanded access to health care, education, and social services, as well as discursive commitments to dismantling racial and gender oppression. However, for the first several years of the revolution, continuities rather than change defined state approaches to women's reproduction. Physicians and revolutionary police continued to investigate impoverished and rural women, many of whom were of African descent, for a range of reproductive events, from suspected criminal abortion to spontaneous miscarriage. The 1965 informal adoption of a more liberal interpretation of women's health marked a watershed: formal criminal investigations of abortion and miscarriage stopped at this time. Although abortion was not formally decriminalized until a new penal code was instituted in 1979, the informal interpretive shift effectively decriminalized abortion in Cuba.

In the context of expanded access to contraception, and to medical care more generally, as well as major revolutionary social reforms such as universal childcare and maternity protections, this important change afforded unprecedented reproductive autonomy to Cuba's most vulnerable women. However, expanded access to abortion does not necessarily translate to more equitable reproductive experiences for women and their families. Scholars have raised important challenges to the triumphalist narrative that the revolution abolished colonial racial disparities through more equitable access to education, healthcare, housing, food, and social services.[7] More research is needed to understand the extent to which the de facto decriminalization of abortion influenced historic racial disparities in women's reproductive experiences.

Whatever extent the revolution may have alleviated racial disparities in women's reproductive lives, market-oriented reforms introduced in response to the Special Period reversed many of the gains.[8] The disintegration of the Soviet Union, and the ensuing collapse of Soviet subsidies to Cuba, brought on a period of intense economic crisis known as the Special Period. In response, the revolutionary government implemented economic adjustments, including the liberalization of private enterprise, tourism, and remittances, as well as the establishment of a dual-currency economy. These reforms drove growing economic disparities in post-Soviet Cuba, in which access to foreign currency through work in the tourism industry or via remittances from relatives living abroad enabled some Cubans to attain significantly higher standards of living than most. The widening gap translated most obviously into disparate access to nutrition, a key determinant of maternal and fetal health. Additionally, many important revolutionary services aimed at reducing the burden of reproduction on women contracted with austerity measures, contributing to declining fertility and increased pregnancy termination.[9] These trends underscore what scholars of reproductive justice have argued regarding the insufficiency of abortion for guaranteeing women's autonomy in reproductive decision-making.[10]

Dorothy Roberts argues that reproduction has historically served as a mechanism of racial inequality, but that it also offers a possible route to liberation.[11] Certainly, the evidence presented here confirms that, in Cuba, racial inequality defined women's experiences of reproduction, as did legal status under slavery. Though much of this book underscores the almost insurmountable weight of structures of racial and gender oppression, it does so with the hope of illuminating potential pathways toward a more just and equitable society. In emphasizing the oppressive power of medicalization, charity, and criminalization, it also anticipates the potential for those same assemblages to be redesigned for more just ends, allowing women and people with uteruses to enjoy greater bodily autonomy and to engage or not with reproduction on their own terms.

NOTES

ABBREVIATIONS

AHMT, JIT	Archivo Histórico Municipal de Trinidad, Juzgado de Instrucción de Trinidad
Anales	*Anales de la Academia de Ciencias Médicas, Físicas y Naturales de la Habana*
ANC, FCB	Archivo Nacional de la República de Cuba, Fondo Casa de Beneficencia
ANC, GSC	Archivo Nacional de la República de Cuba, Fondo Gobierno Superior Civil
ANC, RCJF	Archivo Nacional de la República de Cuba, Fondo Real Consulado de la Junta de Fomento
ANC, ME	Archivo Nacional de la República de Cuba, Fondo Miscelánea de Expedientes
APHC, JIC	Archivo Provincial Histórico de Cienfuegos, Juzgado de Instrucción de Cienfuegos
exp.	*expediente* (an archival item within a *legajo*)
leg.	*legajo* (a bundle of archival items)

INTRODUCTION. Centering Women in Cuba's Demographic Dilemma

1. De la Fuente, *Havana and the Atlantic*, 85.

2. Funes Monzote, *From Rainforest to Cane Field*; Moreno Fraginals, *Sugarmill*; Curtin, *Rise and Fall*.

3. Knight, *Slave Society in Cuba*, 22; Reid-Vázquez, *Year of the Lash*, 16, 17.

4. For an account of the Haitian Revolution, see Dubois, *Avengers of the New World*; For an account of the impact of the Haitian Revolution on Cuba during the early nineteenth century, see Ferrer, *Freedom's Mirror*; González-Ripoll Navarro et al., *El rumor de Haití*.

5. Slave imports to Cuba by individual year and broad regions of embarkation, Slave-Voyages Trans-Atlantic Slave Trade Database, www.slavevoyages.org/voyagesK6Yugs RW, accessed October 23, 2017; Bergad, García, and Barcia, *Cuban Slave Market*, 27.

6. Knight, *Slave Society in Cuba*, 22; Reid-Vázquez, *Year of the Lash*, 16, 17.

7. Naranjo Orovio, "El temor a la 'africanización.'" Also see Reid-Vázquez, *Year of the*

Lash, 22–23. For an account of the development of one of these white colonies, see Lucero, *Cuban City, Segregated*.

8. Saco, *Colección de papeles científicos*, 2:129–47; Saco, *La supresión del tráfico*.

9. Saco, *Ideario reformista*, 32.

10. Corwin, *Spain*; Murray, *Odious Commerce*.

11. I use the term "women" to denote people with uteruses, who often, but not always inhabited their social words in ways understood to be feminine in their cultural and temporal contexts. Pregnancy, childbearing, and motherhood were central to this social construct, even when bodies understood to be female refused, struggled, or failed to meet those expectations, and even when people's physical and experiential truths transcended binaries of sex and gender.

12. Helg, *Our Rightful Share*; Lucero, *Revolutionary Masculinity and Racial Inequality*; Guridy, *Forging Diaspora*; Pappademos, *Black Political Activism*; Benson, *Antiracism in Cuba*.

13. On honor and marriage in colonial Latin American societies, see Seed, *To Love, Honor, and Obey*; Socolow, "Amor y matrimonio"; Lavrín, *Sexuality and Marriage*; O'Phelan Godoy et al., *Familia y vida cotidiana*; Lyman L. Johnson and Lipsett-Rivera, *Faces of Honor*; Germeten, *Violent Delights, Violent Ends*. These insights have framed studies of nineteenth-century Cuba and other parts of Latin America. See Martínez-Alier, *Marriage, Class and Colour*; Martinez-Alier, "Elopement and Seduction." Also see Suárez Findlay, *Imposing Decency*; Sloan, *Runaway Daughters*; Twinam, *Public Lives, Private Secrets*; María Elena Martínez, *Genealogical Fictions*; Twinam, *Purchasing Whiteness*.

14. González and Premo, *Raising an Empire*; Twinam, *Public Lives, Private Secrets*.

15. Twinam, "Church," 166; González, "Down and Out in Havana," 103. The institution was founded as the Real Casa de Expósitos, pejoratively called the Casa Cuna. Later, it was expanded to include an internal maternity ward, and merged with the Casa de Beneficencia in the 1850s, becoming the Casa de Beneficencia y Maternidad.

16. See, for example, Jaffary, *Reproduction and Its Discontents*; Roth, *Miscarriage of Justice*.

17. Martínez-Alier, *Marriage, Class and Colour*.

18. On mulata women's racial improvement through sex with white men, see Andreo García and Abao, "Vida y muerte"; also see Fraunhar, *Mulata Nation*.

19. Barcia Zequeira, *La otra familia*.

20. Morrison, *Cuba's Racial Crucible*; Perera Díaz and Meriño Fuentes, "African Women."

21. See, for example, Berry and Harris, *Sexuality and Slavery*.

22. Meriño Fuentes and Díaz, "La madre esclava."

23. Cowling, *Conceiving Freedom*.

24. Paugh, *Politics of Reproduction*.

25. Paton, "Maternal Struggles," 263.

26. Roth, "From Free Womb to Criminalized Woman," 274–75; Santos, "Mothering Slaves"; Cowling, *Conceiving Freedom*.

27. Morgan, *Laboring Women*; Cowling et al., "Mothering Slaves."

28. On the dearth of criminal cases against enslaved women in Brazil, see Roth, "From Free Womb to Criminalized Woman," 269–86, 274–75.

29. Turner, *Contested Bodies*; Bush, *Slave Women in Caribbean Society*.
30. Barcia Zequeira, *Oficios de mujer*; Franklin, *Women and Slavery*. On wet nursing in the United States, see Jones-Rogers, "[S]he could ... spare."
31. Jaffary, *Reproduction and Its Discontents*; Few, *For All of Humanity*; Carrillo, "Nacimiento y muerte"; Warren, *Medicine and Politics*; Cordova, *Pushing in Silence*; Cooper Owens, *Medical Bondage*; Fraser, *African American Midwifery*; Paier, "Gender as Pathology"; Leavitt, *Brought to Bed*.
32. Reid-Vázquez, *Year of the Lash*; Finch, *Rethinking Slave Rebellion in Cuba*. Also see Finch, "Scandalous Scarcities"; Barcia, *Oficios de mujer*.
33. On French influence in Latin American medicine, see Warren, "Between the Foreign and the Local."
34. Tomich, *Politics of the Second Slavery*.
35. Jenkins Schwartz, *Birthing a Slave*; Cooper Owens, *Medical Bondage*.
36. Roth, *Miscarriage of Justice*.
37. Briggs, "Race of Hysteria."
38. Stepan, *Hour of Eugenics*.
39. Sippial, *Prostitution*.
40. García González, Álvarez Pelaez, and Naranjo Orovio, *En busca*.
41. Rodríguez, *Right to Live in Health*.
42. DeBarros, *Reproducing the British Caribbean*.
43. See, for example, Blum, *Domestic Economies*; Milanich, *Children of Fate*.
44. Clark, *Gender, State, and Medicine*; Mooney, *Politics of Motherhood*; Ramm and Gideon, *Motherhood*.
45. On white immigration during this period, see Moya, *Cousins and Strangers*; Foote and Goebel, *Immigration and National Identities*. On homiculture and puericulture interventions in the region, see Otovo, *Progressive Mothers, Better Babies*; García González, Álvarez Pelaez, and Naranjo Orovio, *En busca*.
46. Briggs, *Reproducing Empire*; Kluchin, *Fit to Be Tied*; López, *Matters of Choice*; Stern, *Eugenic Nation*; Stern, "Hour of Eugenics"; O'Brien, "Pelvimetry."
47. Bliss, *Compromised Positions*; Ruggiero, *Modernity in the Flesh*; Guy, *Sex and Danger*. On the white slave trade, see Guy, *White Slavery and Mothers*.
48. Barcia Zequeira, *La otra familia*; Lucero, "Entre esclavos y comerciantes."
49. Stoler, *Carnal Knowledge and Imperial Power*.
50. Fanon, *Black Skin, White Masks*, esp. 24–63.
51. On abortion, see Necochea López, *History of Family Planning*; Kimball, *Open Secret*; Roth, *Miscarriage of Justice*; Jaffary, *Reproduction and Its Discontents*; on contraceptive, see Briggs, *Reproducing Empire*, and Bourbonnais, *Birth Control*; Soto Laveaga, *Jungle Laboratories*.
52. Hynson, *Laboring for the State*.
53. Brodie, *Contraception and Abortion*; Gordon, *Moral Property of Women*; Schoen, *Choice and Coercion*; Siegel Watkins, *On the Pill*; Flavin, *Our Bodies, Our Crimes*; Reagan, *When Abortion Was a Crime*.
54. Pacino, "Creating Madres Campesinas"; Htun, *Sex and the State*; Smith and Padula, *Sex and Revolution*.
55. Morrison, *Cuba's Racial Crucible*.

56. Lucero, *Cuban City, Segregated*, 27–54.
57. Torres Pico, *Los expósitos*, 77, 89.
58. Roberts, *Killing the Black Body*, 6.
59. Bergallo, *Justicia, Género y Reproducción*; Davis, "Obstetric Racism"; Gurr, *Reproductive Justice*; Price, "What Is Reproductive Justice?"; Ross and Solinger, *Reproductive Justice*; Russell, *Assisted Reproduction of Race*.
60. Ferrer, *Insurgent Cuba*.
61. Lucero, *Revolutionary Masculinity and Racial Inequality*.

CHAPTER 1. Women's Reproduction in Law and Public Policy

1. Provencio Garrigós, "Las madres cubanas."
2. Franklin, *Women and Slavery*, 21–23.
3. Twinam, *Public Lives, Private Secrets*; Martínez, *Genealogical Fictions*; Twinam, *Purchasing Whiteness*.
4. Seed, *To Love, Honor, and Obey*; Lyman L. Johnson and Lipsett-Rivera, *Faces of Honor*.
5. Arrazola et al., *Enciclopedia española*, 460–61.
6. Alfonso X, *Las Siete Partidas*, vol. 4, title 23, law 4.
7. Alfonso X, *Las Siete Partidas*, vol. 7, title 33, law 12.
8. Alfonso X, *Las Siete Partidas*, vol. 4, title 23, law 5. On monstrous births in the early modern Spanish Empire, see Barragán and Martín-Estudillo, "Monstrous Births." For later explorations in Latin America, see Jaffary, "Monstrous Births and Creole Patriotism"; Few, "That Monster of Nature."
9. Alfonso X, *Las Siete Partidas*, 136–38.
10. Montanos Ferrín and Sánchez-Arcilla, *Estudios de historia*, 139–40.
11. *Las leyes de Burgos*.
12. Alfonso X, *Las Siete Partidas*.
13. *Las leyes de Burgos*.
14. De las Casas, *Brevísima relación*, 19–20.
15. Ibid., 15.
16. On the challenge of determining fertility and mortality from skeletal remains, see Wood et al., "Osteological Paradox."
17. La Rosa Corzo and Jaramillo, *Costumbres funerarias*, 39–40.
18. Fernández de Oviedo, *Crónica de las Indias*, 26v, 38v, 132, 151; López de Gómara, *Historia general de las Indias*, chapters 29, 32, 33; De la Fuente, "Población libre y estratificación social," 18; López de Gómara, *Historia general*, chapters 29, 32, 33; De las Casas, *Brevísima relación*.
19. De la Fuente, *Havana and the Atlantic*, 3.
20. De las Casas, *Brevísima relación*, 32, 84. For similar commentary on Indigenous fertility in conquest-era New Spain, see Whitmore and Robinson, *Disease and Death*, 17, 28, 45.
21. La Rosa Corzo and Jaramillo, *Costumbres funerarias*, 40–45.
22. De las Casas, *Brevísima relación*, 40; Wright, *Early History of Cuba*, 15.
23. López de Gómara, *Historia general de las Indias*.

24. On Spanish discussions of the juridical implications of conquistadores' atrocities, see Brading, *First America*, 79–101.

25. On the racialized gender implications of criminal accountability in rape cases, see Crenshaw, "Mapping the Margins."

26. Le-Roy y Cassá, "Apuntes para la historia," 340–41.

27. See, for example, Rodríguez Ferrer, *Naturaleza y civilización*, 437. José Beato, Luis Montané, among others have also repeated this assertion. Le-Roy y Cassá, "Apuntes para la historia," 340–41.

28. De Gordón y de Acosta, "Medicina indígena de Cuba"; Le-Roy y Cassá, "Apuntes para la historia," 340.

29. Bachiller y Morales, *Cuba primitiva*, 347; Le-Roy y Cassá, "Apuntes para la historia," 341.

30. Valcárcel Rojas, *Archaeology of Early Colonial Interaction*, 57–62; Anderson-Córdova, *Surviving Spanish Conquest*, 52–53.

31. De la Fuente, "Población libre y estratificación social," 18–19.

32. De la Fuente, *Havana and the Atlantic*, 3.

33. See Borucki, Eltis, and Wheat, *From the Galleons to the Highlands*.

34. "Carta del Licenciado Vadillo," in Real Academia de Historia, *Colección de documentos*, 252.

35. "Carta de los oficiales reales," July 18, 1534; "Carta del gobernador Manuel de Rojas," November 10, 1534; "El oficial real Hernando de Castro," December 10, 1534, all in Real Academia de Historia, *Colección de documentos*, vol. 4, 211, 325, 354, 358–60.

36. Marrero, *Cuba*, 217.

37. Altman Source, "Marriage, Family, and Ethnicity."

38. *Recopilación de leyes*, book 7, title 5, law 6.

39. Given the condition of archives in Cuba, there might be other surviving criminal court cases involving infanticide or abortion, and it is probable that some records either did not make it into the archives, were destroyed, or were misplaced since. However, my research did not turn up any criminal cases involving abortion or infanticide prior to the 1830s.

40. O'Brien, "Many Meanings of *Aborto*."

41. Ibid.; Few, Tortorici, and Warren, *Baptism through Incision*; Rigau-Pérez, "Surgery at the Service."

42. Montanos Ferrín and Sánchez-Arcilla, *Estudios de historia*, 175–76.

43. Carlos IV, *Novísima Recopilación*, vol. 10, title 5, law 2.

44. Montanos Ferrín and Sánchez-Arcilla, *Estudios de historia*, 162–64.

45. Mata, *Vade mecum de medicina*, 192–93.

46. Le-Roy y Cassá, "Apuntes para la historia," 341.

47. García Goyena, *Código criminal español*, 73.

48. Chelala-Aguilera, *Natalidad, mortalidad, y aborto*, 156–59. In Cuba, women reportedly also attempted to provoke abortions by ingesting concoctions made with local herbs, including "retoño de aguacate," "anon root and green mango leaves," "Chinese parsley root," leaves and cuttings of "yamagua," "caja de palo," "aguedita," "cascos de mulo," and "Espino cerval." Another folk remedy involved mustard footbaths. Chelala-Aguilera, *Natalidad, mortalidad, y aborto*, 156–59.

49. Jaffary, *Reproduction and Its Discontents*, 33.
50. "¡Mujeres, Mujeres, Mujeres!" *El Siglo*, May 7, 1865; "Esencia Pura de Zazaparrilla de Honduras," *Diario de la Marina*, June 1, 1862, 4.
51. Chelala-Aguilera, *Natalidad, mortalidad, y aborto* 156–59.
52. Stampa Braun, "Las corrientes," 47–78.
53. O'Brien, "Many Meanings of *Aborto*," 6; Jones, *Soul of the Embryo*; Connery, *Abortion*; Mata, *Tratado de medicina*, 389–90.
54. On later theorizations of female criminality in Cuba, see Bronfman, "Allure of Technology."
55. Martínez-Alier, *Marriage, Class and Colour*, 106–19; Franklin, *Women and Slavery*, 47–55.
56. Twinam, *Public Lives, Private Secrets*.
57. On Cuba, see Martínez-Alier, *Marriage, Class and Colour*; Martinez-Alier, "Elopement and Seduction." On honor other colonial Latin American societies, see Seed, *To Love, Honor, and Obey*; Sloan, *Runaway Daughters*; Lavrín, *Sexuality and Marriage*; Lyman L. Johnson and Lipsett-Rivera, *Faces of Honor*; Germeten, *Violent Delights, Violent Ends*.
58. Lyman L. Johnson and Lipsett-Rivera, *Faces of Honor*; Sloan, *Runaway Daughters*, 105–15; Seed, *To Love, Honor, and Obey*.
59. The sonnet, titled "El aborto," was translated from a French version dating back to the rule of French monarch Louis XIV, though the original poem was recorded in Latin and was subsequently translated into numerous European languages. It gained popularity in Spain's New World empire, the Spanish translation being attributed to both Colombian and Venezuelan authors, including José María Gutierrez and Vicente Tejera. Calderón, "Un soneto célebre," 1434–35. Calcaño, *Parnaso venezolano*, 17–18. García Goyena and Aguirre, *Febrero*, 227–28.
60. For an exploration of discourses of motherhood, and the notion of natural maternal sentiments, see Provencio Garrigós, "Las madres cubanas."
61. Montanos Ferrín and Sánchez-Arcilla, *Estudios de historia*, 151.
62. On abortion and infanticide in viceregal Mexico, see Jaffary, "Reconceiving Motherhood."
63. For a discussion of patriarchy in colonial Cuba, see Franklin, *Women and Slavery*, 2–5.
64. Marrero, *Cuba*, 2–3, 5, 21.
65. Huguet-Termes, "Madrid Hospitals and Welfare."
66. Certificado expedido por Félix Iznaga, Registrador de Propiedad del Mediodía, March 22, 1906. Archivo Judicial, Juzgado de Primera Instancia del Sur. Escribanía de Francisco Abeillé y Santurio, transcribed in Le-Roy y Cassá, *Historia del Hospital*, 155–57.
67. Arrate y Acosta, *La llave del nuevo mundo*, chapter 40.
68. De la Fuente, *Havana and the Atlantic*, 85.
69. Poska, *Gendered Crossings*, 2–3.
70. López Sánchez, *La medicina en La Habana*, 12.
71. Ibid., 13; Actas Capitulares de la Habana (transuntadas), September 5, 1664, vol. 13, f. 250v–251, transcribed in López Sánchez, *La medicina en la Habana*, 87.
72. López Sánchez, *La medicina en La Habana*, 13–14.

NOTES TO CHAPTER ONE   317

73. Le-Roy y Cassá, "Apuntes para la historia," 351–32.
74. Martínez Fortún, "Historia de la medicina."
75. Barcia, *Oficios de mujer*, 30–33.
76. See Roth, "Birthing Life and Death."
77. Fisas, *Historias de las Reinas*, 138–42; Franklin, *Women and Slavery*, 25. Queen Isabel de Braganza died as the result of a failed cesarean section during the delivery of her second child.
78. Few, Tortorici, and Warren, *Baptism through Incision*, 3–5.
79. Actas Capitulares de la Habana (transuntadas), January 16, 1598, vol. 4, f. 427v, transcribed in López Sánchez, *La medicina en la Habana*, 45; Actas Capitulares de la Habana (transuntadas), February 6, 1637, vol. 9, f. 437, transcribed in López Sánchez, *La medicina en la Habana*, 66; Actas Capitulares de la Habana (transuntadas), February 3, 1668, vol. 14, f. 462v-463, transcribed in López Sánchez, *La medicina en la Habana*, 91.
80. Actas Capitulares de la Habana (transuntadas), April 29, 1654, vol. 11, f. 874v–75, transcribed in López Sánchez, *La medicina en la Habana*, 76–78; Marrero, *Cuba*, 143.
81. On the Spanish military presence near the port, and the city walls built in the seventeenth century, see Guadalupe García, *Beyond the Walled City*, 35, 54–55. There was precedent for medical treatment of syphilis with the sixteenth-century establishment of a separate hospital in Spain dedicated to the disease. See Martz, *Poverty and Welfare*, 36.
82. Sánchez, *La medicina en la Habana*.
83. Le-Roy y Cassá, *Historia del Hospital*, 207, 283.
84. Ibid., 231, 278, 285.
85. Actas Capitulares de la Habana (transuntadas), November 7, 1597, vol. 4, f. 418–20, transcribed in Sánchez, *La medicina en la Habana*, 43–45.
86. De la Fuente, *Havana and the Atlantic*, 204.
87. De la Fuente, "Sugar and Slavery," 130–34.
88. Marrero, *Cuba*, 151.
89. El Obispo Fray Evelino Hurtado de Compostela to the King, Havana, October 11, 1699, Archivo General de Indias, Santo Domingo, 150, reproduced in Marrero, *Cuba*, 65–66.
90. Franklin, *Women and Slavery*, 116.
91. Obispo Díaz Vara Calderón to Conde de Medellín, August 6, 1674, Archivo General de Indias, Santo Domingo, 150, doc. 152, reproduced in Marrero, *Cuba*, 179n84.
92. Boyle, *Unruly Women*, 3–5.
93. On institutions of charity as instruments of colonial social order, see Franklin, *Women and Slavery*; Martínez-Vergne, *Shaping the Discourse on Space*.
94. Martz, *Poverty and Welfare*, 41–42.
95. Le-Roy y Cassá, *Historia del Hospital*, 207.
96. For more on the use of the court-ordered coerced labor of women of African descent in Havana's charitable institutions, see Bonnie Lucero, "A Racial Economy of Care: Incarceration, Labor Extraction, and Charity in Cuba's Nineteenth-Century Slave Society," unpublished manuscript, 2021.
97. Real Cédula del 16 de septiembre de 1760, reproduced in Le-Roy y Cassá, *Historia del Hospital*, 305–6.
98. Le-Roy y Cassá, *Historia del Hospital*, 204–5.

99. Ibid., 307–8.
100. Ibid., 279–80. On the Haitian Revolution, see Dubois, *Avengers of the New World*; on the royal slaves, see Díaz, *Virgin*.
101. Constituciones o Reglamento dictado por la Condesa de Santa Clara, Havana, October 5, 1798, reproduced in Le-Roy y Cassá, *Historia del Hospital*, 317–32.
102. Constituciones el Hospital San Francisco de Paula, February 3, 1812, reproduced in Le-Roy y Cassá, *Historia del Hospital*, 309–13.
103. Le-Roy y Cassá, *Historia del Hospital*, 375.
104. Constituciones de la Santa Sínodo Diocesano de Cuba de 1680, Archivo General de Indias, Santo Domingo, 903, reproduced in Marrero, *Cuba*, 35–39; 38. For earlier and later dispositions on slave marriage, see Franklin, *Women and Slavery*, 46; Díaz, *Virgin*, 253; Hall, *Social Control*, 95, 107.
105. Archivo General de Indias, Santo Domingo, 134, doc. 37, cited in Marrero, *Cuba*, 198.
106. "Resolución sobre la libertad de los negros y sus originarios, en el estado de pagando y después ya cristianos, 1681–1683," Archivo General de Indias, Santo Domingo 527, reproduced in Marrero, *Cuba*, 191–98.
107. Ibid.
108. Padrón de la Habana, July 12, 1691, reproduced in Marrero, *Cuba*, 66.

CHAPTER 2. From Unwanted Infants to Useful Vassals

1. De la Torre, *Lo que fuimos*, 92.
2. Arrate y Acosta, *La llave del nuevo mundo*, chapter 42.
3. Zenea, *Historia de la Real Casa*, 15.
4. Ibid., 18–22.
5. Felipe IV, "Prohibición de estudios de Gramática," in Carlos IV, *Novísima Recopilación*, vol. 3, book 7, title 37, law 1, 687; La Reyna Gobernadora, "Aplicación de los niños expósitos y huérfanos al exercicio de la Marina," December 22, 1677," in Carlos IV, *Novísima Recopilación*, vol. 3, book 7, title 37, law 2, 688.
6. Torres Pico, *Los expósitos*.
7. El Obispo Fray Evelino Hurtado de Compostela to the King, Havana, October 11, 1699, Archivo General de Indias, Santo Domingo, 150, reproduced in Marrero, *Cuba*, 65–66.
8. De la Torre, *Lo que fuimos*, 92.
9. In 1823, the Casa Cuna relocated to Reina 109, and later to the corner of Prado and Trocadero in 1833. De la Torre, *Lo que fuimos*, 92n1.
10. Torres Pico, *Los expósitos*, 34–35.
11. Zenea, *Historia de la Real Casa*, 11.
12. Ibid., 18–22.
13. Ibid., 18–22.
14. Twinam, "Church," 180.
15. "Informe del Obispo Compostela al Consejo de Indias," in Marrero, *Cuba*, 65.
16. Actas Capitulares de la Habana (transuntadas), March 17, and 26, 1711, vol. 20, f. 640v–642, transcribed in López Sánchez, *La medicina en la Habana*, 138–39.

17. "Real cédula con motivo del informe presentado por el obispo Gerónimo Valdés de haber fabricado en la ciudad de la Habana una casa para la habitación y crianza de los niños expósitos, excluyendo a los hijos de los esclavos mulatos y morenos. Habana," November 15, 1713, Fondo Antonio Bachiller y Morales, no. 505 (f. 33), Biblioteca Nacional José Martí, Sala de Manuscritos.
18. Ibid.
19. De la Fuente, *Havana and the Atlantic*, 147–70.
20. Ibid., 173.
21. Ibid., 173.
22. Ibid., 15.
23. Zenea, *Historia de la Real Casa*, 15.
24. "Expediente relativo al origen y fundación de la Casa de Benef y Maternidad," 1813, leg. 402, no. 39, ANC, FCB.
25. Carlos III, "Cuidado de los rectores de las casa de expósitos en la educación de estos, para que sean vasallos útiles," June 2, 1788, in Carlos IV, *Novísima Recopilación*, vol. 3, book 7, title 37, law 3, 688.
26. Naranjo Orovio, "La otra Cuba."
27. González, "Down and Out in Havana," 105–6.
28. Esteban de Zayas, January 16, 1814, leg. 402, no. 39, ANC, FCB.
29. Howe, *Trip to Cuba*, 90–91.
30. Twinam, "Church," 170.
31. Archivo del Archdiócesis de la Habana, Libros de Bautismos de la Casa Cuna, book 1, f. 854, cited in Torres Pico, *Los expósitos*.
32. Twinam, *Public Lives, Private Secrets*; Twinam, *Purchasing Whiteness*.
33. "Representación a S.M. por el Escmo. Señor Don Mariano de Arango sobre la fundación de una Casa de Maternidad," October 24, 1825, in Zenea, *Historia de la Real Casa*, 88.
34. Carlos IV, *Novísima Recopilación*, vol. 3, book 7, title 37, law 2, 688n2.
35. González, "Down and Out in Havana," 103.
36. For mortality among expósitos in eighteenth-century Mexico's Casa de Expósitos, see Gonzalbo Aizpuru, "La Casa de Niños Expósitos," 416; Ávila Espinosa, "Los niños abandonados." On Spain, see Fernández Ugarte, "La mortalidad." On the Southern Cone, see Moreno, "La Casa de Niños Expósitos"; Fernández, "Los Niños Expósitos"; Milanich, "Los hijos del azar."
37. Torres Pico, *Los expósitos*, 26–27.
38. "Real cédula," November 15, 1713.
39. Ibid.
40. Torres Pico, *Los expósitos*, 15–26.
41. "Representación a S.M.," 82.
42. Guadalupe García, *Beyond the Walled City*, 55–57.
43. Kuethe, "Havana in the Eighteenth Century," 13.
44. "Real cédula," December 31, 1755, Fondo Antonio Bachiller y Morales, no. 507 (f. 35–38).
45. "Representación a S.M.," 82–83.
46. Ibid., 83.

47. Ibid., 87.
48. Ibid., 85.
49. Ibid., 83–84, 86.
50. Twinam, "Church," 171.
51. Torres Pico, *Los Expósitos*, 42–43, citing ANC, "Libro de carga y data de la administración de la Casa Cuna, correspondiente a 1783," no. 13668, Miscelánea de Libros, Archivo Nacional de Cuba; "Libro de carga y data de la administración de la Casa Cuna, correspondiente a 1782," no. 13727, Miscelánea de Libros, Archivo Nacional de Cuba.
52. Twinam, "Church," 179.
53. Twinam, *Purchasing Whiteness*, 5–6.
54. Ibid., 165–72.
55. Ibid., 169–70.
56. Ibid., 170–71.
57. See, for example, the case of María Ascensión Valdéz, recounted in Franklin, *Women and Slavery*, 118–20.
58. Gabriel B. Paquette, *Enlightenment*; Jennings, *Constructing the Spanish Empire*.
59. Schneider, *Occupation of Havana*. Also see Sherry Johnson, *Social Transformation*.
60. See Kuethe, *Cuba*.
61. Poska, *Gendered Crossings*, 4. On the role of physicians in population management in Bourbon-era colonial Peru, see Warren, *Medicine and Politics*.
62. "Real Cédula de 5 de enero de 1794 de SM y señores del Consejo por la cual se manda a guardar y cumplir el Real Decreto en que se declaran por legítimos para todos los efectos civiles y sin excepción a los expósitos de ambos sexos. Impresa en La Habana en 1835," leg. 401, no. 8, ANC, FCB. Also see Carlos IV, "Los expósitos que sin padres conocidos se tengan por legítimos por todos los oficios civiles, sin que pueda servir de nota la qualidad de tales," in Carlos IV, *Novísima Recopilación*, vol. 3, book 7, title 37, law 4, 688–89.
63. Twinam, "Church," 164.
64. Torres Pico, *Los expósitos*, 44.
65. Twinam, "Church," 174–78.
66. Carlos IV, *Real cédula de Su Magestad concediendo libertad*.
67. SlaveVoyages Trans-Atlantic Slave Trade Database, www.slavevoyages.org/voyages/K6YugsRW; Bergad, García, and Barcia, *Cuban Slave Market*, 27.
68. "Expediente relativo a las informaciones que califica la condición de expósito de José Narciso Bravo," 1796, leg. 128, no. 4, Archivo Nacional de Cuba, Fondo Audiencia de Santo Domingo.
69. Twinam, *Purchasing Whiteness*, 20.
70. "Expediente relativo a las informaciones."
71. Ibid.
72. Ibid.
73. Ibid.
74. Ibid.
75. Ibid.
76. Torres Pico, *Los expósitos*, 44.
77. "Representación a S.M.," 83–84, 86; "Est. progresos y actual estado de la Casa de

NOTES TO CHAPTER TWO 321

Benef extramuros de la Habana, 1813, leg. 392, no. 14850, ANC, GSC; "Reglamento para el establecimiento de las casas de expósitos, crianza y educación de estos," December 11, 1796, in Carlos IV, *Novísima Recopilación*, vol. 3, books 6–7, 689.

78. On the role of the Casa de Beneficencia in the reproduction of colonial patriarchy and racial hierarchy, see Franklin, *Women and Slavery*, 105–11.
79. Wudermann, *Notes on Cuba*, 224–25.
80. "Reglamento para el establecimiento," 692.
81. Ibid., 689.
82. Ibid., 692.
83. Ibid., 691–92.
84. Twinam, "Church," 166.
85. "Expediente relativo al origen y fundación."
86. "Reglamento para el establecimiento," 693.
87. See Barcia Zequeira, *Oficios de mujer*, 143–44, 148. On the commodification of enslaved women's ability to breastfeed, see Franklin, *Women and Slavery*, 128–46.
88. "Reglamento para el establecimiento," 691–92.
89. "Informe del Obispo Compostela," 5:65.
90. "Representación a S.M.," 86.
91. See Suárez y Romero, "Vigilancia de las madres," in *Colección de artículos*, 23.
92. Anonymous correspondence, June 25, 1767, leg. 402, no. 39, ANC, FCB.
93. Jones-Rogers, "[S]he could . . . spare," 339–40.
94. "Expediente relativo al origen y fundación."
95. Roth, "Black Nurse, White Milk."
96. Zenea, *Historia de la Real Casa*, 26–27.
97. "Expediente relativo al origen y fundación."
98. D. Carlos III, "Cuidado de los rectores de la Casa de expósitos en la educación de estos, para que sean vasallos útiles," June 2, 1788, in Carlos IV, *Novísima Recopilación*, vol. 3, book 7, title 37, law 3, 688.
99. "Representación a S.M.," 86; González, "Down and Out in Havana," 103.
100. Sarah L. Franklin's survey of newspaper advertisements turned up only three ads for white wet nurses in the 1840s. Franklin, *Women and Slavery*, 140.
101. "Compra de 100 negras esclavas para torcer el tobaco; compra de 8 esclavos bozales," May 9, 1802, Fondo Soc., vol. 40, no. 20, Biblioteca Nacional de Cuba José Martí, Sala de Manuscritos; "Acuerdo de la compra de cien negras para elaborar tabaco en la casa de beneficencia—1802," July 22, 1802, Fondo Soc., vol. 40, no. 21.
102. "La Caxa de la Casa de Beneficencia su cta. Con el proo. Del uno pr. Mil de la introducción de negros en esta ciudad—1810," 1810, Fondo Soc., vol. 54, no. 14ª.
103. D Lorenzo Marron Pres Cappn Admin de la Real Casa de Expositos por SM ante VS Habana, May 7, 1806, leg. 402, no. 39, ANC, FCB.
104. "Expediente relativo al origen y fundación."
105. Ibid.
106. Ibid.
107. Ibid.
108. Ibid.
109. D Lorenzo Marrón Pres., May 7, 1806.

110. "Expediente relativo al origen y fundación."
111. Ibid.
112. Ibid.
113. "Representación a S.M.," 90.
114. Esteban de Zayas, January 16, 1814.
115. "Representación a S.M.," 90.
116. "Expediente relativo al origen y fundación."
117. Ibid.
118. See, for example, "Expediente criminal sobre haber encontrado el cadáver de un párvulo blanco en el jardín de D Francisco Armenteros," July 20, 1842, leg. 3796, letter Br, ANC/FME; "Dos niños metidos en un jabuco," May 29, 1849, leg. 3490, letter O, ANC/FME; and others in ANC/FME.
119. "Expediente relativo al origen y fundación."

CHAPTER 3. For the "Propagation of Slaves"

1. Tadman, "Demographic Cost of Sugar," 1536. On natural increase in the United States, see Van Woodward, *American Counterpoint*, 91; Fogel, *Without Consent*, 123–26; Genovese, *Roll, Jordan, Roll*, 5. On lack of natural increase in the British Caribbean, see Bush, *Slave Women in Caribbean Society*, 120; On reproduction in the French Caribbean, see Moitt, *Women and Slavery*, 89–99; For comparative study of Caribbean colonies, see Morrisey, *Slave Women*, 100–118.
2. Curtin, *Atlantic Slave Trade*, 29–30; Craton, *Searching for the Invisible Man*, 85–118.
3. de la Sagra, *Historia económico-política y estadística*, 22; Humboldt, *Island of Cuba*, 195–203; Baird, *Impressions and Experiences*, 1:179–81.
4. Higman, *Slave Populations*; Patterson, *Sociology of Slavery*; Lowenthal and Clark, "Slave Breeding in Barbuda"; Bush, *Slave Women in Caribbean Society*, 127; Brown, *Reaper's Garden*.
5. López Denis, "Disease and Society"; Graden, *Disease, Resistance, and Lies*.
6. Gurney, *Winter in the West Indies*, 208. For more on travelers' perceptions of the gender ratio on Cuban plantations, see Finch, "Scandalous Scarcities" Reid-Vázquez, "Tensions of Race."
7. Alfonso X, *Las Siete Partidas*, part 4, title 21, laws 1 and 2.
8. Malagón Barceló, *Código Negro Carolino*; Alfonso X, *Las Siete Partidas*, vol. 4, title 8. law 8.
9. Cowling, *Conceiving Freedom*, 84.
10. De la Fuente, "Slaves," 116.
11. Carlos IV, *Real Cédula de Su Magestad sobre la educación*.
12. Ibid.
13. See for example, Joda Esteve, "El comercio de esclavos."
14. Carlos IV, *Real Cédula de Su Magestad sobre la educación*.
15. Ibid., 3–7. For an English translation, see "Royal Decree" in García Rodríguez, *Voices of the Enslaved*.
16. Carlos IV, *Real Cédula de Su Magestad sobre la educación*.
17. Ibid.

18. On sexual relations and rape by slave owners, see Morrison, "Slave Mothers and White Fathers"; Cowling, *Conceiving Freedom*, 83–84.
19. Erenchún, *Anales de la isla*, 1:1039.
20. Garcia Paz, *Great African Slave Revolt*; González-Ripoll Navarro et al., *El rumor de Haití en Cuba*.
21. "Representación," in Saco, *Historia de la Esclavitud*, 5:106, 5:108.
22. Humboldt, *Island of Cuba*, 229.
23. "Instructivo para suavizar la suerte de los negros esclavos," 1795, leg. 150, exp. 7405, ANC, RCJF
24. Carlos IV, *Real Cédula de Su Magestad sobre la educación*, chapter 2.
25. Humboldt, *Island of Cuba*, 213–14; Alexander, *Transatlantic sketches*, 375.
26. Moreno Fraginals, *El ingenio*; Suárez y Romero, *Colección de artículos*, 205–8.
27. Caballero, "Matrimonio entre esclavos," 320.
28. Ibid., 320.
29. Ibid., 319–23, 320, 322.
30. Arango y Parreño, *Obras*, 2:239–40.
31. See Paugh, *Politics of Reproduction*; Also see Williams, *Capitalism and Slavery*.
32. On enslaved men's military experience, see Barcia Paz, *Great African Slave Revolt*.
33. Real cédula of April 22, 1804, reproduced in *Documentos de que hasta ahora*, 124–25.
34. "Real Orden Reservada de 11 de Abril de 1804," in Arango y Parreño, *Obras*, 2:240–41.
35. Carlos IV, *Real Cédula de Su Magestad sobre la educación*.
36. Bush, *Slave Women in Caribbean Society*, 124–27. Cuban physicians shared these racist views regarding enslaved peoples' sexual deviancy as a cause of infertility. See Dumont, *Memorias sobre la historia médica*, 96–97; Moreno Fraginals, *El ingenio*.
37. Tadman, "Demographic Cost of Sugar," 1541.
38. Bush, *Slave Women in Caribbean Society*.
39. See Dierksheide, *Amelioration and Empire*.
40. See Corwin, *Spain*; Murray, *Odious Commerce*.
41. Number of slaves imported into Cuba by individual year and flag, SlaveVoyages Trans-Atlantic Slave Trade Database, www.slavevoyages.org/voyages/j2HaqTGA.
42. "Representación de la Ciudad de la Habana á las Cortes, el 20 de julio de 1811, con motivo de las proposiciones hechas por D. José Miguel Guridi Alcocer y D. Agustín de Argüelles, sobre el tráfico y esclavitud de los negros; extendida por el Alférez Mayor de la Ciudad, D. Francisco de Arango, por encargo del Ayuntamiento, Consulado y Sociedad Patriótica de la Habana," in Arango y Pareño, *Obras*, 2:194–95.
43. Arango y Pareño, *Obras*, 2:194.
44. Ibid., 2:195.
45. Ibid., 2:197.
46. Ibid., 2:197.
47. Ibid., 2:200.
48. Ibid., 2:200.
49. For commentary on planters' attitudes about enslaved peoples' sexuality, see Humboldt, *Island of Cuba*, 213–14; Alexander, *Transatlantic sketches*, 375.

50. Arango y Pareño, *Obras*, 2:196.
51. Ibid., 2:201–2.
52. Number of slaves imported into Cuba by individual year and flag.
53. Rafael Orozco to Martín de Garay, January 24, 1817, Archivo General de Indias, Santo Domingo, 2828.
54. José Cienfuegos to Martín de Garay, April 14, 1818, Archivo General de Indias, Santo Domingo, 2828.
55. Unknown correspondence, Madrid, February 16, 1818, Archivo General de Indias, Santo Domingo, 1158.
56. Perera Díaz and Meriño Fuentes, "African Women," 892–909. For a broader discussion of the *Dos Hermanos* case, see Meriño Fuentes and Perera Díaz, *Del tráfico a la libertad*.
57. Number of slaves imported into Cuba by individual year and flag; percentage women by five-year increments, SlaveVoyages Trans-Atlantic Slave Trade Database, www.slavevoyages.org/voyages/9AszM1Ve.
58. Arango y Pareño, *Obras*, 2:197.
59. Bergad, García, and Barcia, *Cuban Slave Market*, 62–63.
60. Letter XI. to E W, Esq. Matanzas, March 9, 1828, in Abbot, *Letters*, 42.
61. Ibid.
62. Humboldt, *Island of Cuba*, 229.
63. Steele, *Cuban sketches*, 93.
64. Abiel Abbot to G___ B___, Esq., La Recompensa, St. Marks, April 1828, in Abbot, *Letters*, 142–43.
65. Abiel Abbot to Mrs. E___ A___, March 8, 1828, in Abbot, *Letters*, 55.
66. Abiel Abbot to Unknown, St. Marks, April 13, 1828, in Abbot, *Letters*, 149.
67. Abbot to G___ B___, 142–43.
68. Matrimonios de Color, Archivo de la Santísima Catedral de Cienfuegos, book 1; Bautizos de Color, Archivo de la Santísima Catedral de Cienfuegos, book 1, nos. 19–392.
69. For a survey of "good treatment" policies and debates, see Ghorbal, "La política."
70. On slave prices, see Moreno Fraginals, *El ingenio*, 199.
71. Arango y Pareño, "Representación al Rey sobre la extinción," in Arango y Parreño, *Obras*, 2:655.
72. Ibid., 2:656.
73. Ibid., 2:657.
74. Ibid., 2:655.
75. de Zayas, "Observaciones sobre los ingenios," 264–68.
76. Varela, "Proyecto de decreto sobre la abolición de la esclavitud," reproducido en Ortiz, *Los negros esclavos*, 298–307.
77. "Representación," in Saco, *Historia de la Esclavitud*, 108.
78. "Preliminary Essay," in Humboldt, *Island of Cuba*, 73–76.
79. Moreno Fraginals, *El ingenio*.
80. Turnbull, *Travels in the West*, 146; Moreno Fraginals, *El ingenio*.
81. Bergad, García, and Barcia, *Cuban Slave Market*, 62.
82. Tornero Tinajero, *Crecimiento económico y transformaciones sociales*, 120.
83. Ibid., 121.

84. See Morrison, *Cuba's Racial Crucible*, 59; Meriño Fuentes and Perera Díaz, *Un Café para la microhistoria*, 100.
85. Joda Esteve, "El comercio de esclavos," 114.
86. Carlos IV, *Real Cédula de Su Magestad sobre la educación*, chapter 2.
87. Tornero Tinajero, *Crecimiento económico y transformaciones sociales*, 128.
88. Ibid., 129.
89. Archivo General de Indias, Cuba, leg. 1470, calculated and reproduced in Morrison, *Cuba's Racial Crucible*, 62.
90. de la Sagra, *Historia económico-política y estadística*, 24.
91. Humboldt, *Island of Cuba*, 228–31; Dana, *To Cuba and Back*, 244–58; Alexander, *Transatlantic sketches*, 375; Wudermann, *Notes on Cuba*, 153.
92. Carlos IV, *Real Cédula de Su Magestad sobre la educación*, chapter 2.
93. Craton, *Searching for the Invisible Man*; Gutman, *Black Family*; Dunn, *Tale of Two Plantations*.
94. Kiple, *Caribbean Slave*; Bush, *Slave Women in Caribbean Society*, 131.
95. For a discussion of similar patterns in Rio de Janeiro, see Karasch, *Slave Life*, 138–45; for the British colonies, see Morgan, *Laboring Women*. Also see Bush, *Slave Women in Caribbean Society*, 124–26.
96. ANC, ME contains dozens of these cases.
97. de la Sagra, *Estudio coloniales*, 18–24.
98. Bautizos de Color, Archivo de la Santísima Catedral de Cienfuegos, book 1, no. 169.
99. Franklin, *Women and Slavery*, 128; Barcia Zequeira, *Oficios de mujer*, 143–44.
100. Dirección de la Casa de Beneficencia y Maternidad de La Habana, "Cuenta de los sueldos abonados a las nodrizas internas por la lactancia de los niños expósitos correspondientes al mes de enero de 1874," January 1874, leg. 7, letter J, ANC, ME; Dirección de la Casa de Beneficencia y Maternidad de La Habana, "Cuenta de los sueldos abonados a las nodrizas internas por la lactancia de los niños expósitos correspondientes al mes de febrero de 1874," February 1874, leg. 7, letter G, ANC, ME; Lactancia de expósitos en la casa de beneficencia, 1867, leg. 113, letter I, J, K, L, Ll, M, and N, ANC, ME.
101. "Noticias particulares de la Havana," *Papel Periódico de la Havana*, June 2, 1793, Biblioteca Nacional de España, Hemeroteca Digital; Turnbull, *Travels in the West*, 130.
102. Bush, *Slave Women in Caribbean Society*.
103. Morrison, *Cuba's Racial Crucible*, 67.
104. Tornero Tinajero, *Crecimiento económico y transformaciones sociales*, 123.
105. Ibid., 130.
106. Madden, *Island of Cuba*, 121–22.
107. Ibid., 126.

CHAPTER 4. Preserving White Infant Life

1. *Reglamento general de beneficencia pública*, 11–17.
2. Ibid., 11–13.
3. Gobierno de España, *Código penal español*, art. 612, 124–25.
4. Ibid., arts. 639 and 640, 130–31.
5. *Reglamento general de beneficencia pública*, 11–13.

6. Gobierno de España, *Código penal español*, art. 612, 124–25.
7. "Actas Capitulares de la Habana (transuntadas)," March 17, 1711, vol. 20, f. 640v–41, transcribed in López Sánchez, *La medicina en la Habana*, 138.
8. "Actas Capitulares de la Habana (transuntadas)," March 26, 1711, vol. 20, f. 642, transcribed in López Sánchez, *La medicina en la Habana*, 139.
9. "Noticias sobre medicos y parteros en los anos 1701–1788," Fondo Pérez, no. 917, Biblioteca Nacional José Martí, Sala de Manuscritos.
10. Barcia Zerqueira, *Oficios de mujer*, 43–47.
11. Rosaín, *Examen y cartilla de parteras*.
12. Alonso y Fernández, *Discurso inaugural*.
13. Vives, in Rosaín, *Examen y cartilla de parteras*, ii–iii.
14. Domingo Rosaín to protomedicato, October 20, 1824, in Le-Roy y Cassá, *Historia del Hospital*, 390.
15. Drs. Lorenzo Hernández and Juan Pérez Delgado to Domingo Rosaín, September 1, 1824, in Le-Roy y Cassá, *Historia del Hospital*, 390.
16. Protomedicato to Domingo Rosaín, November 15, 1824, in Le-Roy y Cassá, *Historia del Hospital*, 390.
17. Gobernador, November 26, 1824, in Le-Roy y Cassá, *Historia del Hospital*, 391.
18. Ibid.
19. Vives, in Rosaín, *Examen y cartilla de parteras*, vi–vii.
20. Ibid., xii–xiii.
21. Ibid., vi–vii.
22. Ibid., iv–v.
23. Ibid., vi–vii.
24. Gobernador, November 26, 1824.
25. On education for women and girls in colonial Cuba, see Vinat de la Mata, *Luces en el silencio*. On race and education in the nineteenth century, see Otheguy, "Es de suponer." On sex and education, see Franklin, *Women and Slavery*, 71–101.
26. For a critiques in this vein, see Cañizares-Esguerra, *How to Write a History*; and Sharman, *Deconstructing the Enlightenment*.
27. Domingo Rosaín in his July 6, 1827, letter to the Tribunal del Protomedicato, in Le-Roy y Cassá, *Historia del Hospital*, 388–89.
28. Domingo Rosaín in a letter to the Real Sociedad Patriótica, July 6, 1827, in Le-Roy y Cassá, *Historia del Hospital*, 389.
29. Alonso y Fernández, *Exámenes públicos de obstetricia*; Le-Roy y Cassá, "Apuntes para la historia," 342–43; Alonso y Fernández, *Discurso inaugural*.
30. Alonso y Fernández, *Discurso inaugural*.
31. Domingo Rosaín in a letter to the Real Sociedad Patriótica on July 6, 1827, in Le-Roy y Cassá, *Historia del Hospital*, 389.
32. Le-Roy y Cassá, *Apuntes para la historia*, 12. A similar project developed in Puerto Príncipe, where José de la Luz Castellanos established a midwifery class in the Nuestra Señora del Cármen Women's Hospital.
33. Real Sociedad Patriótica de la Habana, *Memorias*, 2:141.
34. For the United States, see Cooper Owens, *Medical Bondage*; for Brazil, see Féres da Silva Telles, "Pregnant Slaves, Workers in Labour."

35. Francisco Arango y Pareño on behalf of the Sociedad Patriotica, in Le-Roy y Cassá, *Historia del Hospital*, 389.
36. Barcia, *Oficios de mujer*, 74–75.
37. For an analysis of marriage rates among people of African descent in nineteenth-century Cuba, see Morrison, *Cuba's Racial Crucible*, 40–106.
38. Rosaín, *Necrópolis de la Habana*, 341.
39. "Reglamento para las clases de parteras, establecida en el Hospital de San Francisco de Paula, bajo los auspicios de la Real Sociedad Patriótica y dirigida por el doctor D. Domingo Rosaín," September 27, 1827, in *Diario de la Habana*, January 31, 1828, and republished in *Anales*, 39:335–81, esp. 347–48n1.
40. "Parteras matriculadas y habilitadas provisionalmente por el término de un año," *Diario de la Habana*, February 1828, reproduced in Deschamps Chapeaux, *El negro en la economía*, 171.
41. *Gaceta de la Habana*, August 11, 1828.
42. Barcia Zequeira, *Oficios de mujer*, 58–60, 92–95.
43. *Guía de Forasteros*, 1834, 1837, 1840, 1845, cited in Deschamps Chapeaux, *El negro en la economía*, 172–73.
44. Le-Roy y Cassá, "Apuntes para la historia," 347–48; Rosaín, "Discurso."
45. Joaquín José García, *Protocolo de antigüedades*, 2:240.
46. Ibid.
47. "Real órden de 3 de enero de 1844 al gobernador civil de la Habana como vice-real protector de la inspección de estudios de las dos Islas," in Zamora y Coronado, *Biblioteca de legislación ultramarina*, 6:348.
48. Reid-Vázquez, "Tensions of Race," 198; Barcia, *Oficios de mujer*, 78–82.
49. *Guía de Forasteros*, 1834, 1837, 1840, 1845, cited in Deschamps Chapeaux, *El negro en la economía*, 172–73.
50. Real Sociedad Patriótica de la Habana, *Memorias*, 3:236.
51. Ibid., 2:141.
52. Cowley, *Ensayo Estadístico-Médico*, n.p.
53. Ibid., 3–8.
54. Jaffary, *Reproduction and Its Discontents*, 73–74.
55. For a discussion of obstetric interventions in maternal and infant mortality in early twentieth century Rio de Janeiro, see Roth, "Birthing Life and Death." For a discussion of causes of infant mortality in late nineteenth-century Havana, see Le-Roy y Cassá, *La mortalidad infantil en Cuba*.
56. Rosaín, *Exámen y cartilla de parteras*, 20–21; González del Valle, *Manual de Obstetricia*; Sánchez Rodríguez, *Curso de estudio*.
57. "Honorario a que son acreedoras las Parteras, por su asistencia al exercicio de su profesión," in Rosaín, *Exámen y cartilla de parteras*, n.p.
58. Carrillo, "Nacimiento y muerte."
59. *Reglamento general de beneficencia pública*, art. 42, 12.
60. Ibid.
61. Ricafort, *Reglamento de la Real Casa*, 3–4; among the main points of contention was funding the institution. See "Real Cédula," reproduced in Ricafort, *Reglamento de la Real Casa*, 3–8.

62. Zenea, *Historia de la Real Casa*, 11–12.
63. Ibid.
64. Ricafort, *Reglamento de la Real Casa*, 34–38. Also see *Reglamento general de beneficencia pública*, 11–13.
65. Records show that the institution shifted to external wet nurses, as directed by the Ley de Beneficencia. In 1823 Casa Cuna employed four wet nurses (it is possible that these women, likely working inside the institution, had given birth inside the Casa and stayed on as wet nurses to their own children). Inventorio general de bienes del establecimiento de niños expósitos llamada Casa Cuna de la ciudad de la Habana en 26 de mayo 1823, leg. 42, no. 15, Fondo Negociado de Bienes del Estado, Archivo Nacional de la República de Cuba.
66. Ricafort, *Reglamento de la Real Casa*, 24–26.
67. Joaquín José García, *Protocolo de antigüedades*, 2:240.
68. Few, *For All of Humanity*, 98, 115.
69. Ricafort, *Reglamento de la Real Casa*, 36.
70. Zenea, *Historia de la Real Casa*, 11, 13, 15.
71. Ibid., 11–12.
72. Ibid., 17–30.
73. Naranjo Orovio, "El temor a la 'africanización.'"
74. "Representación a S.M. por el Escmo. Señor Don Mariano de Arango sobre la fundación de una Casa de Maternidad," October 24, 1825, in Zenea, *Historia de la Real Casa*, 91–92.
75. Twinam, *Public Lives, Private Secrets*, 59–60.
76. Ibid., 82–86; Lipsett-Rivera, "Slap in the Face of Honor," 192–94.
77. Twinam, "Church," 163–86; Martínez-Vergne, *Shaping the Discourse on Space*, 117–18.
78. Real Sociedad Patriótica de la Habana, *Memorias*, 3:16. The Board of Charity included, among other notable people, two ecclesiastical officials appointed by the bishop, two members of the city council, two businessmen, two property owners, two scholars, and two physicians.
79. Real Sociedad Patriótica de la Habana, *Memorias*, 3:17.
80. "Expediente formado por el Secretario de la Junta de Maternidad sobre lo acordado para evitar el abuso de admitir tantos expósitos de color en la Casa de Beneficencia," 1833, leg. 3578, letter I, ANC, FCB.
81. Francisco Arango y Parreño to President of Casa de Maternidad, April 24, 1836, in Zenea, *Historia de la Real Casa*, 283–84.
82. "Reglamento para el establecimiento de las casas de expósitos," December 11, 1796, in Carlos IV, *Novísima Recopilación*, vol. 3, books 6–7, 692; Ricafort, *Reglamento de la Real Casa*, 39.
83. Libro de matrícula general de expósitos de la casa, book 1 (1840–86) and book 2 (1886–1917), ANC, FCB.
84. Ricafort, *Reglamento de la Real Casa*, 11–14, 59–63.
85. Franklin, *Women and Slavery*, 110–11.
86. Junta de Caridad, February 14, 1833, in "Expediente formado."
87. See, for example, Madden, *Island of Cuba*, 164–67; Turnbull, *Travels in the West*, 62, 146, 288–89; Gurney, *Winter in the West Indies*, 209.

88. José Antonio Verdaguer, February 26, 1833, in "Expediente formado."
89. Excma Sra Presidenta Rosa Arango de Quesada, La Condesa de Gibacoa, La Condesa de Fernandina to Sor Secretario, March 2, 1833, in "Expediente formado."
90. Mariano de Arango, Domingo Aguirre to Junta de Caridad, June 4, 1833, in "Expediente formado." Summaries of the discussions hereafter can also be found in Zenea, *Historia de la Real Casa*, 261–62.
91. Zenea, *Historia de la Real Casa*, 261–62.
92. Ibid., 262.
93. Huguet-Termes, "Madrid Hospitals and Welfare."
94. Mariano de Arango and Domingo de Aguirre to Presidente y Señores Vocales de la Real Junta de Caridad, April 9, 1834, in Zenea, *Historia de la Real Casa*, 262.
95. Ibid., 263.
96. La Condesa de Villanueva and Rosa Arango de Quesada, "Dictamen de las Señoras de la Junta de Piedad sobre las Gentes de Color," November 20, 1833, in Zenea, *Historia de la Real Casa*, 263.
97. Zenea, *Historia de la Real Casa*, 266.
98. Ibid., 267.
99. Ibid., 264.
100. Census of 1827, in Dionisio Vives, *Cuadro estadístico*.
101. Arango y Pareño, *Obras*, 2:200.
102. Ibid., 2:201–2.
103. Ibid., 2:201–2.
104. Ibid., 2:264.
105. Zenea, *Historia de la Real Casa*, 265.
106. Ibid., 265–66.
107. For a similar argument about the racist roots of early feminism, see Newman, *White Women's Rights*.
108. Mariano de Arango and Domingo de Aguirre to Presidente y Señores Vocales de la Real Junta de Caridad, 270.
109. Ibid., 271.
110. Ibid., 273.
111. Ibid., 273.
112. Ibid., 275.
113. Ibid., 274.
114. Ibid., 275.
115. Ibid., 273.
116. Ibid., 277.
117. "Expediente formado"; Mariano de Arango and Domingo de Aguirre to Presidente y Señores Vocales de la Real Junta de Caridad, 276, 279.
118. "Real Cédula de 5 de enero de 1794 de SM y señores del Consejo por la cual se manda a guardar y cumplir el Real Decreto en que se declaran por legítimos para todos los efectos civiles y sin excepción a los expósitos de ambos sexos, Impresa en La Habana en 1835," leg. 401, no. 8, ANC, FCB.
119. Francisco Arango y Parreño to President of Casa de Maternidad, April 24, 1836, in Zenea, *Historia de la Real Casa*, 285–6.

120. "Circular sobre que el inicio depósito de esclavos es en la real Casa de Beneficencia," June 1840, leg. 1061, no. 37790, ANC, GSC; "Real Orden disponiendo el departamento de esclavos en la Casa de Beneficencia," June 12, 1842, leg. 1061, no. 37792, ANC, GSC.

121. "Circular sobre que el inicio depósito"; "Real Orden disponiendo el departamento de esclavos."

122. "Sobre la carta de emancipación entregada por el Gobierno a la negra Paula N 354 del bergantín Negrito," March 30, 1842, leg. 151, no. 7574, ANC, RCJF.

123. "Expediente promovido por D. José Bara subarrendatario del Depósito Judical de esclavos, solicitando eximirse el recibo de párvulos y inútiles," 1844, leg. 152, no. 7646, ANC, RCJF.

124. "Emancipados que fallecieron en el Hospital de la Casa de Depósito de 1824 a 1843," [n.d.], leg. 149, no. 7383, ANC, RCJF; "Sobre fallecimientos de emancipados, 1842–54," [n.d.], leg. 149, no. 7347, ANC, RCJF.

125. "Expediente sobre el fallecimiento de la emancipada Rita de Casia no 212 de la goleta Planeta," April 25, 1845, leg. 148, no. 7286, ANC, RCJF.

126. "Expediente sobre la entrega a D Nicolas Aparicio del párvulo José Eligio hijo de la emancipada Rita n 212," May 10, 1845, leg. 148, no. 7291, ANC, RCJF.

127. "Expediente sobre fallecimiento en el deposito de cimarrones del párvulo Julian, hijo de la emancipada Luiteria no. 346," September 16, 1844, leg. 152, no. 7650, ANC, RCJF.

128. Lactancia de expósitos en la casa de beneficencia. November 15, 1867, leg. 113, letters I, J, K, L, Ll, M, and N, ANC, ME.

129. "Expediente rel a que se consignen desde enero próximo 2,500 pesos del Presupuesto de Emancipados para la Casa de Beneficencia," 1856–57, leg. 12020, no. 47142, ANC, GSC.

130. "Expediente en el que la morena esclava Dolores Villafranca pide sea admitida en la Casa de Beneficencia y de Maternidad, su hijo Manuel," 1850, leg. 3580, letter A, ANC, ME.

131. Ibid., 275.

132. Leg. 3578, letter Ac, ANC, ME.

133. "Sobre la extracción que se hizo de una niña que tenía en lactancia Da. Maria de la Merced Zaldívar por Da. Práxedes Paris," January 20, 1841, leg. 3578, letter G, ANC, ME.

134. Ibid.

135. See, for example, "D Juan Peraza pide se le entregue su nieto D Juan Leandro que se halla en la Benef," 1845, leg. 3483, letter Bj, ANC, ME.

136. "Exp en que Manuel Rodriguez solicita se admita en la Casa de Maternidad a su hija Josefa," July 4, 1841, leg. 3578, letter Aw, ANC, ME.

137. "Expediente sobre la traslación de varios niños del Hospital de S Lázaro a la Casa de Maternidad," July 28, 1841, leg. 3578, letter H, ANC, ME.

138. "Evaristo Zenea Expediente sobre la traslación de varios niños del Hospital de S Lázaro a la Casa de Maternidad," June 11, 1841, leg. 3578, letter H, ANC, ME.

139. Ibid.

140. Ibid.

141. "Expediente sobre la traslación de varios niños del Hospital de S Lázaro a la Casa de Maternidad," July 28, 1841.

142. Tomas O'Naghten, "Expediente sobre la traslación de varios niños del Hospital de S Lázaro a la Casa de Maternidad," October 5, 1841, leg. 3578, letter H, ANC, ME.

143. Ibid.

144. Zenea, *Historia de la Real Casa*, 289.

145. Ibid., 291.

146. Ibid., 292.

147. *Diario de la Marina*, July 10, 1849, 3.

148. "Extractos de varias representaciones presentadas por distinctos individuos en solicitud de que se les admitiesen niños en la Casa de Benef cuyas representaciones fueron remitidas al Rector para su resolución en junta," 1848, leg. 3490, letter N, ANC, ME.

149. "Expediente promovido por la parda Josefa Salgado solicitando si la admiten en la Casa de Beneficencia sus tres nietos," 1848, leg. 3538, letter Bj, ANC, ME. One other reference to the surrender of an infant classified as "parda al parecer" through the torno appears in the registry of surrendered infants. There may have been a separate book kept for infants of color, but does not appear within the archival collection. See "Libro de matrícula general de expósitos de la casa," 1840–86, book 1, ANC, FCB.

150. García Goyena, *Código criminal español*, 2:73.

151. Montanos Ferrín and Sánchez-Arcilla, *Estudios de historia*, 152.

152. García Goyena and Aguirre, *Febrero*, 228.

153. Ibid.

154. The implementation of the 1822 penal code was postponed by royal order until January 1823 in the peninsula, and sixty days thereafter in the overseas colonies, including Cuba. Although some speculate that the penal code did not go into effect, there is evidence that provincial authorities in the peninsula did apply the law. Casado Ruíz, "La aplicación del Código penal," 334; Fraile Foro, "Nuevas aportaciones," 46–50.

155. For a similar argument in twentieth-century Brazil, see Roth, *Miscarriage of Justice*, 157.

156. "Causa formada contra la negra Merced conga por haber ahogado en un arroyo a sus dos hijas Loreto y Margarita," 1839, leg. 1192, letter Y, ANC, ME.

CHAPTER 5. From Regulating Slavery to Policing Enslaved Wombs

1. "Causa formada contra la negra Merced conga por haber ahogado en un arroyo a sus dos hijas Loreto y Margarita," 1839, leg. 1192, letter Y, ANC, ME.

2. Ibid.

3. Ibid.

4. Baró Pazos, "El derecho penal español," 107n8.

5. On low incidence of criminal prosecution of fertility crimes in colonial Mexico and Brazil, see Jaffary, "Reconceiving Motherhood"; Roth, "From Free Womb to Criminalized Woman.""

6. "Expediente contra la negra esclava de nación lucumí por haber dado muerte a su hijo y tratar de suicidarse," 1837, leg. 2266, letter A, ANC, ME.

7. Baró Pazos, "El derecho penal español," 105–6.
8. Franklin, *Women and Slavery*, 138–39.
9. López Valdés, "Hacia una periodización," 34.
10. Murray, "Statistics of the Slave Trade," 144.
11. Madden, *Island of Cuba*, 3.
12. Ibid., 3–4.
13. Turnbull, *Travels in the West*, 556.
14. Ibid., 62.
15. Gurney, *Winter in the West Indies*, 209.
16. Turnbull, *Travels in the West*, 422.
17. Alexander, *Transatlantic sketches*, 375.
18. Humboldt, *Island of Cuba*, 213–14.
19. Turnbull, *Travels in the West*, 62.
20. Ibid., 146.
21. Madden, *Island of Cuba*, 126.
22. Ibid., 164–67; Turnbull, *Travels in the West*, 285, 88–89.
23. Madden, *Island of Cuba*, 162.
24. "Expediente sobre la solicitud de D. Antonio María del Valle de Villafranca para comprar doce negras de las que fueron del Ingenio de Cangre," Abril 18, 1836, leg. 151, no. 7595^a, ANC, RCJF.
25. "Expediente sobre la solicitud de D. Antonio María del Valle."
26. Arango y Pareño, *Obras*, 2:195; Baird, *Impressions and Experiences*, 1:107.
27. "Expediente promovido por el Sr Coronel D Evaristo Carrillo para que la Junta le venda el negro Feliciano, o se le compre una negra que este dice ser su consorte," January 13, 1841, leg. 151, no. 7528, ANC, RCJF.
28. Dumont, *Antropología y patología*, 97.
29. For a critique of this image, see Meriño Fuentes and Perera Díaz, "La madre esclava," 49–59.
30. Real Sociedad Patriótica de la Habana, *Memorias*, 17.
31. "Causa formada contra la negra Merced conga."
32. Ibid.
33. Ibid.
34. "Diligencias practicadas contra la negra Ciriaca de la Rosa por la herida que infirió a su hija Jacinta y el suicidio que intentó," 1832, leg. 127, letter G, ANC, ME.
35. "Expediente sobre el suicidio de la negra carabalí Isabel, esclava de D Pedro Galí que se precipitó al pozo de la casa con su hijito Fernando," Barrio de Guadalupe, 1837, leg. 4362, letter Ñ, ANC, ME.
36. "Expediente contra la negra esclava de nación lucumí."
37. Pérez, *To Die in Cuba*, 143.
38. "Expediente contra la negra esclava de nación lucumí."
39. Ibid.
40. Ibid.
41. Ibid.
42. Ibid.
43. Ibid.

44. Ibid.
45. Ibid.
46. For example, the preponderance of court cases involving enslaved people claiming rights or facing legal consequences date from the late 1830s through the 1860s. See García Rodríguez, *Voices of the Enslaved*.
47. Peiro and Rodrigo, *Elementos de medicina*, 86–87.
48. Leg. 940, exp. 33158, ANC, GSC.
49. Bergad, García, and Barcia, *Cuban Slave Market*, 65.
50. "Encuesta sobre la reforma del sistema higiénico, moral, y alimentar de los siervos," February 23, 1842, leg. 940, exp. 33158, ANC, GSC. Also see transcription in Tardieu, *Morir o dominar*, 206–8.
51. Leg. 940, exp. 33158, ANC, GSC. For biographical details about the planters and transcriptions of their letters, see Tardieu, *Morir o dominar*, 132–38, 208–63.
52. Sebastián I. de Lasa to Captain-General, March 5, 1842, leg. 940, exp. 33158, ANC, GSC.
53. Joaquín Muñoz Izaguirre to Captain-General, March 7, 1842, leg. 940, exp. 33158, ANC, GSC.
54. "The Hacendado Jacinto González Larrinaga Explains His Methods," April 14, 1842, leg. 941, exp. 33186, ANC, GSC, reproduced in García Rodríguez, *Voices of the Enslaved*, 78–79.
55. Sebastián I. de Lasa to Captain-General.
56. Joaquín Gómez to Captain-General, February 28, 1842, leg. 940, exp. 33158, ANC, GSC.
57. José Manuel Carrillo to Captain-General, March 3, 1842, leg. 940, exp. 33158, ANC, GSC.
58. Juan Montalvo to Captain-General, April 8, 1842, leg. 940, exp. 33158, ANC, GSC.
59. Domingo de Aldama to Captain-General, Ingenio de Santa Rosalía, March 18, 1842, leg. 940, exp. 33158, ANC, GSC.
60. Joaquín Muñoz Izaguirre to Captain-General.
61. Ibid.
62. Juan Montalvo to Captain-General, April 8, 1842.
63. Jacinto González Larrinaga to Captain-General, April 14, 1842, leg. 940, exp. 33158, ANC, GSC.
64. José Manuel Carrillo to Captain-General.
65. Ignacio Herrera to Captain-General, March 4, 1842, leg. 940, exp. 33158, ANC, GSC.
66. Juan Montalvo to Captain-General.
67. Rafael O'Farril to Captain-General, February 26, 1842, leg. 940, exp. 33158, ANC, GSC.
68. Domingo de Aldama to Captain-General.
69. José Manuel Carrillo to Captain-General.
70. "Hacendado Jacinto González Larrinaga."
71. Joaquín Muñoz Izaguirre to Captain-General.
72. Domingo de Aldama to Captain-General.
73. Juan Montalvo to Captain-General.
74. Sebastián I. de Lasa to Captain-General.

75. Joaquín Muñoz Izaguirre to Captain-General.
76. Duvergier de Hauranne, "Cuba et les Antilles," 638.
77. Hazard, *Cuba with Pen and Pencil*, 354.
78. Ibid., 354.
79. José Manuel Carrillo to Captain-General.
80. Un Montuno, *Cartilla práctica*, 84–85.
81. Saco, *La supresión del tráfico*, 134–35.
82. "Parecer de la Real Junta sobre el Reglamento de esclavos," in Tardieu, *Morir o dominar*, 265.
83. Marqués de Arcos to Captain-General, May 19, 1842, leg. 940, exp. 33158, ANC, GSC.
84. El Conde de Fernandina to Captain-General, March 12, 1842, leg. 940, exp. 33158, ANC, GSC.
85. Wenceslao de Villa Urrutia, Havana, March 25, 1842, leg. 940, exp. 33158, ANC, GSC.
86. José Manuel Carrillo to Captain-General.
87. Article 7, Reglamento de Esclavos, November 14, 1842, in Ortiz, *Los negros esclavos*, 202.
88. "Excerpts from the Slave Code," November 14, 1842, in García Rodríguez, *Voices of the Enslaved*, 80–81.
89. Reglamento de Esclavos, November 14, 1842, in Ortiz, *Los negros esclavos*, 84.
90. Finch, *Rethinking Slave Rebellion in Cuba*, 1–2. Also see Robert L. Paquette, *Sugar Is Made with Blood*.
91. Captain-General to Presidente de la Junta de Fomento, Havana, February 29, 1844, leg. 943, exp. 33271, ANC, GSC, reproduced in Tardieu, *Morir o dominar*, 264.
92. Reglamento de Esclavos, November 14, 1842, in Ortiz, *Los negros esclavos*, 442–49.
93. El conde de Romero, el conde de Cañonago, and Antonio María de Escovedo to Junta de Fomento, Havana, April 17, 1845, leg. 943, exp. 33271, ANC, GSC, reproduced in Tardieu, *Morir o dominar*, 266.
94. Ibid., 267.
95. Ibid., 268–69.
96. Circulares impresas del Gobierno Superior Civil de la Isla de Cuba, May 31, 1844, leg. 943, exp. 33271, ANC, GSC, reproduced in Tardieu, *Morir o dominar*, 272–75; Barcia Paz, "Powerful Subjects."
97. Dana, *To Cuba and Back*, 251–52.
98. Wudermann, *Notes on Cuba*, 153.
99. Baird, *Impressions and Experiences*, 1:107.

CHAPTER 6. "No Race Can Substitute Black Africans"

1. "Causa criminal por haberse encontrado cerca de la pila de la iglesia de San Felipe el cadáver de un párvulo de color," 1855, leg. 2977, letter E, ANC, ME. For an analysis of this case from a medical-legal perspective, see Lucero, "Interpreting the Remnants."
2. Arts. 327–31, in *Código Penal de España* (1848), 143–46.
3. Chapter 2, title 9, book 2, arts. 336–40, in *Código Penal de España* (1850), 86–87.

4. *Código Penal de España* (1848), 143–44n2.
5. Ibid., 145n1; also see Rosaín, *Examen y cartilla de parteras*, 30–31.
6. *Código Penal de España* (1848), 145n1.
7. "El Gobernador Capitán general de la Isla de Cuba en escrito reservado no 3, fecha 15 de febrero de 1845," in "Expediente general de esclavitud: Falta de mano de obra para la agricultura por la abolición de la esclavitud," 1845–1857, leg. 3548, exp. 1, ANE, Ultramar.
8. "La sección de Ultramar del Consejo Real," December 22, 1846, leg. 3548, exp. 1, ANE, Ultramar.
9. Enriquez, note, January 11, 1853, leg. 3548, exp. 1, ANE, Ultramar.
10. Dana, *To Cuba and Back*, 251–52.
11. On Black women midwives birthing enslaved babies, see Barcia, *Oficios de mujer*, 90–92.
12. Chateausalins, *El Vademecum*, 33–91.
13. Ibid., 33, 69, 68.
14. Ibid., 59.
15. Ibid., 60.
16. Ibid., 62.
17. Ibid., 59–60.
18. Ibid., 65, 426.
19. Arteaga y Quesada and Olivella, "La partonalgina."
20. Chateausalins, *El Vademecum*, 65–66.
21. Ibid., 75.
22. Ibid., 68–69, 80.
23. Ibid., 77, 85.
24. Chateausalins, *El Vademecum*, 79,
25. Ibid., 78–79, 99–100.
26. Ibid., 90.
27. Ibid., 91.
28. Alexander, *Transatlantic sketches*, 374.
29. Auvard, "La antisepsia en la ginecología."
30. Ibid., 92, 90–91, 93.
31. Un Montuno, *Cartilla práctica*, 84–85.
32. *Anales* 50 (1914): 1019.
33. Cantero, *Los ingenios*, 274–75.
34. Ibid., 185.
35. Moreno Fraginals, *El ingenio*.
36. Cantero, *Los ingenios*, 66.
37. Moreno Fraginals, *El ingenio*.
38. Olivares, Fiscal de la Real Audiencia Pretorial de la Habana, August 27, 1853, leg. 948, exp. 33,486, ANC, GSC.
39. Murray, "Statistics of the Slave Trade," 147.
40. Olivares, Fiscal.
41. Ibid.
42. Kathleen López, *Chinese Cubans*; Scott, *Slave Emancipation in Cuba*.
43. Olivares, Fiscal.

44. Ibid.
45. Ibid.
46. "Proyecto de importación de mujeres esclavas en la Isla de Cuba," 1855, leg. 3549, no. 4, ANC, GSC.
47. Ibid.
48. Ibid.
49. Ibid.
50. *Anales* 15 (1878): 267.
51. "Proyecto de importación."
52. Ibid.
53. Joda Esteve, "El comercio de esclavos," 114.
54. Hulbert, *Gan-Eden*, 192.
55. "Expediente criminal por haberse encontrado ahogada en un pozo la negra Juana criolla y su hijo Juan Emeterio de D Antonio Sánchez Arencibia," April 25, 1851, leg. 805, letter O, ANC, ME.
56. "Causa criminal por haberse encontrado."
57. Erenchún, *Anales de la isla*, 1:22.
58. "Del Infanticidio," chapter 3, title 9, book 2, art. 336, in *Código Penal de España* (1850), 86.
59. Erenchún, *Anales de la isla*, 1:22.
60. Ibid., 22. Lauderdale Graham, "Honor among Slaves."
61. Lauderdale Graham, "Honor among Slaves."
62. Erenchún, *Anales de la isla*, 1:22.
63. Ibid.
64. See Gloria García, *La esclavitud desde la esclavitud*, 117; Morrison, *Cuba's Racial Crucible*, 136; Cowling, *Conceiving Freedom*, 83–84.
65. Reid-Vázquez, *Year of the Lash*, 16, 17; Knight, *Slave Society in Cuba*, 86.
66. Reid-Vázquez, *Year of the Lash*, 22.
67. de la Sagra, *Historia física y política*, 165.
68. "Expediente Criminal por la Muerte Casual del Parvulito Hijo de la Negra Lorenza Conga," 1864, leg. 809, letter Ñ, ANC, ME.
69. "Expediente criminal contra la negra Isabel Frías, esclava de Rosario de Laza, por ocultación de un feto," 1865, leg. 3026, letter L, ANC, ME. Subsequent details in the text regarding Isabel's case are from this source.
70. For a similar argument in the context of twentieth-century Brazil, see Roth, *Miscarriage of Justice*, 156–67.
71. Un Montuno, *Cartilla práctica*, 82.
72. Bergad, García, and Barcia, *Cuban Slave Market*, 65.
73. Moreno Fraginals, Klein, and Engerman, "Level and Structure," 1216.
74. "Sesión pública ordinaria del 16 de febrero de 1879," Comisión Nacional Cubana de la UNESCO, *Actas*, 80–83; *Anales* 15 (1878): 266.
75. *Anales* 15 (1878): 266.
76. "Sesión pública ordinaria."
77. Melero, "Reseña estadística acerca de la mortalidad," 294.
78. Gallenga, *Pearl of the Antilles*, 123.

79. Paugh, *Politics of Reproduction*; Paton, "Maternal Struggles," 263; Roth, "From Free Womb to Criminalized Woman," 274–75; Santos, "Mothering Slaves"; Cowling, *Conceiving Freedom*.

80. Saco, *La estadística criminal*, quoted in Castellanos, *La delinquencia femenina en Cuba*, 17.

CHAPTER 7. Reconstituting Slavery

1. Scott, *Slave Emancipation in Cuba*, 71–73.
2. Paton, "Maternal Struggles," 258, 263.
3. Roth, "From Free Womb to Criminalized Woman," 274–75.
4. del Valle, "Demografía médica de niños," 373–74; del Valle, "Elementos demográficos de natalidad," 65–66; del Valle, "Mortalidad de la Habana en el verano de 1878," 440; del Valle, "Mortalidad de la Habana en el otoño de 1878," 94–95; del Valle, "Mortalidad de la Habana en el otoño de 1882," 88.
5. For example, Scott, *Slave Emancipation in Cuba*, 73.
6. Cowling, *Conceiving Freedom*, 11.
7. Scott, *Slave Emancipation in Cuba*, 73–75.
8. Aimes, "Coartación," 423. Also see Varella and Barcia, *Wage-Earning Slaves*.
9. Gallenga, *Pearl of the Antilles*, 123–24.
10. Lucero, *Cuban City, Segregated*, 85; Perera Díaz and Meriño Fuentes, *Nombrar las cosas*, 56–57.
11. Morrison, *Cuba's Racial Crucible*, 142.
12. Ibid., 143.
13. Perera Díaz and Meriño Fuentes, *Para librarse de los lazos*, 259–63.
14. "Derechos de sepulture de los hijos de esclavos cuando libres hasta que cumplan la edad de 18 años," June 26, 1871, leg. 4759, exp. 37, Archivo Histórico Nacional, Ultramar.
15. Villanova, *Estadística de la abolición*, 3.
16. Pichardo, *Documentos*, 1:384–85; Scott, *Slave Emancipation in Cuba*, 69.
17. Cowling, *Conceiving Freedom*, 88.
18. Ibid., 86–87.
19. "Exp promovido por la morena Maria de la Cruz Morejon en queja de haber sido tenida en esclavitud siendo libre, e igualmente dos hijos," July 19, 1875, leg. 3484, letter Ap, ANC, ME.
20. Scott, *Slave Emancipation in Cuba*, 80; Cowling, *Conceiving Freedom*, 91.
21. Cowling, *Conceiving Freedom*, 92.
22. Scott, *Slave Emancipation in Cuba*, 135.
23. Cowling, *Conceiving Freedom*, 93.
24. Piña y Peñuela, *Topografía médica*, 109; Valdés Castro, *Memoria sobre la lactancia*, 8–20.
25. For wet nurse ads from mid-century Havana, see Franklin, *Women and Slavery*, 140; Camacho, "Los criaderos de esclavos," 11.
26. "Informe relativo," *Anales* (1878): 49–53; Valdés Miranda, *Apuntes sobre la lactancia artificial*; Valdés Castro, *Memoria sobre la lactancia*, 6–8; Le Riverend, *Memoria sobre la leche*.

27. Ricafort, *Reglamento de la Real Casa*, art. 120; Zenea, *Historia de la Real Casa*, 253.
28. "Papeletas del alta y baja de los departamentos y de raciones distribuidas en el mes de octubre de 1867," leg. 113, letter O, ANC, ME.
29. "Papeletas del alta y baja de los departamentos y de raciones distribuidas en el mes de noviembre de 1867," leg. 113, letter Ñ, ANC, ME.
30. "Lactancia de expósitos en la casa de beneficencia," leg. 113, letters I, J, K, L, Ll, M, and N, ANC, ME.
31. "Papeletas del alta y baja de los departamentos y de raciones distribuidas en el mes de diciembre de 1867," leg. 113, letter F, ANC, ME.
32. "Dirección de la Casa de Beneficencia y Maternidad de La Habana. Cuenta de los sueldos abonados a las nodrizas internas por la lactancia de los niños expósitos correspondientes al mes de enero de 1874," leg. 7, letter J, ANC, ME.
33. "Dirección de la Casa de Beneficencia y Maternidad de La Habana. Cuenta de los sueldos abonados a las nodrizas internas por la lactancia de los niños expósitos correspondientes al mes de febrero de 1874," leg. 7, letter G, ANC, ME.
34. "Exp promovido por la morena Francisca criolla sobre su libertad y la de sus hijos," n.d., leg. 3484, file AD, ANC, ME.
35. On petitions by enslaved mothers following the Moret Law, see Cowling, *Conceiving Freedom*, 87–94; Meriño Fuentes and Perrera Díaz, "La madre esclava," 53.
36. The enslaved woman Marilina Conga was placed as a wet nurse in the Casa, with her own one-month-old baby in October 1867. No other enslaved babies were listed in that record. "Papeletas del alta y baja de los departamentos y de raciones distribuidas en el mes de octubre de 1867," leg. 113, letter O, ANC, ME.
37. Ariza, "Bad Mothers."
38. Meriño Fuentes and Perrera Díaz, "La madre esclava," 52; Zenea, *Historia de la Real Casa*, 265.
39. Hidalgo Valdés, *Real Casa de Beneficencia*, 70–71.
40. For an analogous example, see Martínez-Alier, *Marriage, Class and Colour*, 84.
41. "Expediente sobre el sistema que ha de seguirse para clasificar los niños expósitos en la clase a que pertenecen," 1865, leg. 389, no. 35, ANC, FCB.
42. Ibid.
43. "Lactancia de expósitos en la casa de beneficencia."
44. "Papeletas del alta y baja de los departamentos y de raciones distribuidas en el mes de octubre de 1867," leg. 113, letter O, ANC, ME.
45. "Papeletas del alta y baja de los departamentos y de raciones distribuidas en el mes de noviembre de 1867."
46. Papeletas del alta y baja de los departamentos y de raciones distribuidas en el mes de diciembre de 1867."
47. Ibid.
48. *Anales* 23 (1886): 355–59.
49. Ibid., 358.
50. Ibid., 355–59.
51. Ibid., 357.
52. The documents are missing from ANC, FCB.

53. "Libro de matrícula general de expósitos de la casa," book 1 (1840–86) and book 2 (1886–1917), ANC, FCB.
54. C. C. Coppinger, "Expediente formado a instancia del director solicitando se coloquen los niños de color que se hallan en el período de lactancia en distinto local del que ocupan los blancos," July 8, 1886, leg. 389, no. 20, ANC, FCB.
55. Ibid.
56. Ibid.
57. Ibid.
58. Plá, *La Raza de Color*.
59. Morrison, *Cuba's Racial Crucible*.
60. Plá, *La Raza de Color*, 31–35.
61. *Ordenanzas para el gobierno*, 7–8.
62. "Libro de matrícula general", book 2, no. 2354, July 20, 1886.
63. "Libro de matrícula general," book 2, no. 2588, August 9, 1896.
64. Libro de matrícula general," book 2, October 23, 1886.
65. "Expediente criminal contra la morena Caridad González Betancourt por parricidio frustrado," 1888, leg. 2778, letter C, ANC, ME.
66. Cassia Roth makes a similar argument for early twentieth-century Brazil, where physicians and jurists often conflated abortion/infanticide with miscarriage and stillbirth (*Miscarriage of Justice*, 157–76).
67. "Diligencias sumarias formadas por encontrarse abandonado el cadáver de una criatura recién nacida en la puerta del Cementerio de Espada," 1878, leg. 2281, letter S, ANC, ME.
68. See, for example, "Expediente criminal por el hallazgo del cadáver de un niño recién nacido," 1880, leg. 2285, letter M, or "Causa por haberse encontrado en el mar el cadáver de un niño sanguinolento, Escribano Joaquín Gussiñer," 1885, leg. 2956, letter Ab, both in ANC, ME.
69. Delfín, "Estadística demográfica del año 1892," 69–75, quoted in Swiggett, *Proceedings*, 437.
70. De la Torriente, *Estudio sobre la riqueza*.
71. Plá, *La Raza de Color*, 27–36.

CHAPTER 8. From the Art of Midwifery to the Science of Obstetrics

1. Rodríguez, *Right to Live in Health*, 4–6.
2. Le-Roy y Cassá, "Apuntes para la historia," 349.
3. Rodríguez, *Right to Live in Health*, 6–7.
4. At least ten Cuban medical students, including José Beato Dolz and Gabriel M. Landa, published dissertations in France between 1855 and 1889.
5. Lucero, *Revolutionary Masculinity and Racial Inequality*; Ferrer, "Rustic Men, Civilized Nation."
6. Prados Torreira, *Mambisas*; Guadalupe García, "Urban Guajiros."
7. Lucero, *Revolutionary Masculinity and Racial Inequality*, 47–74.
8. Arteaga, *Sífilis hereditaria*.

9. Le-Roy y Cassá, "Apuntes para la historia," 362.
10. Ibid., 356.
11. Ibid., 363.
12. Weiss Verson, "La situación de la vulva."
13. Le-Roy y Cassá, "Apuntes para la historia," 365–66; Weiss Verson, "New Curette," 359–60.
14. Le-Roy y Cassá, "Apuntes para la historia," 365–66.
15. *Anales* 3 (1866): 10.
16. "Cuestiones de obstetricia," *Anales* 10 (1873): 59–62.
17. "Informe en un caso de supuesto infanticidio," *Anales* 22 (1885): 99–102; "Informe sobre infanticidio," *Anales* 38 (1901): 75–83.
18. Roth, *Miscarriage of Justice*, 157, 176.
19. Mata, *Tratado de medicina*, 2:395.
20. Ibid., 2:392.
21. Ibid., 2:391.
22. "Informe en causa de infanticidio," *Anales* 8 (1871): 164–66.
23. "Consulta sobre el valor científico de un reconocimiento judicial en caso de infanticidio," *Anales* 16 (1879): 285–86.
24. "1º Informe en causa contra Da. S.M. y otros (¿), por infanticidio," *Anales* 32 (1895):111–15.
25. "2º informe en causa contra Da. S.M. por infanticidio," *Anales* 32 (1895): 116–20.
26. "Informe sobre infanticidio," *Anales* 27 (1891): 548–52.
27. "Informe sobre infanticidio," *Anales* 24 (1887): 330–31.
28. "Informe médico-legal en cuestión de infanticidio," *Anales* 6 (1870): 222–23.
29. "Informe médico-legal en causa por infanticidio," *Anales* 30 (1893): 193–206.
30. Le-Roy y Cassá, "Informe médico legal."
31. "Informe sobre el reconocimiento médico-legal de un feto," *Anales* 30 (1894): 527–34.
32. "Informe sobre infanticidio," *Anales* 38 (1901): 75–83.
33. For more on this point, see Lucero, "Interpreting the Remnants."
34. Assorted jail records, box 61, no file, U.S. National Archives II, Records of the Military Government of Cuba, record group 140, entry 3.
35. Jaffary, *Reproduction and Its Discontents*, 5–7.
36. "Expediente criminal por hallazgo del cadáver de una niña en una jaula, Escribanía de Castro," 1876, leg. 2863, letter G, ANC ME.
37. Names have been changed.
38. "Muerte de la morena M.M. a consecuencia del parto; intervención de una intrusa," *Anales* 25 (1889): 535–47; "Informe en un caso de muerte a consecuencia del parto. Observaciones a dicho informe por el Dr. Núñez," *Anales* 20 (1894): 393–95, 419.
39. "Informe en un caso de muerte," 393–95, 419.
40. Ibid.
41. Ibid.
42. Casuso y Roque, *Profilaxia de la fiebre puerperal*, 4–11.
43. Ibid.; "Reglamento de desinfección para las comadronas," *Anales* 27 (1890): 659–65, 658–59.
44. *Anales* 27 (1891): 628.

45. Ibid., 490.
46. "Informe en causa seguida por muerte," 158.
47. Casuso y Roque, *Profilaxia de la fiebre puerperal*, 3–4.
48. Ibid., 4–11; "Reglamento de desinfección," 659–65.
49. "Informe en causa seguida por muerte," 158–62.
50. Madrigal Lomba, "Dr. Gabriel Casuso Roque."
51. Casuso y Roque, "Asepsia puerperal," 654–56; Casuso y Roque, "Consideraciones sobre algunos casos operados," 338; Casuso y Roque, "Histerectomías," 105–6.
52. "Informe en cause seguida por muerte," 158–62.
53. Le-Roy y Cassá, "Apuntes para la historia," 351–52.
54. Ibid., 352–54.
55. *Anales* 27 (1891): 491.
56. Auvard, "La antisepsia en la ginecología."
57. *Anales* 27 (1891): 491.
58. Ibid., 628.
59. Farnot and Rios, "Mortalidad materna," 72–73.
60. Lugones Botell, "La cesárea en la historia."
61. *Anales* 13 (1876): 251, 254–66.
62. Ibid., 141.
63. Le-Roy y Cassá, "Presentación de tronco," 74–80.
64. Otovo, *Progressive Mothers, Better Babies*, 139; Jaffary, *Reproduction and Its Discontents*, 68–70.
65. *Anales* 28 (1891): 94–97, 95; Reyes Zamora, *La semi-anestesia*; Arteaga Quesada and Ramírez Olivella, "La partonalgia," 277–87.
66. Thanks to the anonymous reviewer who provided this information. Jaffary, *Reproduction and Its Discontents*, 85; Prescot, "Dissertation"; Colmeiro, *Curso de Botánica*, 804.
67. Gómez de la Maza, *Ensayo de Farmacofttología cubana*, 44; Creus y Manso, *Del uso del cornezuelo*, 41–42; Cebrian Villanova, *Del cornezuelo de centeno*.
68. *Ginecopatía, obstetricia, y pediatría* (Barcelona) 14, no. 4 (1901): 106–15.
69. On cervical dilation, see Sánchez de Bustamante, "Contribución al estudio"; on dilation and curettage, see Weiss Verson, "New Curette," 359–60; on uterine injection, see Weiss Verson, *Accidentes provocados*.
70. *Ginecopatía, obstetricia, y pediatría* (Barcelona) 14, no. 4 (1901): 106–7.
71. *Anales* 61 (1924–25): 689.
72. Weiss Verson, "New Curette," 359–60.
73. *Código Penal de España* (1850), 145n4.
74. O'Brien, "Many Meanings of *Aborto*," 8.
75. Weiss Verson, "Método y técnica," 651.
76. Documentation of this case provides only initials for the sake of anonymity. I have given names for readability.
77. "Obstetricia," *Anales* 21 (1884): 427–28.
78. Ibid.
79. Beato Dolz, "Ampliación de un informe."
80. Vargas Machuca and Donoso, "Informe químico."
81. Martínez, *Aborto ilícito*, 201.

CHAPTER 9. Birthing a Better Nation

1. I owe this phrasing about the war to Foner, *Spanish-Cuban-American War*.
2. Pérez, *War of 1898*.
3. Lucero, *Revolutionary Masculinity and Racial Inequality*.
4. Pérez, *Cuba between Empires*; Benjamin, *United States*.
5. See, for example, Pérez, *On Becoming Cuban*; Guerra, *Myth of José Martí*; Moore, *Nationalizing Blackness*. Some important exceptions are Bronfman, *Measures of Equality*; Sippial, *Prostitution*; Rodríguez, *Right to Live in Health*.
6. García González, Álvarez Pelaez, and Naranjo Orovio, *En Busca*, 265–442.
7. Willcox, Gannett, and Sanger, *Report on the Census*, 714–17.
8. Ibid, 86–87.
9. Ibid., 714–17.
10. Ibid., 72.
11. *Secretaría de Agricultura*, 88.
12. Briggs, *Reproducing Empire*, 81–89.
13. Le-Roy y Cassá, "Informe acerca de un aparato.
14. Chelala-Aguilera, *Natalidad, mortalidad, y aborto*, 155.
15. Le-Roy y Cassá, "Informe acerca de un aparato."
16. Ibid.
17. Coronado, "Consulta médico legal."
18. Ibid.
19. Ibid.
20. On the racial boundaries of elite status in early republican Cuba, see Pappademos, *Black Political Activism*, 19; Helg, *Our Rightful Share*, chapter 4.
21. Hollerbach and Díaz-Briquets, *Fertility Determinants in Cuba*, 21.
22. Fosalba, "El problema de la población," 743.
23. Barnet, "Consideraciones," 43.
24. Ramos, "Mortalidad infantil en Cuba," 113.
25. Ibid.
26. Ramos, "La homicultura en Cuba," 39.
27. Ibid.
28. Lebredo, "Causas y medios," 210.
29. Le-Roy, "Apuntes sobre las funciones sexuales," 363–65.
30. Ibid., 364; de la Sagra, *Historia física y política*, 74–77, 121–22; and "Fecunidad de las cubanas" in Rodríguez Ferrer, *Naturaleza y civilización*, 436–38.
31. Le-Roy y Cassá, "Apuntes sobre las funciones sexuales," 362–63.
32. Le-Roy y Cassá, *Desenvolvimiento de la sanidad*, 89. Barnet, *Manual de práctica sanitaria*, 1052–73.
33. Le-Roy y Cassá, "Apuntes sobre las funciones sexuales," 362.
34. Ramos, "La homicultura en Cuba," 24, 27.
35. Ibid., 23–24.
36. Betancourt, *Algunos accidentes*.
37. Ramos, "La homicultura en Cuba," 49–50.
38. Stepan, *Hour of Eugenics*, 63–101.

39. Ibid., 76–83. On puericulture in Brazil, see Otovo, *Progressive Mothers, Better Babies.*
40. Hernández and Ramos, *La homicultura*, 47–49.
41. Ibid., 16–18.
42. Duque, *La terapéutica de la sífilis*; Duque, *La prostitución*; Duque, *Estudios sobre enfermedades venéreas.*
43. Hernández, "La homicultura," 16–18.
44. Hernández and Ramos, *La homicultura*, 18.
45. Ramos, "La homicultura en Cuba," 51–54.
46. Suárez, "Notas sobre los trabajos," 12.
47. Suárez, "Informe del Sr. Secretario," 57–58.
48. In Hernández and Ramos, *La homicultura*, 12.
49. Ramos, "Servicio de higiene infantil," 614.
50. Menocal, "Decree No, 441," July 18, 1913, in Taboadela, *Report of the Work*, 5–6.
51. Hollerbach, Díaz-Briquets, and Hill, "Fertility Determinants in Cuba," 9–10.
52. Le-Roy y Cassá, *Desenvolvimiento de la sanidad*, 75.
53. Ramos and Hernández, *La homicultura*, 18.
54. Ibid., 47–49.
55. Secretaría de Sanidad y Beneficencia, *Concursos de Maternidad e Infancia*, n.p.
56. Ibid.
57. Ibid.
58. Secretaria de Sanidad y Beneficencia, *Servicio de Higiene Infantil*, 10.
59. Ibid., 12.
60. José Agustín Martínez, *Aborto ilícito*, 271; "Exp relativo a la Moción del Dr. Candido Hoyos sobre la supresión del torno y el cambio del apellido Valdés en la casa de Beneficencia y Maternidad," September 11, 1936, leg. 189, exp. 38, AN, FCB.
61. "Para nuestros hijos cuando tengan dieciocho años. Consejos de un Médico, por el Profesor Fournier, Introducción y traducción del *Dr.* Gonzálo Aróstegui, Sesión del 12 de julio de 1903," *Anales* 40 (1907): 95–126.
62. José Agustín Martínez, *Aborto ilícito*, 287–89; Lebredo, "Causas y medios." Also see María Gómez Carbonell's 1936 eugenics bill (Chelala-Aguilera, *Natalidad, mortalidad, y aborto*, 65–67).
63. Lebredo, "Causas y medios."
64. Ramos, "Servicio de higiene infantil."
65. Ibid. Also see Lebredo, "Causas y medios."
66. Ramos, "La homicultura en Cuba," 23–24, 27, 35.
67. On the experience of single mothers, see Barcia, *Capas populares y modernidad.*
68. Barnet, "Consideraciones," 42–43; Ramos, "Mortalidad infantil en Cuba," 113.
69. Agramonte, "Nota," 905–7; Guiteras, "Sobre mortalidad infantil"; Ramos, "Mortalidad infantil en Cuba"; Sánchez de Fuentes, "Mortalidad infantil," 223, 292.
70. Chelala-Aguilera, *Natalidad, mortalidad, y aborto*, 129.
71. Marqués de Armas, *Ciencia y poder en Cuba*, 60–64; Chelala-Aguilera, *Natalidad, mortalidad, y aborto*, 142.
72. Taboadela, *Report of the Work*, 18–25.
73. Valdés, "Mortalidad infantil"; Agramonte, "Nota," 903–4, 907.

74. Fosalba, "El problema de la población."
75. Taboadela, *Report of the Work*, 18–25.
76. Ibid., 7–9.
77. Guiteras, "Sobre mortalidad infantil."
78. Fosalba, "El problema de la población," 697–98.
79. "Exp rel al proyecto para la creación de un depto. Cuna o creche y el acuerdo de la junta de gobierno," 1902, leg. 399, no. 53, ANC, FCB.
80. Olmsted and Gannett, *Cuba*, 212; Willcox, Gannett, and Sanger, *Report on the Census*, 157.
81. Willcox, Gannett, and Sanger, *Report on the Census*, 143.
82. Le-Roy y Cassá, *Desenvolvimiento de la sanidad*, 89.
83. "Exp rel al proyecto."
84. "Libro matrícula general de la casa," 1886–1917, book 2, ANC, FCB.
85. "Exp formado para compeler al Ayuntamiento de esta ciudad a que abone a la Real Casa las dietas que devenguen los niños vecinos de este termino que en ella han ingreso, cubierto como esta el no de personas que el Asilo puede sostener con sus propios recursos 1897," leg. 285, no. 35, ANC, FCB.
86. "Libro matrícula general."
87. "Weyler re combo instituciones benéficas," 1896, leg. 402, no. 249, ANC, FCB.
88. "Exp formado con motivo de haberse participado a esta casa que los niños a ella enviadaos por el Gob Americano corra su pago en lo adelante por es del Ayuntamiento," April 5, 1900, leg. 285, no. 39; "Exp formado para la admisión de algunos niños hasta cubrir el numero de 366 personas que como promedio ha venido sosteniendo la Casa," September 26, 1901, leg. 285, no. 38; "Expediente formado por un acuerdo de la Junta Piadosa de Maternidad pretendiendo que se suspenda la admisión en la Casa de niños en lactancia procedentes del Ayuntamiento y que no se den a criar fuera los expositos," 1906–11, leg. 285, no. 20, all in ANC, FCB.
89. "Exp rel al proyecto."
90. Ibid.
91. Similar arguments about the public benefit of moralization campaigns emerged in debates about charity in Puerto Rico, and especially about regulating prostitution. Martínez-Vergne, *Shaping the Discourse on Space*; Suárez Findlay, *Imposing Decency*; Sippial, *Prostitution*; Ruggiero, *Modernity in the Flesh*; Guy, *Sex and Danger in Buenos Aires*.
92. "Exp rel al proyecto."
93. Juan R O'Farrill to director of Casa de Maternidad, October 15, 1903, leg. 399, no. 53, ANC, FCB.
94. See, for example, "Expediente formado por un acuerdo."
95. "Exp relativo a la Moción."
96. Private institutions—including Dr. Delfín's Granja La Caridad (Havana); Colegio La Ciudad Infantil for boys (Calabazar); Asilo Truffin (Marianao), Colegio La Domiciliaria, La Sagrada Familia, El Buen Pastor, and San Vicente de Paúl, for girls; Asilo y Creche del Vedado, operated by Sra. Lili Hidalgo de Cunill, and Asilo Menocal for babies of both sexes and girls (Cerro)—collectively served between 600 and 750 children. Additional correctional and preventative institutions housed another 700 children.
97. Public institution outside of Havana included Asilo de Camaguey, Asilo Católico

de Cárdenas, Asilo y Casa de Beneficencia de Matanzas, Casa de Beneficencia y Asilo de Niños de Santiago de Cuba, and Asilos de Guantánamo y de Holguín.

98. Plazaola, "La beneficencia en Cuba," 124–26.

99. Among these women were Lila Hidalgo de Cunill, Ofelia Rodríguez Arango de Herrera, Juanita Cano de Font, Mina Pérez Chamont de Truffin, María Herrera de Seva, y Antonia Prieto de Calvo, Berta Machado de Sánchez, (married to Rafael Jorge Sánchez), Ángela Elvira Machado de Obregón, Dalia Suárez de Fernández Quevedo, Hortensia García de San Pedro, and the Srta Caridad Coello (inspector of Creches and Asylums).

100. Secretaría de Sanidad y Beneficencia, "Comision nacional."

101. *Ordenanzas y Reglamento de la Casa de Beneficencia y Maternidad de la Habana* (Havana: Imprenta Escuela de la Casa de Beneficencia y maternidad, 1917), leg. 294, exp. 9, ANC, FCB.

102. Stepan, *Hour of Eugenics*, 63–101.

CHAPTER 10. Abortion in Law and Medicine

1. "Comunicación oral sobre el incremento del número de abortos provocados," *Anales* 49 (March 28, 1913): 848.

2. "Consideraciones sobre aborto criminal, con motivo de una comunicación oral del Dr. Tomás V. Coronado," *Anales* 52 (July 9, 1915): 121–22.

3. Ibid.

4. *La Discusión*, January 13, 1911.

5. On physicians' antiabortion remarks in Brazil and Peru, see Roth, *Miscarriage of Justice*, 108–13, and Necochea López, *History of Family Planning*, 52–53.

6. Roth, *Miscarriage of Justice*, 111.

7. Stoner, *From the House*, 142.

8. Ramos, "Servicio de higiene infantil."

9. Ibid.

10. Ramos, "Los abortos criminales en Cuba," 25.

11. "Comunicación oral sobre el incremento," 849.

12. Ramos, "Los abortos criminales en Cuba," 25.

13. On obstetric intervention in cases of pelvic deformities, see Cañizares, *Influencia*. Physicians continued to perform such procedures when the fetus was deemed to be dead or montruous. See Ruiz Casabó, "Un caso más de anencefalia," 217–22.

14. "Comunicación oral sobre el incremento," 849.

15. Le-Roy y Cassá, "Vómitos incoercibles," 49–80.

16. Ramos, "Los abortos criminales en Cuba," 25.

17. "Comunicación oral sobre el incremento," 850.

18. Benítez Pérez, "La trayectoria del aborto," 87–104, 92.

19. "Comunicación oral sobre el incremento," 848–49.

20. Ibid., 850.

21. Ramos, "Mortalidad infantil en Cuba."

22. Ramos, "Servicio de higiene infantil."

23. "Consideraciones sobre aborto criminal."

24. "Comunicación oral sobre el incremento," 848.
25. "Consideraciones sobre aborto criminal."
26. "Consideraciones obstétricas, médico-legales y sociale s sobre el aborto," *Anales* 49 (March 28, 1913): 850–51.
27. Ibid., 851.
28. Ibid., 849–50.
29. "Consideraciones sobre aborto criminal," 119–20.
30. Ibid., 121.
31. Ramos, "Servicio de higiene infantil."
32. "Muerte de la morena M.M. a consecuencia del parto; intervención de una intrusa," *Anales* 25 (1889): 535–47; "'Obstetricia' Sesion pública ordinaria del 8 de febrero de 1885," *Anales* 21 (1884): 427–28.
33. Ramos, "Servicio de higiene infantil."
34. Ibid.
35. "Comunicación oral sobre el incremento," 850.
36. Ramos, "Servicio de higiene infantil."
37. "Consideraciones sobre aborto criminal," 121.
38. Ibid., 122.
39. "Comunicación oral sobre el incremento," 848–49.
40. Secretaria de Justicia, *Memoria de estadística judicial*, 253.
41. "Expediente sobre el aborto de Josefa López Partieles de un feto de cinco meses al cual enterró en el patio de su casa, provocado por una caída," September 29 to December 23, 1927, leg. 1, exp. 17, AHMT, JIT.
42. Castellanos, *La delinquencia femenina*, tables 110 (1914–18), 116 (1919–23), 119 (1926), 121 (1924–27).
43. Stoner, *From the House*, 147.
44. Álvarez Torres, "Las prácticas malthusianas," 47.
45. On Cuba's sugar economy during the Great Depression, see Pollitt, "Cuban Sugar Economy."
46. Large bundles of these letters can be found in leg. 405, ANC, FCB.
47. Mrs. L. S. Houston, Presidenta de la Rama Caridad Humanitaria del International Sunshine Society to Dr. Ramón M Alfonso, Director de la Casa de Bene y Matern, Marzo 3, 1930, in "Exp conteniendo correspondencia del Director de la Casa de Benef con diferentes personas y entidades. Dr. Aurelio Gómez Miranda. Enero a octubre 1930," leg. 405, exp. 19, ANC, FCB.
48. Contesta March 6, 1930, in "Exp conteniendo correspondencia."
49. Juan Parés, Teniente de Policía Nacional, Quinta Estación, San Lázaro 219 to Reverenda madre superior de las Hermanas de Caridad, June 10, 1931, in "Exp cartas firmadas por Aurelio gomez miranda director de la casa de benef dirigida a diversas personas otras enviadas a el, enero a nov 1931," leg. 405, exp. 23, ANC, FCB.
50. Victoria P. vda de Portuondo to Sr. Aurelio S. Miranda, February, 20, 1931, in "Exp cartas firmadas."
51. "Exp relativo a la Moción del Dr. Candido Hoyos sobre la supresión del torno y el cambio del apellido Valdés en la casa de Beneficencia y Maternidad," September 11, 1936, leg. 189, exp. 38, ANC, FCB.

52. Chelala-Aguilera, *Natalidad, mortalidad, y aborto*, 334–35.
53. Ibid., 335–36.
54. Martínez, *Aborto ilícito*, 254–55.
55. Dr. Rubio to Chelala, February 9, 1937, in Chelala-Aguilera, *Natalidad, mortalidad, y aborto*, 327.
56. Ibid., 327; Chelala-Aguilera, *Natalidad, mortalidad, y aborto*, 339.
57. *El Mundo*, September 18, 1936, 8.
58. Report by Dr. Antonio Ruiz de León, Judge of the Audiencia de Matanzas, in Chelala-Aguilera, *Natalidad, mortalidad, y aborto*, 337–38.
59. The sample preserved in the Archivo Histórico Municipal de Trinidad, though likely incomplete, suggests an increase in negative reproductive outcomes and abortions linked to economic crisis.
60. "Expediente sobre la denuncia de Serafin Sánchez Lago contra Ramona González, por haber enterrado la criatura que dio a luz en una fosa," December 31, 1931, to January 13, 1932, leg. 74, exp. 2056, AHMT, JIT.
61. Ibid.
62. Ibid.
63. "Expediente sobre la denuncia de Alberto Borges y Rodríguez porque su concubina Rosa Hernández Quevedo, abortó sin asistencia médica sufriendo una gran infección de pronóstico grave," March 21 to April 13, 1934, leg. 1, exp. 21, AHMT, JIT.
64. "Expediente sobre la denuncia del Doctor Antonio María Guzmán contra la comadrona Eladia Mirabal, por haberle provocado aborto a Felicia Alfonso Gabilla con un aparato insertado," March 4 to March 19, 1930, leg. 1, exp. 18, AHMT, JIT.
65. "Expediente sobre la denuncia de María González Gaspar contra el Dn Antonio M. Guzmán, por haberle provocado aborto a Juana Jorge González," May 26 to June 3, 1930, leg. 1, exp. 19, AHMT, JIT.
66. "Expediente sobre la denuncia de Rafael Martínez contra Hermogenio Cruz por divulgar del honor de su hija, Catalina Martínez, diciendo que la misma había abortado," May 15 to June 4, 1931, exp. 20, AHMT, JIT.
67. Chelala-Aguilera, *Natalidad, mortalidad, y aborto*, 337.
68. Vieites, *El aborto*, 36.
69. Vieites, *Proyecto de un Código Penal*; Martínez, *Aborto ilícito*, 202–3.
70. Vieites, *El aborto*, 48.
71. Ibid., 46.
72. Ibid., 47.
73. Stoner, *From the House*, 177–78.
74. Ibid., 177–78, 167. On race and domestic workers, see Hicks, "Hierarchies at Home."
75. Rodríguez Acosta, *La tragedia social*, 22–23.
76. Chelala-Aguilera, *Natalidad, mortalidad, y aborto*, 65–67.
77. Ibid., 348–51.
78. Martínez, *Aborto ilícito*, 211.
79. Ibid., 208–9. Also see Martínez, "Serie de Conferencias."
80. Martínez, *Aborto ilícito*, 208–9.
81. Ibid., 211.
82. Ibid., 212.

83. Ibid., 212.
84. Tejera, *Código de represión criminal*; Martínez, *Aborto ilícito*, 204–5.
85. Tejera, *El aborto criminal*, 8.
86. Ibid., 11–16.
87. Ibid., 9.
88. Ibid., 65.
89. Ibid., 60.
90. Rubio to Chelala, 332.
91. Martínez, *Aborto ilícito*, 341.
92. Ibid., 343–44.
93. Llaca y Argudín, *Repertorio judicial* (1939), 217.
94. Llaca y Argudín, *Repertorio judicial* (1941), 184.
95. On women's rights in the constitution of 1940, see Prats García, *Mujer y familia*; Stoner, *From the House*, 185–92.
96. Castellanos, *La odontología legal*.
97. "Expediente sobre la denuncia de Zoila Argüelles Entenza, sobre un aborto que tuvo debido al trato que le daba su esposo José Candelario Bosch," August 21 to September 13, 1937, leg. 1, exp. 22, AHMT, JIT.
98. "Expediente sobre la demanda presentado por Adriano Rodríguez Gutiérrez, por haber encontrado a una niña abandonada en la finca 'Cedro Seco,' metida dentro de un saco al parecer producto de un aborto," August 3, 1940, leg. 1, exp. 23, AHMT, JIT.
99. "Expediente sobre la demanda presentado por Antonio Blanco González, referente al aborto de Brígida Medina, matando la criatura," July 17 to September 9, 1941, leg. 1, exp. 24, AHMT, JIT.
100. Cases dating to the 1950s exist in the Municipal Historical Archive of Trinidad. An additional sample of criminal abortion cases exists in the Provincial Historical Archive of Santa Clara, dating to the 1940s and 1950s.
101. Álvarez Torres, "Las prácticas malthusianas," 47–49, 69–71.
102. Lowry Nelson, "Cuban Population Estimates."
103. Álvarez Torres, "Las prácticas malthusianas," 47–49, 69–71.
104. Case 1558, Delito Aborto, November 15, 1961, to February 17, 1962, APHC, JIC.
105. Ibid.
106. Malthus, *Essay*, 13, 60–65.
107. Cervantes-Rodríguez, *International Migration in Cuba*; Shnookal, *Operation Pedro Pan*.
108. Case 533, Delito Aborto, Juzgado Municipal de Cruces, April 25, 1961, to June 1, 1961 APHC, JIC.
109. Case 393, Delito Aborto, Juzgado de Instrucción de Cienfuegos, June 25, 1963, APHC, JIC.
110. Ibid.
111. Case 307, Delito Aborto, Juzgado de Instrucción de Cienfuegos, March 6–15, 1962, APHC, JIC.
112. Case 53, Delito Aborto, Juzgado de Instrucción de Cienfuegos, January 15–26, 1963, APHC, JIC.
113. See, for example, case 569, Delito Aborto, Juzgado de Instrucción de Cienfuegos,

March 24–25, 1960; case 579, Delito Aborto, Juzgado de Instrucción de Cienfuegos, April 16, 1960, both in APHC, JIC.

114. Hynson, *Laboring for the State*, 39–90, 41–42.

115. On the increase in criminal prosecution for abortion, see Roth, "From Free Womb to Criminalized Woman," and Jaffary, "Reconceiving Motherhood"; Reagan, *When Abortion Was a Crime*.

116. Andaya, *Conceiving Cuba*, 36–40; Randall, *Cuban Women Now*.

117. Smith and Padula, *Sex and Revolution*.

118. Andaya, *Conceiving Cuba*, 42.

119. Hynson, *Laboring for the State*.

CONCLUSION. Protection, Correction, or Liberation

1. Alberdi, *Bases y puntos de partida*.

2. Lavrín, *Sexuality and Marriage*, 3–4.

3. Malthus, *Essay*, 60–65.

4. For an overview of Malthusian ideas in the British Caribbean, see Paugh, *Politics of Reproduction*, 14.

5. Ross and Solinger, *Reproductive Justice*, 177; Fried, "Politics of Abortion," 88–90; Cunningham et al., *Youth at Risk*, 210–16.

6. Martínez-Alier, *Marriage, Class and Colour*; Morrison, *Cuba's Racial Crucible*.

7. Benson, *Antiracism in Cuba*. Also see Sawyer, *Racial Politics in Post-Revolutionary Cuba*; De la Fuente, *Nation for All*, 259–341.

8. Blue, "Erosion of Racial Equality"; Hansing and Hoffmann, "When Racial Inequalities Return."

9. Andaya, *Conceiving Cuba*, 3–4, 68–92.

10. Gerber Fried, *From Abortion to Reproductive Freedom*; Ross and Solinger, *Reproductive Justice*; Briggs, *How All Politics Became Reproductive Politics*; Bloomer, Pierson, and Claudio, *Reimagining Global Abortion Politics*, 107–26; Roberts, *Killing the Black Body*; López, *Matters of Choice*; Jennifer Nelson, *Women of Color*; Hinojosa Hernández and Upton, *Challenging Reproductive Control*.

11. Roberts, *Killing the Black Body*, 6.

BIBLIOGRAPHY

Archives and Libraries

Archivo Nacional de la República de Cuba, Havana
Fondo Audiencia de Santo Domingo
Fondo Casa de Beneficencia
Fondo Gobierno Superior Civil (ANC, GSC)
Fondo Miscelánea de Expedientes (ANC, ME)
Fondo Real Consulado de la Junta de Fomento
Miscelánea de Libros

Biblioteca Nacional de Cuba José Martí, Havana
SALA DE MANUSCRITOS (MANUSCRIPTS ROOM)
Fondo Antonio Bachiller y Morales
Fondo Soc.
Fondo Pérez
SALA DE LIBROS RAROS Y VALIOSOS
(RARE AND VALUABLE BOOKS ROOM)

Archivo Provincial Histórico de Cienfuegos, Cuba
Juzgado de Instrucción de Cienfuegos

Archivo de la Santísima Catedral de Cienfuegos, Cuba
Bautizos de Color
Matrimonios de Color

Archivo Histórico Municipal de Trinidad, Cuba
Juzgado de Instrucción de Trinidad (AHMT, JIT)

Archivo General de Indias, Sevilla, Spain
Santo Domingo
Ultramar

Archivo Histórico Nacional, Madrid, Spain
Ultramar

National Archives at College Park, Md.
Military Government of Cuba (record group 140, entry 3)

Database
SlaveVoyages Trans-Atlantic Slave Trade Database

Periodicals

Anales de la Academia de Ciencias Médicas, Físicas y Naturales de la Habana (1864–1927)
Carteles (1919–58)
Diario de la Marina (1842–66)
Diario de la Habana (1828–49)
El Siglo (1865)
Gaceta de la Habana (1828)
Ginecopatía, obstetricia, y pediatría (Barcelona) (1901)
La Discusión (1911)
Nueva Revista Cubana: Periódico Quincenal de Ciencias, Derecho, Literatura, y Bellas Artes (1877–82)
Papel Periódico de la Havana (1793)
Puck (1898)
Salubridad y Asistencia Social (1915)
Sanidad y Beneficencia (1909–17)

Published Primary Sources

Abbot, Abiel. *Letters written in the interior of Cuba, between the mountains of Arcana, to the east, and of Cusco, to the west, in the months of February, March, April, and May, 1828.* Boston: Bowles and Dearborn, 1829.

Agramonte, Arístides. "Nota acerca de la pasteurización de la leche." *Anales de la Academia de Ciencias Médicas, Físicas y Naturales de la Habana* 50 (February 13, 1914): 903–11.

Alberdi, Juan Bautista. *Bases y puntos de partida para la organización política de la República Argentina.* 1852; rpt., Buenos Aires: La Cultural Argentina, 1915.

Alexander, James E. *Transatlantic sketches, comprising visits to the most interesting scenes in North and South America, and the West Indies. With notes on Negro slavery and Canadian emigration.* London: R. Bentley, 1833.

Alfonso X. *Las Siete Partidas.* Ca. 1265; rpt., Barcelona: Imprenta de Antonio Belgnes, 1844.

Alonso y Fernández, Francisco. *Discurso inaugural que para la apertura del curso de obstetricia ó arte de partear, pronunció en el museo anatómico de la Habana, el 20 de Siemptiembre de 1830.* Havana: Imprenta Fraternal, 1830.

———. *Exámenes públicos de obstetricia ó arte de partear que han de celebrarse en el Museo de Anatomía Descriptiva perteneciente al Hospital Motilitar de San Ambrosio*. Havana: Imprenta de P. Nolasco, 1825.

Álvarez Torres, Alfredo. "Las prácticas malthusianas y sus consecuencias." *Carteles* (Havana) 17 (1957): 47–49, 69–71.

Arango y Parreño, Francisco de. *Obras del Excmo. Señor D. Francisco de Arango y Parreño*. Havana: Howson y Heinen, 1888–89.

Arrate y Acosta, José Martín Félix de. *La llave del nuevo mundo: La Habana descripta*. 1827; rpt., Havana: Impr. de las viudas de Arazoza y Soler, 1830.

Arrazola, Lorenzo, Pedro Sainz Andino, Miguel Puche y Bautista, José Romer Giner, Vicente Valor, Mariano Antonio Collado, and Ruperto Navarro Zamorano. *Enciclopedia española de derecho y administración: Ó Nuevo teatro universal de la legislación de España é Indias*. Madrid: Tipografía General de D. Antonio Rius y Rosell, 1848.

Armas, Frank de. *Essai sur la rétention da placenta: Thèse pour le Doctorat en Médecine des Facultés de Montpellier*. Montpellier: Cabirou Frères; 1889.

Arteaga, Serapio. *Sífilis hereditaria*. Havana: La Propaganda Literaria, 1877.

Arteaga y Quesada, Julio F., and José M. Ramírez Olivella. "La partonalgina." *Anales de la Academia de Ciencias Médicas, Físicas y Naturales de la Habana* 52 (1915): 277–87.

Auvard, Pierre Victor Adolphe. "La antisepsia en la ginecología y en la obstetricia." Translated by Gabriel Casuso y Roque and Rafael Weiss. *Progreso Médico* (1891, 1892).

Bachiller y Morales, Antonio. *Cuba primitiva: Origen, lenguas, tradiciones e historia de los indios de las Antillas mayores y las lucayas*. Havana: Librería de Miguel de Villa, 1883.

Baird, Robert *Impressions and Experiences of the West Indies and North America in 1849*. 2 vols. Edinburgh: William Blackwood and Sons, 1850.

Barnet, Enrique B. *Manual de práctica sanitaria*. Havana: n.p., 1905.

———. "Consideraciones sobre el estado sanitario en Cuba." *Anales de la Academia de Ciencias Médicas, Físicas y Naturales de la Habana* 50 (May 28, 1913): 34–43.

Baró Pazos, Juan. "El derecho penal español en el vacío entre dos códigos (1822–1848)." *Anuario de historia del derecho español* 83 (2013): 105–38.

Beato Dolz, José. "Ampliación de un informe en caso de tentativa de aborto. Discusión del informe por los Dres. Mestre, Finlay, J.I. Torralbas, Machado, Valdés, Santos Fernández, Delgado y Gutiérrez." *Anales de la Academia de Ciencias Médicas, Físicas y Naturales de la Habana* 22 (1884): 102–4.

———. *Del'etat puerpéral. Thèse pour le Doctorat en Médecine des Facultés de Paris*. Paris: A. Parent, 1862.

Betancourt, Alfonso. *Algunos accidentes teratológicos de la guerra*. Havana: Imprenta de F. Xiques, 1899.

Caballero, José Agustín. "Matrimonio entre esclavos." In *José Agustín Caballeros: Obras*. Havana: Imagen Contemporánea, 1999.

Calcaño, Julio. *Parnaso venezolano: colección de poesías de autores venezolanos desde mediados del siglo XVIII hasta nuestros días*. Caracas: El Cojo, 1892.

Calderón, Próspero. "Un soneto célebre." *Páginas Ilustradas* 3, no. 90 (1906): 1434–35.

Cañizares, Manuel J. *Influencia que los diferentes vicios de conformación de la pelvis, tienen sobre la gestión y el parto*. Havana, 1872.

Cantero, Justo G. *Los ingenios: colección de vistas de los principales ingenios de azúcar de la isla de Cuba*. Havana: Litografía de Luís Marqués, 1857.
Carlos IV. *Novísima Recopilación de las leyes de España*. Madrid: Real Academia de Jurisprudencia y Legislación, 1805.
———. *Real cédula de Su Magestad concediendo libertad para el comercio de negros con las islas de Cuba, Santo Domingo, Puerto Rico, y provincia de Caracas, a españoles y extrangeros, bajo las reglas que se expresan*. Madrid: Imprenta de la Viuda Ibarra, 1789.
———. *Real Cédula de Su Magestad sobre la educación, trato y ocupaciones de todos sus dominios de Indias é Islas Filipinas baxo las reglas que se expresan*. Madrid: Imprenta de la Viuda Ibarra, 1789.
Cartaya, Pedro María. *Des vomissements incoercibles pendant la grossesse, de leur traitement, surtout au point de vue de l'avortement provoqué. Thése pour le Doctorat en Médecine des Facultés de Paris*. Paris: Rignoux, 1855.
Castellanos, Israel. *La delinquencia femenina en Cuba*. Havana: Ojeda, 1929.
———. *La odontologia legal en la investigacion de la paternidad*. Havana: Cultural, 1943.
Casuso y Roque, Gabriel. "Asepsia puerperal: Observaciones por los Dres. Tamayo, Santos Fernández, Lavin, Horstmann." *Anales de la Academia de Ciencias Médicas, Físicas y Naturales de la Habana* 27 (1891): 654–56.
———. "Consideraciones sobre algunos casos operados." *Anales de la Academia de Ciencias Médicas, Físicas y Naturales de la Habana* 30 (1893): 338.
———. "Histerectomías por la vía abdominal y vaginal." *Anales de la Academia de Ciencias Médicas, Físicas y Naturales de la Habana* 33 (1896): 105–6.
———. *Profilaxia de la fiebre puerperal: reglamento para las comadronas*. Havana: Imprenta de A. Álvarez y Compañía, 1891.
Cebrian Villanova, Cristino. *Del cornezuelo de centeno y su utilidad en obstetricia: memoria leida por el alumno en el ejercicio de grado de doctor*. Madrid, 1881.
Centro de estadística. *Noticias estadísticas de la isla de Cuba, en 1862*. Havana: Imprenta del gobierno, 1864.
Chateausalins, Honorato Bernard de. *El Vademecum de los hacendados cubanos, ó guia práctica para curar la mayor parte de las enfermedades*. Havana: Depósito de Libros, 1854.
Chelala-Aguilera, José. *Natalidad, mortalidad, maternidad, y aborto*. Havana: Instituto de Ciencias Médicas y Educacionales, 1937.
Código Penal de España: Sancionado por SM en 19 de marzo de 1848 y comentado por D.J.S y D.A. de B. Barcelona: Imprenta de D. Ramón Martín Indar, 1848.
Código Penal de España: Edición oficial reformada. Madrid: Imprenta Nacional, 1850.
Colmeiro, Miguel. *Curso de Botánica ó elementos de organografía, fisiología, metodología y geografía de las plantas: Metodología, cuadro de las familias con las propiedades y usos, Geografía botánica*. Vol. 2. Valparaiso y Lima: Casa de los Señores Calleja y Compañía. 1857.
Comisión Nacional Cubana de la UNESCO. *Actas de la Sociedad Antropológica de la Isla de Cuba*. Havana: ECAG, 1966, 80–83.
Coronado, Tomás V. "Consulta médico legal por infanticidio." *Anales de la Academia de Ciencias Médicas, Físicas y Naturales de la Habana* 44 (1907): 524–37.

Cowley, Ángel J. *Ensayo Estadístico-Médico de la Mortalidad de la Diócesis de la Habana Durante el Año de 1843*. Havana: Imprenta del Gobierno y Capitanía General por S.M., 1845.

Creus y Manso, Juan. *Del uso del cornezuelo de centeno en obstetricia: conferencia dada en el Ateneo de internos de la Facultad de Medicina de Madrid*. Madrid: Imprenta de F. Maroto é Hijos, 1878

Dana, Richard Henry. *To Cuba and Back*. Boston: Houghton, Mifflin, 1859.

De Gordón y de Acosta, Antonio. "Medicina indígena de Cuba: Su valor histórico." *Anales de la Academia de Ciencias Médicas, Físicas y Naturales de la Habana* 31 (October 28, 1894): 279–316.

de la Sagra, Ramón. *Estudio coloniales con aplicación a la Isla de Cuba*. Vol. 1, *De los Efectos de la Supresión en el tráfico negrero*. Madrid: D. Dionisio Hidalgo, 1845.

———. *Historia económico-política y estadística de la Isla de Cuba, o sea de sus progresos en la población, la agricultura, el comercio, y las rentas*. Havana: Imprenta de las Vuidas de Arazoza y Soler, 1831.

———. *Historia física y política: Relación del último viaje del autor*, 2 vols. Paris: Hachette, 1842–43.

de las Casas, Bartolomé. *Brevísima relación de la destrucción de las Indias*, Edición y notas José Miguel Martínez Torrejón. Prólogo y cronología Gustavo Adolfo Zuluaga Hoyos. Medellín: Editorial de la Universidad de Antioquia, 2011.

De la Torre, José María. *Lo que fuimos, lo que somos, o La Habana antigua y moderna*. Havana: Imprenta de Spencer y Compañía, 1857.

De la Torriente, Celestino. *Estudio sobre la riqueza de Cuba*. Havana: Imp. El Telégrafo, 1878.

del Valle, Ambrosio. "Demografía médica de niños de raza blanca y de color, de 1876, en La Habana." *Nueva Revista Cubana. Periódico Quincenal de Ciencias, Derecho, Literatura, y Bellas Artes* 1 (1877): 373–74.

———. "Elementos demográficos de natalidad y mortalidad de la Habana en 1877, comparados con el año anterior." *Nueva Revista Cubana* 3 (1877): 65–66.

———. "Mortalidad de la Habana en el verano de 1878." *Nueva Revista Cubana* 3 (1877): 440.

———. "Mortalidad de la Habana en el otoño de 1878." *Nueva Revista Cubana* 3 (1879): 94–95.

———. "Mortalidad de la Habana en el otoño de 1882." *Nueva Revista Cubana* 12 (1882): 88.

de Zayas, Andrés. "Observaciones sobre los ingenios de esta isla." In *Memorias de la Sociedad Económica de La Habana*. Havana: Imprenta del Gobierno y Sociedad Económica por S.M., 1836.

Dionisio Vives, Francisco. *Cuadro estadístico de la siempre fiel isla de Cuba correspondiente al año de 1827*. Havana: Impresores de Gobierno y Capitanía, 1829.

Documentos de que hasta ahora se compone el expediente que principiaron las cortes extraordinarias sobre el tráfico de la esclavitud de los Negros. Madrid: Imprenta de Repulles, 1814.

Dumont, Henri. *Antropología y patología comparadas de los negros esclavos. 1876*; rpt., Havana: n.p., 1922.

———. *Memorias sobre la historia médica y quirúrgica de las regiones intertropicales de América: Islas de Cuba, y Puerto Rico, Méjico, Santómas, Guayana, etc.* Havana: Imprenta La Antilla, 1875.

Duque Perdomo, Matías. *Estudios sobre enfermedades venéreas.* Havana: Impr. Montalvo Cárdenas, 1925.

———. *La prostitución: Sus causas, sus males, su higiene.* Havana: Rambla, Bouza y Compañia, 1914.

———. *La terapéutica de la sífilis.* Havana: Imprenta Mercantil, 1904.

Duvergier de Hauranne, Ernest. "Cuba et les Antilles: II. Matanzas, une plantation." *Revue des Deux Mondes* 65, no. 3 (1866): 619–54.

Erenchún, Félix. *Anales de la isla de Cuba: Diccionario administrativo, económico, estadística, y legislativo.* 4 vols. Havana: Imprenta La Antilla, 1855–56.

Fernández de Oviedo, Gonzalo. *Crónica de las Indias: Primera Parte* (1547). Madrid: Imprenta de la Real Academia de la Historia, 1851.

Figueroa, Bernardo. *Des obstacles que le col utérin peut apporter á l'accouchement. Thése pour le Doctorat en Médecine des Facultés de Paris.* Paris: A. Parent; 1872.

Fosalba, Rafael J. "El problema de la población en Cuba." *Anales de la Academia de Ciencias Médicas, Físicas y Naturales de la Habana* 45 (April 16, 1909): 693–751.

Gallenga, Antonio Carlo Napoleone. *The Pearl of the Antilles.* London: Chapman and Hall, 1873.

Gálvez Alfonso, Federico. *De l'opération cesarienne. Thése pour le Doctorat en Médecine des Facultés de Paris.* Paris: Rignoux, 1855.

García, Joaquín José. *Protocolo de antigüedades, literatura, agricultura, industria, comercio &.* 2 vols. Havana: Imprenta de D. Vicente de Torres, 1845.

García Goyena, Florencio. *Código criminal español según las layes y prácticas vigente comentado y comparado con el Penal de 1822, el francés y el inglés.* 2 vols. Madrid: Librería de los Señores Viuda de Calleja e Hijos, 1843.

García Goyena, Florencio, and Joaquín Aguirre. *Febrero, o Librería de jueces, abogados y escribanos, comprensiva de los códigos civil, criminal y administrativo, tanto en la parte teórica como en la práctica con arreglo en un todo a la legislación hoy vigente.* Madrid: I. Biox, 1842.

García Rijo, Mariano. *De la folie puerpérale. Thése pour le Doctorat en Médecine des Facultés de Paris.* Paris: A. Parent, 1879.

Gobierno de España. *Código penal español, decretado por las cortes en 8 de junio, sancionado por el rey, y mandado promulgado, en 9 de junio de 1822.* Madrid: Imprenta Nacional, 1822.

Gómez de la Maza, Manuel. *Ensayo de Farmacofitología cubana. Resumen de las propiedades medicinales, con especialidad de las recientemente estudiadas, de muchas plantas indígenas o de cultivo. Nuevos productos. Precedido de un prólogo del doctor F. I. Vildósola.* Havana: La Propaganda Literaria, 1889.

González del Valle, Ambrosio. *Manual de Obstetricia para el uso de nuestras parteras, ilustrado con figuras litografiadas.* Havana: Imprenta y Librería de A. Graupera, 1854.

Guiteras, Juan. "Sobre mortalidad infantile." *Sanidad y Beneficencia* 10 (1913): 429–45.

Gurney, Joseph John. *A winter in the West Indies, described in familiar letters to Henry Clay, of Kentucky.* London: J. Murray, 1841.

Hazard, Samuel. *Cuba with Pen and Pencil.* Hartford: Hartford Publishing Company, 1871.
Hernández, Eusebio. "La homicultura." *Sanidad y Beneficencia. Boletín Oficial de la secretaría* 4, no. 2 (1910): 9–12.
Hernández, Eusebio, and Domingo F. Ramos. *La homicultura.* Havana: La Moderna Poesia, 1911.
Hollerbach, Paula E., and Sergio Diaz-Briquets, eds. *Fertility Determinants in Cuba.* Washington, D.C.: National Academy Press, 1983.
Howe, Julia Ward. *A Trip to Cuba.* Boston: Ticknor and Fields, 1860.
Hulbert, William Henry. *Gan-Eden: or, Pictures of Cuba.* Boston: John P. Jewett and Company, 1854.
Humboldt, Alexander von. *The Island of Cuba, with notes and a preliminary essay by J. S. Thrasher.* New York: Derby & Jackson, 1856.
Kokly, Federico. *De la ligature et de la section du cordon ombilical. Thése pour le Doctorat en Médecine des Facultés de Paris.* Paris: A. Parent; 1875.
Landa, Gabriel M. *Considérations sur un cas d'expusión partielle de la caduque pendant la grossesse non suivie d'avortement. Thése pour le Doctorat en Médecine des Facultés de Paris.* Paris: A. Parent, 1883.
Las leyes de Burgos de 1512 y Leyes de Valladolid de 1513: reproducción facsimilar de los manuscritos que se conservan en el Archivo General de Indias (Sevilla) en las Secciones de Indiferente General leg. 419, lib. IV y Patronato, legajo 174 ramo 1, respectivamente/ análisis histórico y transcripción paleográfica por Ma. Luisa Martínez de Salinas; estudio jurídico institucional por Rogelio Pérez Bustamante. Burgos: Fundación para el Desarrollo Provincial, 1991.
Lebredo, Mario G. "Causas y medios de reducir la mortalidad infantil en cada término municipal." *Sanidad y Beneficencia* 18 (1917): 209–33.
Le Riverend, Julio J. *Memoria sobre la leche.* Havana: Imprenta de El Artista, 1849.
Le-Roy y Cassá, Jorge E. "Apuntes para la historia de la Obstetricia en Cuba: Discurso pronunciado en su recepción solemne de Académico de número." *Anales de la Academia de Ciencias Médicas, Físicas y Naturales de la Habana* 39 (1902–3): 336–74.
———. "Apuntes sobre las funciones sexuales en la mujer cubana." *Anales de la Academia de Ciencias Médicas, Físicas y Naturales de la Habana* 46 (1909): 358–69.
———. *Desenvolvimiento de la sanidad en Cuba durante los últimos cincuenta años, 1871–1920.* Havana: La Moderna Poesia, 1922.
———. *Historia del Hospital San Francisco de Paula: Historia de la ermita, iglesia y hospital de San Francisco de Paula, en la ciudad de la Habana, y de los que en ellos han intervenido.* Havana: Impr. El Siglo XX, 1958.
———. "Informe acerca de un aparato titulado 'Infecundador de señoras.'" Sesión del 27 de septiembre de 1903.: *Anales de la Academia de Ciencias Médicas, Físicas y Naturales de la Habana* 40 (1907): 145–47.
———. "Informe médico legal en causa por infanticidio." *Anales de la Academia de Ciencias Médicas, Físicas y Naturales de la Habana* 47 (1910): 102–6.
———. *La mortalidad infantil en Cuba: notas demográficas. Trabajo presentado a la Academia de Ciencias Médicas, Fisicas y Naturales de la Habana en la sesión del 27 de marzo de 1914.* Havana: Imp. y Libreria de Lloredo y Ca., 1914.

———. "Presentación de tronco: Ruptura uterina: Operación de Porro." *Revista Progreso Médico* 48 (1900): 74–80.

———. "Vómitos incoercibles de las mujeres embarazadas." Doctoral diss. Havana: Establecimiento Tipográfica, 1892.

Llaca y Argudín, Francisco, ed. *Repertorio judicial: Revista mensual fundad bajo los auspicios del colegio de abogados de la Habana.* Havana: Rambla, Bouza y Compañia, 1939.

———, ed. *Repertorio judicial: Revista mensual fundad bajo los auspicios del colegio de abogados de la Habana.* Havana: Rambla, Bouza y Compañia, 1941.

López de Gómara, Francisco. *Historia general de las Indias.* Amberes: Casa de Juan Steelsio, 1554.

Madden, Richard Robert. *The Island of Cuba: its resources, progress, and prospects, considered in relation especially to the influence of its prosperity on the interests of the British West India colonies.* London: Partridge & Oakey, 1853.

Malagón Barceló, Javier, *Código Negro Carolino (1784). Código de legislación para el gobierno moral, político y económico de los negros de la isla Española.* Santo Domingo: Ediciones Taller, 1974.

Malthus, Thomas. *An Essay on the Principle of Population, as it Affects the Future Improvement of Society with Remarks on the Speculations of Mr. Godwin, M. Condorcet, and Other Writers.* 1798; rpt., Bellingham, Wash.: Electronic Scholarly Publishing, 1998. www.esp.org/books/malthus/population/malthus.pdf.

Martínez, José Agustín. *Aborto ilícito y derecho al aborto: historia y definición del aborto, el aborto en la legislaciones penales contemporáneas y el aborto en Cuba.* Havana: Jesús Montero, 1942.

———. "Serie de Conferencias sobre el Código de Defensa Social." In *Ciclo organizado por el Colegio de Abogados de la Habana.* Havana: Jesús Montero, 1939.

Mata, Pedro. *Tratado de medicina y cirugía legal.* 2d ed. 2 vols. Madrid: Don Joaquín y Suárez, 1846.

———. *Vade mecum de medicina y cirugía legal.* Madrid: Imprenta de la Calle Padilla, 1844.

Melero, Marcos de J. "Reseña estadística acerca de la mortalidad de la Isla de Cuba." *Anales de la Academia de Ciencias Médicas, Físicas y Naturales de la Habana* 15 (1878): 287–95.

Olmsted, Victor H., and Henry Gannett, eds. *Cuba: Population, History and Resources 1907.* Washington, D.C.: U.S. Bureau of the Census, 1909.

Ordenanzas para el gobierno de las casas reunidas de beneficencia y maternidad. Havana: Imprenta del Gobierno y Capitanía General, 1888.

Pichardo, Hortensio. *Documentos para la historia de Cuba*, 4 vols. Havana: Editorial de Ciencias Sociales, 1977.

Piña y Peñuela, Ramón. *Topografía médica de la isla de Cuba.* Havana: Del Tiempo, 1855.

Plá, José. *La Raza de Color. Necesidad de instruir y moralizar a los individuos de color y de fomentar el matrimonio entre los patrocinados.* Matanzas: El Ferrocarril, 1881.

Plazaola, Fernando de. "La beneficencia en Cuba." In *Trabajos presentados por los médicos cubanos al intercambio sanitario de la Liga de Naciones celebrado en la Habana del 1º al 10 de marzo de 1925,* 121–26. Havana: Imprenta El Siglo, 1925.

Prescot, Oliver. "A Dissertation on the Natural History and Medical Effects of Secale Cornutum, or Ergot, read at the annual meeting of the Massachusetts Medical Society, June 2, 1813." *Medical Physics Journal* 32 (1814): 90–99.
Ramos, Domingo F. "La homicultura en Cuba." *Sanidad y Beneficiencia* 4 (1910): 13–43.
———. "Los abortos criminales en Cuba." *Prensa Médica* 6, no. 3 (1915): 24–26.
———. "Mortalidad infantil en Cuba: Sus causas, distribución geográfica, y medios profilácticas que deben realizarse." *Sanidad y Beneficencia* (1915): 113–89.
———. "Servicio de higiene infantil: enteritis infantil—aborto criminal." *Salubridad y Asistencia Social* 13 (1915): 614–30.
Real Academia de Historia. *Colección de documentos inéditos relativos al descubrimiento, conquista, y organización de las antiguas posesiones españolas de ultramar.* 25 vols. Madrid: Tipografía Sucesores de Rivadeneyra, 1885–1932.
Real Sociedad Patriótica de la Habana. *Memorias de la Real Sociedad Patriótica de la Habana. Redactadas por una comisión de su seno.* 8 vols. Havana: Oficina del Gobierno y Capitanía General, 1836–39.
Recopilación de leyes de los reynos de las indias: mandadas imprimir y publicar por la Majestad Católica del rey Don Carlos II, nuestro señor Madrid: Impr. por Ivlian de Paredes, 1681.
Reglamento general de beneficencia pública decretado por las Cortes Extraordinarias en 27 de diciembre de 1821, y sancionado por S. M. Leon: Reimpreso por D. Pablo Miñon, 1822.
Reyes Zamora, Antonio. *Contribution á l'étude des présentations de l'extrémité pelvienne. Thése pour le Doctorat en Médecine des Facultés de Paris.* Paris: A. Parent, 1877.
———. *La semi-anestesia en el parto natural o fisiológico.* Havana: Imprenta Militar, 1878.
Ricafort, Mariano. *Reglamento de la Real Casa de maternidad, dispuesto por su Junta de Gobierno.* Havana: Real, 1833.
Rodríguez Acosta, Ofelia. *La tragedia social de la mujer.* Havana: Editorial Génesis, 1933.
Rodríguez Ferrer, Miguel. *Naturaleza y civilización de la grandiosa Isla de Cuba.* 2 vols. Madrid: Imprenta de J. Noguera a cargo de M. Martínez, 1876–87.
Rosaín, Domingo. "Discurso en la inauguración de esta clase." *Revista Médica Cubana* 2, no 3 (February 1, 1903).
———. *Examen y cartilla de parteras, teórico práctica.* Havana: Oficina de Don José Boloña, impresor de la Real Marina, 1824.
———. *Necrópolis de la Habana: Historia de los cementerios de esta ciudad: con multitud de noticias interesantes.* Havana: "El Trabajo," 1875.
Ruiz Casabó, Manuel. "Un caso más de anencefalia." *Anales de la Academia de Ciencias Médicas, Físicas y Naturales de la Habana* 40 (1907): 217–22.
Saco, José Antonio. *Colección de papeles científicos, históricos, políticos, y de otros ramos sobre la Isla de Cuba.* 3 vols. Paris, Impr. de d'Aubusson y Kugelmann, 1858–59.
———. *Historia de la Esclavitud, Ensayo introductorio compilación y notas de Eduardo Torres-Cuevas.* 6 vols. Havana: Imagen Contemporánea, 2006.
———. *Ideario reformista.* Havana: Secretaría de Educación, 1935.
———. *La supresión del tráfico de esclavos africanos en la isla de Cuba: examinada con relación a su agricultura y su seguridad.* Paris: Impr. de Panckoucke, 1845.
Sánchez de Bustamante, Alberto. "Contribución al estudio de la distocia cervical—Tres

casos de tabicamiento transversal del cuello—dilatador de Bossi." *Anales de la Academia de Ciencias Médicas, Físicas y Naturales de la Habana* 40 (1904): 336–45.

Sánchez de Fuentes, Alberto. "Mortalidad infantil en Cuba: sus causas, distribución geográfica y medidas profilácticas que deben adoptarse." *Sanidad y Beneficencia* 13 (1915): 211–307.

Sánchez Rodríguez, Isidro. *Curso de estudio para las que se dedican al ejercicio de comadronas*. Havana: Imp. de Barcina, 1850.

Sánchez Toledo, Domingo. *Recherches microbiologiques sur l'utérus après la parturition physiologique*. Paris: Maisonneuve; 1888.

Secretaría de Agricultura, Industria y Comercio breve reseña para la exposición universal de St. Louis, Missouri, U.S.A. Havana: Imprenta Rambla y Bouza, 1904.

Secretaria de Justicia, República de Cuba, *Memoria de estadística judicial. Quinquenio del 1909 al 1913*. Havana: La Mercantil, 1915.

Secretaría de Sanidad y Beneficencia. "Comision nacional para la protección de la maternidad y la infancia." In *Cinco años de labor sanitaria y de beneficencia pública*, 316–20. Havana: La Propagandista, 1931.

———. *Concursos de Maternidad e Infancia, 1931–1932*. Havana: Imprenta Nueva, 1931.

———. *Servicio de Higiene Infantil: Concurso Nacional de Maternidad*. Havana, 1920.

Steele, James W. *Cuban sketches*. New York: G. P. Putnam's sons, 1881.

Suárez y Romero, Anselmo. *Colección de artículos*. Havana: Establecimiento Tipográfico La Antilla, 1859.

Swiggett, Glen Levin, ed. *Proceedings of the Second Pan American Scientific Congress*. Vol. 9. Washington, D.C.: Government Printing Office, 1917.

Taboadela, José Antonio. *Report of the Work Done by the Department in Favor of the Protection of Infancy from May 20, 1913 to Date*. Havana: La Moderna Poesia, 1914.

Tejera, Diego Vicente. *Código de represión criminal*. Havana, 1936.

———. *El aborto criminal*. Havana: Jesús Montero, 1938.

Turnbull, David. *Travels in the West; Cuba, with notices of Porto Rico, and the slave trade*. London: Longmans, 1840.

Un Montuno. *Cartilla práctica del manejo de ingenios o fincas destinadas a producir azúcar*. Irún: Imprenta de la Elegancia, 1862.

Valdés, Juan B. "Mortalidad infantil: Sus causas, medios para prevenirlas y combatirlas." In *Séptima Conferencia Nacional de Beneficencia y Corrección de la Isla de Cuba*, 99–115. Havana: Moderna Poesía, 1908.

Valdés Castro, Justino. *Memoria sobre la lactancia*. Havana: Barcina, 1856.

Valdés Miranda, Manuel. *Apuntes sobre la lactancia artificial en relación con las haciendas de la Isla de Cuba*. Havana: Imprenta del Gobierno, 1842.

Vargas Machuca, M., and C. Donoso. "Informe químico sobre unos polvos empleados como abortivos." *Anales de la Academia de Ciencias Médicas, Físicas y Naturales de la Habana* 22 (1885): 127–29.

Varona Suárez, Manuel. "Informe del Sr. Secretario de Sanidad y Beneficencia al Honorable Presidente de la República, March 25, 1911." In *Homicultura*, edited by Hernández and Ramos. Havana: La Moderna Poesía, 1911.

———. "Notas sobre los trabajos de los dres. E. Hernández y D. F. Ramos." In *Homicultura*, edited by Hernández and Ramos. Havana: La Moderna Poesía, 1911.

Vieites, Moisés. *El aborto a través de la moral y de la ley penal*. Madrid: Editorial Reus, 1933.

———. *Proyecto de un Código Penal*. Havana: P. Fernández, 1926.

Villanova, Manuel. *Estadística de la abolición de la esclavitud en la Isla de Cuba*. Havana: Imprenta de Soler, 1885.

Weiss Verson, Gaspar Rafael. *Accidentes provocados por las inyecciones intrauterinas*. Havana: Propaganda Literaria, 1894.

———. "Método y técnica del parto prematuro artificial." *Anales de la Academia de Ciencias Médicas, Físicas y Naturales de la Habana* 45 (1909): 651–61.

———. "A New Curette and a Dilating Uterine Sound." *American Journal of Obstetrics and Diseases of Women and Children* 26 (1892): 359–60.

———. "La situación de la vulva. Su influencia en el parto, en las lesiones del periné y en las deformaxiones del cráneo fetal." *Revista de Ciencias Médicas* 5, nos. 34–35 (1888).

Willcox, Walter Francis, Henry Gannett, and Joseph Prentiss Sanger. *Report on the Census of Cuba, 1899*. Washington, D.C.: Government Printing Office, 1900.

Wood, James W., George R. Milner, Henry C. Harpending, and Kenneth M. Weiss. "The Osteological Paradox: Problems of Inferring Prehistoric Health from Skeletal Samples." *Current Anthropology* 33, no. 4 (1992): 343–58.

Wudermann, John George. *Notes on Cuba: Containing an Account of Its Discovery and Early History; a Description of the Face of the Country, Its Population, Resources, and Wealth; Its Institutions, and the Manners and Customs of Its Inhabitants; with Directions to Travellers Visiting the Island*. Boston: J. Munroe and Company, 1844.

Zamora y Coronado, José María. *Biblioteca de legislación ultramarina en forma de diccionario alfabético*. 6 vols. Madrid: Imprenta de J. Martín Alegría, 1844–46.

Zenea, Evaristo. *Historia de la Real Casa de Maternidad de esta Ciudad, en la cual se comprende la antigua Casa Cuna, refiriendose sus fundaciones, deplorarle estado y felices progresos que después ha tenido hasta el presente, escrita por Don Evaristo Zenea, abogado de la real audiencia del distrito y vocal secretario de la junta que gobierna este asilo de piedad*. Havana: Oficina de D. José Severino Boloña, Impresor de la Real, 1838.

Secondary Sources

Aimes, Hubert H. S. "Coartación: A Spanish Institution for the Advancement of Slaves into Freedmen." *Yale Review*, February 1909, 412–31.

Altman, Ida. "Marriage, Family, and Ethnicity in the Early Spanish Caribbean." *William and Mary Quarterly* 70, no. 2 (2013): 225–50.

Andaya, Elise. *Conceiving Cuba: Women, Reproduction, and the State in the Post-Soviet Era*. New Brunswick, N.J.: Rutgers University Press, 2014.

Anderson-Córdova, Karen F. *Surviving Spanish Conquest: Indian Fight, Flight, and Cultural Transformation in Hispaniola and Puerto Rico*. Tuscaloosa: University of Alabama Press, 2017.

Andreo García, Juan, and Alberto José Gullón Abao. "'Vida y muerte de la Mulata': Crónica ilustrada de la prostitución en la Cuba del XIX." *Anuario de Estudios Americanos* 54, no. 1 (1997): 135–57.

Araújo Ariza, Marília Bueno de. "Bad Mothers, Labouring Children: Emancipation, Tutelage, and Motherhood in São Paulo in the Last Decades of the Nineteenth Century." *Slavery and Abolition* 38, no. 2 (2017): 408–24.

Ávila Espinosa, Felipe. "Los niños abandonados de la Casa de Niños Expósitos de la Ciudad de México, 1767–1821." In *La familia en el mundo iberoamericano*, edited by Pilar Gonzalbo Aizpuru and Cecelia Rabell, 265–310. Mexico City: Instituto de Investigaciones Sociales, Universidad Nacional Autónoma de México, 1994.

Barcia Paz, Manual. *The Great African Slave Revolt of 1825: Cuba and the Fight for Freedom in Matanzas*. Baton Rouge: Louisiana State University Press, 2012.

———. "Powerful Subjects: The Duplicity of Slave Owners in Nineteenth-Century Cuba." *International Journal of Cuban Studies* 7, no. 1 (2015): 99–112.

Barcia Zequiera, María del Cármen. *Capas populares y modernidad en Cuba, 1878–1930*. Havana: Fundación Fernando Ortiz, 2005.

———. *La otra familia: Parientes, redes y descendencia de los esclavos en Cuba*. Havana: Casa de las Américas, 2003.

———. *Oficios de mujer: Parteras, nodrizas y "amigas": Servicios públicos en espacios privados (siglo XVII–siglo XIX)*. Santiago de Cuba: Editorial Oriente, 2015.

Barragán, José P., and Luis Martín-Estudillo. "Monstrous Births: Authority and Biology in Early Modern Spain." In *Writing Monsters: Essays on Iberian and Latin American Cultures*, edited by Adriana Gordillo and Nicholas Spadaccini. Special issue, *Hispanic Issues On Line* 15 (Spring 2014): 12–25.

Benítez Pérez, María Elena. "La trayectoria del aborto seguro en Cuba: Evitar mejor que abortar. *Novedades en Población* 10, no. 20 (2016): 87–104.

Benjamin, Jules R. *The United States and the Origins of the Cuban Revolution: An Empire of Liberty in an Age of National Liberation*. Princeton, N.J.: Princeton University Press, 1992.

Bergad, Laird W., Fe Iglesias García, and María del Cármen Barcia. *The Cuban Slave Market, 1790–1880*. New York: Cambridge University Press, 1995.

Bergallo, Paola, ed. *Justicia, Género y Reproducción*. Buenos Aires: Libraria, 2010.

Benson, Devyn Spence. *Antiracism in Cuba: The Unfinished Revolution*. Chapel Hill: University of North Carolina Press, 2016.

Berry, Daina Ramey, and Leslie M. Harris, eds. *Sexuality and Slavery: Reclaiming Intimate Histories in the Americas*. Athens: University of Georgia Press, 2018.

Bliss, Katherine Elaine. *Compromised Positions: Prostitution, Public Health, and Gender Politics in Revolutionary Mexico City*. University Park: Pennsylvania State University Press, 2010.

Bloomer, Fiona, Claire Pierson, and Sylvia Estrada Claudio. *Reimagining Global Abortion Politics: A Social Justice Perspective*. Bristol: Policy Press, 2020.

Blue, Sarah A. "The Erosion of Racial Equality in the Context of Cuba's Dual Economy." *Latin American Politics and Society* 49, no. 3 (2007): 35–68.

Blum, Ann. *Domestic Economies: Family, Work, and Welfare in Mexico City, 1884–1943*. Lincoln: University of Nebraska Press, 2009.

Borucki, Alex, David Eltis, and David Wheat, eds. *From the Galleons to the Highlands: Slave Trade Routes in the Spanish Americas*. Albuquerque: University of New Mexico Press, 2020.

Bourbonnais, Nicole. *Birth Control in the Decolonizing Caribbean: Reproductive Politics and Practice on Four Islands, 1930–1970*. New York: Cambridge University Press, 2016.

Boyle, Margaret. *Unruly Women: Performance, Penitence and Punishment in Early Modern Spain*. Toronto: University of Toronto Press, 2014.

Brading, David A. *The First America: The Spanish Monarchy, Creole Patriots and the Liberal State, 1492–1867*. New York: Cambridge University Press, 1991.

Briggs, Laura. *How All Politics Became Reproductive Politics: From Welfare Reform to Foreclosure to Trump*. Berkeley: University of California Press, 2018.

———. "The Race of Hysteria: 'Overcivilization' and the 'Savage' Woman in Late Nineteenth-Century Obstetrics and Gynecology." *American Quarterly* 52, no. 2 (2000): 246–73.

———. *Reproducing Empire: Race, Sex, Science, and U.S. Imperialism in Puerto Rico*. Berkeley: University of California Press, 2003.

Brodie, Janet Farrell. *Contraception and Abortion in Nineteenth-Century America*. Ithaca, N.Y.: Cornell University Press, 1994.

Bronfman, Alejandra. "The Allure of Technology: Photographs, Statistics and the Elusive Female Criminal in 1930s Cuba." *Gender and History* 19, no. 1 (2007): 60–77.

———. *Measures of Equality: Social Science, Citizenship, and Race in Cuba, 1902–1940*. Chapel Hill: University of North Carolina Press, 2004.

Brown, Vincent. *The Reaper's Garden: Death and Power in the World of Atlantic Slavery*. Cambridge, Mass.: Harvard University Press, 2008.

Bush, Barbara. *Slave Women in Caribbean Society*. Kingston, Jamaica: Heinemann, 1990.

Camacho, Jorge. "Los criaderos de esclavos: Medicina, cuerpos y sexualidad en los ingenios de Cuba." *Hispanófila* no. 188 (2020): 3–18.

Cañizares-Esguerra, Jorge. *How to Write a History of the New World: Histories, Epistemologies, and Identities in the Eighteenth-Century Atlantic World*. Stanford, Calif.: Stanford University Press, 2002.

Carrillo, Ana María. "Nacimiento y muerte de una profesión: Las parteras tituladas en México." *Dynamis* 19 (1999): 167–90.

Casado Ruíz, José Ramón. "La aplicación del Código penal de 1822." *Anuario de derecho penal y ciencias penales* 32, no. 2 (1979): 333–44.

Cervantes-Rodriguez, Margarita. *International Migration in Cuba: Accumulation, Imperial Designs, and Transnational Social Fields*. University Park: Pennsylvania State University Press, 2010.

Clark, Kim. *Gender, State, and Medicine in Highland Ecuador: Modernizing Women, Modernizing the State, 1895–1950*. Pittsburgh: University of Pittsburgh Press, 2012.

Connery, John. *Abortion: The Development of the Roman Catholic Perspective*. Chicago: Loyola University Press, 1977.

Cooper Owens, Deirdre. *Medical Bondage: Race, Gender, and the Origins of American Gynecology*. Athens: University of Georgia Press, 2017.

Cordova, Isabel M. *Pushing in Silence: Modernizing Puerto Rico and the Medicalization of Childbirth*. Austin: University of Texas Press, 2017.

Corwin, Arthur F. *Spain and the Abolition of Slavery in Cuba, 1817–1886*. Austin: University of Texas Press, 1967.

Cowling, Camillia. *Conceiving Freedom: Women of Color, Gender, and the Abolition of*

Slavery in Havana and Rio de Janeiro. Chapel Hill: University of North Carolina, 2013.

Cowling, Camillia, Maria Helena P. T. Machado, Diana Paton, and Emily West, eds. "Mothering Slaves: Motherhood, Childlessness and the Care of Children in Atlantic Slave Societies." Special issues of *Slavery and Abolition: A Journal of Slave and Post-Slave Studies* 38, no. 2 (2017) and of *Journal of Women's History* 27, no. 6 (2018).

Craton, Michael. *Searching for the Invisible Man: Slaves and Plantation Life in Jamaica.* Cambridge, Mass.: Harvard University Press, 1978.

Crenshaw, Kimberlé. "Mapping the Margins: Intersectionality, Identity Politics, and Violence against Women of Color." *Stanford Law Review* 43, no. 6 (1991): 1241–99.

Curtin, Philip D. *The Atlantic Slave Trade: A Census.* Madison: University of Wisconsin Press, 1968.

———. *The Rise and Fall of the Plantation Complex: Essays in Atlantic History.* 2d ed. New York: Cambridge University Press, 1998.

Cunningham, Wendy V., Linda McGinnis, Rodrigo García Verdú, Cornelia Teslius, and Dorte Verner. *Youth at Risk in Latin America and the Caribbean: Understanding the Causes, Realizing the Potential.* Washington, D.C.: World Bank, 2008.

Davis, Dána-Ain. "Obstetric Racism: The Racial Politics of Pregnancy, Labor, and Birthing." *Medical Anthropology* 38, no. 7 (2019): 560–73.

DeBarros, Juanita. *Reproducing the British Caribbean: Sex, Gender, and Population Politics after Slavery.* Chapel Hill: University of North Carolina Press, 2014.

De la Fuente, Alejandro. *Havana and the Atlantic in the Sixteenth Century.* Chapel Hill: University of North Carolina, 2008.

———. *A Nation for All: Race, Inequality, and Politics in Twentieth-Century Cuba.* Chapel Hill: University of North Carolina Press, 2001.

———. "Población libre y estratificación social, 1510–1770." In *Historia de las Antillas,* tomo I: *Historia de Cuba,* edited by Consuelo Naranjo Orovio, 17–28. Madrid: CSIC, 2009.

———. "Slaves and the Creation of Legal Rights in Cuba: Coartación and Papel." In *Slavery and Antislavery in Spain's Atlantic Empire,* edited by Josep M. Fradera and Christopher Schmidt-Nowara, 659–92. New York: Berghahn Books, 2013.

———. "Sugar and Slavery in Early Colonial Cuba." In *Tropical Babylons: Sugar and the Making of the Atlantic World, 1450–1680,* edited by Stuart B. Schwartz, 125–62. Chapel Hill: University of North Carolina Press, 2004.

Deschamps Chapeaux, Pedro. *El negro en la economía habanera del siglo XIX.* Havana: UNEAC, 1971.

Díaz, María Elena. *The Virgin, the King, and the Royal Slaves of El Cobre Negotiating Freedom in Colonial Cuba, 1670–1780.* Berkeley: University of California Press, 1999.

Dierksheide, Christa. *Amelioration and Empire: Progress and Slavery in the Plantation Americas.* Charlottesville: University of Virginia Press, 2014.

Dubois, Laurent. *Avengers of the New World: The Story of the Haitian Revolution.* Cambridge, Mass.: Harvard University Press, 2004.

Dunn, Richard S. *A Tale of Two Plantations: Slave Life and Labor in Jamaica and Virginia.* Cambridge, Mass.: Harvard University Press, 2014.

Fanon, Franz. *Black Skin, White Masks.* New York: Grove, 1967.
Farnot, Ubaldo, and Norma Eneida Rios. "Mortalidad materna en las primeras décadas del siglo XX." *Revista Cubana de Salud Pública* 39, no. 1 (2013): 69–83.
Féres da Silva Telles, Lorena. "Pregnant Slaves, Workers in Labour: Amid Doctors and Masters in a Slave-Owning City (Nineteenth-Century Rio de Janeiro)." *Slavery and Abolition* 27, no. 6 (2018): 924–38.
Fernández, N. S. "Los Niños Expósitos de Buenos Aires, 1779–1823." *Sociales y Virtuales* 2, no. 2 (2015).
Fernández Ugarte, María. "La mortalidad entre los ninos expósitos de Salamanca (1700–1725)." In *Enfance abandonnée et société en Europe, XIVe–XXe siècle*, 591–608. Rome: Publications de l'École Française de Rome, 1991.
Ferrer, Ada. *Freedom's Mirror: Cuba and Haiti in the Age of Revolution.* New York: Cambridge University Press, 2014.
———. *Insurgent Cuba: Race, Nation, and Revolution, 1868–1898.* Chapel Hill: University of North Carolina Press, 1999.
———. "Rustic Men, Civilized Nation: Race, Culture, and Contention on the Eve of Cuban Independence." *Hispanic American Historical Review* 78 no. 4 (1998): 663–86.
Few, Martha. *For All of Humanity: Mesoamerican and Colonia Medicine in Enlightenment Guatemala.* Tucson: University of Arizona Press, 2015.
———. "'That Monster of Nature': Gender, Sexuality, and the Medicalization of a "Hermaphrodite" in Late Colonial Guatemala." *Ethnohistory* 54, no. 1 (2007): 159–76.
Few, Martha, Zeb Tortorici, and Adam Warren. *Baptism through Incision: The Postmortem Cesarean Operation in the Spanish Empire.* University Park: Pennsylvania State University Press, 2020.
Finch, Aisha K. *Rethinking Slave Rebellion in Cuba: La Escalera and the Insurgencies of 1841–1844.* Chapel Hill: University of North Carolina, 2015.
———. "Scandalous Scarcities: Black Slave Women, Plantation Domesticity, and Travel Writing in Nineteenth-Century Cuba." *Journal of Historical Sociology* 23, no. 1 (2010): 101–42.
Fisas, Carlos. *Historias de las Reinas de España: La Casa de Borbón.* Barcelona: Editorial Planeta, 1991.
Flavin, Jeanne. *Our Bodies, Our Crimes: The Policing of Women's Reproduction in America.* New York: New York University Press, 2009.
Fogel, Robert W. *Without Consent or Contract: The Rise and Fall of American Slavery.* New York: Norton, 1989.
Foner, Philip S. *The Spanish-Cuban-American War and the Birth of American Imperialism.* New York: Monthly Review Press, 1972.
Foote, Nicola, and Michael Goebel, eds. *Immigration and National Identities in Latin America.* Gainesville: University Press of Florida, 2014.
Fraile Foro, Emilio de Benito. "Nuevas aportaciones al estudio sobre la aplicación práctica del Código Penal de 1822." *Foro, Nueva época* 8 (2008): 41–68.
Franklin, Sarah L. *Women and Slavery in Nineteenth-Century Colonial Cuba.* Rochester, N.Y.: University of Rochester Press, 2012.

Fraser, Gertrude Jacinta. *African American Midwifery in the South*. Cambridge, Mass.: Harvard University Press, 1998.

Fraunhar, Alison. *Mulata Nation: Visualizing Race and Gender in Cuba*. Jackson: University Press of Mississippi, 2018.

Fried, Marlene. "The Politics of Abortion: A Note." In *Markets and Malthus: Population, Gender and Health in Neo-liberal Times*, edited by Mohan Rao and Sarah Sexton, 84–102. Los Angeles: Sage, 2010.

Funes Monzote, Reinaldo. *From Rainforest to Cane Field in Cuba: An Environmental History since 1492*. Chapel Hill: University of North Carolina Press, 2008.

García, Gloria. *La esclavitud desde la esclavitud: La visión de los siervos*. Mexico: Centro de Investigación Científica "Ing. Jorge L. Tamayo," 1996.

García, Guadalupe. *Beyond the Walled City: Colonial Exclusion in Havana*. Berkeley: University of California Press, 2015.

———. "Urban Guajiros: Colonial Reconcentración, Rural Displacement, and Criminalization in Western Cuba, 1895–1902." *Journal of Latin American Studies* 43, no. 2 (August 2011): 209–35.

García González, Armando, Raquel Álvarez Peláez, and Consuelo Naranjo Orovio, eds. *En busca de la raza perfecta: eugenesia e higiene en Cuba (1898–1958)*. Madrid: Consejo Superior de Investigaciones Científicas, 1998.

García Rodríguez, Gloria. *Voices of the Enslaved in Nineteenth-Century Cuba*. Translated by Nancy L. Westrate. Chapel Hill: University of North Carolina Press, 2011.

Genovese, Eugene D. *Roll, Jordan, Roll: The World the Slaves Made*. New York: Vintage, 1974.

Gerber Fried, Marlene. *From Abortion to Reproductive Freedom: Transforming a Movement*. Boston: South End Press, 1990.

Germeten, Nicole von. *Violent Delights, Violent Ends: Sex, Race, and Honor in Colonial Cartagena de Indias*. Albuquerque: University of New Mexico Press, 2013.

Ghorbal, Karim. "La política llamada del 'buen tratamiento': Reformismo criollo y reacción esclavista en Cuba (1789–1845)." *Nuevos Mundos* (2009). https://doi.org/10.4000/nuevomundo.57872 .

Gonzalbo Aizpuru, Pilar. "La Casa de Niños Expósitos de la Ciudad de México: una fundación del siglo XVIII." *Historia Mexicana* 31, no. 3 [123] (1982): 409–20.

González, Ondina E. "Down and Out in Havana: Foundlings in Eighteenth Century Cuba." In *Minor Omissions: Children in Latin American History and Society*, edited by Tobias Hecht, 102–13. Madison: University of Wisconsin Press, 2002.

González, Ondina E., and Bianca Premo, eds. *Raising an Empire: Children in Early Modern Iberia and Colonial Latin America*. Albuquerque: University of New Mexico Press, 2007.

González-Ripoll Navarro, Ma. Dolores, Consuelo Naranjo Orovio, Ada Ferrer, Gloria García Rodríguez, and Josef Opatrný. *El rumor de Haití en Cuba: Temor, raza y rebeldía, 1789–1844*. Madrid: CSIC, 2004.

Gordon, Linda. *The Moral Property of Women: A History of Birth Control Politics in America*. Urbana: University of Illinois Press, 2002.

Graden, Dale T. *Disease, Resistance, and Lies: The Demise of the Transatlantic Slave Trade to Brazil and Cuba*. Baton Rouge: Louisiana State University Press, 2014.

Guerra, Lillian. *The Myth of José Martí: Conflicting Nationalisms in Early Twentieth-century Cuba.* Chapel Hill: University of North Carolina Press, 2005.

Guridy, Frank Andre. *Forging Diaspora: Afro-Cubans and African Americans in a World of Empire and Jim Crow.* Chapel Hill: University of North Carolina, 2010.

Gurr, Barbara. *Reproductive Justice: The Politics of Health Care for Native American Women.* New Brunswick, N.J.: Rutgers University Press, 2014.

Gutman, Herbert G. *The Black Family in Slavery and Freedom, 1750–1925.* New York: Vintage, 1976.

Guy, Donna J. *Sex and Danger in Buenos Aires: Prostitution, Family, and Nation in Argentina.* Lincoln: University of Nebraska Press, 1991.

———. *White Slavery and Mothers Alive and Dead: The Troubled Meeting of Sex, Gender, Public Health, and Progress in Latin America.* Lincoln: University of Nebraska Press, 2000.

Hall, Gwendolyn Midlo. *Social Control in Slave Plantation Societies: A Comparison of St. Domingue and Cuba.* Baltimore: Johns Hopkins University Press, 1972.

Hansing, Katrin, and Bert Hoffmann. "When Racial Inequalities Return: Assessing the Restratification of Cuban Society 60 Years after Revolution." *Latin American Politics and Society* 62, no. 2 (2020): 29–52.

Helg, Aline. *Our Rightful Share: The Afro-Cuban Struggle for Equality, 1886–1912.* Chapel Hill: University of North Carolina Press. 1995.

Hicks, Anasa. "Hierarchies at Home: A History of Domestic Service in Cuba from Abolition to Revolution." PhD diss., New York University, 2017.

Hidalgo Valdés, Leyma. *Real Casa de Beneficencia de La Habana: Luces y Sombras de Una Institución (1794–1865).* Barcelona: Linkgua Ediciones, 2006.

Higman, B. W. *Slave Populations of the British Caribbean, 1807–1834.* Baltimore: Johns Hopkins University Press, 1984.

Hinojosa Hernández, Leandra, and Sarah De Los Santos Upton. *Challenging Reproductive Control and Gendered Violence in the Américas: Intersectionality, Power and Struggles for Rights.* Lanham, Md.: Lexington Books, 2018.

Hollerbach, Paula E., Sergio Diaz-Briquets, and Kenneth H. Hill. "Fertility Determinants in Cuba." *International Family Planning Perspectives* 10, no. 1 (1984): 12–20.

Htun, Mala. *Sex and the State: Abortion, Divorce, and the Family under Latin American Dictatorships and Democracies.* New York: Cambridge University Press, 2010.

Huguet-Termes, Teresa. "Madrid Hospitals and Welfare in the Context of the Hapsburg Empire." *Medical History Supplement* 29 (2009): 64–85.

Hynson, Rachel. *Laboring for the State: Women, Family, and Work in Revolutionary Cuba, 1959–1971.* New York: Cambridge University Press, 2020.

Jaffary, Nora E. "Monstrous Births and Creole Patriotism in Late Colonial Mexico." *Americas* 68, no. 2 (2011): 179–207.

———. "Reconceiving Motherhood: Infanticide and Abortion in Colonial Mexico." *Journal of Family History* 37, no. 1 (2012): 3–22.

———. *Reproduction and Its Discontents in Mexico, 1750–1905.* Chapel Hill: University of North Carolina Press, 2016.

Jenkins Schwartz, Marie. *Birthing a Slave: Motherhood and Medicine in the Antebellum South.* Cambridge, Mass.: Harvard University Press, 2010.

Jennings, Evelyn. *Constructing the Spanish Empire in Havana: State Slavery in Defense and Development, 1762–1835*. Baton Rouge: Louisiana State University Press, 2020.

Joda Esteve, Beatriz. "El comercio de esclavos a Cuba (1790–1840): Una proporción femenina." *Anuario Colombiano de Historia Social y de la Cultura* 41, no. 2 (2014): 107–30.

Johnson, Lyman L., and Sonya Lipsett-Rivera, eds. *The Faces of Honor: Sex, Shame, and Violence in Colonial Latin America*. Albuquerque: University of New Mexico Press, 1998.

Johnson, Sherry. *The Social Transformation of Eighteenth-Century Cuba*. Gainesville: University Press of Florida, 2001.

Jones, David Albert. *The Soul of the Embryo: An Enquiry into the Status of the Human Embryo in the Christian Tradition*. New York: Continuum International, 2004.

Jones-Rogers, Stephanie. "'[S]he could . . . spare one ample breast for the profit of her owner': White Mothers and Enslaved Wet Nurses' Invisible Labor in American Slave Markets." *Slavery and Abolition* 38, no. 2 (2017): 339–40.

Karasch, Mary C. *Slave Life in Rio de Janeiro, 1808–1850*. Princeton, N.J.: Princeton University Press, 1987.

Kimball, Natalie L. *An Open Secret: The History of Unwanted Pregnancy and Abortion in Modern Bolivia*. New Brunswick, N.J.: Rutgers University Press, 2020.

Kiple, Kenneth F. *The Caribbean Slave: A Biological History*. New York: Cambridge University Press, 1984.

Kluchin, Rebecca. *Fit to Be Tied: Sterilization and Reproductive Rights in America, 1950–1980*. New Brunswick, N.J.: Rutgers University Press, 2009.

Knight, Franklin W. *Slave Society in Cuba during the Nineteenth Century*. Madison: University of Wisconsin Press, 1970.

Kuethe, Allan J. *Cuba, 1753–1815: Crown, Military and Society*. Knoxville: University of Tennessee Press, 1986.

———. "Havana in the Eighteenth Century." In *Atlantic Port Cities: Economy, Culture, and Society in the Atlantic World, 1650–1850*, edited by Franklin W. Knight and Peggy K. Liss, 13–39. Chattanooga: University of Tennessee Press, 1991.

La Rosa Corzo, Gabino, and Rafael Robaína Jaramillo. *Costumbres funerarias de los aborígenes de Cuba*. Havana: Editorial Academia, 1995.

Lauderdale Graham, Sandra. "Honor among Slaves." In *The Faces of Honor: Sex, Shame, and Violence in Colonial Latin America*, edited by Lyman L. Johnson and Sonya Lipsett-Rivera, 201–28. Albuquerque: University of New Mexico Press, 1998.

Lavrín, Asunción, ed. *Sexuality and Marriage in Colonial Latin America*. Lincoln: University of Nebraska Press, 1989.

Leavitt, Judith. *Brought to Bed: Childbearing in America, 1750–1950*. New York: Oxford University Press, 1988.

Lipsett-Rivera, Sonya. "A Slap in the Face of Honor: Social Transgression and Women in Late-Colonial Mexico." In *The Faces of Honor: Sex, Shame and Violence in Colonial Latin America*, edited by Lyman L. Johnson and Sonya Lipsett-Rivera, 179–200. Albuquerque: University of New Mexico Press, 1998.

López, Iris. *Matters of Choice: Puerto Rican Women's Struggle for Reproductive Freedom*. New Brunswick, N.J.: Rutgers University Press, 2008.

López, Kathleen. *Chinese Cubans: A Transnational History*. Chapel Hill: University of North Carolina Press, 2013.
López Denis, Adrián. "Disease and Society in Colonial Cuba, 1790–1840." PhD diss., Brown University, 2007.
López Sánchez, José. *La medicina en La Habana, 1550–1730*. Havana: MINSAP, 1970.
López Valdés, Rafael L. "Hacia una periodización de la historia de la esclavitud en Cuba." In *La esclavitud en Cuba*, 11–41. Havana: Editorial Academia, 1986.
Lowenthal, David, and Colin Clark. "Slave Breeding in Barbuda: The Past of a Negro Myth," *Comparative Perspectives on Slavery in New World Plantation Societies* 292: 1 (1977): 510–35.
Lucena Salmoral, Manuel. "La instrucción sobre educación, trato y ocupaciones de los esclavos de 1789; Una prueba del poder de los amos de esclavos frente a la debilidad de la Corona Española." *Estudios de historia social y económica de América* 13 (1996): 155–78.
Lucero, Bonnie A. *A Cuban City, Segregated: Race and Urbanization in the Nineteenth Century*. Tuscaloosa: University of Alabama Press, 2019.
———. "Entre Esclavos y Comerciantes: Mujeres Negras como Intermediarias en la Economía Colonial Cienfueguera." In *Emergiendo del silencio: Mujeres negras en la historia de Cuba*, edited by Oilda Hevia Lanier and Daisy Rubiera Castillo, 177–204. Havana: Editorial de Ciencias Sociales, 2016.
———. "Interpreting the Remnants of Women's Reproductive Crises: Physicians, and the Shifting Legal Terrain of Infanticide in Nineteenth-Century Cuba." *Journal of Latin American Cultural Studies*, 2021. https://doi.org/10.1080/13569325.2021.1941817.
———. *Revolutionary Masculinity and Racial Inequality: Gendering War and Politics in Cuba*. Albuquerque: University of New Mexico Press, 2018.
Lugones Botell, Miguel. "La cesárea en la historia." *Revista Cubana Obstetricia y Ginecología* 27, no. 1 (2001).
Madrigal Lomba, Ramón. "Dr. Gabriel Casuso Roque: Multifacética personalidad patriótica y científica." *Revista Médica Electrónica* 29, no. 6 (2007):
Marqués de Armas, Pedro. *Ciencia y poder en Cuba: Racismo, homofobia, nación (1790–1970)*. Madrid: Editorial Verbum, 2014.
Marrero, Levi. *Cuba: Economía y sociedad*. 12 vols. Madrid: Editorial Playor, 1971–85.
Martínez, María Elena. *Genealogical Fictions: Limpieza de Sangre, Religion, and Gender in Colonial Mexico*. Stanford, Calif.: Stanford University Press, 2008.
Martinez-Alier, Verena. "Elopement and Seduction in Nineteenth-Century Cuba." *Past and Present* 55 (May 1972): 91–129.
———. *Marriage, Class and Colour: A Study of Racial Attitudes and Sexual Values in a Slave Society*. New York: Cambridge University Press, 1974.
Martínez Fortún, José A. "Historia de la medicina en Cuba. Siglo XVI a primera mitad del XVIII." *Cuadernos de Historia de la Salud Pública* 96 (2004).
Martínez-Vergne, Teresita. *Shaping the Discourse on Space: Charity and Its Wards in Nineteenth-Century San Juan, Puerto Rico*. Austin: University of Texas Press, 1999.
Martz, Linda. *Poverty and Welfare in Habsburg Spain: The Example of Toledo*. New York: Cambridge University Press, 1983.
Meriño Fuentes, María de los Ángeles, and Aisnara Perera Díaz. *Del tráfico a la libertad:*

El caso de los africanos de la fragata Dos Hermanos *en Cuba (1795–1837)*. Santiago de Cuba: Editorial Oriente, 2014.

Meriño Fuentes, María de los Ángeles, and Aisnara Perera Díaz. "La madre esclava y los sentidos de la libertad. Cuba 1870–1880." *Historia Unisinos* 12, no. 1 (2008): 49–59.

Meriño Fuentes, María de los Ángeles, and Aisnara Perera Díaz. *Un café para la microhistoria: Estructura de posesión de esclavos y ciclo de vida en la llanura habanera (1800–1886)*. Havana: Editorial de Ciencias Sociales, 2008.

Milanich, Nara B. *Children of Fate: Childhood, Class, and the State in Chile, 1850–1930*. Durham, N.C.: Duke University Press, 2009.

———. "Los hijos del azar: Ver nacer sin placer, ver morir sin dolor. La vida y la muerte de los párvulos en el discurso de las élites y en la práctica popular." *Contribuciones Científicas y tecnológicas de Universidad de Santiago de Chile* 25, no. 114 (1996): 79–92.

Moitt, Bernard. *Women and Slavery in the French Antilles, 1635–1848*. Bloomington: Indiana University Press, 2001.

Montanos Ferrín, Emma, and José Sánchez-Arcilla. *Estudios de historia del derecho criminal*. Madrid: Dykinson, 1990.

Mooney, Jadwiga Pieper. *The Politics of Motherhood: Maternity and Women's Rights in Twentieth-Century Chile*. Pittsburgh: University of Pittsburgh Press, 2009.

Moore, Robin. *Nationalizing Blackness: Afrocubanismo and Artistic Revolution in Havana, 1920–1940*. Pittsburgh: University of Pittsburgh Press, 1998.

Moreno, José Luis, "La Casa de Niños Expósitos de Buenos Aires, conflictos institucionales, condiciones de vida y mortalidad de los infantes 1779–1823." In *La política social antes de la política social (Caridad, beneficencia y política social en Buenos Aires, siglos XVII a XX)*, edited by José Luis Moreno, 91–128. Buenos Aires: Trama Editorial/Prometeo libros, 2000.

Moreno Fraginals, Manuel. *El ingenio: Complejo económico-social cubano del azúcar*. 3 vols. Havana: Editorial de Ciencias Sociales, 1978.

———. *The Sugarmill: The Socioeconomic Complex of Sugar in Cuba, 1760–1860*. New York: Monthly Review Press, 1976.

Moreno Fraginals, Manuel, Herbert S. Klein, and Stanley L. Engerman. "The Level and Structure of Slave Prices on Cuban Plantations in the Mid-Nineteenth Century: Some Comparative Perspectives." *American Historical Review* 88, no. 5 (December 1983): 1201–18.

Morgan, Jennifer. *Laboring Women: Reproduction and Gender in New World Slavery*. Philadelphia: University of Pennsylvania Press, 2004.

Morrison, Karen Y. *Cuba's Racial Crucible: The Sexual Economy of Social Identities, 1750–2000*. Bloomington: Indiana University Press, 2015.

———. "Slave Mothers and White Fathers: Defining Family and Status in Late Colonial Cuba." *Slavery and Abolition* 31, no. 1 (2010): 29–55.

Morrissey, Marietta. *Slave Women in the New World: Gender Stratification in the Caribbean*. Lawrence: University Press of Kansas, 1989.

Moya, Jose C. *Cousins and Strangers: Spanish Immigrants in Buenos Aires, 1850–1930*. Berkeley: University of California Press, 1998.

Moya Pons, Frank. *Después de Colón: Trabajo, sociedad y política en la economía del oro*. Madrid: Alianza, 1986.

Muller, Dalia Antonia. *Cuban Emigrés and Independence in the Nineteenth-Century Gulf World.* Chapel Hill: University of North Carolina Press 2017.
Murray, David R. *Odious Commerce: Britain, Spain, and the Abolition of the Cuban Slave Trade.* New York: Cambridge University Press, 1980.
———. "Statistics of the Slave Trade to Cuba, 1790–1867." *Journal of Latin American Studies* 3, no. 2 (1971): 131–49.
Naranjo Orovio, Consuelo. "El temor a la 'africanización': Colonización blanca y nuevas poblaciones en Cuba (el caso de Cienfuegos)." In *Las Antillas en la era de las Luces y la Revolución*, edited by José Antonio Piqueras, 85–122. Madrid: Siglo XXI, 2005.
———. "La otra Cuba, colonización blanca y diversificación agrícola," *Contrastes: Revista de Historia* 12 (2001–3): 5–20.
Necochea López, Raúl. *A History of Family Planning in Twentieth-Century Peru.* Chapel Hill: University of North Carolina Press Books, 2014.
Nelson, Jennifer. *Women of Color and the Reproductive Rights Movement.* New York: New York University Press, 2003.
Nelson, Lowry. "Cuban Population Estimates, 1953–1970." *Journal of Interamerican Studies and World Affairs* 12, no. 3 (1970): 392–400.
Newman, Louise Michele. *White Women's Rights: The Racial Origins of Feminism in the United States.* New York: Oxford University Press, 1999.
O'Brien, Elizabeth. "The Many Meanings of *Aborto*: Pregnancy Termination and the Instability of a Medical Category over Time." *Women's History Review* 30, no. 6 (2021): 952–70.
———. "Pelvimetry and the Persistance of Racial Science in Obstetrics." *Endeavor* 37, no. 1 (2013): 21–28.
O'Phelan Godoy, Scarlett, Fanni Muñoz Cabrejo, Gabriel Ramón Joffré, and Mónica Ricketts Sánchez-Moreno, eds. *Familia y vida cotidiana en América Latina, siglos XVIII–XX.* Lima: Instituto RivaAgüero and IFEA, 2003.
Ortiz, Fernando. *Los negros esclavos.* Havana: Editorial de Ciencias Sociales, 1975 [1916].
Otheguy, Raquel Alicia. "'Es de suponer que los maestros sean de la misma clase': What a Nineteenth-Century Teaching Application Reveals about Race, Power, and Education in Colonial Cuba." *Cuban Studies* 49 (2020): 174–92.
Otovo, Okezi T. *Progressive Mothers, Better Babies: Race, Public Health, and the State in Brazil, 1850–1945.* Austin: University of Texas Press, 2016.
Pacino, Nicole. "Creating Madres Campesinas: Revolutionary Motherhood and the Gendered Politics of Nation Building in 1950s Bolivia." *Journal of Women's History* 27, no. 1 (2015): 62–87.
Paier, Hanni Jalil. "Gender as Pathology: Disease, Degeneration, and Medical Discourse in Late Nineteenth-Century Colombia." *Revista CS10* (2012): 243–76.
Pappademos, Melina. *Black Political Activism and the Cuban Republic.* Chapel Hill: University of North Carolina Press, 2011.
Paquette, Gabriel B. *Enlightenment, Governance, and Reform in Spain and Its Empire, 1759–1808.* Basingstoke: Palgrave Macmillan, 2008.
Paquette, Robert L. *Sugar Is Made with Blood: The Conspiracy of La Escalera and the Conflict between Empires over Slavery in Cuba.* Middleton, Conn.: Wesleyan University Press, 1988.

Paton, Diana. "Maternal Struggles and the Politics of Childlessness under Pronatalist Caribbean Slavery." *Slavery and Abolition* 38, no. 2 (2017): 251–68.

Patterson, Orlando. *The Sociology of Slavery: An Analysis of the Origins, Development, and Structure of Negro Slave Society in Jamaica.* New York: Humanities Press, 1969.

Paugh, Katharine. *The Politics of Reproduction: Race, Medicine and Fertility in the Age of Abolition.* New York: Oxford University Press, 2017.

Peiro, Pedro Miguel de, and José Rodrigo. *Elementos de medicina y cirujía legal, arreglados a la legislación española.* Madrid: Imprenta de la Compañía general de Impresores y Libreros, 1841.

Perera Díaz, Aisnara, and María de los Ángeles Meriño Fuentes. "The African Women of the *Dos Hermanos* Slave Ship in Cuba: Slaves First, Mothers Second." *Women's History Review* 27, no. 6 (2018): 892–909.

Perera Díaz, Aisnara, and María de los Ángeles Meriño Fuentes. *Nombrar las cosas: Aproximación a la onomástica de la familia negra en Cuba.* Guantánamo: El Mar y la Montaña, 2006.

Perera Díaz, Aisnara, and María de los Ángeles Meriño Fuentes. *Para librarse de los lazos, antes buena familia que buenos brazos: Apuntes para la manumisión en Cuba (1800–1881).* Santiago de Cuba: Editorial Oriente, 2009.

Pérez, Louis A., Jr. *Cuba between Empires, 1878–1902.* Pittsburgh: University of Pittsburgh Press, 1983.

———. *On Becoming Cuban: Identity, Nationality, and Culture.* Chapel Hill: University of North Carolina Press, 2012.

———. *To Die in Cuba: Suicide and Society.* Chapel Hill: University of North Carolina Press, 2005.

———. *The War of 1898: The United States and Cuba in History and Historiography.* Chapel Hill: University of North Carolina Press, 1998.

Pollitt, Brian H. "The Cuban Sugar Economy and the Great Depression." *Bulletin of Latin American Research* 3, no. 2 (1984): 3–28.

Poska, Allyson M. *Gendered Crossings: Women and Migration in the Spanish Empire.* Albuquerque: University of New Mexico Press, 2016.

Prados Torreira, Teresa. *Mambisas: Rebel Women in Nineteenth-Century Cuba.* Gainesville: University Press of Florida, 2005.

Prats García, Ariadna. *Mujer y familia en la sociedad cubana 1889–1918.* Madrid: Editorial Verbum, 2019.

Price, Kimala. "What Is Reproductive Justice? How Women of Color Activists Are Redefining the Pro-Choice Paradigm." *Meridians* 10, no. 2 (2010): 42–65.

Provencio Garrigós, Lucía. "Las madres cubanas no son madres sino a medias: Discurso teórico y disciplina de la maternidad." In *Dimensiones y diálogo americano contemporáneo sobre la Familia en la época colonial* edited by Francisco Chacón Jiménez and Ana Vera Estrada, 321–67. Murcia: Editum, 2010.

Ramm, Alejandra, and Jasmine Gideon. *Motherhood, Social Policies and Women's Activism in Latin America.* New York: Palgrave Macmillan, 2019.

Randall, Margaret. *Cuban Women Now: Interviews with Cuban Women.* Toronto: Women's Press, 1974.

Reagan, Leslie. *When Abortion Was a Crime: Women, Medicine, and Law in the United States, 1867–1973*. Berkeley: University of California Press, 1997.
Reid-Vázquez, Michelle. "Tensions of Race, Gender, and Midwifery in Colonial Cuba." In *Africans to Spanish America: Expanding the Diaspora*, edited by Sherwin K. Bryant and Rachel Sarah O'Toole, 186–205. Urbana: University of Illinois Press, 2012.
———. *The Year of the Lash: Free People of Color in Cuba and the Nineteenth-Century Atlantic World*. Athens: University of Georgia Press, 2011.
Rigau-Pérez, José G. "Surgery at the Service of Theology: Postmortem Cesarean Sections in Puerto Rico and the Royal Cédula of 1804." *Hispanic American Historical Review* 75, no. 3 (1995): 377–404.
Roberts, Dorothy. *Killing the Black Body: Race, Reproduction, and the Meaning of Liberty*. New York: Pantheon, 1997.
Rodríguez, Daniel. *The Right to Live in Health: Medical Politics in Postindependence Havana*. Chapel Hill: University of North Carolina Press, 2020.
Ross, Loretta, and Rickie Solinger. *Reproductive Justice: An Introduction*. Berkeley: University of California Press, 2017.
Roth, Cassia P. "Birthing Life and Death: Women's Reproductive Health in Early Twentieth-Century Rio de Janeiro." *História, Ciências, Saúde* 25, no. 4 (2018): 921–41.
———. "Black Nurse, White Milk: Breastfeeding, Slavery, and Abolition in 19th-Century Brazil." *Journal of Human Lactation* 34, no. 4 (2018): 804–9.
———. "From Free Womb to Criminalized Woman: Fertility Control in Brazilian Slavery and Freedom." *Slavery and Abolition* 38, no. 2 (2017): 269–86.
———. *A Miscarriage of Justice: Women's Reproductive Lives and the Law in Twentieth-Century Brazil*. Stanford, Calif.: Stanford University Press, 2020.
Ruggiero, Kristin. *Modernity in the Flesh: Medicine, Law, and Society in Turn-of-the-Century Argentina*. Stanford, Calif.: Stanford University Press, 2004.
Russell, Camisha. *The Assisted Reproduction of Race*. Bloomington: Indiana University Press: 2018.
Santos, Martha S. "Mothering Slaves, Labor, and the Persistence of Slavery in Northeast Brazil: A Non-Plantation View from the Hinterlands of Ceará, 1813–1884." *Women's History Review* 27, no. 6 (2018): 954–71.
Sawyer, Mark Q. *Racial Politics in Post-Revolutionary Cuba*. New York: Cambridge University Press, 2010.
Schneider, Elena A. *The Occupation of Havana: War, Trade, and Slavery in the Atlantic World*. Chapel Hill: University of North Carolina Press, 2018.
Schoen, Johanna. *Choice and Coercion: Birth Control, Sterilization, and Abortion in Public Health and Welfare*. Chapel Hill: University of North Carolina Press, 2005.
Scott, Rebecca J. *Slave Emancipation in Cuba: The Transition to Free Labor, 1860–1886*. Pittsburgh: University of Pittsburgh Press, 1985.
Seed, Patricia. *To Love, Honor, and Obey in Colonial Mexico: Conflicts over Marriage Choice, 1572–1821*. Stanford, Calif.: Stanford University Press, 1988.
Sharman, Adam. *Deconstructing the Enlightenment in Spanish America: Margins of Modernity*. Cham: Springer, 2020.

Shnookal, Deborah. *Operation Pedro Pan and the Exodus of Cuba's Children*. Gainesville: University of Florida Press, 2020.

Siegel Watkins, Elizabeth. *On the Pill: A Social History of Oral Contraceptives, 1950–1970*. Baltimore: Johns Hopkins University Press, 2001.

Sippial, Tiffany A. *Prostitution, Modernity, and the Making of the Cuban Republic, 1840–1920*. Chapel Hill: University of North Carolina Press, 2013.

Sloan, Kathryn. *Runaway Daughters: Seduction, Elopement, and Honor in Nineteenth-Century Mexico*. Albuquerque: University of New Mexico Press, 2008.

Smith, Lois M., and Alfred Padula. *Sex and Revolution: Women in Socialist Cuba*. New York: Oxford University Press, 1996.

Socolow, Susan Migden. "Amor y matrimonio en la América Latina colonial." In *Cuestiones de familia a través de las fuentes*, edited by M. Mónica Ghirardi, 19–57. Córdoba, Argentina: Universidad Nacional de Córdoba, 2006.

Soto Laveaga, Gabriela. *Jungle Laboratories: Mexican Peasants, National Projects, and the Making of the Pill*. Durham, N.C.: Duke University Press, 2009.

Stampa Braun, J. M. "Las corrientes humanitarias del siglo XVIII y su influencia en la concepción del infanticidio como delictum exceptum." *Anuario de derecho penal y ciencias penales* 6, no. 1 (1953): 47–78.

Stepan, Nancy Leys. *The Hour of Eugenics: Race, Gender, and Nation in Latin America*. Ithaca, N.Y.: Cornell University Press, 1991.

Stern, Alexandra Minna. *Eugenic Nation: Faults and Frontiers of Better Breeding in Modern America*. 2d ed. Berkeley: University of California Press, 2015.

———. "'The Hour of Eugenics' in Veracruz, Mexico: Radical Politics, Public Health, and Latin America's Only Sterilization Law." *Hispanic American Historical Review* 91, no. 3 (2011): 431–43.

Stoler, Ann Laura. *Carnal Knowledge and Imperial Power: Race and the Intimate in Colonial Rule*. Durham, N.C.: Duke University Press, 2002.

Stoner, K. Lynn. *From the House to the Streets: The Cuban Woman's Movement for Legal Reform, 1898–1940*. Durham, N.C.: Duke University Press, 1991.

Suárez Findlay, Eileen. *Imposing Decency: The Politics of Sexuality and Race in Puerto Rico, 1870–1920*. Durham, N.C.: Duke University Press, 1999.

Tadman, Michael. "The Demographic Cost of Sugar: Debates on Slave Societies and Natural Increase in the Americas." *American Historical Review* 105, no. 5 (2001): 1534–75.

Tardieu, Jean Pierre. *"Morir o dominar": En torno al reglamento de esclavos de Cuba (1841–1866)*. Madrid: Iberoamericana Vervuert, 2003.

Tomich, Dale W., ed. *The Politics of the Second Slavery*. Ithaca: State University New York Press, 2016.

Tornero Tinajero, Pablo. *Crecimiento económico y transformaciones sociales: Esclavos, hacendados y comerciantes en la Cuba Colonial (1760–1840)*. Madrid: Ministerio de Trabajo y Seguridad Social, 1996.

Torres Pico, José M. *Los expósitos y la sociedad colonial: La Casa Cuna de La Habana, 1710–1832*. Havana: Editora Historia, 2013.

Turner, Sasha. *Contested Bodies: Pregnancy, Childrearing, and Slavery in Jamaica*. Philadelphia: University of Pennsylvania Press, 2017.

Twinam, Ann. "The Church, the State and the Abandoned: Expósitos in Eighteenth-Century Havana." In *Raising an Empire: Children in Early Modern Iberia and Colonial Latin America*, edited by Ondina E. González y Bianca Premo, 163–86. Albuquerque: University of New Mexico Press, 2007.

———. *Public Lives, Private Secrets: Gender, Honor, Sexuality, and Illegitimacy in Colonial Spanish America*. Stanford, Calif.: Stanford University Press, 1999.

———. *Purchasing Whiteness: Pardos, Mulattos, and the Quest for Social Mobility in the Spanish Indies*. Stanford, Calif.: Stanford University Press, 2015.

Valcárcel Rojas, Roberto. *Archaeology of Early Colonial Interaction at El Chorro de Maíta, Cuba*. Gainesville: University Press of Florida, 2016.

Van Woodward, C. *American Counterpoint: Slavery and Racism in the North/South Dialogue*. New York: Oxford University Press, 1983.

Varella, Claudia, and Manuel Barcia. *Wage-Earning Slaves: Coartación in Nineteenth-Century Cuba*. Gainesville: University of Florida Press, 2020.

Vinat de la Mata, Raquel. *Luces en el silencio: Educación femenina en Cuba (1648–1898)*. Havana: Editora Política, 2005.

Warren, Adam. "Between the Foreign and the Local: French Midwifery, Traditional Practitioners, and Vernacular Medical Knowledge about Childbirth in Lima, Peru." *História, Ciências, Saúde—Manguinhos* 22, no. 1 (2015): 179–200.

———. *Medicine and Politics in Colonial Peru: Population Growth and the Bourbon Reforms*. Pittsburgh: University of Pittsburgh Press, 2010.

Whitmore, Thomas M., and David J Robinson. *Disease and Death in Early Colonial Mexico: Simulating Amerindian Depopulation*. Boulder, Colo.: Westview, 1992.

Williams, Eric. *Capitalism and Slavery*. 1944; rpt., Chapel Hill: University of North Carolina Press, 1994.

Wright, Irene A. *The Early History of Cuba, 1492–1586*. New York: Macmillan, 1916.

INDEX

abandonment, 198–199, 201–206, 232, 259, 275–277. *See also* children; *expósitos*
abolition, 74–75, 82–83, 191–192, 198–199, 201
abortions: 1850 code, 165–166; abortifacients, 36, 227–228, 230; access to, 275, 292–293; alternatives, 52–53; antiabortionism, 230–231, 265–271, 292; artificial premature birth, 228–229; charges as retaliation, 296; clandestine, 278; constitution (1940), 289; cornezuelo de centeno (abortifacient), 227–230; decriminalizing, 210–212, 264, 299, 309; the Depression and, 277–279; described, 293–294; devices, 235–236; dilation and curettage, 228–229; equated to murder, 287–288; eugenics and, 284; extreme pelvic narrowness, 228–229; fetal autopsies, 217; hospital, 278; investigations and prosecutions of, 161, 165–166, 181–183, 229–230, 262, 273, 277–289, 293–299; legal defenses, 283; legal interventions, 252; male perception of, 265, 274–275, 288; Malthusian practices, 292, 294, 295, 297; medical attitudes toward, 265–266, 272; methods of, 36, 228, 230, 264; midwives and, 269–272, 278; numbers of, 262, 264, 269; paternalism and, 272; physicians and, 98, 227–231, 266–267, 297–298; population and, 262–263, 265, 270–271, 288, 292; poverty exemption, 285–286; "prácticas maltusianas," 295; promiscuity and, 236; revolutionary period, 298–299; Siete Partidas, 27, 28, 30–36; Social Defense Code, 263, 285–287, 289, 308; surgical advances, 266, 268; therapeutic, 236, 265–267; in twentieth century, 263, 274–275, 277–283, 292–295; whiteness and, 231

Abreu, Rosalía, 245
Academia de Parteras (Midwives' Academy), 49, 105, 106
Academy of Medical, Physical, and Natural Sciences of Havana, 211–214, 221, 224, 226, 229, 230
Acea, Felipa, 293
adultery, 26, 37, 45, 60, 81. *See also* marriage
African descendants / Blacks: ancestry records, 95; Black republic, 80, 82; captives of *Dos Hermanos* (ship), 87; Código Negro Español (Spanish Black Code), 77; "corrupt" white children, 129; deterring infant abandonment among, 121; educational opportunities, 104; *emancipadas*, 46, 125; enslaved/free status of, 180, 182–184; *expósitos* excluded from care, 72; female hospital staff, 52–53, 67; fertility crimes, 205–206, 274; forced labor, 46; Free Trade in Slaves Act, 77; hospital patients, 46; infants/children unwanted, 51, 52, 65, 72, 121–123, 203, 216, 218; marriage rates among, 26, 203–204; midwives, 41, 100–107, 219–220; polygamy and, 81, 83, 85; as preferred labor source, 175–176; pregnancy and poverty, 27, 206; as settlers, 33; women hypersexualized, 305; women's morals, 124, 127–128, 203–207; working mothers, 253. *See also* slavery; wet nurses
Africanization, 61, 63, 80, 82, 182
Agramonte, Aristedes, 270, 272
agriculture, 54, 79
Aguirre, Domingo de, 122–123
Aguirre, Joaquín, 135
Agustín Martínez, José, 286

INDEX

Alberdi, Juan Bautista, 301
Aldama, Domingo de, 155–157
Alfonso X of Castile, 27
Alonso y Fernández, Francisco, 101, 105
al parecer blanco (white-passing), 51, 198, 201
Álvarez, 110
Amelia, Dolores, 200
amelioration, 75, 83, 88–89, 93, 138, 158–159, 190
amenorrhea, 32, 35–36, 93, 169
Ana Josefa, 55
Anatomical Museum, 105
Andaya, Elise, 299
animation, 34–35
antinatalism, 83, 95–96. *See also* pronatalism
antisepsis/asepsis, 112, 114, 170, 223–226, 235–236, 266
antiseptics, 223–226, 235–236
antislaving treaties, 86–90, 140–145
Apostolicae Sedis moderation, 36
"apprentices," 191–195, 201, 207
Aragón, Polonia, 220
Arango, Mariano de, 122, 130
Arango y Parreño, Francisco, 79, 80, 84–85, 89, 106, 124
Arcos, Marqués de, 159
Argentina, 245
Aristotle, 34
Arteaga y Quesada, Serapio, 209–210
artificial premature birth, 210, 228–229
asepsis/antisepsis. *See* antisepsis/asepsis
asphyxiation, 215
autopsy, 211, 213–215, 221

Bacuranao, 29
Bahía Honda, 92
Bañón, Antonia, 39
baptism, infant, 27, 34–35, 41, 102, 132–133, 193, 198, 200
Barales, Isabel, 62
Barga, Agüeda de, 100
Barnet, Enrique, 243, 252–253
barracoons, 81, 90–91
Basallo, Tranquilina, 215
bastards, as term, 60
Batabanó, 95
Batista, Fulgencio, 292
Bauta, 92
Beaterio, 54
Bejucal, 110
Berta Machado, 260

Betancourt, Alfonso, 245
birth. *See* childbirth
bitch, son of a, as term, 60
bohiques (healers), 32
Bourbon reforms, 59
Bravo, Antonio, 62
Bravo, José Narciso, 61–63
Brazil, 167, 191, 198, 207, 245, 263
breastfeeding: accommodations, 156, 158, 160, 170–171; Casa de Maternidad, 115, 196–197, 199–200, 204; educational campaign, 253; enteritis, 71, 173; freedom through, 76; ill children, 131; Indigenous/Native peoples, 28; medicalization of, 253–254; nutrition, 170–171; white women, 67–68; working and, 252–253. *See also* wet nurses
breech births, 114, 209, 216, 226
"breeding," 167, 173–174
Britain, 61, 74–75, 82–84, 96
Brouardel, Hippolyte, 217

Caballeros, José Agustín, 81
Cabanas, 92
calidades (qualities), 102
Camille, Paul, 217
Cano, 111
Cañongo (Count), 162
Cárdenas, 110
Caribbean, 30, 33, 59, 63, 74, 83, 233
Carlos II, king of Spain, 54
Carlos III, king of Spain, 68, 76
Carlos IV, king of Spain, 61
Cármen Alfonso, María del, 106–107
Carrillo, Ana María, 114
Carrillo, José Manuel, 155, 157, 158
Casa Cuna (Cradle House), 52–58, 68–71, 115
Casa de Beneficencia: admission requirements, 119; African-descended babies, 122–123, 130–133; infant surrender and police intimidation, 258–259; intake forms, 120–121; *parteros* (male midwives), 101; *partus sequitur ventrem* (child's status), 125; racial segregation, 199–205, 257–259; reforms/regulations, 63–69, 198, 202; *torno* (turnstile/wheel), 276–277; wealthy women and pregnancy, 117; wet nurses, 196–197; white babies and, 204; working mothers and, 256
Casa de Expósitos, 51–52, 59–60, 64–65, 69–71, 97, 115, 198, 304
Casa de Mendigos (Paupers' House), 119

Casa de Recogidas, 106, 184, 185, 218
Casa de Refugio, 97, 114
Casas, Bartolomé de las, 29–30, 32
Casas, Isabel, 194, 195
Castellanos, Israel, 289
Castillo, Francisca del, 132
Castillo y Sucre, Rafael del, 47
castration, 48
Casuso Roque, Gabriel, 223–226, 246
Catholic Church: *Apostolicae Sedis moderationi*, 36; assistance for white women, 114; baptism, infant, 27, 34–35, 41, 102, 132–133, 193, 198, 200; defines "soul," 34–35; excommunication, 34; ignores Casa funding problems, 56; Immaculate Conception, 26; "moralizing" slaves, 80; Pope Pius IX, 36; reproduction, women's Christian duty, 303
Cayo Salinas, 29
celibacy, 85, 143
cesarean sections, 41, 112, 226, 229
charitable institutions: abandoned infants, 51; advance colonial order, 45; Charity Board, 119–123; charity boundaries, 48, 119–123, 304; colonialism, 52, 56–57, 64; consolidated, 114–115; ill, criminals, laborers, 49; moralization campaigns, 344n91; Piety Board, 121; regulating, 63–66, 97; state-run, 39–44. *See also specific institution*
Charity Board, 119–123
chastity, 26, 37
Chateausalins, Honorato Bernard De, 168–172, 174
Chávez, Paula de, 124
Chelala-Aguilera, José, 278, 282–283
childbirth: artificial premature birth, 210, 228–229; birth defects, 27, 35, 245; birth rates, 94, 124, 174–176, 181, 183, 206; breech births, 114, 209, 216, 226; cesareans, 41, 112, 226, 229; delivery complications, 112–114, 209, 212, 220, 227–228; enslaved women and, 75, 78, 84–85; extreme pelvic narrowness, 228, 229; female attendants, 36, 40–41, 113; at home, 113, 279–280; hygienic conditions, 171–173, 206, 222, 225–226, 253–255; medical management, 167–171; mortality rates, 109–112; multiple births, 32; Native women and pain, 32; obstetrics, 209–212; out-of-wedlock, 203–204; stillbirths, 101, 109–113, 135; surgery, 41, 112, 170, 226, 229. *See also* midwifery/midwives
child care, 157–160, 172–173, 253, 256–258, 260

children: abandoned, 52, 54, 58–60, 65–66, 130–133, 201, 275–278; caring for, 157–160, 172–173, 253, 256–258, 260; Casa de Maternidad, 115; child's status follows mother's, 33; custody rights, 97, 130, 193–195; Departmento de Expósitos (Dept. of Abandoned Children), 52; girls prepped for marriage, 44, 64, 72, 73; (il)legitimate, 37, 60–64, 204, 231; from illicit sex, 51; man of the cradle, 53–54; Native population, 29–30; orphans, 63–64, 72–73; *partus sequitur ventrem* (child's status), 33, 75, 84, 122, 125, 191–192, 197; puericulture, 256–260, 284–285; from rape, 79; redeeming impoverished, 260; slavery and, 33, 76–78, 88, 94–95, 129–130, 193–194, 198; "that which is born follows the womb," 75; unwanted = useful vassals, 54; Valdés surname, 52; white "corrupted" by Black, 129. *See also expósitos*; infants
chloroform, 227
cholera, 107, 141, 196
Christian duty, 303
Cienfuegos, 88, 92–94, 110, 143, 266–267, 297–298
Cienfuegos, José, 86
Ciriaca de la Rosa, 148–149, 152
coartadas/coartación (purchasing freedom), 76
código negro carolino (manumission prohibited), 76
Código Negro Español (Spanish Black Code), 77
Colegio de Niñas San Francisco de Sales, 44, 64, 101–106
Colegio de Niños San Ambrosio, 64
colonialism: anticolonial struggle, 191, 208, 209; charitable institutions, 52, 56–57, 64; demographics, 53, 60; *expósito* legal category, 72–73; fertility/reproduction and, 28, 32, 34, 37–38, 48–49, 71–72, 301; honorable societal paths, 26; introduces slavery, 33; Junta de Colonización Blanca, 79; legal whiteness, 61–63; Little War, 208; medicine, 40–45; pronatalism, 48, 64, 75; racial purity, 51, 60, 102; slavery and, 47–48; Ten Years' War, 208; War of Independence, 208
comadre de partera (midwife), 100. *See also* midwifery/midwives
comadrones, 101
Comité Revolucionario Cubano, 245
Committee for the Abolition of the Slave Trade, 75

Committee for the Defense of the Revolution (CDR), 296, 297
Compostela, Diego Evelino Hurtado de, 51
conception. *See* reproduction
Conga, Marilina, 196
Conga, Merced, 138–139, 146–148, 152
conquistadors, 28–31, 302
Consejos a las Madres de Familia, 257–258, 260
Conspiración de la Escalera (Ladder Conspiracy), 108, 161
Consulado de la Havana, 79
contraception, 235–236, 284, 292. *See also* fertility: controlling
Convento San Basilio, 63
Convento Santa Teresa, 52
convulsions, 220
Coppinger, Cornelius, 201–204
cornezuelo de centeno (abortifacient), 227–230
Coronado, Tomás V., 217, 237–242, 262, 267–271
Cowley, Ángel J., 109
Cowley, Rafael, 212
Cowling, Camillia, 192
Cradle House, 52. *See also* Casa Cuna
crèches, 260
Creole elites, 61, 63, 79, 80, 82
crimes/criminals: abortion, 98, 165–166, 284, 292; Casa de Recogidas, 106; court, 211–215, 217, 220–221, 230; *depositadas*, 46–47; evidence, 198, 211–215, 217, 218, 225, 230; fertility crimes, 205–206, 211, 217–219, 273–274, 277–278, 289–292; fetal autopsies, 217, 221; forensic investigation in infanticide case, 212–218; framing of enslaved, 149–151; gender breakdown, 189; homicide, 48, 220, 222, 225; *honoris causa*, 134–136, 181; infanticide, 27–30, 34, 52–53, 64, 72, 98, 134–136, 146–147; insanity defense, 140, 146–148, 153; *lesa patria* crimes, 235–236; National Revolutionary Police, 293; parricide, 27, 98, 205; police reports, 135; Somerset case, 74; women prisoners, 48. *See also* abortions; infanticide
Crucet, León, 130, 132
Crucet, Salustiana, 130–131, 132
cuarentena (quarantine), 156
Cuban Revolution, 245, 263, 296–299, 302
culpability: midwifery/midwives, 99, 220–227, 230, 231, 270–271, 280–281; physicians, 230, 231; wet nurses, 67–70
curanderos (midwives), 223
custody, 97, 130, 193–195

decrees. *See* laws/reforms/decrees
Delfín, Manuel, 206
Departmento de Expósitos (Dept. of Abandoned Children), 52
depositadas, 46–47
Depósito de Cimarrones, 109, 129
depósitos, 46, 128
Depression, the, 275–279
Díaz Vara Calderón, Gabriel (bishop), 45
dilation and curettage, 228–229
disabilities, 27, 35, 245
diseases: asepsis/antisepsis, 112, 114, 170, 223–226, 235–236, 266; cholera, 107, 141, 196; leprosy, 41–42, 130–132; measles, 41; mortality rates, 109–113; neonatal tetanus, 112, 165, 171–173, 215, 223, 262; smallpox, 41, 42; syphilis, 112, 251; tuberculosis, 42, 112; yellow fever, 41–42. *See also* medicine
disguises, 116
divorce, 44–45
docimasia (lung test), 166, 212, 215–216
Domínguez, Irene, 200
Dos Hermanos (ship), 87
dowries, 44, 64
Dumont, Henri, 146
Duque Perdomo, Matías, 246

ecclesiastical authorities, 39, 42–43, 45, 50, 56, 97
eclampsia, 112
economy, 79–86, 275–279, 309–310
education, 40, 44, 63–64, 101–106
emancipadas, 46, 125, 128, 191, 196–197, 199, 275
embryos, 35–36, 265, 287–288
encomienda system, 30
Enlightenment era, 59, 104
ensoulment, 34–35
Erenchún, Félix, 181–182, 184, 187
Escovedo, Antonio María de, 162
Esperanza, 213
Espírito Santo, 93, 95
Essay on the Principle of Population (Malthus), 303
eugenics, 284, 287
Europeans, 40
excommunication, 34
exhaustion, 220
expósitos (exposed ones): breastfeeding of *expósitos*, 68; Casa de Expósitos, 51–52, 59–60, 64, 69–71, 97, 115, 198, 304; court case, 61–63;

defining, 50–51, 59–61; deterring abandonment, 121; females neglected, 54; *hombres buenos*, 60; legal rights, 72; precarious situations, 59; racial boundaries, 51, 60, 72, 201; registering, 97; worthiness, 58–63
extreme pelvic narrowness, 228–229

Feliciano, 145
feminism, 123–126, 284, 308
Fernandina, Countess de, 124
Fernandina, Count of, 159
Fernando, 149
Fernando III (Castilian monarch), 27
fertility: abortions, 98, 165–166; of Black women, 203–204, 206; "breeding," 167, 173–174; colonialism and, 32, 34, 37–38, 48–49, 71–72, 301; color balance and, 243; controlling, 36, 134–136, 233–236, 238–241, 284, 303; embryo versus fetus, 35–36; fertility crimes, 205–206, 211, 217–219, 273–274, 277–278, 289–292; legal intervention, 280–282; *lesa patria* crimes, 235–236; medical management, 167–174; men's obligations, 289; "owner" controls, 89, 140–141, 148, 152–153, 161, 181–182; population control and, 285–286; preserving, 209, 227, 231; rates of, 29–30, 94, 174–176, 181, 183; reproduction, women's Christian duty, 303; Republic and, 243; sterility, 93; "unfertilizer of women," 235–236; whites', 34. *See also* abortions; infanticide
fetuses, 27, 34–36, 76, 117, 214, 219, 225, 229
Few, Martha, 117
fidelity, 26, 37, 45, 60, 81. *See also* marriage
Flores, María de, 55
Fosalba, Rafael, 243
Fource, Eugenio, 185
France/French territories, 63, 80, 82, 87, 101–105, 168, 208, 245
Franklin, Sarah, 121
freedom, 33, 53, 76, 87
Free Trade in Slaves Act, 77, 91–92
Free-Womb law, 90, 191–194, 198, 201, 207
Frías, Isabel, 184–188
Fuentes, Juana de, 62
Fuero Juzgo, 27

García, Cástula, 196
García, Leocadia, 194
García Herreros, Manuel, 84
García Oña, Antonio, 153

gender, 42–47, 77–82, 90–91, 122, 141–145, 176–179, 183
generational slavery. *See* slavery: generational
Gertrudis, 129
Giménez Lanier, Manuel, 285–286
gobernar es poblar ("to govern is to populate"), 301
Gobierno, Junta de, 203
Gobierno Superior Civil, 153
Gómez, Joaquín, 155
Gómez, José Miguel (president), 247
Gómez Carbonell, María, 284–285
González, Francisco, 208, 229–230
González Larrinaga, Jacinto, 156
González Olivares, Ignacio, 174
Gordón, Antonio de, 32
Governing the Management of Slaves (1844 ordinance), 162–164
Goyena, Florencio García, 135
gracias al sacar (permission to [leave racial impurity]), 58–59
Grande Rossi, Federico, 269
Guamutas, 110
Guanabacoa, 110
Guanajay, 111
Guardia, Vicente de la, 223
Guarro, Joaquín, 107
Guerrita de Agosto, 242
Guía de Forasteros, 107
Güines, 110
Gutiérrez, Nicolás José, 105
Gutiérrez de la Concha, José, 176
gynecology, 208, 211, 224. *See also* obstetrics

Haitian Revolution, 80, 82
Havana, 39, 40, 53, 57–61, 79, 94, 177–178
healers (*bohiques*), 32
health care, 42, 208. *See also* hospitals; medicine
hemorrhages, 113
Heredia, Tomás de, 57
hermanos de leche (milk siblings), 76
Hernández, Eusebio, 245–246, 247–248, 262
Hernández, Natalia, 196
Herrera, Ignacio, 156
Hispaniola, 33
hombres buenos, 60
homiculture, 233, 245–251, 259–261, 263–264
honor: Black mothers, 127; Casa de Maternidad, 116; chastity threatened, 37; fertility control and, 37, 134–136; *honoris causa*, 98–99, 102,

honor (*continued*)
117, 134–136, 152, 181, 303; infanticide and, 38, 50; morality, 44–49, 124, 127–129, 196, 203, 207, 344n91; paths to, 26; race and, 38–39; wealthy women and pregnancy, 117

hospitals: convalescence institutions, 42; *depositadas*, 46; enslaved/incarcerated women, 105–106, 146–147, 152–153, 185; Hospital Número Uno, 270; Hospital Real de S. Felipe y Santiago, 39–40; "hysteria" treatments, 46; living quarters, 46; *maestras*, 46; male patients, 42; maternal/infant death and abandonment, 49; Mercedes Hospital, 270; moral function of, 44–49; relief and confinement, 45; San Ambrosio Military Hospital, 101, 105; San Francisco de Paula Charity Hospital for Women, 28, 39–40, 42, 44–49, 69–71, 146–147, 152, 185; San Juan de Dios hospital, 39–40, 69–71; San Lázaro hospital, 42, 130; visitors, 47

Huter (physician), 235–236

hydrostatic tests, 166, 212, 215–216

hygiene, 171–173, 206, 222, 225–226, 247–248, 253–255

hysteria, 46

Iberian law, 303
Iberian Peninsula, 60, 74
Iberian tradition, 123
"idiocy" defense, 147, 153
Immaculate Conception, 26
imperialism, 261
inbreds, 60
incest, 26, 60, 303
indemnification, 195
Indigenous/Native peoples, 28–32
Infant Hygiene Service, 247–248, 253–255
infanticide: cases, 210–218, 231; criminal process, 138–139, 146–148, 152, 165–166, 179–182, 185–189, 273; exceptions, 98, 135; fetal animation, viability, 34–36; forensic investigation, 212–218; Havana, 1907, 238–241; maternalism and, 38, 50; poverty and, 237; race/class and, 135, 237, 241–242; *reglamentos* for, 64; Siete Partidas, 27–31; sonnet, 38, 316n59; state intervention, 52; by third party, 134
infants: abandoned temporarily, 65–66; baptism, 27, 34–35, 41, 102, 132–133, 193; Black infants, 88, 95, 197–199, 201, 203, 206–207, 210, 223; care of, 157–160, 172–173; caring for several, 71; childcare and working, 256; conquistadors' violence toward, 28–31; deaths, 210–211, 214, 219, 223–225, 229; enslaved or free status of, 180; enteritis, 71, 252–253; *expósitos*, 50, 58–60, 72; identifying race, 239–241; Indigenous/Native peoples, 29–30; infant tetanus, 109–110, 112, 113, 165, 171–172; inheritance/rights, 27, 35; mixed-race, 55; more care when placing, 68; mortality, 56–57, 67–70, 108–115, 208–210, 224, 243–245, 248, 255; multiple births, 32; National Commission for the Protection of Maternity and Infancy, 260; National Maternity and Infancy Competitions, 248–251; neonatal tetanus, 109–110, 112, 113, 165, 171–173, 223, 248; nurses and, 253; premature, 93–94; puerperal septicemia, 226; race and poverty, 290; racial restrictions on admission of, 198–201, 203, 204; state intervention, 259; stillbirths, 101, 109–113, 135; "that which is born follows the womb," 75; *torno* (turnstile/wheel), 54–55, 121; unintentional deaths, 183; "useful vassals," 68; welfare campaigns, 261; wet nurses and, 67–71. *See also* children

inferiority, 46
inheritance/rights, 27, 35
insanity defense, 140, 146–148, 153
Instituto de Homicultura Nena Machado, 259–260
Isabel, 149

Jaffary, Nora, 112
Jamaica, 191, 207
Jaruco, 110
Jesús, María y José, Havana, 93, 215
Jesús del Monte, Havana, 48, 224, 260
Jibacoa, Havana, 93, 110
Jimenez, Amparo, 273
Jimenez, Antonio, 39
José Antonio, 200
José Eligio, 129
Josefa, 150
Josefa (Pita), 273
Juan Emeterio, 180
Juana, 180
Julián, 129
Junta de Caridad (Charity Board), 119–123
Junta de Colonización Blanca, 79
Junta de Fomento, 129

Junta de Patrocinados, 195
Junta de Piedad (Piety Board), 121
Junta Superior de Sanidad de la Isla de Cuba, 109

kidnapping, 37
Knaus-Ogino method, 292

labor/work: of Black women, 49, 51, 55, 67, 72; after childbirth, 156, 158, 160, 170–171; children born to enslaved mothers, 76; *depositadas*, 46; feed, not work, enslaved children, 78; forced, 32, 46, 47–48; Indigenous/Native peoples and, 30, 32; in mines, 29; pregnancy and, 28; slave hours, 74; slavery instituted, 33; supply of, 44, 303; tiered poverty relief, 123; unfree, 46, 72, 123, 207; women of color and childcare, 72
lactation, 95, 115, 186, 196. *See also* breastfeeding; wet nurses
Ladder Conspiracy, 161
La Divina Pastora sugar mill, 90–91
Laredo Brú, Federico, 286
Lasa, Sebastián I. de, 155
Las Pozas, 111
La tragedia social de la mujer (Rodríguez Acosta), 284
laws/reforms/decrees: 1789 code (Spanish Black Code), 77–82, 86, 91–92, 96, 140, 186; 1789 royal decree (Free Trade in Slaves Act), 61, 179; 1794 royal decree (*expósito* legitimacy), 59–60, 62; 1804 royal decree (slavery reproduction), 82–84, 86–87, 140; 1817 Antislaving Treaty, 86–90, 125, 140; 1835 Antislaving Treaty, 141; 1842 royal order (midwifery training), 107, 160, 208; 1842 slave code, 160–164, 179; 1844 Ordinances Governing the Management of Slaves, 162–163, 166, 169, 175, 179; 1850 code (infanticide, abortion), 165–166; abortion, 82; abortion, 252, 283; begging/vagrancy, 39; care in placing infants, 68; children's freedom, 33; *código negro carolino* (manumission prohibited), 76; Código Negro Español (Spanish Black Code), 77; colonial and whiteness, 61; criminal charges in killing enslaved, 48; excommunication, 34; *expósitos*, 59–63, 68, 72; fertility control, 134–136; Free Trade in Slaves Act (1789), 77–82, 91–92; Free-Womb law, 90, 191–194, 198, 201, 207; Fuero Juzgo, 27; generational slavery, 75–76; Gobierno Superior Civil, 153; *gracias al sacar* (permission to [leave racial impurity]), 58–59; *hombres buenos*, 60; implementation gaps, 31, 34, 48, 65, 96; infanticide, 27–28, 30, 34; legal medicine committee, 212–217, 221–222, 230; Ley de Beneficencia Pública de España (Spanish Law of Public Beneficence), 97, 114; Leyes de Burgos, 28, 30–31; Leyes Nuevas (New Laws of the Indies), 32, 33, 41–42; *Librería de jueces, abogados y escríbanos*, 135; metropolitan, 30, 59, 82–86, 128; midwifery, 41, 99–108; midwifery training, 107, 160, 208; Moret Law, 165, 191–195, 197, 198, 199, 207; National Revolutionary Police, 293; ordinance of 1844 (Governing the Management of Slaves), 162–164; *partus sequitur ventrem* (child's status), 33, 75, 84, 122, 125; Patronato law, 191, 195, 201, 207; penal codes, 98–99, 102, 117, 134–136, 139, 152, 165–166; pregnancy termination, 35; pronatalist reforms, 75, 302; quarantines, 41–42; Real Audiencia de Santo Domingo, 63; Reglamento de esclavos de Cuba (1842), 160–164, 179; *reglamentos* for Casas de Expósitos, 64; Siete Partidas, 27–35, 75–76, 82–86, 139, 186–187; slavery, 61, 77–92, 96, 125, 140–141, 160–163, 166, 169, 175, 179, 186; Social Defense Code (1936), 263, 285–287, 289, 308; suing for insult or offense, 60; Toro (Bull Laws), 35; wet nursing, 66–67. *See also* crimes/criminals
Lebredo, Mario, 244
legitimacy, 37, 58–60, 62, 204, 231
Leocadia, 165
leprosy, 41–42, 130–132
Le-Roy y Cassá, Jorge, 236, 244, 262, 266, 267–268, 271–272
lesa patria crimes, 235–236
Ley de Beneficencia Pública de España (Spanish Law of Public Beneficence), 97, 114
Leyes de Burgos, 28, 30–31
Leyes Nuevas (New Laws of the Indies), 32, 33, 41–42
Little War, 208
Lorenza, 183–184
Lucumí, Teresa, 149–152
Luisa, 165–166, 180–181
Luiteria, 129

384   INDEX

Macuriges, 95, 111
Madden, Richard, 142–144
maestras, 46
Magdalene house, 45
Malthus, Thomas Robert, 295; *Essay on the Principle of Population*, 303
Malthusian practices, 292, 294, 295, 297, 303. *See also* abortions
man of the cradle, 53–54
Manuel, 129–130
manumission, 53, 76
Margarita, 145
María, 39
María Candelaria, 55
María Caridad, 205
María Manuela, 58–59
Marqueti, Merced, 130, 132
marriage: adultery, 26, 37, 45, 60, 81; Blacks, 26, 203–204; divorced women hospitalized, 44–45; dowries, 44, 64; of enslaved, 75, 78–82, 88, 92, 203–204; fertility and rates of, 244–245; fidelity, 37; girls prepped for, 44, 64, 72, 73; informal unions, 204; interracial, 26–27; legitimacy of children, 37, 58–60, 62, 204, 231; as moralization tool, 203–204; partner selection, 26; polygamy, 81, 83, 85; promotion of, 167; remarrying, 27; sex outside, 26–27, 37, 45, 81, 97
Martínez, José Agustín, 231, 288
Martínez Bandujo, Candita Gómez Calas de, 285
Marxism, 308
masturbation, 81
Matanzas, 95
maternalism, 38, 50, 127–128, 145–146, 149, 150, 169, 212
Maternidad de María Santísima y San José, 115
maternity wards, 114–119
matrifeticultura, 251–252
matrinaticultura, 252–255
measles, 41
medicine: abortifacients, 36, 227–228, 230; Academia de Parteras Santa Lutgarda, 106; alkaloids, 220, 227–230; asepsis/antisepsis, 112, 114, 170, 223–226, 235–236, 266; chloroform, 227; docimasia (lung test), 166, 212, 215–216; *Ensayo estadístico de la mortalidad en la diócesis de la Habana: Año 1843*, 109; *Examen y cartilla de parteras, teórico práctica* (midwife training), 101; folk remedies, 36; forensic investigation in infanticide case, 212–218; hydrostatic tests, 166, 212, 215–216; Junta Superior de Sanidad de la Isla de Cuba, 109; legal medicine committee, 212–217, 221–222, 230; medical professionalization, 208; *Medicina indígena de Cuba y su valor histórico*, 32; midwives refer cases to doctors, 114; morphine, 227; mortality rates, 109; Museo Anatómico de La Habana (Anatomical Museum), 105; obstetrics, 40, 100–101, 105, 208–211, 219, 225–231, 245–246; patriarchal protection and, 108–115; penicillin, 112; Real Tribunal del Protomedicato (medical board), 40, 100–101; Real y Pontificia Universidad de San Gerónimo de la Habana, 40; sulfa drugs, 112; Superior Board of Medicine and Surgery, 132; United States, 208, 228, 292–293; unregulated, 40. *See also* diseases; physicians
men: castrated, 48; escape consequences of illicit sex, 37–38; hospital patients, 42; initiate *expósito* cases, 59; man of the cradle, 53–54; "owner's" preference for, 141–145, 178–179; paternity, 27, 33, 95; perpetrate abortion, 28, 31; population, 40; postgenitocultura, 248. *See also* gender
Méndez, Soledad, 62
Méndez Capote, Fernando, 267, 268
Menocal, Antonia María, 115
menstruation, 32, 35–36, 93, 169
Mercedes Hospital, 270
mestizos, 206, 239–241, 249–250, 274. *See also* pregnancy
metritis, 109–110, 112
metropolitan law, 30, 59, 82–86, 128
metrorragia, 109–110, 112
Mexico, 245
Middle Passage, 93, 125
midwifery/midwives: abortifacients, 36, 227–228, 230; Academia de Parteras (Midwives' Academy), 49, 105, 106; African-descended women, 41, 52–53, 101–107, 219–220; antisepsis, 223, 224; *calidades* (qualities) lacking, 102; culpable, 99, 220–227, 230, 231, 270–271, 280–281; dependence on, 86; *Examen y cartilla de parteras, teórico práctica*, 101; *Guía de Forasteros*, 107; hostility toward, 210, 218–219; as "interlopers," 218; laws/regulations, 41, 99–108; Museo Anatómico de La Habana (An-

atomical Museum), 105; obstetric knowledge limited, 112; obstetrics school, 97, 105; origins of, 36; outrage over, 227; parteros (male midwives), 101; physicians and, 101–106, 167–169, 172, 210, 218–227, 271–272, 280–281, 304; professionalization, 208; *recibidoras* (unlicensed midwives), 223–224, 226–227; "reckless endangerment," 225; refer cases to doctors, 114; regulation of, 253–254, 304; training/licensing, 100, 105, 106–107, 113–114, 116, 222–226
Miguel, 129
Milanés, Teresa, 218
milk purity, 254–255
milk siblings, 76
Ministerio de la Hacienda, 86
Miranda, Martina, 219–220
miscarriages, 36, 192, 210, 212, 228–230. *See also* pregnancy
miscegenation, 27, 38
mixed-races. *See* race
Montalvo, Juan, 155, 156, 157
Montané, Luís, 217
morality, 44–49, 80, 124, 127–129, 196, 203–207, 344n91. *See also* honor
morenos, 39, 128, 130, 219–220
Moret Law, 165, 191–195, 197, 198, 199, 207
morphine, 227
Morrison, Karen Y., 95
mortality: *Ensayo estadístico de la mortalidad en la diócesis de la Habana: Año 1843*, 109; of enslaved, 74, 80, 93; of Indigenous/Native peoples, 29–30; infant/child, 56–57, 67–70, 108–115, 189, 208–210, 224, 243–245, 248, 255; maternal, 209, 210, 223–226; rates of, 42, 93, 200, 206; septicemia, 223–225; wet nurses blamed, 67–70
mulatas, 39, 226
mulaticas, 55
Muñoz Izaguirre, Joaquín, 155
"murderous mother" trope, 145–146, 149, 169
Museo Anatómico de La Habana (Anatomical Museum), 105

National Commission for the Protection of Maternity and Infancy, 260
National Maternity and Infancy Competitions, 248–251
National Revolutionary Police, 293
Nava, Mariana, 41

negligence, 222, 224–225
Negrito (ship), 129
negrophilia, 202
neonatal death, 192, 206, 210, 212
neonatal tetanus, 112, 165, 171–173, 215, 223, 262
New Laws of the Indies, 32, 41–42
Nieves, María de la Luz, 185
Ninfa (ship), 129
Nuestra Señora de Belén Iglesia, 51–52
Núñez de Villavicencio Palomino, Enrique, 246, 247
nurseries/child care, 157–160, 172–173, 253, 256–258, 260
nurses, 253. *See also* wet nurses

O'Brien, Elizabeth, 229
obstetrics, 208–211, 219, 225–231, 245–246. *See also* childbirth
O'Donnell, Leopoldo, 162–163, 167
O'Farrill, Juan Manuel, 80, 90
O'Farrill, Juan R., 258
O'Farrill, Rafael, 156
O'Gavan, Juan Bernardo, 121
ordinances, 163–164, 204. *See also* laws/reforms/decrees
orphans, 63–64, 72–73
Otherness, 31, 232, 242

pardo (mixed race), 62
parricide, 27, 98, 205
parteros (male midwives), 101
partus sequitur ventrem (child's status), 33, 75, 84, 122, 125, 191–192, 197
paternity, 27, 33, 95
Paton, Diana, 191
patriarchy, 37–44, 97, 108–115, 137, 210, 231, 308
patrimatricultura, 251
Patronato law, 191, 195, 201, 207
Paula, 129
Paupers' House, 119
Pedro Antonio, 62
pelvic narrowness, extreme, 228, 229
penal codes, 98–99, 102, 117, 134–136, 139, 152, 165–166. *See also* laws/reforms/decrees
penicillin, 112
Peraza, Trinidad, 200
Perico, 29
Peru, 32–33, 263
perversion, 81, 85

phenotypes, 61, 121, 240
physicians: abortion and, 227–231, 266–267, 297–298; Agramonte, Aristedes, 270, 272; Agustín Martínez, José, 286; authority of, 211; Barnet, Enrique, 243, 252–253; Betancourt, Alfonso, 245; convictions of white women, 212, 218; Coronado, Tomás V., 237–242, 262, 267–269; culpability, 230, 231; disagreement among, 212; Duque Perdomo, Matías, 246; forensic medical investigations, 212–218; Giménez Lanier, Manuel, 285–286; Grande Rossi, Federico, 269; Hernández, Eusebio, 245–248, 262; Huter, Arzt., 235–236; intervene in reproductive control, 235–236; Laredo Brú, Federico, 286; Le-Roy y Cassá, Jorge, 236, 244, 262, 266–268, 271–272; Martínez Bandujo, Candita Gómez Calas de, 285; medical establishment protects, 222–223; Méndez Capote, Fernando, 267, 268; midwives and, 167–169, 172, 210, 217–227, 280–281, 304; Núñez de Villavicencio Palomino, Enrique, 246, 247; obstetrics training, 208; physician shortage, 40; Pinard, Adolphe, 245, 246; population growth, 235, 237; race certifications, 199; Ramos, Domingo, 243–247, 265, 267, 271; research on maternal outcomes, 209; Varona Suárez, Manuel, 246; wet nurses and, 253–254, 304. *See also* medicine; midwifery/midwives
Piedra, Buenaventura, 149–150
Piety Board, 121
Pinard, Adolphe, 245, 246
Pinar del Río, 92, 111
Pita (Josefa), 273
Plá, José, 203, 207
Planeta (ship), 129
Platt Amendment, 302
polygamy, 81, 83, 85. *See also* marriage
population: abandoned infants, 58; Africanization, 61, 63, 80, 82, 182; Africans versus Natives, 33; Black versus white, 117, 124; Cuba versus Puerto Rico, 234–235; effects of Spaniards arrival, 32–33, 48; enslaved, 49, 74, 77–82, 90–91, 122, 191; *Essay on the Principle of Population*, 303; exodus, 295; fertility and, 243–245; by gender, 40, 53, 74; "to govern is to populate," 301; growth and illicit conception, 303; Havana in eighteenth century, 57; Havana in sixteenth century, 40; Indigenous/Native peoples, 29–30; Jesús del Monte, 49; manumitted, 53; "quality" of, 243–244, 262–263, 265, 270–271; racialization of, 302; state intervention, 174–179; valuable resource, 301; wartime, 234; whites, 34, 39, 54, 243; working women, 256

Portugal, 84
postgenitocultura, 248
Poveda, María Pilar, 108
poverty, 39–44, 50, 63–67, 119–125, 204–206, 260, 275–279, 303
prácticas maltusianas, 295
pregnancy: aborting, 28, 30–36, 52; accountability and outcome, 226; anonymity and, 116; artificial premature birth, 228; Casa de Maternidad, 115; cesareans, 41, 112; childbirth and, 212; *coartadas*, 76; complications of, 112–113, 228; eclampsia, 112; embryo versus fetus, 35–36; of enslaved, 83–85; extreme pelvic narrowness, 228–229; fetal death, 214, 219, 225, 229; hemorrhages, 113; medical management, 167–170; midwives culpable, 99; miscarriages, 36, 192, 210, 212, 228–230, 279–280; moral/material interests in, 301; National Commission for the Protection of Maternity and Infancy, 260; national maternity insurance, 284; out-of-wedlock, 26–27, 37, 97, 115; paternity, 27, 33, 95; poor outcomes, 206, 211–219, 227, 231; poverty and, 27, 206; propriety and fear, 236; protections, 28, 88–90; quickening, 35; secret, 52–53, 103, 115–116, 196, 252, 265–266, 268; slave codes, 154–156
premature birth, 210, 228–229
procreation. *See* reproduction
prógonocultura, 248–251
promiscuity, 83, 124, 127–129, 170–171, 204, 236, 251, 307. *See also* morality
pronatalism: antinatalism, 83, 95–96; coercion and, 90–96; colonialism, 48, 64, 75; critics of, 81; harnessing reproductive power, 75, 302; inconvenient, 84; metropolitan law and, 82–86; pronatalist measures, 191–193; race and, 210; slavery and, 122, 141–142, 159, 163–164, 175, 190
prostitution, 42, 45, 275, 344n91
puericulture, 256–260, 284–285
puerperal septicemia, 223, 225–226
Puerto Rico, 107, 139, 165, 234–235

quarantine, 41–42, 156
Quemado de Palma, 110
Quivicán, 111

race: Black women, white infants, 51, 67, 72; boundaries of *expósitos* category, 62, 72, 304; in criminal cases, 146–147, 181–182; determining, 132–133, 198–201, 204; feminism and exclusion, 123–126; *gracias al sacar* (permission to [leave racial impurity]), 58–59; honor and, 38–39; interracial sex, 26–27, 182–183; marriage and, 26–27; mestizos, 206, 239–241, 249–250, 274; mixed races, 39, 120–121, 129–130; morenos, 39, 128, 130, 219–220; mulatas, 39, 226; mulaticas, 55; *Ordenanzas para el gobierno de las casas reunidas de Beneficencia y Maternidad*, 204; Otherness, 31, 232, 242; *pardo* (mixed race), 62; phenotypes, 61, 121, 240; race war, 263; racial designations, 204; racial integration, 202; racial purity, 51, 58–60, 102; seemingly white, 59, 121; segregation, 42, 46–47, 64, 78, 80–81, 106, 202–204; white-passing, 51, 55; worthiness, 45–46, 49, 58–63, 103, 126, 203, 277. *See also* African descendants / Blacks; whites
Ramírez, Amancia, 296–297
Ramírez, Gracia, 39
Ramos, Domingo, 243–247, 265, 267, 271
rape, 37, 79
Real Audiencia de Santo Domingo, 63
Real Casa de Maternidad, 187
real cédula (royal decree). *See* laws/reforms/decrees
Real Factoría de Tabaco, 68–69
Real Hacienda, 47
Real Junta de Fomento de Agricultura y Comercio. *See* Royal Development Board
Real Sociedad Económica, 105, 106
Real Sociedad Patriótica de la Habana, 105, 106, 108
Real Tribunal del Protomedicato (medical board), 40, 100–101
Real y Pontificia Universidad de San Gerónimo de la Habana, 40
recibidora (unlicensed midwives), 223–224, 226–227
recogidas (removed), 44, 46
reforms. *See* laws/reforms/decrees

refugees, 47
refugiadas, 196
Reglamento de esclavos de Cuba (1842), 160–164, 179
reglamentos, 64
religion, 143. *See also* Catholic Church
reproduction: *bohiques* (healers), 32; castration, 48; colonialism and, 32, 34, 37–38, 48–49, 71–72, 301; controlling, 36, 75, 263, 302; enslaved women's, 76, 78, 80, 83; fertility rates, 29–30; illicit conception, 26, 303; importing enslaved cheaper than, 85–86; incentivizing, 75, 88–89; maternal health, 93–94; "natural" and Antislaving Treaty, 86–90; poverty and, 303; Royal Development Board, 89; San Francisco de Paula Charity Hospital for Women, 28; state intervention, 52; sterility, 93; uterus bearer not owner, 117; violence toward, 48; whites', 33, 34; women's Christian duty, 303. *See also* pregnancy; pronatalism
Revolution, Cuban, 245, 263, 296–299, 302
Rita, 129, 149
Roberts, Dorothy, 19, 310
Rodríguez, Antonia, 196
Rodríguez, Daniel, 208
Rodríguez, Manuel, 130
Rodríguez, Petrona Josefa, 130
Rodríguez Acosta, Ofelia, 284
Romero, Blasa, 100
Romero, Elena Muñoz, 218
Rosaín, Domingo, 101–102
Roth, Cassia, 263
Royal Development Board, 79, 80, 89, 128, 144–145, 159, 161–162
Rubio, Luis Alberto, 278, 288

Saco, José Antonio, 159, 189
Sagra, Ramón de la, 183
Sainz, Manuel, 129–130
Sales y Valdés, Francisca, 55
San Agustín Convent, 105
San Ambrosio Military Hospital, 101, 105
San Antonio de los Baños, 110
Sancti Spíritus, 110
San Francisco de Paula Charity Hospital for Women, 28, 39–40, 44–49, 69–71, 101, 146–147, 152, 185
sanitation, 171–173, 246–247

San Juan de Dios hospital, 39–40, 69–71
San Juan de los Remedios, 110
San Lázaro hospital, 42, 130
San Leopoldo, 219
San Miguel sugar mill, 90–91
Santa Cruz de Oviedo, Estéban, 173–174
Santa Cruz de Oviedo y Muñoz, Antonio, 173
Santa María del Rosario, 110
Santiago, 110
Santiago de Cuba, 62, 63, 92
Santo Fernández, Juan, 245
"seasoning," 74
secrecy: pregnancy, 52–53, 103, 115–116, 196, 252, 265–266, 268; slavery, 88
Secretariat of Sanitation and Beneficence, 246–247
seduction, 37, 117
segregation, 42, 46–47, 64, 78, 80–81, 106, 202–204
Seven Years' War, 61
sex: abstinence, 81, 305; Blacks hypersexualized, 305; Blacks "morally depraved," 124, 127–128; celibacy, 85, 143; chastity threatened, 26, 37; enslaved women and, 80; illicit, 37–38, 51, 80; incest, 26, 60, 303; interracial, 26–27, 182–183; masturbation, 81; menstruation, 32; out-of-wedlock, 26–27, 37, 58–60, 62, 204, 231; perversion, 81, 85; promiscuity, 129; prostitution, 42, 45, 275, 344n91; rape, 37, 79; seduction, 37, 117; sexual deviance, 81, 85; sodomy, 81; "stain of," 26; venereal diseases, 42, 112, 251; virginity, 26, 37. *See also* marriage
Sibarimar, 92
Siete Partidas, 27–35, 75–76, 82–86, 139, 186–187
slavery: abolition, 74–75, 82–84, 191–192, 198–199, 201; amelioration, 75, 83, 88–89, 93, 138, 158–159, 190; antislaving treaties, 86–90, 140–145; "apprentices," 191–195, 201, 207; Brazil, 167, 191, 198, 207; breastmilk and, 68; "breeding," 167, 173–174; Britain prohibits, 74–75; brutality against enslaved, 48, 93; Casa Cuna purchases women, 68–69; castration, 48; Catholicism and "moralizing" slaves, 80; charges in killing enslaved, 48; children and, 33, 76–78, 88, 94–95, 129–130, 193–194, 198; *coartadas/coartación* (purchasing freedom), 76; *código negro carolino* (manumission prohibited), 76; Código Negro Español rules on slavery, 77; Committee for the Abolition of the Slave Trade, 75; Conspiración de la Escalera (Ladder Conspiracy), 108; *Dos Hermanos* (ship), 87; economic dependence on, 74, 84, 86, 96; *emancipadas*, 46, 128; enslaved and marriage, 75, 78–82, 88, 92, 203–204; enslaved and pregnancy, 83, 88–90; enslaved elderly, 77; enslaved framed for crimes, 149–151; enslaved mothers, 94, 192–198, 204–207; enslaved population, 49, 74, 77–82, 90–91, 122, 191; enslaved segregated, 78, 80–81; enslaved's legal status, 192; exclusion after slavery, 201–205; familial preservation, 93–94, 96; Free Trade in Slaves Act, 77, 91–92; gender ratios, 53, 75, 77, 79–82, 86, 122, 143; generational, 75–76, 125, 191, 195, 198, 205, 207; hospitals and, 45, 47–48, 105–106; importing cheaper than reproduction, 85–86, 122; institution of, 197, 207; "Instructivo para suavizar la suerte de los negros esclavos" (Guide to improve the lot of the Black slaves), 80; introduced, 33; manumission, 53; maximizing before restricted, 83; Middle Passage, 93, 125; morbidity, 74, 93; Moret Law, 207; *Negrito* (ship), 129; *Ninfa* (ship), 129; "owner" controls fertility, 89, 140–141, 148, 152–153, 161, 181–182; "owners" of females taxed, 78; *Planeta* (ship), 129; pronatalism fails at self-sustaining populations, 85–86, 122; racial exclusion after, 201–205; replacing enslaved, 83; restrictions on, 160–165, 179; "seasoning," 74; secrecy, 88; slave rebellion, 63, 80, 108; Slave Trade Act, 84, 96; Slave Voyages Trans-Atlantic Slave Trade Database, 92; St. Domingue rebellion, 63; sterility of enslaved, 93; taxation, 78, 79, 81, 86–87; United States, 84, 142, 178; unrestricted trade, 61, 71, 91–92; value of female enslaved, 85; working hours, 74. *See also* Moret Law
smallpox, 41, 42
Social Defense Code, 263, 285–287, 289, 308
social welfare, 275
Sociedad Económica, 79, 81–82
sodomy, 81
Somerset case, 74
souls, 34–35, 41
Spain: Anglo-Spanish antislaving treaty, 90, 96; charitable institutions, 97; conquistador violence, 28–31, 302; Fernando III (Castilian monarch), 27; fetal viability laws, 35; Iberian Peninsula, 60, 74; king refuses to fund Casa

INDEX 389

Cuna, 56; metropolitan laws, 30, 59, 82–86, 128; Ministerio de la Hacienda, 86; New Spain, conquest of, 32–33; population, 48; pronatalism, 96; slavery and, 61, 74–77, 84; Spanish-American War, 232; Spanish Black Code, 77; Spanish colonization and white fertility, 53; Spanish Empire and infanticide, 27, 38, 165; Spanish Law of Public Beneficence, 97, 114; Spanish penal code *honoris causa*, 98; Spanish penal code of 1848, 165; Treaty of Versailles, 47; violence toward Native families, 28–31. *See also* laws/reforms/decrees
Special Period, 309–310
status, 33, 45, 59–60, 84, 115, 119, 122
St. Domingue, 47, 63
Stepan, Nancy Leys, 261
sterility, 93
stillbirths, 101, 109–113, 135, 192, 210, 212. *See also* childbirth
strangulation, 213–214, 216
suicide, 30, 138
sulfa drugs, 112
Superior Board of Medicine and Surgery, 133
Superior Board of Sanitation, 224
surgery, 41, 112, 133, 170, 226. *See also* childbirth; medicine
syphilis, 112, 251

taxes, 56, 78, 79, 81, 86–87
Tejera, Diego Vicente, 287–288
Tenochtitlán, 33
Ten Years' War, 208
Teresa, 152
tetanus, infant, 109–110, 112, 113, 165, 171–172
Tomás, 199
torno (turnstile/wheel), 54–55, 121
Toro (Bull Laws), 35
Torres Pico, José, 51
Torriente, Celestino de la, 207
Treaty of Versailles, 47
Trinidad, 90–91, 110
Trist, Nicholas, 142
tuberculosis, 42, 112
Turnbull, David, 142, 143
Twinam, Ann, 60

United States: abortion laws, 308; Cuba and, 228, 232–234, 242, 245, 257; medicine, 208, 228, 292–293; slavery, 84, 142, 178

Valdés, Gerónimo, 52, 56, 115
Valdés, Jerónimo, 154
Valdés, Serapio, 219
Valdés surname, 52
Valencia y García, Pablo, 209
Valle, Ambrosio González del, 212, 226
Valle, Fernando González del, 208
Varela, Félix, 90
Varona Suárez, Manuel, 247
Velázquez, Diego, 33
Vélez Herrera, Ramón, 149
venereal diseases, 42, 112, 251. *See also* diseases
Versailles, Treaty of, 47
Vieites, Moisés, 283–284
Villa Clara, 110
Villafranca, Dolores, 129–130
Villa Urrutia, Wenceslao de, 159–160
violence, 28–31, 37, 48, 79, 212–213, 215
virginity, 26, 37
Vives y Planes, Francisco Dionisio, 102–104
vulvar lesions, 224

War of Independence, 208, 234, 257
Weiss Verson, Gaspar Rafael, 229
West Indies, 83
wet nurses: advertisements for, 94, 321n100, 337n25; Barales, Isabel, 62; caring for several babies, 69, 71; Casa de Maternidad, 196–197; culpable, 67–70; demographics of, 196–197; dependence on, 68, 196; enslaved, 94, 157, 192–198, 207; for ill children, 131; internal, 196, 198; regulation of, 253–254, 304; salaries, 67, 70; unhygienic conditions, 203
whites: abortions and, 231; breastfeeding, 67–68; children "corrupted" by Blacks, 129; colonialism, 61, 79; economic prosperity and, 54; *expósitos*, 60, 62, 72, 198, 201; fertility crimes, 274; girls prepped for marriage, 44, 64, 72, 73; honor and, 38–39; immigration, 243; infanticide cases, 211–214, 216, 218; infants, 51, 67–70, 195–197, 200, 203–204; Junta de Colonización Blanca, 79; as medical authority, 169; mortality, 210; others' reproduction, 33; patriarchy protects women, 37, 210, 231; population, 34, 39, 54, 63, 124–125, 301; "seemingly white," 59, 121; wealthy women and pregnancy, 117; whiteness, 61–63, 199, 203–205, 231; whitening, 261, 289; white-passing, 51, 55; worthiness, 103

women: abused as "savages," 31; Black hospital staff, 52–53; Blacks "morally depraved," 124, 127–128, 203–207; Black women hypersexualized, 305; childbirth attendants, 36, 40–41, 113; childcare and working, 256–258; child's status follows mother's, 33; *coartadas/coartación* (purchasing freedom), 76; corrupt but deserve grace, 303; *depositadas*, 46–47; divorced, hospitalized, 44–45; educational opportunities, 44, 104; *emancipadas*, 46; enslaved, 68–69, 77; girls prepped for marriage, 44, 64, 72, 73; honorable colonial path, 26; hospitals and slavery, 45, 47–48; "hysteria" treatment, 46; infanticide charges and race/wealth, 135, 237, 241–242; liabilities, 54; manumission prohibited if mothers, 76; maternalism, 38, 50, 127–128, 145–146, 149, 150, 169, 212; mestizo, 206; morals of, 44–49, 80, 124, 127–129, 196, 203–207, 344n91; objectification of, 236; patriarchal protection of, 37–44, 97, 108–115, 137, 210, 231, 308; population, 40, 53, 74, 256; pregnancy threats, 99–100; prisoners, 47; reproduce slaves, 75; reproduction Christian duty, 303; right to motherhood, 252; San Francisco de Paula Charity Hospital for Women, 28, 39–40, 44–49, 69–71, 101, 146–147, 152, 185; sexual threats, 26, 37; unwed, pregnant, 26, 37, 52; value of, 85, 144–145, 178, 182; wayward, 44–49; womanhood, 26

work. *See* labor/work

worthiness, 45–46, 49, 58–63, 103, 126, 203, 277

Yaguaramas, 92–93

yellow fever, 41–42

Zayas, Andrés de, 89–90

RACE IN THE ATLANTIC WORLD, 1700–1900

*The Hanging of Angélique: The Untold Story of
Canadian Slavery and the Burning of Old Montréal*
    BY AFUA COOPER

*Christian Ritual and the Creation of
British Slave Societies, 1650–1780*
    BY NICHOLAS M. BEASLEY

*African American Life in the Georgia Lowcountry:
The Atlantic World and the Gullah Geechee*
    EDITED BY PHILIP MORGAN

*The Horrible Gift of Freedom:
Atlantic Slavery and the Representation of Emancipation*
    BY MARCUS WOOD

*The Life and Letters of Philip Quaque,
the First African Anglican Missionary*
    EDITED BY VINCENT CARRETTA AND TY M. REESE

*In Search of Brightest Africa: Reimagining the Dark
Continent in American Culture, 1884–1936*
    BY JEANNETTE EILEEN JONES

*Contentious Liberties: American Abolitionists in
Post-emancipation Jamaica, 1834–1866*
    BY GALE L. KENNY

*We Are the Revolutionists: German-Speaking Immigrants
and American Abolitionists after 1848*
    BY MISCHA HONECK

The American Dreams of John B. Prentis, Slave Trader
    BY KARI J. WINTER

*Missing Links: The African and American Worlds of
R. L. Garner, Primate Collector*
    BY JEREMY RICH

Almost Free: A Story about Family and Race in Antebellum Virginia
    BY EVA SHEPPARD WOLF

*To Live an Antislavery Life:
Personal Politics and the Antebellum Black Middle Class*
    BY ERICA L. BALL

*Flush Times and Fever Dreams:
A Story of Capitalism and Slavery in the Age of Jackson*
    BY JOSHUA D. ROTHMAN

Diplomacy in Black and White:
John Adams, Toussaint Louverture, and Their Atlantic World Alliance
    BY RONALD ANGELO JOHNSON

Enterprising Women:
Gender, Race, and Power in the Revolutionary Atlantic
    BY KIT CANDLIN AND CASSANDRA PYBUS

Eighty-Eight Years: The Long Death of
Slavery in the United States, 1777–1865
    BY PATRICK RAEL

Finding Charity's Folk: Enslaved and
Free Black Women in Maryland
    BY JESSICA MILLWARD

The Mulatta Concubine: Terror, Intimacy, Freedom,
and Desire in the Black Transatlantic
    BY LISA ZE WINTERS

The Politics of Black Citizenship: Free African Americans in
the Mid-Atlantic Borderland, 1817–1863
    BY ANDREW K. DIEMER

Punishing the Black Body:
Marking Social and Racial Structures in Barbados and Jamaica
    BY DAWN P. HARRIS

Race and Nation in the Age of Emancipations
    EDITED BY WHITNEY NELL STEWART
    AND JOHN GARRISON MARKS

Vénus Noire: Black Women and Colonial Fantasies
in Nineteenth-Century France
    BY ROBIN MITCHELL

City of Refuge: Slavery and Petit Marronage
in the Great Dismal Swamp, 1763–1856
    BY MARCUS P. NEVIUS

An American Color: Race and Identity in
New Orleans and the Atlantic World
    BY ANDREW N. WEGMANN

Maroons in Guyane: Past, Present, and Future
    BY RICHARD PRICE AND SALLY PRICE

Almost Dead: Slavery and Social Rebirth in
the Black Urban Atlantic, 1680–1807
    BY MICHAEL LAWRENCE DICKINSON

Race and Reproduction in Cuba
    BY BONNIE A. LUCERO

www.ingramcontent.com/pod-product-compliance
Lightning Source LLC
Chambersburg PA
CBHW010720300426
44116CB00017B/2951